Praise for Garry Wills's
Head and Heart

"*Head and Heart* is a major contribution to the national debate over separation of church and state and ought to be read by anyone perplexed by the current interplay of religion and politics."
—Tim Rutten, *Los Angeles Times*

"Garry Wills, one of America's best journalists and historians of the last half century, has always enjoyed taking familiar subjects and staring at them long and hard until they look strange and new. In *Head and Heart* he invited readers to reconsider American religious history, challenging the conventional wisdom on many issues while synthesizing much of the finest recent scholarship."
—Patrick Allitt, *The New York Times Book Review*

"Only someone who has made Wills's own hard intellectual and moral journey . . . would have come to appreciate American history as a grand oscillation, maybe even a dialectic, between Enlightenment (head) and Evangelism (heart)." —John Leonard, *Harper's Magazine*

"The book has . . . a bravado sorely lacking in more standard histories. Wills calls them as he sees them, and he delivers his calls with all the nuance of a World Series umpire." —*The Washington Post*

"Garry Wills is in many ways the ideal man to explain American religion to Americans. . . . Wills has written a significant book, and it ought to be widely read." —Alan Wolfe, *The New Republic*

"*Head and Heart* is essential reading for any student of history and politics who wants to understand the role of religion and any student of faith and religion who wants to understand its role in the wider culture."
—Kevin Horrigan, *St. Louis Post-Dispatch*

"Vintage Wills—a strong interpretive framework, vigorous prose and big, provocative arguments." —*Kirkus Reviews*

"His case for seeing abortion as a nonreligious issue is as cogent as it is refreshing." —*Booklist*

ABOUT THE AUTHOR

Garry Wills has written many acclaimed works on religion and on American history, including *Lincoln at Gettysburg*; *Cincinnatus: George Washington and the Enlightenment*; *What Jesus Meant*; *What Paul Meant*; and *What the Gospels Meant*. His works have received many awards, including the Pulitzer Prize. He studied for the priesthood and took his doctorate in the classics. He is now Professor of History Emeritus at Northwestern University and is a frequent contributor to the *New York Review of Books* and other publications.

HEAD
AND
HEART

A HISTORY OF CHRISTIANITY IN AMERICA

Garry Wills

PENGUIN BOOKS

PENGUIN BOOKS

Published by the Penguin Group

Penguin Group (USA) Inc., 375 Hudson Street, New York, New York 10014, U.S.A.

Penguin Group (Canada), 90 Eglinton Avenue East, Suite 700, Toronto,
Ontario, Canada M4P 2Y3 (a division of Pearson Penguin Canada Inc.)

Penguin Books Ltd, 80 Strand, London WC2R 0RL, England

Penguin Ireland, 25 St Stephen's Green, Dublin 2, Ireland (a division of Penguin Books Ltd)

Penguin Group (Australia), 250 Camberwell Road, Camberwell,
Victoria 3124, Australia (a division of Pearson Australia Group Pty Ltd)

Penguin Books India Pvt Ltd, 11 Community Centre,
Panchsheel Park, New Delhi – 110 017, India

Penguin Group (NZ), 67 Apollo Drive, Rosedale, North Shore 0632,
New Zealand (a division of Pearson New Zealand Ltd)

Penguin Books (South Africa) (Pty) Ltd, 24 Sturdee Avenue,
Rosebank, Johannesburg 2196, South Africa

Penguin Books Ltd, Registered Offices:
80 Strand, London WC2R 0RL, England

First published in the United States of America by The Penguin Press,
a member of Penguin Group (USA) Inc. 2007
Published in Penguin Books 2008

1 3 5 7 9 10 8 6 4 2

Copyright © Garry Wills, 2007
All rights reserved

THE LIBRARY OF CONGRESS HAS CATALOGED THE HARDCOVER EDITION AS FOLLOWS:
Wills, Garry, ——
Head and heart : American Christianities / by Garry Wills.
p. cm.
Includes bibliographical references and index.
ISBN 978-1-59420-146-2 (hc.)
ISBN 978-0-14-311407-9 (pbk.)
1. United States—Church history. I. Title.
BR515.W494 2007
277.3—dc22   2007012631

Printed in the United States of America
Designed by Marysarah Quinn

To Anthony Benezet

AMERICAN SAINT

CONTENTS

PART FIVE: RELIGIOUS NATION

KEY TO BRIEF CITATIONS

A   Sydney Ahlstrom, *A Religious History of the American People*, 2nd ed. (Yale University Press, 1972)

J   Thomas Jefferson, *Papers*, ed. Julian Boyd et al. (Princeton University Press, 1950–)

JP   Merrill D. Peterson, ed., *Thomas Jefferson: Writings* (Library of America, 1984)

JM   James Madison, *Papers*, ed. William T. Hutchinson et al. (University of Chicago Press, 1962–)

M   Cotton Mather, *Magnalia Christi Americana, or: The Ecclesiastical History of New-England*, 2 vols. (Silas Andrus and Son, 1855)

MM   Martin E. Marty, *Modern American Religion*, 3 vols. (University of Chicago Press, 1986–96)

W   Cotton Mather, *The Wonders of the Invisible World: An Account of the Tryals of Several Witches Lately Executed in New-England* (John Russell Smith, 1862)

Since most of the people treated in this book,

through most of the history covered, cited

the Bible in the King James Version,

I shall use it throughout.

❖

INTRODUCTION

W HEN THE DALAI LAMA was scheduled to speak at the Field
Museum in Chicago, he told those arranging the session that he
did not like to give formal addresses; he preferred a more lively format.
So he asked to be questioned by several people onstage with him, to
whom he could give impromptu answers. I was chosen as one of his three
interrogators. Meeting with us ahead of time, he said: "Please ask hard
questions." If people were too deferential to him, he explained, the event
would be boring, for him as well as for the audience. He did not want to
know the questions beforehand, which would dampen the spontaneity.

I tried to think of something difficult to ask, but the only thing I
could come up with was this: "If you were restored to your country, what
would you do in a different way?" He answered: "I would disestablish the
religion. The American system is the proper one." As we left, I said to
him, "For that, don't you first need to have an Enlightenment?" He
smiled: "Ah! That's the problem." He was soon writing a book that called
on Buddhists to confront the issues of modern science and reason, as
they had not in the past.[1]

He was striving for that condition America had been blessed with at
its founding.

ENLIGHTENED RELIGION

W ITHOUT THE eighteenth-century Enlightenment, with its emphasis on reason, benevolence, tolerance, and secular progress,

there would have been no Disestablishment of religion in America. Without it, there would have been no escape from the theological monopoly that governments had always imposed, no rapid proliferation of the sects that multiplied as soon as Disestablishment occurred. Without the Enlightenment, Franklin's humanitarian efforts and Jefferson's intellectual projects would have had no purchase on the citizenry. Without it, Pennsylvania's Quakers could not have challenged the Bible's sanctioning of slavery. It was a great stroke of fortune that the American republic was shaped at the moment when the Enlightenment was having its full effect on the men who did the shaping. Political freedom and religious freedom arrived together, nudging each other forward. Before then, it had been assumed that a national throne and a national altar must be in alliance, to command the necessary acquiescence of the ruled. The United States rid itself of both throne and altar in one inclusive gesture.

Though there was no official religion for the nation, the framers had an Enlightened religion.[2] Those who have a different kind of religion said in the past and say now that this is no religion at all, simply a cult of reason. It is true that some leaders of the Enlightenment in France were hostile to religion, but that was not true of the main and most numerous followers of Enlightenment in America. They were friendly to religion and were religious themselves. Even the most secular of them, Tom Paine, believed in a personal God, in divine providence, and in the afterlife.

Enlightened religion was such a strong force in all the founding period that it might almost be considered the typical American religion. It is true that this form of belief has assumed the moral leadership of the nation at certain crucial times, and one of its forms—Transcendentalism—set much of the intellectual tone of the nineteenth century. But it has rarely been the religion of the mass of Americans. One reason Enlightened religion had such unchallenged sway in the late eighteenth century was that the other characteristic form of American religion—Evangelicalism—was its lowest ebb in just that period. Yet it came roaring back in the early nineteenth century, and has been adhered to by most Americans in succeeding ages.

EVANGELICAL RELIGION

ENLIGHTENED RELIGION professes a belief in "the laws of nature and of nature's God." It holds that reason is the tool for understanding those laws, and that humane conduct is what those laws teach. Evangelicals, by contrast, emphasize an experiential relationship with Jesus as their savior, along with biblical inerrancy and a mission to save others. Theirs is the religion of that characteristic American institution, the revival. The emphasis of Enlightened religion is on the head. The emphasis of Evangelicals is on the heart. These form the two poles of American religion in the dominant (Protestant) culture. The intellectual and the experiential forms of religion tug against each other, though they are not mutually exclusive. That is why I refer to them as two poles of religious attraction, not as two separate religions.

It is true, of course, that America is a land of many religious traditions, not just two. But the two emphases I single out have had the greatest impact on the general religious ethos. They are not separate churches, but strong tendencies in many churches. The two poles are not formal bodies of doctrine. They are two force fields, each with its own tendency and emphases. This is empirically observable in studies of different epochs in our history. Over and over we find historians identifying a conflict between these two strands, the Enlightened and the Evangelical. At different times they are identified by different terms— liturgical vs. pietist, ecclesial vs. revivalist, high church vs. low church, elite vs. populist, rational vs. emotional, studied vs. spontaneous, Modernist vs. Fundamentalist, immanent vs. apocalyptical, and so on. It is tempting but risky to think of the two strands politically—as liberal vs. conservative. In fact, some of the early proponents of Enlightenment, like the Reverend Samuel Johnson, were politically conservative. In the Civil War, an Evangelical like John Brown was radical and the elite class of the South was reactionary. In our time, Evangelicals have been radical enough to commit civil disobedience over abortion. It is too simple, and will uselessly heat discussion, to think of this as a permanent fight between liberals and conservatives.

People have at various times expressed the antagonism of these two forces. In 1853, a prominent minister could complain of "an impression, somewhat general, that an intellectual clergyman is deficient in piety, and that an eminently pious minister is deficient in intellect."[3] Sydney Ahlstrom described the same phenomenon a century later:

> Americans have in effect been given the hard choice between
> being intelligent according to the standards prevailing in their
> intellectual centers, and being religious according to the
> standards prevailing in their denominations.[4]

Sidney Mead thought the two forces incompatible:

> I have concluded that the two stand in a relation of mutual
> antagonism, and are perhaps logically mutually exclusive. This
> is to say that practically every specific of traditional orthodoxy
> in Christendom is intellectually at war with the basic premises
> upon which the constitutional and legal structures of the
> Republic rest.[5]

That is far too pessimistic. In fact, the constitutional framework has done just what Jefferson and Madison said it would—fostered and protected religion. The extraordinary religiosity of America—unparalleled throughout the developed world—is part of the continuing legacy of that legal separation. Besides, the two are not absolute opposites—there are rational Evangelicals and pious Enlightened figures. The two cross-pollinate and are at their best when that happens, as we shall see in figures like Anthony Benezet, Abraham Lincoln, Martin Luther King, Cesar Chavez, and Dorothy Day. Historians of Evangelicalism—men like Mark

Noll and Richard Carwardine—rightly insist that there was a strong element of Enlightenment for most of the time in most of the churches they study. This is revealed by Evangelicals' original adherence to republicanism, to common-sense epistemology derived from the Scots, and to their own version of Disestablishment (no favored sect, but support for religion in general).

Before I begin the story of the conflict between the Enlightened head and the Evangelical heart, two conditions need fairly lengthy introductions, one before the Enlightenment arrived and the other setting up the Enlightened condition that would be the basis of future conflict with Evangelicalism. These two conditions are Puritanism (taken up in Part One) and Disestablishment (treated in Part Two). They would both echo on throughout our religious history.

PURITANS

THE TENSION BETWEEN Enlightenment and Evangelicalism cannot occur, naturally, before there is an Enlightenment. The dominant religious culture of the colonies, in both the Congregational North and the largely Anglican South, was Calvinist. This was a religious culture in which there was no obvious polarity between intellect and emotion. Both were recruited to serve the biblical culture. There was never a more intellectual leadership in religion than among the Puritans, but the logical energies of the school were devoted to a narrow and circular labor to reconcile Calvinist theology and biblical literalism. The emotional component of the movement was seen in the requirement that each church member undergo an experiential conversion. That private and personal epiphany would itself be subject to a later and technical scrutiny by the community, closing the circle of intellectual-experiential and individual-communal completeness that was the strength of Puritanism.

None of this process was leavened by Enlightenment values of tolerance, intellectual openness, or pluralism. The Puritans hanged Quakers, exiled Dissenters, silenced heretics and burnt their books. Yet so deep was the formative impact of Puritanism on American history that vestiges of Puritanism lingered on after the Enlightenment came. These traces would continue to show up in Enlightened figures like Emerson as well as in Evangelical figures like Billy Sunday. It would be very hard to overstate the importance of Puritanism in American culture. It is in our bones. In the words of three outstanding historians:

> In the most influential American churches Puritan categories
> were commonplace until the mid-nineteenth century. Except
> for a number of remarkable southern politicians, almost every
> prominent American thinker before World War I was either
> born in New England or educated there. As late as the early
> decades of the twentieth century many American literary
> figures were still wrestling with the vestiges of the Puritan
> heritage. And even more pervasive than such influence on
> American ideas was the Puritan impact on American values.
> While Puritanism could not claim to have single-handedly
> shaped the American conscience, it certainly helped define its
> most distinctive traits.[6]

DISESTABLISHMENT

THE SECOND CONDITION I dwell on in the early sections is Disestablishment of the church. It is important to be clear about the meaning this had in the minds of its first articulators, since that meaning has been contested ever since the passage of the First Amendment. It is frequently misunderstood or misrepresented. This is not surprising. Disestablishment was a stunning innovation. No other government had been launched without the protection of an official cult. This is the only original part of the Constitution. Everything else—federalism, three branches of government, two houses of the legislature, an independent judiciary—had been around for a long time, in theory and in practice.

But Disestablishment was not a thing with precedents. Our Constitution never mentions God—an omission that was startling, and highly criticized, at the time.[7] Various attempts at an amendment to place God in the Constitution were undertaken in both the nineteenth and the twentieth centuries. They have failed.

Some find Disestablishment so objectionable that they feel the framers did not really mean it. They might not favor a specific sect, but they *had* to think a government should support religion. After all, some of the states had an established religion, or they had religious tests for holding office. It has even been claimed that Disestablishment at the federal level was meant to *protect* establishment at the state level. Jefferson and Madison would not have agreed at all, as we shall see.

It is probable that the great break with history signified by Disestablishment could have taken place at no other time in American history than the founding era. Almost all the framers of our government were Deists. Their influence was not, for a crucial period, countered by a strong Evangelical counterweight. This goes against a myth fondly held by modern Evangelicals—that America was founded in a time of deep religiosity and that this religious fervor has been cooling ever since. The truth is exactly the opposite. The Evangelical scholar Mark Noll calls the period 1750–90 the time (the *only* time in our history) of great Evangelical decline.[8] That is when churchgoing hit an all-time low of 17 percent of the population. The surge in religion came *after* Disestablishment (I shall argue that it came in part *because* of Disestablishment), and it has been on the rise ever since, as the following chart shows.

Some mistake the state of religion at the founding because the Revolution followed on the Great Awakening, the wave of revivals that shook the colonial culture in the 1730s and 1740s. But you will notice that Noll marks Evangelical decline from the 1750s, a quarter of a century before the founding period. The blaze of the Awakening quickly faded, to the dismay of its great sponsor Jonathan Edwards. As the historian John Murrin notes, "Evangelical elation had declined sharply in 1742."[9]

RATES OF RELIGIOUS ADHERENCE, 1776–2000
(Percent of the Population)

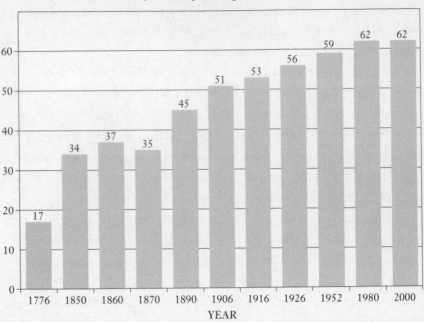

Source: Roger Finke and Rodney Stark, *The Churching of America, 1776–2005* (Rutgers University Press, 2005).

The conservatives' myth of religious beginnings has such a strong hold on the popular conception of our history because it is buttressed by secularists who say the same thing in hope that the first group says in fear— that America was religious at the outset but that reason, science, and progress have made us less religious year by year. Both myths are wrong. Both present the exact opposite of what actually occurred. But I am getting ahead of my story. Before engaging the main struggle between the head and the heart, it is time to ponder the importance of Puritanism and Disestablishment, along with their attendant circumstances.

The growth of religious denominations is the clearest proof that America's system, which the Dalai Lama admires and many other nations have imitated, is the great protector of religion, not its enemy. Even the

Evangelical pole of our religious sentiment recognizes some degree of separation of church and state, and a far greater commitment to toleration of others' beliefs than existed before the Enlightenment. Though Evangelicals have the greatest numbers in America, we remain an Enlightened nation.

PART ONE

Pre-Enlightenment Religion

�֍

I | PURITANS

1 | MARY DYER MUST DIE

O N JUNE 1, 1660, Mary Dyer was led out of the women's detention house in Boston and conducted by an armed guard to the Commons, to the hanging tree (an elm), for execution. A Quaker woman in her forties, she was the mother of six and the wife of a respected colonial official in Rhode Island. Her husband petitioned the Massachusetts authorities to spare her, but they had spared her once before. Now they judged that such reprieves could stretch out forever if they did not cut the process off. She, like other Quakers, had been banished by law from the Massachusetts Bay Colony on pain of death, and she repeatedly defied the law. She would be the third Quaker to die for defying it, while a fourth member of the Friends was already scheduled to follow her to the gallows.

This was not her first trip to the tree. Seven months earlier, she had been led out from the detention house to join with two other Quakers, William Robinson and Marmaduke Stephenson, on their way to a triple execution. She walked between the men, her comrades, hand in hand, with the jauntiness that Protestants had learned from *Foxe's Book of Martyrs.* This insouciance angered the crowd. Some cried that she should be ashamed, old as she was, to be holding hands in public with two younger men. She answered that she was glad to be entering eternal life in such good company.

Execution was a formal ritual. Preachers warned the condemned not to face their Maker unrepentant. Their pleas were studied and polished. Later, some of them would be published. The dramatic occasion was an opportunity to bring even the bystanders to repent their sins. If the condemned persons submitted to these last-minute pleas, that would be an occasion for rejoicing. But these Quakers were prepared with counter-sermons, declaring the righteousness of their cause. Such dueling theatrics held audiences in thrall.

Mary stood below the tree as each of her friends mounted a ladder with rope knotted around his neck. The other end of the rope was affixed to the designated tree limb; each man was urged to confess his sins. When it became clear that they were going to use the moment to voice their damnable heresy, the military escort drowned out their words with drums. Then the ladder was withdrawn from each man, and one after the other fell to the rope's length.

It was Mary's turn. She had so far only watched, with her own rope knotted around her neck. Now she was told to climb the ladder, while men on another ladder went up to tie her hands and legs at the top, and to bind her skirt around her, before fastening a cloth over her face. She was about to be "turned off" just like her friends. Again there was an attempt to exact a confession. It was hoped that she, being a woman, would be cowed by the sight of her friends thrashing at the ropes' ends. Then, it was planned, she would be freed, as an example to other Quakers, that they too could avoid this ordeal by recanting. But if she did not recant, she would be freed anyway, this first time out. They had gone through this charade, even sending her up the ladder, to exact a renunciation from the tree.

But that was the extent of their resolve. There were already grumblings in neighboring colonies over the persecutions in Massachusetts—the objections had even reached England, where they would soon prompt a royal intervention. The Massachusetts authorities realized that the first execution of a woman would intensify criticism of their actions, especially since this woman was a mother, a former member of the Boston church, and the wife of an influential man. So the governor, John Winthrop, feigned that he had yielded, at the last minute, to a plea for mercy from one of Dyer's sons. Actually, her pardon had been signed beforehand, but it was hoped that she would "earn" it by renouncing her errors.

When Mary was told, through the covering on her face, that she was being spared, she refused to accept the favor. She did not want a pardon for herself, but an end to the persecution of Quakers. She stood there, still inviting death, until bystanders began to shout, "Pull her down!" Men could never get her to do the right thing. They took her back to prison, where she continued to assert that she would not accept a pardon from the men who killed her friends. "I rather choose to die than live, as [a gift] from you as guilty of their innocent blood."

There was nothing to do but put her on a horse and lead her to the colony's boundary, hoping she would go home to her husband, who might persuade her to remain there. Instead she went to stay with some fellow Quakers on Long Island, and in seven months she showed up again in Massachusetts. This time a new governor, John Endecott, meant to put an end to the problem she kept thrusting upon them. If she persisted, Mary Dyer must die. She was taken back to the hanging tree. After she went up the ladder, a captain of the military escort told her she could be spared again if she showed repentance. When she refused, he told her, "You are guilty of your own blood." This was the formal position of the colony. If people were told that returning after banishment meant death, then they were in effect committing suicide if they came back.[1]

She answered: "Nay, I came to keep blood guiltiness from you, desiring *you* to repent the unrighteous and unjust law of banishment upon pain of death made against the innocent servants of the Lord. Therefore my blood will be required at your hands who willfully do it."

When she refused to hear the pleas of the Congregational minister who approached her, a mocking bystander asked if she would rather have an elder (a Presbyterian "heretic") pray for her. "I know never an elder here." She desired no grace from a "priest" (Congregationalist) *or* elder.[2] Would she let *anyone* pray for her? "I desire the prayers of all the people of God." A bystander shouted that she must not think there were any people of God present. "I know but few here," she agreed. Asked again if she would accept an elder, she shot back: "Nay, first a child, then a young man, then a strong man, before an elder of Christ Jesus." Before she could say more, the ladder was removed.[3]

Quakers had been presenting petitions to King Charles II ever since his restoration to power two years earlier. He sent an instruction to Massachusetts, telling its rulers to stop executing his subjects for their religious opinions. Before that could reach the colony, a fourth Quaker, William Leddra, was hanged on March 14, 1667. This episode flies in the face of our grade-school understanding of American history. We were taught as children that Pilgrims and Puritans fled to the New World to escape religious repression under the British monarch and find tolerance for their views. But here we see the King championing tolerance and the colonists engaged in repression. That is just the first of many apparent contradictions to be found in the story of Mary Dyer. I put it here, at the beginning of my book, because it contains the seeds of many things that must be understood in the early stages of our history. What happened to Mary Dyer was not an anomaly but part of a pattern, one to be found in New England's treatment not only of Quakers but of Presbyterians and Baptists, of Roger Williams and Anne Hutchinson, of "Antinomians" and "witches." If we are to trace the rise of Enlightened religion in America, we must see first what pre-Enlightenment religion looked like, and that is a subject best pondered in the fate of Mary Dyer. Her treatment is related to a number of topics—six, to begin with: (1) tolerance, (2) the relation of church to state, (3) a general excess of supernaturalism, (4) fear of the devil, (5) expectation of the End Time, and (6) America's providential role in history. I take up each in order.

1. AGAINST TOLERANCE

THE FOUNDERS OF the New England colonies did not come to America to protect any variety in religious practice, or to assert the primacy of the individual's conscience. Far from it. They came to set up the one true faith where corrupt versions of it could not intrude. The only religion recognized as authentic, as what God wills, was the Covenant of Grace, under which God's chosen were predestined to salvation, making their church a collection of "visible saints." Those not consciously saved in this way could not be communicating members of the church, nor could they be voting members of the community. These outsiders had to attend and support the true church even if they were not full members of it. Pastors and governors all had to be communicating members of the church. As Samuel Willard wrote in 1681 against Baptists claiming that New England should be a haven for religious freedom:

> I perceive they are mistaken in the design of our first planters,
> whose business was not tolerating but were professed enemies of
> it, and could leave the world professing they died no libertines.
> Their business was to settle and (as much as in them lay) secure
> religion to posterity according to that way which they believed
> was of God.[4]

Or as Nathaniel Ward put it in 1645: "I dare take upon me to be the herald of New England so far as to proclaim to the world, in the name of our colony, that all Familists, Antinomians, Anabaptists, and other Enthusiasts shall have free liberty—to keep away from us."[5]

The crime of Mary Dyer was to enter the community without submitting to its rulers, whose authority was based on the one true religion. Even to bring a Quaker book into the community was forbidden. So, even more, was the expression of Quaker views with an attempt to win followers. Ship captains were severely fined if they so much as carried Quakers to the colony's shores—and also fined for bringing Quaker books, pamphlets or sermons, or any expressions of religious views other than the one true view. The same ban applied to Presbyterians, Baptists, and believers in any but the authorized faith. When church members strayed from the truth as that was officially expounded, they were expelled from the church. If they persisted in their errors, the civil magistrates could (and should) expel them from the colony. If they refused to go, they were to be whipped, maimed (ears cropped or tongues bored), or otherwise subdued. If they kept returning, there was no way to end such "rebellion" but by death.

Tolerance, in this setting, was sedition. It was treachery to the truth. Mere "opinion" was not a thing to be honored where *certainty* of salvation was the credential for membership in the ruling community. The Cambridge pastor Thomas Shepard, who was prominent in condemning the "heretic" Anne Hutchinson, said that tolerance of different religions was "the foundation of all other errors and abominations in the churches of God."[6] As Richard Mather (father of Increase Mather and grandfather of Cotton Mather) put it in 1657:

> Believe not them that think a man may be saved in any religion,
> and that it were good to leave all religions free, and that opinions
> have no great danger in them. These are but the devils of Satan,
> that so pernicious errors might more easily be entertained, as
> not being greatly suspected. . . . If you believe that sheep may do
> well enough though wolves be let in amongst them, then may
> you believe that false doctrine and they that teach it are in no
> ways dangerous to the souls of men.[7]

By this standard, Mary Dyer was one of the "devils of Satan." Mather's grandson Cotton said that Dyer was crazy, but that the devil drove her mad. Her insistence on returning to the colony when she knew it meant death was an affliction visited upon the Quakers by Satan: "'They must needs go whom the devil drives'—these devil-driven creatures did but the more furiously push themselves upon the government" (M 2.524).[8]

The doctrinal reason for condemning Quakers was their reliance on an "inner light" that let them sit too loose to the literal guidance of the Gospels. Further proof of their diabolic assistance came from the fact that intense waiting for the inner light led some at their gatherings to quiver and shake, giving them the name Quakers and earning Cotton Mather's condemnation: "The quaking which distinguished these poor creatures was a symptom of diabolical possession" (M 2.528). When the first Quaker women arrived in Boston in 1656, the mere fact that they were women preachers was enough for the magistrates to put them in prison and subject them to a strip search for signs of the devil's mark on witches.[9]

It would be a mistake to look for religious tolerance in seventeenth-century New England. Toleration, when it did come, was forced on the Puritans from the very authority they had fled. Though they had been cheered when the papalizing monarch Charles I was overthrown and Protestant Oliver Cromwell came to power, Cromwell needed to hold together all forms of religious dissent in order to oppose the monarchy. This led him to tolerate the differences between Puritans, Presbyterians, Baptists, and others, to the disgust of the New England clergy. In their eyes, Cromwell had sold out the cause of Reform at the very moment of its triumph.

When the monarchy was restored, Charles II could not afford to unsettle his countrymen by reversing the toleration measures already in place. That is why he came to the defense of the Quakers in New England, and threatened to take away the Massachusetts Charter that enabled its governors to quash religious differences. In his letter of June 28, 1662, Charles told local authorities in Massachusetts that they could no longer limit the vote to church members, or restrict communion to those consciously saved. This went against what the colonists took to be their authority under the Charter granted them in 1629. But it was always dangerous for the Massachusetts settlers to bring up that Charter in England. They had brazenly taken it with them to the New World, where they vastly expanded its authority. The Charter simply set up a joint stock company for trade and landholding (similar to the Hudson's Bay Company and the Virginia Company).[10] It did not authorize a separate government. While he was at it, the King decided to recall the Charter. Despite strong local resistance in the colony, the Charter was revoked in 1686, when all the Northern colonies were gathered into a single Dominion of New England governed by the King's appointee, Sir Edmund Andros.

A year after this disaster, King Charles died and was succeeded by James II. Though James was of Catholic sympathies (or, rather, because he was), he too had to issue a Proclamation of Indulgence tolerating all dissent. Increase Mather was sent to London to bargain with the new King for a restoration of the Massachusetts Charter. Before that could happen under James, the Glorious Revolution of 1688 overthrew the King and brought in William and Mary to reassert Protestant rule. The colonies took this opportunity to have their own local revolution, over-throwing the regime of Edmund Andros.

Though William granted a new Charter to Massachusetts, he also issued an Act of Toleration, under which all forms of Protestant (but not Roman Catholic) worship were to be allowed. The new Charter made the governor a royal appointee with expanded powers. The local church in Massachusetts had to submit to this new arrangement even while trying to circumvent it. Thus the pure intolerance of New England was gradually eaten away by royal acts from abroad, running from Cromwell's inclusion of all forms of dissent to Charles II's letter of 1662 to James II's Proclamation of Indulgence to William of Orange's Act of Toleration. Tolerance was the accomplishment of kings.

The immediate pressures for broadening the acceptance of religious views were pragmatic and conciliatory, but a core of principle was also being formed. The impact of the Enlightenment was already being felt in works like John Locke's *A Letter Concerning Toleration* (1689). The pre-Enlightenment religion of America was being challenged at many levels. But many Congregationalists dug in their heels against this tendency. As late as 1708 Samuel Sewall, the judge of the Salem witches, was still refusing to grant permission for a Quaker meetinghouse to be estab-lished in Massachusetts, since "I would not have a hand in setting up their devil worship."[11] Intolerance dies hard, when it dies at all.

2. CHURCH AND STATE

RETURNING TO 1620, to Mary Dyer, we must ask what authority the Puritan church had for the treatment of heretics. The leaders of the Bay Colony would have said that the church had no authority but to stigmatize heretical error. Punishment was left to the state, which had a different mandate. Even from the outset, New England professed a separation of church and state. John Winthrop had called, on the immigrants' ship *Arbella,* for "a due form of government *both* civil and ecclesiastical" (emphasis added). There had to be a civil government, since not all "cohabitants" of the colony were to be full (communicating) church members—in fact, most were finally outside the church. These "unchosen" were not covered by the Covenant of Grace but by the Covenant of Works—that is, by the laws of nature given in God's original relationship to Adam. The church, therefore, identified and guided its own, but could not dictate to those outside its body of visible saints. The civil authorities did that. The churches did not bear the sword of punishment. The sword belonged to secular magistrates, who could not be pastors or ministers. John Cotton put the distinction this way: "Man by nature being a reasonable and sociable creature, capable of civil order, is or may be the subject of civil power and state, but man by grace called out of the world to fellowship with Jesus Christ and with His people is the only subject of church power."[12]

Technically, then, Mary Dyer was not hanged as a heretic but as a disturber of the temporal peace—just as Anne Hutchinson and Roger Williams were not expelled from the colony for their religious views but for their insubordination to the temporal authority. The charge against the Quakers was more plausible than that against "Antinomians" like Hutchinson. The first Quakers were not the peaceable figures they became by the eighteenth century. They were religious radicals who had not yet adopted the general code of pacifism that George Fox eventually fostered in them. They denied the power of king and priest, and frequently disturbed church and secular gatherings, first in Europe, then around the world (as far as Palestine and Barbados). Their refusal to doff their hats, their familiar "thee" and "thou" to those in places of authority, and their refusal to take customary oaths were deliberately subversive in intent. Some even resorted to the form of witnessing called "going naked for a sign." The ancient prophets Samuel (I Samuel 19.24) and Isaiah had both prophesied in a naked state: "My servant Isaiah hath walked naked and barefoot three years for a sign and wonder upon Egypt and upon Ethiopia" (Isaiah 20.3). The Quaker William Simpson had set a famous example of this witness in England. Others followed his lead, so that one publication claimed: "In all great towns Quakers go naked on market days through the town."[13] In Massachusetts, the Quaker women Lydia Wardel and Deborah Wilson "came stark naked as ever they were born into our public assemblies, and they were (baggages as they were) adjudged unto the whipping post for that piece of devilism" (M 2.527).

One has to admit that the Quakers posed a terrible problem for the magistrates, whose first impulse was to throw the troublemakers into jail. People just flocked to hear them at their places of detention. Curiosity was piqued when the prisoners proclaimed fasts and periods of sexual abstinence. There were no remote places for long-term incarceration. Jail was just a holding place for those about to be tried or sentenced. When the Quakers were placed in the stocks, they turned them into pulpits for preaching their message. When they were stripped to the waist, both women and men, and savagely whipped in public, they just returned for more of the same. Some were maimed, beginning with the cropping of one ear—they came back to expose the other ear.[14]

Dragged to the border of the colony and thrown over it, they circled back to re-enter at another place. Death seemed the only thing left for dealing with them. Other repressive measures simply backfired, as when a seventeen-year-old girl, Provided Southwick, went about loudly protesting her parents' imprisonment and was put in the stocks, which created sympathy for her.[15] Earlier, an eleven-year-old, Patience Scott—the niece of Anne Hutchinson and the daughter of Catherine Scott, who helped lead Roger Williams into the Baptist denomination— went to jail with two Quakers she admired. The General Court could do nothing but bluster ineffectual pieties over the girl:

The Court, duly considering the malice of Satan and his
instruments—by all means and ways to propagate error and
disturb the truth and bring in confusion among us—that
Satan is put to his shifts to make use of such a child, not
being of the years of discretion, nor understanding the
principles of religion—judge meet so far to slight her as a
Quaker as only to admonish her according to her capacity
and so discharge her, Captain Hutchinson undertaking to
send her home.[16]

When the magistrates sent Lawrence and Cassandra Southwick into
exile, "the General Court demonstrated the extent to which it has lost
control of the problem by ordering the sale of the Southwick children.
No buyers were found."[17]

Other colonies agreed with Massachusetts that the Friends were a
pest—in 1657, four colonies made a joint petition that Rhode Island
make common cause to exclude Quakers from the whole region; but the
Rhode Island legislature made a common-sense response that Massachusetts would come in time to live with.

And as concerning these Quakers (so called) which are now
among us, we have no law among us whereby to punish any for
only declaring by words, etc. their minds and understandings
concerning the things and ways of God as to salvation and an
eternal condition. And we, moreover, find that in those places
where these people aforesaid in our colony are most of all
suffered to declare themselves freely, and are only opposed by
arguments in discourse, there they least of all desire to come;
and we are informed that they begin to loath this place, for they
are not opposed by the civil authority, but with all patience and
meekness are suffered to say any their pretended revelations
and admonitions, nor are they like or able to gain many here to
their way; and surely we find that they delight to be persecuted
by civil powers, and when they are so, they are like to gain

more adherents by the conceit [opinion] of their patient
sufferings than by consent to their pernicious sayings.[18]

The civil power in Massachusetts was, at that point, sadly lacking in
secular prudence. But the temporal arm was not really acting on its own.
Though the governor and other offices could not be clergymen, they had
to be communicants of the congregation, and only other communicants
could vote for them. The state, moreover, was authorized to exact taxes
for support of the churches (even from noncommunicants) and to compel attendance at the many services (even by noncommunicants) and to
support church doctrine as a condition of temporal order. Heresy, if not
technically a crime, was most often treated as one: when the church
adjudged a person heretical it was often doing, in effect, what the religious Inquisition did in Spain—turning a person over to the secular
authorities to carry out a punishment.

In the case of Mary Dyer, it was the governor of the colony, John
Winthrop, who exhumed the misshapen fetus of her miscarriage, to
show that she had had devilish intercourse.[19] In fact, as was already mentioned, the secular authorities strip-searched the first women Quakers to
reach the colony, looking for devil's marks upon them. Cotton Mather
invoked a pagan parallel for Dyer's case, the Pythian priestess who was
"possessed with a demon" (M 2.523). The Massachusetts separation of
church and state was a sheer formality, since the state was always acting
for and with the church.

The same pattern emerged from a surprising quarter in the 1670s,
from Rhode Island of all places. The colony, remember, had told the
Boston authorities not to get so wrought up by the Quakers. In 1660,
Roger Williams had written rather condescendingly to John Winthrop,
using the case of his friend Catherine Scott to show him how to handle a
problem.

Sir, my neighbor, Mrs. Scott, is come from England; and
(what the whip at Boston could not do) converse with friends
in England and their arguments, have, in a great measure,

drawn her from the Quakers, and usually from their meetings. Try the spirits. There are many abroad, and must be, but Lord will be glorious in plucking up whatever his holy hand hath not planted.[20]

But in the next decade Williams himself showed deep panic over the Quakers. The sect used its welcome in the colony to become so prosperous and powerful that Williams's own faction in the legislature tried to restrict its freedom of speech.[21] Then, when the Quaker leader George Fox came from England to America, Williams challenged Fox to a public dispute, and when he got no response, said that "this old Fox thought it best to run for it."[22] When other Quakers came forward to debate him, Williams published his own account of the encounter as *George Fox Digg'd Out of His Burrowes* (a double pun, on the names of Fox as a fox and of his supporter Edmund Burrough as a lair)

Williams, while not outlawing opinion as such, followed the Massachusetts example of turning religious offenders over to the secular arm as disturbers of the peace. He called for "a due and moderate restraint and punishing of these incivilities"—he lists such "incivilities" as interrupting meetings, using "thee" and "thou," preventing speakers from addressing them, and "the unnatural preaching of their women in public assemblies."[23] That the Quakers were notorious troublemakers he proved from the fact that "their ugly child and daughter, Rantism, rose from their bowels and practiced nakedness of men and women in the streets and in their religious meetings."[24] Their nakedness was an especial danger to social good order, since it might break out at any time, women exposing themselves in the very churches:

> I demanded of them how it should be known that it was the voice and command of God, the God of holiness, and not the command of the unclean Spirit? For I told them that, under that cover that one of them might be so commanded and sent in such a posture and behavior amongst men, why might not ten or twenty, yea, all the women in this present assembly, be so

stirred up as it were by the Spirit of God, to the horror and
amazement of the whole country, yea of the whole world?[25]

Nor were their views on the inner light mere opinions. They were the
promptings of the devil.[26] He agreed with Cotton Mather that their quaking was a sign of diabolical possession: "Such shaking, motions, ecstasies,
etc. were known to be the frequent working of Satan upon his servants in
all ages."[27] He repeatedly compares the Quakers to the papists, who were
the one sect excluded even by the Act of Toleration. He thought that
Catholics go beyond the Gospel in claiming that the Holy Spirit makes
special revelations to the pope, and Quakers go beyond it in claiming special revelations to individuals, making every person his or her own pope.
Quakers were "as simple and monstrous and blasphemous as the papists in
their foolish, monstrous and bloody transubstantiations."[28]

Edmund Morgan wonders at Williams's "unusual anger" and even
"hatred" for Quakers, opining that it might have come from his sense
that the inner light was a caricature version of his own belief in the
supremacy of conscience.[29] Roger Williams is considered a prophet of
the separation of church and state in the United States Constitution (a
matter to be treated later); but even he shows how difficult was such a
separation in seventeenth-century New England. Three important
Christian scholars have concluded that the separation of church and
state among the Puritans was nugatory or illusory:

Although sincere efforts were made to keep church and state
technically separate, in fact it was the state that established the
church in the colonies, saw to it that only true religion was
taught, required church attendance, banished dissenters, and
even called church synods. In Massachusetts Bay the voting
franchise was limited to church members, with the corollary that
only church members were eligible for public office. Behind all
the practical confusion of church and state was the overriding
presumption that New England was the New Israel.[30]

3. ULTRA-SUPERNATURALISM

ONE REASON it was so hard to separate church and state before the Enlightenment is that it was just as hard to separate the spheres of the natural and the supernatural. The Puritans believed in natural law. It was the sphere of the Covenant of Works between God and Adam, as opposed to the Covenant of Grace between Jesus Christ and the saved. But it was hard to keep these two spheres apart, since both God and the devil so often and dramatically crossed the barrier between them, intruding in both. The Puritans tended to see all events as (on the one hand) divine blessings or punishments, or (on the other hand) as diabolical temptations or afflictions. Cotton Mather devoted a whole book of his seven-book *Magnalia Christi Americana* to "Remarkables of the Divine Providence Among the People of New England." He tried to distinguish lightning and thunder loosed by Satan and that sent by God (M 22.361–62)—a difficult matter since God sometimes uses the devil as his agent to punish sinners (W 45–46). Devils could act on their own initiative, and they had power over nature, reshaping its "plastic" stuff to override natural law.[31] In his own life, Mather traced the continual divine incursions into his psyche that he called "particular faiths," allowing him to prophesy events.[32] At one point, a resplendent angel appeared to him.[33] But he also experienced diabolical interventions.

In a world so porous to supernatural visitations, people found confirmation of their hopes or fears in any blessing or disaster. After Anne Hutchinson had been expelled from the Bay Colony for her heresies, she was killed by marauding Indians, which John Winthrop took as a divine confirmation of the colony's judgment on her: "God's hand is the more apparently seen herein, to pick out this woeful woman, to make her and those belonging to her an unheard-of heavy example."[34] For the way both sides interpreted events as divine judgments, consider two readings of a single episode. When the crowd that returned from the first Quaker hangings broke down a bridge with its numbers, John Davenport, the founder of the New Haven township, saw the collapse as a divine judgment on the Quakers, but the Quakers said that it showed how God was punishing their persecutors.[35]

In fact, Quakers declared that Governor Endecott died early as a punishment for condemning Mary Dyer and that John Norton, a minister who supported the death penalty for Quakers, was struck down by a stroke after his grandchildren died sudden deaths.[36] Another judge, Samuel Sewall, feared that a similar divine vengeance would be visited upon him. After he repented his part in the execution of witches on "spectral" evidence, he feared that God would strike down his children in retaliation for what he had done to the women victims. This invocation of "signs" was so common that Roger Williams noted an eclipse of the sun on the day of his first debate with the Quakers as a proof that God was backing him up.[37]

To prove the diabolical nature of Mary Dyer, Governor Winthrop dwelt with grim satisfaction on the monstrous nature of her stillborn child, which, as we have seen, he had disinterred six months after its secret burial, as part of the proceedings against her friend, Anne Hutchinson (whose miscarriage was also dug up).

> [It was] so monstrous and misshapen as the like hath scarce
> been heard of. It had no head, but a face which stood so low
> upon the breast as the ears (which were like an ape's) grew
> upon the shoulders. The eyes stood far out, so did the mouth;
> the nose was hooking upward; the breast and back was full of
> sharp prickles, like a thornback; the navel and all the belly, with
> the distinction of the [female] sex, were where the lower part
> of the back and hips should have been, and those back parts
> were on the side [where] the face stood. The arms and hands,
> with the thighs and legs, were as other children's, but instead of
> toes it had upon each foot three claws, with talons like a young
> fowl. Upon the back, above the belly, it had two great holes like
> mouths, and in each of them stuck out a piece of flesh. It had
> no forehead but, in the place above the eyes, four horns,
> whereof two were above an inch long, hard and sharp; the
> other two were somewhat shorter.[38]

Winthrop adds further "evidence" of diabolical intervention. The midwife at the delivery "was notorious for familiarity with the devil," and the bed shook violently at the moment of the delivery (appropriately for a "quaking" mother). Winthrop cannot let go of his fascination with the devilish birth, calling it in another place "a woman child, a fish, a beast, and a fowl all woven together in one, and without an head."[39] He links Dyer's baby with Anne Hutchinson's miscarriage, which is equally or more "monstrous":

> She brought forth not one (as Mistress Dyer did) but—which was more strange, to amazement—thirty monstrous births (or thereabouts) at once; some of them bigger, some lesser, some of one shape, some of another; few of any perfect shape, none at all of them (as far as I could ever learn) of human shape. . . . And see how the wisdom of God fitted this judgment to her sin everyway, for look! as she vented misshapen opinions, so she must bring forth deformed monsters; and as about thirty opinions in number, so many monsters; and as those were public and not in a corner mentioned, so this is now come to be known and famous over all these churches and a great part of the world. And though he that runs may read their sin in these judgments yet behold! the desperate and stupendous hardness of heart in these persons and their followers, who were so far from seeing the finger of God in all these dreadful passages that they turned all from themselves upon the faithful servants of God that labored to reclaim them.[40]

He concludes of the two portents:

> This loud-speaking providence from heaven in the monsters did much awaken many of their followers (especially the tenderer sort) to attend God's meaning therein; and made them at such a stand that they dared not slight so manifest a sign from heaven.[41]

The providential view of life is clear in works like Increase Mather's history of King Philip's War, where setbacks are divine punishments and victories are divine blessings.[42] The sufferings of the people, whether from plague, quake, fires, or crime—all of them expressed God's anger, prompting "Jeremiad" sermons, calling for the people to repent their sins if they wanted to end God's punishment.

4. SATAN'S REALM

THOUGH GOD was thought to work miracles of deliverance for his people, the devil seemed to be the most active agent in the minds of Puritans. Few shared Cotton Mather's privilege of seeing an angel, but many saw evidence of Satan at work all around them. Since the devil was the Prince of This World, his minions policed the whole of nature with furious energy, but with special attention to God's chosen people in New England. Cotton Mather's views were widely shared: "I believe that never were more Satanical devices used for the unsettling of any people under the sun than what have been employed for the extirpation of the vine which God has here planted" (W 13). The air was clogged with devils, far outnumbering the human inhabitants of New England. "The devils are so many that some thousands can sometimes at once apply themselves to vex one child of man. . . . They swarm about us, like the frogs of Egypt, in the most retired of our chambers. . . . We are poor travelers in a world which is as well the devils' field as the devils' jail, a world in every nook whereof the devil is encamped" (W 44, 63). Satan had many allies pressing upon the Puritans' settlements and undermining them from within—the Indians' false gods, the Jesuit missionaries working with the Indians, the witches collaborating with those alien forces, the "Familists" and Antinomians and Quakers posing as godly people, each a kind of Antichrist. This galaxy of evil obsessed the Puritan psyche (see next chapter). "I believe that never was a poor plantation more pursued by the wrath of the devil than our poor New England" (W 74).

If we now think the reaction to Mary Dyer was overwrought, we must remember that her foes saw her backed by the tremendous power of the devils prompting her. Only that can explain the way people felt that they had to kill her in self-defense, before she killed their spiritual condition. She was only one person, but her sponsors were "legion." As the Bay Colony magistrates put it:

> The Quakers died not because [of] their other crimes, however
> capital, but upon their superadded presumptuous and
> incorrigible contempt of authority, breaking in upon us
> notwithstanding their sentence of banishment made known to
> them. Had they not been restrained, so far as appeared, there was
> too much cause to fear that ourselves must quickly have died.[43]

A similar fear of entertaining hell's energies in the colony made magistrates expel Anne Hutchinson. According to Governor Winthrop, since "Satan seemed to have commission now to use his utmost cunning to undermine the kingdom of Christ here," therefore "the Court saw now an inevitable necessity to rid her [Hutchinson] away, except we would be guilty not only of our own ruin but also of the Gospel's."[44]

5. THE END TIME

A HYPERTROPHIC ACTIVITY of evil was expected in the colonies because the world was racing to an end. Cotton Mather wrote, "He [Satan] knows he hath but a short time" (W 57). The leaders of the Reformation had predicted that the end was near "when his [Satan's] antichristian vicar, the seven-headed beast on the seven-hilled city, shall have spent his determined years" (W 57). "We are entering into the seventh day of the Romish Jericho."[45] Martin Luther was so sure that history was coming to an end that he rushed to complete his translation of Daniel before that could happen.[46] Even the great scientist Isaac Newton had used the biblical books of Daniel and Revelation to work out complicated chronologies for the approaching Apocalypse.

The biblical signs were eagerly sought and found. Cotton Mather heard the end approaching in a drumbeat of plagues, catastrophes, fires—and especially of earthquakes, produced by "the energy of the devil in the earth" (W 60). His father, Increase, specialized rather in the interpretation of aerial phenomena—comets, lightning, eclipses, storms.[47] David Hall refers to such works as "portent-mongering."[48] It is not surprising that a foreign visitor to Boston in 1699 found men there "running melancholy-mad about some mystery of the Revelation."[49]

6. AMERICA'S MISSION

THE PURITANS were especially interested in the completion of God's plan because they were given the starring role in it. They were to be what Edmund Morgan has called "the millennial headquarters." God had assigned them what Samuel Danforth, in his Election Sermon of 1670, called a special "errand into the wilderness." "Wilderness" was a theologically charged term for them. It did not mean an uninhabited place. It meant the devil's lair. Being sent into it made the Puritans the advance guard of God's army in the showdown battle. Jesus had been taken into the wilderness to be tempted by the devil (Matthew 4.1). It is the place to which the devil drives the possessed (Luke 8.29). It is where an exorcised devil goes (Matthew 12.43). It is the resort of devil-terrorists (Acts 21.38). Richard Mather said that the people of God must go through the wilderness to reach Canaan.[50] His grandson Cotton put it this way: "The wilderness through which we are passing to the promised land is all over filled with fiery flying serpents" (W 63). "The New Englanders are a people of God settled in those parts which were once the devil's territorie" (W 143).

> It is written concerning our Lord Jesus Christ "that he was led into the wilderness to be tempted of the devil," and the people of the Lord Jesus Christ, "led into the wilderness" of New England, have not only met with a continual temptation of the devil there—the wilderness having always had serpents in it—but also they have had, in almost every new luster [lustrum] of years, a new assault of extraordinary temptation

upon them, a more than common "hour and power of
darkness." (M 2.490)

When John Winthrop told the first settlers of the Bay Colony that
they were to be "as a city upon a hill," where "the eyes of *all people* are
upon us," he meant that America would be the completion of the Reformation, a pattern of what a pure church should be at the fulfillment of
time. Cotton Mather opined that God had sent these people to this place
in order that "He might there, *to* them first and then *by* them, give a spec-
imen of many good things which He would have His churches elsewhere aspire and arise unto ... to consider the light which, from the
midst of this 'outer darkness,' is now to be darted over unto the other
side of the Atlantic Ocean" (M 1.27). Samuel Sewall asked why "the heart
of America may not be the seat of the New Jerusalem."[51] America would
thus be a "God-City" (*Theopolis*):

> Our glorious Lord will have an holy city in America, a city
> the streets whereof will be pure gold. We cannot imagine that
> the brave countries and gardens which fill the American hemi-
> sphere were made for nothing but a place of dragons. We
> may not image that when the kingdom of God is come and
> his will is done on earth as it is done in heaven—which we
> had never been taught to pray for if it must not one day be
> accomplished—a balancing half of the globe shall remain in
> the hands of the devil, who is then to be chained up from
> deceiving the nations.[52]

Samuel Sewall made his own collection of signs in *Phaenomena Quaedam
Apocalyptica ad Aspectum Novi Orbis Configurata: Some Few Lines Towards a
Description of the New Heaven as It Makes to Those Who Stand upon the New
Earth* (1697). In a later book on Revelation, Sewall says that the angel who
puts his left foot on earth and his right foot on the sea is putting the former on Europe and the latter [the favored one] on America, as the land
of the sea.[53] These millennial hopes for America were not restricted to

this side of the ocean. In England, the great religious poet George Herbert expressed a broader Protestant hope for the end of history coming in the New World.

> *Religion stands on tip-toe in our land,*
> *Ready to pass to the American strand.*
> *When height of malice, and prodigious lusts,*
> *Impudent sinning, witchcrafts, and distrusts*
> *(The mark of future bane) shall fill our cup*
> *Unto the brim, and make our measure up;*
> *When Seine shall swallow Tiber—and the Thames,*
> *By letting in them both, pollutes her streams—*
> *When Italy of us shall have her will*
> *And all her calendar of sins fulfill;*
> *Whereby one may foretell what sins next year*
> *Shall both in France and England domineer;*
> *Then shall religion to America flee.*
> *They have their times of Gospel, ev'n as we.*[54]

Herbert and many others hoped that the Reformation, Revelation, and the End Time would all be culminated and vindicated in a new land where God was at last worshiped as he had prescribed. The stakes were high. So were the hopes. So were the costs—as Mary Dyer learned.

2 | THE PURITAN PSYCHE

THE EARLY SETTLERS of New England faced many foes, visible and invisible. These enemies were leagued with one another against God and against his chosen people. This made for high spiritual drama in their lives, an exciting drama but also a terrifying one. Like Protestants everywhere, they faced this struggle in an almost naked state, stripped of many of the protections that their medieval forebears had worn. Keith Thomas, the most acclaimed scholar of the occult, notes that Roman Catholic practice had supplied believers with many shields against devils and their evil power—guardian angels, patron saints, exorcism, sacramental confession, holy water, priestly blessings, crucifixes and other sacred images. Protestant believers had rejected all of these as superstitions, but had retained the dark magic they were meant to counter.

Increase Mather found every form of superstition a way of interacting with the devil, not of defying him. The supposed protections against the devil, in Mather's eyes, were tools of the devil. Even the hanging of lucky horseshoes over doors was a hellish act.[1] Thomas describes the Protestant situation:

> Men thus became accustomed to Satan's immediacy. . . . It
> seemed that God had given Satan a free rein. . . . Protestantism
> forced its adherents into the intolerable position of asserting
> the reality of witchcraft, yet denying the existence of an
> effective and legitimate form of protection or cure.[2]

That is why Catholic countries did not have witch executions on the
scale of Protestant realms. The Catholic Inquisition burned heretics, but
it did not, for the most part, hang witches.

> In England, witch prosecution and the Reformation arrived
> together. For what the religious changes in the mid-sixteenth
> century did was to eliminate the protective ecclesiastical magic
> which had kept the threat of sorcery under control. It was
> because of the popular faith in such remedies that so few
> instances of positive *maleficium* had been alleged in the Middle
> Ages, even though the belief in witchcraft was already in
> existence. In medieval England a man need not be hurt by
> witches, so long as he observed the prescriptions of the
> Church. If he did not, he would not be likely to complain.
> Faith in ecclesiastical magic was thus the obstacle to witch
> prosecution.[3]

New England did not have a monopoly on the fear of witches. Old
England had a longer and bloodier record. If cases in Scotland are
added to the English tally, nearly a thousand people were executed as
witches.[4] Nor were American witch trials limited to New England.
Witches were executed in Virginia and Maryland in 1659, and trials and
penalties occurred in New York, Pennsylvania, and the Carolinas.[5] Yet
there is no denying that seventeenth-century New England was witch-
obsessed, with an exceptionally virulent spasm in Salem Village during
the year 1692. In Salem, nineteen witches (five of them men) were
hanged, and one (another man) was pressed to death. In the rest of New

England, an additional fourteen (two of them men) were hanged. There were also people scheduled or likely to be executed who either died in jail or escaped, and convictions on lesser forms of witchcraft led to whippings, exile, and fines. So execution was just the tip of the iceberg. The general miasma of fear and accusation can be measured from the fact that there were about 160 witch accusations brought in the small village area of Salem, and over 130 brought in the rest of New England.[6]

The Puritan psyche was ghoul-haunted in a way that is hard for us to imagine now. That is why David Hall finds, in the vast diaries of Samuel Sewall, a constant insecurity and fear of dark forces.

> Versed in matters of theology, Sewall almost never used the language he was trained in as a Harvard student. He thought in terms of wonders and life-crises; he yearned to protect his family and New England even as he struggled to accept the lesson of affliction. It is this yearning for protection that, from start to finish, unifies the diary and emerges as the substance of religion.[7]

Sewall yearned for security, but he had been deprived of the ancient means of assuring it. The same was true for many of his fellows. The dark forces compassing them round left regenerate souls with only their own individual status as "saved" to rely on—putting great pressure on their inner resources of conscience and faith (see the next chapter). The major factors in their mental cosmology can be represented as concentric circles pressing in on them from all directions.

The outermost ring, that of Satan, is not a separate, far less a distant, element in this scheme. He pervades all five of the other concentric rings—pervades everything but the core of chosen ones living in grace. The most distant of these five rings also has a relation to the rest, since paganism was the paradigm of false religion as that was defined for the Puritans by their favorite church father, Augustine.

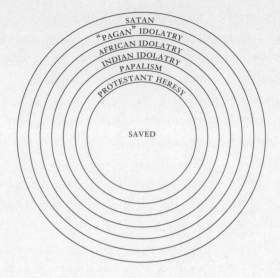

I. "PAGAN" IDOLATRY

IN AUGUSTINE's *City of God,* Books VI–X, paganism is not simply an erroneous belief. The idols of paganism were devils, and religion, when it was not directed to the true God, was a field of diabolic activity. Wooing people from such false beliefs was an act not only of charity but of self-defense. The devil, left unchecked, would ravage believers in the true religion, converting it to idolatry—just as the Gospel had been corrupted into the multiple idolatries of papal Rome. Each of the other rings in the psychological "cosmos" of the Puritans contained a variant of devil worship. But for paganism in the old (Augustinian) sense, the clearest modern variant was Islam, the "false belief" that was menacing Europe in the Turkish incursions. Defeating the Turks was thus almost as important as defeating the Whore of Babylon. Indeed, Protestants had considered them the two outstanding (and cognate) embodiments of the Antichrist. Luther taught that "the spirit of Antichrist is the Pope, his flesh is the Turk."[8]

Protestant eschatology found many references to the Turks in Revelation. For John Bale and George Fox, they were the Beast from the Abyss (Revelation 11.7). Since that figure had already been assigned to the pope,

Catholics and Turks jostled along together toward the End Time, competitor-collaborators in evil. They were, as Bale put it, "the cruel, crafty, and cursed generation of Antichrist—the pope with his bishops, prelates, priests, and religious in Europe; Mahomet with his doting dousepers [paladins] in Africa, and so forth in Asia and India."[9] Thus the defeat of the Turks was one of the eschatological signs that New Englanders anticipated. It was their principal reason for studying the progress of European nations in their struggle with Islam.

Almost as distant as the Turkish threat was, for New Englanders, the "false religion" of the Jews. Admittedly, all forms of Christianity were poisoned with anti-Semitism, and Protestant settlers brought that poison with them to America.[10] But the Puritans' anti-Semitism lacked special virulence. Their sense of themselves as God's chosen people made them see many parallels between their own history and that of the Jews. The crossing of the Atlantic and the advance into the wilderness were constantly called their own Exodus and crossing of the Red Sea and passage toward Canaan. Many of the learned ministers of New England knew Hebrew, and they pored over the Jewish Scripture as carefully as over the New Testament. The Puritans were optimistic about the prophesied conversion of the Jews as an imminent sign of apocalypse. Increase Mather wrote two works predicting it—*The Mystery of Israel's Salvation Explained and Applyed* (1669) and *A Dissertation Concerning the Future Conversion of the Jewish Nation* (1704). Samuel Sewall linked the two great apocalyptic signs, "Turks going down" and "Jews call'd."[11] Though the devil was still at work in the Jewish religion, Puritans felt that his hold on them was weaker than on any of the other forms of devil worship they had to contend with.

Some modern neoconservatives, cultivating their ties to modern Israel, find a "Hebraic foundation" for America in the founding period. While it is true that the Puritans considered themselves "the new Israel," they thought that meant a replacement of the old Israel, not an embrace of it. It is silly to argue, with Michael Novak (of the American Enterprise Institute), that Americans were saluting the Jews of their day by taking names like Abraham and Rebecca. In the same vein, Novak claims that the Declaration of Independence has four references to God under his "Hebrew names"—the names being unmistakably Deist terms like "nature's God," "creator," "supreme judge of the world," and "divine providence"![12] Besides, as Roger Williams said, the turning of Massachusetts into God's singular instrument was a form of idolatry, a judgment with which Christian scholars now concur. A national covenant, they say, distorts the message of Jesus, who said the Spirit will not dwell in a single house (John 4.21–24).[13]

2. AFRICAN IDOLATRY

THE RELIGION that slaves brought with them out of Africa was, in Protestant eyes, an idolatry (that is, a form of devil worship). That is why converting slaves was an act not only of charity toward them but of protection on the settlers' part. The Christianizing of slaves has been looked at, in our times, as a form of spiritual imperialism—depriving them of their heritage. Jon Butler even calls the "death of the African gods" a spiritual holocaust.[14] Albert Raboteau describes the systematic efforts to suppress African religion as one of the means of "slave control."[15]

Of course, the record of dealing with the religion of slaves was as contradictory as all the other aspects of that damnable business. Since so many considered blacks subhuman, the ability to impress them with religious truth was doubted, even when it was considered desirable. Cotton Mather put it bluntly: "Their stupidity is a discouragement. It may seem unto as little purpose to teach as to wash an Ethiopian."[16] Teaching them would challenge racist stereotypes that made it easier to treat them as property. That is why the missionary effort was never as straightforward with blacks as it was with Native Americans.

But Mather also knew that letting devil worship continue in America was dangerous. The Africans were, after all, "vassals of Satan" and "servants of Iniquity."[17]

A roaring lion who goes about seeking whom he may devour
[1 Peter 5.8] hath made seizure of them. Very many of them do

with devilish rites actually worship devils, or maintain a
magical conversation with devils. And all of them are more
slaves to Satan than they are to you [slaveholders], until a faith
in the Son of God has made them free indeed. Will you do
nothing to pluck them out of the jaws of Satan the Devourer?[18]

Mather assures masters that conversion of their slaves "dulcifies and
mollifies" them.[19] Indeed, with his customary ultra-supernaturalism, he
warns them that, if rebellious slaves trouble them, God may be using
them to punish the owners for not converting their charges.[20]

Even in the less devil-haunted colonies, the fear of African religion
was a constant threat. There were many fears that associated the devil
with blackness—including the myths of the mark of Cain and the curse
of Ham (both arising from misreadings of the Bible). Like Mather,
Samuel Sewall felt he had to refute the idea that blacks were under the
curse of Ham.[21] Even the devils that haunted the woods during the
witch craze in Massachusetts were called "black men," a tradition that
Hawthorne recalled in *The Scarlet Letter.*

3. INDIAN IDOLATRY

FOR THE COLONISTS in general, and not merely for those in New
England, the conversion of American Indians was an official prior-
ity. Protestant England felt that as the End Time approached, the
Gospel had to be preached throughout the world. That was as true of the
Virginia settlements as of the New England ones. In the Charter of 1606,
King James declared that he was incorporating the Virginia Company
for "propagating of Christian religion to such people as yet live in dark-
ness and miserable ignorance of the true knowledge and worship of
God."[22] Two years later, the introduction to Captain John Smith's *True
Relation* said that the Virginia settlement was dedicated "to the erecting
of true religion among infidels, to the overthrow of superstition and
idolatry, to the winning of many thousands of wandering sheep unto
Christ's fold who now, and till now, have strayed in the unknown paths

of paganism, idolatry, and superstition."[23] Not only Virginia, but Massachusetts and Connecticut, had in their early documents a declaration of the duty to propagate the true religion to "the barbarous natives" (as a statement of Yale's trustees put it in 1701).[24]

The Virginians were not the active proselytizers that New Englanders were. But the official position was that Indian religion was idolatrous, and therefore under diabolic influence. That is why John Rolfe felt he had to defend at length his marriage to Pocahontas. In his famous letter to Sir Thomas Dale, he grants "her manners barbarous, her generation accursed"—that is why he thinks of his engagement to her as "a dangerous combat." But he sees the outcome as "a holy work" since it involves "converting of one unregenerate to regeneration," a project whose success is foreseen because of "her desire to be taught and instructed in the knowledge of God."[25] There is no doubting the religious sincerity of Rolfe, and Perry Miller warned against taking too lightly the early Virginians' religious commitments.[26]

Concern over the religion of the Indians was keener in New England because the proximity of the devil was more sharply feared. The idolatry of black Africans was less frightening—they had been captured and taken away from the original arena of their dark rites. Indians, by contrast, were the incumbents of the land, with idolatries in their native place of power, under the Lord of the Wilderness. The founders of Harvard felt an urgency to convert the Indians, "who have ever sat in hellish darkness adoring the devil himself for the God . . . [to cause] our very bowels yearning within us to see them go down to hell by swarms without remedy." Yet even while trying to convert them, one had to stay away from contamination by them: "We are wont to keep them at such a distance (knowing they serve the devil and are led by him) as not to embolden them too much or trust them too far."[27] As Cotton Mather put it: "The devils are stark mad that the House of the Lord our God is come into these remote corners of the world, and they fume, they fret prodigiously."[28] The Indians were the instruments of these devils' revenge. "The Indian powaws [conjurors] used all their sorceries to molest the first planters here" (W 74). "That the powaws, by the infernal spirits, often killed persons, caused lameness and impotency, as well as showed their art in performing things beyond human (by diabolic) skill—such who have conversed much among them have had no reason to question" (M 2.426).

When Roger Williams argued that the settlers had no right to the land they had seized, John Winthrop answered that the Indians were the true usurpers: "If we had no right to this land, yet our God hath right to it, and if he be pleased to give it us (taking it from a people who had so long usurped upon him and abused his creatures) who shall control him or his terms?"[29] The "abuse of creatures" is the making of idols. The necessity of countering the devil's claims was a matter of self-reproach for New Englanders when they felt they had neglected it. The preachers of jeremiads blamed the colonies' afflictions on lack of zeal to convert more Indians. Increase Mather said that it was one of the things that brought on King Philip's War.[30]

The colonists were sometimes drawn into contests between the native gods and the Christian God—as when desperate men in drought-stricken Connecticut asked a friendly Indian, Unkas, to have his sorcerers bring them rain. Increase Mather tells how Unkas tried, but his "powaws" were unsuccessful.

> He therefore sent westward to a noted powaw, to try his skill, but neither could that wizard, by all his hideous and diabolical howlings, obtain showers. Whereupon he (i.e., Unkas) applied himself to Mr. Fitch, the faithful and able teacher of the church in Norwich, desiring that he would pray to God for rain. Mr. Fitch replied to him that if he should do so, and God should hear him, as long as their powaws were at work, they would ascribe the rain to them and think that the devil whom the Indians worship, and not God, had sent that rain. And therefore he would not set himself to pray for it until they had done with the vanities and witcheries. Unkas and his son Orinico declared that they had left off powawing, despairing to obtain what they desired. Mr. Fitch therefore called his church

together, and they set themselves by fasting and prayer to ask
of the Lord rain in the time of the latter rain, and behold! that
very night and the next day, He that said to the small rain and
the great rain of his strength, "Be thou upon the earth," gave
most plentiful showers, inasmuch as the heathen were affected
therewith, acknowledging that the God whom we serve is a
great God, and there is none like unto him.[31]

As if the Indians' own idolatry were not enough, it was—to the Puritans' horror—combined with the papistry of the French Canadians, whose Catholic missionaries were spreading that contamination from the Old World to the New World. The most feared of all Catholics, the Jesuits, were especially active in the Indian territories. The Indians they converted were, according to Increase Mather, "twofold more the children of Hell than they were before."[32] One Jesuit was hated with special fervor—Sebastian Rasle (or Rale). He began his missionary work in 1689, and he became a political target for New Englanders because he kept telling the Indians that British purchases of their land were invalid—the men who sold it (often bribed with drink or trinkets) had no right to sell what belonged to the whole people. In 1724, after many years of conflict with this brilliant priest, a party was sent out from Massachusetts to capture or kill him.[33] It brought back his scalp for bounty.[34]

The narratives of Indian captivity were so spellbinding to New Englanders because the captives were taken into the devil's own lair. The story of their ordeal and rescue was a modern version of Daniel going into the lions' den, of Joseph's time in bondage, or of the Israelites' captivity in Egypt. During their period of bondage, they were tempted to take part in devilish rites, to marry ungodly spouses, or even to adopt the religion of the Jesuits.[35] When a captive came back with his or her (usually her) faith strengthened by the ordeal, the community took inspiration from the story. Increase Mather wrote the introduction to the most famous such tale, Mary Rowlandson's *The Sovereignty and Goodness of God* (1682), and Cotton Mather praised the way Rowlandson defied the diabolic rites she witnessed.

Almost as famous in her own time as Mary Rowlandson was Hannah Duston, whose feats were celebrated by Cotton Mather and later remembered in the writings of John Greenleaf Whittier, Henry Thoreau, and Nathaniel Hawthorne. Duston saw her newborn baby killed in an Indian raid, during which she and the infant's nurse were taken off to captivity. With the help of another captive, a young boy, she took a hatchet one night and killed ten sleeping Indians, six of them children. After fleeing, she remembered that she could get a bounty for the scalps of any Indians killed, so she went back to cut off the ten scalps (the children's included). She was acclaimed and rewarded in her home community of Haverhill, Massachusetts, and Mather compared her feat to that of the Jewish heroine Jael, who drove a stake through the head of the sleeping Sisera (Judges 4.21), a feat celebrated in the Song of Deborah:

> *Blest above women shall Jael,*
> *the wife of Heber the Kenite be,*
> *blessed shall she be above women in the tent.*
> *He asked water, and she gave him milk,*
> *she brought forth butter in a lordly dish.*
> *She put her hand to the nail*
> *and her right hand to the workman's hammer;*
> *and with the hammer she smote Sisera,*
> *she smote off his head,*
> *when she had pierced and stricken through his temples.*
> *At her feet he bowed, he fell, he lay down;*
> *at her feet he bowed, he fell;*
> *where he bowed, there he fell down dead.* (Judges 5.24–27)

Mather celebrates the triumph of Hannah in the very words of Deborah's song:

> She heartened the nurse and the youth to assist her in this
> enterprise; and all furnishing themselves with hatchets for the
> purpose, they struck such home blows upon the heads of their

sleeping oppressors that, ere they could any of them struggle
into any effectual resistance, at the feet of these poor prisoners
they bowed, they fell, they lay down; at their feet they bowed,
they fell; where they bowed, there they fell down dead. (M 2.636)

We may find it hard to sympathize with this young mother who
scalped six children—certainly Hawthorne did not condone her.[36] That
may be because we do not grasp the importance the diabolic plays in
her story. Hannah was dealing with what Mather calls "devils in flesh"
(M 2.566). What is more, these devils had tried to force her to say the
Romish prayers *three times a day* (M 2.635). (Though Mather did not know
it, the priests had obviously taught Indians the three daily hours of the
Angelus prayer.) Furthermore, the Indians taunted her, daring her to
show that her God could deliver her. No wonder the warlike spirit of the
holy murderesses of Scripture rose up in her, the spirit of Jael, or of
Judith beheading Holofernes. At least, that is the way her home community understood what she and her coadjutors did:

> Cutting off the scalps of the ten wretches, they came off,
> and received fifty pounds from the General Assembly of the
> province as a recompense of their action. Besides which, they
> received many presents of congratulations from their more
> private friends. But none gave them a greater taste of bounty
> than Colonel Nicholson, the Governor of Maryland, who,
> hearing of their action, sent them a very generous token of
> his favor. (M 2.636)

These Puritans were a hard lot. But they felt they had to be when dealing
with the devil.

The way the concentric circles of concern I have traced "bled" into
one another helps explain the great witch scare of Salem in 1692. This
has been explained in all kinds of ways, no one of them entirely satisfy-
ing to historical curiosity. A neglected aspect of the case is the way the
Indian threat pervaded it. Yet Frederick Drake rightly lists as an element

causing the witch panic the fact that "American Puritans were openly confronted with the Indians as positive instruments of Satan's power and determination to conquer New England for himself."[37] There was a fear that the devils at work with the witches were the same as those using the Indians. There were strong clues of this for the suspicious New Englander. One of the accused who died in prison, Sarah Osborne, said that she "either saw or dreamed that she saw a thing like an Indian, all black, which did pinch her in her neck."[38]

It was natural to fear a confederacy between the external foes (Indians) and "an enemy within," a "fifth column" of collaborators with the outside threat, lurking perhaps in "sleeper cells." What, for instance, if those returning from captivity had been "programmed" to do their bidding? A case of that was suspected in Boston when Mercy Short came back from Canada. Her parents and three siblings had been murdered when she was kidnapped, at age fifteen, from Salmon Falls, New Hampshire. After her ransom two years later, she was an unstable young woman who had visions of the devil as "a tawny man," and she told Cotton Mather and others that in her visions of devil gatherings she saw Indian sagamores present.[39] Mary Toothaker, another accused witch, also saw the devil "in the shape of a tawney man."[40]

Indians flit in and out of the witch crisis. Since one of the illusions was the devil's ability to take on a person's "spectral" appearance, Cotton Mather thought it important to record that "spectral" Indians had been seen (M 2.620–23). And two decidedly unspectral Indians were at the very center of the story—John and Tituba, the married slaves of Samuel Parris. When Parris's daughter and her cousin were thought to be afflicted with witchcraft, John and Tituba helped a woman bake a "witch pie" with some of the girls' urine, to be tested on a dog (whose response would determine whether they were bewitched).[41] When Tituba was indicted for witchcraft (along with Sarah Osborne), she became a great source of information on other witches in the community—a process somewhat like modern "turning state's evidence" which let "confessing" witches save their lives by sending others to their death. Tituba gave examiners extensive information on other witches, their "familiars," their night rides.[42]

It might be asked why a woman, an Indian, a slave, should have been so readily believed in a society prejudiced against all three. But the very fact that she was an Indian meant that she was more privy than others to the devil's activity. In the fear of an "enemy within," those who knew about the external foe using the inner cells were especially valuable. There is a parallel with the fear of an internal Communist threat during the time when the Soviet Union was a menacing outer peril. One of the confessing witches, William Barker, told how witches from Connecticut had planted what we would now call "sleeper" agents—307 of them!—in Massachusetts.[43] Mary Toothaker gave what looked like confirming testimony when she said that there were 305 secret witches in the country.[44] It is easy to see how such reports would have inflamed suspicion—one thinks of those who in the 1950s "thought there was a Communist under every bed." Tituba was trusted as an Indian just as ex-Communists were favorite informers during the McCarthy era. They knew the face of the enemy. They had been to hell and back. A similar line of thought let confessing witches send others to death in 1692. Satan strengthened each of the concentric circles in the Puritan psyche by its interplay with the others—of Indians with the papacy, and of witches with Indians.

4. PAPALISM

ANTI-CATHOLICISM has a long but not a unitary history in America. It would take many different forms. Enlightenment anti-Catholicism, evident in John Adams or Thomas Jefferson, opposed the authoritarian unity of European church and state—which was not exactly the complaint of the Puritans, with their own blend of church and state. The Enlightenment also feared Rome's opposition to reason, science, and free thought—manifested in the silencing of Galileo and the burning of Giordano Bruno. This, too, could not be quite as shocking to the Puritans, who were no slouches at heresy hunting themselves. Nativist anti-Catholicism, by contrast, would exploit ethnic hatreds for the Irish, the Italians, the Germans. Then a more populist objection to Catholicism arose, a democratic revulsion from the monarchical airs of the hierarchy. This was exasperated by chauvinist views of what is "un-American." Some of this resentment fed on ignorance and appealed to the uneducated. Nothing could be farther from the highly educated anti-Catholicism of colonial New England.

Puritan anti-Catholicism, despite some emotional sympathies with later kinds of bias, was deeply different from them. Far from being anti-theological, like that of Jefferson, it was super-theological. It was central to the whole structure of Puritan thought. It was its organizing principle. The Reformation's very raison d'être was a break with the usurpations and corruptions of the papal system. The early Protestants had to defend this rupture by a constant defining of their differences from the past. And this centrality of Rome in their thinking was echoed and emphasized by the importance of Rome to the future. The Apocalypse was as much defined by the defeat of the papacy as was the Reformation itself. Puritans agreed with the Protestant preacher William Fulke that "there are more Antichrists than the Pope, although he be the chief that sitteth in the temple of god."[45] As such, Rome and the pope were the leading figures in Revelation. They were the Beast from the Abyss, the Scarlet Woman, the animal with seven heads (for the seven hills of Rome), or the Great Babylon. Christ could not come again but by the defeat of this diabolical institution. Satan had minions among black Africans and Native Americans. But his real stake in history was on the seven hills of Rome. All his eggs were in that basket. Reading Scripture properly meant, for New England, seeing the importance of that dark kingdom and the even greater importance of its overthrow.[46]

Peter Lake claims that papalism was so central to the psyche of Puritans that they needed it for self-definition:

> Certainly to many, if not most, educated Protestant English
> people of the period popery was an anti-religion, a perfectly
> symmetrical negative image of true Christianity. Anti-Christ
> was an agent of Satan, sent into the Church to corrupt and take
> it over from within. . . . Since the Protestant analysis of popish
> anti-Christianity proceeded through a series of binary

oppositions, every negative characteristic imputed to Rome
implied a positive cultural, political, or religious value which
Protestants claimed as their own exclusive property. Thus the
Protestants' negative image of popery can tell us a great deal
about their positive image of themselves.[47]

The need to distinguish themselves from the Catholic past led to a fear
that crypto-papalism would seep back into their ecclesiastical polity.
Roger Williams said that it had never been entirely expelled, that those
Puritans who kept up ties with the Anglican Church, with its bishops
and sacraments and canonized saints, were papists at heart.

No charge was hurled with greater intent to wound than the charge
that other Puritans were crypto-Catholics. It was noted in the preceding
chapter that Roger Williams accused George Fox and the Quakers of
papalism. John Winthrop said the same thing of Anne Hutchinson, and
she said it of him.[48] Both had a kind of logic to their views. Winthrop
said that in departing from Scripture and claiming a direct and certain
revelation to her, Hutchinson was doing what the pope did when he
went beyond Scripture and claimed an infallible revelation from his tradition. Hutchinson, in response, said that Winthrop relied on virtuous
works rather than faith, as the papists did on their automatically working
sacraments. Once such accusations were leveled, it was hard to the point
of impossibility to return the discussion to irenic channels—especially
when we recall what was the essential point, that to be a papist was to be
in league with Satan himself. Mutual suspicion was self-perpetuating.
After all, Antichrist would look plausibly like the real Christ. Was
Antichrist already present in the citadel of the visible saints?

The polarizing discourse on Rome meant that honest disagreements
among the Puritans would be structured around that polarity. The tensions in the community could most easily be cast in those terms. The radical individualism of the need for a conversion experience could be seen
as abandoning Scripture as the sole source of revelation. On the other
hand, the need for social solidarity, at odds with the entirely personal
nature of salvation, could be seen as going back to church structure on

hierarchical lines—that would be the charge brought against those who introduced a "halfway covenant." For some that was a half a covenant with hell (that is, with Rome). Once more, the concentric circles acted together in their siege on the Puritan psyche.

5. PROTESTANT HERESY

THOUGH EVERY DEPARTURE from true belief was felt to be least inchoately papal, Protestantism had been in existence long enough, by the seventeenth century, to spawn its own spectrum of heretical beliefs. If it was thought that these moved toward papalism, it was still important to see just what steps or half-measures were involved. They had to be identified in order to define the true church in opposition to them. Most of these came from Europe, though Americans added a few of their own. The European heresies had pullulated in the breakup of the old order by the Lutheran wars and the Cromwell revolution. Christopher Hill has chronicled the rich undergrowth of different sects springing up in the seventeenth century—Familists, Ranters, Diggers, Seekers, Socinians, Arminians, Antinomians, Anabaptists, Muggletonians, Fifth Monarchists, Libertines, Brownists, and Burrowists, Grindletonians, and Sabbatarians.[49] Americans would contribute such heretical sects of their own as the Gortonites, the Keithites, the Dunkers, the Rogerenes, the Ephrata Society— and later on, the Millerites and Hicksites.[50] Many such names were already being thrown about in Puritan polemic. Each deviation had to be renounced as soon as it was clearly recognized, not because of some theoretical regard for consistency of doctrine but because here, as in all the other concentric circles of peril, the devil was active in every departure from the true church or Scripture. It was imperative not only to argue against heretics but, in John Winthrop's words (used of Anne Hutchinson), to "give them up to Satan."[51]

At the center of all these snares, the individual soul had only its own consciousness of being saved to protect it. The precariousness of that isolated center was what gave the Puritan conscience its particular quality. It is time to examine that conscience.

3 | THE PURITAN CONSCIENCE

THE PURITAN conscience was at times a blend of the anarchic and the authoritarian—a combination that would show up again in later aspects of American history. On the one hand, this conscience lies at the root of America's radical individualism. What could be more anarchically lonely than the private task of undergoing a conversion to assure one of final salvation? No one else could help in this task. In fact, you could not help yourself. That would be a matter of salvation by your own endeavor or good works. No, the experience had to be a passive reception of predestination by God's free and autonomous choice. On the other hand, what could be more authoritarian than the power of the congregation to decide whether one had undergone that conversion, as a condition of membership in its company?

CONVERSION

SINCE THE all-important conversion was usually expected to occur in one's adolescence, the hope for it added to the other stresses of that time. Later sociological studies would find that religious conversion most often occurs then; but those studies took place when other factors were allowed *or stimulated* to play a role in the event—family encouragement, peer pressure, group rituals like revivals.[1]

Puritan diaries, even (or especially) those of people certifiably pious, show a high degree of anxiety that the conversion had not yet occurred, or was only ambiguous in its occurrence. Once a person had built up enough assurance to go before the congregation and testify to the conversion, doubts seeped back into the conscience of the believer—they were even recommended, to establish a kind of "fail-safe" rechecking that one had "really" been saved. Indeed, smugness was a form of pride that would almost guarantee that the conversion had not been genuine. That is why men like Jonathan Edwards had recurrent doubts about their status as "regenerate."[2] Edmund Morgan points out the paradoxes involved, which were the source of the Puritans' endless self-scrutiny:

> Lifelong anxiety and self-deprecation became the hallmarks of
> the American Puritan. He made a virtue of uncertainty until he
> came to identify feelings of assurance about salvation as signs of
> its absence. The only way to be sure was to be unsure. . . .
> Puritanism required a believer to find certainty in uncertainty—
> required him (or her) to rely for salvation on unmerited,
> predestined saving grace while spending a lifetime doing
> unrewarded good works; required him to search his soul for the
> Holy Spirit but denied him access to direct revelation; required
> him to be pure but told him he could not be. The strain
> produced by straining to contain these contradictions was never
> small, and it was easy to fall into heresy by pursuing one
> requirement at the expense of its opposite. The strain was
> doubly hard for anyone with [Cotton] Mather's intellectual
> energy and enlarged ego, and in his secret flirtations with heresy
> we can see the temptations that led many other Puritans astray.[3]

Some have thought that the Puritans were a smug people. One might expect them to be, since each full member of the Congregationalist

Church had an "assurance" that he or she was predestined for salvation. Without that assurance, one could not become a member. This sense of being individually chosen by the Holy Spirit, who signaled his choice in the conversion experience, might lead to self-satisfaction. Why worry about one's fate when it was sealed? But it did not work that way. The best study of this subject, *The Puritan Conversion Narrative* by Patricia Caldwell, shows that continuing fear and doubt haunted the very people who had been singled out for salvation.

The account a Puritan had to give of his or her conversion was consciously patterned to contrast with the mere recitation of the Creed by Catholics. That was denounced as "popish mumbling": "Is there any papist so ignorant but can say the common Creed?"[4] One must have a sincere and deep acceptance of the Lord as the only teacher of truths in the heart. The promptings of a priest or other guide are no substitute for that individual grasp of the meaning of salvation. But this ideal led to many difficulties. How does one judge one's own experience? What if a person is fooling himself or herself? After the assurance was reached, what if the person fell into sin? Samuel Sewall, who was always insecure about his salvation, felt he must not have been saved after all if he could so grievously offend God by voting for the death of witches on insubstantial arguments.

And if a person was a dubious judge of his or her own experience, how were the examiners who admitted them into membership to weigh that experience? Certain signs were in practice agreed upon, offering what Edmund Morgan called a "morphology of conversion." But once these signs were established, did they not amount to a prompting of the individual, who knew that these signs must be produced? More signs were added or invented in order to make sure that the ones already adduced were adequate. Thomas Hooker, who led a group out of Massachusetts in 1636 to found the Connecticut Colony, took the practice of requiring conversion accounts with him. He wrote extensively on the stages of conversion, which he thought included at least seven items:

1. Contrition for one's sins
2. Humiliation at one's sins

3. A call from God

4. Justification, by imputation of Christ's merits

5. Adoption by the Spirit

6. Sanctification, producing virtuous acts

7. Glorification, the completion of salvation in heaven[5]

Hooker wrote prolifically on these stages—four thousand pages in all.[6] He seemed to provide a kind of checklist by which one could judge one's own or others' sense of salvation; but he also gave an open-ended or indeterminate quality to the process—if one did not continue to grow in "sanctification," then the earlier stages must not have "taken."[7]

In fact, John Cotton argued that Hooker's theology of "stages" took away the "assurance" of conversion as an infallible sign of predestination. It was *too* open-ended, both fore and aft. Before, the preparation involved human effort to bring on one's salvation. And afterward, the separation between justification and sanctification made a person try to prove his justification by engaging in virtuous acts ("sanctification"). In either case, one was relying on human "works" for salvation—which, in Cotton's eyes, made Hooker papistical: "Whatsoever is of grace is not of works, and whatsoever is of works is not of grace."[8] Cotton argued that virtuous acts were no indication of salvation—a message his fervent disciple and friend Anne Hutchinson took up as a way of condemning the majority of colony ministers for preaching a Covenant of Works, not the Covenant of Grace. Cotton had been a pulpit superstar in England, where Hutchinson first heard him, before following him to Massachusetts with her husband and children.

ANTINOMIANISM

COTTON CAUSED a great sensation when he came to Boston in 1633. When he took the second place (teacher, behind the pastor) in Boston's First Church, a flood of new members came in.[9] He became the favorite preacher of the laity in Boston, to the dismay of other ministers, whose preaching was accused of encouraging virtuous "works" as if they availed for salvation. Hutchinson gathered a circle of women (and later of men) in her home to expound Cotton's theology. This seemed to teach that grace made virtuous acts irrelevant, the Puritans' very definition of Antinomianism ("above-the-law-ism"). In this period of Cotton's early influence, he either introduced or made uniform the practice of exacting a sure account of conversion as the condition for membership in the church.[10] Cotton had the support not only of the charismatic Anne Hutchinson and her brother-in-law, the minister John Wheelwright, but of the new young governor of the colony, Henry Vane. Their faction was strong in Boston's First Church. The faction even tried to place Wheelwright as a second teacher there, to squeeze out of action the hostile pastor, John Wilson. John Winthrop, a member of that church, rallied opposition to such an unheard-of innovation as a second teacher.

Since Congregationalism was based on the primacy of the laity in the church, the majority of ministers opposing Cotton seemed outgunned by the overwhelming lay support for him. But the ministers had John Winthrop with them (the former and future governor), as well as Thomas Hooker, who came back from Connecticut to join in the fray. After Cotton allowed Wheelwright to give a Fast Day sermon in the church on January 19, 1637, that sermon was called subversive. About the ministers who opposed Cotton, Wheelwright said, "We must kill them with the word of the Lord."[11] On March 9, the General Court of Massachusetts found Wheelwright guilty of "contempt and sedition" for stirring up trouble in the church (a secular verdict, like convicting Mary Dyer for disturbing the peace).

The legislators were striking at Cotton and Hutchinson through Wheelwright, the most vulnerable of the "free grace" theologians. But the supporters of all three would not let the matter rest there. They fought Wheelwright's conviction by the General Court with a petition, hoping for help from their ally Henry Vane, who was still governor at the time. But at a raucous session of the General Court in May 1637, held outside Boston to reduce the influence of the Cottonites, John Winthrop replaced

Vane as governor, and Winthrop pressed the war on Antinomians with fervor. Cotton was the second target after Wheelwright. Hutchinson would be the third. Either Cotton would be discredited, ending Hutchinson's influence, or Cotton would be forced to disavow Hutchinson, destroying her influence. The latter is what happened.

Cotton had tried to head off controversy by issuing sixteen points of "clarification" in January 1637—but the ministers, in a document called "The Elders Reply," called his explanations inadequate. He wrote a lengthy response to this response, but the disagreements were simply multiplying in an orgy of scholastic quibbles. A momentous step was therefore taken: the individual congregations, which had prized their autonomy to this point, called for the colony's first general synod in August 1637. Critics of such gatherings called them "Presbyterian." Nonetheless, the synod issued a list of eighty-two errors alleged to have been made by the Antinomians. Thomas Hooker, back from Connecticut for the occasion, defended his "stages" theology of conversion, and Cotton had to disown some of his own past statements. As Hooker's biographer Sargent Bush writes: "There is more than a little appearance of a return [from Connecticut] to win vindication for his [Hooker's] principles—a vindication implied in the thoroughness of Cotton's defeat."[12] Cotton had not only to back down himself, but to join the ministers in their attack on his own followers.

Now the way was clear to go after Anne Hutchinson, who had offended in the first place by being a woman preacher, against the pseudo-Pauline verse 1 Timothy 2.12: "I suffer not a woman to teach, nor to usurp authority over the man, but to be in silence." Hutchinson made it easier for Cotton to disown her by claiming not only assurance of her salvation by direct revelation of it, but other revelations that had been made to her by the Holy Spirit—including this prophecy of the General Court's fate: "For this you go about to do to me, God will ruin you and your posterity and this whole state."[13] Cotton himself addressed her at her trial in the harshest terms: "Your opinions fret like a gangrene, and spread like a leprosy, and infect far and near, and will eat out the bowels of religion."[14] Cotton told the court that she must be exiled immediately: "For you to

propound terms of delay, what rule have you for it when in point of practice there hath been a present proceeding as in Acts 5—as soon as ever
Ananias had told a lie, the church cast them out?"[15] Only then could
Winthrop congratulate the community for making "Satan lose the opportunity of making choice of so fit an instrument [as Hutchinson]."[16] On this
Cotton and Hooker could at last agree. Hooker, who followed the trial
from his home in Hartford, said that he and his wife experienced a violent
shaking of their house during the proceedings, which showed the devil's
opposition to those who would judge Anne (M 2.519–20), and he sighed
with relief that she was "cast out as unsavory salt, that she may not continue a pest to the place."[17]

Cotton was defeated so thoroughly that he considered joining John
Davenport in a move out of Massachusetts Bay Colony.[18] But Winthrop,
whose aim was always to hold the fractious community together, urged
him to stay on, in his chastened condition, and help the colony recover
from this Antinomian episode. Thomas Shepard, one of Hutchinson's
most heated prosecutors, did not trust Cotton's recantation: "Mr. Cotton
repents not, but is hid only. . . . He doth stiffly hold the revelation of our
good estate still, without any weight of word or work."[19] Cotton Mather,
John Cotton's grandson, named for him and always his defender, quotes
Cotton's rationale for staying on:

> When in a private conference with some chief magistrates and
> elders, I perceived that my removal upon such difference was
> unwelcome to them, and that such points need not to occasion
> any distance (neither in place nor in heart) amongst brethren, I
> then rested satisfied in my abode amongst them, and so have
> continued, by the grace of Christ, unto this day. (M 1.267)

The condemnation of Hutchinson could not end the problem that
lay beneath the controversy—how did the regenerate soul know it was
chosen? One of the key issues dividing Hooker and Cotton was whether
sanctification occurred at the same time as justification. If it did, then
evidence of later unholy acts would mean that justification had not

occurred. Nor could the matter of "preparation" be resolved entirely. In fact, Roger Williams would go further than Hutchinson in saying that no "works" can usefully precede conversion. He even forbade clergy from making it their intention to convert others when they preached—that would be usurping the role of the Holy Spirit, who alone can convert and save.[20]

Another troublesome issue arose in the course of the Antinomian controversy. As we have seen, a synod—a regional council—had been called to cure the Antinomian infection. Was the cure worse than the illness? Some felt that calling a synod was a departure from the New England Way, undermining the right of each congregation to choose its own ministers and supervise its own doctrinal affairs. A synod was at least a partial lapse toward Presbyterianism (rule by elders), as one could see from the document the ministers (from different congregations) wrote against Cotton, "Reply of the Elders." And Presbyterianism was itself a regression toward the hierarchical and "popish." As Milton wrote, "New presbyter is but old priest writ large." Thomas Hooker, who would preside over this First Synod in 1637, was initially against calling it, but he defended the exceptional meeting as merely advisory to the congregations, with no power to compel agreement from them.[21] This difficulty in conscience would arise when later synods were called. When a drought occurred just before the opening of the synod of 1662, the ultra-supernaturalist fear was that God was expressing his displeasure with synods in general.[22]

BAPTISM

BUT THE MOST nagging fear that plagued the Puritan conscience was the relation of conversion to baptism. If membership in the church was granted only to those who could testify to their personal conversion, what was the point of baptizing infants? They would not be saved before their conversion as adults. Thomas Hooker tried to explain baptism as a kind of pre-preparation for conversion, an act that "establisheth the heart," making it "capable" for later acts of preparation—which just involved baptism in all the other controversies over "preparation." Hooker said that infant baptism sets a seal on the child, aiming him toward conversion, without itself effecting conversion. Such a child has no sanctifying holiness, but a kind of "federal holiness," as part of the saved *community* without being individually saved.[23] Since all the first Puritans to land in Massachusetts had been baptized as infants in the Anglican Church, and since they did not formally renounce their membership in that body (whose head, the King, had given them their Charter), they refused to let Anabaptists enter the colony. (They were called *Ana*baptists, "*re*baptizers," since they counted their own infant baptism as invalid and repeated the sacrament when they were adults capable of conversion. When Anabaptists had children of their own, they would not give them a "first" baptism, and they would properly be known thenceforth simply as Baptists.)

Simply excluding Anabaptists would not solve the deeper problem of "pedobaptism" (infant baptism) among the Saints. They continued the practice of their Anglican forebears, but soon ran up against a new problem. What if infants baptized in Massachusetts grew up with their parents expecting their first "seal" to be completed by an experiential conversion, but no conversion occurred? Such adults could not be admitted to communion. And if these unconverted adults wanted *their* children baptized? Strict teaching forbade this. As Thomas Hooker put it: "The predecessors [grandparents] cannot convey this right without the next [immediate] parents. . . . Apostasy takes off the federal holiness of the children."[24] Others were just as adamant: "That practice, that exposeth the blood of Christ to contempt, and baptism to profanation, the church to pollution, and the commonwealth to confusion, is not to be admitted."[25]

Others invoked the typology of circumcision, and said that Abraham's *seed* had been given the promise: "I will establish my covenant between me and thee and thy seed after thee in their generations" (Genesis 17.7). Since the Covenant of Grace had for its "type" (forebear) the covenant with Abraham, a minister, Peter Bulkeley, argued that children of the Saints were "within the covenant."[26] If they were not, membership of the church might dwindle drastically in a generation or two. Faced with this anguishing prospect, Hooker confessed to being swayed, but he still insisted on principle:

> I shall nakedly profess that if I should have given way to my affection, or followed that which suits my secret desire and inclination, I would have willingly wished that the scale might have been cast upon the affirmative [for allowing baptism], and that such persons [the nonmembers], many whereof we hope are godly, might enjoy all such privileges which might be useful and helpful to them and theirs.[27]

Despite theses tuggings at his heartstrings, Hooker would not desert what he called the "main-pillar principle" of church membership.

This was an issue that tore families apart. Richard Mather was one of the early advocates of allowing such baptisms, but his son Increase opposed them. Thomas Shepard was for a time against the baptisms, but his son Thomas Jr. was for them. Solomon Stoddard was a strong advocate for allowing the baptisms, but his grandson Jonathan Edwards would reverse that policy when Stoddard died and Edwards succeeded to his pulpit in Northampton. The issue was so divisive that individual churches could not resolve the problem. The General Court took the drastic step of calling for another synod, but this time the matter was not dealt with as decisively as the Antinomian crisis had been.

Richard Mather wrote a resolution that favored baptizing the children of unregenerate parents, but the body excised it from the synod report, which was called the Cambridge Platform of 1637, because of opposition from an intense minority of the delegates.[28] Ten years later, the ministers made another try, calling a "ministerial assembly" to deal with the matter. Twenty-one ministers there endorsed a recommendation to allow the baptisms, written by Richard Mather, but only four churches acted on it.[29] The wrangling worked its way toward still another synod, that of 1662, which seemed to settle the matter in favor of allowing the extended baptisms. But individual churches repeated Hooker's argument that synods could only be advisory.

Somewhat surprisingly, the ministers had thought they were responding to a demand by the laity that their children be baptized, but the greatest resistance to the new policy came from laypeople. The ingrained
conservatism of the community made it fear innovation, and a minority
of the pastors played on this, keeping alive the controversy. The objection
was not simply to the baptism policy, but to the synodal authority that
was obtruding it. This was too Presbyterian for lovers of Congregationalist orthodoxy. "Although the Synod established a new orthodoxy, most
churches refused to accept it."[30] The issue died down only when Presbyterian values spread in the church. Even after it had died down, it flared
up again when the fervor of the Great Awakening made people yearn for
the old purity. Thus the issue continued to divide Puritans well into the
eighteenth century.[31]

PURITY

CRITICS OF extended baptism called the decree of the synod of 1662
by a derisory name, "the Halfway Covenant." This was meant to be
a contradiction on the face of it, since the covenant was with Christ, and
there could be no half Christ. But as often happens with religious short-
hand, the name stuck and is now the regular way of referring to the history of this issue. The name has an unintended applicability, because
there was much about Puritanism that was halfway. Roger Williams had
attacked the Congregationalists for only halfway separating themselves
from the Church of England. Puritans (another derisory name that
stuck) had arisen in England because of their quest to purify the English
church of its corruptions. America's Puritans thought they could accomplish this by going to a new arena, where they would be beyond the reach
of Archbishop Laud and other high-church protectors of "papal" taint.
Though they did not formally renounce the church of their homeland,
they set out to create an entirely different ecclesiastical procedure. In
England, there were bishops, who appointed priests, who said Mass. In
Massachusetts (and Connecticut), there were pastors and teachers, who

were elected and disciplined by their lay congregations, who presided over meals of fellowship. In England, the King was the head of the church, there was one church, and anyone who was baptized, acknowledged the Creed, and went to Mass was a member of that church. In New England, civil magistrates had no authority over the church, and no religious leader had authority in any but his own congregation, and only those who could establish their saved status belonged to a congregation.

These differences between the churches of Old England and of New England were salient, however they had been papered over with formal professions of "nonseparation." It seemed to the Puritans that they had purified their own churches. But Roger Williams set out to purify the Puritans. They still took an oath of allegiance to the King as head of the church as well as head of state. They still baptized infants, though they claimed that only adult conversion merited entry into the congregation. They still used the civil magistrates to enforce religious duty. They still punished dissent. They still seized land by grant of the King. They still honored popish idols like the red cross in their flag. When New England Puritans visited Old England, they attended Mass there. They were only halfway separated from the Laudian Antichrist in London. As Roger Williams told his old fellows in Massachusetts: "I first withdrew communion from yourselves for halting between Christ and Antichrist."[32]

This critique stung the New Englanders. It made Cotton Mather, in an etymological frenzy, call Williams an "autocatacritic," or self-contradicting scold (M 2.498). But it was the Bostonians who were self-contradicting, and that is what made them wince under his scolding. There was much that was halfway about Puritanism. Its private conversion and public vindication were halfway between Quaker inner light and Presbyterian communal judgment, or halfway between private revelation and infallible excommunication. Its ultra-supernaturalism was halfway between superstition and rationality—Cotton Mather defended belief in witches since it kept people aware of the supernatural: "Since there are witches and devils, we may conclude that there are also immortal souls" (W 16). Their separation-entanglement of church and state was halfway between constitutionalism and theocracy. In their treatment of the Bible, they were halfway between literalism and allegory. In their treatment of natural knowledge they were halfway between obscurantism and Ramist logic chopping. How on earth did they hold their odd world and their odder selves together?

By intense intellectual effort.

4 | THE PURITAN INTELLECT

G IVEN ALL THE forces pressing in upon the Puritan psyche (those traced in chapter 2) and all those conflicts rending the Puritan conscience from within (those traced in chapter 3), it is a wonder the Puritan soul did not simply explode. But "Puritans" were a tough people—odd, but tough. And very, very intelligent. Some people are misled by later associations of the term "Puritan." It is thought, for instance, that believers in the literal sense of the Bible must be ignorant— as must believers in miracles (what I have called ultra-supernaturalism), as must doomsayers proclaiming the world's end. The Puritans believed all those things, but they were very far from ignorant. In fact, religious historian George Marsden plausibly argues that "Early New England had been ruled, perhaps more than any culture in history, by the educated."[1]

There has probably never been a ministerial class in America as learned as were the pastors and teachers of New England. Most of their founding divines had attended an English university—a hundred at Cambridge, thirty-two at Oxford. The leading Cantabrigians, thirty-five of them, had come from Emmanuel College, the hotbed of Puritanism. As Cotton Mather wrote: "If New England hath been in some respects

Emmanuel's land, it is well; but this I am sure of, Emmanuel College contributed not a little to make it so."[2] New England's prolific theologians did not exist in a scholarly backwater. Some had European reputations. John Cotton and Thomas Hooker had completed the seven postgraduate years that gave them the highest degrees in divinity. Hooker, during his sojourn in Holland, was praised by William Ames, as great a Puritan authority as any then living, for being "without an equal at preaching or disputing."[3] Cotton's adversary Thomas Edwards was giving him high praise when he called him "the prime man of them all in New England."[4] Roger Williams had been a protégé of the leading legal scholar of the time, Sir Edward Coke. These men were part of the great trans-Atlantic scholarly conversation, and the New Englanders contributed more than their share to it—over a third of them published at least one theological tract.[5] Some of these were simply a published sermon, but many were bulky commentaries, topped by Cotton Mather's seven-volume *Magnalia*. Mather takes the prize for productivity—he published 458 books—but Thomas Shepard, with fewer titles to his name, wrote more pages, and John Eliot was not far behind.[6] Mather's father published 108 books, and—as has already been noticed—Thomas Hooker wrote four thousand pages just on the subject of conversion.

These were not casual productions but deeply learned works. It was expected of a pastor in New England that he know both the biblical languages, Hebrew and Greek. It was a matter of special importance and pride for Protestants to master the Bible in its original words, to distinguish themselves from Roman Catholics, who were ordered by the papacy to stick to the Vulgate Latin Bible, a mere translation of the originals. Hebrew was more intensely studied at Harvard than at Oxford. In fact, "the most distinctive feature of the Harvard curriculum was the emphasis on Hebrew and kindred languages."[7] Roger Williams, who had little good to say of the Quakers he debated, had to grant that one of them, John Stubbs, "was learned in the Hebrew and the Greek"—as was Williams himself, as a good product of Pembroke College at Cambridge.[8] It was desirable for Reformers also to know German (the language of Luther) and French (the language of Calvin). Latin they would need for reading fathers like Augustine, legal texts, and such rules of Protestant faith as William Ames's *Medulla Theologiae.*

The New Englanders were not reclusive scholars or university professors, but working pastors, who preached to their congregations three times a week, as well as on special occasions. The pastors' formidable array of talent was increased by a good deal of intermarrying, mentoring, and pulpit sharing in the pastorate, so that they turned a massive artillery of learning on any subject that moved them. Though they professed the "plain style" of preaching, they did not talk down to their audiences, who were expected to listen to hours on end of biblical exegesis and controversial theology. The whole community's pride in its literacy was proclaimed in the clear glass windows with which they had replaced the stained glass of Anglican cathedrals, the better to read one's Bible and the Psalter during services.

The preachers' plain style was not a matter of being simple for the simple folk. Like the Puritans' plain dress, it was meant to draw attention to the essentials. It was opposed to the gaudy rhetoric of Anglican preachers (Lancelot Andrewes and John Donne, for instance). Puritan preachers expounded the sense of Scripture, breaking it down into heads and subheads as was taught by the Renaissance logician Peter Ramus.[9] The ideal of their rhetoric was enshrined in the famous case of John Cotton, as it was memorialized by his grandson. Cotton won his first fame as an orator at Emmanuel College.

> One thing among the rest which caused a great notice to be taken of him throughout the whole university was his funeral oration upon Dr. Some, the master of Peter House, wherein he approved himself such a master of Periclean or Ciceronian oratory that the auditors were even ready to have acclaimed *Non vox hominum sonat* [a more than human voice is speaking]. And that which added unto the reputation that raised for him was an university sermon wherein, aiming more to preach self than Christ, he used such florid strains of words above the words of wisdom, as extremely recommended him to the most, who

relished the wisdom of words above the words of wisdom,
though the pompous eloquence of that sermon afterwards gave
such a distaste unto his own renewed soul that with a sacred
indignation he threw his notes into the fire. (M 1.255)

Cotton underwent a conversion while teaching at Cambridge, and
his new self had to be expressed in a new style. Mather's report of this
conversion is worth quoting at some length, since there is no better
explanation of the way a new religion demanded a new rhetoric. Here is
the profound spiritual import of the plain style.

> Some time after this change upon the soul of Mr. Cotton, it
> came unto his turn again to preach at St. Mary's and, because he
> was to preach, an high expectation was raised through the whole
> university that they should have a sermon flourishing, indeed,
> with all the learning of the whole university. Many difficulties
> had Mr. Cotton in his own mind now what course to steer. On
> the one side, he considered that if he should preach with a
> scriptural and Christian plainness, he should not only wound his
> own fame exceedingly but also tempt carnal men to revive an
> old cavil, that religion made scholars turn dunces, whereby the
> name of God might suffer not a little. On the other side, he
> considered that it was his duty to preach with such plainness as
> became the oracles of God, which are intended for the conduct
> of men in the paths of life and not for theatrical ostentations and
> entertainments, and the Lord needed not any skill of ours to
> maintain his own glory. Hereupon Mr. Cotton resolved that he
> would preach a plain sermon, even such a sermon as in his own
> conscience he thought would be most pleasing unto the lord
> Jesus Christ, and he discoursed practically and powerfully but
> very solidly upon the plain doctrine of repentance.
> The vain wits of the university, disappointed thus with
> a more excellent sermon, that shot some troublesome
> admonitions into their consciences, discovered their vexation

at this disappointment by their not humming, as according to
their sinful and absurd custom they had formerly done; and the
vice chancellor, for the very same reason also, graced him not
as he did others that pleased him. Nevertheless, the satisfaction which he enjoyed in his own faithful soul abundantly
compensated unto him the loss of any human favor or honor;
nor did he go without many encouragements from some
doctors then having a better sense of religion upon them, who
prayed him to persevere in the good way of preaching which
he had now taken.

    But perhaps the greatest consolation of all was a notable
effect of the sermon then preached. The famous Dr. Preston,
then a fellow of Queen's College in Cambridge and of great
note in the university, came to hear Mr. Cotton with the same
itching ears as others were then led withal. For some good
while after the beginning of the sermon, his frustrated expectation caused him to manifest his uneasiness all the ways that
were then possible, but before the sermon was ended, like one
of Peter's hearers, he found himself "pierced to the heart." His
heart within him was now struck with such resentments of his
own interior state before the God of heaven that he could
have no peace in his own soul till, with a wounded soul, he
had repaired unto Mr. Cotton, from whom he received those
further assistances wherein he became a spiritual father unto
one of the great men in his age. (M 1.256)

    The ministers were proud of their learning and wanted to keep its
heritage alive, as we can read in an early (1643) mission statement by
Harvard College: "One of the next things we longed for and looked after
was to advance learning and perpetuate it to posterity, dreading to leave
an illiterate ministry to the churches when our present ministers shall lie
in the dust."[10] Their hope that they would not be succeeded by an illiterate ministry in later America has, perhaps, not been entirely realized. I
have said that these were working pastors, not professors. But they were,

after all, university men, who knew that learning has to be continually renewed and deepened. So it is not surprising that the first touchstone universities of America, Harvard and Yale, were founded in New England. This is one of the principal reasons for Puritan eminence in the colonial period. There was an abundance of religious exercises and leaders in the other colonies. But none had the intense reflection on what they were doing that the Puritan divines did. Only in New England could a profound training in theology be found on these shores. The College of William and Mary was not set up to train clergy—American Anglicans had to rely on ministers who were ordained at Oxford or Cambridge and wanted to travel to America (few qualified ones did). The newcomer Presbyterians and Baptists had to rely on immigrant products of Edinburgh or Glasgow.

The New England colleges were not established purely for the spread and preservation of knowledge. Nothing was entirely separate from Gospel concerns in that culture. The schools were set up as bastions of orthodoxy against challenges from within the society—Harvard to counter the Antinomians, Yale to oppose tendencies typified in the Halfway Covenant. In Massachusetts, the charter for a college was authorized in 1636, while Sir Henry Vane was governor, and it was destined for Salem, which was hospitable to the Antinomians. But when Winthrop came in the next year, the site was changed to Newtown (Cambridge), the bastion of the conservatives, where they had held the General Court meetings and the synod that condemned Antinomians. Thomas Shepard, the Newtown pastor and one of the prime prosecutors of Anne Hutchinson, boasted that he brought the college to his town, where he became its informal chaplain, "because this town (then called Newtown) was, through God's great care and goodness, kept spotless from the contagion of [Antinomian] opinions."[11] Cotton Mather considered the founding of Harvard in Cambridge one of the wonderful providences to the colony:

> Within a year after the gathering of the church at Cambridge
> and the ordaining of Mr. Shepard in that church, the country

was miserably distracted by a storm of Antinomian and
Familistical opinions . . . and from the countenance hereby
given to immediate and unwarranted revelation, 'tis not easy to
relate how many monsters, worse than African, arose in these
regions of America. But a Synod assembled at Cambridge,
whereof Mr. Shepard was no small part, most happily crushed
them all. The vigilancy of Mr. Shepard was blessed, not only
for the preservation of his own congregation from the rot of
these opinions, but also for the deliverance of all the flocks
which our Lord had in the wilderness. And it was with respect
unto this vigilancy, and the enlightening and powerful ministry
of Mr. Shepard that, when the foundation of a college was to be
laid, Cambridge rather than any other place was pitched upon
to be the seat of that happy seminary, out of which there
proceeded many notable preachers who were made such, very
much, by their sitting under Mr. Shepard's ministry. (M 1.385–86)

The concern for orthodoxy that arose in response to the Antinomians
was later echoed in the reaction to the Halfway Covenant. John Davenport, an early overseer of Harvard and one of the fiercest opponents of
the Halfway Covenant, tried to start a college in the city he had founded,
New Haven. In 1656, he began a collection of books (over a hundred of
them) that would later serve as the basis for the Yale library.[12] Interest in
his project came partly from a concern that Harvard was losing its old
orthodoxy. In 1654, Henry Dunster had been forced to resign as Harvard's
president because of his views on baptism.[13] Writing in 1935, Samuel Eliot
Morison said of this scandal: "The news that President Dunster had
become an 'antipaedobaptist' created much the same sensation in New
England as would be aroused in the country today if President Conant
should announce his adherence to communism."[14] Concern over Harvard's "latitudinarian" ways was revived in 1701 when Increase Mather was
forced to resign as president. That year both Increase and Cotton Mather
sent detailed suggestions for a Connecticut college to James Pierpont,

who was promoting the project in Connecticut's General Court. That legislative body issued the charter for what would become Yale on November 6, 1701. The Mather letters had proposed that the new academy be a "school of the churches," to keep religion pure.[15]

Both Harvard and Yale would survive as private universities, but they were authorized and partly funded by the state, which makes it understandable that their goals should be conservative. But this is an example of the paradox of the Puritan intellect—that it was formed to defend a pre-Enlightenment religion but would forge tools later useful to the Enlightenment. The intellectual skills developed in the seventeenth century proved adaptable to the tasks of the eighteenth century. The subtlety, rigor, and erudition expended in exploring doctrines like the Trinity, the Incarnation, predestination, justification (by imputed merit), the stages (or lack of them) in conversion, transubstantiation, or covenant did not lapse or fade when different concerns came into view. And the traits that went along with such energetic busyness of the mind would perdure in new and sometimes surprising ways. It is true that there are what Sacvan Bercovitch called "Puritan origins of the American self." Admittedly, the Puritans of New England were different from people in the Middle Colonies and the South. But they were exaggerations of what was present elsewhere. All the most influential early colonizers from England were products of the Reformation (Catholics and Jews were a minority factor). They all believed that they had escaped the popish Antichrist. They were in some measure chiliastic and providential, with a belief in individual salvation and historic vindication. They were alert to the devil's power and to supernatural intrusions into the natural order. Puritans took these common traits to a new level of intensity. They not only accepted such things but pondered them obsessively.

In doing this, they set the terms of discourse. They did more thinking, preaching, educating, printing than anyone else. They sucked up the intellectual oxygen of the continent. Even those who would differ from them or react against them did so on the terms they had set. As Edmund Morgan wrote:

> The men and women who settled New England took them-
> selves very, very seriously, not only as individuals but as
> a group engaged in a historic mission. That is why they were
> both so irritating and so influential. Posterity has accepted
> them, despite numerous protests, at their own evaluation of
> themselves. . . . Long before 1860 New Englanders laid claim
> to the national consciousness and gave their own past as a
> legacy to the nation, whether the nation wanted it or not.[16]

We will find what he says confirmed over and over in the course of this book. Here it is enough to sketch, in a preliminary way, how Puritan concepts affected American traits for the rest of our history. Partly this was just a matter of what was said of nineteenth-century Whigs in England, with their "dropping of the Puritan tenets but retention of the Puritan tone."[17] But it was more than that, too. Pale simulacra of the tenets themselves continue to haunt our history.

1. RELIGIOSITY

AMERICA HAS defied predictions that secularization will dry up religious devotion. Separation of church and state did not endanger this religiosity but protected it. There are many sources of this strong historic fact—other streams than that of the Puritans. But they set much of the style for American religiosity, its biblical rhetoric, its sense of vocation. The jeremiad, that self-castigating sermon based on the sense of American mission, continues down through our history—in Lincoln's Second Inaugural, in William Jennings Bryan's Cross of Gold Speech, in Martin Luther King's oratory. It was apparent in the millennial hopes of the Great Awakening and the chiliastic imagery of "The Battle Hymn of the Republic." It shows up in the hellfire sermons of the revivals, in the question "Are you saved," in "testifying" and "witnessing" to personal conversion. Our political conventions take some of their ritual from the revivals.

2. CHOSENNESS

THE SENSE OF Americans as a people set apart derives a great deal of its depth from the Puritans' belief in themselves as "the new Israel." This would surface again in many guises—Manifest Destiny, American "exceptionalism," Ronald Reagan's invocation of Winthrop's "city on a hill," the claim that we bring "clean hands" to situations dirtied by European colonialism. This language is not derived solely from Puritans. But they sounded those notes loud and long, and the echoes had a long reverberation.

3. WILDERNESS

THE PURITANS had an errand "into the wilderness," that place where they would win the New World for Christ, facing down the devil in his element, doing what would later be described as "taming the West." Cotton Mather said that it was the Puritans' task to turn American geography into "Christianography."[18] The mystical meaning of the wilderness would continue to haunt America in diluted or partly secularized versions—in the myth of the frontier, the idea that freedom is to be found "yonder" in the great spaces, that America's spiritual stature is matched by its vast land, that this is the arena of American soul-making, that virtue, stifled in the city, breathes its natural air in the wilderness. In Emerson's words: "I think we must regard the *land* as a commanding and increasing power on the citizenry, the sanative and Americanizing influence, which promises to disclose new virtues for ages to come."[19] Emerson had "a premonition that here shall laws and institutions exist on some scale of proportion to the majesty of nature."[20] The Reverend Lyman Beecher, father of seven famous Beecher children, had a similar sense of vast space as a spiritual challenge and fulfillment: "All the West is on a great scale, and the minds and the view of the people correspond with these relative proportions."[21]

When Beecher took up the presidency of Lane Theological Seminary in Cincinnati, he called for a great influx of Christian ministers to realize God's purpose in the West, since God "had prepared the West to be mighty and still wieldable, that the moral energy of his word and spirit might take it up."[22] He said that he had come to believe in Jonathan Edwards's claim that "the millennium would commence in America," and that "this nation is, in the providence of God, destined to lead the way in the moral and political emancipation of the world."[23] If God's plan for the West is completed, "the government of force will cease, and that of intelligence and virtue will take its place; and nation after nation, cheered by our example, will follow in our footsteps till the whole earth is free." This view of the salvific West was proclaimed over a half century before Frederick Jackson Turner's hymns to the frontier.

4. ANTI-CATHOLICISM

LYMAN BEECHER demonstrates that another key element in Puritanism would have a long life in America. The Puritans felt a need to convert the Indians before the Jesuits could recruit them for Antichrist. Beecher felt that hordes of Catholic immigrants were spilling into the West, bringing with them Jesuits and other Catholic enemies of freedom. He saw a conspiracy at work: "If the potentates of Europe have no design upon our liberties, what means the paying of the passage and emptying out upon our shores such floods of pauper emigrants?"[24] The mass of these emigrants might be paupers, but Beecher felt that their clergy were bringing foreign gold to buy American land in the West.[25] Americans had brought the Reformation to America, "and fought the colonial battles with Canadian Indians and French Catholics," while the Jesuits had been formed to abort the Reformation.[26] Cotton Mather thought the struggle with the Jesuits was fearsome since they had the devil on their side. Beecher, too, considered the contest for control of the West an uneven one, where only God could make the good prevail:

> The ministers of no Protestant sect could or would dare to
> attempt to regulate the votes of their people as the Catholic
> priests can do, who at the confessional learn all the private

concerns of their people, and have almost unlimited power
over the conscience as it respects the performance of every
civil or social duty.[27]

I wrote earlier that some later anti-Catholicism was a matter of sheer
ignorance, as opposed to the theological depth of the Puritans' eschatological struggle with the pope as Antichrist. Beecher was clearly not
ignorant, but his opposition to the enemy of the Reformation was a version of the Puritan view only half secularized. He stands in the transition area of principled to obscurantist anti-Catholicism.

5. INDIVIDUALISM

BUT THE ASPECT of the Puritan heritage with the deepest impact
was what Herbert Hoover would call "the American system of rugged individualism." The Puritans' introspection, their self-examination,
the private conversion experience that set off soul from soul by God's
election, the minute scrutiny of the stages of conversion—all this made
the individual prize his or her singular experience. Tocqueville dis-
cerned something like this when he introduced the new word *individualisme* into the analysis of America: "Individualism is a considered and
tranquil trait that inclines each citizen to separate himself from the
crowd of his fellows, withdrawing into the enclave of his family and
friends so that, having formed a little society of his own, he gladly lets
the larger society go its way without him."[28] One coming to that passage
directly after studying the Puritans could well imagine that it was meant
to describe New England, where the individual withdrew into a private
experience of being saved and then joined the elect circle of "visible
saints," separating himself from the unregenerate world, which had to
wallow along toward damnation apart from him and his. And that private
experience of being saved was like the personal assurance that would later
be called "self-confidence" by Emerson—the highest virtue in his eyes.

Yet Tocqueville's initial use of the word was not celebratory. It had
recently been coined in France as a pejorative term, to criticize the atom-

izing forces let loose by the French Revolution. It had been put in wide circulation during the 1820s, by Saint-Simonians, who contrasted it with their ideal of the organic society.[29] Tocqueville noted its recent status: "Our ancestors lacked the word 'individualism,' which we have created for our own use, because in their era there were, in fact, no individuals who did not belong to a group and who could consider themselves absolutely alone."[30] Henry Reeve, Tocqueville's friend and English translator, had to explain why he kept the new word in its Anglicized form. He added a footnote to the first use of the term in his 1840 translation:

> I adopt the expression of the original [*individualisme*], however
> strange it may seem to an English ear, partly because it illus-
> trates the remark on the introduction of general terms
> into the democratic language which was made in a preceding
> chapter, and partly because I know of no English word exactly
> equivalent to the expression.

This is not surprising, given the Europeans' negative use of the term. Tocqueville had distinguished *individualisme* from *égoisme,* but he said that as *individualisme* develops, it circles back into *égoisme*.[31] "Egoism dries up the very seed of every virtue; individualism initially crushes only the impulses to public virtue, but over time it turns on and obliterates every other virtue and at last it disappears into egoism."[32]

This antisocial urge could not be internally corrected, Tocqueville argued. It could be blunted only by some external and countervailing factor—in America, by the individual's partial re-entry into society by way of voluntary associations, which served as buffers between the individual and the state.[33] After Tocqueville, the dark sense of individualism prevailed in France, merging with Emile Durkheim's antisocial *anomie*.[34] But Americans soon gave it an almost entirely sunny sense. It was no longer a dark force that needed correction from outside, one crushing public virtue, but was itself the source of all American virtue. After all, concentration on one's own independent state was a sign of being *saved* in New England.

Yehoshua Arieli, the best student of individualism in America, traces the alchemical transformation from a dark European notion into a golden American one, in a chapter called "A European Concept Crosses the Atlantic."

> This concept and the term that described it were of foreign
> origin and part of an ideology which stood in direct opposition
> to the system of values accepted in America. It was therefore
> necessary to transform the concept of individualism from one
> loaded with a negative meaning into one which meant more
> and more an ideal and principle of the American way of life.[35]

It took a while for the positive meaning to catch on. Noah Webster first defined the word in his *American Dictionary* of 1847 as "an excessive or exclusive regard to one's personal interest; self-interest; selfishness." Other early dictionaries defined it as "egoism."[36] But it quickly altered its meaning to reflect American idealizations of private salvation. Arieli says that association with Protestant values, and especially with Puritan values, helped recast the word's content.[37] According to Professor John Williamson Nevin of Marshall College, writing in 1848, "Individualism itself was an offspring of the Reformation."[38]

Of course, the Calvinist thought that *God* lifted him by the bootstraps up into the company of the saved, while the Emersonian thought he lifted *himself* by the bootstraps. From this we get the "rugged individualism" that would make Americans say one must do everything for oneself, not expecting a handout or a hand up from others, and especially not from government. This is the myth that was embodied in Horatio Alger stories with titles like *Making His Way, Helping Himself, Struggling Upward,* or *Bound to Rise.* There was a ghostly hint of the predestinarian God in millionaires who finally rewarded the self-helping heroes of Alger's stories—but the lesson meant to be read is that the "self-made man" was not only a possible but the most desirable ideal. As Chesterton scoffed, self-made men do not choose their maker wisely.

Though there were a few isolated critics of the ideal of individualism—notably Orestes Brownson—Arieli traces the process by which individualism was identified with everything good in America, so that all factions had to lay claim to their own versions of individualism. It was ideologically unchallengeable. Opposing it became unpatriotic. It was identified with frontier values, with the free market, with freedom itself. In 1851, Mark Hopkins, the president of Williams College, wrote that "the value which Christianity puts upon the individual ... must overturn all systems of darkness and mere authority."[39] Lord Bryce could rightly say in 1888: "Individualism, the love of enterprise, and the pride in personal freedom have been deemed by Americans not only their choicest, but their peculiar and exclusive possessions."[40] That is how Arieli explains the extraordinary fervor with which Herbert Spencer's Social Darwinism was accepted by almost every sector of American society.

It was, then, under the threefold assault of progressivism, radical democracy, and socialism that the Spencerian version of individualism combined with the Gospel of Wealth and the Cult of Success was formulated and propagated. There was a conscious effort to create through individualism an ideological identity between the nation, democracy, and industrial enterprise. Individualism made competitive private enterprise and American identity part of one pattern, through which the new elite hoped to stabilize its own position inside the framework of democracy. This group considered individualism not only an ideology which gave wider significance to its activities, but also a system of values which expressed the aspirations and the sense of identity of the American nation as a whole. This accounts for the fact that not only the Republican party but also the Democrats under Bryan and Wilson, the Rooseveltian Progressives, and even the Populists, Single Taxers, and labor leaders were committed to the concept of individualism as a national ideal.[41]

There was an altered eschatological vision, that of progress, separating the regenerate (the new visible saints) from the unregenerate, and Spencer defined it: "In the competition among individuals of the same kind, survival of the fittest has from the beginning furthered production of a higher type."[42]

It is fascinating to see how eschatology, the wilderness, and the mission impulse were translated into the language of individualism. Converting the Indians became a matter of instilling individualism into them by removing them from tribes. This was the judgment of four Episcopal bishops, working with the Indian Rights Association in the 1880s. John T. Oberly, superintendent of Indian schools at the Department of the Interior, told a conference on Indian rights "that the first essential thing in the attempt to solve the Indian problem is agreement that the Indian is a man and that he should have individualism." Lyman Abbott and Senator Dawes added their voices to the urgent mission of breaking down the tribes to make each Indian man stand on his own two feet.[43]

None of the five traits just described was the same as its pre-Enlightenment foreshadowing. But none of them was entirely disconnected from them, either. Intellectual and moral activity as intense as that the Puritans engaged in was not to be dissipated easily or overnight. Puritanism died hard. In some ways, it did not die at all.

II | PRELUDES TO ENLIGHTENMENT

5 | Precursors: Samuel Sewall, Roger Williams

E RAS IN HISTORY have soft edges. They are retrospective constructs. People living through the Middle Ages did not know they were doing so, and they could have no sense of when Late Antiquity faded out and the Renaissance began to dawn. Nonetheless, looking back, we can tell that one time was in large ways different from another, and we try to give labels that will indicate that difference. The Enlightenment is a large and complex historical shift. It eases away from Reformation concerns toward Early Modern ones. It has a jagged approach, rapid in some places, slower in others. There is no one *click* that shifts us out of one period into the other. But looking over the large field of events, we can say that certain things that characterized the pre-Enlightenment period faded off by the Enlightenment's high period in the eighteenth century.

Concretely, much of the social consensus around the killing of Mary Dyer was missing from the Enlightenment consensus. Ultra-supernaturalism, for instance, which found divine or diabolic intrusions into puzzling events, gave way to natural explanations. Miracles gave way to "special providences" and then to scientific causes. Even things that seem similar in one era are profoundly different in their underlying assumptions—the difference, for instance, between Puritan eschatology and the Enlightenment belief in progress. The range of things subject to human reason and control broadened considerably with the coming of the Enlightenment. The view of human nature was altered when the acceptance or the importance of original sin was diminished.

There were harbingers of the Enlightenment among seventeenth-century Puritans. The reading of the Bible, for instance, was made less literal by a few Puritans. They never did believe *exclusively* in the literal sense of Scripture. They allowed room for "typological" readings—Jewish events as prophetic signs—but they followed Luther in rejecting Catholic forms they considered "allegorical."[1]

Most, for instance, rejected Saint Augustine's claim that apocalyptic prophecies were mere allegories. They left such "poeticizing" of the Bible to Anglican preachers against whom they had adopted the "plain style." Yet some leeway was being given to nonliteral interpretations of what the Bible said. In the Bible, for instance, the sun goes around the earth. But from 1686, when Charles Morton returned from Oxford, the Copernican system was part of the Harvard curriculum. Morton was in some ways a conservative—he taught logic from Aristotle rather than from the more "up-to-date" Peter Ramus. Despite this conservatism in some respects, he taught Galileo's system, however some preachers denounced his disregard for biblical physics.[2]

Departing from the Bible on moral matters was more difficult than on physical ones. Much had been staked on following the Bible literally where morality was concerned. The Bible, after all, was the Puritans' warrant for executing witches (Exodus 22.18) and for many other details of their penal system. One reason that so many godly people owned slaves, even in New England, was that slavery was permitted in both the Jewish and the Christian Scriptures. This would continue to be the case well into the eighteenth century, when Jonathan Edwards, Benjamin Rush, Benjamin Franklin, Aaron Burr, and many other distinguished non-Southerners owned slaves. How could you attack slavery when God allowed it, even commanded it in the case of conquered women (Deuteronomy 20.14; Numbers 31.18)? Fellow Jews should be enslaved for only six years (Exodus 21.2). Jewish law let a man sell himself into slavery (Leviticus 25.39) or sell his daughter as a slave, but only to a fellow Jew (Exodus 21.7). Jews are forbidden to covet another man's slaves or envy him because of them (Exodus 20.17; Deuteronomy 5.21). One might well be tempted to envy Abraham, who had at one point 318 slaves (Genesis 14.14).

The New Testament is no better on slavery. Jesus nowhere criticizes the holding of slaves. In fact, slavery is accepted as a normal part of life in Jesus' parables (Matthew 13.27; Luke 17.7–10; and many other places). Paul tells slaves to be content with their lot (1 Corinthians 7.20–21). 1 Peter 2.18 tells slaves, "Obey your masters." The pseudo-Pauline letters say the same thing (Colossians 3.22, Ephesians 6.5–8; 1 Timothy 6.1–2; Titus 2.9–10). Paul requests (not commands) special treatment for one slave who helped him in prison (Philemon 16), but this is clearly a special case, not a general judgment on slavery.

To all these genuine passages in support of slavery were added two spuriously biblical arguments. For all their phoniness, these arguments had greater appeal to some people in America because they introduced the factor of color. The Bible distinguished two kinds of slavery, for Jews and for non-Jews; but these were all in the broad sense cases of white slavery. It says nothing of black slavery. But Genesis 4.15 (the mark of Cain) and Genesis 9.25 (the curse of Ham) were misread to make the mark and the curse become blackness. Needless to say, there is no reference to blackness in the texts, and the curse was on Ham's son Canaan. But the two myths became a part of the biblical folklore that stigmatized blackness.[3]

Given the massive biblical and pseudo-biblical endorsement of slavery, how was a God-fearing Puritan to oppose the institution? Only by applying humane standards that would not become common until the Enlightenment had done its work. That is why Samuel Sewall deserves consideration as a precursor of the Enlightenment.

SAMUEL SEWALL

S EWALL WAS until recently scorned for his role as a judge in the witch trials. Scholars have used his diary as a rich mine of information on his time. But only recently has the decency of the man been properly emphasized.[4] He was the only judge who publicly confessed his error in the witch trials and publicly repented it. He was also a great promoter of friendship with the Indians—he thought of them as the lost tribes of Israel, so that their conversion and that of the other Jews (both conditions of the End Time) were united and looked more attainable. But the most striking way he stepped outside the constraints of his time is the pamphlet he wrote against slavery, *The Selling of Joseph* (1700).[5]

This booklet, short as it is, had a great impact, far beyond its apparent modesty. It stepped into a spotlight of sorts, emerging from a famous contest Sewall had with his fellow judge John Saffin over the freeing of Saffin's slave, Adam. Saffin had agreed to free Adam after seven years but reneged on the deal. Adam went to court, with Sewall's support, and the process dragged on for years. Sewall, arguing for Adam, reflected on the evils of slavery itself, in a prophetic volume that offers most of the abolitionist arguments before anyone else was bringing them before the public. He used, for instance, what would become some abolitionists' favorite line from the Jewish Scripture, Exodus 21.16: "He that stealeth a man and selleth him, or if he be found in his hand, he shall surely be put to death." This has to do with the kidnapping of a free man, not with the acquiring or selling of a man already enslaved. But abolitionists made "man stealing" their regular term for slavery, since the *original* enslavement, however that occurred, was a case of kidnapping.

Yet even when Sewall uses a Jewish illustration, he does it to introduce an argument from humane natural reason. The title of the book, for instance, refers to Genesis 37.28, where Joseph's brothers sell him into slavery for twenty pieces of silver. In Jewish law, parents could sell children, but siblings could not. Nor could parents or siblings sell Jews to foreigners. But that is not what Sewall is interested in. He looks at the transaction in terms of basic justice. "For he that shall in this case plead alteration of property [commercial transaction] seems to have *forfeited a great part of his own claim to humanity.* There is no proportion between twenty pieces of silver and liberty" (emphasis added). "Claims to humanity" is an Enlightenment argument. Here it is used to trump biblical exegesis.

Sewall begins with the Puritan distinction between the covenant with Adam and the Covenant of Grace—that is, between the sphere of civil and church law. The former is the realm of natural law, and Sewall sees there what Jefferson would see as part of "the laws of nature and of nature's God":

> It is most certain that all men, as they are the sons of Adam, are coheirs, and have equal right unto liberty and all other outward comforts of life. God hath given the earth with all its commodities unto the sons of Adam (Psalm 115.16) "and hath made of one blood all nations of men, for to dwell on all the face of the earth, and hath determined the times before appointed and the bound of their habitation, that they should see the Lord, forasmuch then as we are the offspring of God" . . . so that originally and naturally there is no such thing as slavery.

Sewall argues that the slave trade instills a sinful cruelty in its perpetrators:

> It is likewise most lamentable to think how, in taking Negroes out of Africa and selling of them here, that which God has joined together men do boldly rend asunder—men from their country, husbands from their wives, parents from their children. How horrible is the uncleanness, mortality (if not murder), that the ships are guilty of that bring great crowds of these miserable men and women.

He addresses a natural-reason argument for slavery, that conquerors in a war have the right (even the duty in Jewish history) to kill their victims.

This right of victors to dispose of vanquished lives means that they can impose the lesser penalty of servitude instead of execution. Since many black slaves come to America after being captured and sold in the wars between Africans themselves, clear title, it can be claimed, comes from the rights of conquest. But he objects: "Every war is upon one side unjust. An unlawful war can't make lawful captives." So there is a fifty-fifty chance, even granting the conquest argument, that the conquerors selling the slaves do not have clear title. (Sewall was, after all, a judge.) "And by receiving we are in danger to promote and partake in their barbarous cruelties." He offers an illustration of his point in local terms:

> I am sure, if some gentlemen should go down to the Brewsters
> to take the air and fish, and a stronger party from Hull should
> surprise them and sell them for slaves to a ship outward bound,
> they would think themselves unjustly dealt with, both by
> sellers and buyers. And yet 'tis to be feared we have no other
> kind of title to our Nigers.

Sewall faces directly the Jewish warrant for slavery only twice—first, when quoting the pseudo-argument from Ham's curse. He first says, rightly, that Canaan was cursed, not Ham, and that "blackamores" are commonly derived from Ham's other son, Cush. But even if God had cursed blacks, that does not give men the authority—here again the judge speaks—to execute the curse:

> Of all offices, one would not beg this—videlicet, uncall'd for to
> be an executioner of the vindictive wrath of God, the extent
> and duration of which is to us uncertain. If this ever was a
> commission, how do we know but that it is long since out of
> date [the judge knows about statutes of limitation]? Many
> have found it, to their cost, that a prophetical denunciation of
> judgment against a person or people would not warrant them
> to inflict that evil.

The second scriptural argument for slavery he notes is Abraham's possession of slaves (318 of them, remember). His first response to this is legal: we do not have the bill of sale to explain the transaction. "Until the circumstances of Abraham's purchase be recorded, no argument can be drawn from it." But even if we had such a document, Sewall says, the New Testament moves off from and way beyond the Jewish Scripture (here he was taking on the whole Puritan establishment):

> God expects that Christians should be of a more ingenuous and
> benign [this last a magic term in the coming Enlightenment]
> frame of spirit. . . . For men obstinately to persist in holding
> their neighbors and brethren under the rigor of perpetual
> bondage seems to be no proper way of gaining assurance [the
> result of Puritan conversion] that God has given them spiritual
> freedom. Our blessed Savior has altered the measure of the
> ancient love song, and set it to a most excellent new tune, which
> all ought to be ambitious of learning.

Here he cites Matthew 5.43–44, replacing the old standard ("Love thy neighbor, and hate thine enemy") with a new one ("Love your enemies"). He had just quoted the Golden Rule and he ends with a citation from the great authority William Ames, who also uses it. Sewall quotes the original Latin (from *Casus Conscientiae*), since much was expected of the reader. Here is the translation:

> Slavery voluntarily contracted among Christians is, on the part
> of the slave undergoing it, partly licit because compelled; but,
> on the part of the master in the transaction, acquiring and
> possessing the slave, it can hardly be made licit, since it does
> not fit this overriding rule: "As you would be treated by others,
> so treat them" (Matthew 7.12). And slavery inflicted as a
> punishment cannot be considered just except for some grave
> crime that merits otherwise the ultimate penalty, since liberty,

by common agreement, is the nearest thing to life itself, and is
often preferred to it by many people.

In breaking the hold of Scripture over the issue of slavery, the Golden
Rule would prove the clincher for many later abolitionists. No one
would wish to be enslaved himself, so how can he enslave others and
keep the Golden Rule? Sewall had earlier given a concrete instance of
that rule in action. Why do we condemn Algeria for taking Americans
captive—Sewall had worked to free one such prisoner, William Gee—if
we do the same thing to Africans?

Sewall includes some other arguments, like a lawyer giving a variety
of reasons to a jury. If it is said that bringing slaves to America is bringing them to Christianity, he denies that one can do wrong to bring about
good. God used the selling of Joseph to his own ends, but that did not
excuse the brothers who sold him. There are some practical arguments
of varying force—that "as many Negro men as there are among us, so
many empty places there are in our train bands [militia]"; that the slave
trade brings in people who "can never embody with us"; and that slaves
occasion "temptations their masters are under to connive at the fornication of their slaves, lest they should be obliged to find them wives or pay
their fines [for the crime of fornication]."

It is an explosive little bundle of arguments, to be unfolded in the
eighteenth century by the Quaker abolitionists who tore down the scriptural arguments for slavery. Sewall, though unusually brave in his public
airing of humane views, probably spoke for a number of less prominent
or articulate Puritans with consciences troubled by slaveholding. Saffin
issued a quick and angry reply to Sewall, backing his legal arguments
with racist doggerel. The tenor of the reply is signaled in the full title of
the book: *A Brief and Candid Answer to a Late Printed Sheet Entitled* The
Selling of Joseph, *Whereunto Is Annexed a True and Particular Narrative by
Way of Vindication of the Author's Dealing with and Prosecution of His Negro
Manservant for His Vile and Exorbitant Behavior Toward His Master and His
Tenant Thomas Shepard, Which Hath Been Wrongfully Represented to Their*

Prejudice and Defamation (1701). Sewall had the better arguments as well as better manners. He is a shining precursor of Enlightenment.

ROGER WILLIAMS

THE OTHER precursor is better known. Indeed, he has become a kind of saint of Enlightened values, mocked as such by the Jesuit theologian John Courtney Murray, who said that proponents of a separation of church and state always invoke "Master Roger." That is how Williams is almost invariably considered now, as a prophet of the First Amendment. It is a commonplace to compare him, incessantly, with Jefferson, though the comparison is deeply misleading. It is true that Williams described a "hedge" separating church and state, where Jefferson spoke of a "wall." But Williams claimed the hedge did not work, and Jefferson said that the wall did work.

In his own time, Williams was more often reviled than revered. John Winthrop drove him out of Massachusetts. Cotton Mather considered him an "incendiary," and said his mind was like a windmill whose vanes spin so wildly that their friction burns down their housing (M 2.495). Perry Miller of Harvard, the most influential twentieth-century student of Puritanism, was not much kinder to him—Winthrop was Miller's hero, and he sided with him against Williams. In a strictly historical perspective, said Miller, Williams is revealed as "a relatively minor character," known in his own time "as a divisive and inflammatory character."[6] Since he had "made himself a menace to their [the Puritans'] society; rationally he could and should be silenced . . . the banishment of Williams makes perfect sense."[7] Williams established a settlement at Providence that became a haven of religious tolerance, but only—Miller believes—because he became a total relativist: "Out of his typological meditations, bizarre as they may have been, he emerged with a generous conviction that no man could say for certain what is ultimate truth."[8] Miller believed that Williams could tolerate any views because there are no true ones.

It is customary to say that the only difference between Williams and Jefferson is that Williams wanted a separation of church and state to protect the church, while Jefferson wanted to protect the state.⁹ Perry Miller agrees with that commonplace: "He [Williams] would build a wall of separation between state and church, not to prevent the state from becoming an instrument of 'priestcraft,' but in order to keep the holy and pure religion of Jesus Christ from contamination by the slightest taint of earthly support."¹⁰ Like most of those treating Williams, Miller thinks that he was talking about a *functioning* separation of the church from the state. Luckily, Miller's eminent student Edmund Morgan of Yale saw the more striking truth. Williams was saying that separation between church and state, in the present stage of history, *does not exist*—and cannot.

We saw earlier that Williams tried to purify the Puritans by withdrawing from their compromises with Anglicanism. This led to his being exiled and setting up a new settlement. But once he had begun his withdrawing, he could find no point at which to stop doing so. He separated himself from his own baptism as a child when he was rebaptized—but shortly after that he withdrew from the Baptists.¹¹ He could pray, he said, only with the godly, but he found it harder and harder to find any godly people. He thought he might end up praying only with his wife.¹² He was the opposite of Samuel Johnson, who, when some people objected to the mad poet Christopher Smart for asking people to pray with him in the street, said, "I'd as lief pray with Kit Smart as with anyone."¹³ Williams would not pray with Kit Smart, or with anyone else. But then he set about systematically to undermine his own godliness.

We saw earlier that he felt he could not preach the Gospel. He once dreamed of missionary work among the Indians, but now declared that there was no true church to bring them into.¹⁴ He denied his own ordination, since that had come through the tainted church of his day. Antichrist now reigned in all the churches. There was no clear successor to the pure original church, which might validly ordain and preach. Since oaths were a form of prayer, they could not be administered—that would be a way of praying with the ungodly. Even grace before meals was impossible, since that would be praying with the ungodly members of one's own family.[15]

How, he was asked, did the church originally find members? It did so because Christ had directly commissioned apostles to spread the Gospel. But after the church became the Antichrist in the fourth century under Constantine, there were no more men who could claim to be commissioned by the first apostles or their successors. The Reformers could not reform because they had no direct authority from Christ. It was not enough simply to *remember* the primitive church. One needed to be authorized directly by it, and there was no getting around the intervening corruption, to claim such authorization.

> In the poor small span of my life, I desire to have been a diligent and constant observer, and have been myself many ways engaged in city, in country, in court, in schools, in universities, in churches, in Old and New England, and yet cannot in the holy presence of God bring in the result of a satisfying discovery that either the begetting ministry of the apostles or messengers to the nations, or the feeding and nourishing ministry of pastors and teachers, according the first institution of the Lord Jesus, are yet restored and extant.[16]

The church is *no longer extant.* Morgan calls this part of his own book "The Extinction of the Church."

Though there was a saintly, seeking quality in Williams that made him very appealing, he progressively painted himself into a corner. The world he was constructing in his mind looks, at first, very bleak. With the true church gone, there is no garden left, just wilderness. For this is the key point in his famous garden-wilderness argument, *that there is no longer any separation between them.* Look carefully at the most famous statement on the matter.

> The faithful labors of many witnesses of Jesus Christ, extant to the world, abundantly proving that the church of the Jews

under the Old Testament in the Type, and the Church of the
Christians under the New Testament in the Antitype, were
both separate from the world; and that when they have opened
a gap in the hedge or wall of separation between the garden of
the church and the wilderness of the world, God hath ever
broke down the wall itself, removed the candlestick, etc., and made
his garden a wilderness, *as at this day* [emphasis added].[17]

Jefferson would describe a situation in which church and state coexist, but separately. Williams is not describing coexistence, because one of the two has gone *out of* existence. The wilderness has rushed through the gap in the wall and extinguished the garden. That is the point of the second image in the passage. To remove the candle is a reference to Revelation, where "the seven candlesticks which thou sawest are the seven churches" (King James Version 1.20). To the church at Ephesus God says, "I will come unto thee quickly, and will remove thy candlestick out of his place, except thou repent" (2.5). The "etc." in Williams's passage means that we are supposed to remember the rest of the phrase, "removed the candlestick *out of his place.*" A church disappears when God removes its candlestick. The church will revive only at the Millennium, when Christ comes again and commissions new apostles to spread the Gospel through the last time. Until then, there can be no apostles or preachers, only what Williams called himself, one of the "witnesses to prophesy in sackcloth against the Beast [the regnant Antichrist]."[18]

But here is the paradox. If the garden is entirely gone and all we have is wilderness, we must live by wilderness rules—that is, by the natural covenant with Adam, from before the coming of grace. Williams no less than Enlightenment Deists recognizes only secular rules for the world. That is why Morgan notes that Williams writes little about high theology, the Trinity, the mystery of redemption, the Resurrection, and so on. Rather he looks to the organization and conduct of the community, which is no longer ruled by visible saints.[19] There *are* no visible saints. Thus he can criticize Quakers—as, indeed, he does all other sects—but he cannot exile them, as the Congregationalists did him. He must advocate their "correction," a punishment for things like public nakedness, disrupting meetings, and other forms of disturbing the peace—secular crimes. He has validated a secular world by going as far off from it as possible, then finding that there is nothing else left for him to come back to. Far from protecting the church from the world (as most people say he did), he has eliminated the church. This makes him far more radical in his secularism than Jefferson would ever be. Jefferson never meant to eliminate the church. Williams is also more anticlerical than Jefferson, who criticized "priests" while recognizing some valid ministries, like that of the Unitarian minister Joseph Priestley. Williams recognized no clerical ministers at all.

The danger of claiming that Williams endorsed a separation of church and state in the real world around him can be seen in the legal scholar Mark De Wolfe Howe's discussion of Williams. He concludes that since Williams believed in a separation that "favored" religion, as opposed to Jefferson, a tradition can be traced back to Williams of a "de facto establishment" of religion in general, as opposed to an establishment of one denomination.[20] It is hard to imagine any argument that could be more at odds with Williams's view of things. If he denied legitimacy to every actual religious institution of his time, it was on grounds that would have been even harsher on "religion in general." That would be Antichrist pretending to be Christ, the worst kind of blasphemy in his eyes. And for any state to claim that it was sanctioned by God was blasphemy in his eyes. Even the churches were no longer sanctioned by God (they were under Antichrist), so how could the "wilderness" claim to be the "garden"?

Williams explained why secular values must guide the world with the analogy of travelers on a ship:

> There goes many a ship to sea, with many hundred souls in one
> ship whose weal and woe is common, and is a true picture of a
> commonwealth, or a human combination, or society. It hath
> fallen out sometimes that both papists and Protestants, Jews and
> Turks, may be embarked in one ship, upon which supposal I

affirm that all the liberty of conscience that ever I pleaded
for turns upon these two things—that none of the papists,
Protestants, Jews, or Turks be forced to come to the ship's
prayers or worship, if they practice any. I further add that I never
denied that, notwithstanding this liberty, the commander of the
ship ought to command the ship's course, yea and also command
that justice, peace, and sobriety be kept and practiced, both
among the seamen and all the passengers. If any of the seamen
refuse to perform their services, or passengers to pay their
freight; if any refuse to help, in person or purse, towards the
common charges or defense; if any refuse to obey the common
laws and orders of the ship concerning their common peace
or preservation; if any shall mutiny and rise up against their
commanders and officers; if any should preach or write that
there ought to be no commanders or officers, because all are
equal in Christ, therefore no masters nor officers, no lawyers nor
orders, nor corrections nor punishments—I say I never denied
but, in such cases, whatever is pretended, the commander or
commanders may judge, resist, compel and punish such
transgressors according to their deserts and merits.[21]

The officers of such a ship should not be chosen for their piety, and they
obviously have no authority to instill, monitor, or compel piety in
others. They are better at what they do because there is a secular emphasis on their competence at it.

A Christian captain, Christian merchant, physician, lawyer,
pilot, father, master—and so, consequently, magistrate, etc.—is
no more a captain, merchant, physician, lawyer, pilot, father,
master, magistrate etc. than a captain, merchant, etc. of any
other conscience or religion.[22]

In the secular realm—which is the entire realm of worldly matters—
Williams reaches in his own way the attitude of Jefferson with regard to

the secular competence of the state (one of the key elements of the Enlightenment). Williams said a good captain need not hold true beliefs himself or enforce them in others. He also said that the state has no jurisdiction over religious opinion, and therefore could not enforce "the First Table" (the first four of the Ten Commandments, often depicted on the left tablet of the two stones that Moses brought down from the mountain, the commandments having to do with the honoring of God).

In summary, Williams and Jefferson can sometimes say the same thing, but for very different reasons and with very different effect. Jefferson said: "It does me no injury for my neighbor to say there are twenty gods or no god. It neither picks my pocket nor breaks my leg."[23] And Williams said: "A false religion and worship will not hurt the civil state, in case the worshipper break no civil law."[24] But Williams was no advocate of a separate church in the present order, which he held to be impossible. That is why Jefferson is a true Enlightenment figure and Williams is only a precursor of Enlightenment.

6 | Spur to Enlightenment: The Great Awakening

O NE OF THE MOST praised and studied events in colonial history is the emotional upheaval known as the Great Awakening (1730s–40s). This religious turmoil has been hailed as a precursor of the Revolution and even of the Enlightenment. The most influential historian of American Puritanism, Perry Miller, held that the leading theologian of the Awakening, Jonathan Edwards, practically *was* the American Enlightenment—the first American to understand Locke's epistemology, "the last great American, perhaps the last European, for whom there could be no warfare between religion and science, or between ethics and nature." He "entered abruptly into modernity" and reduced hell to a "footnote."[1]

Miller claimed that "unlike other New England pastors, Edwards was willing to come down from his pulpit and mix with the people."[2]

A self-professed follower of Miller, Alan Heimert, took this last claim and argued at length that the Jonathan Edwards Awakening was the great liberating force in American history, one that led to and through the Revolution, to culminate in Jeffersonian and Jacksonian democracy.[3] Jefferson would have been astonished to hear that his old foes the New England Calvinists somehow "begat" him, and historians have been just as incredulous. Sidney Mead wrote: "Heimert's genealogy of Jacksonian democracy is about as plausible as the 'begat' passages in the Gospels of Matthew and Luke and apparently has about the same relation to historical evidence."[4]

Less enthusiastic followers of Perry Miller think that the Awakening made possible the Revolution, without making wild claims about Jefferson and Jackson. But they have been convincingly refuted by the Princeton historian John Murrin.[5] All such claims run into the embarrassing fact that the Awakening cooled as fast as it had arisen. What it led to was not the Revolution but what Evangelical historian Mark Noll calls the great decline in Evangelicalism (1750–90).

> The revivals of the 1730s and 1740s did produce a dramatic
> interest in religion, to which numerous observers attest. Yet
> after the fires of revival cooled, membership additions dipped
> below earlier averages, and by the 1750s many churches that
> had benefited from the revivals were barely adding enough new
> members to replace those who died.[6]

It is hard to believe that the Revolution was manned out of these depleted ranks. It is true that the Awakening, while it lasted (and Jonathan Edwards lamented that it did not last long), had some social effects that may have contributed, in largely unmeasurable ways, to later developments. But other factors were working in the same direction. We are told that the network of Awakeners drew the colonies together. But that was happening in other, more powerful ways, in the political situation after the French and Indian War and in the forging of colonial resistance to British tax policy. The revivals broke down some class barriers and democratized certain aspects of church life, but that seems to have led to the Evangelical decline as much as to any positive political activism. Alan Heimart shows that some people stirred by the Awakening took part in the Revolution. But as Murrin argues, there is no reason to think they would not have done that even if the Awakening had never occurred.

The Awakening did play a preparatory role for the Enlightenment—not as a precursor of it but as a provocation. The Enlightenment was spurred by the *reaction* to the Awakening. As we shall see in the next chapter, early leaders of the Enlightenment were spurred to special activity as a way of countering what they took to be the fanaticism ("enthusiasm" in the eighteenth-century usage) of the Awakeners. This reaction lasted longer and was more pervasive in its effect than the emotional spasms of the Awakening. What has been attributed to the impact of the Great Awakening is derived more properly from the more vast and lasting effect of the Second Awakening (1800–30), which had to start from scratch after the founding period. That was the movement that created America's religious culture for the nineteenth and twentieth centuries. Nonetheless, the Great Awakening was a striking event during its heated moment, and it must be studied if only because so many misconceptions are still entertained about it, and especially about Jonathan Edwards's supposed embodiment of Enlightened values.

The Awakening seemed radical, if not mad, to many who observed it. In churches where pastors had been elected for their learning, to minister to a single congregation, the idea of itinerant preachers moving in through the parishes, calling people out of their settled church existence, was shocking. New Englanders especially were not used to seeing lay preachers, boy preachers, even women preachers travel from town to town.[7] These evangels preached unconventionally, often outside churches, on weekdays as well as the Sabbath, sometimes at night so workers could get to the sermons. The movement was ecumenical, at least so far as most Protestant sects were concerned. The Awakening was preached by Dutch Reformed men like Theodorus Frelinghuysen, Presbyterians like William Tennent and his sons, Anglicans like George Whitefield, and Congregationalists like Jonathan Edwards.

Not the least important aspect of the Awakening was, thus, the way it challenged, however chaotically, the monopoly of New England over religious teaching. Though Jonathan Edwards was from New England, the seeds of the Awakening were sown in the Middle Colonies, especially New Jersey, where fresh winds of piety were carried from Westphalia by Theodorus Jacobus Frelinghuysen, from Scotland and Ireland by William Tennent and Gilbert Tennent, and from England by George Whitefield.

At first, some pastors welcomed the sudden outpouring of religious fervor. They thought that the stimulus to conversion would fill their churches. But when the crowds spilled out into the streets and fields, and emotional paroxysms began to seem more authentic than the staid rituals of regular service, they had second and severer thoughts. George Whitefield, when he came (four times) from England, especially upset some of them—at last disturbing even his earlier supporter Jonathan Edwards:

> As soon as the itinerant left the region, Edwards delivered a
> series of sermons warning his congregation against being
> deceived by the enthusiasm that Whitefield so facilely
> generated. . . . When Edwards had frankly chided Whitefield
> for following spiritual "impulses," the itinerant seemed not
> at all convinced and rather coolly let the subject drop.[8]

Yet Whitefield was a wonder of the day. He fascinated Benjamin Franklin, who followed his exploits in his newspapers. Once, when a throng filled the streets around Philadelphia's Market Square to hear Whitefield, Franklin calculated that his strong voice and clear diction were audible to thirty thousand people in the open air.[9] Franklin said of the Great Awakening in general: "Never did the people show so great a willingness to attend sermons. Religion is become the subject of most conversation. No books are in request but those of piety."[10] Charles Chauncy, the influential pastor of the First Church in Boston and a critic of the new movement, marveled at the "disposition to be perpetually hearing sermons, to the neglect of all other business."[11]

As the new devotion grew, old-style pastors became ever more alarmed. They denounced these religious Pied Pipers as biblically (and otherwise) unlearned. Chauncy wrote that the new preachers were "most commonly raw, illiterate, weak and conceited young men or lads."[12] The

Awakeners, for their part, denounced the old order as lacking what Gilbert Tennent called the "experience of a special work of the Holy Ghost upon their own souls."[13] He compared them to "the letter-learned and regular Pharisees," and said that "their discourses are cold and sapless, and as it were freeze between their lips."[14] The unauthorized preachers were criticized for lacking a college training in theology. They made this an occasion for attacking the colleges. Tennent remarked on "the public academies being so much corrupted."[15] Whitefield said of Harvard-trained pastors: "As for the universities, I believe it may be said, their light is become darkness."[16] James Davenport tried to inspire a student insurrection against the president of Yale as an ungodly minister.

The attacks on clergy became more virulent. Whitefield wrote, "I am verily persuaded, the generality of preachers talk of an unknown, unfelt Christ."[17] Charles Chauncy reported that Gilbert Tennent had said, "Most of the ministers of the town of Boston and the country are unconverted, and are leading their people blindfold to hell."[18] By 1741, things had reached a point where an "inspired" woman, Bathsheba Kingsley, went door to door in Westfield, Massachusetts, and neighboring towns, telling people that Christ was displeased with their pastors.[19] Disorders led the Connecticut Assembly in 1742 to pass an antivagrancy law by which they could exclude or punish the itinerant preachers.[20]

James Davenport was the most defiant of the well-known Awakeners. A man of distinguished family, descended from the founder of New Haven, he had graduated at the top of his class at Yale and was given a parish in Southold, Long Island. But as a zealous follower of Whitefield, he became an itinerant preacher, and for a while almost equaled Whitefield's drawing power as an orator of force and imagination. He was hauled into court for his extremist statements. Yet some of these can be paralleled in the sermons of the respected leaders of the Awakening. This passage, for instance, resembles one in the most famous speech of Jonathan Edwards:

> He saw hell flames slashing [plashing] in their faces, and that
> they were now! now! dropping down to hell ... Lord! Thou

knowest that there are many in that gallery and in these seats
that are now dropping down to hell![21]

And here is Jonathan Edwards:

Your wickedness makes you as it were heavy as lead, and to
tend downwards with great weight and pressure towards hell;
and if God should let you go, you would immediately sink and
swiftly descend and plunge into the bottomless gulf.[22]

Davenport went beyond words. In Connecticut he caused turmoil at
Yale and was expelled from the colony. He proved just as unruly in Massachusetts, where he was again arrested, adjudged not quite sane, and
deported to Long Island. But he returned to Connecticut to set up an
independent church in New London, where in 1743 he publicly burned
the books of Puritan divines like Increase Mather and of his current
enemies, including Charles Chauncy, pronouncing that dead men like
Mather were in hell and that living authors like Chauncy were hurrying
there: "The smoke of the torments of such of the authors of the above-
said books as died in the same belief as when they set them out was now
ascending in hell in like manner as the smoke of these books rises."[23] He
denounced the whole ministerial establishment as "bound in one bundle
to persecute all true lovers of Christ."[24]

Some Puritans had burnt the books of heretics in the early days. But
burning the works of respected men was an assault on all the great
respect for learning that had been built up in New England. This was too
much even for Davenport's close followers. They sheepishly submitted
to fines for "profaning the Sabbath." These defections shocked Davenport into a recantation. He publicly confessed to wronging the ministers
he had attacked, confessing "Satan and my evil heart" had led him astray
at a time when illness had weakened him.[25] But his antics, and those of
others, were used by Chauncy to impeach the whole Awakening.

Despite the emotional excesses at the revivals—the screams and
leapings and self-abasements—this was not just a populist movement. It

had learned defenders—the "Log College" men in New Jersey who created the future Princeton. The Awakening would indirectly lead to the founding of other colleges—Brown (1760), Rutgers (1764), and Dartmouth (1769). The movement had some learned pastors and lay leaders, men like Thomas Prince, Benjamin Colman, Joseph Bellamy, Thomas Foxcroft, Aaron Burr Sr., Jonathan Dickinson, and Jonathan Edwards. For that matter, Edwards alone would seem to signal that the movement he sponsored was on the side of Enlightenment.

JONATHAN EDWARDS

PERRY MILLER's secular championing of Edwards wrests him almost completely out of his Calvinist matrix, creating what has been called a movement of "atheists for Edwards."[26] Miller has especially overplayed the Lockean nature of Edwards's thought. Norman Fiering, in his thorough and respected study of Edwards as a philosopher, concludes: "Edwards himself was no Lockean. On hardly any single point in moral philosophy does he follow Locke, and in logic and metaphysics his differences from Locke are fundamental."[27] Fiering finds that Edwards was a determinist, opposed to both the "libertarians" and the "humanitarians."

Edwards was brilliant and original, but brilliant in finding new ways to defend the old views. He was a strict Calvinist. When he succeeded to the pulpit of his famous and powerful grandfather Solomon Stoddard, he reversed the liberal positions Stoddard had pioneered—things like baptizing the children of "unconverted" parents, enlarging access to the Lord's Supper. Much of his congregation resented or resisted these moves, but he did not give them a "democratic" hearing, as Miller supposes. He said that giving every man a say would be as absurd as giving every woman a say. Natural reason might support such a position but the Bible outlaws it.[28] One of the reasons Edwards welcomed the Awakening was that it seemed to solve, in a wholesale way, the problem of qualifying people as saved before they could take communion. If whole new waves of converts were being created, Edwards could get a crowded communion service without adopting his grandfather's latitudinarian ways. He applied the old John Cotton view that salvation comes in a rush of the Spirit, though he allowed Thomas Hooker's "preparationism" to the extent that hellfire preaching can ready the soul for reception of the Spirit.

Edwards was far from the Enlightenment in many of his attitudes and actions. He was entirely untroubled in conscience while buying and using slaves. Beyond owning them himself, he publicly defended a fellow minister for owning them.[29] In this he was far less Enlightened than Samuel Sewall had been before him and than his own son Jonathan Jr. would be after him. Slaves bothered him less than what has been called the "bad books crisis." In 1744, when he deplored the fading enthusiasms of revival, he took the occasion of a sermon to name off in public a list of young men he was summoning for punishment. Some of them had learned from medical texts (the "bad books") about menstruation and teased young girls with this information. The young men named had not all done this—some just knew of it, but that was enough for Edwards to publicly excoriate them. The parents, many of them prominent citizens, were furious with Edwards for this pillorying in the Hester Prynne style. They fought the public confession he was demanding, but he backed down only partially and reluctantly, causing lasting animosity toward him.[30]

Edwards was at one with his Puritan forebears in expecting the imminent arrival of the Millennium. In fact, he at first took the Awakening itself as a miraculous overture to the great thousand-year reign. He was as obsessive as Cotton Mather in looking for signs of it, but here too he used new techniques for measuring the matter. He kept elaborate timetables, quantifying the losses of Catholic troops around the world as a principal indicator that Antichrist's reign was coming to an end.

> Edwards accordingly transferred into a notebook detailed reports, mostly from Boston newspapers, that had to do with defeats of Catholic forces, which might be interpreted as drying up the wealth that supplied Babylon for Rome. Whenever the British captured French ships—a staple of the early entries— Edwards copied down the number of men and guns captured.

No friend of learning for its own sake, Edwards included as one
of the first evidences of God's work a report from Vienna of a
Jesuit library, "one of the best-chosen and most curious in
Europe," that was struck by lightning and burned.[31]

In order to hasten the coming of the Millennium, Edwards adopted
what may seem a caricature of the Enlightenment delight in quantifying
measures. He proposed to the Scots that they enter into a "Concert of
Prayer" for the coming of Christ. They would all pray together at predetermined times, to beat down the Antichrist with a concentrated barrage
of impetration.[32] Here is a return to one of the prime notes of pre-
Enlightenment religion, its ultra-supernaturalism. Edwards sees miracles
at work all around him. When the British colonial forces took the French
bastion at Louisbourg in 1745, that was a proof that God had intervened,
and he did it because of the Great Awakening, which had purified the
people: "Sin above all things weakens a people at war."[33] Franklin, a genuine figure of the Enlightenment, scoffed at these prayers fired off like
artillery to batter down the foe.

> Some seem to think forts are as easy taken as snuff.... You have
> a fast and prayer day for that purpose; in which I compute five
> hundred thousand petitions were offered up to the same effect
> in New England, which, added to the petitions of every family
> morning and evening, multiplied by the number of days since
> January 25th [the date for beginning the expedition], make
> forty-five millions of prayers; which, set against the prayers of
> a few priests in the garrison to the Virgin Mary, give a vast
> balance in your favor.... I believe there is a Scripture in what
> I have wrote, but I cannot adorn the margin with quotations,
> having a bad memory, and no concordance at hand.[34]

The way Edwards put a kind of pseudo-Enlightenment technique to
the service of old Calvinist dogma can be seen in his use of the Millennium to answer those who called for a more "benevolent" God. Sure,

souls were being sent by the thousands into hell now. But when the Millennium (the thousand-year reign of Christ) comes, there will be a thousand years of good people multiplying in great numbers, with no infant mortality or other things to depress population. They will likely double their numbers every fifty years, leaving a million saved by the end of the period. A disciple of Edwards, working further with the numbers in consultation with Edwards, figured that eventually there would be only one or so people damned for every seventeen thousand saved.[35] *That* shows the benevolence of God. It also shows a reductio ad absurdum of Enlightenment social science methods.

So we come to the damned. It was wishful thinking that made Miller (and, it must be said, some others) claim that Edwards reduced hell to a footnote. He tried to minimize hell, but only numerically (and, even then, only with the help of a millennial numbers game), not psychologically. Hell was at the center of Edwards's psychology of religion. Fiering was right when he wrote: "Edwards was the most famous fire and brimstone preacher in the eighteenth century and possibly the most famous in the entire history of western civilization."[36] Though Miller claimed in his biography that Edwards did not make a big deal of hell, in another place he chose the following passage as a *representative* sample of Edwards's rhetoric:

> How dismal will it be, when you are under these racking
> torments, to know assuredly that you never, never shall be
> delivered from them; to have no hope; when you shall wish that
> you might but be turned into nothing, but shall have no hope of
> it; when you shall wish that you might be turned into a toad or
> a serpent, but shall have no hope of it; when you would rejoice
> if you might but have any relief, after you shall have endured
> these torments millions of ages, but shall have no hope of it;
> when, after you shall have worn out the age of the sun, moon,
> and stars in your dolorous groans and lamentations, without
> any rest day or night, or one minute's ease, yet you shall have
> no hope of ever being delivered; when, after you shall have

worn out a thousand more such ages, yet you shall have no
hope, but shall know that you are not one whit nearer to the
end of your torments, but that still there are the same groans,
the same shrieks, the same doleful cries, incessantly to be made
by you, and that the smoke of your torment shall still ascend
up forever and ever; and that your souls which have been
agitated with the wrath of God all this while, yet will still
exist to bear more wrath; your bodies, which shall have been
burning and roasting all this while in these glowing flames, yet
shall not have been consumed, but will remain to roast through
an eternity yet, which will not have been at all shortened by
what shall have been passed.[37]

Edwards was not unique in this use of hellfire; he was just better at it,
and more insistent on it. Gilbert Tennent rejoiced that his fellows were not
like the cold and donnish pastors that had not "felt" religion: "They have
not the courage or honesty to thrust the nail of terror into sleeping souls."[38]
Hooker had said that "humiliation" was one of the preparatory stages of
conversion—but that was when the unregenerate soul was expected to
inflict the dread reflection on his or her own self. The Awakeners flogged
the sinners publicly. Here is Edwards in his most famous sermon:

The God that holds you over the pit of Hell, much as one
holds a spider or some loathsome insect over the fire, abhors
you, and is dreadfully provoked; his wrath towards you burns
like fire; he is of purer eyes than to bear to have you in his sight;
you are ten thousand times so abominable in his eyes as the
most hateful venomous serpent is in ours. You have offended
him infinitely more than ever a stubborn rebel did his prince,
and yet 'tis nothing but his hand that holds you from falling
into the fire every moment.[39]

The Enlightenment would bring a certain optimism about human
capacities and nobility. But sermons like this are meant to beat that down

as pride. The effect such words had on some is registered in the memo-ries of young women from that time. One woman said, "I am unclean from the crown of my head to the soles of my feet. I am full of wounds, bruises, and putrifying sores." Deborah Prince said, "By nature I am half a devil and half a beast; I know that in me, that is in my flesh, dwells no good thing." A young convert from Rhode Island said she was "so defiled that I pollute all I touch."[40] Given this kind of response, it is not surpris-ing that some suicides and attempted suicides occurred after Edwards's hellfire sermons, including that of his own uncle. George Marsden even says that "the suicide craze effectively brought the conversions to an end" for the year 1735.[41] And no wonder. Edwards taught that, since the saved were conscious of their salvation, the damned must know their own condition just as well. "So he preached, as he believed he must, that those who despaired were indeed unworthy."[42] With his ultra-supernaturalist approach, he used the suicides to say that Satan was warning others in the way he took off one of his own. It would hardly work against others' despair to hear their pastor's ghoulish warning of how Satan works, how some people "had it urged upon 'em, as if somebody had spoke to 'em, 'Cut your own throat, now is good opportunity, now, NOW.'"

Why were the Awakeners so focused on hell? It came from the heart of their doctrine. As Joseph Bellamy wrote, "Till the infinite evil of sin is seen, an incarnate God dying on a cross is an incredible story."[43] *Infinite* evil. Edwards had said in his famous sermon, "You have offended him *infinitely*." The Reformers had accepted the explanation for the Incarna-tion given by Anselm of Canterbury in the eleventh century. Adam's original sin had offended the infinite God, and there was no way finite man could undo such an offense. The infinite God had to become man and pay the debt. Then his merits could be "imputed" to the saved.

One of the strong points of this theology is the tight interlocking of all its components: original sin, offended Father, redeeming Son, and Spirit bringing sanctification. Each depended on the other. Remove even one and the whole system falls apart. Without original sin, there could be no reason for the first coming of Christ. Without an angry Father, there would be no need for the sacrifice of his Son. Without the suffering of the

Cross, there would be no justification. Without the sending of the Spirit, there would be no sanctification. Without an infinite offense there would be no reason for the infinite suffering of the damned. Without the interaction of all these elements, there would be no reason for the Puritans' endless theorizing on the nature and process of conversion.

The meshing of all these parts meant that the damnation of many souls must be seen not as the flaw in a cosmic system but as its vindication. God's honor is upheld in his power to punish. The saved will not only acknowledge this but delight in it. As an admirer of Edwards writes:

> The misery of the damned is a manifestation of divine
> goodness because it enhances the saints' enjoyment of God; the
> saints' vision of God's hatred and wrath toward others "raises
> their sense of the riches and excellency of his love to them." If
> it did not, there would be "a visible defect, an inharmonious-
> ness between God's eternal punishment and the saints"
> enjoyment of God's glory.[44]

There was a cruelty built into the Puritans' theological system.

> The great creator that made all these stars, and is the creator of
> this great system of bodies, has been murdered, and his blood
> has been wickedly shed in this system, and on this earth, and
> no wonder that this breaks down the whole frame, and fetches
> all down in vengeance and in fury on this earth.[45]

Central to this whole complex is the existence of the Trinity. That is why, as we shall see, a key ingredient—perhaps *the* key ingredient—in the arrival of Enlightened religion was a denial of the Trinity. Thus Unitarianism was the spearhead of the religious Enlightenment. It rejected the idea of a vengeful God. It disliked human sacrifice of any kind, to say nothing of God sacrificing a member of his own Trinity. Of course, there are ways of denying the wrath of God without denying the dogma of the Trinity. There can be Enlightened Trinitarians. But the mesh of dark truths in which the dogma had been so tightly embedded made it culturally important to break the whole scheme apart. Besides, as the early Unitarians emphasized, the doctrine of the Trinity is explicit only in the early creeds and councils of the church, not in the New Testament itself. What then happens to the Reformers' appeal only to the Bible (*sola scriptura*)? The creeds and councils are part of "tradition," which the Reformers rejected.[46]

The logical power of the Puritans came from the total control they established over their imprisoning intellectual task. Their system was perfect, but it was a dwarf perfection. It let in little air or light. It did not breathe. G. K. Chesterton talks of this combination of "a logical completeness and a spiritual contraction." He wrote: "A small circle is quite as complete, as infinite as a large circle; but though it is quite as infinite, it is not so large. . . . A bullet is quite as round as the world, but it is not the world."[47] The best example of this small completeness is the tight reasoning of the Calvinists on the Trinity. There can be a view of the Trinity that, like Augustine's, invites people into a mystery, makes them part of the conversation of God with himself, suggesting that the inmost secret of the universe is a *social* one. As Chesterton says, it inverts the scriptural text "It is not good for man to be alone" (Genesis 2.18) and says that "It is not good for God to be alone."[48] But the Trinity in the Puritans' hand became a way of making it possible for God to punish God, not to enjoy the company of God.[49]

The deepest *cultural* way, then, in which Edwards fought off the coming of the Enlightenment was his dogged defense of the Trinity. He was especially fierce against Jonathan Mayhew, whom we shall meet as an early figure of the Enlightenment, for undermining the concept of the Trinity.[50] Those who try to save Edwards by shearing off this or that unpalatable part of his teaching do not understand the first thing about him—his abiding devotion to the entire apparatus of Calvinism as his intellectual cosmos. Creation, predestination, Incarnation, atonement, particular election, last judgment, heaven, and hell—it is the whole package or nothing. Which is why some would decide, when the Enlightenment arrived, to take nothing.

It is hard to see, therefore, how Edwards could be considered as a major figure in the American Enlightenment. Despite the current interest in him, he had no great impact on American religious practice or thought. His attempts to return to strict control of baptism and the Lord's Supper were rejected by his own community. His own son Jonathan Edwards II did not follow him on these matters or other things. As for his thought, even a fervent admirer of Edwards like Sydney Ahlstrom agrees (and regrets) that he had no followers who understood him:

> He did not have a single disciple who was true to his essential
> genius. His three most dedicated followers, Joseph Bellamy,
> Samuel Hopkins, and Jonathan Edwards, Jr., were all men of
> another type and temperament. Even when they were true to
> the letter, they proved themselves to be of another spirit, at
> once more congenial to their age and less able to transcend
> it than Edwards had been. What is more surprising, the
> Edwardsean spirit was really never infused into the life and
> thought of his church. (A 310)

Mark Noll, another Edwardsean, agrees that his so-called heirs, the leaders of what was called the "New Divinity," departed from him in the direction of Enlightenment, softening his doctrines on depravity and atonement and divine benevolence. Their thought on these matters put Joseph Bellamy "closer to his liberal contemporary Charles Chauncy than to his mentor, Edwards." Bellamy and Samuel Hopkins were "Janus-faced" as they moved away from Edwards. "The difference was that Edwards had translated the new languages back into the old dogma, while Bellamy and Hopkins had begun the process of translating the old dogma into a new language . . . a language of rights, reason, and universal moral intuitions."[51]

But if Edwards had little role to play in bringing on the religious Enlightenment, another group of Awakeners has a better claim to have done that—the "New Side" Presbyterians of New Jersey. Their work, after all, laid the foundations of Princeton University.

THE NEW SIDE

I HAVE ALREADY mentioned Theodorus Jacobus Frelinghuysen and the Tennents as collaborators with George Whitefield in preaching the Awakening. They deserve a closer look. The first stirrings in the 1720s of what became the Awakening were in Frelinghuysen's parish at Raritan, New Jersey. Frelinghuysen was a critic of the conventional Dutch Reformed ministers. He thought them lax and cold formalists who could not deliver "soul searching" sermons to ignite the fires of conversion. He had a great impact on the other Awakeners, who included his five minister sons and his two minister sons-in-law. Frelinghuysen was so intent on breaking with formalisms, in response to the Spirit, that he banned the saying of the Lord's Prayer at service, since that was the rote recitation of a formula and therefore "popish."[52] Gilbert Tennent, one of the "big three" of the Enlightenment (along with George Whitefield and Jonathan Edwards) credited Frelinghuysen with showing him the way to preach.[53] Frelinghuysen and the Tennents prepared the way for the response Whitefield received when he came to America in 1740. They were among the first to welcome him into their churches. Whitefield called Frelinghuysen "the beginner of the great work" of the Awakening.

William Tennent, Gilbert's father, ran into the problem of an untrained ministry outside of New England. The Presbyterian Synod of Pennsylvania refused to accept pastors who had not been educated at Harvard, Yale, or one of the European universities. Tennent already had disagreements with the Synod over subscription to the Westminster Confession of 1647. The Synod made this a test for the acceptance of ministers. Tennent opposed this formalism, which let in candidates he considered unsuitable on other grounds. He had been educated at Edinburgh himself, but he thought a new generation should be educated in the new spirituality of the heart. So he set up his own theological school in 1735 at the Neshaminy River in Pennsylvania. Gilbert, his oldest son, was already ordained by then and under the influence of Frelinghuysen, but William trained his three younger sons in the school, along with other men (including Samuel Finney and Samuel Blair) who formed the nucleus of the Awakening's forces in Pennsylvania.

Tennent's critics mocked his school as the "Log College," and the Pennsylvania Synod refused to recognize its graduates. After some Log College men were rejected in the Synod sessions of 1739 and 1749, a formal break occurred in 1741, when the Subscribers (to the Westminster Confession) expelled all the Log College men and their supporters. The Synod was said to be upholding the "Old Side" in the dispute, which made the expelled members the New Side. The New Side began from a weak position, aggravated by their ties to John Davenport, whose excesses had come under wide criticism (over the burnt books of 1743), and weakened as well by a dispute some of them were having with the traveling Count Zinzendorf, whose Moravian settlement the Log College men considered "Antinomian."

There was disagreement in the Awakeners' ranks when Whitefield at first supported Zinzendorf.[54] But the Tennents found an ally against Zinzendorf in New Jersey—Jonathan Dickinson, who had his own troubles with the Old Side. He and others joined with the Tennents to form their own synod in New York, whose early aim was to form a larger establishment than the Log College. The first sessions of what would become the College of New Jersey met in Dickinson's Elisabeth Town home in 1747. With the help of the pro-Awakening governor of New Jersey, Jonathan Belcher, a broad charter was given to the college and a new site found for it, at Princeton. Belcher raised money for the college and donated his library of four hundred books to it when he died in 1757.

The college suffered the extraordinary bad luck of losing its first five presidents at a young age—Dickinson at fifty-nine, Aaron Burr Sr. at forty-one, Jonathan Edwards at fifty-four, Samuel Davies at thirty-seven, and Samuel Finley at thirty-seven. All but Edwards (who served less than a year) were New Side Presbyterians, one of them (Finley) a graduate of the Log College. The loss of such distinguished men was frustrating— the four Presbyterians among them had accounted for 20 percent of the Presbyterian works published between 1706 and 1789.[55] The Old Side tried to capitalize on these troubles of its foe by opening its own schools, but these went nowhere. Then they tried to take over Princeton at the death of President Finley in 1766, when no obvious New Side candidate was available to replace him. Now the New Side, which had fought the Synod over calling in men from European universities, reached out to Scotland for a product of Edinburgh University, John Witherspoon. With his presidency, Princeton became a pillar of the Enlightenment in America. But the New Side had slithered into that position almost *malgré lui*. In conflicts with the Old Side, the Tennents had said that reason and happiness were false lights, impeding the power of the Spirit to move human feelings.[56] The New Side men were orthodox Calvinists, believers in the Trinity, predestination, and atonement. It was not the Awakening that fostered the Enlightenment, but the reaction against the Awakening.

PART TWO

ENLIGHTENED
RELIGION

❖

III | UNITARIANS

7 | AGAINST THE AWAKENING

I TOUCHED BRIEFLY on the paradox of the Awakening in my last chapter. Though some consider it a liberalizing force in America, the real breakthrough toward liberal thought came from opposition to the Awakening. The overthrow of Calvinism by the Unitarians came from the socially conservative sector, among Anglicans and among those Harvard professors Cotton Mather called "Catholicks."[1]

This goes against some people's preferences or presuppositions, and historians of religion greet the development with surprise, and sometimes with regret. The Awakening was more powerful for what it helped its opponents do than for any lasting impact on its adherents. George Marsden says, "The Awakening, like all radical renewal movements, created a liberal backlash among those whom it had judged spiritually cold.... The Calvinist Awakening thus had the ironic consequence of undermining the structure of Calvinist orthodoxy, especially around Boston."[2] Sydney Ahlstrom puts it this way:

> The Great Awakening thus became the single most important
> catalyst of the "Arminian" [free will] tradition which had been
> growing surreptitiously and half-consciously since the turn of

the [eighteenth] century. One can, in fact, regard Charles Chauncy's critique of the Awakening, *Seasonable Thoughts on the State of Religion in New England* (1745), as a primary document in the rise of Unitarianism. When this book appeared, both Harvard and Yale were considered seminaries of Puritan learning; but thereafter Harvard became increasingly a bastion of liberal thought. (288)

Leonard Trinterud laments that the enemy of the New Side was rationalism, and that the enemy prevailed: "The New Light was snuffed out."[3] E. Brooks Holifield joins this chorus:

> By mid-century, a few colonial theologians, some Anglican and some Congregatiönalist, often reacting against the seeming excesses of the revivals, opened the way toward a theology that defined the virtuous life as a clearer sign of religious devotion than the experience of conversion itself.[4]

That Anglicans played such a leading role in the American Enlightenment is less surprising than might have been supposed. The Anglicans in America, some of whom had stayed loyal to the established church in England, were considered conservative. But developments in England had made for rapid and highly liberal developments in the church there, developments that spread to this continent. The old high-church tradition of Archbishop William Laud had been overthrown by the Parliaments of the eighteenth century, making a liberal theology possible. Latitudinarian views, skeptical and eudaemonist, welcomed the Enlightenment, and favored Unitarian attacks on the Trinity. This tendency was reflected in the American missionary arm of the British Society for the Propagation of the Gospel, which preached a rational religion of nature.[5]

Americans adopting these notions saw the Awakening as a case of the Spirit gone mad. Many agreed with John Locke on the nature of "enthusiasm"—"the habit of giving unreasonable assent to religious propositions."[6] This Enlightenment view of enthusiasm was also expressed in Lord Shaftesbury's "A letter Concerning Enthusiasm" (1711)—a work Jefferson read carefully and took notes from (J 1.548–49).[7] Once men recoiled from emotional excess, they looked more carefully at how reason could be used to guide religion into more acceptable paths. One of the first tasks they gave reason was to conclude, with Locke, against the Trinity, that "the existence of more than one God is contrary to reason."[8]

Unitarianism had, in the seventeenth century, been the secret creed of leading intellectuals like Milton, Newton, and Locke. They had to keep their views to themselves, since denial of the Trinity had been a heresy that led to execution between 1548 and 1612, and it was still condemned in the 1689 Act of Toleration. In America, too, men were cautious in revealing their opposition to the Trinity. Most of those maneuvering toward that position were attacked, in the first place, as Arminians, since the Puritans were obsessed with that heresy as something their fellows could easily slide into unless they kept their guard up against it.[9] Arminianism was at the far pole from Antinomianism. The former was said to give too much play to human virtue, while the latter gave it none. Calvinist believers in the elect held a middle ground between these two, fending off their opposite assaults.

Arminianism and Antinomianism were both condemned by Calvinists at the Synod of Dort (1618–19), which Puritans accepted, along with the Westminster Confession, as their rule of orthodoxy. Although some Arminians could and did retain the doctrine of the Trinity, the men reacting against the Awakening, although called Arminians, were in many cases going further in their attack on the whole cluster of Calvinist beliefs. They rightly saw that the Trinity was at the very center of those views, and they began, timorously at first, to reject belief in a triune God. In doing this, they laid the foundation for much of later American religion. Their importance would be hard to overstate, since they are the forebears of Universalists, Deists, Transcendentalists, and many forms of liberal Protestantism. Unitarianism is the most common form of Enlightened religion. Some, when they hear the word Unitarian, instantly equate it with the formal Unitarian churches that arose at the beginning of the nineteenth century, but the denial of the Trinity had a wider and looser ambit.

LOCKE

FOR UNITARIANS of the Enlightenment, the most influential religious text was John Locke's work *The Reasonableness of Christianity*, which he was careful to issue anonymously. Although this document was denounced by the orthodox as atheistic in intent, it is a sincere profession of faith in Enlightened Christianity by a practicing Anglican. In fact, Locke protests against those who would make "Jesus Christ nothing but the restorer and preacher of pure natural religion, thereby doing violence to the whole tenor of the New Testament."[10] He believes that Adam fell, but not into the total depravity described by the Calvinists. Adam's sin did make him lose Paradise (that is, immortality), and the risen Jesus restores that for his followers. Jesus is a mediator who sponsors those who believe in him, pardoning their faults (30)—faults which remain with them, since they are not "washed clean in the blood of the lamb": "By the law of faith, faith is allowed to supply the defect of full obedience; and so the believers are admitted to life and immortality, *as if* they were righteous" (30, emphasis added). That is: here is no "substitution" or "imputation" of Christ's merits to the chosen, as in Calvinist Atonement.

Locke's Jesus, though he is not God, is the Messiah foretold in the Jewish Scriptures. He proved that by his miracles, including the Resurrection.

> The evidence of Our Savior's mission from heaven is so great, in the multitude of miracles he did before all sorts of people, that what he delivered cannot but be received as the oracles of God and unquestionable verity. For the miracles he did were so ordered by the divine providence and wisdom that they never were, nor could be, denied by any of the enemies or opposers of Christianity. (57)

Locke, unlike Hume and others (including Jefferson), defended a belief in miracles because they are not contrary to reason, just outside its purview. As he put in *An Essay Concerning Human Understanding:*

> (1) *According to reason* are such propositions whose truth we can discover by examining and tracing those ideas we have from sensation and reflection, and by natural deduction find to be true or probable.
>
> (2) *Above reason* are such propositions whose truth or probability we cannot by reason derive from those principles.
>
> (3) *Contrary to reason* are such propositions as are inconsistent with or irreconcilable to our clear and distinct ideas. Thus the existence of one God is according to reason; the existence of more than one God is contrary to reason; the resurrection of the dead above reason.[11]

In *Reasonableness,* he explains what is beyond but not contrary to reason this way:

> It is enough to justify the fitness of anything to be done by resolving it into the "wisdom of God," who has done it; though our short views and narrow understandings may utterly inca- pacitate us to see that wisdom, and to judge rightly of it. We know little of this visible, and nothing at all of the state of that intellectual, world wherein are infinite numbers and degrees of spirits, out of the reach of our ken or guess; and therefore know not what transactions there were between God and our Savior in reference to his kingdom. We know not what need there was to set up a head and chieftain in opposition to the prince of this world, the prince of the power of the air, et., whereof there are more than obscure intimations in Scripture. And we shall take too much upon us if we shall call God's wisdom or providence to account; and pertly condemn for needless all that our weak and perhaps biased understanding cannot account for. (56)

Locke was not an Arian like Milton, but a Socinian.[12] Arian Unitarians considered Jesus a superior being created before heaven and earth. The Socinians thought he was simply a very virtuous man inspired by the Holy Spirit—and Locke says that Jesus can impart the Spirit to strengthen his followers (76).

Locke's Jesus gathers into one system what were scattered moral teachings in the ages that preceded him.

> Such a body of ethics, proved to be the law of nature from
> principles of reason and reaching all the duties of life, I think
> nobody will say the world had before Our Savior's coming. . . .
> These incoherent apothegms of philosophers and wise men,
> however excellent in themselves and well intended by them,
> could never make a morality whereof the world could be
> convinced, could never rise to the force of a law that mankind
> could with certainty depend on. . . . Our Saviour found
> mankind under a corruption of manners and principles which
> ages after ages had prevailed, and must be confessed was not in
> a way or tendency to be mended. (62–64)

God had to supplement the teachings of nature with a revelation, through Scripture and through Jesus, that would reach everyone, high and low, with authority. "And if the poor had the gospel preached to them, it was, without doubt, such a gospel as the poor could understand, plain and intelligible; and so it was, as we have seen, in the preachings of Christ and his apostles" (77).

Shocking as this book was to members of old orthodoxies, it clearly issued a *religious* teaching. Enlightened religion was religion, and that is how it took shape in America as a reaction to the Awakening. The reaction was forming in two main arenas, the Congregational pulpits and lecterns of Boston and Harvard, typified by Charles Chauncy and Jonathan Mayhew, and the Anglican parishes of New York and the University of Pennsylvania, typified by Samuel Johnson and William Smith. Though these centers went forward *pari passu* in theology, their different social milieus and political policies make it hard to keep them associated in their Unitarianism. The Congregationalists supported the American Revolution (with misgivings) while the Anglicans opposed it. And similar as their thought became over time, these two groups drew on different sources for their Enlightenment. The New Englanders looked to Dissenting Arians in England like Thomas Emlyn, Samuel Clarke, and John Taylor. Jonathan Mayhew was also close to the English Unitarians Richard Price and Joseph Priestley. Johnson and Smith, on the other hand, owed their principal impetus to one man, the Anglican bishop George Berkeley.

In Boston, Jonathan Mayhew at the West Church initially raced ahead of his friend Charles Chauncy at the First Church, ridiculing old Calvinist doctrines. This made Mayhew a byword with many of the orthodox as the very type of a modern infidel.[13] But Chauncy quietly moved even further out from orthodoxy—so far that he was afraid, for years, to publish his most daring speculations.[14] His own book *On the Benevolence of God* forced him to the conclusion that God would not create men with the aim of consigning them to eternal torture. He thus became a Universalist, believing that all human beings will finally be saved, perhaps after a series of purgations. (The New Englanders, who had mocked the Catholic doctrine of Purgatory, were thus letting it in by a back door.) John Adams would in time adopt a similar view of God's benevolence: "Now, my friend, can prophecies or miracles convince you or me that infinite benevolence, wisdom, and power created and preserves, for a time, innumerable millions to make them miserable forever for his own glory?"[15]

Chauncy and Mayhew were joined in their attack on the Awakening by their eminent friend Ebenezer Gay, of the First Parish in Hingham, Massachusetts, who preached at Mayhew's ordination. Gay organized the 1745 Weymouth Testimony, which condemned George Whitefield for the way he "disparaged human reason and rational preaching." Gay welcomed into his pulpit the visiting English Unitarian William Hazlitt Sr. (father of the famous essayist), who preached there over forty times.[16] Hazlitt, along with Joseph Priestley's son William, helped bring the

British Enlightenment to America—Hazlitt, for instance, persuaded some to omit the Trinitarian doxology from church prayers.[17] The triumph of Enlightened Unitarians was signaled in 1759, when Gay was appointed to give the prestigious Dudleian Lecture at Harvard. The title of his sermon was "Natural Religion as Distinguished from Revealed Religion."[18] Gay's successor at First Parish was Henry Ware, whose appointment as president of Harvard would kick off the great Unitarian controversy of the nineteenth century. Gay, unlike his friends Chauncy and Mayhew, opposed the Revolution.

Chauncy argued not only with Jonathan Edwards over the Awakening but with his fellows of the Enlightenment Samuel Johnson and William Smith over the idea of initiating an episcopal see in America. The New Englanders opposed popular democracy, even though they supported the Revolution, but they were not as elitist as the Anglicans, who took the Tory side. Samuel Johnson, the president of King's College (later Columbia), died just before the Revolution. William Smith, the president of the College of Philadelphia, tried to straddle the problem of separation from England. He wrote an anonymous attack on Tom Paine's *The Crisis*, hoping for reconciliation with the King. This was not acceptable to the Pennsylvania Assembly, which closed his college in order to shut him up.

The Anglicans' adoption of Enlightened religion began before the Great Awakening, but the earliest pioneers would prove just as harsh as Chauncy and Mayhew when the Awakening arrived. The Anglicans began with the great "Yale apostasy" of 1722, when Yale's rector, two of its tutors, and four local ministers with connections to Yale signaled their conversion from the Congregational to the Anglican Church at the Yale commencement of that year. They had been stirred to this by study of a new theology in books donated to Yale by Jeremiah Dummer. The rector was Timothy Cutler, and one of the ministers was Samuel Johnson, who had recently been a Yale tutor. The board of trustees summoned the seven apostates to the college library and asked them to declare their intentions. When they did so, Cutler and the tutors were suspended. Governor Gordon Saltonstall summoned the seven apostates and the trustees of the college to a confrontation in his office. Benjamin Franklin wrote in his newspaper, "All the people are running mad."[19] Henry May said: "The effect in the colony was similar to that which might have been produced in 1925 if the Yale football team had suddenly joined the Communist party."[20] Four of the seven then backed away from their resolve to leave the Congregational Church; but three of them, including the most important figures, Johnson and Cutler, set sail for England to be ordained as Anglican priests.

On their return to America, Johnson and Cutler went to parishes where they could preach their latitudinarian Anglicanism. Johnson founded a community in Stratford, Connecticut (the first Anglican church in that state), and Cutler was given Boston's Christ Church (which had been Old North Church). Cutler stayed in his parish, but Johnson would be wooed away to the new King's College in New York. Johnson read deeply in matters philosophical as well as theological, but was most profoundly impressed by Bishop George Berkeley's idealistic philosophy. He was therefore thrilled to learn that Berkeley had come to America in 1720, and was staying at Newport. Johnson frequently visited Berkeley for long talks. He learned not only more about Berkeley's epistemology but about his scheme for founding a university in Bermuda. Though that plan fell through, Berkeley's progressive views on education would influence his disciple's later career as university president.

The most direct fruit of Johnson's work with Berkeley was his magnum opus, *Elementa Philosophica*, the first philosophy textbook published in America, which brought Berkeleian ideas to a new audience.[21] Benjamin Franklin published the book in Philadelphia. Johnson's friend William Smith edited the English edition of the work and introduced it into the curriculum of the College of Philadelphia. Smith had developed some of Berkeley's educational philosophy into an ideal school scheme published as *Mironia* (1753). The actual college he would lead grew from one of Franklin's projects, the Philadelphia Academy. Franklin first offered the post of rector there to Johnson. When Johnson turned it down, Franklin extended the offer to Smith, who accepted it—he became provost of the college when it opened in 1756. Meanwhile, Johnson had accepted the presidency of the new King's College in New York in 1754. Though both men were high church in their liturgy, they held an Enlightened religion. They ignored or played down the doctrine of the Trinity, and emphasized the role of reason in their preaching and teaching.[22] Smith's institution gave great support to Philadelphia's burgeoning scientific interests, in the American Philosophical Society, the medical school, and the astronomical projects of David Rittenhouse. Enlightened religion was now as firmly anchored in the Middle Colonies as in New England.

Another anchor was provided at an unlikely place. The College of New Jersey had been founded to support the Awakeners. When the fifth of its short-lived presidents died in 1766, the trustees looked to Scotland for a good Calvinist to lead the "New Light" school, and they thought they had found their man in John Witherspoon. They were fooled by the fact that Witherspoon had won acclaim by defending tradition in Scotland against moderate Calvinists, satirizing their appeal to worldly views in a best-selling attack, *Ecclesiastical Characteristics* (1753). They did not know that in the decade since that book appeared Witherspoon had absorbed the whole spirit of the Scottish Enlightenment, which he would bring with him to make Princeton a center of Enlightenment education in America. He lost little time in ridding Princeton of its New Light faculty members, and introduced the Scottish Common Sense philosophy of Thomas Reid, which, in college after college, "became the official philosophy of nineteenth century America."[23] Half of the "most laudable authors" he recommended to his students were avatars of the Scottish Enlightenment, including Francis Hutcheson, David Hume, Lord Kames, Thomas Reid, and Adam Smith.[24]

Though Princeton was nominally Presbyterian, Witherspoon made it pluralist in fact (to the chagrin of some trustees), so that it drew students from all parts of the colonies, from New England to the Carolinas. Witherspoon trained much of the founding generation, which made him the most influential educator in American history. A list of those who passed under his tutelage is astounding:

> Among these were twelve members of the Continental
> Congress; five delegates to the Constitutional Convention; one

U. S. president (Madison); a vice president (the notorious
Aaron Burr); forty-nine U. S. representatives; twenty-eight
U. S. senators; three Supreme Court justices; eight U. S. district
judges; one secretary of state; three attorneys general; and two
foreign ministers. In addition to these national officeholders,
twenty-six of Witherspoon's graduates were state judges;
seventeen were members of their state constitutional
conventions; and fourteen were delegates to the state
conventions that ratified the Constitution.[25]

Witherspoon was an Enlightened philosopher, but also a sincere Christian minister, a champion of "supernatural rationalism."[26] He down-
played the Trinity, but constantly praised the role of Jesus as the
mediating savior.[27]

Witherspoon was fortunate. He flourished at the time when Americans were receptive to the Enlightenment. This helps explain how he
became "the most admired and even loved, of college presidents in the
Revolutionary era."[28] During his time of influence, the French as well as
the British Enlightenment was welcomed on these shores. The alliance
with France during the Revolution led to great admiration for French
letters, including the writings of Voltaire (his *English Letters* were particularly well received).[29] Victory with the help of the French navy led
St. George Tucker, the Deist from Virginia, to an exultant cry in 1781:

Let every aged parent, every tender mother, every helpless
orphan, every blooming virgin, and every infant tongue unite
and with one voice cry out, God save Louis the Sixteenth![30]

All this would change drastically when Louis XVI was beheaded and
the excesses of the French Revolution caused American Federalists to
sour not only on the French Enlightenment but on Enlightenment itself.
Where Lafayette had been feted on these shores, Citizen Genet was
despised. That explains the different treatment given an Enlightened
minister like Witherspoon and an Enlightened minister like Joseph

Priestley. The famous discoverer of oxygen came to America in 1794, hounded out of England, where his laboratory had been destroyed by rioters because of his sympathy with the French. His religious views differed little from Witherspoon's and not at all from Locke's. Like Locke, Priestley thought Jesus the Messiah foretold by the prophets and confirmed by miracles—he believed in the Resurrection and an afterlife, and he argued these points with his friend Thomas Jefferson.[31] But Priestley was treated as an infidel and atheist. John Adams's secretary of state, Timothy Pickering, wanted to deport him under the Alien and Sedition Acts, but Adams, who admired Priestley's work, said no to Pickering. Adams wrote of Priestley as "this great, this learned, indefatigable, most excellent and extraordinary man. . . . Glory to his soul. For I believe he had one; and one of the greatest."[32]

The reaction to the Enlightenment, which would flower out into the Unitarian controversy and then into the Second Great Awakening, was begun in the 1790s by men like Timothy Dwight at Harvard. It would soon become commonplace to charge that a Unitarian was no better than a Deist, a Deist no better than a Jacobin, and a Jacobin no better than an atheist. This was the burden of attacks on Jefferson in the election of 1800. But meanwhile the Enlightenment had done its work. It had founded the nation, and drafted the Constitution, and passed the First Amendment. And in the labors of the Quakers, it had begun the long struggle to end slavery in America.

8 | QUAKERS

QUAKERISM WAS, for many, especially for the French, the supremely Enlightened religion. This seems unexpected—that the philosophes would admire a group that boasted of no philosophers. In fact, the Quakers had many of the traits condemned by the Enlightened as "enthusiastic." The importance of the Quakers lay precisely in this combination of Enlightened and populist values. They were egalitarian, down-to-earth, and unpretentious, with some of the traits of the Awakeners, against whom the Enlightened had reacted. But the Quakers' enthusiasm, the openness to the Spirit that had made them quake, was cooled by sobriety and plainness. They were, said Jefferson, the only nonpersecuting Christians, who had learned tolerance without any need for Locke's instruction: "I believe, with the Quaker preacher, that he who steadily observes those moral precepts in which all religions concur will never be questioned, at the gates of heaven, as to the dogmas in which they all differ."[1]

Quakers adhered to that highest of Enlightenment virtues, benevolence. They share the benevolent features that set the Enlightened God apart from Calvin's vindictive Deity. They had immediate access to this approachable God through their "inner light." Tom Paine wrote: "The religion that approaches the nearest of all others to true deism, in the moral and *benign* part thereof, is that professed by the Quakers" (emphasis added).[2] The famous philosophe Abbé Raynal wrote of the Quakers: "May it please heaven to cause all nations to adopt their principles; men would then be happy, and the globe not stained with blood."[3] Patrick Henry called them "a people whose system imitates the example of him whose life was perfect."[4] The French abolitionists (Amis des Noirs) celebrated the Quakers, and their founder, Brissot de Warville, visited them in America.[5] Joseph Priestley, when he came to America, wrote under the pseudonym "A Quaker in Politics." To be like a Quaker was an Enlightenment boast.

Benjamin Franklin, when he went to France, affected the plain dress of Quakers, since Voltaire had taught the French to admire George Fox and William Penn. Voltaire praised much in England during his visit there, from the British Constitution to the learned societies; but he especially admired the English Quakers. He devoted four of his *Lettres philosophiques* (1734) to Quakers, ironically feigning to be a shocked Christian who finds Quakers living the faith that others distorted.

The note is struck in his first letter on the sect. When he learns that the Quakers have no baptism, he objects that Jesus was baptized. The Quaker mildly asks Voltaire if he is circumcised. No, comes the answer. "Yet Jesus was circumcised."[6] Voltaire admires the openness of the man who takes him to a London meeting. Women as well as men can speak in the Spirit. There is no hierarchy, priesthood, or ceremonial liturgy. This is a life close to nature, with none of the artificial distinctions created by human striving after power—so it is no wonder that American Indians ("these savages, falsely so-called") were drawn to the Quakers.[7] Voltaire finds much of what Rousseau admired in "the noble savage" in the plainness, simplicity, and lack of ceremonial artifice of Quakers. It therefore saddened him to predict a decline of Quakerism from the innocence of nature to the corruptions of "civilization." Since their refusal to fight or to take oaths sealed them off from military and political office, Voltaire maintained, all their energies were channeled into trade, and the wealth gained in consequence was a lure to their descendants.[8]

Voltaire especially admired William Penn and his American colony, the most just in the world. The Quakers of Pennsylvania enjoyed a reputation for benign administration that stood far off from the early Quaker incursions into Massachusetts and Rhode Island. The rude naturalism that had shocked John Winthrop and disgusted Roger Williams gave place by the eighteenth century to the pacifism and tolerance that philosophes praised. There was no more "going naked for a sign" in the staid Quakerism of Philadelphia.

In fact, the very moderation of the Quakers slowed an initial opposition to slavery. Since many Quakers owned slaves, especially in Barbados, there was an inhibition against criticizing fellow Friends. Even when George Fox visited Barbados, he did not outright oppose slavery. He "cautioned" (the Quaker word for admonishing) that slaves should be treated well, taught Christianity, and perhaps released after a productive time of service that repaid their initial cost.[9] Even this mild instruction angered men holding large slave contingents. When Quakers were accused of encouraging slaves to rebel against their condition, Fox was at pains to say he had no such thing in mind.[10] The Quakers continued their large-scale acquisition of slaves, as Friends became more prosperous and felt they needed slave service to match their competitors. William Penn himself owned slaves, and bequeathed some to his widow. When indentured white slaves made trouble for the overseer of Penn's manor in 1686, Penn told him to get black slaves instead, "for then a man has them while they live."[11]

Despite the involvement of Quakers in slaveholding, some Quakers suffered qualms of conscience. This was a matter of Quaker self-scrutiny. Cadwalader Morgan, for instance, a Pennsylvania farmer, felt it necessary to buy a slave to help work his land. But after a period of unease, he decided that he could not beat a man if he refused to labor.[12] The more brutal aspects of slavery were renounced by various Quaker meetings— for example, the practice of branding a slave's cheek with his owner's initial. Quakers were urged to "labor with" (counsel) any Friends who treated slaves ferociously. Practical problems, too, were considered. The growing number of slaves raised fears of rebellion, so that in 1698 the

Philadelphia meeting asked Friends in Barbados to "forbear sending any Negroes to this place, because they are too numerous here."[13] From a similar motive, the Quaker-controlled Pennsylvania Assembly in 1712 imposed prohibitive tariffs on the importation of slaves, but the Privy Council in London vetoed this action, to keep up the lucrative slave trade.[14]

Quaker meetings found it for a long time impossible to demand that Friends cease importing, buying, or holding slaves. The ideal of Quaker government was to move by consensus, by persuasion, by consultation with other meetings, both in London and in the colonies. To maintain harmony, managers of the Quaker press refused to give authors permission to print divisive literature, and criticism of slaveholding Friends was considered extremely divisive. That is why the first Quaker-inspired attack on slavery was issued by dissident followers of George Keith, who had been disowned by his Quaker fellows.[15] If Friends tried to petition their meetings for action against slaves, they were for a long time ignored, as happened with a petition to the Germantown meetings in 1688.[16] When others tried to write against slavery, they were forbidden. If they defied the order, they were disowned by their meetings. This happened to William Southeby in 1711, to John Farmer in 1718, and to Ralph Sandiford in 1729.[17]

BENJAMIN LAY (c. 1681–1759)

ONE MAN the Quakers in America could not read out of meeting, since Benjamin Lay had already been disowned in his native England, for denouncing what Milton had called "hireling ministers."[18] After spending several years at sea, Lay settled in Barbados, where he ran a shop which gave out food to slaves on Lord's Day (Quaker Sunday). After he caught some slaves stealing other items of his merchandise, he whipped them. Disgusted at what he had done, he became an ardent opponent of slavery, causing masters on the island to revile him. Removed to Pennsylvania in 1730, he built an austere cave house in Abington, where he lived ascetically with his wife, Sarah. The two were like little gnomes in the forest. Lay was five-foot-seven tall, but stooped and hunchbacked, and his wife was of a similar shape. Lay denounced Quakers who held slaves. He interrupted their meetings, as the original Quakers had interrupted religious services in England and New England. He stood barefoot in the snow outside the meetinghouse to protest the living conditions of the slaves. Quakers were forced to post guards to keep him out of their meetings, or to remove him if he got in.

His most famous bit of guerrilla theater occurred in 1738, at the annual meeting in Burlington, New Jersey. He wore a military coat and sword under his plain Quaker cloak, and carried a hollowed-out Bible in which he had placed a bladder of red pokeberry juice. In the middle of the service he threw off his cloak, pulled his sword, and stabbed the Bible, sprinkling its "blood" over bystanders as he told them that they were fake pacifists—they waged war on mankind and defiled the Bible when they captured and held slaves.[19] At another time, he lured the favored child of a slaveholding Quaker to his house and kept him there while the parents searched frenziedly. Then he returned the child, saying, "You may now conceive of the sorrow you inflict upon the parents of the Negro girl you hold in slavery, for she was torn from them by avarice."[20] Though his wife supported Lay's efforts, she took no part in his more dramatic gestures, so she was not excommunicated. She remained a minister in the Abingdon meeting.

Banned from meetings, Lay went into the marketplace to keep up his demonstrations, once throwing his wife's teacups from a balcony, smashing them on the ground, to protest the use of tea leaves harvested by slaves.[21] He also inveighed against capital punishment, the lack of religious education for poor children, and cruel penal practices. He was much admired by Benjamin Franklin, who helped shape his massive and rambling attack on slavery into publishable form as *All Slavekeepers That Keep the Innocent in Bondage, Apostates Pretending to Lay Claim to the Pure and Holy Christian Religion* (1737). Other Quakers, men like Anthony Benezet, took inspiration from Lay's abolitionism, and he was admitted into the Quaker cemetery when he died in 1759.

In the 1750s, the protests of a Lay moved into the Quaker mainstream, as meetings finally began to forbid the holding of slaves by Friends. The leading figures in this great shift were John Woolman and Anthony Benezet. These two accomplished what Samuel Sewall tried to do as early as 1700—they broke down the defense of slavery from the Bible. This was an Enlightenment project that could best be carried on, in America at least, by people who were clearly religious. It was hard for anyone to claim that the saintly Woolman and Benezet had no reverence for God or for his word. Woolman is the better known now, since his *Journal* is one of the recognized classics of spirituality in American literature.

JOHN WOOLMAN (1720–1772)

WOOLMAN GREW UP among slaveholding Quakers in Holly, New Jersey. His work as a notary made him draw up wills and bills of sale for the disposition of slaves, a task his conscience rebelled against. In 1746, when he went as a missionary into Virginia, the plight of the slaves haunted him, as did the callousness of their Quaker masters: "I saw in these southern provinces so many vices and corruptions increased by this trade and this way of life that it appeared to me as a dark gloominess hanging over the land; and though now many willingly run into it, yet in future the consequences will be grievous to posterity."[22] He had completed a powerful antislavery work, which would appear as *Some Considerations on the Keeping of Negroes: Recommended to the Professors of Christianity of Every Denomination,* during the 1740s. But he knew he could not get approval for it from the overseers of the press, and he did not want to publish it at the cost of being disowned. He preferred to work within the meeting by gentle persuasion.

Events and the cooperation of Anthony Benezet strengthened his hand in the 1750s. The coming of the French and Indian War (1755–60) forced Quakers back on their bedrock principles and drove them out of public office. The major breakthrough on the issue of slavery was beginning to occur. In 1753 Woolman wrote the epistle critical of slavery that was issued by the Philadelphia meeting, his *Epistle to the Friends in Virginia.* By this time Benezet had become the leading figure on the board of overseers of the press—so in 1754 it authorized the printing of Woolman's book from the 1740s. That same year, the meeting issued as its own another antislavery letter written by Woolman.

Woolman's writings show us what ingenuity he used in his persuasive campaign to bring Quakers around to abolitionism. Some of his humane arguments can be observed in the second version of *Some Considerations* (1762). He creates what we would call "thought experiments." Imagine, he writes, that instead of buying or inheriting a slave, you went to Africa and personally captured the slave, wrenching him from his family by violence. Would your attitude toward holding him be different? Or imagine that Africans had come of their own will to these shores, bringing goods to trade—but they were first robbed of their merchandise, then taken captive and put up for sale. Would you buy the stolen goods? If you would not buy the stolen goods, how can you buy the stolen *persons* themselves? Or imagine that a slave family has worked as hard as the white family owning it, while living far more cheaply. Does not the slave family deserve a proportion of the profits earned? And if the white family cannot pay what the black family deserves, does it not deserve (even more) its freedom from such a form of indirect theft?

He appeals to the pacifism of Quakers to see slavery as the result of wars waged to take the slaves in the first case:

> Should we meditate on the wars which are greatly increased by
> this trade, and on that affliction which many thousands live in
> through apprehension of being taken or slain; on the terror and
> amazement that villages are in when surrounded by these troops
> of enterprisers; on the great pain and misery of groaning,
> dying men who get wounded in those skirmishes; we shall
> necessarily see that it is impossible to be parties in such a trade,
> on the motives of gain, and retain our innocence.[23]

The 1750s sorely tried Quaker consciences, since the French and Indian War led to demands that they serve in the Regulators (the volunteer army formed because Quaker dominance had precluded the creation of a regular militia). Some Quakers served, under threat of confiscation of their property; but Woolman was a leader in the call to live up to the Gospel command to "turn the other cheek." At the beginning of the war, he wrote *An Epistle of Tender Love and Caution* (1755), urging Friends to refuse payment of any taxes levied to support the war. In 1758, the Philadelphia meeting faced the challenge head-on, calling for all its members to resign from political office, ending Penn's experiment in Quaker government. In this renewal of their own body of principles, they also condemned slaveholding for the first time. (Earlier meetings had criticized the slave trade, but stopped short of a ban on "slave keeping.") Benjamin Lay, ill with what would kill him the next year, rejoiced that his cause had finally prevailed, and exclaimed, "Now I can die in peace."[24]

Woolman had set the stage for this development by visiting Friends who owned slaves, going house to house with his patient counseling. When he had to stay overnight in a home where slaves were owned, he left payment for any services they had rendered him during the stay, refusing to accept uncompensated slave labor.[25] He pioneered the idea of compensation for labor wrested from the slaves during their captivity. He calculated that the labor of "a healthy, industrious slave" was worth at least fifty pounds a year for every year the man was over twenty-one. The longer such a slave is held, the higher would interest mount on such a sum due him (a motive for freeing him as soon as possible). And the slave's heirs should inherit this money: "Where persons have been injured as to their outward substance and died without having recompense, their children appear to have a right to that which was equitably due to and detained from their fathers."[26]

This was just an extension of the consideration that made him pay for work that slaves had performed for him in slave owners' homes. He probably did not expect any scheme of compensation to be adopted. But he hoped to shame people into *at least* freeing the slaves, if only without paying damages. He was also arguing against the policy of some (Quakers and others) to allow slaves to purchase their own freedom. If slaves deserved reparation, they should not have to pay money to those who owed *them*.

Woolman also witnessed the mistreatment of Indians by Quakers and others, and he traveled deep into Indian territory, as a peacemaker, trying to renew the Enlightened policies of Penn. In this effort he displayed none of the arrogance or condescension of some missionaries. He wanted to learn as well as teach:

> Love was the first motion, and then a concern arose to spend some time with the Indians, that I might feel and understand their life and the spirit they live in, if haply I might receive some instruction from them, or they be in any degree helped forward by my following the leadings of Truth amongst them. And as it pleased the Lord to make way for my going at a time when the troubles of war were increasing, and when by reason of much wet weather traveling was more difficult than usual at that season, I looked upon it as a more favorable opportunity to season my mind and bring me into a nearer sympathy with them.[27]

As the time came for Woolman to make his first long journey into Indian country, reports of captures and massacres came back from the territory. A friend had volunteered to go with him; but now Woolman worried about exposing his friend to danger.

> On his account I had a sharp trial, for as the journey appeared perilous, I thought if he went chiefly to bear me company and we should be taken captive, my having been the means of drawing him into these difficulties would add to my own afflictions. So I told him my mind freely and let him know that I was resigned to go alone, but after all, if he really believed it to be his duty to go on, I believed his company would be very comfortable [comforting] to me. It was indeed a time of deep exercise [spiritual effort], and Benjamin appeared to be so fastened to the visit that he could not be easy to leave me; so we went on.[28]

Despite some terrifying encounters, the Quakers soon won the Indians' attention and protection, as unarmed men led by the Spirit. Woolman remained a warm advocate for wise policies in Indian relations.

Woolman cared for all living things. One of his formative spiritual experiences occurred when he was a boy. When he saw a robin flying wildly around its nest to protect its young, he began idly to throw stones at it. One of these, to his horror, killed the bird, and he pledged to protect living things. He was a vegetarian, who would not eat animals killed for food.[29] When he sailed for England in 1772, to visit Friends and join in their work, he protested the way animals were treated on shipboard.

He resolved to protect young boys abused while they served as shipboard apprentices.

> The present state of the seafaring life in general appears so opposite to that of a pious education, so full of corruption and extreme alienation from God, so full of examples the most dangerous to young people that, in looking toward a young generation, I feel a care for them, that they have an education different from the present education of lads at sea.[30]

In England, he refused to travel by stagecoach or to send mail by stage, because of the mistreatment of the horses and the postboys.

> Stagecoaches frequently go upwards of a hundred miles in fourteen hours, and I have heard Friends say in several places that it is common for horses to be killed with hard driving, and many others driven till they grow blind. . . . Some boys who ride long stages suffer greatly in winter nights, and in several places I have heard of their being froze to death. . . . I heard in America of the way of these posts and cautioned Friends in the General Meeting of Ministers and Elders at Philadelphia, and in the Yearly Meeting of Ministers and Elders at London, not to send letters to me on any common occasion by post.[31]

Woolman died in England, so he did not have the great funeral that Philadelphians would give to Benezet. Only when his journal was published posthumously did people at large learn of his spiritual depths, of the universality of his love for all men and women.

ANTHONY BENEZET (1713–1784)

W OOLMAN'S GREAT ally in all his projects was Anthony Benezet, a person now less famous than Woolman but more influential in his day, not only in the colonies but in Europe and the Caribbean. Benezet was born in France, to Huguenot parents who fled persecution, going first to Rotterdam and then to London (in 1716), where they converted to Quakerism. The family emigrated to Philadelphia in 1731, and Anthony worked with his merchant brothers before becoming a schoolteacher. He taught for years in Philadelphia's Quaker school, but then founded his own schools, first a girls' school and then a school for poor blacks, offering them free education by begging support from Friends. His experiments in pedagogy led him to write innovative textbooks tailored to his students' needs—a primer, a grammar, and a spelling book.

He was known for his gentle teaching methods. Since, like Woolman, he would kill no animals, not even a mouse, two of his students tried a trick on him. They left on his desk a live mouse in a toy pillory, with a sign saying it was being punished for stealing cheese. We get an idea of Benezet's psychological tactics from the "punishment" he gave the boys. He let them out of class early, saying that they "wisely and mercifully imprisoned the mouse, rather than put it to death—they should go out at four o'clock that afternoon."[32]

Benezet became a community hero, whom visitors sought out as a famous Philadelphia institution. French visitors, seeking confirmation of their high regard for Quakers, regularly wrote home about the famed philanthropist. Baron Cromot du Boug said: "He is small, old and ugly, but his countenance wears the stamp of a peaceful soul and the repose of a good conscience." Francois Jean Chastellux described "an old Quaker, with a diminutive figure and humble and scanty physiognomy." Benezet was pressed into service for endless worthy causes, overseeing schools and hospitals and libraries.[33] When the Acadians were expelled from Nova Scotia, three British ships brought 454 of them to the Philadelphia harbor. The Assembly, not knowing what to do with them, ordered them held on the ships until their fate could be settled. Benezet, who spoke the Acadians' French, was sent on board to see to their provisioning. He pled their cause to the Assembly, and when they were allowed to come onshore to a sequestered part of town, Benezet raised the funds to house them. Patience with supporting the newcomers ran thin among Philadelphians, and the authorities decided to send their children into homes as indentured servants, but Benezet fought this move and wrote a petition for them to the King of England.

Benezet begged so doggedly for the displaced persons that people learned to avoid him if they saw him coming. The rich Quaker Israel Pemberton complained: "It's tiresome to hear Anthony always saying the same thing."[34] When Benezet realized he could no longer get money from some people, he put up others to do the begging—and he kept at this wearisome task for over a decade. A woman who was in his girls' school told how he took in the Acadian girls for education. The Marquis de Barbé-Marbois, present in Philadelphia, remembered the situation:

> He gathered them together, although he was as poor as they;
> he consoled them, encouraged them, went from door to door
> begging bread for them, made the parents of his young
> Pennsylvanian pupils subscribe help for them, importuned
> the government of Pennsylvania to grant them the means of
> subsistence, addressed request after request to the King and
> Parliament of England, until generous obstinacy had obtained
> some help for these unfortunates, whom he calls his children.[35]

Benezet, like Woolman, took up the cause of the Indians, especially of the Christian (Moravian) Indians threatened in the area of Bethlehem and

Nazareth. He traveled to the peace conferences and helped get support for treaties. He intervened in the French and Indian War when Christian Indians were caught between opposite armies. He attacked the Pennsylvania Assembly when it offered rewards for Indian scalps.[36] Benezet wrote incessantly to support the poor and oppressed. The prominent physician Benjamin Rush, a close friend of Benezet, once saw him in a dream walking along in characteristic fashion. "In one hand he carried a subscription paper and a petition; in the other he carried a small pamphlet on the unlawfulness of the African slave trade, and a letter directed to the King of Prussia upon the unlawfulness of war."[37]

His works were translated into French and German and were widely reprinted in England. The most important of these dealt with slavery. Through them he influenced and collaborated with the leading abolitionists in England and France. He corresponded with Raynal, and wrote an introduction to the abbé's treatise on slavery.[38] He prevailed on the Philadelphia painter Benjamin West, the head of the British Academy of Art, to present antislavery materials to Queen Charlotte.[39] Benezet's two most important writings on slavery were a shorter and a longer description of the conditions of slave capture in Africa. He compiled these from wide reading and from reports gathered in the harbor of Philadelphia. He kept up on slave statistics and circulated them to friends like Benjamin Rush and Benjamin Franklin. Two thousand copies of his shorter account were shipped to England.[40]

His work on Africa impressed John Wesley, the father of Methodism, who incorporated much of it in his own *Thoughts on Slavery* (1774).[41] The shorter African account so struck Thomas Clarkson, as a student at Cambridge, that he devoted his life to the abolitionist cause.[42] Granville Sharp used Benezet's work in his own famous efforts for the slaves.[43] Franklin inserted paragraphs from Benezet in the British newspapers.[44] Benezet made himself an international clearinghouse for information about slavery and for agitation against it. He reprinted much of the material reaching him and cycled it out to all his network of collaborators. These men published, adapted, abridged, embroidered one another's works, in a spirit of generous cooperation. Benezet included passages from Woolman in his own work, as Wesley included passages from Benezet. Benezet asked others to add to or alter his own work to fit the circumstances of their situation—he even bound in blank pages for them to fill up.

Benezet did not succeed with all those he approached. George Whitefield, the great Awakener, was a friend of Benezet's father, and Anthony himself became close to Whitefield during his campaigns in America. But Whitefield owned a plantation in Georgia from which he supported his school and orphanage there, and slaves worked the plantation. Benezet praised Whitefield for his great services to religion, but argued that he would immeasurably increase the good he was doing if he gave up his slaves. Whitefield was unmoved. But when Whitefield died, Benezet persisted in his gentle efforts, writing to the Countess of Huntington, the benefactor to whom Whitefield had left the Georgia orphanage, with its slave support system, asking her to free the blacks. She answered politely but evasively.[45]

Benezet had no better success with the Society for the Propagation of the Gospel (SPG), the missionary arm of the Anglican Church in America, which instructed its ministers not to criticize slavery, lest they be denied access to Southern plantations when they tried to proselytize the slaves. Benezet's protest against this policy was answered with a call for him to shut up:

> [The Society] cannot condemn the practice of keeping slaves
> as unlawful, finding the contrary very plainly implied in the
> precepts given by the apostles, both to masters and servants,
> which last were for the most part slaves; and if the doctrine of
> the unlawfulness of slavery should be taught in our colonies,
> the Society apprehend that masters, instead of being
> convinced of it, will grow more suspicious and cruel, and
> much more unwilling to let their slaves learn Christianity; and
> that the poor creatures themselves, if they come to look on this
> doctrine, will be so strongly tempted by it to rebel against their
> masters that the most dreadful consequences to both will be

likely to follow; and therefore, though the Society is fully
satisfied that your intention in this matter is perfectly good, yet
they must earnestly beg you not to go further in publishing
your notions, but rather to retract them, if you shall see cause,
which they hope you may on further consideration.[46]

Facing such resistance, Benezet nonetheless made great headway
with his publications. That is because he addressed a whole cluster of
rationalizations of slavery based on slaves' prior condition in Africa. The
rationalizations claimed that slaves were so benighted in their native
lands that even servitude in the New World was preferable to that state;
or that they were legitimate prize of war to their fellow Africans, their
lives forfeit to their captors, so that purchasing them actually saved their
lives; or that they were incapable of self-government in any case; or that
teaching them the Christian Gospel is the most that can be done for
their own good.

That such ideas could be held even by devout figures is seen in a letter
that George Whitefield wrote to John Wesley, refusing to yield to abolitionist pleas. Whitefield argued that providence had provided for the
removal of "the poor Ethiopians" for the "great end" of teaching them
Christianity. Besides, considering the savage condition they were found
in, servitude was an improvement. "Though liberty is a sweet thing to
such as are born free, yet to those who never knew the sweets of it slavery,
perhaps, may not be so irksome." Whitefield claimed that he was actually
helping them: "I should think myself highly favored if I could purchase a
good number of them in order to make their lives comfortable. . . . I trust
many of them will be brought to Jesus, and this consideration, as to us,
swallows up all temporal inconveniences whatsoever."[47]

Against this kind of argument, Benezet musters a great deal of
painstakingly gathered information on the African situation, especially
in his longer (162-page) work *Some Historical Account of Guinea, Its Situation, Produce, and the General Disposition of Its Inhabitants, with an Inquiry into
the Rise and Progress of the Slave Trade, Its Nature and Lamentable Effects*
(1771).[48] Far from being incapable of self-government, blacks in Africa

possessed articulated political and religious structures, maintained order and stability, successfully worked an agricultural economy, and excelled in various crafts. To establish these facts, Benezet drew on reports by Portuguese, Dutch, French, and English colonial agents, administrators, merchants, and travelers—as well as on the work of scientific academies.

There may have been some bias in reports of colonial agents wanting to maintain investments in the colonies—some of the material resembles an earlier literature that sang the praises of America in order to promote colonization. But the distortion was not nearly as great as that of people trying to represent Africa as a bloody chaos from which it was an act of charity to extract people. The argument that slaves were captives taken in indigenous wars by other Africans is met by ample testimony that Europeans fomented, encouraged, and expanded the kinds of conflict that gave them their desired captives (169, 190). That is why warfare was most intense near European ports (152).

Benezet shared the Enlightenment temptation to think of "primitive" people as having natural virtue, but this was closer to the truth than the picture of Africans as subhuman beings, rescued by noble civilizers. As for taking blacks to the comforts of civilization and the light of the Gospel, Benezet documents the horrors of the ships taking blacks to the "seasoning" places in the West Indies and the death rate even after they were arrived there. The statistics provide irrefutable testimony to the inhumanity of the slave trade (182, 189, 197–98).

If spreading the Gospel were the real aim, that could be done much more effectively by preaching and teaching Africans in Africa, where the preachers did not wear the dread garb of whip-wielding tyrants. Some argued that taking slaves from Africa was justified by the fact that Africans themselves held slaves. But Benezet shows that the conditions of African slaves were far less brutal than those in the "Christian" countries—and if slavery is wrong, the task of a Christian is to teach that fact to the Africans, not use their milder form of servitude to justify a harsher one (172–73). Europeans claim a higher state of civilization; but they degrade both the Africans and themselves in showing their own depths of savagery. Benezet is especially eloquent on the damage slaveholding wreaks on the master (173–80).

Benezet shredded the hypocrisies that even men like Whitefield indulged in. He documented by patient research the unjustifiable activities of the slave captors, purchasers, exploiters, and sellers. Throughout his works on slavery, he condemns the practice both from Enlightenment and from Christian principles—in the terms of this book, both from head and from heart. He quotes Locke and Montesquieu on the natural right to liberty: "The law of nature gives each human being an equal right to freedom."[49] He says that Abraham's holding slaves is irrelevant for Christians, who have a new covenant with Christ. The text he dwells on repeatedly is Matthew 7.12: "As you would have others do unto you, so do you unto them for that is the law and the prophets."

> *Enlightened* Christians . . . are commanded to do unto others as they would have others do unto them—not to a part only, to those of their own religion or color, but to all men. Wherefore no Christian can keep a slave, or be accessory thereto, without in some degree incurring the guilt of breaking his Lord's command, unless he is willing himself and posterity should be slaves [emphasis added].[50]

A Christian, that is, should treat every child "as thou would desire a child of thine should be treated in the like circumstances."[51] Lincoln put this in his typical commonsensical way: "As a 'good' thing, slavery is strikingly peculiar in this, that it is the only good thing which no man ever seeks the good of *for himself*."[52]

When Benezet died, huge crowds conducted him to his burial, people high and low, white and black.

> At the interment of Anthony Benezet's remains, which took place two days after his death, the greatest concourse of people that had ever been witnessed on such an occasion in Philadelphia was present, being a collection of all ranks and

professions among the inhabitants; thus manifesting the
universal esteem in which he was held. Among others who paid
that last tribute of respect were many hundred black people,
testifying by their attendance and by their tears the grateful
sense they entertained of his pious efforts in their behalf.[53]

The scene brings to mind Benjamin Rush's dream, where blacks run
toward Benezet upon his appearance in their haven.[54] Rush quotes a vet-
eran officer of the Revolution who said at the funeral: "I would rather be
Anthony Benezet in that coffin than George Washington with all his
fame."[55] The only one who was not convinced of Benezet's greatness was
Benezet himself, who said on his deathbed: "I am dying, and feel
ashamed to meet the face of my Maker, I have done so little in his
cause."[56] Benezet seems to me the one unquestionably authentic American saint.

The Quakers made possible all later forms of abolition by proving
that one can be a sincere Christian and yet defy the scriptural endorse-
ments of slavery. If reason says slavery is wrong, then it is wrong no matter what the Bible says. They also proved that Enlightened religion is
indeed a religion. They are stellar exemplars of both religion and
Enlightenment.[57] And they prevailed. At the beginning of the eighteenth
century slavery was legally recognized and actually practiced in all the
Northern colonies. At the end of the century, only one state was still a
holdout, and New Jersey would fall in line in 1804. Much of this was a
result of ferment around the Revolution, but the all-important religious
assault on the biblical support for slavery was needed to supplement
Enlightenment values. Benezet and Woolman had a foot in each camp,
and their moral arguments would serve as the basis for nineteenth-
century abolitionism, giving ammunition for a second assault on the
Bible arguments as they were upheld in the South. One of the greatest
moral episodes in American history was played out in the meeting-
houses of eighteenth-century Philadelphia.

9 | DEISTS

THE REACTION TO the Great Awakening provided an American Unitarian boost that made Deism the religion of the educated class by the middle of the eighteenth century. Legal scholar William Lee Miller writes that the chief founders of the nation were all Deists—he lists Washington, Franklin, Adams, Jefferson, Madison, Hamilton, and Paine, though many more leaders of the founding era could be added (Benjamin Rush, John Witherspoon, David Rittenhouse, Philip Freneau, Joel Barlow, Aaron Burr, James Wilson, Gouverneur Morris, Tench Coxe, to name some).[1] Their agreement on the question of God crossed political and geographical lines. Federalist and Republican, North and South, an Adams and a Jefferson, a Hamilton and a Madison—all were professed Deists. The word has become a loaded one. Many people, from the outset, made it a bogey, a term of denigration for any "unbelief" they were targeting. Ezra Stiles, Yale's president during the Revolution, complained:

> [Timothy Dwight] brings in the Roman Catholics and a
> number of Protestant erroneous divines as subserving the
> cause of Deism. . . . Calvinists think Arminians and Arians and

Socinians subserve Deism. Arians and Socinians think Calvinists, President [Jonathan] Edwards, and New Divinity all
subserve Deism. The Church of England think dissenters, and
dissenters [think] the church of England [subserve Deism].[2]

The main point to begin with is that none of the men listed by
Miller, or comparable figures, was an Evangelical in the pre-Enlightened
or resistant-to-Enlightened sense. They all believed in Enlightened
(Unitarian) religion. "Perry Miller was correct when he pointed out in a
book review that the founding fathers were of a 'liberality' of spirit
which must forever and properly remain a scandal to the rank and file of
professing American Christians."[3]

PAINE

SOME MAY wonder at Miller's inclusion of Paine with the others.
He is often thought to be the American Voltaire, an enemy of reli-
gion in a sense that none of the others was. But Paine insisted on his own
Deism, which is obviously not atheism. Deism, like theism, is simply
"God-ism" (from *Deus* in Latin, *Theos* in Greek). In fact, Paine wrote his
most reviled book, *The Age of Reason*, in France, where he opposed the
extremism of some French Revolutionaries. As he said to Samuel
Adams, "The people of France were running headlong into atheism, and
I had the work [*The Age of Reason*] translated and published in their own
language to stop them in that career"—the book "inculcates this rever-
ential fear and love of the Deity."[4] Paine regularly wrote that God had
favored the American war for independence:

> I have as little superstition in me as any man living, but my
> secret opinion has ever been, and still is, that God almighty
> will not give up a people to military destruction, or leave
> them unsupportedly to perish, who had so earnestly and so
> repeatedly sought to avoid the calamities of war, by every

decent method which wisdom could invent. Neither have I
so much of the infidel in me as to suppose that he has relin-
quished the government of the world and given us up to the
care of devils; and as I do not, I cannot see on what grounds the
king of Britain can look up to heaven for help against us.[5]

He thought belief in God a matter of common sense, for all whose minds
were not perverted (as those of French atheists had been).

It is certain that, in one point, all nations of the earth and all
religions agree. All believe in a God. . . . The belief of God, so
far from having anything of mystery in it, is of all beliefs the
most easy, because it arises to us, as is before observed, out of
necessity. . . . The only idea man can affix to the name of God
is that of a *first cause*, the cause of all things. And incomprehen-
sibly difficult as it is for man to conceive what a first cause is, he
arrives at the belief of it from the tenfold greater difficulty of
disbelieving it.[6]

The moral code for Deists is derived from watching the benign operation of God in the universe.

[God says] "Learn from My munificence to all to be kind to
each other." . . . The practice of moral truth, or in other words a
practical imitation of the moral goodness of God, is no other
than our acting towards each other as he acts *benignly* towards
all. . . . The only idea we can have of serving God is that of
contributing to the happiness of the living creation that God
has made. . . . The moral duty of man consists in imitating the
moral goodness and *beneficence* of God manifested in the
creation toward all his creatures [emphasis added].[7]

This emphasis on a benign God is the keynote of the Enlightenment's
escape from the vindictive God of Calvinism. It is also one of the

weaknesses of the Enlightenment, as even Voltaire knew in his satire on Dr. Pangloss. Enlightenment optimism sees little but the good in creation, neglecting the evils of plague, earthquake, and other natural disasters. (Human evils like torture, revenge, and persecution it attributes to false religion). Jefferson had this same optimism; but so, in varying degrees, did the other Deists. Even John Adams, often a satirist of French philosophes, was a Pangloss when he put on his Deistical hat: "The love of God and his creation—delight, joy, triumph, exultation in my own existence (though but an atom, a molecule organic, in the universe)—are my religion. Howl, snarl, bite, ye Calvinistic, ye Athanasian divines, if you will."[8] Adams could be as harsh on his Calvinist ancestors as was Jefferson. In fact, he rejected both Anglicanism and Presbyterianism as "too Calvinistical for me" and proudly professed his Unitarianism.[9] This optimism is what will always make some Evangelicals consider Enlightenment figures shallow, insufficiently aware of tragedy and the darkness of original sin. But it was so stamped on the nation by its founders that few American leaders can succeed without an optimistic bearing—and even Evangelical leaders have adopted some of the Pangloss rhetoric.

Paine himself was not a halfhearted theist. He believed in spiritual reality, the soul, and the afterlife. In this he was unlike Jefferson, who, as a thorough materialist, thought that even God was simply the most subtly refined form of matter. Paine says:

> Every man is an evidence to himself that he did not make
> himself; neither could his father make himself, nor his grand-
> father, nor any of his race; neither could any tree, plant, or
> animal make itself; and it is this conviction, arising from this
> evidence, that carries us on, as it were by necessity, to the belief
> of a first cause eternally existing, of a nature totally different to
> any *material* existence we know of [emphasis added].[10]

Though Jefferson believed in an afterlife, Paine is more emphatic on the point: "The belief of a future state is a *rational belief,* corroborated by facts visible in the creation" (emphasis in the original).[11]

> I trouble not myself about the manner of future existence. I
> content myself with believing, even to *positive conviction,* that
> the power that gave me existence is able to continue it, in any
> mode and manner he pleases, either with or without this body
> [emphasis added].

This complex of beliefs is what Paine defines as Deism. Though scornful of most of the Bible, he admires the book of Job and the nineteenth Psalm because they "are true *deistical* compositions; for they treat of the Deity through his works" (emphasis in the original).[12] Before the corruptions of priestly religion, "Adam, if there were such a man, was created a deist."[13] Paine admires Quakers because "they are rather deists than Christians."[14] Because "creation is the bible of the deist . . . the only religion that has not been invented, and that has in it every evidence of divine originality, is pure and simple deism."[15]

> Were man impressed as fully and as strongly as he ought to be
> with the belief of a God, his moral life would be regulated by
> the force of that belief. He would stand in awe of God and
> of himself, and would not do the thing that could not be
> concealed from either. To give this belief the full opportunity
> of force, it is necessary that it acts alone; this is deism.[16]

Given Paine's robust belief in a theistic creed and a theistic morality—belief in spirit and soul and afterlife—what has made so many in his time and later consider him "godless" and the enemy of religion? Well, he scoffed at the Bible and all churches. Unlike Locke (though like Jefferson) he placed no credence in miracles or prophecy. Like all the Unitarians, he denied the Trinity. But he went further in mocking the stories of God told in both Jewish and Christian Scripture:

> The Jews have made him the assassin of the human species
> [at the Flood], to make room for the religion of the Jews; the

Christians have made him the murderer of himself [at the
Crucifixion], and the founder of a new religion to supercede
and expel the Jewish religion.[17]

He was gleefully satirical on things like the Virgin Birth (Mary was
"debauched by a ghost"), the Incarnation ("the amphibious idea of a
man-god"), the Atonement ("to make an excuse to himself for not executing his supposed sentence upon Adam"), and the Resurrection.[18]

Like most Unitarians, he has respect for "the real Jesus," the one on
whom miracle and mystery were foisted by his followers. But his Jesus is
not the *best* moral model that Jefferson took him for:

> Nothing that is here said can apply, even with the most distant
> disrespect, to the *real* character of Jesus Christ. He was a
> virtuous and an amiable man. The morality that he preached
> and practiced was of the most benevolent kind; and though
> similar systems of morality had been preached by Confucius,
> and by some of the Greek philosophers many years before, by
> the Quakers since, and by many good men in all ages, it has
> never been exceeded by any.[19]

Paine found Jesus' teachings flawed in just that area where Jefferson
would find them most sound.

> When it is said, as in the testament, *if a man smite thee on the right
> cheek, turn to him the other also,* it is assassinating the dignity of
> forbearance and sinking man into a spaniel. *Loving of enemies* is
> another dogma of feigned morality . . . to love in proportion to
> the injury, if it could be done, would be to offer a premium for
> crime . . . this doctrine would imply that he [God] loved man
> not in proportion as he was good, but as he was bad [emphasis
> in the original].[20]

JEFFERSON

IBEGAN WITH Paine, to give what might be called the "leftwardmost" example of a Deist. Jefferson is sometimes treated as if he were "no better than Paine" (who was in fact his friend). But they differed on many things. Jefferson held that Jesus taught a morality superior to that of all other men, even to that of his favorite Greek philosophers, Epicurus and Epictetus. This was not a view Jefferson had accepted early in his life, when he took the stance of Viscount Bolingbroke. He copied out in his commonplace book Bolingbroke's condemnation of the New Testament's ethical system as inferior to the wisdom "of Tully, of Seneca, of Epictetus."[21] Later in life, Jefferson repudiated this view. He not only decided that Jesus' was the supreme moral code, but he made his own abbreviated New Testament a kind of spiritual bedside reading, to end his day in moral meditation. It was only after he had established Jesus' views as his highest guide that he confided to a friend: "I never go to bed without an hour or half hour's previous reading of something moral, whereon to ruminate in the intervals of sleep" (JP 1417).[22]

Jefferson changed his attitude toward Jesus' moral standard in the 1790s, when he was embroiled in the heightening animosities of partisan politics. Trying to temper his own emotions, he noticed what he thought the most striking thing about Jesus' teaching—that earlier moralities had enjoined love for one's friends but Jesus commanded that one love one's enemies. Some say that Jefferson was misrepresenting the "pagan" moralists, but he obviously felt a personal need, in this period of intense conflict, to find a calming influence on his own attitudes, and he found it in Jesus. This was a religious "conversion" to an *intimate* pacifism to match his Enlightenment *politics* of pacifism.

Jefferson could not have changed his mind on Jesus' ethics unless he had learned to disregard any claim of Jesus to be divine. That change was effected by the writings of Joseph Priestley. In his Bolingbroke days,

Jefferson thought that Jesus was deluded by his followers into thinking
he was God—one who, having "set out without pretensions to divinity,
ended in believing them" (JP 803). But he was convinced by Priestley
that such pretensions to divinity were foisted upon the "real" Jesus by
those who distorted his message in the Gospels, and by later metaphysi-
cians who imposed a Greek (mainly Platonic) mysticism on the New
Testament. This led to doctrines of the Trinity, Transubstantiation, and
other "nonsense."

Priestley framed his argument in works like *An History of the
Corruptions of Christianity* (two volumes, 1782) and *An History of the Early
Opinions Concerning Jesus Christ* (1786), which impressed both Adams and
Jefferson. Jefferson asked Priestley to write a brief summary of Jesus'
teachings (the kind of thing he undertook himself when Priestley did
not produce one that met his need). Adams, who had heard of this
project but thought Priestley died without completing it, wrote: "I
regret—oh, how I regret—that he did not live to publish this work!"[23]
Both Adams and Jefferson felt themselves freed from the "Platonic"
aspects of the Gospels by Priestley's work. Jefferson wrote:

> I have read his [Priestley's] *Corruptions of Christianity* and *Early
> Opinions of Jesus,* over and over again; and I rest on them, and on
> Middleton's writings, especially his letters from Rome and to
> Waterland, as the basis of my own faith.[24]

Adams and Jefferson, like Priestley, were especially critical of the Trinitarian "corruptions" of Christianity. We have already seen what Adams
thought of the Trinity.

> Had you and I been forty days with Moses on Mount Sinai,
> and admitted to behold the divine Shekinah, and there told
> that one was three and three one, we might not have had the
> courage to deny it, but we could not have believed it.[25]

Though Jefferson was careful not to mock religion in public, on the subject of the Trinity he adopted Shaftesbury's advice that ridicule was needed to purify religion:

> Ridicule is the only weapon which can be used against
> unintelligible propositions. Ideas must be distinct before
> reason can act on them; and no man had a distinct idea of the
> Trinity. It is the mere Abracadabra of the mountebanks calling
> themselves the priests of Jesus.[26]

He called the Trinity "the hocus-pocus phantasm of a god like another Cerberus with one body and three heads."[27]

Both Adams and Jefferson were confident that Unitarianism had finally prevailed against Trinitarian mysticism. Adams wrote to his son: "We Unitarians, one of whom I have had the honor to be for more than sixty years, do not indulge our malignity in profane cursing and swearing against you Calvinists, one of whom I know not how long you have been."[28] He also denied that Unitarianism was a recent thing, tracing it (correctly) back into the so-called Arminian days of Jonathan Mayhew.[29] Jefferson also rejoiced in the triumph of Unitarianism, the one form of Christianity he approved of, and one he thought appropriate for a republic. "I trust there is not a young man now living in the U.S. who will not die an Unitarian."[30] And the truth was prevailing not only in America: "I remember to have heard Dr. Priestley say that if all England would candidly examine themselves and confess, they would find that Unitarianism was really the religion of all."[31]

For Jefferson, both Unitarian and Deist meant "monotheist." That is why he called all Jews Deists. "Their system was Deism, that is, the belief of one only God. But their idea of him, and of his attributes, were degrading and injurious."[32] He proposed to "take a view of the *Deism* and ethics of the Jews, and show in what a degraded state they were, and the necessity they presented of a reformation" [emphasis added].[33] Jesus accomplished that reformation.

Moses had bound the Jews to many idle ceremonies,
mummeries and observances of no effect toward producing the
social utilities which constitute the essence of virtue. Jesus
exposed their futility and insignificance. The one instilled in
his people the most anti-social spirit toward other nations; the
other preached philanthropy and universal charity and
benevolence.[34]

The Jesus whom Jefferson adopted as his guide was the reformer of
monotheism who confirmed belief in an afterlife. "He taught, emphatically, the doctrine of a future state; which was either doubted or disbe-
lieved by the Jews; and wielded it with efficacy as an important
incentive, supplementary to the other motives to moral conduct."[35] The
seriousness with which Jefferson took his own religious views can be
seen in his effort to promote the writings of Priestley, and to elicit from
him an even more emphatic work on the superiority of Jesus' teachings
to those of any other moralist. When Priestley did not make that case as
powerfully as Jefferson wished, he decided to do it himself, and to back
up his point with a presentation of the Gospels in their "pure" state. This
led him to three ambitious works.

1. SYLLABUS OF AN ESTIMATE OF THE MERIT OF THE DOCTRINES OF JESUS, COMPARED WITH THOSE OF OTHERS (1803)

JEFFERSON CONSIDERS the three main bodies of moral teaching, that
of the philosophers, of the Jews, and of Jesus.

The *philosophers* were "truly great" in achieving "tranquility of mind,"
but they did this by precepts "related chiefly to ourselves." They were
deficient in "developing our duties to others." They had not "embraced
with benevolence the whole family of mankind."

The *Jews* were sound Deists (monotheists), but their ethics "were not
only imperfect, but often irreconcilable with the sound dictates of reason and morality, as they respect intercourse with those around us."

Jesus, however, corrected the flaws in both the other systems:

> His moral doctrines relating to kindred and friends were
> more pure and perfect than those of the most correct of the
> philosophers, and greatly more so than that of the Jews.
> And they went far beyond both in inculcating universal
> philanthropy, not only to kindred and friends, to neighbors
> and countrymen, but to all mankind, gathering all into one
> family, under the bonds of love, charity, peace, common
> wants, and common aids. A development of this head will
> evince the peculiar superiority of the system of Jesus over
> all others.[36]

Jefferson shared his *Syllabus* with Benjamin Rush, who had requested
an account of Jefferson's beliefs; but the document was kept secret,
to be confided only to a select few, with instructions to keep it to
themselves. Jefferson knew he had to avoid all public discussion of his
religious views, which would just lead to endless explication and
defense.

2. THE PHILOSOPHY OF JESUS OF NAZARETH, EXTRACTED FROM THE ACCOUNT OF HIS LIFE AND DOCTRINES AS GIVEN BY MATTHEW, MARK, LUKE, AND JOHN, BEING AN ABRIDGEMENT OF THE NEW TESTAMENT FOR THE USE OF THE INDIANS, UNEMBARRASSED WITH MATTERS OF FACT OR FAITH BEYOND THE LEVEL OF THEIR COMPREHENSION (1804)

IN ORDER TO recover the true Jesus from the corrupted Gospels, Jefferson assembled his own purified text, cutting out the sayings of
Jesus he thought authentic from printed New Testaments, and pasting
them into his own book. The resulting volume is now lost, but it has been

reconstructed convincingly by Dickinson W. Adams, using Jefferson's title page and list of passages to be used, along with the surviving copies of the New Testament from which Jefferson scissored his passages.[37] Jefferson said that the parts originally derived from Jesus were "as easily distinguishable as diamonds in a dunghill."[38] This was done by paring away all references to miracles, prophecies, the Resurrection, or anything else supernatural. The Jesus who emerges from this slimming process is the wisest of all human beings, but not divine.

Jefferson originally meant to run his excerpts, side by side, in their Latin and English forms. But under the burden of business as president, he simplified his task and assembled all his excerpts in one tongue, English. He was able to do this, he claimed, as "the work of one or two evenings only," though Eugene R. Sheridan points out that he had undoubtedly prepared for the actual scissoring by long consideration of the Gospels.[39] The result was a collection of "forty-six pages of pure and unsophisticated doctrines, such as were professed and acted on by the *unlettered* apostles, the Apostolic fathers, and the Christians of the first century" [emphasis in the original].[40] The emphasized "unlettered," like the title page saying that there was nothing beyond the comprehension of "Indians," is an attack on the supposedly learned Federalists who accepted all the Platonisms of a corrupt Christianity.

Since Jefferson kept this, like all his religious statements, guardedly private, one may ask how he could envisage its being used by Indians. How would they learn of it? Michael Novak, in his attempt to baptize the Founders into a devotion of his own dye, says that this proves the Evangelical religiosity of Jefferson. "He did not plan to send [the Indians] a volume of Locke; he planned to send the moral teachings of the New Testament."[41] Actually, it has been well known to scholars from the time of Henry Adams that, as Adams wrote in 1890, Jefferson's friends understood how he would "use the mask of Indian philanthropy to disguise an attack on conservatism."[42] That is one of the ways he kept his religious views private. "Indian" was a code word for "Federalist."

3. THE LIFE AND MORALS OF
JESUS OF NAZARETH, EXTRACTED
TEXTUALLY FROM THE GOSPELS IN
GREEK, LATIN, FRENCH, AND ENGLISH (1820)

AT LAST, in his retirement, after correspondence on religious matters with Adams and with Francis Adrian Van der Kemp, Jefferson was able to create what he considered the definitively true New Testament, in four languages, two ancient and two modern. For this, he did not restrict himself to what he considered authentic sayings (as he had in *The Philosophy of Jesus*), but added accounts of the life of Jesus, as that had been lived in its natural manifestations. This amounted to his own profession of faith. It, along with the *Syllabus* and *The Philosophy of Jesus*, proves what he said to those he let into his religious views—"I am a Christian, in the only sense in which he [Jesus] wished anyone to be, sincerely attached to his doctrines, in preference to all others."[43] He thanked Charles Thomson for his translation of the four Gospels with a letter saying: "*I* am a *real Christian*, that is to say, a disciple of the doctrines of Jesus, very different from the Platonists, who call *me* infidel and *themselves* Christians and preachers of the gospel, while they draw all their characteristic dogmas from what its Author never said at all" [emphasis in the original].[44] The Deism of Jefferson was a religion, just not the kind many people wanted (or want) to recognize.

OTHER FOUNDERS

ENOUGH HAS already been said about Adams to make his Deism manifest. Like Jefferson, he accepted Priestley's account of the corruption of the New Testament, and adhered to "Christianity reduced to its primitive simplicity."[45] He hated to see the corrupt version of Christianity being spread by missionaries:

> We have now, it seems, a National Bible Society to propagate King James's Bible through all nations. Would it not be better

to apply these pious subscriptions to purify Christendom
from the corruptions of Christianity than to propagate those
corruptions in Europe, Asia, Africa and America?[46]

A committed foe of the Trinity, Adams of course denied that its Second
Person could become man:

[Europeans] all believe that Great Principle which has
produced this boundless universe, Newton's universe and
Herschel's universe, came down to this little ball to be spit
upon by Jews; and until this awful blasphemy is got rid of, there
never will be any liberal science in the world.[47]

Franklin agreed with Jefferson and Adams in holding to a Unitarian
faith in God and the afterlife. On Jesus he said: "I think the system of
morals and his religion, as he left them to us, the best the world ever saw
or is likely to see; but I apprehend it has received various corrupting
changes, and I have, with most of the present Dissenters in England,
some doubts as to his Divinity, though it is a question I do not dogmatize
upon."[48] Franklin did not dogmatize on anything. Henry May perfectly
caught the spirit of this quintessential Enlightenment figure:

Like the aged Voltaire, and unlike any other American I can
call to mind, Franklin was relaxed in his skepticism—without
the belligerence of the village infidel, the arrogance of the
skeptical aristocrat, the self-torture of a Mark Twain, or the
adolescent show-off manner of a Mencken. One of the great
figures of the Skeptical Enlightenment in the world, he
shared—but only occasionally showed—the sadness which
pervaded it.[49]

Alexander Hamilton was a rational believer who gave up churchgoing but died in the Anglican sacraments—which did not by his time
commit one to a firm belief in the Trinity.[50] Even Samuel Johnson was

evasive on the topic, as were men like Benjamin Rush and John Wither-spoon. Once Enlightened religion came to America, the Trinity lost its function as explaining the sacrifice of the Son to the Father. Even those who profess a belief in it in later times hold it in such an attenuated form that it is rarely reflected on.[51] Evangelicals often hold a form of what might be called "Jesusism" or (in the case of Pentecostals) "Spiritism"—emphasis on one or other Person of the Trinity, to the neglect of the other two.

WASHINGTON

ONE FOUNDER is often thought of as "something more than a Deist," though there is nothing in his writings to indicate that that is the case. The director of Washington's home at Mount Vernon, James Rees, told me that people often inquire why there are no marks of religion in the building—no crucifix, or holy picture, or prayer dis-played, or any religious symbol at all, though Washington was very shrewd about symbolism and carefully chose signs of peace, republican-ism, and agrarian virtue for his home. Jordan has to tell them that Wash-ington was not a devout man in the way they want him to be. The famous nineteenth-century engraving of him kneeling in prayer at Valley Forge is a fiction, though bloggers on the Religious Right protested when it was removed from a classroom. Other treatments of that scene include a stained-glass window in the United States Capitol's meditation chapel.

The same people who think Jefferson was *not* religious contrast him with Washington, though Jefferson thought and wrote about religion far more than Washington did. The reverence toward Washington as rever-ent is not based on history or scholarly treatments of the man but on early mythmongering, including the extraordinarily popular (and fanci-ful) biography by Parson Weems, which ran through twenty-nine edi-tions during its author's lifetime, and extended to many dozens more after he died.[52] The impact of the book itself was magnified by the inclu-sion of excerpts from it in the *Eclectic Readers* published by William

Holmes McGuffey (another parson), which were used by generations of schoolchildren. This, along with more pretentious works—like Timothy Dwight's epic *The Conquest of Canaan,* which presented Washington as Moses—prolonged the cult of Washington, a cult already strong enough in 1815 that Marcus Cunliffe can quote a foreign visitor from that year as saying that "every American considers it his sacred duty to have a likeness of Washington in his house, just as we have the image of God's saints."[53]

There is a heavy investment by some modern conservatives in the idea that Washington was devout. This belief has endured despite the work of scholars who show it to be groundless. Washington never himself invoked the name of Jesus or of Christ in prayer—he referred to Jesus only once, speaking to some Indians.[54] He normally used terms for God that were the common parlance of other Deists—"governor of the universe," or "architect of the universe," or "author of the universe," terms that Thomas Paine would have been quite comfortable with.[55] As Joseph Ellis points out, there were no clergy called for or prayers said as Washington was dying. "There were no ministers in the room, no prayers uttered, no Christian rituals offering the solace of everlasting life. . . . He died as a Roman stoic rather than a Christian saint."[56]

Michael Novak, grasping at straws, asserts that Washington on his deathbed must have prayed with his wife when no one was looking, though she never mentioned that afterward.[57] If anything like that occurred, it would almost certainly have been mentioned, since there was great concern expressed at the time about Washington's "godless" death. The Reverend Samuel Miller of New York shared with others "the doubt clouding his own mind as to Washington's piety." How was it possible, he asked, for a true Christian, in the full exercise of his mental faculties, to die without one expression of distinctive belief or Christian hope?

Washington attended church, as all public men were expected to do—and as Jefferson did—but he did not take the Anglican communion. The Washington scholar Marcus Cunliffe called his religion "a social performance."[58] The pastor of the church Washington attended as president, Bishop William White, said that Washington regularly left the service before communion, leaving his wife behind to receive it. When White complained of this, Washington just stopped attending on communion Sundays.[59] This, too, was widely noticed. Dr. James Abercrombie, the assistant rector of Christ Church in Philadelphia when Washington was in that city, said of Washington: "I cannot consider any man as a real Christian who uniformly disregards an ordinance [taking communion] so solemnly enjoined by the divine Author of our holy religion, and considered as a channel of divine grace."[60] In Bishop White's words:

> I do not believe that any degree of recollection will bring to
> my mind any fact which would prove General Washington to
> have been a believer in the Christian revelation, further than
> as may be hoped from his constant attendance on Christian
> worship.[61]

Madison, who was close to Washington in their long collaboration, told Jared Sparks:

> He did not suppose that Washington had ever attended to the
> arguments for Christianity, and for the different systems of
> religion, or in fact that he had formed definite opinions on the
> subject.[62]

Michael Novak says that Washington must have been a religious man since as president he addressed Jewish citizens with respect and as general he told his soldiers not to antagonize Canadian Catholics.[63] He would been a stupid politician to act otherwise. We are left with William Lee Miller's unchallengeable statement that all the major founders of our country were Deists, however unhappy that makes people who ask for a different theology.

DEISTS' FLAWS

IT IS one of this book's theses that Enlightened religion was a blessing to this country—that it was a necessary corrective to the pre-
Enlightenment religion that hanged Mary Dyer, condemned Anne
Hutchinson, and banished Roger Williams. That does not mean that we
must approve everything connected with Enlightenment religion or
condemn everything connected with Evangelical religion. Both have
had their flaws. The failings of the American Enlightenment were the
same that can be found in the European Enlightenment, including anti-
Semitism and anti-Catholicism. Rationalist religion rejected what it
considered the superstitions of the established faiths tied to secular
power, as the Jewish theocracy and the Catholic monarchies had been.

Anti-Semitism was clearly present in men like Montesquieu and
Voltaire. We have seen already Jefferson's condemnation of the Jewish
religion—its "degraded state," "anti-social spirit," and so forth—as
needing reform by Jesus. Though Americans were not as harsh toward
Jews as Europe had been, it is impossible to claim that the general prejudice shown by philosophes did not reach these shores. Martin Marty has
stated that only special pleading can make the early years of the Republic significantly responsive either to Jews or to Catholics.[64] America
began Protestant and was overwhelmingly Protestant for a long time.
Mark Noll notes that as late as 1860 over 95 percent of the houses of worship in America were Protestant.[65]

It is absurd to deny the prejudice of the Deists. Even Peter Gay, a cel-
ebrant of the Enlightenment, does not (cannot) deny its anti-Semitism.[66]
The anti-Catholic posture of the Enlightenment was an adaptation to the
Age of Reason of the Puritan belief in Rome as the Antichrist. John
Adams began his writing career with an attack on the canon law of the
Catholic Church. He is probably the one who pressured Jefferson to
put a reference to Catholic tyranny in the Declaration of Independence,
and he wrote many things to this effect: "A free government and the
Roman catholic religion can never exist together."[67] Yet what Marty calls

"special pleading" led the Jesuit John Courtney Murray to argue that America was really founded on Catholic principles—an idea that would have made Adams and Jefferson snort with derision.[68] Christian scholars have denied that America is a Christian nation—so, a fortiori, it is not a Catholic nation.[69]

The Deists are not often allowed to speak for themselves. When they are not being denounced as infidels, men like Michael Novak dress them up as crypto-Evangelicals, crypto-Jews, or crypto-Catholics. But enough. Whatever their faults, the Deists delivered us from the horrors of pre-Enlightenment religion, title enough to honor. They also founded this country.

IV|
DISESTABLISHMENT

10 | BEYOND TOLERANCE

ONE OF THE GREATEST achievements of the Enlightenment was the Disestablishment of religion. America was the first and best example of this, setting a model that would be aspired to by others (including the Dalai Lama). To appreciate the scale of this achievement, we should look at the gradual way religious freedom emerged in the run-up to the Enlightenment.

There are two basic approaches to the problem of religious freedom, from the top down and from the bottom up. The top-down approach sees religious freedom as something granted by the government, which tolerates (within limits) some forms of dissent. We saw in an earlier chapter how this kind of tolerance was adopted pragmatically by Cromwell and imposed coercively on American Puritans. Cromwell had to give rein to various forms of dissent in order to forge an alliance against the monarchy. Then Kings Charles and James had to continue this dispensation, in order to woo the freed sects back to their restored monarchy. The Puritans in America had to submit, against their will, to this form of toleration.

The trouble with a top-down religious freedom is that it is granted at the discretion of state authority, and is invariably limited. Usually, only some Dissenters are given an exemption from the established church's demands (Catholics were excluded from the freedom of dissent granted by Cromwell, Charles, and James). Even those given religious freedom often have to pay some price for the privilege—perhaps by supporting the established church with their taxes, or by exclusion from state-supported offices, colleges, and privileges. The fight for religious freedom then becomes an attempt to nibble away at these limits. Even John Locke, a pioneer in the cause of religious freedom, did more to extend the areas of dissent than to recognize the rights of Dissenters.

The logic of establishment is simple, and still appeals to many in America. The argument is that a nation must honor God in order for God to bless and protect it. Dissent is a dangerous thing in this frame of reference. What if the Dissenters have a form of religion, or irreligion, that offends God—will he continue his favor? The Puritans were sure that he would *not* continue his protection if dissent from their own true church was allowed—they held that such Dissenters were agents of Satan. Other Protestants feared the Antichrist only in papists. Locke did not fear the devil in any religion, but he feared anarchism as the inevitable result of atheism, and he denied the right to hold that extreme of dissent.

The only way to establish a right of dissent not granted by the state was to start from the bottom up, from the rights of each individual, and especially the rights of conscience. One expression of this view could invert establishment, producing not Disestablishment but a kind of anti-establishment. This holds that religion in general has been an enemy of freedom and it should be discouraged if not quashed. Voltaire was of that school—*"Écrasez l'infâme"*—and so were some leaders of the French Revolution. True governmental neutrality toward religion is hard to achieve. America must continually strive to maintain it. The striving for it had to go through several stages, first aspiring toward tolerance and then moving beyond tolerance. What distinguished the Enlightenment is the relative speed with which it first moved toward tolerance and then moved beyond it. Locke supplied a starting point.

LOCKE

JOHN LOCKE'S *Letter Concerning Toleration* is as much a landmark of Enlightened religion as is his *The Reasonableness of Christianity.* Jefferson read both works carefully and made extensive notes on them (J 1.544–50). Locke makes such a strong argument for the separation of church and state that one might think his title a misnomer. "Toleration" seems a condescending term, implying the right to grant (and therefore the right to withhold) some toleration of dissent. In fact, Locke had not broken entirely with establishment values. He was offering a kind of masked establishment, not of a particular religion but of religion in general. He saw the state as necessarily theistic, and therefore obliged not to tolerate atheism.

The opening pages of Locke's book show how far from Jefferson he was—though Jefferson, like most Enlightenment figures, learned from the book. Locke initially presents toleration as a specifically *Christian virtue.* Since Jesus said that one must love one's enemies, turn the other check, and do good to everyone, it is against the Christian ethos to coerce, oppress, or punish others for their views. Locke begins:

> Since you are pleased to inquire what are my thoughts about the *mutual* toleration *of Christians* in their different professions of religion, I must needs answer you, freely, that I esteem that toleration to be the chief characteristic mark of *the true church.* . . . Whosoever will list himself *under the banner of Christ* must, in the first place and above all things, make war upon his own lusts and vice. . . . If *the Gospel* and the apostles may be credited, no man can *be a Christian* without charity, and without that faith which works not by force, but by love [emphases added].[1]

There is an obvious problem with this approach. If toleration is a specifically Christian virtue, rather than a right of each individual conscience, what does one do with people who are not Christian? Perhaps Locke is just offering his views as specifically Christian in order to win over people who are prejudiced toward that religious position. But is it not odd to begin an argument against prejudice by appealing to prejudice? When Locke begins the body of his argument, he bases it on the nature of things, not on theology. That might suggest that the opening was deceptive. But at the end he will return to the tone of the opening, with some cavils that place his book back in the school of mere toleration.

The heart of Locke's argument depends on two definitions. He defines the state as the holder of a monopoly of force deployed to protect the civil interests of society. "Civil interest I call life, liberty, health, and indolency [non-wounding, from *dolor*] of body" (15). The church, by contrast, is a voluntary society in which men join "in order to the public worshipping of God, in such a manner as they judge acceptable to him and effectual to the salvation of their souls" (23). The state has no competence to decide what a man considers the proper means to please God and save his soul. And the church has no competence to use force for any means, and especially not to affect others' civil interest. So far so good— and Locke will use words that both Jefferson and Madison echo in their own works. Religious error does not of itself disturb another's civil interest—or if it does, it must be checked because of the civil interest injured, not because of the religious error involved: "If any man err from the right way, it is his own misfortune, no injury to thee; nor therefore art thou to punish him in the things of this life because thou supposest he will be miserable in that which is to come" (33). But what if the civil power obtrudes itself into the realm of conscience, commanding something the subject considers immoral?

The subject must not violate his own conscience—but on the other hand, he may not oppose the magistrate with force, which belongs to the civil authority and no one else: "Such a private person is to abstain from the actions that he judges unlawful and he is to undergo the punishment, which is not unlawful for him to bear; for the private judgment of any person concerning a law enacted in political matters, for the public good, does not take away the obligation of that law, nor deserve a dispensation" (83). This presages Martin Luther King's philosophy of nonviolent civil disobedience, which enjoins accepting the penalty for breaking the law.

As with his *Reasonableness*, Locke impressed his age with a powerful rhetoric:

> But now, if I be marching on with my utmost vigour in that
> way which, according to the sacred geography, leads straight
> to Jerusalem, why am I beaten and ill used by others because,
> perhaps, I wear no buskins; because my hair is not of the right
> cut; because, perhaps, I have not been dipped [baptized] in the
> right fashion; because I eat flesh upon the road, or some other
> food which agrees with my stomach; because I avoid certain
> by-ways which seem unto me to lead into briars or precipices;
> because, amongst the several paths that are in the same road,
> I choose that to walk in which seems to be straightest and
> clearest; because I avoid to keep company with some travelers
> that are less grave, and others that are more sour, than they
> ought to be; or, in fine, because I follow a guide that either is
> or is not clothed in white and crowned with a mitre? (47)

Locke says much that anticipates Jefferson and Madison. Things like: "Truth certainly would do well enough if she were once left to shift for herself" (79). Or: "Faith only, and inward sincerity, are the things that procure acceptance with God" (55). But differences emerge clearly toward the end of Locke's book, when he sets the limits to toleration, under three principal heads.

1. A religion that holds as part of its theology something that is a violation of others' civil interest cannot, to that extent, be tolerated.

The examples Locke gives point directly to Roman Catholics, who reportedly held that "faith is not to be kept with heretics" and that "kings excommunicated forfeit their crowns and kingdoms" (89–91). The first breaks the civil protection of contracts, and the second breaks the civil duty of obedience to civil authority—and Rome had notoriously invoked both those maxims in the past, when justifying rebellion against the reign of Elizabeth I.

2. *A religious body that is subject to a foreign prince should not be tolerated by the prince of the country in which they dwell.*

This, too, is obviously directed against Catholics, with their allegiance to the secular ruler of the Vatican state—though once again Locke does not spell that out. To avoid, perhaps, being too inflammatory where open enmities had caused great turbulence in the past, he deftly gives as his example the Mahometans who were "bound to yield blind obedience to the mufti of Constantinople" (93). Locke is still invoking a civil offense to justify denying tolerance, but the result was the same, to deny tolerance to Roman Catholics. In this, he followed the example of both Acts of Tolerance (1649 and 1689).

Jefferson indirectly took Locke's position on Catholics in the Declaration of Independence. After the French and Indian War, when England absorbed Canada into the empire, the English faced the same difficulty that Kings Charles and James did when they regained power over a population with elements that did not recognize the established church. In Canada, the resisters were French Catholics. Rather than try, ineffectually, to enforce submission to the Church of England, the government granted tolerance to Catholic worship by the Quebec Act (1773). The Puritans' fear of the Antichrist flared up again in New England. They did not want to be in a British Empire that recognized Roman idolatry in a neighboring part of the empire.

This became one of the grievances lodged against England in the first Continental Congress of 1774. The royal government was guilty of "erecting a tyranny there [in Canada], to the great danger, from so total a dissimilarity of religions, law, and government to the neighboring British colonies, by the assistance of whose blood and treasure the said country was conquered from France."[2] This was also an item in the petition to the King issued by the Congress, which complained of his "establishing an absolute government and the Roman Catholic religion throughout those vast regions that border on the westerly and northerly boundaries of the free Protestant English settlements."[3]

Jefferson included this among the grievances he listed in the 1775 document drafted for the Continental Congress, "Declaration of the Causes and Necessity for Taking up Arms," where he wrote: "They [Parliament] have erected in a neighboring province, acquired by the joint arms of Great Britain and America, a tyranny dangerous to the very existence of all these colonies" (J 1.200).[4] Though he did not include this grievance in his rough draft of the Declaration of Independence, his committee (persuaded perhaps by John Adams, since this was a matter important to Massachusetts) submitted the Declaration with these words: "For abolishing the free system of English laws in a neighboring province, establishing therein an arbitrary government, and enlarging its boundaries so as to render it at once an example and fit instrument for introducing the same absolute rule into these colonies" (J 1.431).[5]

Those who had not been following the controversy might not see that the problem here was the recognition of a Catholic regime. Congress and Jefferson were using Locke's argument, that Catholics are subject to a tyrannical regime (Rome) which offers a threat to the civil interest of the British. This is not, in theory, a contradiction of Locke's separation of church and state. But can the same be said of the third exception to Locke's scheme of toleration?

3. Locke says that atheists must not be tolerated.

> Lastly, those are *not at all to be tolerated* who deny the being of God. Promises, covenants, and oaths, which are the bonds of human society, can have no hold upon an atheist. *The taking away of God, though but even in thought, dissolves all.* Besides, also, those that by their atheism undermine and destroy all religion, can have no pretence of religion whereupon to challenge the privilege of a toleration [emphases added]. (93)

Those last four words—*"privilege* of a *toleration"*—show that Locke has not broken out of the old top-down framework, in which tolerance is a privilege, instead of a right, one that can be granted or withheld by government. This attitude, which clearly emerges here, was implicit in earlier formulations along the way—for example, "These religious societies I call churches, and these I say the magistrate ought to *tolerate*." The passage also shows that Locke's tolerance is not given to the individual conscience but to religion. If the individual has no religion, he has no "standing," as the lawyers say, to plead for tolerance. That is given *only* to religion. The irreligious "can have no pretence [claim] of religion whereupon to challenge [assert] the privilege of toleration." This presents a kind of catch-22, with a man wanting freedom of conscience without being able to win it without first submitting to religion.

Locke would argue, of course, that he is not punishing belief (or the lack thereof) but an affront to the civil interest. If a man does not believe in God, he cannot be forced to swear an oath to God to guarantee his loyalty to the state. But this argument violates the separation of church and state that Locke had earlier called for. Now the stability of the *state* depends on a *religious* bond. This amounts to a religious test for citizenship. One may not have to believe in a particular religion, but one must believe in God—that is, in religion generally considered. Later attacks on the Jeffersonian separation of church and state can thus appeal back to Locke, and say that religion in general can be established by the state. That is why Jefferson's view, not Locke's, was put by Madison in the Constitution.

Locke's denial of rights to atheists because they could not take oaths, keep promises, or enter covenants would bedevil American politics for some time. Remember that Roger Williams forbade the taking of oaths because it was a form of prayer with the unregenerate. Others would resist taking oaths, notably the Quakers. This was one source of the animosity against them, even though a compromise was reached allowing them to make promises (thus meeting Locke's test of accountability). South Carolina stated the duty of citizens "to bear witness to the truth," but added this accommodation: "Every inhabitant of this state, when called to make an appeal to God as a witness to truth, shall be permitted to do it in that way which is most agreeable to the dictates of his own conscience." But even with this leeway in the mode of calling on God, it was necessary that God be somehow invoked, to avoid Locke's strictures against atheism. Atheists would not be allowed to hold office in several American states.

Locke was a truly liberating force in the early days of the Enlightenment. I point to certain shortcomings in his work simply to show how original were Jefferson and Madison, who completed the Enlightenment project that Locke only began. In his notes on Locke's *Letter,* Jefferson summed up all three of Locke's exceptions to toleration in one sentence of his own, and then added this comment: "It was a great thing to go so far (as he himself says of the Parliament who framed the Act of Toleration), but where he stopped short, we may go on." Then he added a footnote to his own comment:

> Will not his own excellent rule be sufficient here, too?—to punish these as civil offences, e.g., to assert that a foreign prince has power within this commonwealth, is a misdemeanor. The other opinions may be despised [dismissed]. Perhaps the single thing which may be required to others, before toleration to them, would be an oath that they would allow toleration to others. (J 1.551)

Jefferson clearly meant to "go on" from Locke—and he did.

Other expressions of religious toleration in the American colonies, apart from Jefferson's and Madison's, were as limited as Locke's. Roger Williams denied the right of the state to persecute people for their beliefs, and he declared that individual conscience must be respected. But he too thought more in a top-down way than from a bottom-up belief in the rights of individuals. He had a low opinion of the way people had used their freedom of conscience—the mass of them had been submitting to Antichrist for many centuries. He said that the state had no competence to decide on or defend the true religion, for two reasons: because there was no true religion left in his day, and because, even if there were, the depraved generality of mankind could not define and impose it. "If this be not to pull God and Christ and Spirit out of heaven and subject them unto natural, sinful, inconstant men, and so consequentially to Satan himself, by whom *all* people naturally are guided, let heaven and earth judge" (emphasis added).[6] The garden gone, all was wilderness—to be governed by the rules of natural law in the absence of supernatural covenant.

Perry Miller denied that Roger Williams had a continuing legacy: "As for any direct influence of his thought on the ultimate achievement of religious liberty in America, he had none."[7] That is not literally true. The Baptists continually honored his defense of their freedom from repression. Though he had been a Baptist for only a short time himself, he was a friend to the Baptists in Rhode Island, and the most distinguished Baptist leader of the eighteenth century, Isaac Backus, celebrated his work and tried to emulate him, so far as that was possible to one who did not believe that the true church had disappeared. Backus is rightly honored, himself, as a champion of religious freedom. But he, too, thought in a top-down way. He was less liberal than Locke. Locke demanded only that the government be theist itself and exclude atheists. Backus demanded that the state be Christian and exclude non-Christians. It should enforce religion by things like fast days and Sabbatarianism. It was only monetary subvention that he prohibited.

Most of the state constitutions written immediately after the Revolution supported Christianity in some way, often imposing some form of religious test for holding office. South Carolina was typical. Its 1778 document supported the "Christian Protestant religion," since "the Christian religion is the true religion." Even Virginia at first continued the support for the established Anglican (now Episcopal) religion, though concern for Dissenters' rights was voiced well before the Revolution. In 1769, the House of Burgesses had appointed a Committee for Religion to look into this matter (JM 1.170). In 1772, a bill was brought "allowing a free toleration to His Majesty's *Protestant* subjects in this colony" (emphasis added; JM 1.525–26). In 1774, petitions from Baptists and Presbyterians were received. Nothing came of these attempts, but friends to them seized the opportunity of rewriting Virginia's Constitution in 1776 to bring about Disestablishment of the Anglican Church. These attempts also failed, but they laid the groundwork for later success. Three men were important in this sustained effort—Thomas Jefferson, George Mason, and James Madison. In chronological order, these were their moves:

1. Jefferson's first attempt (1776)

From Philadelphia, where he was in the congressional session that passed the Declaration of Independence, Jefferson tried to participate in the drafting of a new Constitution for Virginia. He bombarded the legislators with suggestions, sending at least three drafts of a Constitution. All three included a provision for freedom of religion (J 1.344, 353, 363). The one included in the first draft set the pattern: "All persons shall have full and free liberty of religious opinion, nor shall any be compelled to frequent or maintain any religious service or institution, but seditious behavior to be punishable by civil magistrate according to the laws already made or hereafter to be made" (J 1.344). George Mason, the principal author of the Virginia Constitution, took careful note of Jefferson's suggestions.

2. Mason's attempt (1776)

Mason took Jefferson's religion clause from the body of the Constitution and put its equivalent in his Declaration of Rights preceding the Form of Government. Jefferson had not used the word "toleration," but Mason did. His comments on disturbing the peace and on Christian forbearance show that he is closely modeling his passage on Locke:

> That religion, or the duty which we owe our divine and
> omnipotent Creator, and the manner of discharging it, can
> be governed only by reason and conviction, not by force or
> violence, and therefore that all men should enjoy the fullest

> *toleration* in the exercise of religion according to the dictates of
> conscience, unpunished and unrestrained by the magistrate
> unless, under color of religion, any man disturb the peace, the
> happiness, or safety of society or of individuals. And that it is
> the mutual duty of all to practice *Christian* forbearance, love,
> and charity toward each other [emphases added]. (JM 1.172–73)

Though this was a Lockean form of *Christian* tolerance, it was an
advance on the kinds of dissent allowed in most colonies, and it
influenced the state constitutions of Massachusetts and Pennsylvania
when it was instantly and widely published—even though, as it was
passed, Mason's Declaration lost the word "tolerance" when the Virginia
Assembly accepted Madison's better term, the "free exercise" of
religion.

3. Madison's first attempt (1776)

Madison, a new member of the Assembly to which this bill was submitted, objected to the term "toleration," and he asked Patrick Henry, a
weightier legislator, to sponsor a change, substituting "free exercise of
religion" for "fullest toleration":

> That religion or the duty we owe to our Creator, and the
> manner of discharging it, being under the direction of reason
> and conviction only, not of violence or compulsion, all men are
> equally entitled to the full and free exercise of it according to
> the dictates of conscience, and therefore that no man or class of
> men ought on account of religion to be invested with peculiar
> emoluments or privileges, nor subjected to any penalties or
> disabilities unless under etc.

When Patrick Henry was asked the meaning of "his" amendment, he
said it would not exclude special emoluments to the Episcopal Church
(JM 1.171), which gutted the obvious meaning and sank the amendment.
So the battle for Disestablishment in Virginia was still to be won.

4. Madison's second attempt (1776)

Madison submitted another change, keeping most of Mason's language, still putting "free exercise" in place of "fullest toleration," but removing the denial of "emoluments" to any religion.

> That religion, or the duty which we owe to our Creator, and the manner of discharging it, can be directed only by reason and conviction, not by force or violence, and therefore that all men are equally entitled to enjoy the free exercise of religion, according to the dictates of conscience, unpunished and unrestrained by the magistrate, unless the preservation of equal liberty and the existence of the state are manifestly endangered. And that it is the mutual duty of all to practice Christian forbearance, love, and charity toward each other. (JM 1. 174–75)

This was an improvement on Mason, but it still did not disestablish the Episcopal Church. Madison was not satisfied.

5. Jefferson's second attempt (1776)

Back in Virginia, Jefferson brought a measure to the legislature "For Disestablishing the Church of England and for Repealing Laws Interfering with Freedom of Worship." Debate over this measure Jefferson later called "the severest contests in which I have ever been engaged" (JP 34). Edmund Pendleton and Robert Carter rallied support for the church properties, though Dissenters were exempted from paying for them, and the state salaries of ministers were suspended pro tem (J 1.527–28).

6. Jefferson's third attempt (1777)

Placed on a committee for revising the laws of Virginia, Jefferson drew up "A Bill for Establishing Religious Freedom," which was not taken up by the Assembly until 1779, when Jefferson could not participate in the debates since he had been elected governor. The bill did not pass because at that time debate over religion was concentrated on a "General Assessment" for state support of the different churches.

7. Madison's third attempt (1785)

Madison joined the General Assessment debate with an anonymous pamphlet, *Memorial and Remonstrance Against Religious Assessments*. This was his major statement on religious freedom.

8. Madison's fourth attempt (1786)

Jefferson's 1777 bill was brought again to the Assembly. Jefferson was in France at the time, but Madison steered it through with minor amendments. It was ratified early in 1787. Only then was the Anglican Church disestablished in Virginia.

Since these last four steps led to victory, I shall treat them in more detail in the following chapters, especially the third attempts by Jefferson and by Madison, the former's Statute, the latter's *Remonstrance*.

11 | JEFFERSON'S STATUTE

JEFFERSON'S 1776 EFFORT to disestablish the Anglican Church, when he was a member of the Virginia Assembly, survives for us in the outline of his talk on that occasion, a list of abbreviated arguments. He begins by reciting all the grisly laws for the punishment of heretics that Virginia had inherited from England. This is proof that the old order must be expunged.

> Gentlemen will be surprised at details of these persecuting
> statutes. Most men imagine persecution unknown to our lands.
> Legal status of religion little understood. . . . Happily, the spirit
> of times in favor of rights of conscience. (J 1.536)

Then he discusses religion as a *right* to worship God.

> Individual cannot surrender [this] right—answerable to
> God. . . . God requires every [religious] act according to
> belief, yet belief founded on evidence offered to his mind,
> as things appear to him, not to another. Objection: Other
> men's understanding better? Answer: His own understanding,

whether more or less judicious, only faculty [given by God].
(J 1.537)

Next he defends free inquiry.

> Is religion of state expedient? Purpose must be uniformity.
> Is uniformity desirable? If ever could be obtained, would be
> by suffocating free enquiry. All improvements in religion or
> philosophy have been from setting up private judgment against
> public—venturing despite uniformity. Monkish impositions,
> ignorance, darkness [are] supported on ruins of enquiry.
> Glorious Reformation [had] effect of shaking off public
> opinion. Philosophy reformed by free enquiry (Galileo,
> Newton). (J 1.537–38)

He runs through the sad history of established religions.

> Is uniformity attainable? By Inquisition. By lesser punish-
> ments—burning heretics, fines, imprisoning, abjuration.
> Constraint may produce hypocrites, not prevent sentiment.
> Experience has proved unattainable—millions burnt, tortured,
> fined, imprisoned, yet men differ. In Roman Catholic countries,
> most infidelity. (J 1.538)

Finally, he argues that religion will be the beneficiary of freedom.

> Advantage to religion to put all on [equal] footing. Strengthens
> church, oblige its ministers to be industrious, exemplary [like
> the] Northern clergy. Whether dependence or independence
> most likely to make industrious? Lawyers, physicians. Chris-
> tianity flourished three hundred years without establishments.
> Soon as established, decline from purity. Betrays want of
> confidence in doctrines of church to suspect that reason or

intrinsic excellence insufficient without secular prop. Gates of
hell shall never prevail. (J 1.538–39)

That is the second time he has quoted Matthew 16.18 on the gates of
hell. The first was in answer to an earlier question. "Objection: Religion
will decline if not supported? Answer: Gates of hell shall not prevail"
(J 1.537). Both these places were added to his notes by Jefferson, using
different ink. Was he just trying to disarm Christian legislators in the
Assembly by a feigned reliance on the Christian Scripture? There are
other things in these notes that make them (in an eighteenth-century
expression) "squint toward" Protestantism. He contrasts the "glorious
Reformation" with the imposed uniformity of Mohammedans and
Roman Catholics.

Admittedly, Jefferson is throwing together a variety of appeals, like a
lawyer trying to sway a jury of people who respond to different
approaches. He refers, for instance, to the preface of the state's Constitution, George Mason's text as improved by James Madison: "The Declaration of Rights is freedom of religion" (J 1.539). But we have seen that
George Mason's document did not go beyond toleration. It did not disestablish the Anglican Church, and that Disestablishment is exactly
what Jefferson is pleading for in this place. Since these are only notes, we
do not know how Jefferson would have expanded them in delivery. He
may have argued, for instance, that the Virginia Declaration of Rights
implied in logic more than it stated explicitly.

THE STATUTE

To GET Jefferson's argument for religious freedom entirely spelled
out and put in order, we have to turn to his proposed revisal of the
laws, to what he called on his tombstone THE STATUTE OF VIRGINIA FOR
RELIGIOUS FREEDOM, but what was first known as "A Bill for Establishing
Religious Freedom" (J 2.45–46). As Jefferson wrote it, the bill has only

three paragraphs, each containing just one sentence. But the first paragraph, giving the grounds for the legislative act, is a monstrously long sentence. For the purpose of analysis, I break it down into four headings containing fifteen arguments.[1]

Here is the shape of the first paragraph.

A. *The duties and rights of conscience*

Jefferson begins with the individual's relationship with God, antecedent to any state intrusion on this tie. Since sincere belief is required to pay God homage, the structure of the mind and its way of arriving at belief, without any external coercion, form the basis of all genuine religion.

Well aware

[1] that the opinions and belief of men depend not on their own will, but follow involuntarily the evidence proposed to their minds;

[2] that almighty God hath created the mind free, and manifested his supreme will that free it shall remain, by making it altogether insusceptible of restraint;

[3] that all attempts to influence it by temporal punishments, or burthens, or by civil incapacitations, tend only to beget habits of hypocrisy and meanness;

[4] and are a departure from the plan of the holy author of our religion, who being lord both of body and mind, yet chose not to propagate it by coercion on either, as was in his Almighty power to do, but to extend it by its influence of reason alone

B. *Benefit to the churches*

Moving from the individual duty of religion to the social protection of it, Jefferson looks to the best way of preserving the vigor of church life. Imposing one church deprives all others of their liberty, encourages insincerity in the laity, laxness in the clergy, loss of some citizens' services, and political manipulation of the one church.

[5] that the impious presumption of legislators and rulers, civil as well as ecclesiastical, who, being themselves but fallible and uninspired men, have assumed dominion over the faith of others, setting up their own opinions and modes of thinking as the only true and infallible [ones], and as such endeavoring to impose them on others, hath established and maintained false religions over the greatest part of the world and through all time;

[6] that to compel a man to furnish contributions of money for the propagation of opinions which he disbelieves and abhors, is sinful and tyrannical;

[7] that even the forcing him to support this or that teacher of his own religious persuasion is depriving him of the comfortable [satisfying] liberty of giving his contributions to the particular pastor whose morals he would make his pattern, and whose powers he feels most persuasive to righteousness;

[8] and is withdrawing from the ministry those temporary rewards which, proceeding from an approbation of their personal conduct, are an additional incitement to earnest and unremitting labors for the instruction of mankind;

[9] that our civil rights have no dependence on our religious opinions, any more than our opinions in physics or geometry; that therefore the proscribing any citizen as unworthy the public confidence by laying upon him an incapacity of being called to offices of trust and endorsement, unless he profess or renounce this or that religious opinion, is depriving him injuriously of those privileges and advantages to which, in common with his fellow citizens, he has a natural right;

[10] that it tends also to corrupt the principle of that very religion it is meant to encourage, by bribing, with a monopoly of worldly honors and emoluments, those who will externally profess and conform to it

C. Health of the state
Establishment weakens government by diverting it from its proper functions.

[11] that, though indeed those [clergy] are criminal who do
not withstand such temptation, yet neither are those
[politicians] innocent who lay the bait in their way;

[12] that the opinions of men are not the object of civil
government, nor under its jurisdiction;

[13] that to suffer the civil magistrate to intrude his powers
into the field of opinion and to restrain the profession or
propagation of principles on supposition of their ill
tendency is a dangerous fallacy, which at once destroys all
religious liberty, because he, being of course judge of the
tendency, will make his opinion the rule of judgment, and
approve or condemn the sentiment of others only as they
shall square with or differ from his own;

[14] that it is time enough for the rightful purposes of civil
government for its officers to interfere when principles
break out into overt acts against peace and good order

D. Truth's sway
Religion should not fear truth, or the search for it, since truth is its ally.

[15] and, finally, that truth is great and will prevail if left to
herself; that she is the proper and sufficient antagonist to
error, and has nothing to fear from the conflict unless, by
human interposition, disarmed of her natural weapons, free
argument and debate; errors ceasing to be dangerous when
it is permitted feely to contradict them.

The structure of the argument gives the lie to what is commonly said
of Jefferson, that he was trying to protect the state from religion. The
longest section in this statute (section B as I have called it) is dedicated
to the preservation of the freedom, purity, and vigor of the church. He

had observed and criticized the intellectual and moral torpor of the Anglican clergy in Virginia, which stultified his own college, William and Mary, and would lead him to found the University of Virginia on principles of free inquiry. The churches would be the first to suffer by the imposition of a single religion—very likely a false one, as in the past establishments of Mohammedan or Catholic belief (argument number 5). He contrasts such false religion with what he calls "our religion" in argument number 4. Those more familiar with the stereotype of Jefferson than with his own words must wonder if he is being sincere when he talks of his statute as protecting the true religion from false ones. Surely he did not think there is such a thing as true religion?

But we know that he did. He said often and emphatically that Christian monotheism of the Unitarian sort was what he admired and what he wanted people like Joseph Priestley to promulgate. More than that, he said that Unitarianism was prevailing in America and Europe and would be the religion of the future. Some people, of course, deny that what Jefferson believed was a religion. He claimed it was, since he thought that Jesus taught, with a power no one else did, the need to love one's enemies and the reality of an afterlife. These were not obvious truths of the natural order. But whether he was right or not, he was arguing that true religion would be the beneficiary if freedom of conscience were protected.

Some might find it contradictory for Jefferson to have said, in his final years, that his statute did not protect or promote Christianity. He claims to be reporting what happened when the Virginia legislature passed his statute on religious freedom. He was not there, and he does not say what report he was following.

> The bill for establishing religious freedom, the principles of
> which had, to a certain degree, been enacted before [in Mason's
> Virginia Declaration of Rights as amended by Madison], I had
> drawn in all the latitude of reason and right. It still met with
> opposition; but, with some mutilations in the preamble, it was
> finally passed, and a singular proposition proved its protection of
> opinion was meant to be universal. Where the preamble declares

that coercion is a departure from the plan of the holy author of
our religion, an amendment was proposed, by inserting the word
"Jesus Christ," so that it should read "a departure from the plan
of Jesus Christ, the holy author of our religion." The insertion
was rejected by a great majority, in proof that they meant to
comprehend, within the mantle of its protection, the Jew and the
Gentile, the Christian and Mahometan, the Hindoo, and infidel
of every description. (JP 40)

Madison reported no such amendment in his letter to Jefferson
describing passage of the bill (M 8.473–81), and there is no mention of it
in the legislative record (J 2.552)—and, of course, Jefferson's own draft
talks of "our religion" as opposed to "false religions." In any case, no religion would be given state protection or endorsement—and that is what
Jefferson considered the best way of giving "our religion" a free and pure
way of vindicating itself. The same chance would be given all other religions, so there is no real contradiction between the statute and Jefferson's later claim that every religion would be equally free.

State neutrality on the subject of religion is guaranteed in the second
paragraph of the statute, another single sentence:

We the General Assembly of Virginia do enact that no man
shall be compelled to frequent or support any religious worship,
place, or ministry whatsoever, nor shall be enforced, restrained,
molested or burthened in his body or goods, nor shall otherwise
suffer, on account of his religious opinions or belief; but that all
men shall be free to profess, and by argument to maintain, their
opinions in matters of religion, and the same shall in no wise
diminish, enlarge, or affect their civil capacities. (J 2.546)

These are sweeping provisions. They seem to answer matters of dispute
that have arisen later on the national scale. For instance: if taxpayers are
required to support religious schools not of their own choosing, does
that not mean they are "burthened in their goods" because of their reli-

gious opinions? In that case they are "compelled ... to support any ... religious place or ministry *whatsoever*," against the statute. These provisions certainly anticipate the absolute wall of separation that Jefferson and Madison would later champion.

The third paragraph of the statute, its third and last sentence, addresses one of Jefferson's own problems. He would later say, and apparently already thought, that one generation does not have the power to bind another. Here he makes it clear that this provision is an exception. A matter that is part of what he called in the Declaration of Independence "the laws of nature and of nature's God" cannot be rescinded by human fiat. He puts religious liberty up among those sacred laws, eternally untouchable by anyone following natural reason on the matter of natural right.

> And though we well know that the Assembly, elected by the people for the *ordinary* purposes of legislation only, have *no* power to restrain the acts of succeeding Assemblies, constituted with powers equal to our own, and that therefore to declare this act irrevocable would be of no effect in law; yet we are free to declare, and do declare, that the rights hereby asserted are of the natural rights of mankind, and that if any act shall be hereafter passed to repeal the present or to narrow is operation, such act will be an infringement of natural right [emphasis added].

In other words, *no* interference of the state with religion is to be allowed. Jefferson would say as much during his presidency, in his famous letter to the Danbury [Connecticut] Baptist Association of January 1, 1802.

LETTER TO DANBURY

IN THIS LETTER, Jefferson refers to the First Amendment subsequently carried through Congress by Madison, not to his own statute. But he certainly, then as before and later, saw the two enactments as affirming the entire separation of church and state. Some have tried to separate the letter to the Baptists from the Virginia and the federal laws, claiming that the letter is a later and peripheral comment, prompted by political concerns of the moment, not a statement of basic principle that should be used as an aid in interpreting the First Amendment. But in fact Jefferson was expressing his long-standing and continuing view of religious freedom, one that he shared with Madison, who wrote the First Amendment.

The Baptists in Connecticut had voted for Jefferson as president in 1800, when the state's Federalist leaders had portrayed Jefferson as an atheist, a Jacobin, an enemy of good order. The Baptists were waging a campaign to be freed from the need for certificates exempting them from the taxation that supported the Congregationalist churches. For this purpose, they had formed an association of twenty-six Baptist churches in the Connecticut Valley. They wrote Jefferson asking him for his moral support in this campaign. They were under a regime of mere tolerance, not of religious liberty as a right. As they said: "What religious privileges we enjoy (as minor parts of the state) we enjoy as favors granted, and not as inalienable rights." They knew Jefferson could not intervene in state legislation, but they hoped that his expressed views would strengthen their case.

> Sir, we are sensible that the President of the United States is
> not the national legislator, and also sensible that the national
> government cannot destroy the laws of each state, but our
> hopes are strong that the sentiments of our beloved President,
> which had such genial effect already, like the radiant beams of
> the sun will shine and prevail through all these states and all
> the world, till hierarchy and tyranny be destroyed from the
> earth. Sir, when we reflect on your past services, and see a glow
> of philanthropy and good will shining forth, in a course of
> more than thirty years, we have reason to believe that
> America's God has raised you up to fill the chair of state out of
> that good will which he bears to the millions which you preside

over. May God strengthen you for the arduous task [to] which
providence and the voice of the people have called you, to
sustain you and support you in your administration against all
the predetermined opposition of those who wish to rise to
wealth and importance on the poverty and subjection of the
people.

Only implicitly a plea for help, this is expressly the promise of prayers
from a sincere body of believers. As such, Jefferson's primary task was to
acknowledge that pledge thankfully, which he did: "I reciprocate your
kind prayers for the protection and blessing of the common Father and
Creator of man" (JP 510). What more could he say in answer to the Baptists' implicit request that he support them, without having power to do
so by law?

He first considered exemplifying the Baptists' position by defending
a decision for which he was being criticized at the time—his refusal to
give federal endorsement to national proclamations of prayer and fasting. But since such days were common in New England, Jefferson's
attorney general, Levi Lincoln, advised him that it would look too
polemical against the Federalists to bring the subject up in this letter, so
he refrained from doing so. Despite this, some now consider the letter
simply an attack on the Federalists who did not vote for him, on clerical-
ism, and on religion in general.

Instead of defending his own *policy* at the federal level, Jefferson
expressed his understanding of the *law* binding federal officials—which,
as the Baptists had themselves conceded, could not reach to state establishments, though its principles might someday do so.

> Believing with you that religion is a matter which lies solely
> between man and God, that he owes account to none other
> for his faith or his worship, that the legislative powers of
> government reach actions only, and not opinions, I contem-
> plate with sovereign reverence that act of the whole American
> people which declared that their [federal] legislature should

200 | H E A D   A N D   H E A R T

> "make no law respecting an establishment of religion, or
> prohibiting the free exercise thereof," thus building a wall
> of separation between church and state. Adhering to this
> expression of the supreme will of the nation in behalf of the
> rights of conscience, I shall see with sincere satisfaction the
> progress of those sentiments which tend to restore to man all
> his natural rights, convinced he has no natural right in
> opposition to his social duties. (JP 510.)

The first three clauses echo arguments numbers 1 and 2, 3 and 4, and 14 of his Statute for Religious Freedom. The last sentence reflects argument number 15, that the religious liberty is a matter of natural right, above rightful human interference. How, then, can one argue that this letter is an ad hoc comment, not an expression of Jefferson's basic understanding of religious freedom as that was framed in his own bill and in Madison's First Amendment?

Philip Hamburger, a professor at Columbia Law School, calls the letter an attempt to "propagate his [Jefferson's] own profoundly anticlerical vision," a move to "express his own anticlerical attitudes with new intensity and even hatred," an attempt to "undermine the clergy," a text that "elevated anticlerical rhetoric to constitutional law" in expressing "the strength of his animosity" to anyone not accepting "his Republican gospel."[2] Despite this astonishing misreading, Hamburger has become the favorite authority of conservatives who deny that the Founders ever intended a separation of church and state. They think they have found in him a scholar who makes their best case. But look again at the letter. There is no mention, even an indirect one, of clergy in the letter. Jefferson's anticlericalism, which he shared with Adams and other Deists, did not motivate his defense of the natural rights of conscience. Rather, his principled view of natural right led to the anticlericalism—as it did in Madison's attacks on the established clergy. Both men defended the free and purified rights of church and clergy, in arguments number 5 through 10 of Jefferson's Statute and in Madison's *Memorial and Remonstrance.*

Hamburger further says that Jefferson's views were so extreme that the Baptists rejected them. How does he know this? Because they did not publicly print his letter after receiving it.[3] An argument *e silentio* is always suspect. What makes Hamburger think their motive was disagreement with Jefferson? Their own letter had voiced a claim to "inalienable rights," not mere tolerance. There are many possible reasons for their not publishing the letter. They may have thought it would just annoy the Federalist legislature they were trying to influence. They may have thought Jefferson did not directly address their own plight, just restated the limits on federal action. Their twenty-six churches may have differed among themselves on strategy and timing. It is desperate special pleading to pretend to know that the Baptists disagreed with what Jefferson was saying though they never said so.

Hamburger even pretends to know the exactly *why* the Baptists disagreed. He cannot allege that the Baptists objected to the anticlericalism Hamburger finds in the letter, since the Baptists had no love for clerics. One of the Baptist leaders in New England, John Leland, wrote: "May the combination of rulers and priests, church and state, be dissolved and never re-unite"—a statement more overtly anticlerical than anything in Jefferson's letter.[4] Another prominent Baptist, this one from Connecticut itself, Nehemiah Dodge, denounced "the corrupt fruit which has been always springing from a connection of church and state."[5] That would condemn *any* connection, as clearly as Jefferson did. The Danbury Association itself was more outspoken on a corrupt clergy than was Jefferson in his letter. In 1803, it submitted a petition to the legislature claiming that church doctrines "retained much of their primitive purity until the clergy became corrupted by a legal establishment," and that "the Christian religion is not an object of civil government, nor any way under its control."[6] Hamburger claims that the good Baptists rejected the "extremism" of Jefferson's letter; but they sound fully as extreme— indeed, fully as anticlerical—themselves.

Then what motive does Hamburger give the Baptists for not publishing Jefferson's letter? It is Hamburger's own preoccupation, that a separation of church and state might imply a separation of religion from politics. They must, he says, have feared that separation of church and state would mean a separation of religion and politics, so they "*may* have been hesitant to publish" for that reason.[7] This "*may*" (my emphasis) soon becomes an assertion that the Baptists "ignored as a constitutional principle the separation of church and state." Some people can make a statement mean anything they want it to. Hamburger makes a silence mean anything he wants it to.

Hamburger sees nothing but anticlericalism in Jefferson's devotion to religious freedom. But he shows a more patent anti-Jeffersonianism in making anticlericalism the main (though unexpressed) point of the Danbury letter. He even attributes "hate" to Jefferson as his motive. He manages to attack the "irreverent style" of the letter. Can you spot irreverence in it? He can. He says that Jefferson uses the word "reverence" for the First Amendment—a word he can only, in Hamburger's jaundiced view, use as an ironic insult to the reverent people he despised.[8] Some people idolize Jefferson, others demonize him—in both cases, this distracts from a clear reading of his defense of the rights of conscience.

12 | MADISON'S REMONSTRANCE

JEFFERSON ATTRACTED lightning. That is why he is the person most talked about in the area of religious freedom. Madison, because he passed the Statute for Religious Freedom that Jefferson had drafted, is thought of as subservient to him, secondary in importance. Physically, Jefferson towered over the minute Madison by almost a foot. Symbolically, his stature is even greater. But this deflection of primary attention to Jefferson has given an advantage to those who oppose or minimize the separation of church and state, since Madison is the best defender of that constitutional innovation—more consistent than Jefferson, more radical, and more influential. Jefferson revered the First Amendment. Madison wrote it.

Madison's interest in religious freedom started early, well before he met Jefferson, while he was attending John Witherspoon's classes at the College of New Jersey. Madison was impressed by the degree of religious tolerance practiced in New Jersey, and chagrined by the contrast with Virginia, where Baptists were imprisoned and beaten. When he returned to his home, during a time when the Baptists were being persecuted with special vigor, he wrote a friend in words that Philip Hamburger would no doubt think "extreme" and "anticlerical."

> That diabolical hell-conceived principle of persecution rages among some, and, to their eternal infamy, the clergy can furnish their quota of imps for such business. This vexes me the most of anything whatever. There are at this time, in the adjacent county, not less than five or six well-meaning men in close gaol for publishing their religious sentiments, which in the main are very orthodox. I have neither patience to hear, talk, or think of anything, relative to this matter, for I have squabbled and scolded, abused and ridiculed so long about it, to so little purpose, that I am without common patience. So I leave you to pity me and pray for liberty of conscience to revive among us. (JM 1.106)

His time in Princeton had given Madison his first experience of life outside a world of established religion. When most colleges were devoted to an established religion, and to training its ministers, Witherspoon opened the College of New Jersey's doors to all sects and to all regions of the country (which is how Madison, from Virginia, came to be there). The College of New Jersey had originally been dedicated to "New Light" Presbyterianism, but Witherspoon, though himself a Presbyterian minister, got rid of the New Divinity faculty members he inherited, and taught an Enlightened religion that was closer to Deism than to any (even diluted) Calvinism. Witherspoon actively campaigned for new students from all the colonies, and the college welcomed them with a liberal policy statement:

> In the instruction of the youth, care is taken to cherish a spirit of liberty and free enquiry; and not only to permit, but even to encourage, their right of private judgment, without presuming to dictate with an air of infallibility, or demanding an implicit assent to the decisions of the preceptor.[1]

This policy, and the wide catchment area of students attending the college, explains how Witherspoon succeeded in producing so many leaders of the founding era.

When Madison and Jefferson said that religious liberty would produce a more energetic and knowledgeable class of ministers, they had in mind the Enlightened pastors Madison came to know in the orbit of Princeton—he even considered becoming such an Enlightened pastor himself. In Virginia, by contrast, he found "pride, ignorance and knavery among the priesthood" (JM 1.106). His ties with friends from college who went into the ministry were so close that in 1774 he went to Philadelphia to attend the annual Presbyterian Synod (JM 1.113). When a Presbyterian friend visited his father's plantation, the Madisons allowed him to preach in the local pulpit, defying the Anglican establishment (JM 1.136).

Madison always did energetic research into a topic that he meant to deal with, and religious freedom was no different. He asked his friend William Bradford of Pennsylvania to send him information on the religious freedom he experienced there:

> When you have obtained sufficient insight into the constitution
> of your country, and can make it an amusement to yourself,
> send me a draught of its origin and fundamental principles
> of legislation, particularly the extent of your religious tolera-
> tion. Here allow me to propose the following queries: Is an
> ecclesiastical establishment absolutely necessary to support
> civil society in a supreme government, and how far is it hurtful
> to a dependent state? (JM 1.101)

Patriotic as he was toward his native Virginia, Madison envied his friend for living where religion was free. What he imagines as the unshackled state of Pennsylvania in 1774 comes close to what he promises, in his *Memorial and Remonstrance,* will be the state of Virginia when it disestablishes its religion:

> You are happy in dwelling in a land where those inestimable
> privileges are fully enjoyed and [the] public has long felt the
> good effect of their religious as well as civil liberty. Foreigners
> have been encouraged to settle among you. Industry and virtue

have been promoted by mutual emulation and mutual inspec-
tion. Commerce and the arts have flourished, and I cannot help
attributing those continual exertions of genius which appear
among you to the inspiration of liberty and that love of fame and
knowledge which always accompany it. Religious bondage
shackles and debilitates the mind, and unfits it for every noble
enterprise, every expanded prospect. (JM 1.112–13)

Madison feels that the American colonies escaped a terrible fate in not
having everywhere the establishment that held Virginia in thrall:

If the Church of England had been the established and general
religion in all the northern colonies, as it has been among us
here, and uninterrupted tranquility had prevailed throughout
the continent, it is clear to me that slavery and subjection
might and would have been gradually insinuated among us.
Union of religious sentiments begets a surprising confidence,
and ecclesiastical establishments tend to great ignorance and
corruption, all of which facilitate the execution of mischievous
projects. (JM 1.105)

Madison was well prepared, by long study of the problem, to make
his first contribution as a young member of the Virginia legislature—his
successful effort to remove "toleration" from Mason's draft of Virginia's
Declaration of Rights and substitute "religious liberty." And that experience prepared him for his next great work, the composition of his *Memorial and Remonstrance Against Religious Assessments* (1785). The occasion has
already been mentioned—the proposal to collect taxes for a multiple
establishment, to be distributed proportionally for the support of any
Protestant ministers. The injustice of this was clear to the supposed beneficiaries, the Baptists and Presbyterians, who petitioned against it. And
it would give different treatment to those, such as the Quakers and Mennonites, who had no ordained ministers.

Since Madison was well known to his peers for having thought clearly and deeply on religious freedom, two of them—George Mason and George Nicholas—urged him to draw up a petition stating the grounds for rejecting the general assessment. Madison made it a condition that he remain anonymous, so Mason and Nicholas had themselves to solicit signatures for the petition before presenting it to the legislature. They succeeded in getting thirteen copies of the petition into circulation, which accumulated 1,552 signatures. Though another petition received more signatures (4,889), Madison's arguments were the ones built to last. They are the best exposition of the thought that would lie behind his drafting of the First Amendment. In fact, they are the best arguments for the separation of church and state that have ever been written. The document deserves the most careful study. Such a reading would have prevented many later misunderstandings of the First Amendment. It is time to savor a major piece of well-argued eighteenth-century prose. It lies at the very heart of what Enlightened religion means—and it is a religious argument, not (as some modern Evangelicals claim) an antireligious one.

THE *REMONSTRANCE*

T HE PETITION (JM 8.298–304) begins with a brief paragraph stating the aim of its signers and explaining its title. The undersigned act "to remonstrate against it [the assessment], and to declare the reasons by which we are determined." When Madison goes on to declare the reasons, he numbers them 1 through 15. It is a lengthy document, but supremely important. I take the reasons one by one, supplying a brief title for each paragraph, breaking each down into smaller units, italicizing the key phrases, then adding a comment.[2]

NO COGNIZANCE

1. We remonstrate because we hold it for a fundamental and undeniable truth "that religion, or the duty which we owe to

our Creator, and the manner of discharging it, can be directed only by reason and conviction, not by force or violence." The religion, then, of every man must be left to the conviction and conscience of every man; and it is the right of every man to exercise it as these may dictate. This right is in its nature an unalienable right.

It is unalienable, because the opinions of men, depending only on the evidence contemplated by their own minds, cannot follow the dictates of other men.

It is unalienable, also, because what is here a right towards men is a duty towards the Creator. It is the duty of every man to render to the Creator such homage, and such only, as he believes to be acceptable to him.

This duty is precedent, both in order of time and in degree of obligation, to the claims of civil society. Before any man can be considered as a member of civil society, he must be considered as a subject of the Governor of the Universe. And if a member of civil society, who enters into any subordinate association, must always do it with a reservation for his duty to the general authority, much more must every man who becomes a member of any particular civil society, do it with a saving of his allegiance to the Universal Sovereign.

We maintain, therefore, that in matters of religion, no man's right is abridged by the institution of civil society, and that *religion is wholly exempt from its cognizance.*

True it is, that no other rule exists, by which any question which may divide a society can be ultimately determined, but the rule of the majority; but it is also true that the majority may trespass on the rights of the minority.

The words quoted in the first sentence are from the Virginia Declaration of Rights. Madison had argued in the Assembly that assessment went against the spirit of that document (JM 8.299).

I mentioned in an earlier chapter that mere "toleration" is a top-down approach to religious liberty, as opposed to a bottom-up starting point in individual rights. Madison seems to contradict this claim, since he begins from the very-top-down, from God and every man's duty to worship him. But I earlier meant that tolerance comes from the top of any earthly realm. When Madison says that the duty to God can be paid only by a convinced and uncoerced individual conscience, he cuts out the middle-man of any political authority from which a societally top-down toler-ance can be derived. If the individual conscience cannot sincerely be convinced of the duty to obey God, the duty may still be there, but not in a way that the state can enforce—the only sanction is God's authority, which no political regime may usurp or pretend to mimic.

By beginning with God and the individual conscience, Madison, like Jefferson, makes religion a presocietal right, one neither given, revealed, nor enforced by any earthly power. The state must not be allowed to intrude on the intimate obligation of any man toward his maker. It may not, therefore, have *any cognizance* of the matter. Madison uses the legal term "cognizance" to mean the right to judicial notice. A thing beyond cognizance is outside legal jurisdiction. Jefferson used it in this sense when he said that a court "declined cognizance" of a case.[3] Madison thought that religion should be so far outside governmental purview that he was reluctant (as we shall see) to let religious ministers be counted in the census. He opposed tax exemption for churches and official chaplains. All of them would put religion within governmental cognizance.

ENCROACHMENT

2. [We remonstrate] because, if religion be exempt from the
authority of the society at large, still less can it be subject to
that of the legislative body. The latter are but the creatures and
vicegerents of the former. Their jurisdiction is both derivative
and limited. It is limited with regard to the co-ordinate
departments.
      More necessarily is it limited with regard to the constituents.

The preservation of a free government requires not merely
that the metes and bounds which separate each department of
power be invariably maintained, but more especially that
neither of them be suffered to overleap the great barrier which
defends the right of the people.

The rulers who are guilty of such an *encroachment* exceed
the commission from which they derive their authority, and are
tyrants.

The people who submit to it are governed by laws made
neither by themselves nor by an authority derived from them,
and are slaves.

Since the tie between creator and creature precedes the forming of
civil society, it is a fortiori outside the purview of government, which is
the creature of civil society—outside its legislative power, which Madison
called the supreme power in a republic (*Federalist* No. 51). Even that
supreme power is a limited one, hedged by coordinate departments of
government and by accountability to its electors. Its powers do not extend
farther than the populace itself or society itself, and religion lies beyond
the sphere of all three. Encroachment on that sacred sphere breaks all the
limits of a government's respect for the freedom of its citizens.

NO SLIGHT INFRINGEMENTS

3. [We remonstrate] because it is proper to *take alarm at the first
experiment* on our liberties. We hold this prudent jealousy to be
the first duty of citizens, and one of the noblest characteristics
of the late revolution. The free men of America did not wait
till usurped power had strengthened itself by exercise and
entangled the question in precedents. They saw all the consequences in the principle, and they avoided the consequences by
denying the principle.

We revere this lesson too much soon to forget it. Who does

not see the same authority which can establish Christianity, in exclusion of all other religions, may establish with the same ease any particular sect of Christians, in exclusion of all other sects; that the same authority which can force a citizen to contribute three pence only of his property for the support of any one establishment may force him to conform to any other establishment in all cases whatsoever?

Madison is answering the argument that the general assessment does not notably deprive any Protestants of much freedom, since the funds will be distributed to all authorized Protestant ministers. He rightly says that the principle of free conscience must be looked at, not a minimizing view of first consequences.

EQUAL TREATMENT

4. [We remonstrate] because the bill violates that equality which ought to be the basis of every law and which is more indispensable, in proportion as the validity or expediency of any law is more liable to be impeached. If "all men are by nature equally free and independent," all men are to be considered as entering into society on equal conditions, as relinquishing no more, and therefore retaining no less, one than another of their natural rights.

Above all are they to be considered as retaining an "*equal title to the free exercise of religion* according to the dictates of conscience." Whilst we assert for ourselves a freedom to embrace, to profess, and to observe the religion which we believe to be divine origin, we cannot deny an equal freedom to those whose minds have not yet yielded to the evidence which has convinced us.

If this freedom be abused, it is an offence against God, not against man. To God, therefore, not to man must an account of it be rendered.

As the bill violates equality by subjecting some to peculiar burdens, so it violates the same principle by granting to others peculiar exemptions. Are the Quakers and Mennonists the only sects who think a compulsive support of their religions unnecessary and unwarrantable? Can their piety alone be entrusted with the care of public worship? Ought their religions to be endowed above all others with extraordinary privileges by which proselytes may be enticed from all others? We think too favorably of the justice and good sense of these denominations to believe that they either covet pre-eminence over their fellow citizens or that they will be seduced by them from the common opposition to the measure.

The quotations in the second and third sentences are, once again, from the Virginia Declaration of Rights. Madison is calling the legislature back to the principle behind its own constitutional commitment.

The assessment would not treat all believers equally. Protestants would be favored over non-Protestants. Quakers would be exempt from any assessment. The state would decide who gets what.

CANNOT JUDGE OR ADVANCE RELIGION

5. [We remonstrate] because the bill implies either that the civil magistrate is a *competent judge* of religious truth, or that he may employ religion as an engine of civil policy.

The first is an arrogant pretension falsified by the contradictory opinions of rulers in all ages and throughout the world.

The second, an unhallowed perversion of the means of salvation.

Those who say that Madison, like Jefferson, was not interested in keeping religion free from corruption by the state, but the state free from corruption by religion, do not notice that he first takes up the former subject, with emphasis. History shows that magistrates have enforced false religions (as Jefferson put it). And they did it to suit their own projects (as "engines of civil policy"), putting sacred things to profane use.

RELIGION DOES NOT NEED IT

6. [We remonstrate] because the establishment proposed by the bill is not requisite for the support of the Christian religion. To say that it is, is a contradiction to the Christian religion itself, for every page of it disavows a dependence on the powers of this world.

It is a contradiction to fact, for it is known that this religion [Christianity] both existed and *flourished, not only without the support of human laws, but in spite of every opposition from them,* and not only during the period of miraculous aid [in the era of Jesus], but long after it had been left on its own evidence and the ordinary care of Providence.

Nay, it is a contradiction in terms, for a religion not invented by human policy must have pre-existed, and been supported, before it was established by human policy.

It is, moreover, to weaken in those who profess this religion a pious confidence in its innate excellence and the patronage of its Author, and to foster in those who still reject it a suspicion that its friends are too conscious of its fallacies to trust it to its own merits.

Christianity grew and flourished before it was given state support—indeed, when it was persecuted by state power. Its believers should have faith that it is capable of such independence still. Again, Madison is thinking first of the pure state of religion.

CORRUPTS RELIGION

7. [We remonstrate] because experience witnesseth that
ecclesiastical establishments, instead of maintaining the purity
and efficacy of religion, have had a contrary operation. During
almost fifteen centuries has the legal establishment of Christianity been on trial. What have been its fruits? More or less in all
places, pride and indolence in the clergy; ignorance and servility
in the laity; in both, superstition, bigotry and persecution.

Enquire of the teachers of Christianity for the ages in
which it appeared in its greatest luster. Those of every sect
point to the ages *prior to its incorporation with civil policy.* Propose
a restoration of this primitive state, in which its teachers
depended on the voluntary rewards of their flocks—many of
them predict its downfall. On which side ought their testimony
to have greatest weight, when for or when against their interest?

Madison agreed with Priestley and other Enlightenment figures that
the purity of Christian belief and practice was corrupted when Constantine made it a state religion. All the abuses of power through the Middle
Ages reflected the entanglement of the spiritual with the worldly. Those
calling for a return to that system are trying to reap worldly rewards from
it. This is the third insistence on the primacy of religious considerations
in the separation of church and state.

STATE DOES NOT NEED IT

8. [We remonstrate] because the establishment in question
is not necessary for the support of civil government. If it be
urged as necessary for the support of civil government, only as
it is a means of supporting religion, and it be not necessary for
the latter purpose, it cannot be necessary for the former. If

religion be not within the cognizance of civil government, *how can its legal establishment be necessary* to civil government?

What influence in fact have ecclesiastical establishments had on civil society?

In some instances, they have been seen to erect a spiritual tyranny on the ruins of the civil authority.

In many instances, they have been seen upholding the throne of political tyranny.

In no instance, have they been seen the guardians of the liberties of the people. Rulers who wished to subvert the public liberty may have found an established clergy convenient auxiliaries.

A just government, instituted to secure and perpetuate it, needs them not. Such a government will be best supported by protecting every citizen in the enjoyment of his religion with the same equal hand which protects his person and his property, by neither invading the equal rights of any sect nor suffering any sect to invade those of another.

Only here does Madison reach what critics of separation say was his first concern. After arguing that state support is not necessary for the survival of religion, he adds that state support is not necessary for the survival of the *state.* This is the point on which modern opponents of the separation of church and state are most upset. They like to quote passages like this, from Washington's Farewell Address:

> And let us with caution indulge the supposition that morality can be maintained without religion. Whatever may be conceded to the influence of refined education on minds of peculiar structure, reason and experience both forbid us to expect that national morality can prevail in exclusion of religious principle.[4]

Madison certainly agreed with that sentiment; but he held that those wanting state support for religion get things backward. They think that the state must give support to religion, so that religion will support *it*. The impetus comes from government. He argues that religion will best support morality if it is free and pure, working up from its independent and spontaneous roots, not down from favors done in the political sphere. If religion needs a crutch supplied by government, government will set the terms of that support, blocking the genius of the religious initiative and inspiration.

DISCOURAGES IMMIGRATION

9. [We remonstrate] because the proposed establishment is a departure from that generous policy which, offering an *asylum to the persecuted* and oppressed of every nation and religion, promised a luster to our country and an accession to the number of its citizens.

What a melancholy mark is the [assessment] bill of sudden degeneracy! Instead of holding forth an asylum to the persecuted, it is itself a signal of persecution. It degrades, from the equal rank of citizens, all those whose opinions in religion do not bend to those of the legislative authority.

Distant as it may be in its present form from the Inquisition, it [the bill] differs from it only in degree. The one is the first step, the other the last, in the career of intolerance. The magnanimous sufferer under the cruel scourge in foreign regions, must view the bill as a beacon on our coast, warning him to seek some other haven where liberty and philanthropy, in their due extent, may offer a more certain repose from his troubles.

At a time when the United States is a goal for immigrants and there is great pressure to keep them out, this may seem an odd argument for religious freedom. But there was a deep concern in the early days of the Republic that America was a place of degenerating energies in a primitive setting. Both Franklin and Jefferson mounted propaganda on the growth of population in the New World. Alexander Hamilton in his *Report on Manufactures* said that people with talent and skill would be readier to come to a country that is "under the operation of a more equal government, and—what is far more important than mere religious toleration—a perfect equality of religious privileges."[5] The dream of the early Founders that America would be a haven for those oppressed elsewhere, expressed later in the Emma Lazarus poem on the base of the Statue of Liberty, came true to an extent that would have staggered those who first entertained it, offering what Madison calls here "an asylum to the persecuted." The welcoming of different ethnic groups with different religious commitments played a greater role in that receptivity than we, very often, recognize.

Encourages Emigration

10. [We remonstrate] because it will have a like tendency
to banish our citizens. The allurements presented by other
situations are every day thinning their number. To superadd a
fresh motive to emigration by *revoking the liberty which they now
enjoy* would be the same species of folly which has dishonored
and depopulated flourishing kingdoms.

This is clearly the obverse of the preceding paragraph. Madison considered it powerful enough that he used it in his oral argument before the Assembly against the General Assessment (M 8.198). Madison points to the exodus from European regimes with prescribed creeds as an example to be avoided.

Sows Discord

11. [We remonstrate] because it will *destroy that moderation* and
harmony which the forbearance of our laws to intermeddle
with religion has produced among its several sects.

Time has at length revealed the true remedy. Every relaxation of narrow and rigorous policy, wherever it has been tried, has been found to assuage the disease. The American theater has exhibited proofs that equal and complete liberty, if it does not wholly eradicate it, sufficiently destroys its malignant influence on the health and prosperity of the state.

If, with the salutary effects of this system under our own eyes, we begin to contract the bounds of religious freedom, we know no name that will too severely reproach our folly.

At least let warning be taken at the first fruits of the threatened innovation. The very appearance of the bill has transformed "that Christian forbearance, love, and charity," which of late mutually prevailed, into animosities and jealousies which may not soon be appeased. What mischief may not be dreaded, should this enemy to the public quiet be armed with the force of law?

The quote in the second-last sentence is, once again, from the Virginia Declaration of Rights. Madison contrasts the harmony of states (former colonies) that were tolerant with those, like his own, that had established religions—echoing his early letters to his schoolmate at Princeton. The American experiments show the path of the future, away from the monarchical-papist establishments of Europe.

HAMPERS CHRISTIAN MISSION

12. [We remonstrate] because the policy of the bill is *adverse to the diffusion of the light* of Christianity. The first wish of those who enjoy this precious gift ought to be that it may be imparted to the whole race of mankind.

Compare the number of those who have as yet received it with the number still remaining under the dominion of false religions—and how small is the former! Does the policy of the bill tend to lessen the disproportion? No, it at once discourages those who are strangers to the light of revelation from coming into the region of it, and countenances, by example, the nations who continue in darkness, in shutting out those who might convey it to them.

Instead of leveling, as far as possible, every obstacle to the victorious progress of truth, the bill, with an ignoble and unchristian timidity, would circumscribe it with a wall of defense against the encroachments of error.

This section shows that Madison, like Jefferson, is not simply neutral toward all religions. He sides with the true religion, which he takes to be (Unitarian) Christianity, but he relies on perfect freedom to establish that truth in the free play of believers' consciences confronted with the evidence. Any state favor or coercion will hamper the true religion in the strength that it has over all other contenders. Truth alone will prevail if given its chance.

DISCREDITS GOVERNMENT

13. [We remonstrate] because attempts to enforce by legal sanctions acts obnoxious to so great a proportion of citizens, tend to *enervate the laws* in general and to slacken the bands of society.

If it is difficult to execute any law which is not generally deemed necessary or salutary, what must be the case where it is deemed invalid and dangerous?

And what may be the effect of so striking an example of impotency, in the government, on its general authority?

A bill felt to be violative of conscience is obnoxious (in the eighteenth-century sense of "vulnerable"). All attempts to enforce it just make the state vulnerable too.

MAJORITY SUPPORT NEEDED,
BUT INSUFFICIENT

14. [We remonstrate] because a measure of such singular
magnitude and delicacy ought not to be imposed, without the
clearest evidence that it is called for by a majority of citizens,
and no satisfactory method is yet proposed by which the voice
of the majority, in this case, may be determined, or its influence
secured.

"The people of the respective counties are indeed
requested to signify their opinion respecting the adoption of
the bill to the next session of Assembly." But the representation
must be made equal before the voice either of the representatives or of the counties will be that of the people.

Our hope is that neither of the former will, after due
consideration, espouse the dangerous principle of the bill.
Should the event disappoint us, it will still leave us in full
confidence that a fair appeal to the latter will reverse the
sentence *against our liberties.*

The quotation from the second sentence is from a resolution opposed to the general assessment, asking for a survey of the counties to
see what support the bill had. Madison argues that even this measure is
insufficient, since a tally by counties would not reflect support based on
the populations of the counties. But he goes on to say that even if the
count by population should yield a majority in favor of the bill, that
would not establish the justice of the measure, since this is a matter of
fundamental right, not to be settled by majority vote—the contention of
Jefferson's final paragraph in the Statute for Religious Freedom.

VIRGINIA RIGHTS AND GOD

15. [We remonstrate] because, finally, "the equal right of every citizen to the free exercise of his religion according to the dictates of conscience" is held by the same tenure with all our other rights. If we recur to its origin, it is equally the gift of nature.

If we weigh its importance, it cannot be less due to us.

If we consult the "Declaration of those rights which pertain to the good people of Virginia as the basis and foundation of government," it is enumerated with equal solemnity—or, rather, studied emphasis.

Either, then, we must say that the will of the legislature is the only measure of their authority; and that, in the plenitude of this authority, they may sweep away all our fundamental rights; or that they are bound to leave this particular right untouched and sacred.

Either we must say that they may control the freedom of the press, may abolish the trial by jury, may swallow up the executive and judiciary powers of the state—nay, that they may despoil us of our very right of suffrage and erect themselves into an independent and hereditary Assembly—or we must say that they have no authority to enact into law the bill under consideration. We the subscribers say that the General Assembly of this Commonwealth have no such authority.

And, that no effort may be omitted on our part against so dangerous an usurpation, we oppose to it this remonstrance, earnestly praying—as we are in duty bound—that the Supreme Lawgiver of the Universe, by illuminating those to whom it is addressed, may (on the one hand) turn their councils from every act which would affront his holy prerogatives, or violate the trust committed to them, and (on the other) guide them

into every measure which may be worthy of his blessing [and]
may redound to their own praise, and may establish more
firmly the liberties, the prosperity, and the happiness of the
Commonwealth.

The two quotes at the outset of this section are paraphrases of
George Mason's Declaration of Rights, circling back to the Virginia
commitment to religious freedom. Madison is upset that the state should
veer from its initial commitment to the rights of conscience, for which
he had fought as a freshman legislator. He ends, as he began, with God—
with prayer at the end, as with the duty of worship at the beginning.
That makes it absurd to say that he, or Jefferson, was primarily motivated
by an antireligious (or anticlerical) animus. He spoke for the freedom of
religion, not the freedom from religion. The same would be true of his
work for the First Amendment, which followed the defeat of Virginia's
general assessment.

13 | FIRST AMENDMENT

ELIEVERS IN AMERICA as a Christian nation do not much like
Jefferson the Deist. But they like his Declaration of Independence
because of its reference to "the laws of nature and of nature's GOD."
Though this was not a legislative document, it is more useful to them
than the supreme legislative document of the United States, the Constitution, which (as we saw earlier) does not mention God at all. Even as
late as 1812, Timothy Dwight could issue this lament:

> We formed our Constitution without any acknowledgment of
> God, without any recognition of His mercies to us as a people,
> of his government, or even of his existence. The Convention
> by which it was formed never asked, even once, his direction or
> his blessing upon their labors. Thus we commenced our
> national existence, under the present system, without God.[1]

A year later another lament was issued by Chauncey Lee:

> Can we pause and reflect for a moment, with the mingled
> emotions of wonder and regret, that that public instrument

which guarantees our political rights and freedom and
independence—our Constitution of national government,
framed by such an august, learned and able body of men,
formally adopted by the solemn resolution of each state, and
justly admired and celebrated for its consummate political
wisdom—has not the impress of religion upon it, not the
smallest recognition of the government or the being of
God, or of the dependence and accountability of men—be
astonished, O Earth!—nothing by which a foreigner might with
certainty decide whether we believe in the one true God, or in
any God.[2]

To some of its critics, the Constitution seemed not only godless but anti-God, since Article 6, Section 3 forbids any religious test for holding office—though all but two states (Virginia and New York) required such a test. An atheist might become president of the new government! In order to remedy this, a movement was mounted during the Civil War to rewrite the prologue to the Constitution, declaring America a Christian nation. In wartime, God's protection is felt to be needed. It was also during the Civil War that Salmon P. Chase, secretary of the Treasury, put "In God We Trust" on America's money. In the Cold War, "Under God" was added to the Pledge of Allegiance. Americans have recurrently expressed uneasiness at having a "godless Constitution."

Those maintaining the concept of a Christian nation like to point out that Benjamin Franklin once suggested to the Philadelphia Convention that a minister be brought in to lead an opening prayer for each session. The diplomatic Deist was trying to calm passions that had blown up. His suggestion is less important than the deftness with which it was dismissed. Hamilton said that sending out for aid would be a signal of trouble. Another man said that there were no funds for paying a minister. No vote was taken on Franklin's suggestion.[3] If the Constitution had recognized God, it would have to have been a Deist's God, as John Murrin has emphasized:

The Federal Constitution was, in short, the eighteenth-century
equivalent of a secular humanist text. The delegates were not a
very orthodox group of men in any doctrinal sense. The only
born-again Christian among them was probably Richard Bassett
of Delaware ... who said nothing at the Convention. ... As a
Methodist, even Bassett was probably an Arminian in theology,
willing—like John Wesley—to give individuals some effective
agency in their own salvation. ... Although the dread of corruption had a genuine affinity for orthodox Christian values, it
drew far more directly from civic humanist sources, the effort
by the seventeenth and eighteenth centuries to understand
why republics had failed in the past and how they could be
constructed to endure. The Convention's answer to this
problem, although not always civic humanist in content and
emphasis, came very close in most particulars to what today's
evangelicals mean by secular humanist.[4]

Such men had little taste for meddling with religion.

I mentioned in the introduction how unprecedented it was to launch
a nation with no officially invoked divine protection. It was so new that
many think the Founders did not really mean it. They seek to minimize
the bold initiative by saying (1) that it was just an afterthought, not really
important, or (2) that it was actually meant to protect religious establishments at the state level, or (3) that it was not based on a matter of principle but was a mere bargain forced on Congress by competing sects, or
(4) that it did not rule out an establishment of religion in general (as
opposed to endorsing one denomination). One hears these arguments to
this day, so it is important to consider them one by one.

1. Unimportant?

IT IS SAID that the separation clause did not really accomplish anything. The grounds for this contention are several: The motion to

include a religious liberty clause was unanimously rejected in the Philadelphia Convention. The defenders of the Constitution as drafted and ratified said such a clause was unnecessary. Madison himself repeatedly made this assertion, and when, nonetheless, he brought the subject up in the First Congress, there was resistance to the idea. When he succeeded in getting his amendment through the Congress, critics of the Constitution said it was too little too late. When the ratification took place, Jefferson reported the result with no enthusiasm. All these facts have led some to say that the First Amendment, as understood in its first passage, was "a dead letter"—to quote the political philosopher Willmoore Kendall, who, with his disciple George Carey, was a vigorous critic of what he considered the "cult" of the First Amendment.[5] John Courtney Murray and Philip Hamburger have held similar views.

Much is made of the fact that Madison initially considered a religious liberty clause in the federal Constitution unnecessary and even dangerous. This seems an odd position for the man who had pressed so urgently for a religious-freedom guarantee in the Virginia State Constitution. But Madison was not alone in his opposition to the bill of freedom. Almost all the Federalists, as defenders of the draft were called at the time, took the same stance—Alexander Hamilton, James Wilson, Roger Sherman, Oliver Ellsworth, Edmond Randolph, among others. The constitutional scholar Leonard Levy writes: "Excluding a bill of rights from the Constitution was fundamental to the constitutional theory of the Framers."[6]

The framers said, as Hamilton put it in The Federalist No. 84: "Why declare that things shall not be done which there is no power to do?" The limited powers of the federal government, they claimed, were such that it could not dream of imposing religion or limiting free speech. Even to discuss the possibility went against the impression the Federalists were trying to create—that neither states nor individuals were menaced by the new government. Seven states already had their own bills of rights—that was the proper level at which to address the problem, since that was where problems had occurred. The Federalists felt (rightly, to some degree) that the clamor for a bill of rights was what Leonard Levy calls "a smokescreen" used by people who wanted to defeat the Constitution.

The Federalists' initial arguments were, in fact, weak. If religious liberty needed no overt protection, why was there a ban on religious tests for holding office? Why were other rights expressly protected in the draft? Besides, the novelty of founding a government without a reference to God looked somehow nefarious. Religion needed protecting. The effectiveness of such objections came close to blocking ratification, and it led to fights over conditional ratification or the calling of a new convention. To prevent these latter maneuvers, Madison and others accepted the idea of including "recommended" amendments in the state reports of ratification—five states made such recommendations in their ratifying statements.

Madison did not like this idea, but he had to accede. "It [the Constitution] would have been certainly rejected had no assurance been given by its advocates that such provisions would be pursued" (JM 12.347). He realized that he would have to honor these requests in the First Congress, especially since his own election to the first House of Representatives was accomplished only after he pledged to support them. Robert Morris jovially claimed: "Poor Madison got so cursedly frightened in Virginia that I believe he has dreamed of amendments ever since. This, however, is ad captandum [*sic*—he is referring to the rhetorical device *ad captandam benevolentiam*, words used to placate a crowd]."[7]

Kendall and others say there was no real desire for the Bill of Rights—Madison ran into objections and delays and little enthusiasm when he tried to prod the first Congress toward action on amendments.. This neglects the fact that the principal opponents of the Constitution wanted to *prevent* passage of amendments, to keep their grievances alive. Madison agreed with Hugh Williamson, who had represented North Carolina at the convention, when the latter wrote him that "the true antis" did not want to see a Bill of Rights pass (JM 12.184). Patrick Henry, who had called for a Bill of Rights, decided, when it was actually offered, that it would "tend to injure rather than to serve the cause of liberty."[8]

Madison was moving quickly to remove this weapon from Henry's hands. He did it, he told Congress, "to give satisfaction to the doubting part of our fellow citizens," assuring the House that the amendments he proposed were "neither improper nor altogether useless" (JM 12.198, 201)—or as he put it in notes for his speech in the House, amendments could be "useful, not essential" (JM 12.193). As he told a friend: "It [the Bill of Rights] will kill the opposition everywhere" (JM 12.347). This does not sound like one ushering in a great constitutional principle. He was acting, we are told, only to flummox his foes. Pierce Butler of South Carolina wrote:

> If you wait for substantial amendment, you will wait longer
> than I wish you to do, speaking *interestedly.* A few *milk-and-water*
> amendments have been proposed by Mr. M[adison], such as
> liberty of conscience, a free press, and one or two general
> things already well secured. I suppose it was done to keep his
> promise with his constituents, to move for alterations; but, if I
> am not greatly mistaken, he is not hearty in the cause of
> amendments.[9]

Robert Morris said that he heard from House members that they had passed the amendments "as containing neither good or harm, being perfectly innocent."[10]

When Jefferson, as secretary of state, reported the final ratification of the Bill of Rights, it was not with a triumphant trumpet blast. He put it third in a list of things in a form letter addressed to each state governor:

> Sir,
> I have the honor to send you herein enclosed two copies,
> duly authenticated, of an Act concerning certain fisheries of
> the United States, and for the regulation and government of
> the fishermen employed therein; also of an Act to establish the
> post office and post roads within the United States; also the
> ratification by three fourths of the legislatures of the several
> states of certain articles in addition and amendment of the
> Constitution of the United States, proposed by Congress to the

said legislatures; and of being with sentiments of the most
perfect respect, your Excellency's [humble servant], etc.
　　Th. Jefferson[11]

Philip Hamburger thinks that even Madison had lost interest in the
separation of church and state by 1789, since he submitted to the Congress's changes in his language, effecting what Hamburger thinks is a
dilution of it. Madison proposed:

> The civil rights of none shall be abridged on account of
> religious belief or worship, nor shall any national religion be
> established, nor shall the full and equal rights of conscience be
> in any manner or on any pretext infringed. (JM 12.201)

Congress gave us this final text:

> Congress shall make no law respecting an establishment of
> religion or prohibiting the free exercise thereof.

Hamburger asks why Madison did not object to this watering down.
In fact, he did object to a change made in his religious provision, as we
shall see. But Hamburger indulges again his taste for mind-reading (as
he had with the Danbury Baptists)—he tells us that Madison was backing off from the "extremism" with which he had defended Jefferson's
"anticlerical" Statute for Religious Freedom, since "he may have learned
some moderation" and "he did not think the precise wording mattered
much."[12] Before discussion of this wild claim, it is necessary to look further at the reasons Hamburger and others dismiss the First Amendment
as unimportant.

2. TO PROTECT STATE ESTABLISHMENTS?

SINCE THE First Amendment simply prevents Congress from any
acts "respecting an establishment of religion," it leaves the states

entirely free to engage in such acts. Since six states still gave state support to Christian denominations, they were free to continue, as they did for some time—Massachusetts, the last holdout, only gave up on establishment in 1833. Willmoore Kendall wrote:

> What the First Amendment in effect does (through the emphasis on Congress) is to *recognize* laws respecting an establishment of religion, or prohibiting the free exercise thereof, or abridging the freedom of speech or of the press, or abridging the right of the people to assemble peaceably and petition for redress of grievances *as a monopoly of the state governments;* that is, what it precisely does *not* do is to "take a stand" on the matters Mr. Justice [Hugo] Black now sees as being at stake in it [emphasis in original].[13]

Kendall even thinks it was the amendment's *intention* to protect the state's power to infringe those rights. There are many problems with that claim—for one thing, one delegate, Benjamin Huntington, felt that the ban on federal action dealing with establishment might *undermine* state establishments, since the federal judiciary might refuse to hear cases of, for instance, the refusal to pay a minister of the state-established church.[14] For another thing, the recommendatory amendments appended to five state ratification notices had three proposals for a religious amendment; but none of the three asked that state establishments be protected. Just the opposite—they asked for a freedom-of-conscience guarantee, just what Madison had in mind.

Madison himself was obviously no champion of religious establishment at the state level. That is what he had fought against in his own state. He thought all states should adopt the principles of Jefferson's Virginia Statute and his own *Remonstrance.* This is not an assumption we have to draw indirectly. There is direct evidence of what he wanted from the states, and it explains why he feared that a Bill of Rights, as drawn up by the First Congress, would not go far enough. This fear sets him apart from the other Federalists who opposed the idea of a Bill of Rights. This is what he wrote to Jefferson in October of 1788:

> There is great reason to fear that a positive declaration of some of the most essential rights could not be obtained in the requisite latitude. I am sure that the rights of conscience in particular, if submitted to public definition, would be narrowed much more than they are likely ever to be by an assumed power [of the federal government]. (JM 11.2 97)

Madison thought his fear had been justified by Congress's drafting of the Bill of Rights—which he called, sadly, "the nauseous project of amendments" (JM 12.346). This was not because of anything that Congress did to his suggested form for the First Amendment (which was the fourth in his original list), but because Congress struck out what he had listed as his own Fifth Amendment: "No *state* shall violate the equal rights of conscience, or the freedom of the press, or the trial by jury in criminal cases" (JM 12.202; emphasis added). *Madison intended to disestablish religion at the state level.* When objections were raised to this, he protested:

> [He] conceived this to be the most valuable amendment on the whole list; if there was any reason to restrain the government of the United States from infringing upon these essential rights, it was equally necessary that they should be secured against the state governments; he thought that if they provided against the one, it was as necessary to provide against the other, and was satisfied that it would be equally grateful to the people. (JM 12.344).

So much for Hamburger's contention that Madison had backed off from his earlier views, had become "moderate," and did not care about the wording of the Disestablishment clause. What Madison feared had come true. The religious freedom clause was *not* drawn up in the latitude he desired. He knew that the threat against religious freedom came at the state level, where establishment took place. But he could not get his fellows to go along with him.

Does the fact that Congress would not back his desired amendment mean that it intended to protect religious establishments? That does not follow. There were many practical objections to Madison's proposal—as there had been to his plan, at the Philadelphia Convention, to give Congress a veto over state laws. That would have been an impossible position to sell to the states, entirely aside from its merits. There is other evidence to show that the Congress was not friendly to establishments, as we find in the next argument advanced against the importance of the First Amendment.

3. NOT A MATTER OF PRINCIPLE?

IT IS OFTEN SAID that the First Amendment did not adopt a deep principle about freedom of conscience. It just recognized that the multiplicity of sects in America made it impossible to adopt a single state religion. John Courtney Murray was especially passionate in advocating this view of the matter. He said that the First Amendment was the product of "social necessity," created by the fact that America's different religions had to live together in peace.[15] William Lee Miller, who participated with Murray in the dialogues held in the 1950s by the Fund for the Republic, noted how scornful the Jesuit was of "theologians of the First Amendment."[16]

It must be remembered that Father Murray, being disciplined at the time by the Vatican, had to defend the American system against papal attacks on secular democracy. He did this by saying that there was nothing substantive in the First Amendment to be condemned. It was just a bargain. He admits that if Madison's views in the *Memorial and Remonstrance* were present in the First Amendment, then papal condemnation would be justified, since Madison's argument in the *Remonstrance* is "an irredeemable piece of sectarian dogmatism," just the kind of sectarianism that popes rightly condemn, since it leads to fascism or communism.[17]

Of course, many people hold that the First Amendment was just a social necessity, without having to resort to Murray's condemnation of secularism. Mark Douglas McGarvie puts William McLoughlin and Louis Hartz in this company, though he notes that at the time of the convention "pluralism was an argument raised against the need for the First Amendment rather than, as some suggest, the reason for its enactment."[18] But those who speak of a freedom imposed by the conditions of pluralism seem to be supported by Madison himself, who said that the multiplicity of sects favored religious freedom, just as the multiplicity of factions could bolster political freedom. As he put it in *The Federalist* No. 51: "In a free government, the security for civil rights must be the same as for religious rights. It consists in the one case in the multiplicity of interests, and in the other in the multiplicity of sects." But he speaks of a security given to religious liberty, not of the reason for it. The reason is the free nature of religious assent, the supremacy of the individual conscience.

This was not Madison's concern alone. Madison consulted the lists of recommended amendments sent by the five states offering them. In none of them is it said that Congress should have limited power in order to protect a state establishment, or to recognize the variety of sects. On the contrary, the three states calling for this restriction all do it in the name of freedom of conscience.

The recommendation from Virginia is not surprising, since Madison helped frame it at that state's ratifying convention. It urged:

> That the religion or the duty which we owe to our Creator, and
> the manner of discharging it, can be directed only by reason
> and conviction, not by force or violence, and therefore all men
> have an equal, natural, and unalienable right to the free exer-
> cise of religions according to the dictates of conscience, and
> that no particular religious sect or society ought to be favored
> or established by law in preference to others.[19]

The recommendation from New York is in the same vein:

> That the people have an equal, natural, and unalienable right,
> freely and peaceably to exercise their religion according to the
> dictates of conscience, and that no religious sect or society
> ought to be favored or established by law in preference of
> others.[20]

New Hampshire is just as firm on the rights of conscience, or on any-thing "touching" religion: "Congress shall make no laws touching religion, or to infringe the rights of conscience."[21] Samuel Livermore, the delegate from New Hampshire, rephrased his state's recommendation in a form which the House accepted, before the Senate had adopted its own form: "The Congress shall make no laws touching the rights of conscience."[22]

How can anyone claim that the First Amendment says nothing about principle when Madison said that he was responding to recommenda-tions that voiced the principle of free conscience? None of the recom-mendations talked about a "bargain" the federal government must strike to protect the various sects, or the establishments already in place.

4. SIMPLY NONPREFERENTIAL, NOT AGAINST RELIGION IN GENERAL?

SINCE ALL THREE of the state recommendations talk of not "favor-ing" or preferring one religion over another, it is often said that this is *all* that the First Amendment requires. Religion in general, or all reli-gions indiscriminately, can be fostered by government. But all three state lists go further and say that *freedom of conscience* must be protected. Jeffer-son's Statute and Madison's *Remonstrance* also said that the government must be nonpreferential, but they do not limit the meaning of religious freedom to that. None of the state petitions said that religion in general should be promoted. Leonard Levy points out that nonpreferential lan-guage was used by people who clearly opposed *any* governmental sup-port for religion, including the Baptist ally of Jefferson, John Leland.

Madison regularly referred to the First Amendment as opposing "religious establishments," the term favored by those who wanted nonpreferentially multiple establishments.[23]

Madison made his understanding of the First Amendment clear in his actions as president and his writings after retiring from the presidency. They prove that he did not become more "moderate," as Hamburger claims, but consistently held and acted on his deepest principles, as enunciated in the *Remonstrance* and the First Amendment. In fact, he became more determined in those principles as time went on, as we shall see.

14 | MADISONIAN SEPARATION

M ADISON WAS NOT perfectly consistent on matters of church and state—any more than Americans in general have been. But this was not because he moderated his principles. He simply saw that, given the novelty of the idea of a "godless Constitution," he would have to yield to popular prejudice at times. His method in accommodating certain realities can be seen in his action at the first Congress. He proposed that the constitutionally mandated census include useful information on the interests of the community—"agricultural, commercial, and manufacturing"—to provide grounds for enlightened legislation. When it was suggested that the learned professions should be listed as well, Madison cautioned that this should not be done in such a way as to make the state favor particular views, as if legislating the truth of scientific theory. He wanted a listing of the learned professions in general, without particular attention to particular callings, and he expressed a special concern at the danger of listing clergymen:

> The gentleman from Massachusetts [Mr. Sedgwick] has asked
> why the learned professions were not included. I have no
> objection to giving a column to the general body [of the

various professions]. I think the work would be rendered
more complete by the addition, and if the decision of such a
motion turned upon my voice, they shall be added. But it may
nevertheless be observed, that in such a character, they can
never be objects of legislative attention or cognizance. As to
those employed in teaching and inculcating the duties of
religion, there may be some indelicacy in singling them out, as
*the general government is proscribed from interfering, in any manner
whatever, in matters respecting religion;* and it may be thought to do
this, in ascertaining who [are], and who are not, ministers of
the gospel. Conceiving the extent of the plan to be useful, and
not difficult, I hope it may meet the ready concurrence of this
house. [JM 13.16; emphasis added]

The italicized clause gives Madison's basic understanding of the First
Amendment. But he grants that a partial or apparent exception can be
allowed, if its dangers are pointed out and avoided. The listing of ministers should not, in his view, lead to political consequences. Only if it is
kept from doing that can the act be constitutional.

FAST AND THANKSGIVING PROCLAMATIONS

JEFFERSON REFUSED to issue prayer day proclamations, as had been
the custom with Presidents Washington and Adams. Madison agreed
with him on this issue, and followed his example in the first part of his
presidency. But he gave in to political pressure for such proclamations
during the War of 1812—war, as we have seen, being a time of inflamed
religiosity. The Congress had called for such a proclamation, and Madison needed support for the war, which was opposed by religious groups
in New England, where Madison, like Jefferson, was suspected of being
a godless Jacobin. But though Madison yielded to the pressure, he tried
(as he put it) to "deaden" the idea that this was anything but a reminder
to citizens that they could, voluntarily and on their own, pray if they

wished to. He is quietly backing off from his proclamation even as he issues it:

> Whereas the *Congress* of the United States, by a joint resolution
> of the two Houses, have signified a request that a day *may* be
> nominated to be observed by the people of the United States
> with religious solemnity as a day of public humiliation and
> prayer, and whereas such a *recommendation* will enable the
> several religious denominations and societies *so disposed* to
> offer, at one and the same time, their common vows and
> adoration to Almighty God on the solemn occasion produced
> by the war in which he has pleased to permit the injustice of a
> foreign power to involve these United States, I do therefore
> *recommend* the third Thursday in August next as a *convenient* day
> to be so set apart for the devout purpose of rendering to the
> Sovereign of the Universe and the Benefactor of Mankind, the
> pubic homage due to his holy attributes [emphasis added].[1]

The Deist terms for God—Sovereign and Benefactor, in this instance—are all Madison would use in the later proclamations of the war period. He said he was following the precedent of President Washington, who had used Deist language in his proclamations, unlike President Adams, who used Christian language. But even the Washington proclamations were political in their conjunction with events—like the wartime atmosphere of the Whiskey Rebellion.

Madison regretted his own lapse from principle, and wrote, after leaving office, his grounds for thinking it unconstitutional. He did not want his action to serve as an excuse for more dogmatic proclamations in the future. His uneasy conscience in the matter was expressed in the "Detached Memoranda" he wrote after leaving office, defending his actions in the realm of religion.[2] He gives the conflicting views of Jefferson and Hamilton on Washington's proclamation as an example of the way religion can be used for political purposes. Here is what he wrote in the Memoranda.

RELIGIOUS PROCLAMATIONS

Religious proclamations by the Executive recommending
thanksgivings and fasts are shoots from the same root with the
legislative acts [on chaplains] reviewed. Although recommendations only, they imply a religious agency, making no part
of the trust delegated to political rulers. The objections to
them are:

1. That governments ought not to interpose in relation to
those subject to their authority but in cases where they can do it
with effect. An *advisory* government is a contradiction in terms.

2. The members of a government, as such, can in no sense be
regarded as possessing an advisory trust from their constituents
in their religious capacities. They cannot form an ecclesiastical
assembly, convocation, council, or synod and, as such, issue
decrees or injunctions addressed to the faith or the consciences
of the people. In their individual capacities, as distinct from their
official station, they might unite in recommendation of any sort
whatever, in the same manner as any other individuals might do.
But then their recommendations ought to express the true
character from which they emanate.

3. They seem to imply, and certainly nourish, the erroneous
idea of a national religion. The idea, just as it related to the
Jewish nation under a theocracy, having been improperly
adopted by so many nations which have embraced Christianity,
is too apt to lurk in the bosoms even of Americans, who in
general are aware of the distinction between religious and
political societies. The idea also of a union of all to form one
nation under one government, in acts of devotion to the God of
all, is an imposing idea; but reason and the principles of the
Christian religion require that all the individuals composing a
nation, even of the same precise creed, and wishing to unite in
a universal act of religion at the same time, the union ought to

be effected through the intervention of their religious not of their political representatives. In a nation composed of various sects, some alienated widely from others, and where no agreement could take place through the former, the interposition of the latter is doubly wrong.

4. The tendency of the practice [is] to narrow the recommendation to the standard of the predominant sect. The first proclamation of General Washington, dated July 1, 1795 (see if this was the first), recommending a day of thanksgiving, embraced all who believed in a supreme ruler of the universe. That of Mr. Adams called for a *Christian* worship. Many private letters reproached the proclamations issued by James Madison for using general terms, used in that of President Washington; and some of them for not inserting particulars according with the faith of certain Christian sects. The practice, if not strictly guarded [against], naturally terminates in a conformity to the creed of the majority, and [to] a single sect if amounting to a majority.

5. The last and not the least objection is the liability of the practice to a subserviency to political views; to the scandal of religion as well as the increase of party animosities. Candid or incautious politicians will not always disown such views. In truth, it is difficult to frame such a religious proclamation, generally suggested by a political state of things, without referring to them in terms having some bearing on party questions. The proclamation of President Washington, which was issued just after the suppression of the insurrection in Pennsylvania, and at a time when the public mind was divided on several topics, was so construed by many. Of this the secretary of state himself, Edmund Randolph, seems to have had an anticipation.

The original draft of the instrument [was] filed in the Department of State (see copies of these papers in the files of James Madison), in the handwriting of Mr. Hamilton, the secretary of the treasury. It appears that several slight alterations only had been made at the suggestion of the secretary of state [Jefferson], and in a marginal note in his hand it is remarked that "In short, this proclamation ought to savor as much as possible of religion, and not too much of having a political object." In a subjoined note in the hand of Mr. Hamilton, this remark is answered by the counter-remark that "A proclamation of a government, which is a national act, naturally embraces objects which are political"—so naturally is the idea of policy associated with religion, whatever be the mode or the occasion, when a function of the latter is assumed by those in power.

During the administration of Mr Jefferson, no religious proclamation was issued. It being understood that his successor was disinclined to such interpositions of the executive, and by some supposed moreover that they might originate with more propriety with the legislative body, a resolution was passed requesting him to issue a proclamation (see resolution in the journals of Congress)

It was thought not proper to refuse a compliance altogether; but a form and language were employed which were meant to deaden, as much as possible, any claim of political right to enjoin religious observances by resting these expressly on the voluntary compliance of individuals and even by limiting the recommendation to such as wished simultaneous as well as voluntary performance of a religious act on the occasion.[3]

How far we have traveled from Madison's time can be seen from the fact that the president no longer waits for special occasions to issue a fast or prayer recommendation. In 1988, President Reagan issued a mandate that every first Thursday in May should be a National Day of Prayer. In the administration of President George W. Bush, this would become a rallying event for Evangelical political lobbying with the administration's blessing and benefit.

CHAPLAINCIES

MADISON WAS concerned with two more religious subjects in his Memoranda—chaplaincies and tax exemption. On the subject of chaplaincies, the Religious Right likes to point out that Madison served on the committee of the House that first set up a chaplaincy there. This was done before the House took up the subject of a Bill of Rights, so the First Amendment did not yet exist. But Leo Pfeffer does not accept that as an excuse for Madison's action.[4] The Constitution *did* exist and its sixth clause says there shall be no religious test for holding federal positions. A religious test existed for choosing chaplains. An atheist can, so far as law goes, serve in the Congress or the other two branches of government. But an atheist cannot serve as chaplain, whose duty it is to pray to God. Perhaps Madison did not see the subject clearly in the opening days of the government, or feel that he could bring his colleagues to agree with him before the First Amendment was framed and debated. At any rate, his later views on what he calls "legal ecclesiastics" are clear and he is anxious to express them. He thought that individual members of the Congress, if they wished for spiritual guidance, should seek it at their own expense, not create a public office with public funds. He later took the same view when he succeeded Jefferson as rector of the University of Virginia, allowing parents of children to fund ministers of their own denominations who would be given access to the campus without university appointment or position. Here are his comments on the matter in the Detached Memoranda:

> Is the appointment of chaplains to the two Houses of Congress
> consistent with the Constitution, and with the pure principle
> of religious freedom?
>
> In strictness the answer on both points must be in the
> negative. The Constitution of the U.S. forbids everything like
> an establishment of a national religion. The law appointing
> chaplains establishes a religious worship for the national
> representatives, to be performed by ministers of religion

elected by a majority of them; and these are to be paid out of the national taxes. Does not this involve the principle of a national establishment, applicable to a provision for a religious worship for the constituent as well as the representative body, approved by the majority and conducted by ministers of religion paid by the entire nation?

The establishment of the chaplainship to Congress is a palpable violation of equal rights as well as of constitutional principles. The tenets of the chaplains elected shut the door of worship against the members whose creed and conscience forbid a participation in that of the majority. To say nothing of other sects, this is the case with that of Roman Catholics and Quakers, who have always had members in one or both of the legislative branches. Could a Catholic clergyman ever hope to be appointed a chaplain? To say that his religious principles are obnoxious, or that his sect is small, is to lift the veil at once and exhibit, in its naked deformity, the doctrine that religious truth is to be tested by numbers, or that the major sects have a right to govern the minor.

If religion consists in voluntary acts of individuals, singly or voluntarily associated, and it be proper that public functionaries, as well as their constituents, should discharge their religious duties, let them, like their constituents, do so at their own expense. How small a contribution from each member of Congress would suffice for the purpose! How just would it be in its principle! How noble in its exemplary sacrifice to the genius of the Constitution and the divine right of conscience! Why should the expense of a religious worship be allowed for the legislature, be paid by the public, more than that for the executive or judiciary branch of the government?

Were the establishment to be tried by its fruits, are not the daily devotions conducted by these legal ecclesiastics already degenerating into a scanty attendance and a tiresome formality?

Rather than let this step beyond the landmarks of power have the effect of a legitimate precedent, it will be better to apply to it the legal aphorism *de minimis non curat lex* [law overlooks slight matters] or to class it *cum maculis quas aut incuria fundit aut humana parvum cavit natura* [among the faults that inattention indulges or about which human nature is too little on guard].[5]

Madison was consistent when he considered chaplains for the armed forces.

MILITARY CHAPLAINS

Better also to disarm, in the same way, the precedent of chaplainships for the army and navy that erect them into a political authority in matters of religion. The object of this establishment is seducing, the motive to it is laudable. But is it not safer to adhere to a right principle, and trust to its consequences, than confide in the reasoning, however specious, in favor of a wrong one? Look through the armies and navies of the world and say whether, in the appointment of their ministers of religion, the spiritual interest of the flocks or the temporal interest of the shepherds be most in view—whether, here as elsewhere, the political care of religion is not a nominal more than a real aid. If the spirit of armies be devout, the spirit out of the armies will never be less so, and a failure of religious instruction and exhortation from a voluntary source, within or without, will rarely happen. And if such be not the spirit of armies, the official services of their teachers are not likely to produce it—it is more likely to flow from the labors of a spontaneous zeal. The armies of the Puritans had their appointed chaplains; but without these there would have been no lack of public devotion in that devout age.

The case of navies with insulated crews may be less within

the scope of these reflections. But it is not entirely so. The chance of a devout officer might be of as much worth to religion as the service of an ordinary chaplain (were it admitted that religion has a real interest in the latter). But we are always to keep in mind that it is safer to trust the consequences of a right principle than reasonings in support of a bad one.[6]

CHURCH PROPERTY

O N CHURCH PROPERTY, Madison did not always get his way, though his own policies and preferences are clear. He opposed having the government incorporate church properties, vetoing the incorporation of the Episcopal Church in the District of Columbia, since the government would be "making a law respecting a religious establishment." He noted that the rules for choosing ministers were part of the incorporation document—and the government could not be involved in that. He feared that in case of disputes over control of the corporate property, with each party claiming to be the true religionists who had incorporated, the government would be entangled in doctrinal matters. He also objected to the government's endorsing private charities connected with religion—what is now called "faith-based" welfare. He wrote of the proposed Anglican corporation:

> Because the bill vests in the said incorporated church an
> authority to provide for the support of the poor and the
> education of poor children of the same, an authority which,
> being altogether superfluous if the provision is to be the result
> of pious charity, would be a precedent for giving to religious
> societies as such a legal agency in carrying into effect a public
> and civil duty.[7]

He also vetoed the grant of land to a Baptist church in the Mississippi Territory. He could act here because the territory was, like the

District of Columbia, in the federal domain. He could not act in the states, since the First Amendment was not yet extended to them by way of the Fourteenth Amendment. But though he could not act in a state, he expressed an opinion after he had left office that the state of Kentucky should not have tried to exempt churches from taxation. As president he could and did veto a bill to give Bible societies an exemption from duties on their imports of religious items. Pfeffer notes that he allowed two other bills for such remittance to pass.[8] Each was strongly supported by a specific state, and though the duties were federal customs, not state ones, perhaps Madison felt he could not oppose the states on this—though he clearly felt that the Constitution required it.

Even aside from constitutional considerations, Madison thought the churches should not be encouraged to acquire too much property, since that would corrupt them and give them political influence. The Detached Memoranda are eloquent on this subject:

> But besides the danger of a direct mixture of religion and civil government, there is an evil which ought to be guarded against in the indefinite accumulation of property from the capacity of holding it in perpetuity by ecclesiastical corporations. The power of all corporations ought to be limited in this respect. The growing wealth acquired by them never fails to be source of abuses. A warning on this subject is emphatically given in the example of the various charitable establishments in Great Britain, the management of which has been lately scrutinized. The excessive wealth of ecclesiastical corporations and the misuse of it in many countries of Europe has long been a topic of complaint. In some of them the church has amassed half perhaps [of] the property of the nation. When the Reformation took place, an event promoted if not caused by that disordered state of things, how enormous were the treasures of religious societies, and how gross the corruptions engendered by them. . . .
>
> Are the United States duly awake to the tendency of the precedents they are establishing in the multiplied incorporations

of religions congregations with the faculty of acquiring property
real as well as personal?[9] Do not many of these acts give this
faculty without limit either as to time or as to amount? And must
not bodies—perpetual in their existence, and which may be
always gaining without ever losing—speedily gain more than
is useful and, in time, more than is safe? Are there not already
examples in the United States of ecclesiastical wealth equally
beyond its object and the foresight of those who laid the
foundations of it? In the United States, there is a double motive
for fixing limits in this case, because wealth may increase not
only from additional gifts, but from exorbitant advances in the
value of the primitive one. In grants of vacant land, and of land
in the vicinity of growing towns and cities, the increase of value
is often such as, if foreseen, would essentially control the
liberality confirming them. The people of the United States owe
their independence and their liberty to the wisdom of descrying,
in the minute tax of three pence on tea, the magnitude of the
evil comprised in the precedent. Let them exert the same
wisdom in watching against every evil lurking under plausible
disguises and growing up from small beginnings. *Obsta principiis*
[block the beginnings].[10]

   The wealth of churches continued to trouble Madison, as we can see
from a letter he wrote as late as 1832:

   An omission of the public authorities to limit the duration of
   their charters to religious corporations, and the amount of
   property acquirable by them, may lead to an injurious
   accumulation of wealth from the lavish donations and
   bequests prompted by a pious zeal or by an atoning
   remorse. . . .
       It may not be easy, in every possible case, to trace the line
   of separation between the rights of religion and the civil
   authority with such distinctness as to avoid collision and

doubts on unessential points. The tendency to a usurpation on
one side or the other, or to a corrupting coalition or alliance
between them, will be best guarded against by an *entire
abstinence* of the government from interference *in any way
whatever*, beyond the necessity of preserving public order and
protecting each sect against trespasses on its legal rights by
others [emphasis added].[11]

Madison never tired of laying out the principle of separation. In 1824
he wrote to Edward Everett, explaining why the University of Virginia
had no chaplaincy.

The settled opinion here [in Virginia] is that religion is
essentially distinct from civil government, and exempt from
its cognizance;
that a connection between then is injurious to both;
that there are causes in the human breast which ensure the
perpetuity of religion without the aid of the law;
that rival sects, with equal rights, exercise mutual censorships
in favor of good morals;
that if new sects arise with absurd opinions or overheated
imaginations, the proper remedies lie in time, forbearance,
and example;
that a legal establishment of religion without a toleration
could not be thought of, and with a toleration is no security
for public quiet and harmony, but rather a source itself of
discord and animosity;
and finally that these opinions are supported by experience,
which has shown that every relaxation of the alliance
between law and religion, from the partial example of Holland
to its consummation in Pennsylvania, Delaware, New Jersey,
etc, has been found as safe in practice as it is sound in theory.
    Prior to the Revolution, the Episcopal Church was
established by law in this state. On the Declaration of

Independence it was left, with all other sects, to a self-support.
And no doubt exists that there is much more of religion among
us now than there ever was before the change; and particularly
in the sect which enjoyed the legal patronage. This proves
rather more than that the law is not necessary to the support of
religion.[12]

It is hard to see how Madison's thought could have been distorted by
so many people. He laid it out clearly and repeatedly. Even before the
First Amendment was applied to the states, and while some states still
had religious establishments, he urged them all to imitate what Virginia
had accomplished in the Statute for Religious Freedom:

Ye states of America, which retain in your constitutions or
codes any aberration from the sacred principle of religious
liberty, by giving to Caesar what belongs to God or joining
together what God has put asunder, hasten to revise and purify
your systems, and make the example of your country as pure
and complete, in what relates to the freedom of the mind and
its allegiance to its Maker, as in what belongs to the legitimate
object of political and civil institutions.[13]

PART THREE

THE ROMANTIC ERA

V |
TRANSCENDENTALISM

15 | SCHISM IN NEW ENGLAND

A s America moved from the eighteenth into the nineteenth century, it experienced a gradual shift from the Enlightenment era to
the Romantic era. The Enlightenment had come to the United States
from England and Scotland, from Newton, Locke, Hume, and Gibbon,
or from France as mediated through British authors. The Romantic era
came largely from Germany, as mediated by British authors like Carlyle,
Coleridge, Byron, and Shelley. The Enlightenment had stressed science
and reason. The Romantic era would rely on inspiration and intuition.
Religion was bound to be affected by this alteration. It showed in both
forms of American religion, the elite and the populist. Among the intellectuals, Romanticism led to a Unitarian turn against doctrine, evanesc-
ing into Transcendentalism and nature mysticism. Among those
engaged in the Second Great Awakening, Romanticism led to a religion
of the heart, of personal redemption, of a highly emotional picture
of Jesus. Among the former, Emerson taught the soul to merge with
the universe. Among the latter, a *Sturm und Drang* atmosphere led to the
churning emotions of revival and to renewed apocalyptic visions.
The climax of the Romantic period came in our most Romantic conflict,
the apocalyptic Civil War.

The Romantic era is mainly studied by literary critics, which may be the reason it is not considered as a larger historical shift, comparable with such great movements in history as the Renaissance, the Reformation, or the Enlightenment. But Isaiah Berlin argued that Romanticism is even more important to modern ways of thinking than are any later developments:

> The importance of Romanticism is that it is the largest recent
> movement to transform the lives and the thought of the
> Western world. It seems to me to be the greatest single shift
> in the consciousness of the West that has occurred, and all
> the other shifts which have occurred in the course of the
> nineteenth and twentieth centuries appear to me in compari-
> son less important, and at any rate deeply influenced by it.[1]

Berlin goes on to trace the effects of Romanticism on later developments as different as Pragmatism, Dada, Bergsonism, Fascism, and Existentialism. This is a large claim, but one he made repeatedly, and in strong terms. Lecturing at Bryn Mawr in 1952, he said that, so far as Romantics were concerned, values were not given in the outer world but created from within by a process of struggle:

> The revolution which ensued from this point of view—the
> transformation of values, the new admiration of heroism,
> integrity, strength of will, martyrdom, dedication to the vision
> within one irrespective of its properties, veneration of those
> who battle against hopeless odds no matter for how strange and
> desperate a cause, as against previous reverence for knowledge,
> skill, wisdom, success, and truth, virtue, happiness, natural
> endowment—was the most decisive in modern times. It was
> certainly the largest step in the moral consciousness of
> mankind since the ending of the Middle Ages, perhaps since
> the rise of Christianity. No step of comparable magnitude has

occurred since—it was the last great "transvaluation of values" in modern history.[2]

Whatever the validity of Berlin's extensive analysis, the importance of the Romantic movement in nineteenth-century America is beyond question. It is apparent in the work of authors like Cooper, Bryant, Hawthorne, Poe, Thoreau, Whitman, and Dickinson. In architecture, it accounts for the revolt against Palladian classicism in the Romanesque revival of H. H. Richardson and the Gothic revival of Ralph Adams Cram. The Romantic cult of nature showed in the paintings of the Hudson Valley School and the Luminists, or in the rural cemetery movement. The Romantic ideal even showed in the styles of political leadership, so different from the rational idealism of the Deist founders. There was a taste for the exotic, the eccentric, the daring—in men like Sam Houston and Davy Crockett, but also in the swashbuckling Andrew Jackson, the depressive Ulysses Grant, the idealistic Robert E. Lee, the melancholy Abraham Lincoln, the lost-cause champion John Calhoun.

But perhaps the deepest influence of Romanticism, though the least noticed one, was on religion. To see the truth of this we must first establish just what Romanticism was. Isaiah Berlin notes the difficulty of finding a definition; but he draws reasonable limits around its origin and first manifestations. The German Romantics were in violent revolt against French logic and rationalism. The Enlightenment held that reason could see regular patterns in nature, certain that all questions had clear and univocal answers so long as enough information was accumulated. The Romantics felt that this was despotically reductive of both elements in this dynamic—of the nature being studied and the human person doing the studying. Nature was more enigma than pattern to these men, and the human person was more than a registering intellect. For Romantics, the human person is less cool mind than aspiring spirit. They held that knowledge is more experiential and agonistic than passive and accommodating. The fiery Romantic is in a struggle with mystery, one where authentic humanity goes beyond discovery and submission to "the laws of nature and of nature's God." The Romantic is Faustian, Promethean, Dionysiac, Dostoyevskian.

For the Enlightenment, myth and legend were simply falsehoods accepted by primitive peoples because they had not the scientific equipment to dispel superstition and illogical surmise. The Romantic thinkers found deeper truths in myth, expansions of possibility, a wisdom of "the primitive." Human creativity pushes out the limits that sterile reason tries to impose. Authentic human response, even erratic response, is more valuable than submission to rules. The exaltation of the visionary can break open nature's recalcitrance, freeing human spontaneity from secondhand and recited reactions to the world. A connection of art with personality disorders is one sign of Romantic willingness to "pay the price" of looking into the abyss and struggling to cope with infinite challenge. Originality is at war with convention, the immediate with the remote. The Self defies the Universe.

The Germans' Romantic movement took many forms, including the cult of superconscious melancholy (as in Goethe's *Werther*), the literature of the *Sturm and Drang* (storm and drivenness) school, and "the *Cenacle*, the little group of Romantics who gathered in Jena—the two brothers Schlegel, for a time Fichte, for a time Schleiermacher in Berlin, and Schelling."[3]

Berlin traces the views of these men back to an Ur-Romantic, Johann Georg Hamann, who deeply influenced Goethe and Herder and Klinger. What Hamann wrote early on would be echoed or asserted individually by figure after figure in the Romantic movement as they arraigned the scientism of the Enlightenment:

> The sciences, if they were applied to human society, would
> lead to a kind of fearful bureaucratization, he thought. He was
> against scientists, bureaucrats, persons who made things tidy,
> smooth Lutheran clergymen, Deists, everybody who wanted to
> put things in boxes, everybody who wished to assimilate one
> thing to another, who wished to prove, for example, that
> creation was really the same as the obtaining of certain data

which nature provided, and their rearrangement in certain
pleasing patterns—whereas for Hamann, of course, creation
was a most ineffable, indescribable, unanalyzable personal act,
by which a human being laid his stamp on nature, allowed his
will to soar, spoke his word, uttered that which was within him
and which would not brook any kind of obstacle. Therefore the
whole of the Enlightenment doctrine appeared to him to kill
that which was living in human beings, appeared to offer a pale
substitute for the creative energies of man, and for the whole
rich world of the senses, without which it is impossible for
human beings to live, to eat, to drink, to be merry, to meet
other people, to indulge in a thousand and one acts without
which people wither and die. It seemed to him that the
Enlightenment laid no stress on that, that the human being as
painted by Enlightenment thinkers was, if not "economic
man," at any rate some kind of artificial toy, some kind of
lifeless model which had no relation to the kind of human
beings whom Hamann met and wished to associate with every
day of his life.[4]

That passage would, *mutatis mutandis,* have been endorsed by Emerson,
or by most other Transcendentalists.

The original Transcendentalists eased their way out of orthodoxy
through a transitional stage as Unitarians. Theodore Parker and Ralph
Waldo Emerson were ordained Congregationalist ministers, part of the
Unitarian group within their church. Not until the Unitarians opted out
or were pushed out of the congregations did the Transcendentalists take
the further step of leaving behind their Unitarian communities.

The open split between Congregationalist and Unitarian churches
occurred by the kind of dialectic process we have observed before. As
the Enlightenment and the First Great Awakening prodded each other
into opposite directions in the eighteenth century, so did the Unitarians
and the Second Great Awakening perform the same dos-a-dos in the
nineteenth. Timothy Dwight, Yale's president, laid the foundation of the

Second Great Awakening in the 1790s, by his attacks on the Unitarians in the congregations. He made his college one center of orthodoxy. A "New Haven Theology" would supply intellectual backing for the Second Great Awakening. Meanwhile, at Harvard, the Unitarians were taking over. Bitter controversy followed on the appointment of Henry Ware as Hollis Professor in 1806. The very next year, Samuel Webber was elected president, and critics reacted with a pamphlet war, led by the irascible geographer Jedidiah Morse, a member of Harvard's board of overseers.

When Morse and others withdrew in protest from the board, they set up a counterschool, Andover Theological Seminary, in 1808, to preserve orthodoxy—Harvard would eventually respond by establishing its own Divinity School in 1816. The antagonists were shaping their identities by mutual recrimination. Ware kept up the war by founding a journal, *The Panoplist,* in 1815, to champion Calvinist orthodoxy. The journal's name reflected Morse's belligerence—it means "the fully armed."

But the old religion was losing its hold. It had discredited itself with intemperate rantings against the "atheism" of Jefferson and the Republicans. It made things worse with its Anglophile resistance to the War of 1812. Henry Adams described what was happening.

> Driven to bay by the deistic and utilitarian principles of
> Jefferson's democracy, they fell into the worldly error of
> defying the national instinct, pressing their resistance to the
> war until it amounted to treasonable conspiracy. The sudden
> peace swept away much that was respectable in the old society
> of America; but perhaps its noblest victim was the unity of the
> New England Church.[5]

Fresh new faces were stepping into Boston pulpits—William Ellery Channing in 1803, when he was only twenty-three; Joseph Stevens Buckminster in 1805, twenty-one; Samuel Cooper Thatcher in 1822, twenty-five. These were Unitarians in what were still Congregationalist churches. "No such display of fresh and winning genius had yet been seen in America as was offered by the genial outburst of intellectual activity in the early days of the Unitarian schism."[6] Combined with the takeover of Harvard, this amounted to a religious revolution.

> In religion, the Unitarian movement in Boston and Harvard
> College would never have been possible in England, where the
> defection of Oxford or Cambridge and the best-educated
> society in the United Kingdom would have shaken Church and
> State to their foundations.[7]

This development was not as simple or rapid as Adams seems to suggest. The schism spread more slowly through the churches than it did through Harvard or Boston's high-profile intelligentsia. Mark DeWolfe Howe described the process:

> A slow series of changes, some legislative, some constitutional,
> and some judicial, told the Congregationalists by 1820, however,
> that in fact the commitment of the Commonwealth was not to
> the faith of their fathers but to the forms of church government
> which the fathers had established. Accordingly, when new
> winds of spiritual doctrine had blown so powerfully as to bend
> the community's mind toward a less upright faith, the state had
> no alternative but to let the new inclination of the public mind
> determine which religious enterprise it preferred. When the
> majority of any parish decided that the Unitarian connection
> was preferable to the Trinitarian faith of the Congregational-
> ists, the meeting house with all that it was and all that it
> symbolized was transferred from Congregational to Unitarian
> hands.[8]

The township church in Dedham tried to resist this process. When the parish board appointed a Unitarian minister, the church members objected that many in the parish were not covenanted and active members of their meeting, where the majority taking the sacrament were

Trinitarians. When the latter were ejected from their building, they absconded with the church records and took the matter to law. The Supreme Judiciary Court of Massachusetts, deciding this case, *Baker v. Fales* (1820), found for the parish board, since it was the incorporated body that paid taxes on the property. Madison had been right in fearing that governmental incorporation of churches would land the state in doctrinal matters.

Howe shows that even multiple-establishment incorporations in other states led to state interference in doctrinal disputes. The Massachusetts court claimed not to be deciding on religious grounds (though its members were mostly Unitarians), simply on the basis of corporation law.[9] But the decision indirectly said that Unitarianism was now the true doctrine of the church in question. This uncomfortable fact led to the political outcome, long delayed, by which Massachusetts finally disestablished religion in the state (1833).

The leading figure in making Unitarianism a separate church was William Ellery Channing. He was raised by his grandfather William Ellery, a signer of the Declaration of Independence. As was already mentioned, he was twenty-three when he took over the Federal Street Church, after turning down an offer from the more prestigious Brattle Street Church. He rallied opponents of Jedidiah Morse's *Panoplist*, preaching against it a sermon called "The System of Exclusions and Denunciation in Religion" (1813). He helped found the Harvard Divinity School in 1816. But what came to be known as Unitarianism's manifesto was a sermon he delivered in Baltimore at the ordination of the historian-minister Jared Sparks in 1819 and published in 1820 as *Unitarian Christianity*. That same year, the year of the Dedham decision, he formed a coordinating body for the Unitarians, who were now a separate denomination, the Berry Street Conference. This would, five years later, lead to the formation of a larger body with national ambitions, the American Unitarian Association.

Channing's pamphlet, *Unitarian Christianity*, was attacked by Leonard Woods, who, like Channing, had graduated at the top of his class at Harvard. But Woods threw in his lot with those who departed from Yale, joining Jedidiah Morse in the foundation of the Andover Theological Seminary. His response to Channing was formidable, but Henry Ware— whose appointment as Hollis Professor had presaged the whole conflict fifteen years earlier—answered Woods, and answered him, and answered him. The exchange of their polemics lasted for four years and became know as the Woods-Ware War (among other titles).

Channing was a literate and humane man, an ardent opponent of slavery, and a lecturer on literature. The tie between Unitarianism and Romanticism was confirmed when Channing visited England and became a good friend of Samuel Taylor Coleridge, whose religious views were very influential in America. Channing's literary and reform interests were passed on to two nephews, two more William Channings, who became Transcendentalists, one joining Emerson in Concord and the other joining Margaret Fuller at Brook Farm. This is ironic, since Emerson had by then become critical of Channing for failing, as he thought, to develop theologically. Channing was a Unitarian of the John Locke stripe, a disbeliever in the Trinity but still a believer in prophecies and miracles establishing that Christ was a higher creature than other humans (though not God). He defended his faith at Harvard in the Dudleian Lecture of 1821, "The Evidences of Revealed Religion." His early followers felt that he had become a conservative—a development frequently observed of leaders as they age. An early follower of Emerson himself—Walt Whitman— would feel the same way later about Emerson.

While Unitarians were separating themselves from Congregationalists, Transcendentalists were separating themselves from Unitarianism. Emerson gave up his pulpit at the Second Church of Boston in 1832, pleading ill health as an excuse but actually because he could not administer the Lord's Supper in good conscience. Orestes Brownson gave up his (Unitarian) pulpit at Canton, Massachusetts, in 1836. George Ripley gave up his Boston pulpit at the Purchase Street Church in 1841. Theodore Parker was driven from his pulpit at West Roxbury in 1845.

In 1836, Emerson, Ripley, and Brownson, along with three other Unitarian ministers (Convers Francis, James Freeman Clarke, and Frederic Henry Hedge), one layperson (Bronson Alcott), and three graduate students from the Harvard Divinity School, formed the Transcendental Club, which held its first meeting at the home of Ripley, who was Emerson's cousin. Francis, as the oldest (forty-one), was made the moderator. They had all, on separate schedules, come to the conclusion that formal Christianity, even of the most liberal kind, was a prison of the spirit, a spirit that had to be freed to seek its own destiny, transcending any one set of doctrines. They held a Kant-inspired idealism and a Romantic view of the self as its own guide. "They were dissatisfied, individually, and as a group, with the present state of philosophy, religion, and literature in America. They looked for hope to Europe, especially to Germany, to Kant in philosophy, to Schleiermacher in religion, and to Goethe in literature."[10] They were soon joined by others, including Theodore Parker, Henry David Thoreau, and Margaret Fuller, a friend of Convers Francis.

The final split between Congregationalists and Unitarians had taken place over the Trinity. The open theological split between Unitarians and Transcendentalists took place over miracles. Emerson, Parker, and Ripley rejected first the miracles in Scripture and then Scripture itself. In 1836, Ripley wrote a review in the *Christian Examiner* attacking miracles; in 1838 Emerson did the same in his notorious Harvard Divinity School address. In 1840, Parker issued a pamphlet under the pseudonym Levi Blodger defending Ripley against Andrews Norton, who had attacked both Ripley and Emerson in print. Norton was known as "the Pope of Unitarianism," who had earned his first reputation as a scathing critic of Calvinists at Andover and Princeton, and as a promoter of his own brand of "liberal Christianity." When he found himself outflanked on the left by pesky radicals, he was furious. Against Emerson, who had been his student at Harvard, he directed *A Discourse on the Latest Form of Infidelity* (1839). Emerson had claimed that all the universe is the only real miracle: "The word 'miracle' as pronounced by Christian churches gives a false impression. It is 'monster.' It is not one with the blowing clover and the falling rain."[11]

The Transcendentalists soon escaped from narrow theological controversy and followed Emerson's discursive lead into belles lettres. They published poetry, social tracts, translations, and nature meditations. They were a group of free spirits who did not organize a formal movement. The Transcendental Club was casual. It met about half a dozen times a year for four years. There were no rules. The members discussed the things they were writing about or exploring, and they were bright enough and diverse enough that Sydney Ahlstrom could claim "the publications of the club members would alone provided an outline for a literary history of the period" (A 600).

Robert Richardson says, "A list of the people who attended reads like a who's who of the liberal intellectuals of the time."[12] People drifted in and out. There were regular attendants, like Theodore Parker, Henry David Thoreau, and Margaret Fuller, and more sporadic visitors like the historian George Bancroft or the future Catholic Isaac Hecker. Women were welcomed—not only Margaret Fuller, but Elizabeth Hoar, Sarah Ripley, Sarah Clarke, and Elizabeth Peabody. The two dozen or so people who moved in this orbit for four years had an amazing impact on the culture.

They extended their reach in 1840, when they began publishing *The Dial*, a journal for their own writings and those of others who shared their insights. It was edited for the first two years by Margaret Fuller, then for the last two by Emerson, with the help of Elizabeth Peabody. Though these thoroughbreds were not liable to run in harness with each other, they did have a "cult of friendship [that] these New Englanders were collectively drawing from Goethe, Bettina [von Armin], and de Stael."[13] The 1840s, as we shall see, was a time of burgeoning "voluntary associations," and the different drives of the Transcendentalists led them to dream of great new transformative organizations.

As Robert Richardson argues, it was a period like the 1960s for radical dreams of changing the world. Margaret Fuller said that her fellows "enjoyed the large plans of the universe which were unrolled."[14] Emerson wrote to his friend Carlyle in England: "We are all a little wild here with numberless projects of social reform. Not a reading man but has a draft of a new community in his waistcoat pocket. I am gently mad myself."[15] In this heady atmosphere, even Emerson, an anti-organization man if there ever was one, considered launching a Transcendentalist free university "without charter, diploma, corporation, or steward." Emerson would teach literature, Parker religious history, Alcott psychology, and Hedge poetry. "What Emerson called 'our university' was one expression of the communitarian impulse that was felt all over America in the early and middle 1840s."[16]

Emerson's social schemes rapidly evanesced, but other Transcendentalists were more activist. Two communes hived off from the movement—George Ripley's Brook Farm and Bronson Alcott's Fruitlands—but they died from a lack of firm rooting in economic fact. Transcendentalists were more effective in their opposition to slavery, following the lead of Theodore Parker as he resisted the Fugitive Slave Act and supported John Brown. Orestes Brownson was an early labor advocate and organizer. Elizabeth Peabody, a follower of the educator Horace Mann, was active in the Kindergarten movement, an important liberal project of the time, and so was Bronson Alcott. Margaret Fuller, with friends she assembled at her home meetings called Conversations, was a powerful early feminist, influencing Emily Dickinson, Louisa May Alcott, and Edith Wharton. Thoreau is still the patron saint of environmentalists. There were few reform efforts of that time or later that did not have a Transcendentalist element in them.

Though the circle radiated energies in all directions and over a long span of time, it was constantly crumbling at the center. Emerson was no disciplinarian, and he could not have controlled such a high-strung company if he had wanted to be one. We can tune in to some of the tensions in the group from Hawthorne's fictional account of his time as a member of the Brook Farm commune, which gave him material for his novel *The Blithedale Romance*. The "Zenobia" of his tale is based on the plain but charismatic Margaret Fuller, who glowed with intelligence (and sometimes with mischief). The narrator of the novel, on first meeting her, feels her sexual force:

> In her quiet moods, she seemed rather indolent; but when
> really in earnest, particularly if there were a spice of bitter

feeling, she grew all alive, to her finger-tips. . . . Her free,
careless, generous modes of expression often had this effect of
creating images which, though pure, are hardly felt to be quite
decorous when born of a thought that passes between man and
woman. . . . One felt an influence breathing out of her, such as
we might suppose to come from Eve, when she was just made,
and her Creator brought her to Adam, saying—"Behold, here
is a woman!"[17]

The other main character, an improbable blacksmith named Hollingsworth, a gentle nurse to the narrator in his illness, is a fanatical philanthropist planning a home to cure the criminal mind, with whom Zenobia
falls in love, but who rejects her. Hawthorne depicts him as one of "those
men who have surrendered themselves to an over-ruling purpose":

They have an idol, to which they consecrate themselves high
priest, and deem it holy work to offer sacrifices of whatever is
most precious, and never once seem to suspect—so cunning
has the Devil been with them—that this false deity, in whose
iron features, immitigable to all the rest of mankind, they see
only benignity and love, is but a spectrum of the very priest
himself, projected upon the surrounding darkness. And the
higher and purer the original object, and the more unselfishly
it may have been taken up, the slighter is the probability that
they can be led to recognize the process by which godlike
benevolence has been debased into all-devouring egotism.[18]

Most critics have agreed that Zenobia is at least partly modeled on
Margaret Fuller.[19] Does Hollingsworth have a prototype? George Ripley was the principal figure at Brook Farm, and he certainly had schemes
for curing a sick society, but it is hard to find his traits in the novel.
Hubert H. Hoeltje thinks Theodore Parker is the source, since
Hawthorne's wife considered Parker a monomaniac.[20] But the fraught
relationship Hawthorne had observed in Fuller was with Emerson. He

watched them with fascination, and he privately described a desiccating idealism in Emerson.

Emerson had felt the sexual energy in Fuller and her friend Caroline Sturgis, who both said they wanted to be closer to him, and accused him of "inhospitality of soul" for not admitting them to greater intimacy. He recoiled from their effort, writing to Sturgis: "I dare not engage my peace so far as to make you necessary to me, when the first news I may hear is that you have found in some haven foreign to me your mate, and my beautiful castle is exploded to shivers."[21] Fuller was insistent, telling Emerson he did not have the courage to accept her devotion. "Did you not ask for a 'large, formidable nature'? But a beautiful foe I am not yet, to you. Shall I ever be?"[22] This is exactly how Zenobia talks of her rejection by Hollingsworth: "Will he never, in many an hour of darkness, need that proud intellectual sympathy which he might have had from me?" The relationship with Emerson is described by Fuller's biographer:

> Margaret [was] always dissatisfied with the inadequate capacity
> for friendship that she found in him. . . . Just as he was congrat-
> ulating himself on the good understanding that existed
> between himself and Margaret, she told him it was superficial
> and "commercial."[23]

Others besides Hawthorne felt that Emerson kept his treasured self-possession only by an emotional distance. In this hothouse atmosphere of temperamental intellectuals, there was competition for the affection of the leader. Fuller felt unappreciated. She wrote of herself: "Mine is a great nature, as yet in many regions an untroddden wild, full of wild beasts and reptiles, not yet tamed and classed, but also of rare butterflies, exquisite and great vegetation respondent to the sun and stars."[24] (One is reminded of Whitman's "I am large, I contain multitudes"—these egos all gulped helium.)

Walt Whitman was another man who had a case, as he put it later, of "Emerson-on-the-brain," but he overcame it. "Who wants to be any man's mere follower?"[25] Whitman was not only an early admirer of

Emerson, but a great beneficiary of his patronage. Whitman's early notes on him are effusive:

> He has what *none* else has; he does what none else does. He pierces the crusts that envelope the secrets of life. He joins on equal terms the few great sages and original seers. . . . His words shed light to the best souls; they do not admit of argument.[26]

F. O. Matthieson quotes Emerson's friend J. T. Trowbridge:

> [Whitman] freely admitted that he could never have written his poems if he had not first "come to himself," and that Emerson helped him to "find himself." I asked him if he thought he could have come to himself without that help. He said, "Yes, but it would have taken longer." . . . He gave his own characteristic expression to the process: "I was simmering, simmering, simmering; Emerson brought me to a boil."[27]

When Emerson sent Whitman warm praise for his just-published *Leaves of Grass,* Whitman rushed it into the newspapers, reprinted it as a broad-side, and distributed it everywhere, with electric results—so much that the letter became "a turning point in the public fortunes of *Leaves of Grass*."[28] David Reynolds says: "Emerson's letter came close to making Whitman. . . . Its glow lingers over *Leaves of Grass* even to this day."[29]

This suggests the power of Emerson's influence. It also makes the beneficiary of it sound ungrateful. As we shall see, Emerson remained a strong presence in Whitman's work. Yet we cannot expect lasting cama-raderie between the emitter of the "barbaric yawp" and the craftsman of precision-tooled aphorisms. Whitman became impatient with Emerson for not exemplifying the spontaneity he praised: "Of *power* he seems to have a gentleman's admiration—but in his inmost heart the grandest attribute of God and Poets is always subordinate to the octaves, conceits, polite kinds, and verbs."[30]

But for all these internal carpings, the Transcendentalists, born out of a succession of schisms, suffered no schism themselves. They were polite to one another in public, mutually supportive most of the time, genuinely interested in one another's work and reputation. The very lack of fixed dogma in Transcendentalism, its thin intellectual atmosphere, meant that most disagreements would be trivial and personal rather than beaten out in hard argument. The New Englanders annoyed each other at times, but in the process they irritated pearls out of each other.

16 | EMERSONIANS

THE ROMANTIC ERA in America has been described, on its literary side, in several ways. Van Wyck Brooks called it *The Flowering of New England*; F. O. Matthiesen called it *The American Renaissance*. These are mainly other names for Transcendentalism, which is not merely literary in its focus or regional in its effect. One could say that Transcendentalism became, for the intellectual strain in our history, *the* American religion of the nineteenth century. This is evident in America's nature mysticism, the frontier cult of a spiritual space, the resistance to dogma, the sense that religion must rise from within, not be imposed from without. This is not to say that Transcendentalism was a majority religion in the nineteenth century. It was not. Far more believers belonged to the revivalist strain of the time. This just re-enacts the split we so often find between Enlightened and populist religion in America.

Yet Transcendentalism was an authentic American faith because, for all its ethereal aspiration, it is not deracinated from the American past or present. Catherine Albanese notes that, despite their resistance to soulless "mechanization" in the circumambient culture, Transcendentalists shared in the nineteenth-century Americans' enthusiasm for energy, speed, and progress.[1] They thought of themselves as having a divine restlessness and forward momentum. Emerson wrote: "When a man rests, he stinks."[2] The nineteenth-century American was always "on the go."

But the most important cultural influence on them was their shared Puritan background—Emerson, after all, had seven generations of Congregational clergyman in his family line.[3] Though some of them sought mystical enlightenment from the East—Emerson and Fuller and Thoreau studying the Vedantic literature of ancient India—what Robert Louis Stevenson said of Thoreau could be said of them all: "It was his ambition to be an oriental philosopher, but he was always a very Yankee sort of oriental."[4]

Henry James said the same thing:

> Transcendentalism could only have sprouted in the soil
> peculiar to the general locality of which I speak—the soil of
> the old New England morality, gently raked and refreshed
> by an imported culture. The Transcendentalists read a great
> deal of French and German, made themselves intimate with
> George Sand and Goethe and many other writers; but the
> strong and deep New England conscience accompanied them
> in all their intellectual excursions.[5]

The group had the Puritan focus on self-scrutiny, a kind of rapt contemplation of their own souls. In James's words:.

> The doctrine of the supremacy of the individual to himself, of
> his originality and, as regards his own character, unique quality,
> must have had a great charm for people living in a society in
> which introspection, thanks to the want of other entertain-
> ment, played almost the part of a social resource.[6]

Of no one is that more true than of Emerson, who was the central figure in the whole movement. Though Parker was the most learned person in the circle, and Ripley the most activist, Alcott the most childlike, Thoreau the most delicate, Fuller the most media-savvy, of them all the most influential, not only on Transcendentalism but on American thought in general, was Emerson. In fact, he may be considered the quintessential American thinker of the nineteenth century—as, say, Jefferson was of the eighteenth century, or John Dewey of the twentieth century, tracing a development from Enlightened to Romantic to Pragmatic.

Emerson said he was all of the future and none of the past. But he could not escape the Puritan spell. It is found everywhere in his thought. To see this, we need only recall the basic tenets of New England's original Congregationalism.

1. The saved were given assurance of salvation.
2. This was done by direct action of God.
3. This led to an ultra-supernaturalism, the constant awareness of a manifest providence everywhere at work
4. Being saved was an entirely private and individual experience.
5. Therefore it was an experience opposed to hierarchy or direction by others.
6. The common experience of being saved set the regenerate apart from the unregenerate.
7. So the regenerate had a special "errand into the Wilderness" that was to transform history.

Each of these tenets has an equivalent in the Transcendentalism of Emerson and his allies.

1. The "assurance" of the saved becomes the "self-confidence" of Emerson's "Idealist": "In self-trust all the virtues are comprehended" (65).[7] "By it man is made the Providence to himself, dispensing good to his goodness, and evil to his sin" (77). "The height, the deity of man is to be self-sustained, to need no gift, no foreign force" (195).
2. This self-trust comes directly from the divine presence, creating a union with it, an equivalent of the Puritan's direct experience of God at

his conversion: "When I stand on the bare ground—my head bathed by the blithe air, and uplifted into infinite space—all mean egotism vanishes. I become a transparent eyeball; I am nothing; I see all; the currents of the Universal Being circulate through me. I am part or particle of God. The name of the nearest friend sounds then foreign and accidental; to be brothers, to be acquaintances, master or servant, is then a trifle and a disturbance. I am the lover of uncontained and immortal beauty" (10).

3. The Idealist, as opposed to the Materialist (as Emerson terms them), sees everything as miracle, sees behind the veil to the wonder everywhere instilled by Nature, by "the perpetual presence of the sublime." What might be called an ultra-naturalism does the former work of ultra-supernaturalism: "The Transcendentalist . . . believes in miracle, in the perpetual openness of the human mind to new influxes of light and power; he believes in inspiration and in ecstasy. He wishes that the spiritual principle should be suffered to demonstrate itself to the end, in all possible applications to the state of man, without the admission of anything unspiritual" (196). "If the stars should appear one night in a thousand years, how would men believe and adore; and preserve for many generations the remembrance of the city of God which had been shown! But every night come out these envoys of beauty, and light the universe with their admonishing smile" (9). "The world is a divine dream" (41). A newer, more benign providence of surprise and miracle leads Emerson to say that "nature's dice are always loaded" (27).

4. Being saved was private and personal. "Everything that tends to insulate the individual—to surround him with barriers of natural respect, so that each man shall feel the world is his, and man shall treat with man as a sovereign state with a sovereign state—tends to true union as well as greatness" (70).

5. The antihierarchical self-government of the Puritans became the radical originality of the Transcendentalist. "Let me admonish you, first of all, to go alone; to refuse the good models, even those which are sacred in the imagination of men, and dare to love God without mediator or veil. . . . Yourself a newborn bard of the Holy Ghost, cast behind you all conformity" (88–89). "Truly speaking, it is not instruction but

provocation that I can receive from another soul. What he announces, I must find true in me or wholly reject, and on his word or as his second, be he who he may, I can accept nothing. On the contrary, the absence of this primary faith is the presence of degradation" (79).

6. The separateness of the saved becomes the separateness of the Idealists: "The good, by affinity, seek the good; the vile by affinity seek the vile. Thus of their own volition souls proceed into heaven, into hell" (77). The unregenerate have lost the light: "When simplicity of character and the sovereignty of ideas is broken up by the prevalence of secondary desires—the desire of riches, of pleasure, of power, and of praise—and duplicity and falsehood take the place of simplicity and truth, the power over nature as an interpreter of will is, in a degree, lost" (22). Even the strength of the community came from that of the individuals composing it, be they the saved Puritans or the Idealistic individuals: "The wise and just man will always feel that he stands on his own feet; that he imparts strength to the state, not receives security from it; and that if all went down he and such as he would quite easily combine in a new and better constitution. Every great and memorable community has consisted of formidable individuals who, like the Roman or the Spartan, lent his own spirit to the state and made it great" (227–28).

7. The errand into the Wilderness becomes the Manifest Destiny of "Young America." The United States, as the first child of the Enlightenment, is free of the old habits and structures that blinkered men in the past. It is born of revolution, and "wherever a [real] man comes, there is revolution" (806). America has fresh land and forests that revive the spirit: "I think we must regard the *land* as a commanding and increasing power on the citizenry, the sanative and Americanizing influence, which promises to disclose new virtues for ages to come" (216–17). Emerson had "a premonition that here shall laws and institutions exist on some scale of proportion to the majesty of nature" (217).

Emerson had resigned from the ministry because he did not know how, in good conscience, to administer the sacrament. But he found a way in his new system.

I dreamed that I floated at will in the great Ether, and I saw this world floating also not far off, but diminished to the size of an apple. Then an angel took it in his hand and brought it to me and said, "This must thou eat." And I ate the world.[8]

Emerson's Eucharist was an absorption of the cosmos into himself. Walt Whitman consumed the world in a similar way, to sing his "song of myself." Whitman's words are Emersonian:

Read these leaves in the open air every season of every year of your life, re-examine all you have been told at school or church or in any book, dismiss whatever insults your own soul, and your very flesh shall be a great poem.[9]

AMERICAN SPACE

ONE OF the themes of the Transcendentalists, as of Whitman, was that America is a new thing, a spacious and special place whose very physical scale energizes the spirit. Whitman wrote in the introduction to *Leaves of Grass*:

The United States themselves are essentially the greatest poem. In the history of the earth hitherto the largest and most stirring appear tame and orderly to their ampler largeness and stir . . . the push of its perspective spreads with crampless and flowing breadth and showers its prolific and splendid extravagance. . . . The largeness of nature or the nation were monstrous without a corresponding largeness and generosity of the spirit of the citizen. . . . [The American bard] responds to his country's space, he incarnates its geography and natural life and rivers and lakes. . . . When the long Atlantic coast stretches longer and the Pacific coast stretches longer he easily stretches with them

north or south. . . . To him enter the essence of the real things
and past and present events—over the enormous diversity of
temperature and agriculture and mines.[10]

There is the root of Hart Crane's line that "leaps from Far Rockaway
to Golden Gate"—of all the sighs toward the frontier, toward the West
as a liberating force. Even Emerson, who was more urban than rural,
knew the power of Thoreau's release into sylvan peace, of the agrarian
dreams of Brook Farm and Fruitlands. He spoke of American space as a
spiritual event:

> The land is the appointed remedy for whatever is false and
> fantastic in our culture. The continent we inhabit is to be
> physic and food for our mind, as well as our body. The land,
> with its tranquilizing sanative influences is to repair the errors
> of a scholastic and traditional education, and bring us into just
> relations with men and things. The habit of living in the
> presence of these invitations of natural wealth is not inoper-
> ative; and this habit, combined with the moral sentiment
> which, in the recent years, has interrogated every institution,
> usage, and law, has naturally, given a strong direction to the
> wishes and aims of active young men to withdraw from the
> cities and cultivate the soil.[11]

Emerson fought off Margaret Fuller's call to leave little Concord for
busy Boston:

> Whatever events in progress shall do to disgust men with cities,
> and infuse into them the passion for country life and country
> pleasures, will render a service to the whole face of this
> continent, and will further the most poetic of all the occupations
> of real life, the bringing out by art the native but hidden graces
> of the landscape.[12]

The Transcendentalists fomented a sense of nature as a divine force. But even here they were true to a Puritan heritage. It is a canard that the Puritans had no aesthetic instinct. It is true that their grim biblical ban on most graven images was inhibiting, but that probably made them all the more alert to the beauty of unadorned nature. Jonathan Edwards had a fine sense of nature's majesty:

> When we are delighted with flowery meadows and gentle
> breezes of wind, we may consider that we only see the
> emanation of the sweet benevolence of Jesus Christ; when we
> behold the fragrant rose and lily, we see his love and purity.
> So the green trees and fields, and singing of birds, are the
> emanations of his infinite joy and benignity; the easiness and
> naturalness of trees and vines are shadows of his infinite
> beauty and loveliness; the crystal rivers and murmuring
> streams have the footsteps of his sweet grace and beauty. . . .
> That beauteous light with which the world is filled on a clear
> day is a lively shadow of his spotless holiness and happiness,
> and delight in communicating himself.[13]

Where Edwards saw Jesus shining through nature, Transcendentalists saw pantheist Spirit. But it both cases, what they saw was divine. Even the judge of Salem witches, Samuel Sewall, looked on God's handiwork with an awe at its beauty, and recorded it in one magnificent sentence:

> As long as Plum Island shall faithfully keep the commanded
> post, notwithstanding all the hectoring winds and hard blows
> of the proud and boisterous ocean; as long as any salmon or
> sturgeon shall swim in the streams of Merrimac, or any perch
> or pickerel in Crane Pond; as long as the sea fowl shall know
> the time of their coming, and not neglect seasonally to visit the
> places of their acquaintance; as long as any cattle shall be fed
> with the grass growing in the Meadows, which do humbly bow

themselves before Turkey Hill; as long as any sheep shall walk
upon Old Town Hill, and from there shall pleasantly look
down upon the River Parker and the fruitful Marshes lying
beneath; as long as any free and harmless doves shall find a
white oak or other tree within the township, to perch or feed
or build a careless nest upon, and shall voluntarily present
themselves to perform the office of gleaners after barley
harvest; as long as Nature shall not grow old and dote, but shall
constantly remember to give the rows of Indian corn their
education by pairs—so long shall Christians be born there and,
being first made meet, shall from there be translated, to be
made partakers of the inheritance of the saints in light.[14]

Passages like those are a bridge that the Transcendentalists created
between the Puritans of their past and environmentalists like Rachel
Carson in the future.

Emerson presented the escape from imprisoning church doctrine as
a release from sermonizing enclosures out into the grandeur of nature:

I once heard a preacher who sorely tempted me to say I would
go to church no more. Men go, thought I, where they are wont
to go, else had no soul entered the temple in the afternoon. A
snow storm was falling around us. The snow storm was real; the
preacher merely spectral, and the eye felt the sad contrast in
looking at him, and then out of the window behind him, into
the beautiful meteor of the snow. He had lived in vain.[15]

This contrast between the dead word of the preacher and the living
gospel of nature is presented dramatically in the work of another student of Asian mysticism, Henry Adams. Adams in old age denied that he
had come under the influence of the Transcendentalists (though his
mother-in-law was one, and she published in *The Dial*).[16] But the worship
of energy, of a spiritual equivalent for the dynamo, bound him to what
Catherine Albanese calls the Transcendentalists' "kinetic" mystique.

The Transcendentalists spoke of spiritual energy as of rushing water, pure fountains, or crystalline springs.[17] In Adams's novel *Esther,* he gives us a heroine who demands authenticity in religion, and does not find it in the fashionable preacher Stephen Hazard, who woos her. Rather, she hears it in the roaring voice of American energy at Niagara Falls:

> She felt tears roll down her face as she listened to the voice
> of the waters and knew that they were telling her a different
> secret from any that Hazard could ever hear. "He will think it
> is the church talking." Sad as she was, she smiled as she thought
> that it was Sunday morning, and a ludicrous contrast flashed
> on her mind between the decorations of St. John's [Hazard's
> church], with its parterre of nineteenth century bonnets, and
> the huge church which was thundering its gospel under her
> eyes.[18]

A scientist friend who is arguing with her at the falls tries to say that truth is a vast thing to which the human spirit is only slowly growing up. She answers him in Transcendentalist mode:

> "Does that mean that the next world is a sort of great reservoir
> of truth, and that what is true in us just pours into it like
> raindrops?"
> "Well," said he, alarmed and puzzled, "the figure is not
> perfectly correct, but the idea is a little of that kind."
> "After all I wonder whether that may not be what Niagara
> had been telling me."

Esther had fled the church Hazard was building because it seemed so artificial, forced, and insincere to her. The story is based on the construction of Henry Hobson Richardson's Trinity Church in Boston's Copley Square. Adams considered that such a Romanesque importation, commissioned by his own cousin Philips Brooks, expressed nothing of the native American reality. It was a type of the inauthentic posturing that the churches had succumbed to. Emerson had seen the same thing, and wrote:

> I think no man can go with his thoughts about him into one of
> our churches without feeling that what hold the public worship
> had on men is gone, or going. It has lost its grasp on the
> affection of the good and the fear of the bad.[19]

Adams sees the same untenable pose in the American minister:

> The strain of standing in a pulpit is great. No human being
> ever yet constructed was strong enough to offer himself long as
> a light to humanity without showing the effect on his
> constitution. Buddhist saints stand for years silent, on one leg,
> or with arms raised about their heads; but the limbs shrivel and
> the mind shrivels with the limbs. Christian saints have found it
> necessary from time to time to drop their arms and to walk on
> their legs, but they do it with a sort of apology or defiance, and
> sometimes do it, if they can, by stealth. [20]

This awkwardness may explain why America has not developed a strong indigenous art style for religion. The only deep and moving *body* of religious art is the Negro spiritual. In other areas, America uneasily borrows from Europe—in Romanesque and Gothic cathedrals, in the stained glass of John LaFarge, or the Holy Land watercolors of Henry Ossawa Tanner. There have been individual religious works of genius—the synagogues of Louis Sullivan or Frank Lloyd Wright. But in general Americans seem to feel like John Wayne, who reportedly said, "I don't much like God when he gets under a roof." Our religious sentiments are expressed by the celebrants of majestic nature—the paintings of the Hudson Valley School or the Luminists, the photographs of Ansel Adams, the bleached landscapes of Georgia O'Keeffe, the seascapes of Albert Pinkham Ryder. Our cathedrals are Yosemite Valley and the Grand Canyon, Monument Valley and the great sequoiahs. This American religion was given us by the

Transcendentalists, by a sensibility formed in large part, even when we do not realize what we are responding to, by the great American thinker Emerson and the great American poet Whitman and the great American naturalist Thoreau. Their heirs are people like John Muir, the founder of the Sierra Club, or Rachel Carson, or Anne Morrow Lindbergh.

LEFT EMERSONIANS

T HE TRANSCENDENTALISTS generally prided themselves on being above politics. They transcended anything so grubby. Thoreau refused to vote as well as to pay taxes. Emerson, after leaving a political meeting, felt he had to be "shampooed and in all other ways aired and purified."[21] As we saw in the last chapter, the Transcendentalists did interest themselves in some high-minded reforms. Bronson Alcott and George Ripley tried out communal living on the Fourier plan, and the group was interested in educational reforms. But in general *The Dial* preferred metaphysics to economics. The group disapproved of slavery, but thought the denouncers of it rather vulgar. Margaret Fuller was scornful of the abolitionist firebrand William Lloyd Garrison:

> While praising the editor's motives, she complained that he had
> "spoiled his mind" with denunciations and, having screamed so
> long at deaf people, could no longer "pitch his voice on a key
> agreeable to common ears."[22]

The great exception to this was Theodore Parker, as committed an abolitionist as could be found, and eventually he brought his fellow Transcendentalists around to his views. The catalyst, oddly, was John Brown's raid and execution. These people who thought Garrison vulgar were able to accept the bloody violences of Brown. Perhaps it was the very quixotic nature of his enterprise that appealed to them. They preferred lofty impossibilities to the compromise and gradualism of ordinary politics. In any case, they became effusive eulogists of Brown. Emerson wrote of Brown's courage in facing death:

> What a contagion belongs to it. It finds its own with magic
> affinity all over the land. . . . Everything feels the new breath,
> excepting the dead old doting politicians, whom the trumpet of
> resurrection cannot wake.[23]

Brown, Emerson felt, made "the gallows as glorious as the cross."[24]

Once roused, Emerson became wholehearted in the antislavery cause, even making amends to Garrison, whom he now called "the Cassandra that has foretold all that has befallen us."[25] He also shed his initial skepticism about Lincoln as just another politician—by 1862 he was greeting him as an angelic dictator:

> Government must not be a parish clerk, a justice of the peace.
> It has, of necessity, in any crisis of the state, the absolute
> powers of a dictator. The existing administration is entitled
> to the utmost candor. It is to be thanked for its almost angelic
> virtue compared with an executive experience with which we
> are familiar.[26]

The dreamers had become radicals.

RIGHT EMERSONIANS

IT IS a mark of Emerson's pervasive influence on American culture that he is a hero to the Right as well as the Left. I knew an editor at the conservative *National Review* who treated his writings as if they were the Bible. The Right reads his praise of self-reliance as a license for the competitive actions of the "self-made man." If John Muir expressed one aspect of Emerson's legacy, Richard Nixon expressed another. Nixon, the neopuritanical striver, had a romantic image of himself as "the man in the arena," digging deep into his own psychic resources. This was another updating of Puritan values, which came down to the twentieth century through many channels, to the capitalists as well as to the Transcendentalists, driving them in very different directions.

Sometimes the Romantic vision of Prometheus defying the universe shrinks to the luck-and-pluck formulas of Horatio Alger. Here is Nixon on the exhilaration of facing crises:

> Two of the most important lessons I have learned from going through the fire of decision is [*sic*] that one must know himself, be able to recognize his physical reactions under stress for what they are, and that he must never worry about the necessary and even healthy symptoms incident to creative activity.[27]

This is the self-celebratory language of CEO memoirs, telling us how the lone individual made his way to the top. It might embarrass Emerson to recognize these men as his descendants. They may be bastard children, bred on a business-culture mother, but they are still his children.

So, less evidently, are the soul-cure and self-help gurus, from Aimee Semple McPherson to Dale Carnegie to Oprah Winfrey. Emerson has a lot to answer for—which is the price, perhaps, of being a central American thinker.

VI | RELIGION OF THE HEART

17 | THE SECOND GREAT AWAKENING

IN THE FIRST HALF of the nineteenth century, while Transcendentalism was arching over the country like a high and beautiful rainbow,
the other American religion was roaring through the land like a gulley
washer. This was what is now called the Second Great Awakening. Historian Mark Noll says it might also be called the Methodist explosion,
since that became America's leading form of religion, almost overnight.
"To the extent that the United States ever experienced a Second Great
Awakening, Methodist expansion was it."[1]

The Methodists were part of a general surge of Evangelicalism that
occurred in the first part of the nineteenth century, when the country
was becoming egalitarian for the first time. Transcendentalists, influential as they were in more rarified intellectual circles, were elitists, not
likely to command a mass following in this period of rough and rising
democracy.

The established churches, Episcopalian and Congregational, were
elitist in organization and membership. At the end of the eighteenth
century these were the major denominations, and Jefferson predicted

that the future belonged to their more liberal Unitarian versions. But he was wrong. The predominance of the Anglicans and Congregationalists faded as the Methodists and Baptists grew exponentially. By 1860, Evangelicals made up at least 85 percent of the American church population.

> The religious wonders of the age were the more aggressively evangelical churches—Presbyterians advancing at or slightly above the [rapid] rate of the general population, Baptists and the new Disciples/Christian Churches far above, and the Methodists off the chart in a class all of their own.[2]

This surge of churches is astonishing, given the multiplication of the whole population: "The population of the United States, less than half of England's in 1775, was growing three times faster than England's in the early 1800s. By 1845, Americans outnumbered the English by five million."[3]

The true religionizing of America began two decades after the Revolution. But when it did begin, it happened at a whirlwind rate.

> The eighteen hundred Christian ministers serving in 1775 swelled to nearly forty thousand by 1845. The number of preachers per capita more than tripled; the colonial legacy of one minister per fifteen hundred inhabitants became one per five hundred. This greater preaching density was remarkable, given the spiraling population and the restless movement of peoples to occupy land beyond the reach of any church organization.[4]

From 1800 to 1860, the Methodists went from 65,000 to 1,744,000 members. (This—like most church attendance numbers from the time, when records were irregularly kept or did not count casual attendees— probably understates the growth.) This was not merely because the whole population was growing. Conversions outraced the general demographics, and they occurred in the relatively new forms of piety. "From nowhere, in a period of very rapid general growth in church affiliation and over a remarkably short span of time, Methodism had become the most pervasive form of Christianity in the United States."[5]

METHODISTS

MARK NOLL uses a vivid comparison to illustrate the massive change. In this period, the United States Post Office was by far the largest federal agency, larger even than the combined federal military services, except in the War of 1812. Yet it was dwarfed by the new evangelical associations.

> By the 1850s the Methodists by themselves—joined together through an interlocking system of personal and epistolary contact—had constructed almost as many churches as there were post offices and employed almost as many ministers as there were postal workers. The largest evangelical denominations were each raising almost as much money per year as the postal service took in. Considered together, the evangelical churches employed nearly double the personnel, maintained nearly twice as many facilities, and raised at least three times the money as the Post Office. Moreover, the churches delivered their message to more people in more places than the postal service delivered letters and newspapers . . . the people of the United States were hearing several more times the number of Methodist sermons each year than they received pieces of mail.[6]

In fact, by 1840, Methodists "were, after the federal government, the nation's largest organization of any kind."[7]

What can explain such growth? Obviously there were large social forces favoring a voluntarist, antihierarchical, largely lay-led, mobile, democratic, indeed populist form of religion. But credit should not be withheld from the strenuous itinerant Methodist preachers, "circuit riders," who braved all conditions in all places to reach previously unchurched people on the frontier or in fields or in small towns. They thought of themselves as the new Saint Pauls, forever traveling and on fire with the Spirit. They went not only from town to town but from camp to camp and even from door to door with the most "hands-on" kind of spiritual exhortation imaginable. "During a particularly ferocious storm it used to be said, 'There's nobody out tonight but crows and Methodist preachers.'"[8]

Isaiah Berlin once casually remarked that he saw nothing Romantic about Methodist preachers. He was not thinking of those who rode out in the early days. Consider, for instance, Lorenzo "Crazy" Dow, a slender reed of a man whose voice was an almost soprano howl, one so frail, so asthmatic, so epileptic, that he could convincingly fake his own death in the middle of a sermon to warn people they should always be prepared for the afterlife—yet year after year he traveled throughout America and England, probably preaching to more people than any other man during his lifetime.[9]

A soberer but certainly no less astonishing man is the Methodists' first and greatest American bishop, Francis Asbury. He brings into focus the amazing fact that Methodism became the great American religion despite the fact that the Methodists' leadership opposed the American Revolution. Their founder, John Wesley, had come to America in 1736, but he left before the Revolution and he opposed it in his writings. The missionaries he sent there withdrew at the time of Independence, since the British Methodists would not split with the Anglican Church. Asbury was the only one sent by Wesley who stayed—and even he refused to take an oath of allegiance to the Revolutionary government or to become (ever) an American citizen.

Like other Methodists, Asbury was hounded as a Loyalist. Yet he survived the Revolution—preaching all through it—and set up the American Methodist Episcopal Church, distinct from the English Wesleyans. This occurred at a Baltimore "Christmas Conference" in 1784. Though made a bishop, Asbury did not indulge in any pomp of office, but kept tirelessly riding the circuit. When age and illness made it impossible for him to do this on horseback, he kept moving in a buggy. He had no residence, no family, nothing to clog or slow him. He was truly Pauline. One of his great followers, Peter Cartwright, explained Asbury's and his own success:

> The Presbyterians and other Calvinistic branches of the
> Protestant Church used to contend for an educated ministry,
> for pews, for instrumental music, for a congregational or state-
> salaried ministry. The Methodists universally opposed these
> ideas; and the illiterate Methodist preachers actually set the
> world on fire (the American world at least) while they were
> lighting their matches.[10]

The circuit riders had such a hard life that they suffered from an early death rate, yet by 1828 over twenty-five hundred had served in what Nathan Hatch calls "this stern fraternity."[11] If any found they could not keep up their itinerancy, they were stripped of full membership in the Methodist Connection. Asbury imposed a discipline that kept the riders a "youth cadre." In 1784 the Methodists had adopted his policy:

> Our grand plan, in all its parts, leads to an itinerant ministry.
> Our bishops are traveling bishops. All the different orders
> which compose our conferences are employed in the traveling
> line; and our local preachers are, in some degree, traveling
> preachers. Everything is kept moving as far as possible; and
> we will be bold to say that, next to the grace of God, there is
> nothing like this for keeping the whole body alive from the
> center to the circumference; and for the continual extension
> of that circumference on every hand.[12]

Asbury played a key role in another major part of the Second Great Awakening, the evangelization of black Americans. A black preacher, Richard Allen, was at his founding Christmas Conference in 1784. Allen was an ex-slave Asbury had taken with him on his rides. Allen preached to both black and to mixed audiences, and in 1785 he was a traveling partner with another key Methodist founder, Richard Whatcoat.[13] In 1787, Allen and another black preacher, Absalom Jones, founded the Free African Society in Philadelphia. When blacks were segregated in the Philadelphia churches, these men set up two black churches in 1794. Jones, who had assisted an Episcopalian bishop, William White, formed Saint Thomas African Episcopal Church. Allen set up Bethel Church.

Asbury, who dedicated Bethel Church, ordained Allen a Methodist deacon. When white Methodists tried to take over Bethel Church, the Pennsylvania Supreme Court ruled that it was the property of the blacks—it was the Dedham case situation, but with the Dartmouth case outcome. In 1816, Allen called a Christmas Conference of his own, and sixty representatives of five black churches created the African Methodist Episcopal (AME) Church, which in 1899 W. E. B. DuBois called "by long odds the vastest and most remarkable product of American Negro civilization."[14]

The Second Great Awakening witnessed the rise of black churches everywhere. In the South, after the itinerant preachers had reached them, racists tried to deny them church membership—which to some extent backfired. When blacks had to tend to their own religious needs, they created "the black church as the first public institution over which blacks exercised control."[15] Preachers in these churches developed their own style of leadership, able to mobilize a community with few other resources. W. E. B. DuBois called the black preacher "the most unique personality developed by the Negro on American soil—a leader, a politician, an orator, a 'boss,' an intriguer, an idealist."[16] The community was generating an original form of leadership that would culminate in Dr. King.

DO-IT-YOURSELF RELIGION

THE METHODISTS, like other Evangelicals, were not simply loners. They rode assigned networks, strategically laid out, and they used camp meetings for their revivals. The camp meeting became an enormous part of American life, following on the famous Cane Ridge Meeting of 1801, which attracted a reported twenty thousand attendees to a remote state (Kentucky) whose largest city held only two thousand at the time. This most famous revival had all the emotional convulsions that would later be more sporadically observed at similar events—swooning, screaming, barking, "jerking." Future stars of revivalism—Barton Stone, who had called the meeting, Peter Cartwright, Lorenzo "Crazy" Dow— were present at Cane Ridge, observing and learning.[17] The rituals of revival were developed all through this period, making it a highly developed art form. Historians have often noted how the revival set styles of America's political campaigning

> The hullabaloo surrounding the political campaigns of the
> era—the torchlight parades, the tent pitched outside town, the
> urgent call for a commitment—was borrowed by political
> campaigners from the revival preachers. Far from being
> irrelevant distractions or mere recreation, the evangelical
> techniques of mass persuasion that we associate with the
> campaigns of 1840 and after actually provide a clue to the
> moral meaning of antebellum politics. Even the practice of
> holding national conventions was borrowed by the parties from
> the cause-oriented benevolent associations. Anti-Masonry,
> which held the first presidential nominating convention in 1831,
> was both an evangelical reform movement (a "blessed spirit" to
> its supporters) and a political party.[18]

In the scattered conditions of the frontier, hiving instincts brought people together for spontaneous effusions that broke down barriers between denominations, between clerical status and laypeople, between preachers and audience. As blacks took over their own religion in the South, so whites did on the frontier. There were too few churches for people to rely on just one venue or one denominational ministry. It was a time for do-it-yourself religion. Later revivals would be criticized as individualistic, interested only in the single person's conversion; but they began as an intensely communal experience.

The camp meeting set the pattern for credentialing Evangelical ministers. They were validated by the crowd's response. Organizational credentialing, doctrinal purity, personal education were useless here—in fact, some educated ministers had to make a pretense of ignorance. The minister was ordained from below, by the converts he made. This was an even more democratic procedure than electoral politics, where a candidate stood for office and spent some time campaigning. This was a spontaneous and instant proclamation that the Spirit accomplished. The do-it-yourself religion called for a make-it-yourself ministry.

The camp meeting was just one manifestation of a general urge to form spontaneous groups in the early nineteenth century, the "voluntary societies" Tocqueville described as an important glue in this country with a minimal government. John Murrin aptly called the government of the period "a midget institution in a giant land."[19] This was a time of mission societies, Bible-distribution clubs, temperance groups, antislavery societies, benevolent organizations (for the orphaned, the blind, the deaf), reading programs, Sunday schools, prison reformers, hospital organizers, women's rights groups. The combined impact of all these associations was immense. As Mark Noll puts it:

> Comparisons are again illuminating. From its beginning to 1818,
> the United States government spent nearly $3.6 million on
> internal improvements (roads, canals, communications). In that
> same span of years the thirteen leading benevolent societies,
> overwhelmingly evangelical in constituency and purpose,
> spent over $2.8 million to further their goals. No broad-based
> movement, not even the political parties, brought together so
> many people committed to so much social construction as did
> the national meetings of the benevolent societies.[20]

There were reasons both economic and psychological for this boom in social clubbing. The loneliness of the frontier, minimal government, social dislocation, the abrasions of industrial society, capitalism's competitive individuality—all these needed some countervailing social cushion. Where social needs were great and social resources not supplied, people had to take on tasks voluntarily. As Tocqueville said: "Where there is a new undertaking, at the head of which you would expect to see in France the government and in England some great lord, in the United States you are sure to find an association."[21] Nothing more connects this development with Romanticism than the brotherhoods and sisterhoods of these groups, both expressing and creating what Tocqueville calls "habits of the heart."[22] In such associations, "Feeling and ideas are renewed, the heart expands, and the human spirit develops only through the reciprocal action of human beings on one another."[23]

Isaiah Berlin should not have made a snap judgment about Methodists as non-Romantic. Transcendentalism was Romantic in its mysticism, but it could not express some aspects of Romanticism as the Methodists could—especially the folk element, the *Volk* of the German Romantics.. The New England sages did not speak for the "common man." America would reflect a very pale and partial Romanticism if the Transcendentalists were its only exemplars. Johann Gottfried Herder expressed another side of Romanticism—regard for the wisdom of the race, the communal myths and ballads, the genius of a nation. The German Romantics were not aristocrats, and their Enlightened enemies were.

> [In the Enlightenment] Montesquieu was a baron, Condorcet was a marquis. Mably was an abbé, Condillac was an abbé, Buffon become a count, Volney was well-born, d'Alembert was the illegitimate son of a nobleman. Helvetius was not noble, but his father had been doctor to Madame [de Pompadour] and he was a billionaire. Baron Grimm and Baron d'Holbach were two Germans who came to live in Paris, one from near Bohemia and one from the Rhineland. There were a number of other abbés: the abbé Galiani was the Secretary at the Neapolitan Embassy; the abbé Morellet and the abbé Raynal were of good origin. Even Voltaire came from the lesser gentry. Only Diderot and Rousseau were commoners, real commoners. Diderot really did come from the poor. Rousseau was a

Swiss, and therefore does not count in this category. They were
no doubt oppositional, but they were oppositional against
persons who came from the same class as themselves. They
went to salons, they glittered, they were persons of high polish,
great education, splendid prose style, and a generous and
handsome outlook on life.[24]

It was far otherwise with the Germans who launched the Romantic
movement, who were comparative outsiders, and proud of that fact:

Lessing, Kant, Herder, Fichte were all very humbly born.
Hegel, Schelling, Schiller, Hölderlin were lower middle-class.
Goethe was a rich bourgeois but attained to a proper title only
later. Only Kleist and Novalis were what would in those days
be called country gentlemen.[25]

In America, the Second Great Awakening was decidedly a movement
of the "common man," consciously so, as we saw from Peter Cartwright's
description of the circuit rider. Gordon Wood accurately says: "As the
Republic became democratized, it became evangelized."[26] The social
improvement groups were a product of the period's growing egalitarian-
ism and a producer of it. Tocqueville presented this as a fulfillment of
the Romantics' yearning for *Bruderschaft* and *Freundschaft*:

When ranks in a nation are roughly equal and everyone
thinks and feels in almost the same way, then each person
can judge everyone else's sensations in an instant; all he has to
do is cast a quick glance at himself. Hence there is no misery
that he cannot readily conceive, or whose extent is not revealed
to him by a secret instinct. No matter if strangers or enemies
are involved; his imagination instantly puts him in their place.
His pity is thereby tinged with something personal, causing
him to suffer when the body of his fellow man is torn to
pieces.[27]

This is no doubt exaggerated, but it should be remembered that the Second Great Awakening overlapped what is known as the Era of Good Feelings after the War of 1812, and it extended into the anti-institutional Jackson era. Tocqueville marveled at how little formal government Americans had, and it is true that the myriad social associations did not expect or ask for governmental support or approval. Church and state were separate at this time because the churches were more vital and powerful than the state. Laissez-faire and social bonding partly converged as people tried to solve problems, on their own initiative but jointly:

> Americans of all ages, all conditions, and all minds are
> constantly joining together in groups. In addition to commer-
> cial and industrial association in which everyone takes
> part, there are associations of a thousand other kinds: some
> religious, some moral, some grave, some trivial, some quite
> general and others quite particular, some huge and others tiny.
> Americans associate to give fetes, to found seminaries, to
> build inns, to erect churches, to distribute books, and to send
> missionaries to the antipodes. This is how they create hospitals,
> prisons, and schools. . . . When Americans have a feeling or
> idea they wish to bring to the world's attention, they will
> immediately seek out others who share the feeling or idea and,
> if successful in finding them, join forces. From that point on,
> they cease to be isolated individuals and become a power to be
> reckoned with, whose actions serve as an example, a power that
> speaks, and to which people listen.[28]

ESCAPING DOCTRINE

THE ANTI-INSTITUTIONAL emphases of frontier Methodism meant that elements in it continually went their own way. It would be a very "splintery" movement, as communities formed their own view of the best way to follow Jesus. Some wanted to take the return to primitive

Christianity further than most Methodists had so far done. The presbytery of elders, which had historically been a rejection of hierarchy, priesthood, and bishops, was too formal for Barton Stone, the pastor at Cane Ridge. Stone was one of six signers of a document his friend Richard McNemar wrote in 1804, *The Last Will and Testament of the Springfield Presbytery.* With the presbytery gone, Christians would not be Presbyterian Christians or Baptist Christians but just plain Christians.

This movement resembled the actions of other former Presbyterians who called themselves just "Disciples of Christ." The Disciples were formed by three men from Scotland, Thomas Campbell, his son Alexander Campbell, and Alexander's convert Walter Scott. In the 1820s, the Christians and the Disciples began to cooperate, and in the 1830s they merged. The "Campbellites" and "Stonites" were plentiful in Mark Twain's Hannibal as he was growing up—in fact, his best friend, Will Bowen, was Barton Stone's grandson, and Stone died in his Hannibal home in 1844. As a boy printer, Twain met Alexander Campbell and set one of his sermons in type.[29] The camp meeting in chapter 20 of *Huckleberry Finn* is a takeoff on Campbellite revivals.

The Disciples of Christ were, in turn, part of a Holiness Movement that expanded on John Wesley's "perfectionism," taking Jesus' words to heart: "Be perfect, then, as your heavenly Father is perfect" (Matthew 5.48). This primitivism was called a Restoration of the original church. It would take many forms—from Phoebe Palmer's movement for women ministers to schismatic Methodisms (the Wesleyan Church or the Free Methodist Church)—and, later on, to the Church of the Nazarene and various Pentecostal groups.

Such frontier movements upset the more traditional guardians of doctrine in the East. Not that the two were ever entirely separate. The Yale revivals, conducted by President Timothy Dwight at the dawning of the new century, created a link with the revivals of the South and West. Yale sponsored the New Haven Theology to which Evangelicals paid at least lip service. It was a Calvinism that made room for freedom of the will—a necessary precondition for the do-it-yourself religions of the West. After all, when a preacher asked that people make a decision for Jesus, the power to choose was essential. But even those who sub-scribed to the New Haven Theology sat very loose to it.

Doctrine was not a chief concern, even for most academics of the period. Congregationalism had been absorbed into Presbyterianism through most of the land, since a Plan of Union in 1801 called for an interchange of pulpits and personnel. (The amalgamate has been called "Presbygationalism.") Serious schools of theology were set up in the West—Lane Theological Seminary, Oberlin College, and Knox College. But they were focused on practical religion and reform—abolition being one of their causes—and their leaders were considered heretics by the remaining strict Calvinists. Yale itself was considered heretical by Bennett Tyler, a former president of Dartmouth, who formed the Theological Institute of Connecticut to fight Yale's "infidelities" (A 420).

CHARLES GRANDISON FINNEY (1792–1875)

WHEN LYMAN BEECHER, a disciple of Yale's Nathaniel Taylor, went to establish Lane Theological Seminary in Cincinnati, he was called heretical for his lax evangelizing ways. Then he accused Charles Grandison Finney of heresy for being even more latitudinarian than himself. In 1827, at a conference in New Lebanon, New York, Beecher said he would block Finney from bringing revivals into New England:

> You mean to come into Connecticut, and carry a streak of fire
> to Boston. But if you attempt it, as the Lord liveth, I'll meet
> you at the state line and call out all the artillerymen and fight
> every inch of the way to Boston, and then I'll fight you there.[30]

But there was no stopping Finney, the most famous evangelist of the time. Beecher himself had eventually to invite Finney into Boston. George Gale, later the founder of Knox College, had promoted Finney for Presbyterian ordination, and later regretted it.

Those who licensed Finney as a preacher recommended that he undergo further study. He later claimed that they offered to pay his way to Princeton Theological Seminary. But he thought the education conventional clergymen received would unfit him. "I plainly told them that I would not put myself under such an influence as they had been under; that I was confident they had been wrongly educated, and they were not ministers that met my ideal of what a minister of Christ should be."[31] He was blazing a trail for the college-shunning preachers who would follow him. "Finney was an ordained layman, and after him there would be no popular evangelist who was a graduate of a first-class university or seminary."[32] Despite this attitude, he was made the president of Oberlin College. He had a higher claim on God's call than did ministers who could read the Bible in its original languages, since he had saved more souls than any man alive. Even so, some of his fans feared he was giving in to the enemy: "Is there not danger of his turning into an intellectualist?"[33]

There was little danger of that. Finney had the highest credentials of the new Evangelical mission—sheer numbers of converts. He had amassed these by a series of innovations that his opponents attacked as the New Measures—prerevival campaigns of publicity, personal testimonies advertised, women's participation, long night sessions, cards signed by the converted (who could then be counted in competitive rankings of converted from each meeting). To top it all, there was the highly effective "anxious bench" up front for people not yet ready to give themselves to Christ, who sat as it were in a pressure cooker while the whole congregation turned up the heat of their fervent prayers for such sinners. Calling people up to the anxious seat was an important step in the development of the revival form. Earlier, people had been urged to show they were ready for conversion by holding up their hands or standing. The "decision for Christ" would become the climax of almost all later revivals, with the converted streaming forward toward the preacher. Finney wrote of his own invention:

When I had called them simply to stand up in the public congregation, I found this had had a very good effect, and so far as it went it answered the purpose for which it was intended. But after all I had felt for some time that something more was necessary to bring them out from among the mass of the ungodly to a pubic renunciation of their sinful ways, and a public committal of themselves to God.[34]

Finney, shrewd and charismatic, was the first man to make of revivals a carefully planned system. Little was to be left to the Spirit. Manipulation of the emotions was perfected. In Weberian terms, Finney routinized the charisma of the Second Great Awakening.

[A revival] is not a miracle, or dependent on a miracle, in any sense. It is a purely philosophical [methodical] result of the right use of the constituted means—as much so as any other effect produced by the application of means. . . . The right use of means for a revival, and a revival, is as philosophically sure as between the right use of means to raise grain, and a crop of wheat.[35]

Finney proudly compared his tactics to those of the political parties:

What do the politicians do? They get up meetings, circulate handbills and pamphlets, blaze away in the newspapers, send their ships about the streets on wheels with flags and sailors, send coaches all over town, with handbills, to bring people up to the polls; all to gain the attention to their cause and elect their candidates. . . . The object of our measures is to gain attention and you must have something new.[36]

Revivals had first influenced political conventions, and now—closing the circle—politics affected the revivals.

Of course, not just anyone can run such a campaign. Finney had important advantages:

His six-foot-two long-armed figure was magnetic and compelling. When preaching, he whirled his arms about; at

Troy, a colleague on the platform spent a nervous five minutes ducking as Finney, describing the Creation, flung world after world into space. In Rochester, in 1831, he was depicting the fall of the sinner to hell. His index finger stabbed at the ceiling, then curved downward, downward, and the back benches rustled as the crowd rose involuntarily to its feet to see the final disappearance.[37]

Finney had, as well, a virtuoso's voice, one that could crack like a whip or pour out syrupy persuasion. And he had a prophet's compelling gaze, "the most impressive eyes—except perhaps for John C. Calhoun's—in the portrait gallery of nineteenth-century America."[38] No wonder Richard Hofstadter opined that the star system was not born in Hollywood but on the sawdust trail of the revivalists. Finney set the mark for others to meet after him—Dwight Moody, Billy Sunday, Billy Graham. This is one of the legacies bequeathed us by an alternative Romanticism, taking up where Transcendentalism left off.

18 | SCHISMS OVER SLAVERY

THE CIVIL WAR was a religious war before it was a military war. The breakup of the nation at its core occurred when the largest Protestant churches could no longer remain united. A great blow ran like some historic cleaver through the Presbyterian, Methodist, and Baptist communities, dividing the country—religiously—into two nations. This happened in the 1830s and 1840s, decades before the military war began. Regional war was already under way.

The shock of this schism had not been expected. During the Second Great Awakening there had generally been good ecumenical relations between the Protestant sects. They attended the same revivals, went to each other's churches, and were beginning to downplay or forget doctrinal points of difference. They shared a conviction that America was a Protestant nation—one nation.

But the Era of Good Feelings did not last. President Jackson's terms (1829–37) were rancorous on several fronts—over dissolution of the Federal Bank, over Indian Removal, and especially over the tariffs of 1828 and 1832, which prompted South Carolina to pass a Nullification Bill. Jackson beat back the threat of secession with his own Force Bill, but bitterness had divided his own cabinet and estranged him from his native state.

There were other sources of enmity that struck closer to religion. America's chronic anti-Catholicism was mounting to meet the influx of Catholic immigrants. One of the areas of ecumenical agreement uniting the Protestant sects was their shared conviction that the Church of Rome was the enemy of their religion and therefore of the United States. I considered earlier Lyman Beecher's call for Protestants to settle and proselytize the West, to exclude Catholic influence there. In the 1830s a spate of spurious "memoirs" of salacious conduct in nuns' convents sold well and widely. (The most famous was *Awful Disclosoures of the Hotel Dieu Nunnery of Montreal, 1836*.) Reports of evil doings inside an Ursuline convent school in Charlestown, Massachusetts, led a mob to burn it to the ground in 1834.[1] In 1837, much of the Irish quarter in Boston was trashed and burned.[2]

In 1844, violence raged for several days in Philadelphia when Saint Michael's Church in a suburb and Saint Augustine's Church in the downtown area were burnt down.[3] Fires and intimidation were used against many Catholics in this period. Four men were killed in anti-Catholic riots in New Orleans. In Lawrence, Massachusetts, fifteen hundred nativists went on a rampage in the Irish workers' section of town, setting fires, destroying property, and beating those who resisted. Efforts were made to keep Irish Catholics from getting to the polls to vote. In Saint Louis, threats turned to action, two men died, and many were wounded.[4]

The anti-Catholic agitation would grow into the 1850s when the American Party (the "Know-Nothings") was formed. In 1854, the party won many state and local offices, and sent seventy-five members to Congress. In 1855, they continued their brief string of victories at the polls. In that same year, riots against Catholic voters in Louisville led to many injuries and twenty deaths as a rooming house was burnt up with boarders in it. A priest was stoned in the street.[5]

The souring mood of the time helps explains why thousands of people believed William Miller's prophecy that the Second Coming of Christ would occur on October 22, 1844. There was nothing new about eschatological predictions in American religion. But most of them had been of the optimist (Postmillennial) variety, the belief that God would bring history to its completion with the triumph of American-style free-dom around the world. In this vein, Jonathan Edwards had counted the setbacks to Catholic power as steps to the fulfillment of God's plan for the world. But Miller preached the less popular and pessimistic premil-lennial idea that the world as currently constituted was irredeemable except by God's punishing intervention—an idea that would become powerful in the twentieth century, but which went against the triumphal chiliasms of the early Republic.

SLAVERY

UNDER ALL these discontents, the deepest cause of unrest and panic was the growing crisis over slavery. There was a long-standing hope and determination in the United States to avoid the subject, one that dated from the drafting of the Constitution. The subject was too painful to be adverted to. Much of the modern world has shared this evasiveness where slavery is concerned, and not only with regard to America. One of the most popular and influential works on classical antiquity was Werner Jaeger's three-volume study of Greek culture, *Paideia*—which shied away entirely from the economic basis of ancient Greek society, the institution of slavery.[6] Jaeger was following the tradition of Victorian classicists, who avoided two topics in the ancient world, slavery and homosexuality.

It was becoming harder in the early nineteenth century to look away from slavery, that elephant in the living room. Abolitionists were attack-ing the institution as the most heinous kind of sin. That would not have had much effect if practical concerns had not kept thrusting unavoid-able decisions upon people—especially the issue of extending slavery into the West. Many hoped the explosive problem could be defused by the Missouri Compromise in 1820, admitting Missouri as a slave state but banning slavery in the rest of the Northwest Territory. But the conflict would not go away. Events kept obtruding it. Two years after the Com-promise, the slave revolt of Denmark Vesey panicked the South (as Nat Turner's uprising would in 1831). The struggle over tariffs started the

306 | HEAD AND HEART

turmoil all over again. South Carolina's Nullification Act of 1832 was formally just about the tariff; but the reason for this was to protect the slave-based economy.

The South made its concern over the matter unmistakable in 1835, when the House of Representatives passed the Pinckney Resolutions, refusing even to hear petitions urging emancipation. This was a clear violation of the First Amendment, which guarantees the right of petition for redress of grievances, but the House renewed it every year for the next nine years. And the Senate adopted a trickier way to avoid discussion of petitions in 1836. Another clear signal that discussion stopped at the cordon sanitaire of the South was given in 1835. The Tappan brothers, Arthur and Lewis, millionaire philanthropists—a kind of American version of the Cheeryble Brothers—sent thousands of antislavery tracts addressed to Southern churchmen.[7] When a packet of these materials arrived in Charleston Harbor, the postmaster of the town refused to deliver them. To prevent any wavering on this point, a mob—led in part by Robert Hayne, the famous 1830 debater against Daniel Webster on states' rights—broke into the post office, removed the tracts, and burnt them on the public parade ground.

President Jackson, born in South Carolina, could not sanction the destruction of the U.S. mail, but he did not want to exacerbate the tensions created when he quashed the Nullification Act three years earlier, so he issued this policy directive to the postmaster general:

> We can do nothing more than direct that those inflammatory
> papers be delivered to none but who will demand them as
> subscribers; and in every instance the postmaster ought to take
> their names down, and have them exposed through the public
> journals as subscribers to this wicked plan of exciting the
> Negroes to insurrection and to massacre.[8]

From this time on, discussion of slavery was suppressed in the South. Those who tried to speak against it were intimidated, beaten, or expelled.[9] Newspapers and printing presses were prevented from publishing abolitionist sentiments. The presses of those who defied the ban were destroyed.[10]

College professors in the South who voiced any criticism of slavery were driven out of their jobs and their town—as was a chemistry professor at the University of North Carolina at Chapel Hill when he spoke well of the presidential campaign of John C. Frémont. After students burned him in effigy, he was fired in response to popular clamor.[11] William Wertenbaker, the librarian at Jefferson's University of Virginia, publicly burned an abolitionist newspaper.[12] Young people were urged not to study in the North, where they could imbibe antislavery views. Academies, seminaries, and schools were set up to keep Southerners where they could be protected from the foreign ideology. Jefferson mentioned this as one motive for founding the University of Virginia. He wrote to William Cabell, his collaborator in creating the university:

> How many of our youths she [Harvard] now has, learning the
> lessons of anti-Missourianism, I know not; but a gentleman
> lately from Princeton told me he saw the list of the students at
> that place, and that more than half were Virginians. [Madison,
> it will be remembered, studied at Princeton.] These will return
> home, no doubt, deeply impressed with the sacred principle of
> our holy alliance of restrictionists [restricting slaves in the
> Missouri territory].[13]

And Jefferson wrote to John Taylor, the ardent defender of slavery: "These [Northern] seminaries are no longer proper for Southern or Western students. The signs of the times admonish us to call them home."[14] Even the cosmopolitan Jefferson was helping the South to seal itself in.

PRESBYTERIAN SCHISM, 1837–38

A CLEAR SIGN that the two parts of the nation could no longer live by the same standards was the separation of Southern from Northern churches of the same denomination. This began with the Presbyterians, who split apart in the General Assembly meetings of 1837 and 1838. Formally, this was not a sectional division, but it was soon recognized to be just that. The declared disagreements were between Old School and New School Presbyterians. The New School followed the comparatively liberal New Haven Theology and collaborated with Congregationalists, in accord with the Plan of Union (1801)—in 1836, Presbyterians and Congregationalists jointly founded Union Theological Seminary in New York. The Old School, still Calvinist, was especially strong in the South, which feared liberalism in all its forms and noticed that New School people were becoming abolitionists. The General Assembly of 1837 expelled the New School members and imposed a ban on any pronouncements having to do with slavery (A 659–61).

Presbyterians in the South denounced New School Presbyterians in the North for their association with abolitionists. According to the *Charleston Observer,* in 1836:

> For there [in the North] Anti-Presbyterianism and Perfectionism and ecclesiastical radicalism, and a host of errors in doctrine and practice, have grown up side by side with the spirit of abolitionism, scattering far and wide their poisonous fruits. The peculiar tenets of fanaticism and the abolition of slavery have been welded together, and together they have marched, till by their joint action they have nearly completed the destruction of the Christian intercourse which once obtained between the North and South.

In Richmond, the *Watchman of the South* proclaimed:

> Here then a revolution has been attempted at two points, an attempt [by the New School] to change our creed, and to pour a flood of abolition into the bosom of the Presbyterian church.[15]

Even the small number of New School Presbyterians in the South gave their position a distinctly sectional defense. To dissociate themselves from the abolitionists, they stressed that their cause was the cause of the South, to protect minority rights—language borrowed from John Calhoun's denunciations of Northern tyranny and foreshadowing future defenses of the Confederacy.[16] Thus, underlying the Old School–New School split was a deeper division, what Sydney Ahlstrom calls "the first great South-North separation" (A 660).

METHODIST SCHISM, 1844

THE METHODIST schism was more momentous, since it involved the largest church in the South (37.4 percent of the churches in what would become the Confederacy).[17] The Methodists had tried to stave off division in 1836 by issuing a statement that recognized the evils of slavery while condemning "modern abolitionism." This did not satisfy Methodist opponents of slavery, some of whom withdrew to form their own Wesleyan Methodist Church in Michigan. Others, in New York, organized the Methodist Wesleyan Connection in 1843, under the leadership of Orange Scott, one of the most ardent ministers in the antislavery cause.

The unavoidable crisis came in 1844. Bishop James Osgood Andrew of Georgia had not owned slaves when he was elected to the episcopacy, but he acquired them by marriage. Some Northerners demanded that he give up either the slaves or his office.[18] Southerners said that the General Assembly had no right to tell a bishop how to care for his flock. The General Assembly of 1844 debated the issues of constitutionality, episcopal rights, and the morality of slavery. The South had let it be known that if Bishop Andrews were deposed—or even if he resigned of his own free will—they would leave the Assembly. After a fortnight of heated debate and a vote along sectional lines—110 to 69—that the bishop desist from exercising his office, the Southerners asked for an amicable parting. For a time the Northerners adopted what would later be called the "let-our-erring-sisters-go" approach. Bishop Leonidas Hamline said: "God forbid that they should go as an arm torn out of the body, leaving a point of junction all gory and ghastly! Let them go as brethren beloved in the Lord, and let us hear their voice, responsive, claim us for brethren" (A 662). The Southern members convened in Louisville and formed the Methodist Episcopal Church, South.

The amity between the separate bodies did not last long. In the 1848 General Conference, the Plan of Separation passed the year before was declared null and void. Partly this was a dispute over property, since vast Methodist publishing interests were at stake. Years of litigation were settled only in 1854, when the Supreme Court divided assets pro rata, indirectly validating the Plan of Separation that the General Assembly had called null and void. (Madison's fears of having the government mix with doctrinal matters were once again justified.)

BAPTIST SCHISM, 1845

THE SEPARATION of Northern and Southern Baptists was not like that of the Presbyterians or Methodists. Baptists had no central ruling authority. Each church was independent. The clash came in, as it were, by the back door. The churches had agreed to pool their resources for two mission societies—the Foreign Mission Board and the Home Mission Society. Both bodies had agreed to be neutral on slavery, in order to keep peace between the sections—the Foreign Mission in 1840, the Home one in 1841. But Northern Baptists were becoming abolitionists, and when, in 1844, Georgia Baptists put up a slaveholder, James Reeve, to be a missionary to the Indians, the Home Society refused to endorse a project being carried out by one who owned fellow human beings. The South, defiant, forced the issue by demanding that a similar thing would not happen with the Foreign Board. When this demand was rebuffed, Baptists in Georgia separated themselves in 1845 as the Southern Baptist Convention. This body would endure and become the largest Protestant denomination in the twentieth and twenty-first centuries.

Thus, fifteen years before the Civil War began, the nation had broken into two camps at a very deep level, and all because of slavery. David Brion Davis says: "Slavery played a central part in the national division of the Presbyterian, Methodist, and Baptist churches, *institutions that had served as the main cultural bridges between North and South...*" (emphasis added).[19] With those bridges gone, how long could the two regions stay united? Not long, some prophesied. The *Charleston Mercury* greeted the Methodist split as "the first dissolution of the Union."[20] When, a year later, the Baptists separated, the *Savannah Republican* said that this event was "intimately connected with our Southern institutions, and perhaps may have a remote bearing on the ultimate political relations of the Northern and Southern portions of the Union." Religion was leading the way and calling on the political leaders to follow.

RELIGION AS THE GUARDIAN OF SLAVERY

A s THE SOUTH sealed itself into a bastion of thought where no adversary voice was allowed, it became more extreme in its defenses of slavery. The Founders' generation in Virginia held that slavery was an evil, but one that could not be quickly escaped. They entertained hopes for some distant elimination of the evil—through colonization abroad, or by diffusion of the institution out through the West (where it would become manageably thinned out), or by graduated emancipations (of the sort Washington accomplished for his own slaves at his wife's death). But by the 1830s, leaders in the South were calling slavery a positive good, something to be made permanent, indeed a divine institution. John C. Calhoun, arguing in 1837 that abolition should not even be discussed in Congress, said:

> Let me not be understood as admitting, even by implication,
> that the existing relation between the two races in the
> slaveholding states is an evil—far otherwise; I hold it to be a
> good, as it has thus far proved itself to be to both, and will

continue to prove so if not disturbed by the fell spirit of abolition.[21]

Calhoun's praise of slavery as a positive good had been voiced earlier by John Taylor (in *Arator,* 1814) and would be repeated by George Fitzhugh in 1854 (in *Sociology for the South*).

Religious leaders in the South wholeheartedly subscribed to this praise of slavery. A region that allowed no criticism of the institution in its newspapers had nothing to fear from its pulpits. Southern clergymen, Catholic as well Protestant, were unanimous in their support of the war—all eleven of the Catholic bishops in the South supported the war (A 673–74). James Silver writes of Southern ministers: "As no other group they sustained the people in their long, costly and futile war for Southern independence."[22] The contrast between Northern and Southern religious figures at this time did not follow the pattern we have seen in other religious separations—where Enlightened religion was the preserve of the socially elite. In this case, two elites faced each other, two social establishments. The antebellum South was like pre-Enlightenment New England, with an educated and influential clergy near the center of its power structure. Just as Jonathan Edwards professed Enlightenment and held slaves, religious leaders in the South were educated slaveholders. Of course, there were poorer Methodist and Baptist preachers in the countryside. Only about half of the clergy could be called affluent. But it was the upper half, the town ministers with pulpits serving the upper classes, that framed the issues and made the arguments followed by the lower half.

In a study of the hundred most influential Southern clergymen of the time, the men he calls "the gentlemen theologians," Brooks Holifield found that their average wealth was $20,000, at a time when the average for a free adult white male in America was $2,500.[23] It is not surprising that these leaders mounted a spirited defense of slavery. They or their families or their principal supporters were deeply involved in the institution.

Three of the five pastors in Athens, Georgia, were slave
owners in 1859; 45 percent of the clergy in Savannah held
slaves in 1855; by 1860 at least 60 percent of the pastors in
Macon, Georgia, were slave owners, as were at least 50 percent
of the ministers in Spartanburg and Beaufort, South Carolina,
and 54 percent in Columbia. Most of the ministerial masters
seem to have held from five to eleven slaves; eight pastors
in Macon, for example, owned a total of forty-nine; nine
ministers in Columbia held ninety-nine. But some had larger
holdings: Basil Manly, Sr., who helped initiate the regional split
within the Baptist Church, owned thirty-eight persons while
he lived at Tuscaloosa; by 1860 Bishop James O. Andrew, who
had been the symbol of the slavery issue in the Methodist
Church, owned twenty-two; and the Episcopalian Stephen
Elliott of Beaufort, South Carolina, represented the small
body of clergymen within the uppermost circles of the
slavocracy; he owned one hundred ninety-nine human
beings.[24]

In the sermons of the South, slavery became not only a good thing
but a divine thing. One of the most famous sermons on slavery was
preached by Benjamin Morgan Palmer to two thousand people at the
First Presbyterian Church on Lafayette Square in New Orleans. It was
called "Slavery a Divine Trust: Duty of the South to Preserve and Perpetuate It." He argued that God gave certain people a mission, and the
mission of the South was to vindicate his ways by protecting the biblical
institution of slavery. "What, at this juncture, is their providential trust? I
answer that it is to conserve and to perpetuate the institution of domestic slavery as now existing."[25]

The South constantly cited all the biblical passages permitting slavery, those that Quakers had discredited in the North a century earlier.
Those texts were used now not simply to say that slavery was allowed
but that it was promoted by Scripture. The "curse of Ham" proved that

Negroes had incurred divine displeasure. All religion could do is show kindness to such defective beings.

> By nature the most affectionate and loyal of all races beneath the sun, they are also the most helpless, and no calamity can befall them greater than the loss of that protection they enjoy under this patriarchal system. Freedom would be their doom; and equally from both they call upon us, their providential guardians, to be protected.[26]

In this era it was the conservatives of the South who invoked a separation of church and state. The preachers could recommend slavery as a biblical institution and offer moral advice on the gentle treatment of slaves, while leaving it to politicians to argue slavery's place in the civil institutions of the polity. This was a tack plantation owners had developed for coping with preachers who wanted to spread the Gospel to slaves on their estates. The missionaries would be given access to blacks only on condition that they discuss the *souls* of their charges, not ever their slave status—that would be "mixing religion with politics."

Most evangelists accepted this as a condition for preaching at all.[27] That was the recommendation, as we saw in discussing Anthony Benezet, of the Society for the Propagation of the Gospel. This was also the line followed by Southern churchmen in their arguments that the General Assembly of the Presbyterians, the General Conference of the Methodists, and the mission societies of the Baptists should not have mixed politics with religion by addressing the subject of slavery in any but a biblically sanctioned way.[28]

But when such a separation did not serve their purpose, the preachers dropped the idea and directly mixed religion and politics.[29] When it came time to secede politically, some preachers offered their break with the Northern churches in the 1830s and 1840s as a model for the politicians to follow. The *Central Presbyterian* of Richmond counseled against submission to the North:

The Southern Presbyterians did not do it. The Southern Methodists did not do it. The Southern Baptists did not do it. And as they are *of* the people, and *with* the people, it is passing strange that their example, given years ago, has not been read with greater profit—an example which serves to show that the same cause which has produced sectional disruption in ecclesiastical brotherhoods may also rend asunder the brotherhood of states.[30]

One way the preachers offered themselves as a model for the politicians was the tactic by which the former had denied that they were schismatics. They said the Northern states had withdrawn from *them*, that they were upholding the true and historic stand of their churches, that those acting against them were *unconstitutional*, violating the standing rules of their denomination.[31] In the same way the South claimed that the North had broken the Constitution, leaving the South to preserve that document in its original intent. "We do not secede—our enemies have seceded."[32]

The nation was de facto divided from the time its principal religious bodies broke apart. In the past, some have claimed that the Civil War was not fought over slavery—the greatest source of divisive bitterness in all our history. Jefferson Davis said that, and so have Confederate defenders ever since. They say it was fought over freedom from an overweening federal power—though it is hard to see how states that had for years suppressed freedom of speech, of the press, of the mails, and of religion can be made the champions of individual liberty (leaving aside the lack of freedom for slaves). Others say it was a matter of economics, of the tariff, of a rural vs. industrial culture—though the plantation owners were in fact entrepreneurs in a market economy. But the elephant in the room remains, and its name is slavery. The breakup of the religious bodies is clear proof of that, years before the war began.

19 | GOD OF BATTLES

EVANGELICALS, like most Americans—like, as we have seen, the Transcendentalists—tried to avoid a hard stand on slavery for as long as they could. The most astonishing example of this is Charles Grandison Finney, the president of Oberlin College, which had a strong antislavery tradition. Finney said that, *yes*, of course, slavery was a bad thing; but let's not go overboard—it must not impede our concentration on revivals.

> Nothing is more calculated to injure religion, and to injure the
> slaves themselves, than for Christians to get into an angry
> controversy on this subject. . . . Great care should be taken to
> avoid a censorious spirit on both sides. . . . A denunciatory
> spirit, impeaching each other's motives, is unchristian,
> calculated to grieve the Spirit of God, and to put down
> revivals. . . . I do not mean by this that the attention of the
> church should be so absorbed by this as to neglect the main
> question of saving souls.[1]

In keeping with this attitude, Finney did not let free blacks sit with whites at his revivals, and he rejected the plea of his rich patrons, the

Tappan brothers, when they proposed a black man for a church board position.[2] While Finney was the president of Oberlin College, an anti-slavery institution funded by the Tappans, he cooled the fires of abolitionism and redirected them to revivalism. As a historian of the school, Robert Fletcher, wrote: "If the antislavery sentiment in Oberlin was so strong and so general, why then did the college contribute so few abolitionist lecturers after 1837? The answer is—the answer to so many queries about Oberlin—*Finney.*"[3]

APOCALYPTIC WAR

B UT MANY of the saved souls in the 1830s were not able to remain "uncensorious" where slavery was concerned. They put their moral attitude in highly censorious language, including that of Harriet Beecher Stowe in *Uncle Tom's Cabin*. They saw the war on slavery as a cosmic event, connected with the Second Coming of Christ:

> This is an age of the world when nations are trembling and
> convulsed. A mighty influence is abroad, surging and heaving
> the world, as with an earthquake . . . O Church of Christ, read
> the signs of the times. Is not this power the spirit of him whose
> kingdom is yet to come, and whose will is to be done on earth
> as it is in heaven? But who may abide the day of his appearing?
> "For that day shall burn as an oven; and he shall appear as a
> swift witness against those that oppress the hireling in his
> wages, the widow and the fatherless, and that turn aside the
> stranger in his right; and he shall break in pieces the oppressor.
> Are not these dread words for a nation bearing in her bosom so
> mighty an injustice? Christians, every time that you pray that
> the kingdom of Christ may come, can you forget that prophecy
> associates, in dread fellowship, the day of vengeance with the
> year of his redeemed? . . . For not surer is the eternal law by
> which the millstone sinks in the ocean than that stronger law

by which injustice and cruelty shall bring on nations the wrath
of Almighty God.[4]

Most of us know the apocalyptic imagery used in the Civil War from
Julia Ward Howe's "Battle Hymn of the Republic," with its New Testament images of final judgment—the winepress of God's wrath (Revelation 14.19), the terrible swift sword loosed from God's mouth (Revelation
18.15), the all-fulfilling trumpet (Revelation 10.7), and so on. The war
against slavery was seen as God's work, to be accomplished in an eschatological showdown with evil. But the hymn singers of the South were
just as sure that they were fighting a cosmic battle on God's side. Henry
Timrod of South Carolina equated the Union soldiers with Satan's evil
out of the North (Jeremiah 1.14):

> *And what if, made with wrongs themselves have wrought,*
> > *In their own teachings caught,*
> > *By their own fears made bold,*
> > *In League with him of old,*
> * *Who long since in the limits of the North*
> > *Set up his evil throne and warred with God . . .*[5]

When the South won battles, said the pastor of Richmond's Third Baptist Church, this was "not to be attributed to the number or skill of our
troops, not to the superiority of our generals, but to the Divine Hand."[6]
The South was so sure of its religious mission that Lincoln became a
kind of Antichrist in its eyes. When he wrote humbly in a fast day
proclamation, the South saw this as the devil quoting Scripture. The
Richmond Daily Dispatch sneered: "A despot humbles himself because his
bloody crimes have not yet produced their desired result. Can anything
more shockingly blasphemous be imagined?"[7] Basil Gildersleeve, the
South Carolinian who would become America's greatest classical
scholar after the war, wrote of "the fit idol of these modern Egyptians,
their god Anubis [the dog god], their chosen chief, Abraham Lincoln."[8]
A Presbyterian preacher said of Lincoln that "the heart of our modern

Pharaoh is so hardened that he will not let Israel go."⁹ These attacks were echoed from afar in the *Times* of London, which called Lincoln "a traitor to his race."¹⁰

The famed Louisiana preacher Benjamin Morgan Palmer, speaking just after Lincoln's election, saw the triumph of abolitionist "hate" as a world-rending event, a continuation of the rage against authority loosed on the world by the French Revolution. Palmer is worth quoting at length because he blends all the Southern themes in an eloquent summary.

> In this great struggle we defend the cause of God and religion. The abolitionist spirit is undeniably atheistic. The demon which erected its throne upon the guillotine in the days of Robespierre and Marat, which abolished the Sabbath and worshiped reason in the person of a harlot, yet survives to work other horrors, of which those of the French Revolution are but the type. Among a people so generally religious as the Americans, a disguise must be worn; but it is the same old threadbare disguise of the advocacy of human rights. From a thousand Jacobin clubs here, as in France, the decree has gone forth which strikes at God by striking at all subordination and law. Availing itself of the morbid and misdirected sympathies of men, it has entrapped weak consciences in the meshes of its treachery; *and now, at last, has seated its high priest [Lincoln] upon the throne,* clad in the black garments of discord and schism, as symbolic of its ends. Under this specious cry of reform, it demands that every evil shall be corrected or society become a wreck—the sun must be stricken from the heaven if a spot is found upon his disc. The Most High, knowing his own power, which is infinite, and his own wisdom, which is unfathomable, can afford to be patient. But these self-constituted reformers, would quicken the activity of Jehovah, or compel his abdication. In their furious haste, they trample upon obligations sacred as any which can bind the conscience.
>
> It is time to reproduce the obsolete idea that Providence must govern man, not that man shall control Providence. In the

imperfect state of human society, it pleases God to allow evils
which check others that are greater. As in the physical world,
objects are moved forward not by a single force but by the
composition of forces, so in his moral administration there are
checks and balances whose intimate relations are comprehended only by Himself. But what reck they of this—those
fierce zealots who undertake to drive the chariot of the sun?
Working out the single and false idea which rides them like a
nightmare, they dash athwart the spheres, utterly disregarding
the delicate machinery of Providence, which moves on, wheels
within wheels, with pivots and balances and springs, which the
Great Designer alone can control. *This spirit of atheism,* which
knows no God who tolerates evil, no Bible which sanctions law,
and no conscience that men can be bound by with oaths and
covenants, has selected us for its victims and slavery for its
issue. Its banner-cry rings out already upon the air: "liberty,
equality, fraternity"—which, simply interpreted, means
bondage, confiscation, and massacre. With its tricolor waving in
the breeze, it waits to inaugurate its reign of terror.

To the South the high position is assigned of defending,
before all nations, *the cause of all religion and of all truth.* In this
test, we are resisting the power which wars against constitutions and laws and compacts, against Sabbaths and sanctuaries,
against the family, the state, and the church; which blasphe-
mously invades the prerogatives of God and rebukes the Most
High for the errors of his administration, which, if it cannot
snatch the reins of empire from His grasp, will lay the universe
in ruin at His feet [emphases added].[11]

As one can tell from this passage, the South, in its devotion to tradition, subordination, and honor, had grown fond of Edmund Burke's
denunciations of the French Revolution as anarchical and atheistic.[12] It
is ironic that the South now saw Jacobins everywhere. Sixty years earlier,
when the Southerner Thomas Jefferson was elected president, New

Englanders saw him as ascending an atheistical and Jacobin throne—exactly the way the Southerner Palmer now saw Lincoln.

Some Northern Evangelicals had their own (opposite) way of using horror at the French infidelities. In that context, Lincoln was not the villain, but the North's old bugbear Jefferson was. Horace Bushnell, the Hartford theologian, said that Jefferson's infidel philosophy—that power is derived from the people, not from God—is what led the Southerners to think they could secede from a government anytime they wanted to. Jefferson the Southerner had caused the war, and it was the North that was fighting on God's side.[13] Bushnell glorified the holy war:

> There is an immense praying too by day and by night in
> all parts of the country; wives, mothers, children, fathers,
> brothers, praying for the dear ones they have sent to the field
> for the commanders, for the cause; soldiers fighting and
> praying together, and many of them learning even in the field
> to pray and catch heroic fire from God. Oh! It is religion, it is
> God! Every drum-beat is a hymn, the cannon thunder God, the
> electric silence, darting victory along the wires, is the inaudible
> greeting of God's favoring word and purpose.[14]

Another Northern preacher who was delighted to claim that "the state is indeed divine" was Henry W. Bellows, famous pastor of the First Unitarian Church in New York. Hoping that the Civil War would overcome "the unhappy alienation of church and state" in America, he argued for "the body of the state ... as essentially and vitally connected with the prosperity and life of the church, as the health of our bodies with the welfare of our spirits." The state should receive "unconditional loyalty," since "the head of a nation is a sacred person." Lincoln was God's chosen: "File at the staple which God fastens to his own throne, in the oaths of office which make a man chief ruler of a people, and you loosen thoughtlessly every link of the chain of law and order, which binds society together."[15]

THE CRY FOR BLOOD

W E HAVE SEEN how the Transcendentalists responded to John Brown's raid. These lofty thinkers became positively blood-thirsty. Theodore Parker said it was not only the right but the duty of slaves to kill their masters: "All the great charters of humanity have been written in blood . . . it is plain, now, that our pilgrimage must lead through a Red Sea, wherein many a Pharaoh will go under and perish."[16] In the apocalyptic time coming, there would be many invocations of blood. The winepress where the grapes of wrath are stored gushes so abundantly in Revelation 14.20 that "blood came out of the winepress, even unto the horses' bridles, by the space of a thousand and six hundred furlongs." That was the apparent inspiration for pastor after pastor to call from the pulpit, as Henry Ward Beecher did, "Give me war redder than blood and fiercer than fire."[17]

Horace Bushnell seemed almost drunk on it: "Blood, blood, rivers of blood have bathed our hundred battlefields and sprinkled the horns of our altars! Without this shedding of blood, how could the violated order be sanctified?"[18] Speaking at the Yale commencement just after the war's end, Bushnell saw the whole war as through a veil of blood.

> According to the true economy of the world, so many of its
> grandest and most noble benefits have and are to have a tragic
> origin, and to come as outgrowths only of blood. . . . As the mild
> benignity and peaceful reign of Christ begins at the principle,
> "Without the shedding of blood, there is no remission," so
> without shedding of blood there is almost nothing great in the
> world. . . . The matter wanted here was blood, not logic, and
> this we have on a scale large enough to meet our necessity . . .
> [creating a] bond of common life which God has touched with
> blood. . . . In these rivers of blood we have now bathed our
> institutions, and they are henceforth to be hallowed in our sight.
> Government is now become Providential—no more a mere

creature of our human will, but a grandly moral affair. The awful
stains of sacrifice are upon it, as upon the fields where our dead
battled for it, and it is sacred for their sakes. The stamp of God's
sovereignty is upon it; for he has beheld their blood upon its gate
posts and made it the sign of his Passover.[19]

Some Northerners, early in the war, gloried in a vision of blood
being spilled as if this were a purifying sacrifice; the more shed, the
more redeeming the effect. Charles Eliot Norton, the Harvard littera-
teur, contemplating the great Northern losses at the first battle of Bull
Run, said the nation should face the prospect that "a million men should
die on the battlefield."[20] Norton wrote to a friend after the battle of
Shiloh: "I can hardly help wishing that the war might go on and on till it
has brought suffering and sorrow enough to quicken our consciences
and cleanse our hearts."[21] Even in the South, where a quick exit from the
Union was desired, some thought that a prolonged conflict was necessary to prove that slavery was a divine institution. A Methodist quoted in
the *Richmond Dispatch* hoped for a war of "ten to fifteen years" to wipe
abolitionism off the face of the earth.[22]

Emerson thought that "one whole generation might well consent to
perish, if by their fall, political liberty and clean and just life could be
made sure to the generations that follow."[23] For Orestes Brownson, the
war was a "thunderstorm that purifies the moral and political atmosphere."[24] The historian Francis Parkman predicted: "Upheaved from its
depths, fermenting and purging itself, the nation will stand at length
clarified and pure in a renewal of strengthened life."[25] Henry James Sr.
felt that the ordeal of war would lift Americans to a "divine-natural
humanity," full of "celestial vigor and beatitude."[26] Such thoughts
inspired even the seventeen-year-old Josephine Shaw, whose brother
Robert Shaw would die in battle leading black soldiers. She wrote in her
diary for August 1861:

This war will purify the country of some of its extravagance
and selfishness, even if we are stopped midway. It can't help

doing us good; it has begun to do us good already. It will
make us young ones much more thoughtful and earnest,
and so improve the country. I suppose we need something
every few years to teach us that riches, luxury and comfort
are not the great end of life, and this will surely teach us that
at least.[27]

The Civil War was a savage and brutal conflict—at one point Southern women made necklaces from the teeth of dead Union soldiers.[28] But
it was, even more than other American wars, a time of heightened,
almost feverish, religiosity. There were many revivals, both in the North
and the South—there was an entire book written to record the revivals
going on in the Southern armies (A 675). Wartime converts to various
Christian faiths were estimated in the hundreds of thousands.[29] Organized efforts showered Bibles and tracts on the soldiers. Ministers,
including Horace Bushnell, played a leading role in the Sanitary Commission (early equivalent of the Red Cross). Josephine Shaw wrote, well
into the war, that "war is exactly like a revival—a direct work of God, so
wonderful are some of the conversions."[30] In 1862, a writer in Philadelphia was surprised to find the war fever so strong precisely in the *religious*
press: "Religion has grown warlike. Men have discovered the Book of the
Wars of the Lord, and congregations are chanting the war psalms now in
all their majesty that would have shocked a year ago."[31] The South was
certain of its alignment with divine purpose, and had included in the
preamble to the Constitution of the Confederated States the words
"invoking the favor and guidance of Almighty God." The importance of
that is underlined by Harry Stout:

> When Confederate lawmakers introduced God explicitly into
> their national constitution, they had no idea of the significance
> this act would later assume. It would not only solidify the
> South's identity as a Christian republic, but also supply a
> surprisingly powerful critique of a "Godless" Northern
> Constitution.[32]

BLACK RELIGION

THE GREATEST triumph in the history of American religion is the fulfillment of black hopes and prayers, down the generations, as they saw Union troops, with their black units, marching to their rescue. This is what they had sung about for years.

> *When Israel was in Egypt's land*
> *(Let my people go),*
> *Oppressed so hard they could not stand*
> *(Let my people go).*

Thomas Wentworth Higginson, Emily Dickinson's friend and her posthumous publisher, who led black troops himself, recorded how his soldiers used spirituals as marching songs:

> *We'll cross de danger water . . .*
> *O Pharaoh's army drownded!*
> *My army cross over.*[33]

During the war, a white Southerner who heard slaves in Alabama singing, "By and by we'll go home to meet Him / Way over in the promised land," did not think they were singing about their death but their liberation. He "seemed to see the mantle of our lost cause descending."[34] A soldier marching with Sherman through Georgia said of the slaves' jubilant greetings, "To them it was like the bondsmen going out of Egypt."[35] When Jefferson Davis abandoned the Confederate capital, the slaves sang, "Thank God A' mighty, I's free at last"—a cry Dr. King would echo throughout his life and in his most famous speech.[36]

Lincoln witnessed the overflow of religious emotion when he entered Richmond after Davis's departure. Accompanied only by ten sailors, he walked down the city street. Blacks had just greeted black soldiers of the Union army who were liberating them. Then they saw the president himself. James McPherson re-creates the moment carefully, since he considers it "the most unforgettable scene of this unforgettable war."

> [Admiral] Porter [in charge of the sailors] peered nervously at
> every window for would-be assassins. But the Emancipator was
> soon surrounded by an impenetrable cordon of black people
> shouting "Glory to God! Glory! Glory! Glory!" "Bless the Lord!
> The great Messiah! I knowed him as soon as I seed him. He's
> been in my heart four long years. Come to free his children
> from bondage. Glory Hallelujah!" Several freed slaves touched
> Lincoln to make sure he was real. "I know I am free," shouted
> an old woman, "for I have seen Father Abraham and felt him."
> Overwhelmed by rare emotions, Lincoln said to one black man
> who fell on his knees in front of him, "Don't kneel to me. That
> is not right. You must kneel to God only, and thank Him for the
> liberty you will enjoy hereafter." Among the reporters from
> Northern newspapers who described these events was one
> whose presence was a potent symbol of the revolution. He was
> T. Morris Chester, who sat at a desk in the Confederate Capitol
> drafting his dispatch to the *Philadelphia Press.* "Richmond has
> never before presented such a spectacle of jubilee," he wrote.
> "What a wonderful change has come over the spirit of
> Southern dreams." Chester was a black man.[37]

The delivery would continue to be seen in religious terms. A visitor to the South described the freed slaves' "devoutness and recognition of God's hand in everything." One black woman said, "God planned dem slave prayers to free us, like he did de Israelites, and dey did." And another: "The children of Israel was in bondage one time, and God sent Moses to 'liver them. Well, I s'pose that God sent Abe Lincoln to 'liver us." After the assassination of Lincoln, a black man told one woman, "Lincoln died for we, Christ died for we, and me believe him de same man."[38] It was a belief made more understandable by the fact that Lincoln was killed on Good Friday.

LINCOLN'S RELIGION

W HAT DID Lincoln make of all the religious pressures exerted on
him? Many wanted him to be a Messiah—not only that black
man kneeling to him but apocalyptics like Bushnell and Bellows. Many
leaders in that position have yielded to the demand. Lincoln resisted it
consistently. A Messiah would presumably know God's will, and Lincoln
repeatedly said that it was unknowable. Nor did he offer himself as a
religious model. He told a Synod of Presbyterians, "I sincerely wish I
was a more devoted man than I am."[39] When a group of Chicago churchmen said that God required him to emancipate the slaves, he replied:

> I hope it will not be irreverent for me to say that if it is
> probable that God would reveal his will to others, on a point so
> connected with my duty, it might be supposed he would reveal
> it directly to me; for, unless I am more deceived in myself
> than I often am, it is my earnest desire to know the will of
> Providence in this matter. And if I know what it is, I will do it.
> These are not however, the days of miracles, and I suppose it
> will be granted that I am not to expect a divine revelation.[40]

That is not how most modern presidents speak. Dwight Eisenhower
told evangelist Billy Graham how religious he was, and added, "Billy, I
believe one reason I was elected President was to lead America in a religious revival" (MM 3.305–6). George W. Bush told another evangelist,
James Robison, "I feel like God wants me to run for president. I can't
explain it, but I sense my country is going to need me. Something is
going to happen. . . . I know it won't be easy on me or my family, but God
wants me to do it."[41]

Some Americans cannot truly admire a person who is not a religious
person—preferably a religious person of their own stripe. So many
people have tried to make a redeemer figure of Lincoln, as we have seen
them doing with Washington. But Lincoln is just as elusive as Washington

on this subject. One of the more sophisticated recent attempts to present a religious side to Lincoln was made by the historian Richard Carwardine. He admits that Lincoln was a religious skeptic in his younger days but thinks his later statements "indicated some movement toward the Evangelical mainstream."[42] But how can anyone be counted an Evangelical who never referred to Jesus by name or said he had a personal relationship with him? Carwardine himself admits: "Christ himself is notably absent from Lincoln's authenticated words."[43] The closest he ever came was in thanking a delegation of freed blacks from Baltimore who gave him a gift Bible. In thanking them, he said, "All the good the Savior gave to the world was communicated through this book."[44]

Carwardine relies on flimsy connections. He had rightly claimed, in an earlier book, that Evangelicalism was the dominant religious culture in the nineteenth century while Lincoln was growing up.[45] But that does not make everyone in Lincoln's age group an Evangelical. Moreover that culture was drenched in biblical terminology, as was Lincoln's prose—but not to the degree that other writers of his day were, who not only echoed the Bible but expressly invoked it. Carwardine reaches for a rare evocation of an Evangelical author like Leonard Bacon, who wrote in 1846, "If those laws of the Southern states, by virtue of which slavery exists there, and is what it is, are not wrong—nothing is wrong." Lincoln said in 1854 that "if slavery is not wrong, nothing is wrong." Carwardine offers no evidence that Lincoln had read Bacon, and in any case the statement is the kind of trope used of many things—yet he says that Lincoln "appears to have acknowledged this debt to a Yankee clergyman."[46]

Carwardine's cherrypicking of sources is clear from the fact that he uses this far-fetched "debt" while never mentioning the widely accepted debt to a clergyman of a very different sort. The Transcendentalist Theodore Parker was a hero to Lincoln's law partner, William Herndon, who had often pushed his writings upon Lincoln. Parker used many variations on the phrase "government of the people, by the people, and for the people."[47] Carwardine does not mention this because the "debt" was not to an Evangelical. Herndon quotes Lincoln's friend Jesse Fell, who elicited from him a campaign autobiography and who had many lengthy discussions with him, and who delivered this judgment: "If, from my recollections on this subject [religion], I was called upon to designate an author whose views most nearly represented Mr. Lincoln's on this subject, I would say that author was Theodore Parker."[48]

The shrewdness of that conclusion is confirmed by Parker's and Lincoln's writings. Parker held that the Declaration of Independence was the central statement of the American ideal, to which the Constitution was only a provisional approximation, one flawed by its tolerance of slavery, its flaws to be worked out by striving toward the ideal of the Declaration:

> The great political idea of America, the idea of the Declaration
> of Independence, is a composite idea made up of three simple
> ones: 1. Each man is endowed with certain unalienable rights.
> 2. In respect of these rights all men are equal. 3. A government is
> to protect each man in the entire and actual enjoyment of all the
> unalienable rights. . . . The American Revolution, with American
> history since, is an attempt to prove by experience this
> transcendental proposition, to organize the transcendental idea
> of politics. The idea demands for its organization a democ-
> racy—a government of all, for all, and by all.[49]

Lincoln wrote of the Declaration in just those terms:

> They [the Founders] meant to set up a standard maxim for free
> society, which should be familiar to all, and revered by all,
> constantly looked to, constantly labored for, and even though
> never perfectly attained, constantly approximated and thereby
> constantly spreading and deepening its influence, and
> augmenting the happiness and value of life to all people of all
> colors everywhere.[50]

Lincoln shared many views with Parker and other Transcendentalists.[51] He heard Emerson lecture and received him in the White House. He knew and was friendly with the Transcendentalist George Bancroft.

But he could not acknowledge an affinity with Parker, since Parker was the most fervent of abolitionists, a supporter of John Brown. It would have been political suicide, in the Illinois of the 1850s, which banned immigration by free blacks, for Lincoln to show any alliance with Parker. Lincoln's career was itself a graduated approximation to the ideal of the Declaration. He temporized with slavery, which leads some now to criticize him. But if he had not done so, he would not have reached a position where he could do something about the ideal. He is an example of what George Bancroft himself wrote: "In public life, by the side of the actual world, there exists this ideal state toward which it should tend."[52]

What is relevant to discussion of Lincoln's religion is that the Transcendentalists were at a far remove from the Evangelicals. The religion of the common man (so called) was Evangelicalism. Lincoln was a champion of the common people, so there is a wish that his religion would be theirs. But it was not. He was aware, as Doris Kearns Goodwin and others have pointed out, that he was an uncommon man with a radically original mind. He was more at home in the conceptual world of the Transcendentalists than in that of the revival preachers. Yet Carwardine completely ignores the Transcendentalists while trying to make improbable ties to Evangelicals.[53]

Since Lincoln became more fatalistic in the later stages of the war, Carwardine thinks he is returning to the Calvinism of the world he grew up in.[54] But Stoics and Deists were fatalistic, too, and were believers in providence. And the Calvinism of the Evangelicals was not at all like Lincoln's attitude toward providence. The Evangelicals concentrated on the salvation of the individual, on knowing whether one was predestined to sanctity. Lincoln went back beyond Calvin to his sources in Jewish Scripture. He thought of the salvation *of a whole people.* This is what the Hebrew prophets were concerned with. It is also what black Americans looked to. Would they *as a people* reach the Promised Land? Would the Ark carry them through?

> *That awful rain she stopped at last*
> *The waters they subsided,*

> *An' that old Ark with all on board*
> *On Ararat she rided.*[55]

The New England Calvinists had to reach an entirely individual and private experience of being saved. The black Evangelicals express a *solidarity* in salvation:

> *O wrestlin' Jacob—Jacob, day's a-breakin',*
> *I will not let thee go!*
> *O wrestlin' Jacob—Jacob, day's a-breakin',*
> *He will not let me go!*
> *O, I hold my brudder wid a tremblin' hand,*
> *I would not let him go!*
> *I hold my sister wid a tremblin' hand,*
> *I would not let her go!*[56]

If Lincoln's religion was not that of the white Evangelicals of his day, it was closer to that of the black Evangelicals, who had given their Bible a different reading from what their masters found in it. Lincoln thought the whole nation was as one in the guilt of slavery and as one in the agony of freeing itself from that sin. In a letter of 1864, he wrote to an emissary from the South:

> Now, at the end of three years' struggle, the nation's condition is not what either party, or any man, devised or expected. God alone can claim it. Whither it is tending seems plain. If God now wills the removal of a great wrong, and wills also that we of the North as well as you of the South shall pay fairly for our complicity in that wrong, impartial history will find therein new cause to attest and revere the justice and goodness of God.[7]

He would rework those words for the Second Inaugural Address:

> Each [side] looked for an easier triumph, and a result less fundamental and astounding. . . . The prayers of both could not

be answered; that of neither has been answered fully. The Almighty has his own purposes. . . . If we are to suppose that American slavery is one of those offences which, in the providence of God, must needs come, but which, having continued through its appointed time, He now wills to remove, and that He gives to both North and South this terrible war, as the woe due to those by whom the offence came, shall we discern therein any departure from those divine attributes which the believers in a Living God always ascribe to Him?

In the Jewish sacred writings, God punishes the whole nation before saving the whole nation.

If God wills that it [the war] continue until all the wealth piled by the bondman's two hundred and fifty years of unrequited toil shall be sunk, and until every drop of blood drawn with the lash shall be paid by another drawn with the sword—as was said three thousand years ago, so still it must be said: "The judgments of the Lord are true and righteous altogether."

The biblical sense of a struggle for freedom that Lincoln sensed in the black religion of his time had no doubt its part in the strong attraction that drew together Lincoln and Frederick Douglass.

The best understanding of Lincoln's religion that I have read is that of the Evangelical Mark Noll. He saw that Lincoln's theological insight into the meaning of the war surpassed that of any churchman, North or South:

The contrast between the learned religious thinkers and Lincoln in how they interpreted the war poses the great theological puzzle of the Civil War. Abraham Lincoln, a layman with no standing in a church and no formal training as a theologian, propounded a thick, complex view of God's rule over the world and a morally nuanced picture of America's

destiny. The country's best theologians, by contrast, presented
a thin, simple view of God's providence and a morally juvenile
view of the nation and its fate.[58]

Though not an elitist in social or political terms, Lincoln was not
only a part of the intellectual elite of his time, but much the most intelligent man in that company. Noll, far from thinking Lincoln leaned
toward the Evangelicals, says that he was free to go deeper into the truth
of history because he avoided the Evangelicals of his day. Others Noll
finds approaching his insights were also far from Evangelical thought—
Emily Dickinson and Herman Melville. What he does not state is that
Dickinson and Melville, too, were influenced by the Transcendentalists.

> Certainly the evangelical juggernaut was working too well for a
> few souls who, if they could not stop wrestling with God, still
> wondered if the energetic God of the Protestant evangelicals was
> adequate for the complexities of the universe or the turmoil of
> their own souls. So Emily Dickinson, Herman Melville, and
> supremely Abraham Lincoln may have been pushed by the
> successes of "American Christianity" into post-Protestant, even
> post-Christian theism. The tragedy of these individuals was that
> to be faithful to the God they found in their own hearts—or in
> the Bible, or in the sweep of events—they had to hold themselves
> aloof from the organized Christianity of the United States and
> from its preaching about the message of Jesus Christ.[59]

"Post-Christian theists" is what most Transcendentalists would have
called themselves. Lincoln, in a time of apocalyptic fanaticisms, was an
example of both Enlightened religion—the religion of Melville and
Dickinson—and of the Evangelical instincts of his black contemporaries:
the religion of Frederick Douglass. Like Anthony Benezet, he combined
the best elements of both head and heart in our religious heritage.

I am drawn back to the mutual fascination experienced by Abraham
Lincoln and Frederick Douglass. Starting from points very distant from

each other, they gravitated insensibly toward each other, as if drawn by a dim perception of each other's depths—a process sensitively traced by James Oakes in his book on the two men, *The Radical and the Republican.*[60] If Lincoln was the Transcendentalist who imbibed the black version of Evangelicalism, Douglass was the Evangelical with a Transcendentalist view of nature. Both men described the struggle against slavery in a biblical rhetoric. This came naturally to Douglass because of his experience of conversion, his role as a Sabbath schoolteacher, and his brief time as a lay preacher.[61] Though Douglass was a fierce critic of the churches for their complicity in slavery, and their hypocrisy on that score, he remained religious all his life, with a deep belief in providence. He always attributed his early assurance that he would be free to God's own blessing on him:

> I may be deemed superstitious, and even egotistical, in
> regarding this event [his transfer to the care of Sophia Auld]
> as a special interposition of divine Providence in my favor. But
> I should be false to the earliest sentiments of my soul if I
> suppressed the opinion. I prefer to be true to myself, even at
> the hazard of incurring the ridicule of others, rather than to
> be false, and incur my own abhorrence. From my earliest
> recollection, I date the entertainment of a deep conviction that
> slavery would not always be able to hold me within its foul
> embrace; and in the darkest hours of my career in slavery, this
> living word of faith and spirit of hope departed not from me,
> but remained like ministering angels to cheer me through the
> gloom. This good spirit was from God, and to him I offer
> thanksgiving and praise.[62]

Douglass remembered fondly his early spiritual awakenings. Teaching the Sabbath school was the sweetest time of his life, and his long hours of prayer and Bible reading with the holy black man Charles Lawson stayed with him: "The advice and the suggestions of Uncle Lawson were not without their influence upon my character and destiny."[63] But he did not just look back to his formation among the Evangelicals. He looked forward to the nature mysticism that connects him with the Transcendentalists he came to know in New England. As a teenager he had been awed by a meteor shower.

> The heavens seemed about to part with its [the shower's] starry
> train. I witnessed this gorgeous spectacle and was awe-struck.
> The air seemed filled with bright descending messengers from
> the sky. It was about daybreak when I saw this sublime scene.
> I was not without the suggestion, at the moment, that it might
> be the harbinger of the coming of the Son of Man.[64]

His sense of space and silence as numinous stayed with him. What he wrote of the silent distances of Egypt, the land of "Abraham and Moses," could have come from Emerson.

> In this wide waste, under this cloudless sky, star-lighted by night
> and by a fierce blazing sun by day, where even the wind seems
> voiceless, it was natural for men to look up to the sky and stars
> and contemplate the universe and infinity above and around
> them; the signs and wonders in the heavens above and the
> earth beneath. In such loneliness, silence, and expansiveness,
> imagination is unchained and man has naturally a deeper sense
> of the Infinite Presence than is to be felt in the noise and bustle
> of the towns and men-crowded cities. . . . The heart beats louder
> and the soul hears quicker in silence and solitude.[65]

In Lincoln and Douglass, two great men provided the measure, each of the other, and they provide a hope and promise not only that black and white in American can know and love each other, but that the two poles of religion considered in this book can complete and confirm each other, as happened in the case of both men. The Transcendentalist-Evangelical and the Evangelical-Transcendentalist bridge many a gap.

20 | RELIGION IN THE GILDED AGE

A S SO OFTEN HAPPENS in a postwar situation, Americans after the Civil War came to see that many of the hopes they had invested in that bloody conflict were disappointed. The apocalyptic showdown did not produce a repristinated world. In the first blush of victory, it is true, all things seemed possible. Phillips Brooks preached from his Boston pulpit:

> We thank thee, O God, for the power of Thy right arm,
> which has broken for us a way, and set the banners of our
> Union in the central city of treason and rebellion. We thank
> Thee for the triumph of right over wrong. We thank Thee for
> the loyal soldiers planted in the streets of wickedness. We
> thank thee for the wisdom and bravery and devotion which
> Thou has anointed for Thy work, and crowned with glorious
> victory. . . . And now, O God, we pray Thee to complete Thy
> work.[1]

Edward Beecher, the abolitionist preacher who had urged his sister to write *Uncle Tom's Cabin,* was giddy with victory: "Now that God has smitten slavery unto death, he has opened the way for the redemption of our whole social system."[2]

But redemption was not so easily achieved. Religious groups rushed to send materials for black schools to the South, but the failure of Reconstruction deprived them of most opportunities. Not only did they meet a doomed-romantic resistance in the South, of which the Ku Klux Klan was just one dramatic symbol, but they were not backed energetically from the North, even by many former abolitionists. Opposition to slavery did not necessarily mean an acceptance of equality. Henry Adams, for instance, who was proud of his family tradition of opposing slavery, was against letting blacks vote after they were freed. He supported Andrew Johnson's limits on Reconstruction.

At first, the South had all its religious certitudes shattered. It had been certain that it was on God's side. Its Constitution put the South explicitly under divine protection—the first words were: "We the deputies of the sovereign and independent States of South Carolina, Georgia, Florida, Alabama, Mississippi, and Louisiana, *invoking the favor of the Almighty God,* do hereby . . ." (emphasis added).[3] As we have seen, this was a deliberate rebuke to the federal Constitution.[4] But at the war's end, having heard from preachers that God's cause would prevail, the South had to meditate on the Book of Job, on how God lets wrong prevail and good men suffer. The editor of the *Southern Presbyterian Review* said that the only religious mistake the South had made was forgetting that God sometimes lets the just suffer and the evil succeed.[5] Southerners would brood for many decades on the degraded position they had been reduced to, while the North took off on a spree of gaudy prosperity. Most whites in the South blamed their plight on the blacks and sought many indirect modes of revenge.

Not only had Southern cities and plantations been gutted. The whole economy was a wreck, with no recovery in sight. David Brion Davis said that emancipation without compensation was the exception in the modern history of slavery, and it had certainly never occurred on the scale of the South's costly emancipations:

> The slaves' value came to an estimated $3.5 billion in 1860 dollars. That would be about $69.4 billion in 2003 dollars. But a more revealing figure is the fact that the nation's gross national product in 1860 was only about 20 percent above the value of slaves, which means that as a share of today's gross national product, the slaves' value would come to an estimated $9.75 trillion. As investment capital, the value of the nation's slaves in 1860 had far exceeded (by perhaps a billion dollars) the cash value of all the farms in the South, including the border states of Delaware, Maryland, Kentucky, and Missouri. In 1860 the Southern slaves were also worth three times the cost of constructing all the nation's railroads or three times the combined capital invested initially in business and industrial property.[6]

The South would remain the most backward part of the country for almost a century. Not only was it crippled within—there was little support or change coming from without. The resources of the government were absorbed in expansion to the West. The tides of immigration did not flow southward, where there were no jobs, so the region stayed sealed off in its own retrospection, not forced to face new developments in the century. A major turning point would come only with the New Deal, in projects like the Tennessee Valley Authority.

Those who, like Emerson and Charles Eliot Norton, thought the war would bring America back to an austere morality saw their country plunge into the luxurious excesses and political corruption of the Gilded Age. The plight of freed blacks, and of the Indians being driven back to make way for Western expansion, was blotted out by dizzy fascination with the explosive changes of the Second Industrial Revolution, in which America's manufacturing equaled that of Great Britain, France, and Germany combined. Cities grew vertiginously. Robert Wiebe describes the push to make everything bigger—factories, city halls, churches, libraries.[7] And there was an urgency to make America itself bigger—first in the West, then in imperial thrusts into Spanish Cuba, Puerto Rico, the Philippines, and other Latin American and Pacific outposts.

NON-EVANGELICAL PREACHERS

WHERE DOES religion fit into this hectic picture? Richard Hofstadter said that the clergy lost status and had to accept lower pay than others in the professions. A number of religious colleges came under lay control.[8] In the 1850s, "of the fifty-four oldest colleges in the United States, fifty-one were presided over by clergymen."[9] The increased professionalism of the time, described by Burton Bledstein, meant that many of the advisory and social roles formerly played by priests and ministers were being handled by new specialists.[10] Ann Douglas adds an important qualifier to Hofstadter's claim. She notes that it was *non-Evangelical* preachers who became less important. (Evangelical revivalists were a different matter.) The non-Evangelical ministers became adjuncts to the prosperous, the confidants of well-to-do ladies. Douglas claims that a "woman's sphere" was created, made up mainly of women, clergy, and the authors of sentimental popular literature. Thus islanded off from the rough masculine world, the women and the clergy were made politically irrelevant, protected from contamination with vulgar things.[11]

There were some important and successful men among the non-Evangelical preachers, including those Sydney Ahlstrom calls "Princes of the Pulpit," men like Henry Ward Beecher and Phillips Brooks (A 738–40). But these, too, were social darlings, favorites of the ladies, whose main job was to comfort the comfortable. Brooks, it may be remembered, was satirized by his cousin Henry Adams in the novel *Esther,* whose heroine rejects the Brooks church for its lack of challenge and authenticity. Brooks and Beecher exemplify what H. Richard Niebuhr criticized in the religion of this time, which tells how "a God without wrath brought men without sin into a kingdom without judgment through the ministrations of a Christ without a Cross."[12] If that is all even the Princes had to offer, no wonder the clergy seemed irrelevant.

So far the stereotype of America's "Victorian age" seems to be confirmed, with its sentimentality, prim respectability, complacency, and its reticence about disquieting things (including sex). This was the time when Anthony Comstock waged his war on vice, as part of which the federal government passed the Comstock Law of 1873, making it a crime to sell, buy, or possess "obscene" literature or contraceptives. Comstock was given official authority by the United States Postal Service to seize mail he considered in breach of that law—as a result of which he destroyed books by the ton.

Comstock was popular and powerful because the Victorians wanted to protect the innocence of an idealized womanhood and childhood. Twain gave a vivid picture of the Victorian home in chapter 17 of *Huckleberry Finn*, where the child of the family has died young and her room is kept as a shrine—as Twain would later keep his own daughter's. The dead child, Emmeline, had lived her short life writing poems about dead people.

> Every time a man died, or a woman died, or a child died, she
> would be on hand with her "tribute" before he was cold. She
> called them tributes. The neighbors said it was the doctor first,
> then Emmeline, then the undertaker—the undertaker never
> got in ahead of Emmeline but once, and then she hung fire on a
> rhyme for the dead person's name, which was Whistler.[13]

The sentimentality of a decadent Romanticism glorified perfect and perishing little children. There was Little Eva of Harriet Beecher Stowe, along with Twain's own Little Eva and Little Willie. These were imitations of Dickens's Little Nell. Ann Douglas describes the whole phenomenon as a "domestication of death."[14] Even Twain gave in to it in his mawkish book *Joan of Arc*.

EVANGELICALS

THE STRIKING thing about the Gilded Age is that this time of clois-
tered piety coexisted with the most crude and corrupt power
struggles for gain. This showed in the ruthless drive to the West, where
Indians were killed who got in the way. It showed in the growth of corrupt city machines, in the "robber barons" who routinely bought politicians, making the Senate a "millionaires' club." It showed in the rationale
supplied by Social Darwinism for the most cutthroat practices of
laissez-faire capitalism. The social dislocations caused by rapid change,
industrialization, urbanization, immigration, a population explosion,
and competitive business left many of the less fortunate stranded or vulnerable to exploitation, not only immigrants and outsiders (like the Chi-
nese working on the railroads), but the native workers in mines and
factories. The unrest of the times reached a crescendo in the large
strikes and riots of the 1880s and 1890s, which were met with brutal
repression by hired agents, state militias, and federal troops responding
to businessmen's calls for help.

Evangelical ministers—at least some of them—could not ignore
these woes, as the Princes of the Pulpit most often did. The Evangelicals
were too close to the victims, to the rural workers who fought back in
populist movements, to the urban poor, to those immigrants not
recruited as foot soldiers of the city machines, to blacks being forced
back into subservience. Some religious groups responded to the needs of
such people—with settlement houses, home missions, soup kitchens,
and urban welfare organizations. The YMCA, Sunday schools, the Salvation Army, and Volunteers of America performed charity services in
an organized way.[15]

But not all Evangelicals were on the side of the poor, even when they
seemed to be. The revivalists, in particular, were more popular with the
exploiters than with the exploited. This was the time of endless revivals
everywhere. They reached their climax at the beginning of the next
century, when there were "650 active evangelists in the field, and 2,200

part-time campaigners," who would give thirty-five thousand revivals between 1914 and 1918, spending $20 million a year to mount them (A748). We have already seen that there were busy revivalists in both the North and the South during the war. Yet the wave of these emotional events swelled after the war, and kept on mounting.

Some have the impression that these revivals were rural or small-town phenomena, but most of them—and certainly the most successful and crowded ones—took place in cities, the bigger the better. Of course, many people in the city had just come streaming in from the country. Robert Wiebe argued that this was an age of anxiety because the values of what he calls "island communities" of self-sufficient and tightly connected personal relations in stable rural villages could not survive in the "distended" networks of the impersonal city.[16] One might therefore try to explain the city revivals, full of the older values, as a way of bridging the difference between provincial and cosmopolitan worlds, bolstering the displaced with comforting memories.

The trouble with this analysis is that the revivals were themselves tools of the new world. To see this we need only take the advice "Deep Throat" gave to Bob Woodward during the Watergate scandal: "Follow the money." The revivals were encouraged and financed by the robber barons, to keep their workers docile, and they were organized to the pattern and rhythms of the urban culture. The best example of this is the most successful evangelist, a model for others of his calling, Dwight L. Moody. As William McLoughlin wrote, "Charles Finney made revivalism a profession, but Dwight L. Moody made it a big business."[17]

MOODY

A T FIRST, this young urban businessman gave up his shoe trade to work for the Salvation Army in the slums of Chicago. He slept in church basements and ate the fare of the poor. He was a favorite of street children and became something of a Chicago institution—even Abraham Lincoln visited his mission, once just before his election as president and once just after.[18] Moody was conducting a religious service for twenty-five hundred when the great Chicago fire of 1871 swept toward the hall where his service was being held. Moody fled to get his wife and children and send them north of the fire. His singing master, Ira Sankey, went to the shore and watched the fire from a boat in Lake Michigan.[19] It was while his and the YMCA's halls were being rebuilt that he accepted an invitation that changed his life. Wealthy and titled Evangelicals in England and Scotland invited him to lead a revival in Great Britain.

Moody's first adventures in a wider sphere came from trips to England for religious conferences in 1867, 1870, and 1872, where he made important acquaintances with wealthy Evangelical Tories, including the Seventh Earl of Shaftesbury. These trips paid off in 1873, when he was invited to give that series of revivals throughout Britain. Moody was following the example of Lorenzo Dow and Charles Finney, who had conducted some of their most successful early revivals in Great Britain. When Moody arrived in 1873, he had a potent ally in his singing master, Ira Sankey, whose popular hymns would become Victorian best-sellers. By the end of his two-year campaign, Moody was preaching in the Royal Opera House, with the first gallery reserved for nobility under the patronage of Lord Shaftesbury, a Tory anti-Darwinist who opposed British liberal moves like the Reform Act of 1867 and the Ballot Act of 1873.[20]

Moody's revivals in Scotland and England made him and Sankey world famous, a staple of the secular as well as the religious press. When he returned to Chicago, the city's newspapers urged their readers to join a moral crusade led by Moody.[21] He quickly got the same kind of wealthy backing that he had received in England. For his major city campaigns, he sought and received support from local business leaders. Churches were not large enough to hold the audiences he drew. In Philadelphia, the head of Wanamaker stores renovated a warehouse so it could seat ten thousand people. In New York, Moody took over P. T. Barnum's Hippodrome. In Boston, a new "tabernacle" had to be built, capable of holding six thousand hearers. Chicago, too, built him a special tabernacle, with seating for eight thousand.[22] From this time on, Moody asked the sponsoring committees to build him a new tabernacle in each city he visited. To finance these large projects, he needed support from the very robber barons who were causing the problems of the poor. He was financed by Jay Cooke in Philadelphia, Cyrus McCormick and George Armour in Chicago, Cornelius Vanderbilt II and J. P. Morgan in New York, Amos A. Lawrence and Joseph Story in Baltimore.[23]

To mount his huge events, Moody had to employ the very kind of "bureaucratization" that was, according to Wiebe, far from the "small-town values" of the past. Even the *Unitarian Review,* which had criticized him for "commercializing" religion, had to admit: "The thorough organization and clear business sense in this movement are to be admired."[24] He had a permanent staff in the dozens. Before coming to a city to revive it, he formed a local executive committee and finance committee to organize resources. Advertisements were taken out in the newspapers and posters were nailed up. He recruited well-drilled teams of ushers, one hundred to two hundred of them, wearing identifying ribbons and carrying long "wands" to conduct people with. Hundreds of local singers were drawn from city churches and rehearsed to join Sankey in his hymns.[25]

There was no more "anxious seat" up front. Instead, "inquiry rooms" were built along the sides of the tabernacles, where Moody and his staff could consult with the converts who came forward at the "call meeting." There the spiritual state of those who had chosen Jesus would be inquired into.[26] Cards signed by the converted kept a tally of Moody's score in each town and made it possible to reach the same people in the future. (Many of his "converts" were repeaters.) Moody's revivals were a managerial prodigy, with the show-biz addition of his own performances and Sankey's tearjerking songs. That is why Moody is such an emblem of the Gilded Age itself. As Richard Hofstadter wrote: "Finney's revivalism belonged to the age of Andrew Jackson and Lyman Beecher; Moody's belonged to the age of Andrew Carnegie and P. T. Barnum."[27]

Moody directed his hearers away from social concerns. As he put it himself:

> When I was at work for the City Relief Society, before the
> [Chicago] fire, I used to go to a poor sinner with the Bible in

one hand and a loaf of bread in the other. . . . My idea was that I
could open a poor man's heart by giving him a load of wood or
a ton of coal when the winter was coming on; but I soon found
out that he wasn't any more interested in the Gospel on that
account. Instead of thinking how he could come to Christ, he
was thinking how long it would be before he got the load of
wood. If I had the Bible in one hand and a loaf in the other, the
people always looked first at the loaf, and that was just the
contrary of the order laid down in the Gospel.[28]

The sins Moody denounced were personal ones—especially the sins
of drunkenness, which led to poor job performance. "I do not believe we
would have these hard times if it had not been for sin and iniquity. Look
at the money that is drank up!" Self-reliance meant having nothing to do
with unions or strikes. "Work your way up to the top of the ladder and
you will like to stay up there; but if you are lifted up there by somebody,
you will be all the time tumbling back." What about the ten-hour day?
(The eight-hour was still far off.)

> Get something to do. If it is for fifteen hours a day, all the
> better; for while you are at work Satan does not have so much
> chance to tempt you. If you cannot earn more than a dollar a
> week, earn that. That is better than nothing, and you can pray
> to God for more.[29]

Though his wealthy supporters were comforted by these words, it is
doubtful that they reached many of the people they were aimed at.
Drunkards and the unemployed were not in attendance. The respectable
middle class, along with some wealthy people, made up his audience.
"He boosted the morale of the regular churchgoers, but he did not reach
the masses and he did not add appreciably to the numerical growth of
the churches."[30]

Moody's theology was even more elusive than that of Charles Finney.
They both decried university learning about God. When a woman said,

"I want you to know that I do not believe in your theology," he replied, "My theology? I didn't know I had any. I wish you would tell me what my theology is."[31] He was, in fact, inconsistent. Though he was technically pessimistic about the world, expecting the Second Coming, he was very worldly about getting ahead: "I don't see how a man can follow Christ and not be successful."[32] He did not, like others, preach hellfire, explaining, "Terror never brought a man in yet."[33] He said he would rather "love people in."

> Christ's teaching was always constructive. . . . His method of
> dealing with error was largely to ignore it, letting it melt away
> in the warm glow of the full intensity of truth expressed in
> love. . . . Let us hold truth, but by all means let us hold it in
> love, and not with a theological club.[34]

"I look upon this world as a wrecked vessel," he said. "God has given me a lifeboat and said to me, 'Moody, save all you can.'"[35] To do that all the theology he needed was "the three *r*'s": *ruin* by sin, *redemption* by Christ, *regeneration* by the Holy Ghost.[36]

THE MOODY EMPIRE

GIVEN HIS rather superficial theology, it is easy to underestimate Moody's continuing importance in American religion, to think of him as a glitzy fad of the Gilded Age. But he may well have been the second most influential revivalist of all. Those who had the most impact would include, at the very least, these seven: George Whitefield, Francis Asbury, Lorenzo Dow, Charles Finney, Dwight Moody, Billy Sunday, and Billy Graham. Among them, I suspect, Francis Asbury had the deepest and most sustained impact, because of the role he had in the explosion and persistence of Methodism in the nineteenth century. But Moody has a strong claim on the second rank. This is not only because of his revivals. It comes from his use of the revivals to build a Bible study empire that absorbed the two most important new Evangelical emphases of his time, the Holiness Movement and Dispensational Premillennialism. His name and sponsorship provided both with a medium of wider diffusion than they could have won on their own. Moody was primarily interested in personal piety, but "his lieutenants—Torrey, Gray, Pierson, Gordon, Blanchard, Erdman, and Scofield—added to that piety a strong interest in ideas."[37] And the ideas that interested them inform Fundamentalism to this very day.

Though Moody did not have a high regard for academic theology, he was quick to support the Bible schools so popular in his time, promulgated by the Sunday schools and the YMCA, and he added his own more lasting variants on them. Given his vast prestige, he was able to set up two centers that still exist, one in the Northeast, near his home (Northfield, Massachusetts), and one in his original base of operations, Chicago. He set up the Northfield Schools (one for boys, one for girls) in 1879 and 1881 to show how a preparatory school could have a Bible-centered curriculum. The schools were also used as sites for Bible conferences, adult programs, and international students' gatherings (which became, in 1887, the Student Volunteer Movement for missionary work).[38]

In 1886 he had established the Chicago Evangelization Society, which became the still-flourishing Moody Bible Institute. This grew out of work Moody started doing with Emmeline (known as Emma) Dryer. After the Chicago fire, he recruited her in 1871 to help build up the YMCA again, as superintendent of the Women's Auxiliary (which would become the YWCA). In 1873 he raised funds for her to begin a school for training women missionaries. In 1883, again with his help, she broadened her scope into a Bible studies program called the May Institute. When there was a call for a more ambitious and permanent Bible study effort, Moody typically challenged Chicago businessmen to put up $250,000 to launch it. When they did, he opened the Evangelization Society,[39] Moody became its president, and in 1889 appointed Reuben A. Torrey as the school's superintendent. Its later growth into a large publishing and broadcasting center was a powerful part of the Evangelical presence in America.

The connections between Moody's network and the burgeoning Holiness Movement and Dispensationalist school were personal and institutional. Moody was the man others wanted to be associated with, in order to spread their own views and contacts. Moody was not only a businessman in the revival business; he was a kind of entrepreneur of the Spirit, encouraging any Protestants he found interested in conversion. The more powerful of the two movements that flowed into his in the 1870s, Dispensationalism, was developed mainly after Torrey succeeded Moody as president of the institute, so it will be considered in the next chapter. Here it is enough to consider the Holiness Movement.

THE HOLINESS MOVEMENT

HOLINESS IN this context refers to Christian perfectionism, which dates back to Wesley and some of his followers. Charles Finney and Asa Mahan taught a version of it at Oberlin College in the 1830s. But its concepts took on new force and definition as a result of annual meetings at Keswick parish in England's Lake District. These began in 1875, when Moody was in England, and he helped promote a Brighton conference which was the immediate inspiration of the Keswick meetings. George Marsden writes: "Although Moody did not follow Keswick terminology precisely, he taught very similar views and made them central in his work. The Northfield conferences especially resemble the Keswick gatherings."[40]

In England, the movement was often called the Higher Life Movement, since an internal second baptism was supposed to lift one above the level of physical life into a life of the Spirit. This was called "the second touch," and it resulted in "entire sanctification." Most Keswick speakers did not think of this as "eradication" of the bodily life, but as a "counteraction" to it. It is not gained by one's own effort but by a total surrender to God's action:

> Self is dethroned. God is enthroned. The sanctification is a
> process, but one that begins with a distinct crisis experience. It
> is analogous to man struggling in the water (lost sinner) who

grasps hold of a rowboat (regeneration), climbs aboard and
rests in the boat itself (sanctification). Then he is in a position
to rescue other struggling men (service).[41]

The process was referred to by key terms loaded with meaning for
the followers—like Victorious Life, or Power for Service. The idea of
surrender had special appeal in the anxious age that, as Wiebe put it, was
searching for order. It promised a release from nagging doubts and anxieties. It could, of course, become mere autosuggestion of the Émile
Coué sort ("Every day in every way I am getting better and better") or
the anodyne formulas of Norman Vincent Peale. The promise of peace
is a powerful part of evangelists' preaching even today. But it had special
force as the nineteenth century was ending. William James seems to have
caught some ripples from it when he wrote of the popularity of "mind
cure" in his 1902 Gifford Lectures:

> The fundamental pillar on which it rests is nothing more than
> the general basis of all religious experience, the fact that man
> has a dual nature, and is connected with two spheres of
> thought, a shallower and a profounder sphere, in either of
> which he may live more habitually.[42]

The mind curers, according to James, think that fear is the thing that
binds one to the lower sphere, and to give up fear lifts one to a higher
plane. He calls this America's "only decidedly original contribution to
the systematic philosophy of life." It may not be that, but it clearly fits
in with the optimism of American culture—and it helps explain the
immense force of Keswickism and related thought at the turn of the
century. It reinvigorated the Oberlin theology. It led to the formation of
new religious bodies, like the Church of the Nazarene, and new colleges,
like the Columbia Bible School, and the establishment of an American
Keswick in Whiting, New Jersey.

This, like many other continuing features of American life, was partly
the responsibility of Moody. His death in the last year of the century was

an occasion of national mourning. It was estimated that he had spoken to 100 million people—and, said his followers, had reduced the population of hell by at least a million.[43] He was indeed "God's Man for the Gilded Age." Martin Marty was not overstating the case when he wrote: "At a critical stage of American religious history, the Chicago-based evangelist could plausibly have been called Mr. Revivalism and perhaps even Mr. Protestant."[44]

PART FOUR

CULTURE WARS

❖

VII | DOOMSDAY OR PROGRESS?

21 | SECOND-COMING THEOLOGY

G EORGE MARSDEN says that Dwight Moody had every typical mark of a Fundamentalist but one. He was irenic, and most Fundamentalists relish—perhaps too much—a fight.

> Moody's contribution to emerging Fundamentalism was both large and complex. Moody was a progenitor of Fundamentalism—it could even be argued that he was its principal progenitor. He believed in biblical infallibility and premillennialism. He did as much as anyone in America to promote the forms of Holiness teaching and the ethical emphases that were accepted by many Fundamentalists. His closest associates had virtually all the traits of later Fundamentalism, and many of them participated directly in organizing the Fundamentalist movement in the twentieth century. Yet Moody himself lacked the one trait that was essential to a "Fundamentalist"—he was unalterably opposed to controversy.[1]

Moody spread a wide tent, not only for the Holiness Movement but for the more important school of Premillennialism, whose most important advocates in America all sheltered under his powerful patronage.

This was a hinge moment in Evangelical history. Most Protestant theologians before the 1880s had been Postmillennialists in their eschatology—that is, they thought that Christ would come again only *after* the thousand-year reign (Millennium), in which Satan is bound and the saints rule (Revelation 20.3). This was an optimistic view of history, in which the Puritans felt that America played a vital role, if not the leading one, bringing the reign of God to a glorious fulfillment. Cotton Mather, Jonathan Edwards, and Samuel Sewall had used prophecies to show that the Antichrist (papal Rome) was being set back and God's progress (the Great Awakening) was being confirmed. This is a view that has pervaded American history, bolstering "exceptionalism," the sense of being a chosen people, indeed the Second Israel.

There had been a few dissenters from this view—*Pre*millennialists, who thought Christ would return *before* the Millennium, and especially before the catastrophes ("the Tribulation") that, on one reading, the Bible said must precede the Millennium. The previously most famous of these Premillennialists in America, as we have seen, was William Miller, with his prediction that Christ would return in the 1840s. When the predicted date passed, Miller's hard-core followers held out for some later vindication, and perpetuated themselves as Seventh-day Adventists or Jehovah's Witnesses. But it went against the grain of America's optimistic spirit to say that all of history was leading straight to disaster.

That is what makes the Premillennialists of the 1880s so striking. They turned the biblical timetable upside down. If, before then, most Evangelicals had been "Postmills," to use the seminary slang, since then most have been, in one degree or another, "Premills." They have expected the coming of Christ *before* all the prophecies of the End Time, whether dire (the Tribulation) or sunny (the Millennium). They adopted the "any moment" concept—Christ's coming is imminent. Be prepared *right now*! Convert others in frenzied urgency! There is little or no time left! It is not surprising that this approach would be plausible.

The first followers of Jesus had expected his early return and an end to history. The church had uncomfortably adjusted to the fact that this did not occur in the lifetime of the original disciples, or of their followers, for decades and then for centuries. It was the genius of the new Premillennialists in the 1880s to come up with reasons for thinking that the doomsday clock, stalled for centuries, would soon start ticking.

These new alarmists, persuasive as they were to many, could not have had their great impact if they had not sheltered under the broad-spread tent of Moody's ecumenical spiritual gathering. Under its shelter, strong personalities were able to turn old energies around. They had such power because the revivalistic Evangelicals did not act within hierarchical structures or creedal continuities. They had acquired the ability to elicit immediate responses to biblical texts, however wrenched from context. Their followers would turn the "Premill" system into a rigid set of rote ideas; but the bracing thing about their first appearance was the willingness of Evangelicals to *throw away* old certitudes and adopt a radical new approach to the Bible. They had Spirit leaders who convinced them to become Spirit-led. And in an America without the resources of an established church, they could rely on the wealth of individual entrepreneurs who responded to their initiatives. They had Moody's all-important sanction to add to their other recommendations. The first of these in rank was Moody's heir apparent at the Moody Bible Institute, Reuben Torrey.

REUBEN A. TORREY (1856–1928)

A S A CHAMPION of Premillennialism, Torrey was far stricter and more consistent than Moody himself. It is not surprising that the openhearted Moody could hold to both the optimistic Holiness creed and the darker Premillennialism. But Torrey made the combination even more anomalous. Moody had met Torrey when the latter was studying at the Yale Divinity School, and later heard good things about his ministry in Minneapolis before he asked him to manage the administration and curriculum of his Chicago Bible School. But Moody, while vaguely accepting Premillennialism, was not a dogged scrutinizer of its details. Torrey was. He had a pedantic personality, as William McLoughlin notes:

> On the street he usually wore a high hat, and he always talked
> as though he had one on. With typical pompous gravity
> he once told a reporter, "I cannot say that I fully advocate
> the old-time style of revival where emotion was the chief
> instrument. . . . I always think of myself as a lawyer when I get
> up to speak and of the audience as a jury.". . . He had absolutely
> none of Moody's humor and gruff humanity, and he com-
> pletely lacked Moody's persuasive personal appeal.[2]

Despite this dour personality, Torrey felt that he should continue the revivals of Moody upon the leader's death. He therefore accepted an invitation to conduct a revival in Australia, keeping up a tradition of launching one's first ambitious campaign abroad. He was surprisingly successful, largely because of the expansive personality and infectious singing of his music partner, Charles McCallom Alexander. In the first decade of the twentieth century, Torrey led revivals in Europe and America. This took him away from the daily running of the Moody Bible Institute (as he had renamed the Chicago school on the death of Moody). In 1912 Torrey became dean of a new Bible school, the Los Angeles Bible Institute, financed by the godfathers of the Premillennials, the oil million-aire brothers, Lyman and Milton Stewart. When the Stewarts launched a famous book series, known as *The Fundamentals,* Torrey was one of the three editors of the project. In all these activities, Torrey energetically advanced the views of Premillennialism's British founder, John Darby.

JOHN NELSON DARBY (1800–1887)

DARBY'S GODFATHER, who gave him his middle name, was a family friend, Lord Nelson. Darby himself trained as a lawyer before he turned to the ministry, as a priest in the established Church of Ireland.

He left that church when the archbishop of Dublin tried to make Darby's Roman Catholic converts swear allegiance to King George IV. He joined others who were discontented with the established church, and they formed a body called the Plymouth Brethren. These men followed a new approach to the Bible and the End Time which Darby spread through Europe and brought to America in seven trips between 1862 and 1877.[3] His reception here was far more cordial and lasting than what he encountered in his home country. There, he had fallen into feuding with the Plymouth Brethren. In America, the Premillennialists did not form a separate church, like the Plymouth Brethren, but remained in their own churches—primarily Presbyterian, Baptist, and Methodist—to act as a saving leaven in each community.

For his followers, Darby was the first person to make sense of the Bible's apocalyptic prophecies. He added an important adjective to the noun Premillennialism—"Dispensational." In a sense, all Christian theology is "dispensational," since it speaks of two testaments or covenants or economies—that under the Jewish revelation and that under the Christian. But Darby made these two discontinuous and autonomous, in a way that was new. One did not succeed the other. They were ruled by different prophetical systems—one of them past, *Israel*, under the law, with all past prophecies applying only to it; and one of them future, the *church*, with its prophecies not to move toward fulfillment until the church was taken up by God before the End Time. Only then would the predicted final catastrophe (the Tribulation) and final resolution (the Millennium) occur. Christ would trigger this new sequence not only by a Second Coming (to take up his church to heaven) but by a Third Coming (to bring his saints back to earth, after the Tribulation, to share his reign in the Millennium). It was the Second Coming, to gather in his saints (which Darby called "the Rapture") that was new, odd, and appealing. It did seem to unlock many scriptural passages. Probably no other man has had a more deeply reorienting impact on American theology than John Nelson Darby.

Many Americans, along with Torrey, enthusiastically worked out the implications of this new system. Following his example, they called this practice "rightly dividing the word," quoting the King James Version's mistranslation of 2 Timothy 2.15. The verb *orthotomein*, which the King James Version rendered as "dividing," actually means to "to cut straight." to forge a direct path—but the Premillennialists fought any new translation of the Bible, since sixteenth-century scholarship gave them the unalterable texts they expounded as interlocking, mutually confirming "facts." Among his followers, the first to take the new system to new audiences was James Brookes, the pastor of the Second Presbyterian Church in Saint Louis.

JAMES H. BROOKES (1830–1887)

B ROOKES SPREAD the Premillennial message through a network of conferences and publications. He founded and edited a periodical, *The Truth.* He wrote and disseminated (with the help of rich friends) over 250 tracts and seventeen books—of which the most successful, *Maranatha, or The Lord Cometh*, ran through ten editions between 1874 and 1889. But his important contribution was the annual Bible conference he ran between 1875 and 1897.

These were known as the Niagara Conferences, though they had been held elsewhere before settling down at their permanent site, Niagara-on-the-Lake in Ontario. Here all the leading Premillennialists met to refine their views and shape strategies for disseminating them. Other conferences modeled themselves on this one, and Brookes himself set up the first International Prophecy Conference in 1877 (later ones were assembled in 1886, 1895, 1901, 1914, and 1918). The Niagara Conferences were as important for Premillennialism as the Keswick meetings had been for the Holiness Movement. One of those attending the Niagara meetings and sending its message around the world was William Blackstone.

WILLIAM E. BLACKSTONE (1841–1935)

A DESCENDANT of William Blackstone, the eighteenth-century legal theorist, William Ewing Blackstone was a successful businessman in Oak Park, Illinois, a Chicago follower of Dwight Moody. He became a backer of Dispensationalist ideas in talks and pamphlets. In 1878 he published one of the most influential books on the subject, *Jesus Is Coming*. This was expanded in later editions of 1888 and 1908, translated into forty-two languages, and freely distributed. He had thousands of copies in various languages stored in Petra, since he thought that during the Tribulation Antichrist would drive unconverted Jews to Petra, where they could read the book and be converted.

ARNO C. GAEBELEIN (1861–1945)

I F BLACKSTONE was the leading Dispensationalist in the Midwest, Arno Gaebelein was his equivalent in the East (New York). He had been born in Germany but came to America at age eighteen. Previously a Lutheran, he became a Methodist minister in America. He was an accomplished linguist and an intellectual networker who coordinated the support of wealthy Evangelicals for Dispensationalism. He worked to evangelize Jews in New York's East Side with the Hope of Israel Mission and the journal *Our Hope*. He decided to revive the Niagara Conferences in 1901, holding them annually at Sea Cliff, the Long Island estate of John T. Pirie, the Chicago millionaire owner of Carson Pirie Scott department store. It was at these conferences that Gaebelein decided to raise money for Cyrus Scofield to devote his full time to a Dispensationalist edition of the Bible, a momentous project.

CYRUS I. SCOFIELD (1845–1921)

T HE NIAGARA conferees and their many allies had their work cut out for them in putting the ideas of John Darby on pages. Darby was a powerful advocate in person, but he left rather hazy sketches of his thought in writing. Ernest Sandeen rightly says: "He left a massive set of *Collected Writings* which are almost uniformly unintelligible."[4] Other men—Torrey, Brookes, Blackstone, Gaebelein—wrote more persuasively about Darby's views, but it was felt that a strict exposition of them, in conjunction with all the Bible verses buttressing the system, was needed—a summa of biblical thought on the matter. The need for this led to the immense success of the Scofield Reference Bible when it appeared in 1909.

Scofield had emerged from a murky background, which he later took pains to conceal. Born in Michigan, he served in the Confederate army before becoming a lawyer and an officeholder in Kansas (state legislator and district attorney). But then he fled his political career, his wife and children, some debts (certainly), alcoholism (probably), and accusations of stealing the campaign funds of his law partner, Senator John Ingalls.[5] After time in a Saint Louis jail, he was born again and came under the influence of James Brookes, the father of the Niagara Conferences. Scofield joined Dwight Moody in one of his revival campaigns. In 1888 he was licensed to preach in Congregational churches and was ordained in 1883. He began a series of Bible studies—in his churches, and by correspondence school, and in a monthly journal. In 1888 he published a Darbyite pamphlet called *Rightly Dividing the Word of God*. In 1895 Moody invited him to become the pastor of the church in East Northfield near Moody's home.

All this time Scofield was attending the Niagara Conferences and other prophecy meetings and refining his theory of the Dispensations. At last he published his magnum opus, his reference Bible, with the prestigious Oxford University Press. It soon became the ruling authority in seminaries, Sunday schools, and Bible conferences. Preachers preached from it. Laymen learned its recondite terminology. The book is dry, pedantic, and certain—a kind of printed papacy, where an infallible meaning is given for any verse in the Bible. Scofield did not rely simply on his notes to give a Dispensationalist structure to the whole Bible. He gave titles to chapters and to subdivisions that sifted material through his interpretive grid. "Unlike most commentators, Scofield combined his notes and the biblical text on the same page, so the former took on much the same authority as the latter; readers often could not remember whether they had encountered a particular thought in the notes or in the text."[6] The book sold in the millions, decade after decade. As late as the 1950s, James Barr interviewed many Evangelicals for a book on Fundamentalism and found over half of those he interviewed were familiar with Scofield's Bible, and many of them were surprised that any views but its could be considered.[7] When Oxford brought out still another edition in 1967, it sold two and a half million copies.

Scofield said that there were seven historical Dispensations clearly spelled out in the Bible—all of whose books, whether poetic, legislative, or historical, whether Psalms or Gospels or Epistles—he read as a single integrated text with a single all-embracing message. Five of the Dispensations preceded the death of Christ. The sixth, the present age, is a kind of "parenthesis" to which no prophecies apply. The prophetic clock will start again when Christ comes for his saints, after which the predicted End Time will occur (Tribulation followed by Millennium). Scofield's method was at once enticing (like a treasure hunt) and stultifying (since it sealed off any but one meaning for the components of the different genres included in the Hebrew and Greek writings). He purported to study Bible "facts" with Baconian straightforwardness—any "allegorizing" of the Scripture allows too many ways of escaping the literal sense, and the literal sense is the only thing that allows fact to be linked with fact in the authoritative structure of Bible truth. For him, Bible truth is the whole truth—anything outside its purview must not be allowed to challenge it. Since Scofield's is a sealed and self-referential system, outsiders, not willing to "crack the code" of this complex set of references, have usually considered it an eccentric system. But to many it is the very center of the meaning of Christianity.

LYMAN STEWART (1840–1924)

ONE OF THE MEN who financed Scofield's research for his great project was Lyman Stewart. Of all the wealthy men who supported Dispensationalism, Lyman Stewart and his brother Milton were the foremost. They had made their money in the Union Oil Company of

California, and they meant to use it for religious purposes. Milton specialized in support for missionary activity in China, while Lyman worked mainly in the United States. It has already been noticed that Stewart set up the Bible Institute of Los Angeles where Reuben Torrey was dean. He also gave money to Occidental College for Bible teachers and their books. Lyman paid for the publication and distribution of William Blackstone's *Jesus Is Coming* (including those thousands of copies in many languages hidden at Petra).[8]

But the brothers are best known for financing a series of twelve books of collected essays called *The Fundamentals,* which appeared between 1910 and 1915. The Stewarts distributed them free to about 3 million leaders. The man they put in charge of the project, A. C. Dixon, was the pastor of Moody Church in Chicago. From the 1880s he had been active in the Dispensationalists' Bible and prophecy conferences. He chose Reuben Torrey to serve on the executive board of *The Fundamentals,* and about half of the sixty-four contributors to the volumes were Dispensationalists.[9] They reflected the list of fourteen fundamental religious truths drawn up at the 1878 Niagara Conference and published as the Niagara Creed, a document Sandeen calls "one of the most significant documents in the history of the Fundamentalist movement."[10] So the Stewarts' project was not primarily a defensive reaction to modernism in the twentieth century but the culmination of a long Darbyite program that began in the 1870s.[11]

THE RAPTURE

I SHOULD NOT leave the Dispensationalists' theology without a look at their most distinctive belief, the Rapture, by which God's saints will be swept up to Christ before the world-rending Tribulation begins. Critics of Dispensationalism—even other Fundamentalists—argued that this belief is a strange one for believers in biblical literalism, since there is no one "proof text" for the idea in the Bible. It emerges, rather, from the whole concatenation of prophecy beliefs. Since the prophecies apply to the Jews, they are the ones who will suffer the Tribulation. Christians have no real role in it. They will not, like the surviving mass of mankind, acknowledge the rule of Antichrist in his time of power, so they will be kept hors de combat. It was the total schema, too, that made Darby always refer to the *secret* Rapture. Not secret in the sense that no one would notice when thousands of people disappeared. But they would not know the explanation, since Jesus would not be seen except by those meeting him "in the air." This *secret* coming of Jesus is in contrast with his final coming in glory, which will manifest his power to all. Once the whole framework was in place, the Dispensationalists searched for biblical texts that can be made to conform with it. The principal one is from Paul's First Letter to the Thessalonians 4.17. The Thessalonians, who expected the imminent return of Christ, worried about their fellow Christians who had already died. Paul assured them that the living and dead would both be swept up to meet the returning Jesus: "Then we, which are alive and remain, shall be caught up together with them [the dead] in the clouds, to meet the Lord in the air; and so shall we ever be with the Lord."

One trouble with use of this passage can be seen in the immediately preceding verse (16): "For the Lord himself shall descend from heaven with a shout, with the voice of the archangel and with the trump of God, and the dead in Christ shall rise first." That is hardly a secret coming. It has the finality of the ultimate coming, which does not fit Darby's sequence of second *and third* comings. This verse also describes Jesus as *descending* from heaven, while Darby wants him to be invisibly remaining in heaven, snatching the chosen up to him while no one else sees him.

The other favorite passage of the Darbyites is Matthew 24.40–41: "Then shall two be in the field; the one shall be taken, and the other left. Two women shall be grinding at the mill; the one shall be taken, and the other left." This is what gives the "left behind" language to the movement, where the "taken" are the chosen and the remaining are the doomed. But this passage, too, takes its meaning from the immediately preceding verse. Describing all the people who refused to hear Noah and join him on the ark, it says: "And [they] knew not until the flood came *and took them all away.*" The section speaks of destruction, not deliverance. To be taken away is to be destroyed. Being left behind, like Noah and his family, is the desirable thing.[12]

Other passages cited have even flimsier connections with a "rapture." The odd thing is that there is a much better verse that could be used to indicate the Rapture, one from the Lord's Prayer. What the King James Version renders as "Lead us not into temptation" (Matthew 6.13) is more properly "Do not carry us into the Trial," where "Trial" (*Peirasmos*) means the apocalyptic ending of time (what the Darbyites call the Tribulation). Jesus tells the disciples in other places to pray that they avoid the Peirasmos (Mark 14.38; Luke 11.4, 22.40, 22.46). Moreover, the next verse of the Lord's Prayer, translated "Deliver us from evil," is seen by parallel usage to be referring to a masculine noun, not neuter (the forms are the same: "Snatch [*rhusai*] us from the Evil One"). And all these passages warn the disciples to "stay awake." The Lord's Prayer is an eschatological prayer, and it could be seen as a prayer to be taken away before the Tribulation (Peirasmos).

Why do the Darbyites not use this passage? There are two reasons. Since they believe not only in the inerrancy of the Bible but in the inerrancy of the King James Version, they do not look for meanings beyond the obvious ones given there. Moreover, Scofield considered the Lord's Prayer a Jewish prayer, not a Christian one. His note on it says: "The Lord's prayer is, dispensationally, upon legal, not church ground; it is not a prayer in the name of Christ; and it makes human forgiveness, as under the law it must, the condition of divine forgiveness, an order which grace exactly reverses." Their system was too rigid to let them find more convincing arguments for it.

Yet the Rapture has been one reason for the success of the Premillennialists. It gives some people comfort to think they may at "any moment" be with Jesus. The imminent Second Coming lets some preachers, who no longer dwell on the horrors of hell, dwell on the horrors of the Tribulation. And it gives others a kind of weird satisfaction to dwell on the horrid fate of those "left behind"—the kind of smug assurance reflected on one bumper sticker: "In case of the Rapture, this car is driverless."

Not all Fundamentalists, of course, are Premillennialists; but most have been affected by them. It would be hard to argue with Timothy Weber's conclusion: "Without millenarianism, there could not possible be a Billy Graham, Oral Roberts, PTL Club, Jerry Falwell and Moral Majority, or any of a myriad of similar personages and movements."[13]

In confirmation of that, two quotes (from a very great many). One, by Jerry Falwell: "If you are saved, you will never go through one hour, not one moment, of the Tribulation."[14] The other, by Billy Graham: "The whole world is hurtling toward a war greater than anything known before."[15] Darbyism is truly the most pervasive of the influences on modern Premillennialism.

22 | SECOND-COMING POLITICS

A COMMON VIEW of religious history in America is that Evangelicals, wounded by ridicule around the Scopes trial in 1925, withdrew
from public life and did not return to the social scene until much later in
the century. There are many things wrong with that scenario. They
never did withdraw entirely. To the extent that they did, it was on principled grounds that predated the trial. The main force driving them
from political activity was Premillennialism. After all, what sense did it
make to engage in ameliorative public action when Jesus could appear
"any moment." The Premillennialists held that the present Dispensation
is not an improvable one; it is doomed. There were some things that
tempered this shrinking away from reform actions, but they too were
a matter of theological commitment—having to do, for instance, with
Israel, with Russia, and (later) with nuclear politics. But the dominant
tropism of the school was toward passivity.

SOCIAL PASSIVITY

THE GENERAL attitude of Premillennialists was stated by the oracle of the school, Cyrus Scofield: "The true mission of the church is not the reformation of society. What Christ did not do, the Apostles did not do. Not one of them was a reformer."[1] Arno Gaebelein opposed social reform as a palliative of the disease that must reach its height, the sooner the better: "Satan, I doubt not, wants to reform his world a little, to help on the deception that men do not need to be born again."[2] As one of the school put it: "A Premillennialist cannot cooperate with the plans of modern social service, for these contemplate many years with gradual improvement, through education as its main avenue for cooperation, rather than the second coming of Christ."[3]

The Fundamentalist distrust of merely human efforts at controlling history has lasted into late-twentieth-century opposition to "world government," to the U.N., to the World Bank, to the Trilateral Commission, to the Council on Foreign Relations, to the Aspen Institute, to the National Council of Churches, to the efforts of science to improve mankind.[4] When President George H. W. Bush proclaimed a New World Order, Pat Robertson wrote a whole book to denounce this as a ploy to create world government, "a new order for the human race under the domination of Lucifer and his followers."[5] The Antichrist in Tim LaHaye's Dispensationalist "Left Behind" series of novels, Nicolae Carpathia, is a social reformer and one-worlder.

Of course, Premillennialists could not entirely disengage from the world, since that is where one has to meet the souls to be saved. Thus the inactivism of the Premillennialist always had exceptions—especially where Temperance was concerned. How could one convert a sinner if he was too drunk to hear the preacher? But even this gave some purists misgivings. After all, drunkenness was one of the signs of the world's end, so perhaps the devil was using Temperance itself "to hinder Christ's return and extend his own probation."[6] Evangelists would be drawn back into worldly reform by various circumstances—especially, as we shall see, by war, when it is difficult for anyone to abstain. But basic principles were always tugging them back toward passivity.[7]

That is why, as Christian liberalism and the Social Gospel arose, the Premillennialists resisted them just as their descendants now denounce "humanism," a swearword among them. Tim LaHaye even condemns Thomas Aquinas for his use of Aristotle: "It is an irony of history that a man who was sainted by his church as a scholar was responsible for reviving an almost dead philosophy, which has become the most dangerous religion in the world today—humanism."[8] Attempts to reform the church were, in their eyes, a way of joining the world in its efforts at self-sufficiency. According to Darby, the real church was simply the number of individual saints in the various denominations. The formal churches were headed toward apostasy, and any compromise with Darwinism, the Higher Criticism of the Bible, or technological improvements was a ploy of the devil. On the other hand, events seen as fulfilling End Time prophecies were objects of intense interest, not from humanitarian or social concerns, but to proclaim the word of God. That was especially true for what the Bible seemed to say about Israel.

ISRAEL

SOME THINK it odd (and recent) for the Religious Right in America to have fastened itself so closely to the state of Israel. But the tie is a very old one. The Premillennialists were for the state of Israel before there was a state of Israel. As the Israeli scholar Jaakov Ariel notes: "Amazingly, premillennialist Christians anticipated the Jewish national restoration.... By the late nineteenth century, American evangelicals came out with proto-Zionist initiatives."[9] The Dispensationalists were forced to this position by the logic of their system. Other Christians can think of "the New Israel" as symbolic or allegorical—as referring to the Christian church, or to the New World (America in general or New England in particular), or to the heavenly kingdom. That position was not possible for Darby or Scofield. Israel was, for them, always and only literal fact. If the Bible says the End Time will take place in Israel, that is the physical place where it *has* to occur—even though such a literal place did not even exist when Darby and Scofield began their studies. If it did not exist yet, then it must come into existence. God had predicted it. So the Premillennialists became the earliest supporters of a restored homeland for the Jews.

In 1891—five years before Theodore Herzl, the father of modern Zionism, issued his first call for a Jewish homeland—William Blackstone presented a petition to United States President Benjamin Harrison asking for the same thing. The petition had over four hundred signatures, many of them of business, political, and social leaders, including J. P. Morgan, Cyrus McCormick, John D. Rockefeller, Congressman William McKinley, the governor of Massachusetts, the mayors of New York and Philadelphia, the Speaker of the House of Representatives, and the Catholic archbishop of Baltimore.[10] Blackstone would present a similar petition to President Woodrow Wilson in 1917, asking him to support the Balfour Resolution for the turning over of British control of Palestine to a Jewish state (Wilson did support it). At that time Blackstone was cooperating with the great American Zionist Louis Brandeis.[11] In gratitude for such efforts, memorial trees were dedicated to Blackstone in Israel on the seventy-fifth anniversary of the petition to President Wilson.[12]

Most of those signing Blackstone's petitions did it, no doubt, from humanitarian motives, protesting especially the treatment of Jews in tsarist Russia. But Blackstone, the author of *Jesus Is Coming,* was spurred to his long and ardent work for a Jewish state in order to help fulfill Bible prophecies—and the same was true of his fellow Dispensationalists. He worked to convert Jews to Christianity, establishing the Chicago Hebrew Mission in 1887, and editing its journal, *The Jewish Era.* He had two motives for this work. Any Jews he could convert would be among those swept up to heaven in the Rapture. And even those he did not convert would learn about Christianity.

That was important because when the Antichrist sets up his rule over Jews during the Tribulation, 144,000 of these Jews will become Christians and resist him, leading to their martyrdom (Revelation 7.3–4).

Somehow these martyrs would have to know enough about Christianity to accept it. That is why Blackstone wanted them to learn about the Gospel before the saved Christians are taken away in the Rapture. It is also why he planted multilingual copies of his book in Petra, where it was predicted that people oppressed by the Antichrist would flee, hoping to escape him.[13] Only the courageous 144,000 would be saved. The rest of the Jews—Darby calculated them at two thirds of the total number— would perish in the final battle of Christ with Antichrist, never to be raised again to life.[14]

Many Jews, unlike Brandeis, thought it wrong to cooperate with Blackstone, implicitly endorsing his conversion efforts. But others took the attitude that would last throughout the next century and be voiced by Lucy Dawidowicz when a televangelist said on his program, "God does not answer the prayers of Jews." She wrote in *Commentary*: "Why should Jews care about the theology of a Fundamentalist preacher? What do such theological abstractions matter as against the mundane fact that this same preacher is vigorously pro-Israel?"[15] Yet it was hard to overlook the fact that many if not most of these first Christian champions of Israel were anti-Semites. The proof is that all but one of them accepted as true the forged slanders of *Protocols of the Elders of Zion*.[16] Some Premillennialists even reprinted the *Protocols* in their journals.

Premillennialists followed the claims of Darby and Scofield that the present age, the "parenthesis" or gap to which no prophecies apply, had happened because the Jews killed the Messiah at his first coming, diverting the whole course of history and putting the Bible promises on hold. Since the Tribulation is to be an entirely Jewish matter (saved Christians having been rapt away), strict Dispensationalists departed from the long Protestant tradition identifying Antichrist with the pope. As Ariel says, "Since the early nineteenth century, and until the publication of *Left Behind*, dispensationalist writers have routinely characterized the Antichrist as a Jew."[17] Jerry Falwell was widely denounced for saying that Antichrist will be a Jew.[18] Scofield took a key step away from the idea that the pope was the principal Antichrist when he wrote that there are two Babylons in the Scripture, ecclesiastical Babylon, in the current Dispensation, headed by the pope, and "political Babylon," of the End Time, headed by the Beast of the Tribulation.[19]

When Henry Ford distributed *Protocols of the Elders of Zion*, Blackstone was the honorable exception among Premillennialists to see that they are inauthentic—he wrote a protesting letter to Ford. But Arno Gaebelein accepted and reprinted the *Protocols*.[20] On the surface this is surprising, since Gaebelein had at first been a friend to many of the Jews he wanted to convert. A skilled linguist, he learned Hebrew and Yiddish so well that he was mistaken for a Jew himself. He and his initial collaborator in the Hope of Israel, Ernest Stroeter, did not insist that their converts give up Jewish law and customs.[21] This was no doubt connected with their concentration on converting Orthodox Jews, the only ones they felt had kept to the Bible. Dispensationalists equated Reform Judaism with liberal Christianity—people who had deserted their own tradition. And of course they had no time at all for secular or assimilated Jews.[22]

Gaebelein wrote several books addressed to Jews—*The Messiah and His People Israel* (1898) and *Hath God Cast Away His People?* (1905). But in time he gave up the attempt to create a Christianized Jewry, which led to a break with Stroeter, who left America to continue his work with Jews in Düsseldorf. Gaebelein now turned his magazine into a general Dispensationalist journal, and wrote books taking an ever harder line against any attempts to better the social situation. A chapter in one of these later books is typically entitled "Down, Down, and Still Going Down."[23] He became increasingly bitter, dwelling on dark visions of the End. This man who had enthusiastically made himself well versed in Jewish history ended up with no Jewish contacts at all.

But the Premillennialists continued to think of Israel as the place where all God's plans for history were centered. They were jubilant, of course, at the 1948 founding of the Jewish state, but they were even more ecstatic at victory in the 1967 war, since that recovered the site of the Temple, which is at the center of their End Times scenario.

In fact, since the French Revolution and the Napoleonic Wars in the last years of the eighteenth century and the beginning of the nineteenth century probably no political-military event has provided so much fuel for the engine of prophecy as the short war between Israel and its neighbors in June 1967, a war that led to the Jews taking over the historical sections of Jerusalem. The dramatic and unexpected Israeli victory [repeatedly compared to David overcoming Goliath], and the territorial gains it brought with it, strengthened the premillennialists' conviction that the State of Israel was created for an important mission in history, and that the Jewish commonwealth was to play an important role in the process that would precede the arrival of the messiah.[24]

With these territorial gains, the Evangelicals asked for more, demanding the restoration of the whole biblical grant of land, saying that God had given it to Jews, and Arabs had no right to it.[25] They urged the rebuilding of the Temple, and raised money for the project, and prayed for the removal of the mosques on Temple Mount (an Australian Dispensationalist even set fire to the El-Aksa Mosque in 1969).[26]

In the last decade of the twentieth century, television and radio preachers, popular writers of Evangelical tracts, and pastors from their pulpits filled the air with talk of Israel and prophecy, so much so that President Reagan, ever a tuning fork for political vibrations in the air around him, told an Israel lobbyist, Thomas Dine, who visited the White House:

> You know, I turn back to your ancient prophets in the Old Testament and the signs foretelling Armageddon, and I find myself wondering if we're the generation that's going to see that come about. I don't know if you've noted any of those prophecies lately, but believe me, they certainly describe the times we're going through.[27]

RUSSIA

THE PROPHECIES concerning Israel were connected, from the beginnings of Dispensationalism, with putative biblical references to Russia.

The prophecies supposedly affecting Russia simply refer to "the north":

> So the king of the north shall come, and cast up a mount, and take the most fenced cities; and the arms of the south shall not withstand, neither his chosen people; neither shall there be any strength to withstand. (Daniel 11.15)

> Out of the north an evil shall break forth upon all the inhabitants of the land. (Jeremiah 1.14)

> And thou [Gog] shalt come from thy place out of the north parts, thou and many people with thee, all of them riding upon horses, a great company, and a mighty army. (Ezekiel 38.15)

These come from different books of the Bible, from different contexts, from different eras, at a time when there was no such country as Russia. But Dispensationalists read the Bible as one work with one meaning, no matter how or when or by whom expressed, so they reached an early accord that north meant Russia. Scofield's note on Ezekiel 38 reads: "That the primary reference is to the northern European powers, headed up by Russia, *all agree*" (emphasis added).

How did this idea arise? It came, clumsily, from false etymologies. In an 1828 German lexicon of the Old Testament by Wilhelm Gesenius, soon translated into English, Hebrew names in Ezekiel 38 were equated with Russian ones—Rosh with Russia, Meshech with Moscow, and Tubal with Tobolsk. They do sound somewhat alike, but they have no real philological connection.[28] Yet Fundamentalists to this day continue to cite these old mistakes in their exposition of Russia's role in God's reign. (They deride science except when they can misuse a science like philology.)

They were pleased when they saw the prophecies were "coming true" as godless Bolsheviks took control of the nation in 1917, making them clearly the biblical Gog. After the Russians built their own nuclear weapons, they were equipped to bring about Armageddon, the world-destroying battle. Cold War anticommunism gave a new lease on life to the Dispensationalists. This is not to say that many took the pure religious view of the matter, but the Premillennialists were given a free and very extensive ride on the broader mood of the Cold War. Once again, Ronald Reagan, who had many Fundamentalists among his California friends, was abreast of the talk. In 1971, while he was governor, he gave reporters a long dinnertime dissertation on prophecies. The part of it concerning Russia was this:

> Ezekiel tells us that Gog, the nation that will lead all of the
> other powers of darkness against Israel, will come out of
> the north. Biblical scholars have been saying for generations
> that Gog means Russia. What other powerful nation is to the
> north of Israel? None. But it didn't seem to make sense before
> the Russian revolution, when Russia was a Christian country.
> Now it does, now that Russia has become communistic and
> atheistic, now that Russia has set itself against God. Now it fits
> the description of Gog perfectly.[29]

When the Iron Curtain came down, the Evangelicals were unwilling to give up their demonization of Russia. Too much of their prophetic theorizing was based on it. When Mikhail Gorbachev liberalized the system, they denounced this as a ruse, and did a letter count of his name, using the Russian numbers for letters, to say that it came to the Beast's number, 666 (Revelation 13–18).[30] In the "Left Behind" novels, worldwide best-sellers for volume after volume, Russia is still the power invading from the north during the Tribulation.

ATOMIC WEAPONS

W HEN AMERICA revealed the destructive potential of the atomic bomb in 1945, this caused misgivings in some people, but the Dispensationalists welcomed it. The time of Tribulation is going to witness destruction on a scale never known before, and the Bomb makes that possible. The *Moody Monthly* boasted in a 1945 issue, "The Bible is ahead of science again." There was a scurry to turn up relevant passages outside of Ezekiel, Daniel, and Revelation, and then a concerted pounce on Zechariah 14.13, as an exact description of death by radiation:

> And this shall be the plague wherewith the Lord will smite all
> the people that have fought against Jerusalem: Their flesh shall
> consume away while they stand upon their feet, and their eyes
> shall consume away in their holes, and their tongue shall
> consume away in their mouth.

They also liked to cite 2 Peter 3.10:

> But the day of the Lord will come as a thief in the night; in
> which the heavens shall pass away with a great noise, and the
> elements shall melt with fervent heat, the earth also and the
> works that are therein shall be burned up.

As usual, Ronald Reagan vibrated to the biblical emanations. At his 1971 dinner seminar on the Bible, he said: "Everything is falling into place. It can't be long now. Ezekiel says that fire and brimstone will be rained upon the enemies of God's people. That must mean that they'll be destroyed by nuclear weapons."[31]

Dispensationalists may have been the only substantial group that looked on the prospect of nuclear war with equanimity. In fact, they resisted attempts at nuclear limitation or elimination, at civil defense programs or bomb shelters. William Ayer, pastor of New York's Calvary

Baptist Church, said in 1947: "The emerging peace program is not God's program, but only a variation of man's international plans, which always come to naught." One of their pastor-professors in Idaho said:

> Although Armageddon will be an awesome and terrifying
> experience for the world, it should be welcomed by the child
> of God as the day of vindication of our holy and sovereign
> Creator. Many beneficial results will be produced by this great
> battle.... What should be the believer's attitude to the
> destruction of the world by fire? First, of all, he should
> welcome it and pray for its nearness.[32]

This insouciance could be accompanied with a certain smugness. The Raptured will not feel the effects of nuclear incineration. One pastor wrote in 1967: "Thank God, I will get a view of the Battle of Armageddon from the grandstand seat of the heavens. All who are born again will see the Battle of Armageddon, but it will be from the skies."[33] This is the true note of Dispensationalism dating back to its founder John Darby, who wrote in 1840: "Let us remember one thing ... we Christians are sheltered from the approaching storm."[34]

A. G. Mojtabai got an intimate sense of this rather ghoulish glee when she interviewed a number of Christian workers in Amarillo, Texas, the home of the Pantex Army Ordnance Plant, which assembles, disassembles, modifies, and repairs all American nuclear warheads— four of them a day when she was there in the early 1980s.[35] Though the citizens there realized they were a prime target for others making nuclear weapons, that did not worry them. One said, "If the Amarillo bomb dropped today, it wouldn't bother me at all."[36] The Christians in Amarillo were ready to be Raptured. They listened to a preacher telling them:

> You know they're spending a fortune on this space program.
> A fortune! If they'd just shut it all down, see, and wait for the
> sound of the trumpet, that, my friend, is going to be one space

program! I've got my name, by the grace and help of God, in
that other astronaut program. You know, the one where you
don't need a big missile over in Florida to put you in the air. . . .
Why don't you do it tonight, Jesus? Do it tonight![37]

A RHETORIC OF ALIENATION

DISPENSATIONALISTS ARE probably the only long-standing major
force in American culture that has taken a dark view of this country and its destiny.[38] Pre-Enlightenment religion held that God had
formed a sacred covenant with the American people. Enlightened religion denied that, but the Deists still believed in a benevolent providence
that, as Tom Paine put it, willed that man be free and blessed American
efforts at liberation. But the break that occurred in the 1870s brought
something unprecedented into the history of American religion—a God
who was angry at America and was targeting it for punishment. It brought
to the fore what Amy Johnson Frykholm calls "a rhetoric of alienation."[39]

This vision of an angry God is not like the jeremiads of the past.
Those were expressions of penitence that sinners had failed the covenant
and pleas that God would restore it. The new form of religion denied
that God ever had a covenant with America. This was closer, in fact, to
the vision of Roger Williams, who said that the garden had never existed
in America, only the wilderness. From the 1870s on, there would be two
great bodies of Evangelicals—one still thinking of America as God's
chosen people, the other thinking of America as God's foe. When most
Americans were boasting of the superiority of America to the godless
Russians, some Dispensationalists were equating this country with
the enemy. A woman interviewed in Amarillo by A. G. Mojtabai, for
instance, said: "We've already adopted half the philosophies of Russia—
abortion, our atheistic thinking is the same as in Russia. We've already
adopted John Dewey, who went to Russia and China. . . . I believe Russia
will take us down from the inside out. They don't need bombs. They're

already doing it in our schools and universities, not over bombs, but over minds in this country."[40]

A preacher in Amarillo regularly substituted "America" for "Babylon" when reading from the Scriptures condemning God's enemies.[41] The same attitude came out very clearly in Dispensationalist reaction to the attack on the World Trade Center and the Pentagon on September 11, 2001. While others were blaming terrorists for the tragedy, Dispensationalist leaders were blaming America. The conservative religious journal *Christianity Today*, in its September 14, 2001, issue, reported with approval Fundamentalist indictments of America as the cause of the attacks. Here is Jerry Falwell, speaking on Pat Robertson's *700 Club* broadcast:

> The ACLU has got to take a lot of blame for this. . . . I really
> believe that the pagans, and the abortionists, and the feminists,
> and the gays and lesbians who are actively trying to make that
> an alternative lifestyle, the ACLU, People for the American
> Way—all of them who have tried to secularize America—
> I point the finger in their face and say, "You helped this
> happen . . . [causing God] to lift the curtain and allow the
> enemies of America to give us probably what we deserve."

Robertson said he totally concurred with what Falwell had said:

> [Terrorism] is happening because God Almighty is lifting his
> protection from us. We have a court that has essentially stuck
> its finger in God's eye. . . . We have insulted God at the highest
> level of government. Then we say, "Why does this happen?"

The editor of *World Magazine* (edited by Marvin Olasky, George W. Bush's adviser on faith-based programs) was also quoted, comparing the fall of the World Trade Center to the way God destroyed the Tower of Babel:

> Now we're being called on to look our idolatry square in the
> face. High on our own Western shelf of false deities have been

the gods of nominalism, materialism, secularism, and pluralism. And it's hard to think of more apt symbols of all those "isms" than the twin towers of the World Trade Center—anchored in the financial capital of the world, and capped as they were with transmitting towers for the major media and entertainment networks. Babel needed just one such tower. New York built two.

This easy acceptance of the horrors of 9/11 may seem inhuman, but we should remember that the Dispensationalists have supped on horrors in all their vivid imaginings of the longed-for Tribulation—from Hal Lindsey's *The Late Great Planet Earth* (called by the *New York Times* the best-seller of all nonfiction books for the entire decade of the 1970s), from *A Thief in the Night* (a movie shown repeatedly at church and youth gatherings through the years), and—especially—from the "Left Behind" series by Tim LaHaye, at least one of whose books has been read by one out of every ten adult readers in America.[42] Each book has a series of catastrophes—in *The Remnant*, Chicago is incinerated by nuclear attack. The gore mounts vertiginously when Jesus comes back with his Raptured saints and slays millions by the power of his words, staining the hem of his robe crimson as he wades through the oceans of blood he sheds:

Rayford watched through the binocs as men and women soldiers and horses seemed to explode where they stood. It was as if the very words of the Lord had superheated their blood, causing it to burst through their veins and skins.

Tens of thousands of foot soldiers dropped their weapons, grabbed their heads or their chests, fell to their knees, and writhed as they were invisibly sliced asunder. Their innards and entrails gushed to the desert floor, and as those around them turned to run, they too were slain, their blood pooling and rising in the unforgiving brightness of the glory of Christ....

The riders not thrown leaped from their horses and tried to control them with the reins, but even as they struggled, their

own flesh dissolved, their eyes melted, and their tongues
disintegrated. As Rayford watched, the soldiers stood briefly
as skeletons in now baggy uniforms, then dropped in heaps of
bones as the blinded horses continued to fume and rant and
rave. [How does a horse rant?] Seconds later the same plague
afflicted the horses, their flesh and eyes and tongues melting
away, leaving grotesque skeletons standing, before they too
rattled to the pavement.[43]

Horror on that scale may indeed be the one thing that can make the
tragedy of 9/11 acceptable.

CULTURE WARS

I HAVE JUMPED ahead of chronological order in this chapter, since I
wanted to introduce the twentieth century as a time of cultural wars.
Things that seemed to break out unexpectedly in the last half of the
century had their powder train laid far earlier. The Dispensationalists
set the tone, since they warred against so much in American life. Not all
of them could keep optimism from breaking in—that is what made
Ronald Reagan, with his sunny temperament, far less extreme than his
own words. But many of the moral conflicts that lay ahead in the twentieth century would take their cues from the fervent past. The Fundamentalists and the liberal Christians began the century at odds with each
other. The conflict then went under the cultural observers' radar for a
while without disappearing. There would be truces called—during the
century's wars, and during the dazed state of comity in the 1950s—but
the culture wars would come roaring back in the Sixties (over racial
integration, Vietnam, and school prayer), the Seventies (over abortion
and feminism), the Eighties (over gay rights and pornography), the
Nineties (over creationism and the Supreme Court), and into the
twenty-first century (over all of the above). It would be a time of warring
absolutes.

23 | THE SOCIAL GOSPEL

A T THE OTHER POLE from Premillennial revivalism was the Social Gospel. The two differed, in some measure, as Populism differed from Progressivism. Populism was a rural movement in the last decades of the nineteenth century to regulate food prices through co-ops and railroad costs. Fundamentalists, despite their social passivity, were close to the plight of the farmers, and gave them religious support, especially in the South. In fact, the Fundamentalists' champion, William Jennings Bryan, was the Democratic and Populist presidential candidate in 1896. The decline of Populism, defeated on the issue of a silver currency, overlapped the rise of Progressivism, which was as centrally urban as Populism had been rural.

Progressivism was a reaction to the dislocations, corruption, and industrialization of the Gilded Age. It sought to bring in reforms like civil service tests, antitrust laws, shorter workdays, and urban hygiene. Both Populism and Progressivism were warmly praised by liberal historians in the early twentieth century.[1]

But in the second half of the century there was a scholarly backlash in some circles. Richard Hofstadter alleged that the Progressives were as much concerned with their own loss of status in the new industrial system as with the plight of the poor.[2] Robert Wiebe said that Progressives were the champions of a middle-class bureaucracy, imposing system on the rapidly changing circumstances of the Gilded Age.[3] If the reputation of Progressivism suffered, then that of the Social Gospel was bound to decline as well, since the latter was simply the religious wing of the former.

> In a sense, reforming clergymen served as the honorary
> chairmen of progressivism. It was still important for most
> Protestants to feel the presence of a Christian justification, and
> Progressives regularly urged the ministers to join them, not as
> advisers but as sponsors who could spread that distinctive aura
> of righteousness about the cause.[4]

So a growing disillusionment with the Progressives was extended to the Social Gospelers. Hofstadter said that the religious ministers involved were worried about their own social status, that the Social Gospel was "an attempt to restore through secular leadership some of the spiritual influence and authority and social prestige that clergymen had lost."[5] (Ironically, Hofstadter was saying the same thing about the Social Gospel that Fundamentalists alleged.) Wiebe said that the Social Gospel was not an independent force of any great consequence: "As Taft left office, they had not accomplished a great deal, but as one of them exulted, 'public opinion . . . has been wonderfully developed of late.'"[6] Martin Marty was also rather dismissive of the Social Gospel, noting that it showed little interest in African Americans, women's rights, or a developing socialism: "It may seem amazing that the Social Gospel in its time connoted something radical, given its programmatic timidity and gentility" (MM 1.225).

Those who think the Social Gospel too tame are usually looking at it simply in its political effects, not in its theology. In the latter field, it made important strides toward modernity. Darwinism had been either rejected by most religious leaders or cautiously worked into a compromised alliance with the Bible. The Social Gospel gave full acceptance to the arguments for evolution. The Higher Criticism of the Bible was boldly carried over from Germany. The study of Christianity as a social program, not simply as a bid for individuals' salvation, left behind a permanent legacy.

Some seem to scorn the Social Gospel because it spoke of the plight of the lower classes, yet the movement was articulated by ministers who were themselves members of an upper middle class. It is certainly true that the earliest advocates of the Social Gospel came from the very churches that had been established in the eighteenth century, the Anglicans and the Congregationalists. Those Social Gospel ministers who lagged and entered later came from the more popular religions— Methodists, Baptists, and Presbyterians, in that order.[7] Some were surprised that Episcopalians, a generally conservative denomination that had not joined early reform efforts like abolitionism, should have jumped into the lead of the Social Gospel; yet the Episcopal Church gave birth to the first and most effective Social Gospel organizations.

In 1887, a group of Episcopal clergy and laity founded the Church Association for the Advancement of the Interests of Labor, led by Bishop F. D. Hogan.[8] The idea that the Social Gospel was tame did not occur to the Episcopal parishioners at Saint George's Church in New York City. The famous naval historian Alfred Thayer Mahan left the church because its pastor, W. S. Rainsford, not only preached concern for the working class but brought members of it onto the vestry board. J. P. Morgan also threatened to leave, until Rainsford persuaded him to stay.[9]

Henry May, in his book on the Social Gospel, explains the apparent anomaly of Episcopal activism from the priests' close acquaintance with developments in the British church. As the Industrial Revolution had hit England earlier and harder than it did America, social awareness grew faster there, moving toward various forms of Christian socialism. The Anglican priest F. D. Maurice sounded a note that became the Social Gospel motto in America when he published *The Kingdom of Christ* (1838). The idea of the kingdom was taken from Lord's Prayer: "Thy kingdom come, thy will be done, *on earth* as it is in heaven." The kingdom on earth must bless the poor, the meek, and the peacemakers. This idea had been elaborated in Germany by Albrecht Ritschl, whose work influenced an American priest, Laurence Schwab, who wrote *The Kingdom of God* in 1897.[10] The Anglicans, like the Congregationalists, were generally more cosmopolitan and educated than many in other denominations, which explains their access to German as well as British thought. Enlightened religion always begins, at least, among the educated.

GLADDEN

CONGREGATIONALIST LEADERSHIP in the Social Gospel is best seen in the early prominence of Washington Gladden (1836–1918). Like many of those who came to the Social Gospel, he had an inner-city ministry which gave him a close-up look at emotional workers' strikes—in his case, the strike at a shoe factory in Adams, Massachusetts (1879); the Hocking Valley coal strike (1884), while Gladden was a pastor in Columbus, Ohio; and the Columbus streetcar strike (1910). At first Gladden followed what had been an earlier religious attitude toward strikes—that workers should be treated fairly but that strikes were an un-Christian form of coercion. A regular bit of advice was that workers discipline themselves to save money for buying shares in their company, ending the distinction between owners and workers. Only after he had seen other forms of pressure fail did Gladden become the first prominent minister to defend unions and the use of strikes. He eventually became a defender of both the American Federation of Labor and the Industrial Workers of the World (the "Wobblies").

Gladden became a leading voice of reform in Columbus, serving one term as alderman there, setting up a settlement house, and acting as mediator in various disputes. Eventually he was called "the First Citizen of Columbus." At the national level, he made the previously moribund National Council of Congregational Churches a center for the study of social problems, setting up committees on labor, industry, and social service, while organizing a series of national conferences. He established friendly relations with Jews as well as Catholics. His attacks on the nativist American Protective Association cost him the presidency of Ohio State University in 1892, but it made him the first Protestant recipient of an honorary degree from Notre Dame University in 1895.

Gladden was not a timid man. During an early stint at a Brooklyn church, he wrote the religion pages of the local paper, where he attacked Boss Tweed. As president of the National Council of Congregational Churches, he turned down a gift of $100,000 from John D. Rockefeller, whose Standard Oil Company oppressed its workers. Gladden said Rockefeller's wealth was held "by no better moral title than the booty of the highwayman."[11] After meeting and admiring W. E. B. DuBois, Gladden became the rare Social Gospel minister who denounced racial segregation.

The contribution of Congregationalists to the learned side of the Social Gospel can be seen in the teaching of Richard T. Ely (1854–1943), a founder of the Christian Socialist movement. After taking his doctorate at the University of Heidelberg, he taught economics at the Johns Hopkins University, where Frederick Jackson Turner and Woodrow Wilson were among his students. Ely then went off to chair the department of political economy at the University of Wisconsin. He was denounced for his socialist views at Hopkins, and tried on similar charges by the board of regents at Wisconsin—his exoneration is counted an early victory for academic freedom. In 1885, he established the American Economic Association, of which Washington Gladden was a charter member.

A lighter contribution by a Congregationalist was the most successful Christian social novel of the time. Proponents of the Social Gospel were fans of Edward Bellamy's *Looking Backward*, and many imitations of it were written with a more heavily Christian emphasis.[12] The one that succeeded best was *In His Steps*, by Charles M. Sheldon, a pastor in Topeka, Kansas, who disguised himself as an unemployed laborer to see how the lower classes were treated. In his novel, he argues that social problems could be solved if people just asked themselves, "What would Jesus do?"

RAUSCHENBUSCH

THOUGH BAPTISTS were generally slower to join the movement than Episcopalians and Congregationalists, the man who earned the greatest Social Gospel fame was a Baptist, the son of a minister from Germany, Walter Rauschenbusch (1861–1918). His father sent him back to Germany for early schooling, but he took his theology degree from Rochester Seminary, where his father was professor of New Testament interpretation. His first ministry was in the Hell's Kitchen sector of New York City, where he championed the cause of poor immigrants. In 1886, he campaigned for Henry George in the New York mayoralty race (George, with his anti-rich tax program, was a favorite with the Social Gospel ministers). Rauschenbusch returned for higher studies to Germany (in economics and theology) and in England (where he became interested in the Fabian Society). Back in America, he helped form the Brotherhood of the Kingdom, before succeeding to his father's faculty position at the Rochester Seminary. In Rochester, he promoted civic causes and worker education. His *Christianity and the Social Crisis* (1907) became a central document for the Social Gospel.

Though no two denominations stood farther apart in their history than the Baptists and the Unitarians, Rauschenbusch with his German training was an ally of the Unitarian minister Francis Greenwood Peabody (1847–1936), who had been trained at the University of Halle. Peabody set up the first department of social ethics at the Harvard Divinity School, an innovation followed at other seminaries. He engaged in fruitful interchanges with Harvard colleagues like William James and Josiah Royce, and he helped found the *Harvard Theological Review*. The scholarly side of the Social Gospel was principally upheld by Ely and Peabody.

Those who think the Social Gospel promoters were not strong enough critics of their time tend to forget what passed as common Christian currency then. They should remember that the largest Protestant church of its time, and the most popular Christian sermon (by far), were the product of Russell H. Conwell, who preached "Acres of Diamonds" over six thousand times, to enormous acclaim. Conwell said that people seek diamonds far off when they have them in their own backyard, if they would only find them by diligence and hope. Those at-hand "diamonds" only need polishing by hard work. Asked why he preached about making money rather than the Gospel, Conwell answered: "Because to make money honestly is to preach the Gospel." He claimed:

> You ought to get rich, and it is your duty to get rich. . . . Ninety-eight out of one hundred of the rich men in America are honest. That is why they are rich. . . . The number of poor who are to be sympathized with is very small. To sympathize with a man whom God has punished for his sins, thus to help him when God would still continue a just punishment, is to do wrong.[13]

In such a world, the Social Gospel *was* radical. But sometimes it was radically wrong. The problem with the Social Gospel was not that it was a status quest (Hofstadter), or a bureaucratic intrusion (Wiebe), or a timorous endorsement of mild liberalism (Marty). The problem was that many of its proponents endorsed the new American imperialism.

CHRISTIAN IMPERIALISM

AMERICA AT the end of the century seemed to be running out of room. Frederick Jackson Turner said that the frontier was closed in the West. Energies that had driven America across the continent to the far West Coast now seemed bottled up. So many were looking for new areas to master. During the nineteenth century, both the old-line form of religion and the revivalist strain had sent thousands of missionaries into Asia, Africa, and Latin America. The government was sometimes called on to protect them, and the notion that the United States should itself spread Christianity was given support by the Social Gospelers. Their belief in progress, in Christianity's beneficial social effect, in an evolution toward higher religious forms, came together to give them their own form of Social Darwinism. In order to promote joint responsibilities in the social arena, they rejected William Graham Sumner's survival of the fittest *individual* as the rationale for laissez-faire competition. But they did believe in progress based on the survival of the fittest *social order*—which meant for them that Christianity was bound to prevail worldwide.

That is why the religious world, but especially its Social Gospel contingent, joined the clamor for Americans to support a rebellion in Cuba against the Old World typified by Spain. Racial and religious prejudices were mobilized against what was seen as an inferior "Latin" power, part of a corrupt papist empire. William Rainsford, the rector of Saint George's Episcopal Church in New York—the man whose care for the working class offended Alfred Thayer Mahan and J. P. Morgan—was quick to join Mahan in a call for America's war with Spain: "This war has not been cunningly devised by strategists. America is being used to carry on the work of God in this war, which no politician could create, control, or gainsay."[14]

JOSIAH STRONG

THE MOST imperialistic Social Gospel preachers were two Congregational ministers, Josiah Strong (1847–1916) and Lyman Abbott (1835–1922). Strong was an energetic organizer of interdenominational conferences with concern for urban problems. His *Our Country: Its Possible Future and Its Present Crisis* (1885) was called by Sydney Ahlstrom "almost certainly the most influential Social Gospel book of the nineteenth century" (A 798). That is a very disturbing judgment, since Strong's book was full of racist and imperial theses. It is true that he argued, like any believer in the Social Gospel, for solving urban problems. But his diagnosis of those problems was nativist. Cities, he claimed, were cesspools because the evils plaguing the nation met there—immigrants, Catholics, drunkards, and socialists.[15]

Each of these evils ratcheted the others up. They contaminated the pure Anglo-Saxon stock that made America the instrument of human perfection. Luckily, the West was the purifying agent that could counter Eastern corruption. Though Strong was an urban reformer, he fit all too well Wiebe's assertion that the Progressives were nostalgic for rural and small-town virtues. That, Strong believed, was where the Anglo-Saxon culture had reached its highest point, uniting the two greatest elements of civilization—a pure Christianity and civil liberty. England, it is true, has Anglo-Saxon blood, but its Christianity is corrupted by a union of church and state, and its civil liberty compromised by the lingering elements of the monarchy.[16] Anglo-Saxons in America have qualities that fit them for evangelizing the world—"money-making power," a "genius for colonizing, and "persistent energy."[17]

> The time is coming when the pressure of population on the means of subsistence will be felt here as it is now felt in Europe and Asia. Then will the world enter upon a new stage of its history—the final competition of races, for which the Anglo-Saxon is being schooled. Long before the thousand millions [of immigrants] are here, the mighty centrifugal tendency, inherent in this stock and strengthened in the United States, will assert itself. Then this race of unequaled energy, with all the majesty of numbers and the might of wealth behind it— the representation, let us hope, of the largest liberty, the purest Christianity, the highest civilization—having developed peculiarly aggressive traits calculated to impress its institutions upon mankind, will spread itself over the earth. If I read not amiss, this powerful race will move down upon Mexico, down upon Central and South America, out upon the islands of the sea, over upon Africa and beyond. And can anyone doubt that the result of this competition of races will be the "survival of the fittest"?[18]

The United States, Strong argued, was "destined to dispossess many weaker races, assimilate others, and mold the remainder until, in a very true and important sense, it has Anglo-Saxonized mankind."[19] This vision of racial domination has ominous resonances for us who live after the Aryan vision of Adolph Hitler. A shiver can be felt when Strong says he is describing "God's final and complete solution of the dark problem of heathenism among many inferior peoples."[20]

Strong's influential book was written, remember, in 1885—thirteen years before the imperialistic war with Spain. Once that war was declared, Strong cheered on all other colonizing ventures in the *Homiletic Review;* in his 1900 book, *Expansion* (in which he thanked Admiral Mahan and Theodore Roosevelt for their advice); and in a 1915 extension of *Our Country* called *Our World: The New World Religion.* But it was his first and most influential book that gave American Christianity its Gospel of empire.

LYMAN ABBOTT

SYDNEY AHLSTROM called Lyman Abbott (1835–1922) the "virtual chaplain of Theodore Roosevelt's Progressivism" (A 788). Abbott was invited by Henry Ward Beecher to help him edit the journal *Christian Union.* When Beecher retired from the editorship, Strong took over the magazine. Then when Beecher died, Strong was elected to succeed him in the prominent Plymouth Congregational Church of Brooklyn. Abbott changed the *Christian Union* into *The Outlook,* which became the most important religious organ commenting on politics. It was entirely devoted to promoting the career of Abbott's friend Theodore Roosevelt, who tried out speeches and articles on Abbott before delivering or publishing them.[21] Contemporaries thought of Roosevelt as Abbott's "obsession."[22] Roosevelt returned the fascination. In fact, when Roosevelt left the presidency, he became an active editor of *The Outlook.* Roosevelt's history of the West glorified the conquest of Native Americans, since they were at a lower stage of civilization than the Anglo-Saxons. Abbott agreed. Supporting the Dawes Severalty Act (1877) for the seizing of Indian lands, he wrote:

> Barbarians have rights which civilized folk are bound to
> respect; but barbarism has no rights which civilization is bound

to respect. In the history of the human race, nothing is more certain than that civilization must conquer and barbarism must be subdued.[23]

Abbott was an ardent imperialist. He called his program "the Imperialism of Liberty." Like Strong, he saw America's destiny in evolutionary terms. Man was rising to higher levels of spirituality, and America was in the vanguard of this process. His talk of a higher self and an indwelling divinity picked up some of the old themes of Transcendentalism. At times he echoed Emerson to the verge of plagiarism: "Religion has to do with the present and the future, not the past—save as it disentangles us from the past for the future."[24] He was able to etherealize even the bloody war for the Philippines. Writing in *The Outlook* in 1900, he called this "a noble stage in the development of human brotherhood."[25] In his memoirs he recalled his words at the time:

> I believe the proudest chapter in our history is that written by the statesmanship of McKinley, the guns of Dewey, and the administration of Taft. There is nothing to repent, nothing to retract: our duty is to go on and complete the work already so well begun. I do not defend or apologize for what we have done in the Philippines. I glory in it.[26]

The war was not supported solely by the Social Gospel camp. Far from it. Evangelicals were even more likely to rejoice at a blow to papal Spain, and they were anxious to have missionaries admitted to the countries from which Spain had excluded them. President McKinley joined them in this missionary impulse. Explaining what he called the "benevolent assimilation" of the Philippines, he told an interviewer:

> When I next realized that the Philippines had dropped into our laps, I confess I did not know what to do with them. . . . I went down on my knees and prayed Almighty God for light and guidance more than one night. And one night late it came to

me . . . that there was nothing left for us to do but to take them all, and to educate the Filipinos, and uplift and civilize and Christianize them, and by God's grace do the very best we could by them, as our fellow men for whom Christ also died.[27]

Theodore Roosevelt, whom McKinley had appointed Undersecretary of the Navy, called it "almost treasonable" for men like Carl Shurz and Harvard president Charles Eliot Norton to oppose forceful seizure of the Philippines—he thought of it simply as an extension of the Progressives' domestic reform program, and of course Lyman Abbott's *The Outlook* supported this stand.[28]

Though the Spanish War was initially fueled with anti-Catholic feelings toward Spain, even the Catholics in America came to support the conquest of the Philippines. The American army at first supported the native revolution against Spain, led by Emilio Aguinaldo. When Aguinaldo had been used to help defeat the Spaniards, his American allies betrayed him and took over the country—but not before the revolution had disestablished the Catholic Church, seizing its properties. By promising to restore those properties, McKinley won an endorsement of his war from Pope Leo XIII. America's Catholic hierarchy swung into line—Abbott even opened the pages of *The Outlook* to Archbishop John Ireland so he could defend the war.[29]

In putting down the native revolution it had first supported, the American forces committed atrocities on a grand scale. The racism that had presented itself to religious leaders at home as caring for natives, who were little better than children, took the form at the front line of indifference to the lives of an inferior people. In 1903, as more atrocities came to light and the cover-ups were failing, the philosopher William James summed up the "benevolent assimilation" this way:

> The material ruin of the Islands, the transformation of native friendliness to execration, the demoralization of our army, from the war office down—forgery decorated, torture whitewashed, massacre condoned, the creation of a chronic

anarchy in the Islands, with ladronism still smoldering, and the
lives of America travelers and American sympathizers unsafe
in the country out of sight of army posts; the deliberate rein-
flaming on our part of ancient tribal animosities, the arming of
Igorrote savages and Macabebe semi-savages too low to have a
national consciousness, to help us hunt the highest portions of
the population down; the inoculation of Manila with a floating
Yankee scum.[30]

Mark Twain, writing two years earlier, was already just as indignant. He
published in the *North American Review* an article called "To the Person
Sitting in Darkness"—a reference to Isaiah 9.2: "The people that walked
in darkness have seen a great light; they that dwell in the land of the
shadow of death, upon them hath the light shined." He tries to explain to
a Filipino how he has been lifted up by the Gospel that was rammed into
him with bayonets. Twain is sardonically grieved that the great blessings
bestowed on the survivors of our conquest are not appreciated by its
beneficiaries:

> We have robbed a trusting friend [Aguinaldo] of his land and
> his liberty; we have invited our clean young men to shoulder
> a discredited musket and do bandit's work under a flag which
> bandits have been accustomed to fear, not to follow; we have
> debauched America's honor and blackened her face before the
> world; but each detail was for the best.[31]

After recounting some of the war atrocities committed in the Philippines, the article closes on this note:

> As for a flag for the Philippine Province, it is easily managed.
> We can have a special one—our States do it: we can have just
> our usual flag, with the white stripes painted black and the stars
> replaced by the skull and cross-bones.[32]

VIII | REVERSALS

24 | Evangelicals Riding High

The early years of the twentieth century were kind to the reputation of Evangelicals, in several areas, especially that of Prohibition, revivalism, and the Great War.

Prohibition

Prohibition was the greatest political triumph of the Evangelicals. Not that it was theirs alone. The Progressives were also promoters of Temperance.[1] No other peacetime cause combined the various Protestant wings as closely as the Temperance campaign. As the prospect of triumph neared, even the Evangelical churches that had split into Northern and Southern bodies experienced a partly recovered unity. The motives for this might be different—some in the North embraced Temperance to stop the Irish and Germans and Poles from drinking, while some in the South wanted to keep liquor out of the hands of blacks—but the cause was the same, and the cause seemed on the verge of triumph. Only war could have a greater unifying effect on the churches.

The Temperance forces had scored some successes even before the Civil War, when eighteen states and even more localities banned the sale of liquor. But the alcohol interests made a great comeback after the war. Brewers and distillers and vintners organized to fight Temperance laws, to lower taxes on liquor, and to oppose antitrust moves against their combinations. There was a great change in the drinking habits of people in this period. Spirits were losing out to beer, since technological changes—pasteurization, refrigeration, new brewing processes, more uniform quality control—made beer easier to make, transport, and store than it had been. It was a better product, more plentiful, and cheaper. But beer, unlike spirits, had to be sold in great quantities to make money. So the brewers worked to open as many saloons as possible, and they organized for vertical integration of the industry, controlling production, distribution, and sale of their product.[2] More and more saloons came to be owned or controlled by a specific brewer, which meant that they had to carry only the brewer's beer, or pay fees to the brewer. The brewers offered free ads, cut rates, and ampler supply to gain control of individual saloons.

A popular impression is that crime and corruption came into the liquor business in the 1920s, when gangs were defying the Prohibition laws. But the liquor industry's criminality was deep and broad during the Gilded Age. The most famous case was that of the Whiskey Ring, which, in collusion with members of the Treasury Department, defrauded the government of millions of dollars in tax revenue. In this case alone, 238 persons were indicted and 110 were convicted. But there were many other cases where liquor money backed candidates and programs meant to block Temperance initiatives. The reform aims of the Progressives were now engaged in a problem that Evangelicals had long made their one political issue. Sometimes the efforts of the Progressives backfired. When they tried to control saloons by increasing the licensing fees for them, that made more saloon owners turn to the producers for loans, protection, or mergers, or tempted them to supplement their income with gambling, drugs, or prostitutes on the premises.[3]

In the joint crusade of the churches, the Progressives supplied the reform justifications for Temperance, but Evangelicals supplied the troops. The latter's indignation over the growth of a whole saloon culture in the Gilded Age soon reached boiling point and stayed at that intensity. The liquor interests were pushing their product in the cities, as those filled up with immigrants from countries where beer, whiskey, and wine were drunk. The result was an explosion of saloons. In 1909 there was one saloon for every five hundred people.[4] "There were more saloons in the United States than there were schools, libraries, hospitals, theaters, or parks, and more certainly than churches."[5]

The sheer number of saloons made any one of them a marginal competitor in a large market. They made up for this by evading closing times, age restrictions, and other government regulations—which meant that they often had to bribe policemen to look the other way, completing a circle of corruption.[6] Besides, the saloon keeper, in touch with the immigrant and worker classes, was often a contact man for the urban machines that controlled so much of the political activity of the time. They became ward heelers, which also gave them protection for their own illegalities.

> The liquor industry became thoroughly involved in political corruption through its connection with the saloon. The root of the trouble here was that the ordinary saloonkeeper, confronted by overcompetition, was practically forced to disobey the liquor laws and to ally himself with vice and crime in order to survive. Unable to make a living honestly, he did so dishonestly.[7]

This growing menace was taken on by groups of Evangelical women. In 1873 and 1874 a Women's Crusade brought hundreds of its members into saloons to sing and pray and plead for the place to shut down. Some of them were in fact closed, at least temporarily, but the main effect of this crusade was to organize women and raise consciousness of the issue.[8] As this crusade sputtered out, a more serious one began. In 1874, the Women's Christian Temperance Union (WCTU) was formed, initially just to agitate against the saloons. But when Frances Willard became the Union's president, she broadened its mandate to include women's suffrage, the Kindergarten movement, prison reform, the eight-hour day, federal aid to education, and other reforms.

FRANCES WILLARD (1839–1898)

SYDNEY AHLSTROM claimed that Willard was "the single most impressive reformer to have worked within the context of the Evangelical churches," and that the WCTU was "the greatest women's organization of the century" (A 868, 870). After taking her degree at the Evanston Women's College, Willard went on to study in France and Germany, then returned to become dean of the Women's College. When the college was incorporated into Northwestern University, whose new president was her former fiancé, the Methodist minister Charles Fowler, Willard was forced out of the college. Fowler could not fire her, since she had tenure, but he undermined her actions in order to control the women's division himself.[9] As Willard later told Dwight Moody, "Dr. Fowler has the will of a Napoleon, I have the will of a Queen Elizabeth."[10]

Willard now shifted her attention to the Temperance Movement, which she always saw as simply the base for action on a wide variety of women's issues. As Secretary of the WCTU, she at first lost her fight to broaden the organization's program out from the single issue of Temperance. She then went to work (in 1877) with Dwight Moody's evangelizing team, where she led women's groups. But soon she objected to this segregated approach to evangelism and Moody objected to her sharing platforms with Unitarians (whom he considered heretics).[11] While giving temperance lectures on her own, she added the call for women's suffrage and became a close friend of Susan B. Anthony and the other leading suffragists.[12]

Willard overcame resistance to the promotion of suffrage in local meetings of the WCTU, in a campaign that led to her election as president of the national Union in 1879. At age forty she had at last found her life's work. She built the WCTU into the first mass organization of women, with twenty-five thousand regular members and twenty-seven thousand auxiliaries. Willard was an exceptional organizer, traveling around to form local units, spearheading legislative drives in the various states, forming political alliances with labor unions and local reform groups. Eventually she extended her work abroad, working with Lady Henry Somerset in England to create the World WCTU. When she could not get either of the two American parties to adopt her programs, she worked with the Prohibition Party in the 1880s to effect a merger with Populists and Christian Socialists, hoping to mount a major third-party initiative.[13] When she maneuvered the WCTU to formal endorsement of the Prohibition Party in 1889, some women, who were Republicans and thought the Union should not be in partisan politics, left the WCTU.[14] Though she did not accomplish all that she hoped, the Prohibition Party won local legislative and electoral victories, thanks to the new energies she brought to it.

WAYNE WHEELER (1869–1927)

B ECAUSE WILLARD'S agenda was a broad one, her Temperance campaign was shoved aside by the more narrowly focused Anti-Saloon League (ASL). In 1893, the ASL was begun in Ohio. Its superintendent was Howard Russell, a Methodist minister who considered the ASL a divine work, the extension of his ministry. By 1895, the organization had become national. Willard had often been thwarted by the way the liquor interests used money to block Prohibition candidates and legislative moves, backing opponents and lobbying around the states as well as in Washington. The Anti-Saloon League used the same kind of tactics in well-financed drives devoted to a single issue. Its base for action was fairly broad to begin with. Temperance had a long and fairly successful history. Before the Civil War, thirteen states had gone dry. After the war, in the excesses of the Gilded Age, that base shrank back to the original Prohibitionist state, Maine. But then momentum built up again, so that in seven years (1907–14) eleven states went dry, along with many other local jurisdictions. By 1917, another twelve states had quickly gone on the wagon.

This meant that three-quarters of the nation, by territory, already had some form of Prohibition. The catch was that this large amount of territory was sparsely populated—it was mainly the rural West and South. Of the thirteen industrial states, only two had adopted Temperance. The imbalance between large dry areas and dense "wet" cities seemed to have reached a stalemate.[15] The dry faction was frustrated, moreover, by the fact that any locale it added to the dry column could be neutralized by the influx of liquor from nearby wet states. An attempt to ban interstate commerce in alcohol was passed by Congress (the Webb-Kenyon Act) in 1913. President Taft vetoed the bill, but Congress overrode him. Yet this was a futile gesture, unenforceable by either the states or the federal government. Moreover, the threat of this law led the distillers and brewers, who had beforehand been at odds, to unite their forces and funds.[16] The League decided that further action at the state level was leading nowhere. A national ban was the only thing that would work. Wayne Wheeler conceived a strategy to bring that about.

Wheeler was the lawyer-lobbyist (he said "agitator") for the ASL. He had begun in the birthplace of the ASL (he was a fellow graduate with Russell from Oberlin). At first he practiced a Fabian strategy—a series of victories at the county level using "local option" to outlaw alcohol. But by 1914 he was in Washington coordinating a nationwide strategy to defeat "wets" at every level. In the congressional elections of that year, he sent out fifty thousand trained speakers to argue for Prohibition candidates.[17] He could not have done this without a broad money-raising operation. He had some wealthy donors, like John D. Rockefeller and S. S. Kresge.[18] But the mass of his resources came from small donations given by millions of people, who pledged to give on a continuous basis from their churches or Bible study groups. The regular fulfillment of their pledges gave Wheeler identifiable troops to get to the polls or to flood nominating conventions and caucuses.

These numbers and this money gave Wheeler the tools he wanted, to counter the money and influence with which the breweries had kept their favored politicians in line. It was uphill work for him. All the brewers needed was neutrality on the liquor issue, while Wheeler had to extract from the the politicians a positive commitment to ban liquor. But he went at his job with a ruthless zeal. He shamelessly shamed candidates before their churchgoing constituents. He targeted men and campaigns with the kind of ruthless efficiency used by later lobbies like the National Rifle Association. He created a whole new meaning for the term "pressure politics." Politicians who had formerly vacillated or evaded the liquor issue were forced to toe the Wheeler line. This was piety with a bludgeon.

> "Wheelerism," as both friends and enemies used the term by 1920, meant the techniques of the hard persuasion. On both state and federal legislative chambers, it meant thousands of telegrams and letters and the threat of political annihilation to a man of soft resolve who was tempted to vote wrong in committee or on the open floor.[19]

By the eve of World War I, the Prohibition movement was a juggernaut that seemed unstoppable. Even the Irish columnist for the *Chicago Journal,* Finley Peter Dunne, made his philosopher-bartender, Mr. Dooley, say:

> "I used to laugh at th' prohybitionists. I used to laugh them to scorn. But I laugh no more; they've got us on the run. I wouldn't be surprised at anny minyit if I had to turn this emporyum into an exchange f'r women's wurruck. Whether ye like or not, in a few years there won't be anny saloons to lure the married man fr'm his home, furnish guests f'r our gr-reat asylums an' jails
>   "I don't believe in this here prohybition," said Mr. Hennessy. "Th' man who dhrinks moderately ought to be allowed to have what he wants."
>   "What is his name?" asked Mr. Dooley. "What novel is he in?"

Prohibition, on the verge of passage anyway, was eased into triumph with the help of preparations for World War I. On June 1, 1914, Josephus Daniels, the Secretary of the Navy, banned alcohol consumption by sailors, to make them readier for combat. On August 10, 1917, as a "war measure," the Lever Food Control Act banned the use of grain by distilleries, cut back the amount of grain and coal available to brewers, and limited the alcohol content of beer to 2.75 percent. Then, on December 18, 1917, the Eighteenth Amendment was passed, banning the manufacture, sale, or transportation of intoxicating liquors. The "wets" in Congress for the first time put a time limit on the states for ratifying the amendment, hoping the amendment could not pass in the prescribed period. But in fact the states were quick to ratify by January 16, 1919. The Evangelicals in America celebrated with nightlong festivities, while bars held wakes, with caskets for their wares. The joy of the dries would prove premature.

BILLY SUNDAY (1863–1935)

N O ONE was happier at the victory of Prohibition than the Reverend Billy Sunday, who claimed that he had single-handedly brought it about. The real credit lay elsewhere—several elsewheres, in fact, beginning with Progressive reformers Frances Willard, Wayne Wheeler, and their many coworkers. But it is true that Sunday kept the fires of the Temperance crusade burning brightly. His most famous sermon, long polished and perfected and frequently performed, was a dramatic and emotionally wrenching hand-to-hand wrestle between Billy Sunday and Demon Rum. And he was not an insignificant figure throughout the last stages of the fight for Prohibition, proving that revivalism was still alive and popular in America. In 1914, Sunday tied for eighth place, along with Andrew Carnegie, in a poll asking the question "Who is the greatest man in the United States?"[20] Woodrow Wilson praised Sunday and received him in the White House.[21] He was praised as well by John D. Rockefeller, Andrew Carnegie, William Jennings Bryan, and Theodore Roosevelt. Reliable statistics say that he preached to over 100 million people.

Sunday was a great athlete and a great showman. He gave up a very successful baseball career, in which he was known for his speed at stealing bases (initially for the Chicago White Stockings). After he was converted, he went to work for the YMCA in 1890. In 1893, he became an assistant evangelist on the team of Wilbur Chapman, who had invented a system he called the "Simultaneous Evangelistic Campaign." He and his assistants, numbering as many as two dozen, would take over all the Protestant pulpits in a town and work up a coordinated revival that reached its climax led by Chapman himself in the main church or large auditorium. Sunday became the advance man for these campaigns, going into towns and arranging for the cooperation of the pastors. He was learning all the tricks of the trade, and he would repay his mentor by regularly stealing from his sermons for the rest of his life.[22]

When Sunday went out on his own, he was slow in building the kind of reputation that star evangelists need. He had to overcome resistance from pastors because he was not a clergyman. He had to seek ordination, though he admitted, "I don't know any more about theology than a jackrabbit knows about ping-pong—but I'm on my way to glory."[23] Part of his appeal was that he said he knew no more than his audience. His only claim was that he had been saved, and they could be too, while most of the learned were damned. "Thousands of college graduates are going as fast as they can straight to hell. If I had a million dollars [he did], I'd give $999,999 to the church and $1 to education."[24] He expected when he got to heaven to move into a mansion with a FOR RENT sign, since "it had been intended for a professor in Union Theological Seminary" who went to hell.[25]

Since Sunday preached to all denominations, his choice of a church to be ordained in was not based on doctrine. He seems to have gone to the most respectable body that would take him—which he decided was the Presbyterians, who had ordained his mentor Wilbur Chapman. Richard Hofstadter quotes what he calls "a bit of Protestant folk lore": "A Methodist is a Baptist who wears shoes; a Presbyterian is a Methodist who has gone to college; and an Episcopalian is a Presbyterian who lives off his investments."[26] Sunday just squeaked by in his bid for clerical status. To the examining board of ministers in Chicago, he answered doctrinal or historical questions with frank admissions that "that's too deep for me," or "I'll have to pass that up." But a friend on the board said that his prowess as a preacher showed that God had ordained him. Later, the Presbyterian scholars at Princeton would be among his harshest critics.[27]

Sunday did not follow Chapman's practice of simultaneously preaching with others. He wanted to be the whole show—except that, like most evangelists, he left the music to a partner, in his case the jaunty trombonist Homer "Rody" Rodeheaver. Unlike other evangelists, Sunday did not call for conversions in the first days of his campaigns but saved the great summons for the last session. It took great skill and dramatic gifts to keep people coming back to the wooden "tabernacle" he raised in each town for the climactic event. He built suspense toward the final day, on which at last he called people to stream down the sawdust trail he had prepared for them—he called his converts "trail hitters." In 1915, when George M. Cohan wrote a musical comedy in which he played a version of Sunday called Billy Holliday, he called it *Hit-the-Trail Holliday*. The only trouble with the show, said drama critic Heywood Broun, was that Cohan was less entertaining than Sunday. "All in all, we believe that Sunday has more of the dramatic instinct than Cohan."[28]

Sunday used his great athleticism as part of his performance—he could compete with Cohan even as a dancer. He dashed about the stage, fell on his knees and pounded the floor, stood on a chair, smashed the chair in a tirade against Satan, and ran to the lip of the stage to denounce a sinner in the audience:

> He would impersonate a sinner trying to reach heaven like a
> ball player sliding for home—and illustrate by running and
> sliding the length of the improvised tabernacle stage. . . .
> Hurling some imprecation at a "boozer," the ex-outfielder
> would leap to the edge of the platform, one leg stretched out

behind him, the other knee bent double, his arm stabbing out
ahead of him, his whole taut, tense body like a javelin held in
rest a few inches off the ground.[29]

Sunday stole most of his sermons and anecdotes from other evangelists, but he spiced things up with his own peppery language. Here is how he told the story of Salome's dance before Herodias:

> When the entertainment was at its height, Herodias shoved
> Salome out into the room to do her little stunt. She said to her:
> "Go like a twin-six [race car]!" She had anklets and bracelets
> on, but she didn't have clothes enough on her to flag a hand car.
> And she spun around on her toe and stuck her foot out at a
> quarter to twelve [imitating the action]. The king let out a
> guffaw of approval . . . and he said, "Sis, you're sure a peach.
> You're the limit. You can have anything you want."

When he told the story of David and Goliath, David "soaked the giant in the coco right between the lamps, and he went down for the count."[30] When he got to the New Testament, Pontius Pilate became "just one of those rat-hole, pinheaded, pliable, stand-pat, free-lunch, pie-counter politicians."[31]

When people objected to this slangy approach to the Bible, Sunday soaked them in the coco:

> Those who abuse me are trying to divert attention from their
> own abusive language and iniquity by saying, "Bill is vulgar,
> and Bill is crude." Oh no, I am not vulgar and crude. You are
> rotten, that is all there is to it. You doped that wrong, my
> friends. . . . Rotten is a good Anglo-Saxon word, and you don't
> have to go to the dictionary to know what it means. . . . "A
> process in the formation of new chemical compounds" is just
> the Bostonese way of saying a thing is rotten. It's the society

way of trying to keep you from holding your nose, because it's
vulgar; but I like "rotten" because it gets over the line quicker.

Even when Sunday was offering the prayer at the end of his sermon, he
remained bellicose:

> Oh, say, Jesus, save that man down at Heron Lake that wrote that
> dirty black lie about me. You'll have a big job on your hands to do
> it, Lord, I'll tell you that before you begin—but go ahead. Better
> take along a pair of rubber gloves and a bottle of disinfectant, but
> if you can save him, Lord, I'd like to have you do it.[32]

His critics were just sissies: "What do I care if some puff-eyed little
dibbly-dibbly preacher goes tibbly-tibbling around because I use plain
Anglo-Saxon words?"[33] He bullied, cajoled, wooed, and sang people to
"hit the trail." In Pittsburgh he told them what God would ask when they
got to heaven: "Are you from Pittsburgh?" "Yes, Lord." "Were you there
when Bill was trying to save the city?" "Yes, Lord." "Did you help him?"
"No, Lord." "Beat it."

For Sunday, as for the Fundamentalists, religion was a private thing, a
state of soul to be worked out between a person and God—only where
the Fundamentalists often shrank back into themselves and held their
peace, Sunday made religion irrelevant by dragging it into the center
ring and turning it into show biz. That suited the powerful just fine.
William McLoughlin argues that Sunday effectively blunted efforts at
social reform.[34] He argued that conversion to Christ would of itself
solve all social problems, especially since one sign of conversion was the
abandonment of alcohol. Helen Keller called him "a monkey wrench
[thrown] in the social revolution."[35] Businessmen supported him, invited
him to their towns, encouraged their workers to attend his revivals. If
workers could stop drinking and be diverted from policy issues, they
would be very happy. An analyst who watched Sunday work in his town
called him "the best strike breaker the country has produced."[36]

WORLD WAR I

JOSIAH STRONG was no longer alive by the onset of the Great War, but the remaining Social Gospel team became cheerleaders—all but Walter Rauschenbusch. His German birth was offered as an excuse for his abstention, but that was not enough to keep his reputation from going into an immediate decline, not to recover for years. Lyman Abbott turned his magazine, *The Outlook,* over to war promotion and justification. In 1918 he wrote a book calling the war *The Twentieth Century Crusade,* since "a crusade to make this world a home in which God's children can live in peace and safety is more Christian than a crusade to recover from pagans the tomb in which the body of Christ was buried."[37] Abbott was willing to accept almost anything that was proposed in the name of the war effort—banning of German music, dismissal of pacifists from uni versity faculties, outlawing of antiwar assemblies, and suppression of *The Masses.*[38] He even accepted, as war measures, things he had previously opposed— Prohibition and women's suffrage.[39]

War generally heightens religiosity, and in America it tends to unite the generations. That was certainly true of the Great War. All churches but the pacifist ones—Quakers and Mennonites—swung into line. Billy Sunday roared that "Christianity and Patriotism are synonymous terms, and hell and traitors are synonyms."[40] He laughed out his propaganda: "If you turn hell upside down, you will find *Made in Germany* stamped on the bottom."[41] As usual, Sunday presented the struggle as his own fight against Satan and the Kaiser: "I today . . . declare war against hell and all its commissaries and all its cohorts. You can't shove your cursed kultur and your damnable Hohenzollernism down our throats. You can't spit on the Stars and Stripes." He prayed that God would "guide the next gunner who sights a U-boat so that his aim will be true."[42]

Other preachers were just as bloodthirsty as Sunday. Henry B. Wright, a professor of divinity at Yale and a YMCA officer, counseled men to go into battle with Jesus at their side:

> I would not enter this work till I could see Jesus himself
> sighting down a gun barrel and running a bayonet through an
> enemy's body.... I discerned through clouds of gas and smoke
> One on foot arrayed in a garb of olive drab which was stained
> with blood and mire, and in His hands a bayonet sword
> attached to a rifle.[43]

Many preachers found in Germany the sources of biblical Higher Criticism, Nietzschean "survival of the fittest" ideas, and other abominations—even that devilish invention, Kindergarten. William Barton, preaching in the First Congregational Church of Oak Park, Illinois, said:

> I place here on the pulpit these four books, Treitschke,
> Nietzsche, Bernhardi, Clausewitz.... I say deliberately that the
> great question to be settled in the present war is whether the
> future is to be dominated by the ideas of these four books, or
> this other one, the Holy Bible, the Gospel of Jesus Christ.[44]

Some preachers equated fighting with spreading the Gospel. As a Baptist minister in California said: "I look upon the enlistment of an American soldier as I do on the departure of a missionary for Burma."[45]

The pressures to conform to calls on patriotism in time of war can be gauged by the conduct of the Premillennialists. At first, as war loomed, the three leading Premillennial journals kept to their traditional stance, that no effort to improve a doomed world can work. Arlo Gaebelein, at *The Outlook,* said that real believers should take no part in "man's plans during 'man's day.'"[46] He opposed making war to save civilization—worldly civilization was not worth saving. This stance prompted a ferocious assault on the Premillennialists from the Modernist theologians at the University of Chicago. Shirley Jackson Case and Shailer Mathews called this stand "treasonous." For a time, the two sides kept up their fire against each other, even accusing the other side of taking German funding for its position.[47] But soon the heat proved too much for the Premillennialists to bear, as all around them caught the war contagion. They softened their stand and began to beat the war drums themselves. This affected their later attitude toward politics. They more rarely treated America as a country lacking any covenant with God. George Marsden says: "This development is so dramatic, and the premillennialists played such a central role in organizing fundamentalism immediately after the war, that a close look at their wartime views is most helpful for understanding the relationship between fundamentalism and its cultural context."[48]

The decade ended with the Evangelicals feeling stronger than ever. The Premillennialists, who had abstained from cooperation with Postmillennial Fundamentalists (that is, others believing in biblical inerrancy), were now aligned with them, first for the war, and then for postwar reforms. They were all called Fundamentalists now, though the Premillennialists were in the strongest position now that they had joined the world's efforts.

> Those who held to this teaching were in command in 1919 at
> the forming of the World's Christian Fundamentals Associa-
> tion. They thereupon challenged all comers with whom they
> had to coexist through the twenties. But precisely because
> they thus had to coexist for the purpose of forming their fac-
> tion, they also had to surrender their general designation
> as Premillennialist and replace it with the more inclusive orga-
> nization name, Fundamentalism. While not all Fundamental-
> ists believed in Premillennialism, those who did were most
> energetic about organizing the movement nationally. While
> Fundamentalists acquired the image of being most at home
> in the Southern Bible Belt, much of the leadership had come
> from the North—from Niagara bible conferences, from pulpits
> in Boston and New York, Philadelphia and Chicago, from bible
> institutions in Chicago and Minneapolis. (MM 2.194)

Premillennialists would hanker back to their passive stance, especially after setbacks like the Scopes trial. Even in 1919, Arno Gaebelein could not go all the way to engagement with the world—he opposed the League of Nations as another example of man's pride trying to arrange the world to its own pattern.[49] But the Russian Revolution made even Gaebelein think that End Time signs were being fulfilled, as "the North" fell under the dominion of atheists. Fundamentalists backed the Red Scare raids of Attorney General A. Mitchell Palmer at war's end. Gaebelein proclaimed that "the Beast lifts the head in our land."[50] When Palmer began to deport "Reds," Billy Sunday said that was not good enough: "I would stand every one of the ornery, wild-eyed IWWs, anarchists, crazy socialists, and other types of Reds up before a firing squad and save space on our ships."[51]

The surge of Fundamentalism was expressed in new alliances, like William B. Riley's Baptist Bible Union. The Presbyterians renewed the 1910 pledge to the Five Fundamentals. "From 1922 to 1925, Fundamentalists were close to gaining control of the Northern Presbyterian and Northern Baptist groups."[52] In deep concern, the famous Modernist theologian Harry Emerson Fosdick preached the widely distributed sermon "Shall the Fundamentalists Win?" (1922). His worry was premature. The Evangelicals did not know what was about to hit them.

25 | EVANGELICALS
BROUGHT LOW

IF THE FIRST DECADE of the twentieth century treated Evangelicals rather well, the second decade sharply devalued them—Prohibition failed, the Scopes trial exposed them to ridicule, and compromising involvement with the Ku Klux Klan and other anti-Catholic efforts made them look bigoted in the campaign against Al Smith, the Democratic candidate for president. It is not true that Evangelicalism went into a total eclipse at this time, but many of its followers retired to lick their wounds. The setback had come, unexpectedly, just as they were savoring their greatest time of influence in a century (since the glory time of the Second Great Awakening).

The first blow came from the very thing that had been their greatest political triumph, the passage of the Eighteenth Amendment. The "noble experiment" they had brought to the nation became a nightmare of nonenforcement, corrupt circumvention, new forms of organized crime, and a selectively higher level of alcohol consumption and other forms of hedonism in the "Roaring Twenties." The problem was not simply that Prohibition had to be revoked. The actions of the Evangelical leaders made the problems of enforcement worse, with the former champion of the law, the Anti-Saloon League (ASL), contributing to the crackup. This came about in the classical way, from overreaching on the part of the conquerors. Two ASL men especially gummed up the works as they tried to be, respectively, the "Dry Boss" and the "Dry Messiah"—Wayne Wheeler and Bishop James Cannon.

WAYNE WHEELER, THE "DRY BOSS"

T HE MAN who muscled the amendment into being did not want to step away from the thing he had created. As he had insisted on overseeing the politics of its passage, he tried personally to oversee its enforcement, beginning with the enabling law itself, the Volstead Act. The Eighteenth Amendment prohibited "the manufacture, sale, or transportation of intoxicating liquors." But that left several matters unresolved.

1. Was *possession* of liquor—as opposed to "sale, transport," etc.—still allowed? Most of the states that had already gone dry did not go what was called "bone dry."[1] They allowed consumption of alcohol, but in regulated amounts or places. Rationing of alcohol, closing of saloons, and limitation of the amount of alcohol in beer and spirits were adopted, but not a total ban on all forms of alcohol consumption. In Virginia, for instances, a measure supported by the ASL allowed liquor to be sold only in towns with a police force that could control it. As we have seen, wartime Prohibition just regulated the production of alcoholic beverages and their alcoholic content. Could peacetime Prohibition do something similar? Congress would have to decide that before the Eighteenth Amendment could go into effect.

2. What is an "intoxicating liquor"? Some were against treating mild beer or wine as intoxicating. Some states, like the federal government under President Wilson, had mandated "near beers" of less than 3 percent alcohol. The wine and beer industries said they would make their products low in alcohol, and they had some supporters in Congress.

3. Enforcement was left to "the Congress and the several states"—but how was Congress going to enforce it, and through what agency or agencies? The Justice Department is the normal enforcer of laws, but some were saying that the Treasury Department should handle this law, because the Internal Revenue Service had data and experience with the liquor industry through its taxation of it.

Wayne Wheeler rushed in to answer all these questions, pressuring the same congressional forces he had maneuvered into passing the amendment in the first place. He said the ban should be total, leaving behind the many experiments in partial Prohibition. This would make the law far more difficult to enforce. He wanted a ban on possession as well as sale. He wanted to set the allowed alcohol level so low—one-half of 1 percent—as to be, in effect, a total ban. And he was determined to lodge enforcement in the Treasury Department, which he had worked with and hoped to control. These measures, drawn up by Wheeler himself, were passed in the Senate.

In the House, however, Minnesota representative Andrew Volstead was determined to draft the legislation. He adopted all but one of the Senate's provisions—he would allow possession as opposed to sale of alcohol. Except on this one point, his plan was so close to Wheeler's that Wheeler would later claim to be the author of the Volstead Act (to Volstead's embarrassment).[2] The act accepted Wheeler's limit on alcoholic content (one-half of 1 percent) as opposed to that of President Wilson and many states (less than 3 percent). The lower figure had been set in the past for taxation purposes by the Internal Revenue Service—the lower amount made for more taxable beverages. Wheeler called this a precedent controlling what was an "intoxicating liquor." If he had lost on this point, the law enforcement problems would have been far less severe in the coming years. Once all liquor was banned, the defiance of the law was bound to be extensive.

The one point on which the Volstead Act departed from Wheeler's agenda—allowing possession but not sale—was self-crippling. It said that private consumption in the home could go on, so long as the liquor had been legally acquired—that is, so long as one was drinking beverages purchased before the act went into effect. But how could the Treasury enforcers (called "T-men" to parallel the FBI's "G-men") verify that anyone's private stock was bought before the ban? Home searches, income surveys, raids on private parties? This raised Fourth Amendment issues of illegal search and seizure. But if homes were to be exempted from intrusive enforcement, how could private parties anywhere be controlled? Speakeasies would claim they were private clubs with a right to the private possession specified in the law.

Obviously when private stocks ran out, they had to be replenished, but owners would keep maintaining that they had bought their bottles long ago. Besides, home brews were not purchased (as alcoholic beverages). If the alcohol was fermented at home, in wine or beer, did that escape the law? The authorities would go back and forth on this issue. As for "bathtub gin," buying raw alcohol to put in it was arguably not the purchase of an "intoxicating liquor"—not until it was processed at home. Endless wrangles were opened up by the legislation itself.

Wheeler compounded the problems when he had the administration accept a crony of his, Roy Haynes, as the Commissioner of Prohibition, on the assumption that he could use him to pressure lawmakers, federal and local, on tough enforcement measures. Wheeler feared that Congress would make changes like accepting "near beer" as legal, so he meant to keep up his lobbying effort on the Senate and House. Here, as elsewhere, Wheeler's strategy backfired. Wheeler did not trust the Secretary of the Treasury, Andrew Mellon, and tried to use Roy Haynes to undermine him. This led to Haynes's being despised by other Treasury personnel. Wheeler then made things worse by exempting Prohibition agents from civil service rules—he wanted to keep bringing in flunkies he could control. Though this was denounced as a "spoils raid," Wheeler was able to keep the exemption in place until his death in 1927.[3] Haynes, for his part, did little to educate the public on liquor issues. On the contrary, he wrote a book, *Prohibition Inside Out,* that glorified T-men and sensationalized bootleggers.[4] Morale and integrity in the Treasury Department were constantly undermined by Wheeler's actions.

Wheeler's methods had been disapproved by some in the Anti-Saloon League even before passage of the Eighteenth Amendment. But his high-handed ways afterward made it necessary for him to become even more manipulative of the ASL itself, rigging its internal elections, shoving aside more moderate voices like that of Ernest Cherrington.[5] Wheeler now became what his own chosen ghostwriter, Justin Steuart, called a "dictator." Wheeler thought of himself as the single-handed enforcer of Prohibition. Milder methods or public education programs he considered betrayals of the true hard line. When T-men were overwhelmed by their task, he advocated bringing in the army and navy.[6] He was unhappy with the exemptions written into the Volstead Act—for alcohol needed in industrial operations, sacramental wine, and medical treatments. He got Haynes to add poisons to the industrial-use alcohol, to prevent its being used in beverages, saying, "The government is under no obligation to furnish people with alcohol that is drinkable . . . The person who drinks this industrial alcohol . . . is a deliberate suicide."[7] When he heard that millions of gallons were being ordered for sacramental wine (M 2.218), he wanted to mount raids on sacristies.

He was willing to work with bigots and fanatics who were angered at defiance of the Prohibition laws. Some ASL local leaders collaborated with the Ku Klux Klan in its search for Catholic violators—though Wheeler himself denounced this.[8]

> Described by a wet editor as a man who "works with the zeal
> of a Savonarola and the craft of a Machiavelli," Wheeler was
> zealous, crafty, and, above all, successful. Another enemy said
> that Wheeler "would make any combination, would cohabit
> with the devil himself, to win."[9]

Against such a ruthless man, violators of the law did not feel that they had ceded the moral high ground to its enforcers. The contradictions in the law and corruption in its enforcement made people feel they had a right to despise and defy it.

THE SCOPES TRIAL (1925)

D URING THEIR POSTWAR EUPHORIA, the Fundamentalists thought they could bring down the principal threat to their principal doctrine—biblical inerrancy. That threat, as they saw it, was Darwin's theory of evolution. They determined that they would ban that theory from school textbooks, and they succeeded in passing laws for that purpose in many legislatures. William Jennings Bryan, the three-time Democratic nominee for president, had every reason to think that this was a winning effort he could help push through to completion. I do not think he was being merely opportunistic. He was in his politics a Progressive, who had championed all kinds of projects the Fundamentalists disapproved of—women's suffrage, the League of Nations, a federal income tax, opposition to capital punishment, and many regulatory reforms. Cause after cause that he promoted would be taken up later and carried through to victory. Edward Larson claims: "Probably no other American, save the authors of the Bill of Rights, could rightly claim credit for as many Constitutional amendments as the Great Commoner."[10] Bryan's campaigns were the most leftist ever conducted by either of the two major parties. Robert Cherny put it this way:

> The middle of Bryan's career, from 1900 to 1910, reveals few instances where he reduced a complex issue to a simple one. His 1908 platform was one of the longest and most complicated up to that time. While he might have dramatically argued that private monopoly was intolerable, he posed a variety of solutions, including government ownership, licensing, and anti-trust action.[11]

But if Bryan did not reduce politics to simplistic formulas, the same thing could not be said of his views on evolution. He thought of it as a relativistic and "Nietzschean" assault on morals, without knowing much about either science or the Bible. He thought such expertise could be swept away by moral urgency and earnest rhetoric. His campaigns had not prepared him for the courtroom or the logic class. Clarence Darrow would give him lessons in both those areas.

As Bryan took the lead against evolution, he was welcomed into the Fundamentalist movement. Billy Sunday wrote to him: "Every time I pick up a paper and find where you are smiting evolution. . . . I feel like reaching out my hand to you and saying, 'God bless you.'" Other religious leaders expressed the same kind of gratitude—President J. D. Eggleston of Hampden-Sydney College and former Arkansas governor Charles H. Brough (MM 2. 192–93). "It was Bryan who did most to bring the evolution controversy to this public stage" (MM 3.83). Frank Norris, pastor of Fort Worth's First Baptist, the largest Protestant church in the United States, cheered Bryan on. In the public eye Bryan became the great champion who could defeat Darwin—a role he assumed without knowing how dangerous it could prove.

Bryan's lack of knowledge in this new arena showed when he started teaching Bible classes in Florida. In the intellectually thin Evangelical culture of the time, this amounted to telling Bible stories and drawing a moral. His false assurance reached even to giving the 1922 Sprunt Lectures at the Union Theological Seminary of Virginia. He worked from the Fundamentalist view that a "scientific" approach to the Bible meant accepting its "facts" at face value. All other approaches were mere "hypotheses." Martin Marty sees how this whole stage of his career betrayed his own past. Darrow came late to his task of taking Bryan apart. Bryan had been working to do that himself:

> In religious debates, Bryan was caustic, which he had not been
> in his years of political controversy. He was supercilious and
> defensive at once against those he called that "cultural crowd,"
> those who dismissed religion as being useful only among the
> "superstitious and ignorant." He retained only a rare glint of
> his old good humor when he said he was "trying to bring some
> of the honesty of politics into the church." In his best popular
> style, Bryan said he would "take the church out of the hands of

the bosses and put it into the hands of worshippers." . . . Bryan
had taken on Darwin with a condescension he rarely showed in
politics. Darwinism represented "tommyrot," a "ridiculous
attempt to explain the unexplainable." It was all "ludicrous":
evolution promoted the basis of Germanic "Superman"
teaching and was thus responsible for the recent war. Bryan
seemed on the verge of reviving the Red Scare when he argued
that Darwinism was also responsible for class struggle.
(MM 2.190–91)

Bryan had so embodied the fight against Darwin that to bring Bryan
down would discredit the entire opposition—or so lawyer Clarence
Darrow of the Illinois bar and journalist H. L. Mencken of the *Baltimore
Sun* believed. And that is exactly what they meant to do. These friends
happened to be together in Richmond, Virginia, when word reached
them that Bryan was going to attack evolution in a Tennessee courtroom.[12] They agreed on the spot to get into the fray, working together,
Darrow before the bench and Mencken before the nation. They succeeded beyond their fondest dreams. The judge allowed the proceedings
to be broadcast on the young medium of radio. Mencken took a team of
journalists to Tennessee, and other famous writers flocked there—
among them Westbrook Pegler and Joseph Wood Krutch.

Legal points counted little in what followed. The recently founded
American Civil Liberties Union, to stop the increasing practice of purging textbooks of Darwinism, had advertised for a volunteer to break
the law against teaching evolution. A young high school teacher named
John T. Scopes had stepped up for the role. The ACLU did not want to
subject their volunteer to a criminal trial, but to a civil trial testing the
ban's constitutionality. Scopes, however, agreed to be arrested and asked
the ACLU to accept Darrow's offer to defend him, over the ACLU's
qualms. The ACLU went ahead, expecting a Tennessee jury to convict
Scopes (as it did) but then to appeal the verdict up to the Supreme
Court. But after Darrow made a fool of Bryan, the Tennessee Supreme
Court voided the conviction on a technicality, precisely to block Darrow

from further appeals. In a sense this did not matter, since the public humiliation of Bryan made national textbook authors continue publishing books with Darwin in them. Yet that, in turn, did not matter either, since schools in the South just refused to teach those sections. (Scopes later admitted that he had not taught that section, either—he was out of school when it came up.)

Even the crucial event in the trial had no legal force. Darrow called Bryan to testify as an expert witness on the Bible. He was counting on Bryan's foolhardy ignorance, and his bet paid off. Bryan accepted the challenge. The judge let the testimony go forward without the jury, pending his decision on its relevance. The jury did not hear Bryan floundering around, trying to defend the literal meaning of Jonah in the whale and other embarrassments—but the whole world heard it, through the radio and through Mencken's lurid accounts. The damage was done. That was all that counted. When Bryan died shortly thereafter of diabetes, Mencken gloated, "Well, we killed the son of a bitch."[13] But he thought he had felled bigger game, Fundamentalism itself, and he was almost right.

But only almost. Fundamentalists shrank back from the limelight, but they were far from dead. They dug in their heels. They were still quietly keeping Darwin from being taught. Much of the nation scorned them, and saw their image in Sinclair Lewis's 1927 portrait of the preacher as charlatan, *Elmer Gantry*. But their Bible institutes continued in business, actually expanding their enrollments and outreach, and their radio preachers polished their techniques and built large audiences without the sophisticated world's notice.[14] The real damage is that they were driven into an intellectual ghetto, confirmed in their narrow ways. Mark Noll points out that the sequestered Evangelical culture protected the childish view of the Bible they celebrated in Bryan. The Scopes episode is a prime example of the danger Noll sees in an Evangelicalism cut off from an openness to reason.[15] The point, for purposes of this book, is that the populist pole of religiosity needs interaction with the elitist pole. One without the other is sterile. That is the real lesson of the Scopes trial.

424 | HEAD AND HEART

JAMES CANNON, THE
"DRY MESSIAH" (1864–1944)

WHEN WAYNE WHEELER died in 1927, James Cannon, the Methodist Temperance leader and stalwart of the ASL, stepped into his shoes, with the same tough attitude on enforcing the Volstead Act that Wheeler had initiated. Like Wheeler, Cannon did not trust the Secretary of the Treasury, Andrew Mellon, and he publicly denounced him for not pouring sufficient funds into quashing violations.[16] He continued the pressure politics of Wheeler, though support for this approach was fading even in the ASL. H. L. Mencken wrote of him that "Congress was his troop of Boy Scouts and presidents trembled whenever his name was mentioned."

Cannon was born in Maryland, where his father, a successful Delaware businessman, had moved during the Civil War to show his support for the South. He transferred his membership from the Methodist Church North to the Methodist Church South. Cannon went to Randolph Macon College in Virginia, a state to which he was fervently devoted through the rest of his life. After studying at Princeton Theological Seminary, Cannon was ordained in the Methodist ministry, and promoted to bishop by 1918. He ran several religious schools and newspapers in Virginia, and the state ASL operation, before becoming the head of ASL's national legislative committee. He was a power in the Democratic Party's Prohibition wing. In 1916 he testified before the Senate to prevent the appointment of Louis Brandeis to the Supreme Court—Brandeis, as a lawyer, once represented the liquor interests.[17] In 1917, he successfully lobbied Congress to include in the Selective Service Act a ban on selling alcohol to military men in uniform and authorizing the president to create zones around military camps that prostitutes could not enter.[18]

As chairperson of the ASL legislative committee, Cannon bargained with President Wilson over provisions of the wartime Prohibition.[19] He also took advantage of anti-German feeling in the war to denounce

German-American brewers as pawns of the Kaiser. He backed Wheeler's "bone dry" approach to the Volstead Act and its enforcement. Though he was happy for America to be fighting Germany, the land of biblical Higher Criticism, he was uneasy about the beer and wine consumed by America's allies. To keep American soldiers out of saloons abroad, he and another ASL minister, E. J. Moore, toured camps in England and France.[20] This well-publicized trip was resented by the military and derided by the press—much as the European tour by Senator McCarthy's aide Roy Cohn, and Cohn's friend David Schine, would be laughed at when they investigated United States Information Agency libraries and personnel for "subversive" literature.[21]

The fact that Cannon took over the main lobbying role in the ASL in 1927 meant that he was in charge of its activities during the 1928 presidential campaign. Though Cannon was a Democratic leader in Virginia, he worked to make Virginia and other Southern states vote for the Republican candidate Herbert Hoover, since the Democrats had nominated Al Smith, a wet, a Catholic, a New Yorker with ties to Tammany Hall. Cannon raised funds for the Hoover effort, and lent it money from the ASL, while churning out propaganda against Smith. The New Yorker, he alleged, drank "from four to eight cocktails a day."[22] Cannon was given the principal credit when traditionally Democratic Virginia voted Republican that year. He accomplished this despite the fact that the Democratic establishment in Virginia—Governor Harry Byrd, U.S. senator Carter Glass, former attorney general John Garland Pollard, all proven dries—campaigned energetically for Smith (Glass had written a Prohibition plank in the Democratic platform and won Smith's agreement to it).[23]

When Smith was nominated by the Democrats, Cannon left their convention and set up an anti-Smith headquarters for the South in Asheville, North Carolina, where he was elected chairman of the anti-Smith campaign. Soon after, he orchestrated a joint statement against Smith by himself and three other Methodist bishops.[24] He joined forces with the Republican boss in Virginia, the exquisitely named C. Bascom Slemp, who channeled Republican funds into Cannon's effort.[25] Cannon traveled and spoke against Smith, focusing on his Catholicism, which he called "the mother of ignorance, superstition, intolerance, and sin."[26] When it was reported that he had called Smith's followers "dirty people," he denied that, but he made "the sidewalks of New York" a refrain in his speeches (playing on the song used at Smith rallies, "East Side, West Side"). He explained to a Maryland crowd what types infest those sidewalks:

> [We want] people like yourselves—English, Scotch, Dutch, and German—people possessing honorable purposes, the kind of people who make good citizens in this land. But that is not the kind of people Governor Smith wants, that is not the type Tammany can control. . . . [Smith wants] the Italians, the Sicilians, the Poles and the Russian Jew. We have been unable to assimilate such people in our national life. . . . He wants the kind of people that you find today on the sidewalks of New York.[27]

Asked why he had attacked Jews, he answered:

> I did not refer to the German, English, or Spanish Jews. They are entirely different types from the Russian Jew. I refer to the Russian Jew who inhabits the sidewalks of New York in multiplied thousands.[28]

Cannon's point was put more directly, but with the same sense, in crude rhymes like the one dedicated to "Al-cohol Smith":

> *Alcohol Al for President,*
> *I stand for whiskey and bad government.*
> *My platform is wet, and I am too,*
> *And I get my votes from Catholic and Jew.*
> *The ignorant wop and the gangster too,*
> *Are the trash I expect to carry me through.*[29]

Though Cannon kept clear of the Ku Klux Klan's efforts against Al Smith, he showed no distaste for cooperating with a wide variety of bigots, including Bob Jones, who said, "I'd rather see a saloon on every corner in the South than see the foreigners elect Al Smith president."[30] Billy Sunday, as usual, made the contest against Smith his own battle with Satan, "to defy the forces of hell—Al Smith and the rest of them."[31] Cannon did nothing to repudiate the wild charges circulated in the anti-Smith campaign—that the Smith White House would have a suite for the pope, that the pope would set up artillery on the heights of Georgetown to terrorize the District of Columbia, that he would bring back the Inquisition.[32]

Cannon campaigned throughout the South against Smith, and deserves much of the credit for the fact that five states from the Solid South broke Democratic ranks for the first time. At this moment he almost justified Mencken's claim that he was "the most powerful ecclesiastic ever heard of in America."[33] This could be considered a triumph for the Evangelicals, though one achieved at the cost of boosting bigotry and the Klan. Besides, many historians now think Hoover would have won without the religious sliming of his opponent—he was immensely popular in 1928. And in fact his election was a Pyrrhic victory, as Johnson's defeat of Barry Goldwater in 1964 was a Pyrrhic victory. In the latter year, Lyndon Johnson was a sure winner in any event, but the loser realigned his party for future victories. Goldwater brought the South into the Republican Party, and Smith brought the immigrants to the fore in the Democratic Party. As David Burner wrote:

> Because of its effect upon Democratic fortunes in the cities,
> the candidacy of Governor Smith, regardless of his personal
> shortcomings as a campaigner, was undoubtedly a significantly
> healthy event in the evolution of the Democracy. . . . Walter
> Lippmann wrote that the chief result of the Smith candidacy
> was the reconstruction of the Democratic party and its
> liberation from Bryan and the South.[34]

428 | HEAD AND HEART

At the very moment of Cannon's triumph against Smith, he plummeted from the peak of ecclesiastical glory. Cannon was simultaneously accused of four things: (1) dealing with an unauthorized brokerage firm (a "bucket shop" in the slang of the day) whose manager went to jail, (2) illegal use of ASL funds in the campaign against Smith, (3) flour hoarding during the war, and (4) adultery with his secretary. He was questioned by several church boards and before a United States Senate committee (he became the first witness ever to stalk out of a Senate hearing). He escaped conviction on any of the charges, by cleverness and bravado.[35] Randolph Hearst, whose papers denounced Cannon repeatedly, had to admit privately that the man was too slippery for him:

> I have come to the conclusion that it will be next to impossible
> to directly pin anything to Bishop Cannon. I am sincere in
> saying that I consider him to have the best brain in America, no
> one excepted. He has without exception foreseen and prepared
> for every attack made upon him.[36]

But Cannon's reputation was ruined beyond repair. In the end, this was another one of the Evangelical low points in this period.

26 | Religion in a Radical Time

THE STOCK MARKET CRASH of 1929 took America overnight from the Roaring Twenties to the Radical Thirties. American incomes fell by 50 percent, 4 million were jobless, euphoria yielded to despair. Some felt that only radical measures could cope with such a disaster, and they lurched toward the far Left or the far Right. When people looked back after two decades, the radicals who had to live down their past were those who veered Left into membership in the Communist Party. But at the time the radical threat was far more insistent from the Right, from admirers of the European dictators or their imitators in America. The United States had always lacked a Left of the sort that European nations lived with. It is only because the dictators were defeated in World War II, while the Soviet Union was still powerful in the postwar period, that Americans of the 1950s forgot the various Mussolini lovers at home and became obsessed with those who had been Stalinists for a season.

The whole capitalist system seemed to have failed in 1929, and Marx looked prophetic. But parliamentary representation also seemed bankrupt, so much so that fascist efficiency had its charms. The rightist Union

Party mounted a campaign in 1936 that was more successful than the leftist Socialist Party—and the latter was not Stalinist, just meliorative, in the Norman Thomas vein. In the early Thirties, many people spoke well of Mussolini—including Will Rogers, Thomas Edison, and Andrew Mellon.[1]

A senator from Pennsylvania said, "If ever this country needed a Mussolini, it needs one now."[2] Many people were saying the same thing to Franklin Roosevelt in the four months between his 1932 election and 1933 inauguration. Walter Lippmann, the ruling journalist, went to Warm Springs, Georgia, Roosevelt's polio spa, to tell him personally what he had written in his column: "A mild dictatorship will help us over the roughest spots in the road ahead."[3]

Even the liberal Catholic magazine *Commonweal*, with a rosy view of Mussolini, editorialized that "the powers of a virtual dictatorship to reorganize the government" may be necessary. William Randolph Hearst created a movie that was a programmatic outline for the new president to follow—he sent the script to Roosevelt to read before the movie could be completed. Called *Gabriel over the White House*, it tells how a president received instructions in a dream from the archangel Gabriel—that he should dissolve the Congress and take all power in to his own hands, executing his opponents. Roosevelt suggested a few mild changes, but wrote Hearst the movie "should do much to help."[4] Another movie appeared simultaneously, *Mussolini Speaks*, narrated by Mussolini admirer Lowell Thomas. It was advertised as "the answer to what America needs." When a Fascist air squadron flew from Italy to the Chicago World Fair of 1933, Roosevelt invited its leader to lunch at the White House.[5] Charles Lindbergh paid even greater compliments to the German Luftwaffe, and was rewarded in 1938 with the Service Cross of the German Eagle by order of Hitler himself.[6] Lawrence Dennis, who wrote *The Coming American Fascism*, was taken as the inspiration for a fascist party in America, the National Party.[7]

When Roosevelt refused to dismiss Congress and take executive control of the country, many of his first followers became disillusioned with him and began to promote their own Fascist schemes. The American Liberty League, financed by the du Pont family, created a number of front organizations—like the Sentinels of Liberty and the Southern Committee to Uphold the Constitution.[8] The German American Bund modeled itself on Hitler's program, as did the Khaki Shirts led by Art J. Smith, and the Black Legion (MM 2.262).[9] The Silver Legion of America, with its troops of Fascist-styled Silver Shirts, was organized by William Dudley Pelley and had fifteen thousand members in 1934 (MM 2.263–65).[10] Gerald B. Winrod, a son of faith healers, had himself been a boy evangelist before he founded the Dispensationalist body, Defenders of the Christian Faith, which had sixty thousand members in 1934. By 1938, he had turned this into a fan club for Hitler. The same year, he ran unsuccessfully for the Senate in Kansas. In 1942 he was indicted by the federal government for sedition (MM 2. 265–66).[11]

Most of those yearnings for a dictator were minor disturbances on the far Right. But several other movements were potentially more dangerous as they converged to make up the Union Party. These were salient events in America's religious history because they were led by two clergymen and two devout laymen. The clergymen were a Catholic priest, Charles Coughlin, and a Disciples of Christ minister, Gerald L. K. Smith. The laymen were a famous physician, Francis Townsend, and a United States congressman, William Lemke.

FATHER COUGHLIN (1891–1979)

CHARLES COUGHLIN was born, educated, and ordained in Canada, in the Basilian religious order. When that order was dissolved, he placed himself under the American diocesan discipline of Bishop Michael J. Gallagher of Detroit. Bishop Gallagher had just returned from the canonization in Rome of the nun Thérèse of Lisieux, known as the Little Flower. He wanted to build a national shrine in her honor, and he assigned this task to Father Coughlin, who was to raise it in a Detroit suburb, Royal Oak. This was not a typical parish—it had a potential outreach to pilgrims from all over the country. But the immediate neighborhood was not prosperous, and Coughlin began broadcasting his Sunday sermons on local radio as a way of raising funds for the shrine. President Roosevelt's Fireside Chats, beginning in 1933, are often credited with pioneering use of the radio for suasive purposes. But the real credit should go to Father Coughlin. Beginning in 1926, Coughlin had, by the time of the Fireside Chats, built a radio audience of 30 million listeners, greater than was reached at the time by radio stars like Rudy Vallee or George Burns and Gracie Allen.[12] He had a warm voice softened by just a touch of Irish brogue. The novelist Wallace Stegner called it "a voice of such mellow richness, such manly heartwarming, confidential intimacy, such emotional and ingratiating charm, that anyone turning past it almost automatically returned to hear it again."[13]

At first, Coughlin just broadcast the sermons he was preaching in his church. But within a year he was receiving four thousand letters a week and had to hire over a hundred assistants to handle them—the basement of his shrine looked like the post office of a medium-sized town. His admirers poured money into the shrine, small donors in great numbers—he once walked into his bank to deposit twenty-two thousand one-dollar bills that he had received in the last few days (MM 2.274). After the crash occurred, people asked him what to do as the Depression deepened. At first, he relied on the social encyclicals of Popes Leo XIII and Pius XI, recommending an activist (corporative) state like that which Mussolini was professing, a living wage for all families, and labor unions modeled on medieval guilds. As the 1932 election neared, he backed the Roosevelt campaign, coining the widely used slogan "Roosevelt or Ruin." Roosevelt, ever the adroit politician, flattered Coughlin and made the priest think of himself as an important adviser, one who deserved much of the credit for his man's election. Now Coughlin was calling the New Deal "Christ's Deal."[14]

But when Roosevelt failed to take the priest's advice—mainly to dissolve the Federal Reserve System and set up a national bank issuing new currency—Coughlin felt that Roosevelt had failed in his duty as an energetic executive. He now called him Franklin Double-Cross Roosevelt. Coughlin's audience, at first mainly Catholic, had become ecumenically anti-Roosevelt—65 percent non-Catholic by 1934.[15] In that year, Coughlin openly became a political leader, with the backing of his bishop. The priest founded the National Union for Social Justice, with *Social Justice* as its periodical. Roosevelt, who had checked on Coughlin's mail rate with James Farley, his postmaster general, urged Catholics in his administration—Farley himself and Joseph Kennedy, the chairman of the Securities and Exchange Commission—to calm Coughlin down.[16] But as the 1936 election neared, Coughlin was reaching out to other anti-Roosevelt forces for an electoral alliance—to Louisiana "Kingfish" Huey Long, to Francis Townsend, the leader of a senior citizen movement, to the agrarian late-Populist William Lemke, and—most ominously—to the anti-Semitic Gerald L. K. Smith.

GERALD L. K. SMITH (1898–1976)

EARLY IN THE ELECTION year 1936, a Democratic committee of the Congress (the Bell Committee) meant to head off a challenge to Roosevelt's reelection from a popular movement led by a retired physician, Francis Townsend, who had sponsored something he called a revolving pension plan. The government was to give a monthly payment of $200 to retired people on condition that they spend it within thirty days, injecting money into the consumption cycle, thus stimulating the production cycle. This was the cure-all for the Depression that millions of people were hoping for. But Townsend had so many faddists in his organization raking money off from it that he found himself unable to respond to harsh questions from the Bell Committee. E. B. White of the *New Yorker* wrote, "When forced to deal with the fundamental problems, he quietly came apart, like an inexpensive toy."[17] But Gerald L. K. Smith was there to put him back together again. Dr. Townsend got up in an anguished state and tried to make his way out of the committee room. One of the congressional inquisitors called, "Stop that man!" but a tall and muscular member of the audience rushed to his side and barreled Townsend out to open air. The man was Smith, and Townsend in gratitude turned over his movement to his rescuer. Smith knew what he wanted to do with it.

Smith was a revivalist who had gone to Louisiana for his wife's health and become a preaching sensation there. Senator Huey Long, glad to find a religious ally in this rising star, recruited Smith to organize nationally for his Share-the-Wealth plan. Smith became Long's enthusiastic acolyte, accompanying him on his trips to Washington and preaching an eloquent sermon at Long's funeral after the senator was assassinated in 1935. Smith tried to take over Long's movement at his death, but the Democratic establishment in Louisiana froze him out. Smith then shopped around for a new mass audience, finding it in Dr. Townsend's following of older citizens. Smith the organizer approached Coughlin and suggested they merge the priest's National Union for Social Justice, his own vestigial Share-the-Wealth movement, Townsend's Old Age Retirement Plan, and the Nonpartisan League of the rural activist William Lemke, U.S. representative from North Dakota.

This was a promising idea in the abstract, though its parts might not fit in practice. Coughlin's audience was mainly urban, largely Eastern, and initially Catholic. Smith's base was Southern, largely rural, and traditionally anti-Catholic, as was Lemke's Midwestern following. The core of Townsend's first following was in his native California. Still, the groups would make a large coalition if they could be coaxed together. Aligning them was a delicate operation, which occurred in Cleveland early in July of the election year 1936. Dr. Townsend held there his convention for the pension plan, with eleven thousand delegates. Simultaneously, Coughlin held his convention of the National Union for Social Justice, with ten thousand delegates. While jockeying to keep emotions under control, Coughlin addressed the Townsendites, and Smith addressed the Coughlinites, and the two organizations were ever so carefully linked to form the Union Party, nominating William Lemke as its presidential candidate. Coughlin was clearly the most popular member of the coalition, but he was ineligible for the presidency because of his Canadian birth. Smith was too divisive a figure—in fact, he would be expelled from the party during the campaign because of his vitriolic remarks. Townsend was considered too old for the effort, and Lemke, as a member of Congress, was considered knowledgeable in the ways of politics.

The numbers of these combined bodies looked formidable, but Roosevelt was not easily panicked. With typical shrewdness he said, "There is no question that it is all a dangerous situation, but when it comes to a showdown, these fellows cannot all lie in the same bed, and will fight among themselves with almost absolute certainty."[18] The Union Party got four times as many votes as Norman Thomas's Socialist Party in this first year of its existence, 1936—but that was only 2 percent of the returns, and it was the high-water mark for the friable coalition. Coughlin's movement shrank back to its original Catholic base, and even that was dissolved under the presidential attention lavished on Catholics by Roosevelt.[19] The electoral challenge from the Religious Right ended as rapidly as it began.

Coughlin and Smith kept themselves in the news only by ever more vicious appeals to anti-Semitism. Both kept company with Henry Ford in his promotion of *Protocols of the Elders of Zion.* Coughlin had pledged that he would give up his radio show if the Union Party lost the election. But he was soon back on the air, claiming that Bishop Gallagher's dying request was that he resume the broadcasts. Coughlin's new bishop, Edward Mooney, silenced him for a year, but Coughlin got back on the air in 1938, continuing until 1942, when the attorney general charged his journal, *Social Justice,* with violation of the Espionage Act, and the postmaster barred its distribution through the mails. Archbishop Mooney finally made Coughlin shut up shop.[20] Smith, without religious superiors to rein him in, rode the anti-Semite trail until his death in 1979, running for a while in every presidential campaign on one or other confected party line. In 1948, when a premature rumor hinted that Dwight Eisenhower would run for president that year, Smith claimed that Eisenhower had Jewish ancestors and tried to organize an opposition with the slogan "Stop Ike the Kike."[21]

CATHOLICS

SYDNEY AHLSTROM claims that Roman Catholics first achieved the ability to influence national policy in the 1930s. Their numbers as immigrants had made them important in urban politics before this, thanks to their role in city machines, unions, and the service industries; but their energies as a group were mainly concentrated in the immense task of servicing their own, establishing dioceses, and building up parish schools. Only in the 1930s were they ready to move out of their chosen "ghettos" to act on the national scene, largely as part of Roosevelt's New Deal. "The New Deal was, in one sense, an enactment of the Bishops' Program [the 1919 Bishops' Program for Social Reconstruction, written by Monsignor John A. Ryan]" (A 1,007). Charles Morris concurs: "The NRA [National Recovery Administration] looked a lot like [Pius XI's] *Quadragesimo Anno*'s 'associations of industries.'"[22] Of course, Catholics had been important on the local scene for many years, thanks to the numbers of Catholic immigrants—Irish, Italian, German, Polish, Lithuanian, and others. They were taken into the city machines of the late nineteenth and early twentieth century. They were given patronage jobs in the urban service industries (such as police, fire, and sanitation). They were ward and precinct operatives and city officials. But the first task of the immigrant church was to set up social services for its own people, create a separate education system, and build functioning parishes. Its concentration on the tasks at hand kept it from larger social roles. It was almost a boast that no American bishop had a college-educated parent.

Although a care for their working-class parishioners made bishops defend unions, there was little other political activity. When a priest joined Walter Rauschenbusch in campaigning for Henry George, he was defrocked for a time (A 791, 834–35). When a priest advocated socialism in 1903, he had to leave the priesthood after being silenced (A 1,003–4). Isaac Hecker and Orestes Brownson tried to create an American form of Catholicism, but they were rebuked by Leo XIII in his encyclical *Testem Benevolentiae* (1899), which condemned "Americanism" for its religious pluralism. Some priests, however, took an earlier encyclical by the same pope, *Rerum Novarum* (1891), as a mandate for social activity. One priest in particular, John A. Ryan, made it his life work to bring to the fore a very different view of "social justice" from that espoused by Charles

Coughlin. He published his doctoral dissertation from Catholic University in Washington, D.C., as *The Living Wage: Its Ethical and Economic Aspects* (1906). It had an introduction by the eminent Social Gospel economist, Richard T. Ely, though it drew from Thomist theories on distributive justice.

Catholics first had the confidence to speak as an American national body during World War I, when they formed the National Catholic War Council (NCWC) to address the cares of Catholic servicemen. At the end of the war, the bishops felt they should continue the body as the National Catholic Welfare Council (NCWC), and Father Ryan wrote their peacetime agenda in what became the Bishops' Program of that year. It called for a minimum wage, the banning of child labor, government insurance for the elderly, and equal pay for women workers. The body changed the last noun in its name from Council to Conference as a way to underscore its consultative (not legislative) nature. Ryan had become the premier voice on social matters for American Catholics. But he caused Al Smith difficulties in 1928 because, liberal as he was on social issues, Ryan was an old-fashioned Catholic in his opposition to the separation of church and state—that is how he avoided the strictures from Rome that John Courtney Murray would incur in the 1950s.

Ryan was early in the field denouncing Father Coughlin as a misinterpreter of what Catholic tradition means by "social justice." Then, when Al Smith tried to run again for president in 1932, Ryan was opposed to him, fearing another flare-up of the anti-Catholicism experienced in 1928. Ryan thought Roosevelt would be better for Catholics, and Roosevelt was happy to reward the priest for his services, appointing him to a board of the National Recovery Administration. When Ryan was made a monsignor in 1934, entitling him to the church title of "Right Reverend Monsignor John A. Ryan," he became popularly known as the Right Reverend New Dealer. He was one of many Catholics Roosevelt was careful to cultivate and appoint to posts in his administration—including James Farley, Thomas Corcoran, and Joseph Kennedy.

Democrats had a strong base in the Catholic urban electorate, but Roosevelt knew he could not count on automatic support from them.

For one thing, the Democrats had the other main part of their base in the South, where anti-Catholic feeling still ran high (the Democrats had rejected an anti-Klan plank in their platform as recently as 1924 and would reject an anti-lynching plank in 1936). Also, Roosevelt beat out Al Smith for the Democratic nomination in 1932, alienating some Catholics who wanted revenge for the mistreatment of Smith in 1928. Roosevelt would face more problems ahead, including Father Coughlin's admirers and some Catholics who, favoring Francisco Franco in the Spanish Civil War, wanted more American help for him. Roosevelt knew enough about the Catholic situation to be especially attentive, later on, to Cardinal Spellman of New York, who was a favorite of the man who became Pope Pius XII.

For Catholics, Roosevelt had his own form of Dutch blarney, quoting the popes' encyclicals or pointing to his own family's Catholic connections—his father's first cousin, a convert to Catholicism, had been the third president of Fordham University, and he had a distant connection with the beatified nun Mother Seton.[23] Roosevelt pleased many Catholics (including Monsignor Ryan) when he steered through repeal of Prohibition in the early days of his administration. He worked with Joseph Kennedy and Francis Spellman, then the bishop of Boston, to achieve close relations with Cardinal Eugenio Pacelli, whom he entertained at Hyde Park when he visited America in 1936. When Pacelli became Pope Pius XII, Roosevelt sent Kennedy to represent America at his coronation. This was a first step toward diplomatic relations with the Vatican. Congress had cut off all ties to the papal state in 1867, and Protestant feeling against renewing them had continued. Roosevelt knew that opening up diplomatic ties with Rome would bring criticism for his move, but it would win deep and enduring support from Catholics.

The president went about this task with typical skill. He put it in the context of the refugee problem that was growing as war spread in Europe during the late 1930s. He argued that a number of the refugees would come from Catholic countries, and handling their problems would be expedited by cooperation with the Vatican. Roosevelt had already picked a man to be his representative in Rome, Myron C. Taylor, the former head of U.S. Steel, whom he sent to the Evian Conference on refugee problems in 1938. Roosevelt admired the way Taylor had handled union difficulties at U.S. Steel, and he appointed him to a committee of the NRA. Taylor was a Protestant, but an Episcopalian, the denomination closest to the Catholics. He owned a villa in Florence, and said that he would reside there, not in Rome. His position was not ambassadorial, under State Department supervision. Roosevelt called him his "personal representative" to the pope. Thus with many subtle nudges and dodges Roosevelt slid this explosive move past his critics. Taylor went to Italy in 1939.[24]

Roosevelt had many Catholic friends to run interference for him. He was close not only to Spellman but to Cardinal Mundelein in Chicago. When Coughlin turned on Roosevelt, Mundelein joined Monsignor Ryan in denouncing him. In 1934, Catholics were upset with the president for not doing more to prevent the killing of priests in Mexico, but Mundelein arranged for Roosevelt to receive an honorary degree from Notre Dame, where Mundelein bestowed the award, muting Catholic protests.[25] When Mundelein died in 1939, his auxiliary bishop Bernard Sheil proved just as firm a Roosevelt supporter, countering Irish Anglophobia when Roosevelt revised the neutrality policy to give aid to Britain.[26] When Al Smith came out for Roosevelt's opponent in 1936, John Ryan headed off Catholic support for their 1928 champion. When Catholics wanted Roosevelt to support Francisco Franco's overthrow of the Spanish government, the hierarchy damped down criticism of the president.

Roosevelt's relations with Spellman were very cordial. He had the churchman as his overnight guest in Washington and Hyde Park. When he invited him for lunch or dinner on a Friday, he made sure that fish was served. Spellman became the first (the only?) priest to celebrate Mass in the White House. His diary for 1936 reads:

> Arrived in Washington at 1:15 in the midst of a snowstorm.
> James Roosevelt at train to meet me and bring me to the White
> House, where I was assigned to the Yellow Bedroom. We

worked in his office on speech that he [James] is to deliver
Saturday night over national hook-up urging Massachusetts to
ratify child labor amendment. Had tea with President and he
was wonderful. He made the cocktails before dinner.... We
saw movies after supper.... [Next morning] said Mass in the
Monroe Room of the White House. It was the first time Mass
was ever said in the White House. Miss LeHand, Miss Tully,
Miss Eben and Miss Hackmeister present. Breakfast after with
them.... Said goodbye to the President in bed. He said he had
intended to get up for Mass.[27]

Roosevelt even explored with Spellman the possibility that he might
be transferred to the diocese of Washington.[28] In a sense, Spellman was
sprung free and given a worldwide mandate when the pope made him
the military vicar of Catholic chaplains during World War II. This let
him roam the world, checking on the armed services. It also gave President Roosevelt the idea of using Spellman's wanderings to carry secret
messages from him to heads of state he met in his travels.[29]

JEWS

JEWS, LIKE the more numerous Catholics, were not able to make a
serious dent in the dominant Protestant culture of America until
the 1930s. Quotas had limited them to certain business enclaves, notably
those of show business, as Catholics were hemmed in by urban limits.
Both were under a quota system in business and educational and governmental opportunities, so that both, for a long time, "had a public presence incommensurate with their actual numbers."[30] That is why it has
not been necessary, so far, to spend much time on their role in the general religious culture. But that situation was changing, and changing rapidly, by the 1930s—and we shall see it changing dramatically in the 1940s
and 1950s. But here it is enough to note that Jews, like Catholics, moved
out onto a larger stage at the time of the New Deal.

Roosevelt's relationships with Jews were just as close as with Catholics. Both were urban parts of his Democratic constituency, but they were also communities he respected and trusted. He made even more Jewish appointments to his administration than Catholic ones, though Catholics made up ten times the population that Jews did. Fifteen percent of FDR's high appointments were Jewish.[31] Naturally, the bigots accused him of having Jewish ancestry, to which he made the wonderful response, "In the dim distant past [my family] may have been Jews or Catholics or Protestants. What I am more interested in is whether they were good citizens and believers in God. I hope they were both."[32] Surprisingly, he had shed his own prejudice more successfully than had his wife, who was initially shocked by his friendship with Henry Morgenthau and disliked the company of Felix Frankfurter (she called "the Jew party appalling").[33]

Roosevelt relied heavily on his principal speechwriter, Samuel Rosenman, the Phi Beta Kappa and summa cum laude graduate of Columbia who put together his brain trust. Rosenman had written speeches for Roosevelt during his campaign for governor of New York and during his tenure of that office in Albany. He performed the same service while Roosevelt was campaigning for and holding the presidency. He gave the Democratic nominee his acceptance speech in Chicago, including the final paragraph, which began, "I pledge you, I pledge myself, to a New Deal for the American people."[34] Roosevelt wrote to him in 1935, after giving one of his speeches to Congress, that he had used ninety-eight and a half percent of Rosenman's draft—"[in Albany] I used to take only ninety-five percent, so your batting average is improving."[35]

Rosenman did much of his work for the president while serving on the New York State Supreme Court, but had to resign from the bench when Roosevelt needed him during the war. He moved into the White House, where he drew up many of the war mobilization plans. He stayed on to work for President Truman, drafting the outline of his Fair Deal program and contributing to America's recognition of the state of Israel—he was a confidential emissary between Truman and Chaim Weizmann.[36]

Rosenman might be called Roosevelt's Jewish Spellman, but Spellman could just as well be called the Catholic Rosenman.

Ben Cohen, a brilliant student of Felix Frankfurter at Harvard Law School, was brought to Washington by Frankfurter and his own mentor, Louis Brandeis, to draft New Deal legislation for Roosevelt. His close work with Thomas Corcoran led *Time* magazine to feature the two of them on a cover with the caption THEY CALL THEMSELVES CATALYSTS. Cohen had worked for the American Zionist movement, and he helped draw up the Palestine Mandate at the Paris Peace Conference. After serving Roosevelt, he stayed on to become a delegate to the U.N. General Assembly under Truman.

While the Thirties showed radical extremes of both the Right and the Left, Roosevelt drew together into the center a truly ecumenical group of Protestants, Catholics, and Jews, presaging what would be a great truce between what were being recognized as the three principal religious traditions of the country. Catholics and Jews achieved a new prominence and respect that would bear fruit in the war years and postwar America, as quotas and barriers came down.

THE JEWISH-CATHOLIC NEOPURITANISM

A N ODD CONNECTION between the two outsider cultures of the 1930s led to their service of the Protestant ethos. Between them, they created a new Puritanism during the Depression. An interesting point about the post-Crash culture is that it did not, as many national crises had, lead to a recoil into religiosity. Though local revivals continued to occur, there was no great nationwide recourse to faith. The best study of this was a survey for the Social Science Research Council in 1937, which found that people did not, on the whole, seek relief from hard times in the churches. It concluded: "At the beginning of the Depression there was an assumption on the part of some church people that, if the Depression continued, the country would experience a series of revivals." But that did not occur (MM 2.251–58). On the other hand, there was a kind of spiritual belt-tightening, more ascetic than revivalistic, a call for people to be less hedonistic and excessive, and this effort brought Jews and Catholics into a cultural coalition.

The Roaring Twenties had led to a binge mentality that people felt they should renounce. This showed in the reaction to an entertainment industry that had spawned scandals like the Fatty Arbuckle trial, the William Desmond Taylor murder, and various divorce, drug, and suicide stories. Some early silent films had glorified the 1920s flappers, drunken parties, high life, adultery, and promiscuity. Hollywood was being denounced by preachers and editorialists as "Sin City," and the movie studios, after trying to cover up a series of scandals, decided they must clean up their image. In 1922, they called on William Harrison Hays, the former postmaster general and chairman of the Republican National Committee, to head up a Motion Picture Producers and Distributors Association (popularly known as the Hays Office) for monitoring the morals of the cinema.

The Hays Office established a "morals clause" in Hollywood contracts that said actors could be dismissed for immoral conduct—a demand that producers welcomed, as a way of controlling their employees.[37] But from his office in New York Hays was a distant monitor of Hollywood, and his vague guidelines for what movies could show (known as his "Don'ts and Be Carefuls") were easily evaded.[38] Local moralists were not pacified, as the studios had hoped, by the Hays façade of respectability. The coming of sound added risqué lines to the risqué situations of the old silents. Catholic priests were especially aggressive in warning their flocks against the bad example being set by depictions of sin on screen.

The Catholic Church had for many years controlled the reading of the faithful with an *Index of Forbidden Books.* Some felt that the mass entertainment medium offered greater "occasion of sin" than did books. One Catholic layman was especially inventive in his opposition to the moral level of the movies. Martin Quigley, the editor of the *Motion Picture Herald,* was busy on three fronts, reflecting his ties with his church's hierarchy, with the bankers who backed movies, and with Roosevelt's government.

1. Quigley persuaded Will Hays to accept a new Production Code in 1930, written by a Jesuit priest, Daniel Lord, who had been used by Cecil DeMille to give Catholic cover to his Bible epics. Father Lord's Production Code was not actively enforced until 1934, when a Catholic layman, Joseph Breen, took charge of the Production Code Administration (PCA). Movie historians divide films into pre-Code, Code, and post-Code (from the 1950s).

2. Quigley tried to use good Catholic relations with the New Deal to get government into the censoring business. He lobbied for Roosevelt's National Recovery Administration, which regulated industries, to include the regulation of moral content in its rules for the movie industry. This effort failed, even before the NRA was declared unconstitutional by the Supreme Court.[39]

3. But Quigley had another string to his bow. With the help of Roosevelt's friend Cardinal Mundelein, he moved the National Catholic Welfare Conference, which had passed the liberal Bishops' Program, to set up a purely Catholic censorship.[40] It created the Legion of Decency, which posted in Catholic churches and diocesan newspapers a grade for every movie's moral content, under three headings: A for "morally unobjectionable," B for "morally objectionable in part," and C for "condemned." Catholics were instructed not to see a C picture themselves ("under pain of sin") and to keep their children away from B pictures. Some priests had their parishes take a pledge to that effect. This solidified the Catholic hold on Hollywood. Joseph Breen of the Code could use the Legion, telling producers who resisted any of his rulings that the Legion of Decency would get them even if he could not. It was a fail-safe system.

Why did the producers put up with this? They did it to avoid what seemed to them even worse alternatives—government supervision, or a multiplicity of contradictory local censoring bodies. At least there was public predictability in their dealings with the Production Code and the Legion of Decency. Before this, Protestant groups and individual Catholic bishops had been even more arbitrary and extreme. Before the

Legion was created, Cardinal Dennis Dougherty of Philadelphia had ordered Catholics to shun *all* movies, causing a 40 percent drop in profits at local theaters.[41] In a time of austerity, it was clear that some form of censorship would be imposed, and the producers wanted one that would give them uniformity and predictability, making it unnecessary to fight censor boards city by city and state by state. Besides, the Code and the Legion would give Hollywood a respectability forfeited in the recent past. In the chastened aftermath of the Twenties, Hollywood wanted to be seen as contributing to a new national mood of uplift. The theaters ran promotions of the NRA during its time in effect. Works like *Gabriel over the White House* and the Frank Capra political films yearned for a new national authority.

There was, besides, a strange feeling of comradeship between Jewish producers and Catholic prelates, leaders of two immigrant groups telling the native born to live up to old Puritan standards. It was a way for both of them to show patriotism. (Louis B. Mayer, of MGM, was so patriotic that he claimed to have been born on the Fourth of July). As Neal Gabler wrote: "Mayer felt a spiritual affinity for Catholicism":

> As his daughter Edith put it, Louis Mayer was "very Catholic
> prone. He loved the Catholics." He was a close friend and a
> great admirer of New York's Cardinal Spellman, with whom
> he dined every time he visited New York, and a large portrait
> of Spellman in his red vestments was the first sight that greeted
> visitors to Mayer's library. Edith remembers being awakened
> abruptly one morning by an urgent call from her father.
> Spellman had come to visit him, and he wanted his daughter to
> come immediately to witness the occasion.[42]

Other moguls who dabbled in Catholicism were Harry Cohn and Jesse Lasky. Cohn was another who felt the tug of Catholicism, though he was too much the cynic to subscribe formally to any faith. Like Mayer, he regarded Cardinal Spellman as a friend and visited him every time he was in New York. Yet Catholicism struck much closer. Cohn's first wife had been a Catholic, and his second wife, Joan, was a converted Catholic who took her religion very seriously—so seriously that Cohn unhesitatingly let her raise their children in the church. "As with Mayer, attraction to Catholicism led to rumors that he would convert, but it is likely that Cohn would have considered this a capitulation, and he was a man who never capitulated."[43]

Lasky's wife, Bess, was convent-educated: "Though she never formally converted, she retained a deep attachment to Catholicism; in her bedroom there were tables covered with rare crucifixes she had collected."[44] The Laskys' interest in Catholicism was later swallowed up in a general spiritualism, her séances, his attraction to the mystical Edgar Cayce.

In the radical decade, there was a return to old values, to a moral righteousness that was a preview of the great religious truce about to occur in the 1940s and 1950s.

PART FIVE

RELIGIOUS NATION

❖

IX | EUPHORIA

27 | THE GREAT RELIGIOUS TRUCE

THE CENTER OF American society had held during the Radical Thirties, despite fringe radicalisms of the Left and Right. World War II would have an even greater unifying effect. Some would look back on it as "the Good War." Then, moral issues seemed clear, though the Holocaust would be only a retrospective justification for the conflict. Even apart from that the German ideology was hateful, and Hitler's treatment of Europe was terrifying. When Mussolini joined with Hitler, he lost his appeal for American Catholics. Japan's sneak attack on Pearl Harbor was a national affront that caused an instantaneous reaction to what Roosevelt called "a day that will live in infamy." America mobilized with a great sense of mission. The draft brought people of all sorts and incomes together—to be a "draft dodger" was universally considered shameful.

Though blacks were still segregated in the armed services, there was integration of another sort. Young men and some women, from North, South, Midwest, and West, mingled with one another on a previously unknown scale, breaking out of their various provincialisms. Efforts at vicarious service on the "home front" were organized to include the whole population. Many normal activities were suspended "for the duration." The entertainment industries held patriotic celebrations, sold war bonds, opened "stage door canteens," and toured military bases. Rationing distributed the hardships. Everyone was asked to do something "for the war effort."

As had happened in most of the previous wars, religiosity soared. The idea that there are no atheists in a foxhole was given concrete expression in many war movies. Heroic chaplains, nicknamed "sky pilots," were celebrated. Songs like "Coming in on a Wing and a Prayer" became popular. All the churches supported the war, and supported one another in the effort. The government paid for large contingents of priests, ministers, and rabbis. Six hundred interfaith chapels were built at military posts (A 949). As we have seen, Cardinal Spellman roamed from camp to camp as military vicar.

In the postwar world, this sense of interfaith amity was sustained and intensified. The integration that had begun in the military was extended as the G.I. Bill brought new students, and new kinds of students, onto colleges. President Truman at last integrated blacks into the military services. Affluence was undergirded by the wartime "conversion" drives of industry, and renewed demand led to quick "reconversion" at the war's end. The result was a great truce between the religious communities that had held themselves aloof from one another.

Some people look constantly for a new religious Awakening in American life. Certain of them were sure they had found one in the 1940s and 1950s. It is quite true that there was a surge of religiosity. It created a boom in church and synagogue attendance. Americans, always religious, were now more adherent to specific denominations. The 1957 census found an astonishing 96 percent of Americans saying they belonged to a church or synagogue (A 952). Church construction was the fourth-largest building activity in the private sphere.[1]

Respect for all religious figures was very high. In 1942, a Roper poll had put religious leaders third when asked (during the war) what leaders contributed most to the national well-being—they came in after political and business leaders. Just after the war, in 1947, the religious leaders were put first.[2] The intellectual respectability of faith was growing. Colleges and universities either established or expanded departments of religious study at this time. In 1950, the leftist journal *Partisan Review* devoted four successive issues to a running symposium on "Religion and the Intellectuals." Of the twenty-nine contributors, five professed their religious faith and ten took positions favoring religion—a slim majority in that least expected place.

Every religious group enjoyed greater esteem. Enlightened religion was honored in elite quarters, as theologians like Reinhold Niebuhr became widely read guides to national life. Evangelical Christians were seen as coming out of the darkness to which they had been consigned since the Scopes trial, and Billy Graham began his spectacular career. Catholics were celebrated in the media, with Bing Crosby movies and the television career of Monsignor (later Bishop) Fulton Sheen appealing to people of all faiths. Jews finally made headway against quotas on their admission to various schools and clubs, and leaders like Abraham Heschel and Arthur Hertzberg spoke across confessional lines, introducing many Christians to the thought of Martin Buber.

This is when Americans at large began to describe their heritage as "Judeo-Christian." It was a Jew, Will Herberg, who defined the new religious situation in terms of "three great faiths" in his book *Protestant—Catholic—Jew*. Politicians like Nelson Rockefeller celebrated the nation as existing under "the brotherhood of man and the fatherhood of God" (reduced by journalists following him to the acronym "Bomfog"). An earlier period was known to historians as the Era of Good Feelings. But the same title could be applied even more justly to the religious atmosphere during Eisenhower's presidency. As president, he said, "Our government makes no sense unless it is founded in a deeply felt religious faith and I don't care what it is." The comment was widely derided as an expression of relativism, but Herberg rightly concluded that Eisenhower was saying he did not care which *of the "three great faiths"* an American professed. "Under God" was added to the Pledge of Allegiance in 1954. The slogan on our money, "In God We Trust," put there in the Civil War, became the nation's official motto in 1956. The American

Legion organized a "Back to God" movement (A 954). Some would have sworn that the national anthem was Kate Smith singing (it seemed everywhere) "God Bless America."

ENLIGHTENED RELIGION

REINHOLD NIEBUHR became the semi-official theologian of World War II, and of the Cold War after it, answering ancient Christian questions about just war. He had earlier been a pacifist, but his time as pastor in a Detroit church made him aware of the need for some kind of compulsion in class and other conflicts. He became an early and ardent opponent of Nazis in the 1930s. (As the son of a German immigrant and the pastor of a German Evangelical church, he had opposed fellow believers who supported Germany in World War I.) He certainly spoke for Enlightened religion, humane and rational; but he made his real mark by reviving one of the doctrines—original sin—that had been repudiated by the Enlightenment. He felt that liberals placed too much trust in human wisdom and virtue, which disarmed them in dealing with evil.

In this way he gave religious backing to the *Realpolitik* of American liberals—to those who formed with him the anti-Communist Americans for Democratic Action: Hubert Humphrey, Arthur Schlesinger Jr., Walter Reuther, and others. His legacy could be felt in the architects of postwar American policy like Dean Acheson and George Kennan, and in the later thinking of Hans Morgenthau and Henry Kissinger.

Niebuhr expressed the union of political and theological concerns in ways that few found fault with in the warm religious atmosphere of the time. He even won an odd following among Evangelicals with a popular prayer—though most people did not know he wrote it. They ascribed it to an astonishing number of other sources, going as far back even as Saint Francis of Assisi. It is the so-called Serenity Prayer, written by Niebuhr during the war for a Sunday service. In his original version, the prayer went: "God, give us the serenity to accept what cannot be changed; give us the courage to change what should be changed; give us the wisdom to distinguish one from the other." Various groups, including Alcoholics Anonymous, have adopted (and adapted) the prayer. This is in itself a testimony to the inclusive religiosity of this period in American history.[3]

EVANGELICALS

THE EVANGELICALS joined the rest of America in the war effort. This was a repetition of what had happened in World War I. Then, the Premillennialists forgot, in some measure, their doctrine that there was nothing to be done with a corrupt age and found reasons to fight the "godless" Germans. Modernists like Shailer Mathews and Shirley Jackson Case had shamed them into the war.[4] The same thing happened on a grander scale with the Evangelicals in World War II. Many of them had given up any hope for American culture after their own repudiation at the Scopes trial. But they were swept along with others in the war effort, rallying to "support our boys" and to boost home morale. This was especially true of a new element in the Evangelical community, the Youth for Christ movement. "Old-time religion" had already created radio preachers during the 1930s, with old-fashioned hymns. But during the war Youth for Christ took over younger styles and developed a new media savvy.

These youth-oriented shows could shock old-fashioned Evangelicals by following secular models. One hymn singer, Torrey Johnson, was called the "religious counterpart of Frank Sinatra." A trumpeter with a religious choir was called a "Harry James of the Sawdust Trail." Women Gospel singers imitated the tight harmony of the Andrews Sisters. And a bright new star appeared in the war rallies: "Billy Graham imitated the clipped speech of Walter Winchell."[5] In the last year of the war Youth for Christ put on a Memorial Day rally in Chicago's Soldier Field that drew seventy thousand people to hear Billy Graham and others.

Patriotism and religion were combined even more closely when William Randolph Hearst ordered his papers to promote the Youth for Christ movement. He became still more energetic in "puffing" Billy

Graham when Graham started his independent Crusades for Christ.[6] Prayer breakfasts for businessmen became fashionable. Bill Bright made a huge success of the Campus Crusade for Christ, and C. Stacey Woods did the same with the Inter-Varsity Christian Fellowship. Evangelicals, whom Mencken had satirized as ignorant louts lurking in the backwoods, were now a vibrant presence in colleges and universities. They also founded an important new journal in 1956, *Christianity Today*. But the best symbol of Evangelicals' remarkable re-emergence on the national scene was the way Billy Graham became the pastor to American presidents, a continuing presence in the White House.

It was Graham's relation to Eisenhower that laid the foundation for all his later presidential services—and the way it came about was deeply symbolic of the whole religious atmosphere of the Fifties. Texas oilman Sid Richardson, a poker pal of Eisenhower's, told his friend during the 1952 presidential campaign that he should consult with a rising religious star named Graham. Eisenhower, when he met Graham, said, "I don't believe the American people are going to follow anybody who's not a member of a church." Not only was Eisenhower not a member. He had never been baptized. What denomination should he adopt? Graham asked what his parents had belonged to, and Eisenhower said the River Brethren. Graham thought Presbyterians would be more acceptable, so Eisenhower was baptized into that church after his election to the presidency (MM 3.305–6).

CATHOLICS

CATHOLICS, who had begun to make a mark on the national scale in the 1930s, prospered after the war. They were becoming assured enough to be self-critical. Their spokespersons looked around in the postwar period and gauged their own shortcomings, as a first step toward overcoming them. An extensive survey done in 1945 found Catholics as a whole less educated than Protestants or Jews.[7] But postwar affluence and the G.I. Bill raised their educational level. Two priests, John Tracey Ellis and Walter Ong, along with the layman Thomas O'Dea, set the agenda for a more rigorous intellectual life in their church.

Young men and women were flocking to the seminaries and convents to become priests and nuns. The number of Catholic converts surged. The most famous of these was probably Thomas Merton, whose account of his conversion, *The Seven Storey Mountain,* was a best-seller in 1948. Fulton Sheen won a number of converts, including Clare Booth Luce, wife of the magazine founder, and Henry Ford II, son of the automobile pioneer.

Paul Blanshard renewed some old nativist charges against Catholicism in his 1949 book, *American Freedom and Catholic Power.* But Catholics' participation in the war effort made it hard to question their Americanness. Catholics held all political offices but the highest one—and that would soon change. There were almost a hundred Catholics in Congress. The previously slow development of intellectual life in the immigrant church changed with the revival of Thomistic studies, which spread beyond Catholics into the program of Robert Hutchins and Mortimer Adler at the University of Chicago. Thomist scholars from abroad—Jacques Maritain and Étienne Gilson—were invited in the 1950s to give the prestigious Mellon Lectures in the Fine Arts. Harvard gave a chair in 1958 to the Catholic historian from England Christopher Dawson. The mystical French paleontologist Pierre Teilhard de Chardin was being studied already, though his vogue in America would expand in the Sixties. Catholic novelists in America (Flannery O'Conner and J. F. Powers) and from England (Graham Greene and Evelyn Waugh) enjoyed a wide audience.

The peak of Catholic prestige and influence came at the end of this postwar period, in two brief reigns as the Sixties began—that of Pope John XXIII (1958–63) and that of President John F. Kennedy (1961–63). The pope addressed two encyclicals to the whole world—*Mater et Magistra* (1961) and *Pacem in Terris* (1963)—and the world responded to them. Robert Hutchins ran an international congress devoted to exploring the promise of *Pacem in Terris.* When the pope opened the Second Vatican Council, Protestant and Jewish observers were welcomed, and the secular press closely followed its proceedings—especially through a learned insider's accounts sent to the *New Yorker*. The Council repudiated the old libel that Jews were Christ killers, and finally recognized the validity of pluralist societies—the old position was that governments should recognize a monopoly of "the one true religion." It was an American, John Courtney Murray, whose views were adopted by the universal church.

John F. Kennedy became a symbol of American pluralism when he was elected the first Catholic to win the presidency, after a speech in Houston to Protestant ministers where he said, "I believe in an America where separation of church and state is absolute." He was echoing the 1947 Supreme Court decision in *Everson v. Board of Education of Ewing Township*, in which Justice Hugo Black, writing for the majority, turned for guidance to Jefferson's letter on the wall of separation.

That decision has been called by some "antireligious," raising the question how it fits into a postwar culture so friendly to religion. The answer, of course, is that it is not antireligious any more than the Establishment Clause—or Jefferson's letter—is antireligious. Black showed this by ruling that the Board of Education could recompense parents for bus expenses in sending their children to parochial schools. He likened this to a community's fire and police protection of such schools, and showed that the state is "neutral" in all such activities. Those trying to make the decision antireligious are hostile to the letter quoted in it—and that would become obvious in the far amore acrid days soon to follow on this religious Era of Good Feeling.

JEWS

AFTER THE WAR, it was just as hard to challenge the Americanness of Jews as of Catholics. As Melvin Konner writes, "550,000 Jews served in the military, of whom 10,500 were killed, 24,000 were wounded, and 36,000 were decorated for bravery."[8] Jews had fought for a country that was fully theirs, but they were also asserting a faith that was

more compellingly theirs in the aftermath of the war. Shock at the revelations of the Holocaust put traditional anti-Semitism on the run. In
America, the influx of famous Jews fleeing European persecution had
already begun to change the attitude of Americans to Jews. How could
one look down on Albert Einstein, Hans Morgenthau, Hannah Arendt,
Ludwig von Mises, Eric Fromm, or Leo Strauss?

Jews, who had become increasingly important to American culture,
rose to new prominence after the war. They were no longer outsiders to
the culture; they seemed to *be* the culture—Aaron Copland, Leonard
Bernstein, Norman Mailer, Saul Bellow, Philip Roth, Joseph Heller, J. D.
Salinger, Arthur Miller, Allen Ginsberg. In New York, the intellectuals
were Irving Howe, Alfred Kazin, Philip Rahv, William Phillips, Nathan
Glazer, Daniel Bell, Lionel Trilling, David Riesman, and Leslie Fiedler.
Jews had always been important in Hollywood, but now they were leaders in all parts of popular culture.

> The impact of Jews extended far beyond high culture. They
> taught Americans how to dance (Arthur Murray), how to behave
> (Dear Abby and Ann Landers), how to dress (Ralph Lauren),
> what to read (Irving Howe, Alfred Kazin, and Lionel Trilling)
> and what to sing (Irving Berlin, Barry Manilow, Barbra
> Streisand). Jonas Salk discovered a way to defeat a crippling
> disease. The Sulzbergers demonstrated how to publish a great
> newspaper, the *New York Times*. Walter Annenberg showed how
> to make a huge fortune with a simple magazine listing television
> programs (*TV Guide*). Norman Lear's impact on TV (*All in the
> Family, Sanford and Son, The Jeffersons,* etc.) is still being felt. It is no
> exaggeration to suggest that during the [postwar] Golden Age,
> Jews, for better or worse, came to play a critical role in defining
> America to other Americans.[9]

Will Herberg noted that "Hansen's Law," named for the student of
immigration Marcus Less Hansen, states that "what the son wishes to
forget, the grandson wishes to remember." There has been a general

attempt to reclaim traditions in the third generation. That was more remarkable among Jews, he argues, since they were reclaiming both a religious and an ethnic heritage in a way more poignant than was the case with Protestants or Catholics.[10]

This reclaiming took place in the postwar period. Sydney Ahlstrom argues that the second generation of Jews drifted further and faster from their roots than other groups, but, "After 1945, however, neither Protestantism nor Roman Catholicism experienced so marked an increase in formal religious identification and institutional support" (A 980). The third-generation experience was deepened by the founding of Israel in 1947. Anti-Semitism receded as the world tried to come to grips with the reality of the Holocaust. Literature about it, journalistic, scholarly, and popular, made a deep impact—for instance, in the writings of Elie Wiesel, in *The Diary of Anne Frank,* in novels like *Exodus* and plays like *Judgment at Nuremberg.*

Jews felt united in new ways. The old split between Sephardic and Ashkenazi Jews had been partially bridged, but now all elements of the Jewish faith—Orthodox, Reformed, Conservative, and Reconstructionist—were united in feeling, just as the "three great faiths" were experiencing a sense of common commitment to religion. Herberg notes that a move of all Jews toward moderate Reform was taking place, and that an approximation of Christian church practice was part of the friendly acculturation in this period.

> The institutional system was virtually the same as in the major
> Protestant churches—the same corporate structure, the same
> proliferation of men's clubs, sisterhoods, junior congrega-
> tions, youth groups, "young marrieds," Sunday school classes,
> discussion circles, adult education projects, breakfasts,
> "brunches," dinners, and suppers. . . . The central place of the
> sermon, congregational singing, mixed choirs, organs, re-
> sponsive readings, abbreviated services, the concluding bene-
> diction, and many other commonly accepted features

obviously reflected the influence of familiar Protestant
practice.[11]

Protestant, Catholic, and Jew were all part of the cheerful bustle of religiosity of the 1940s and 1950s.

The Limits of Good Feeling

O F COURSE, the religious scene in the postwar period was not all
euphoria and fellowship. One reason for the surge in religiosity
was the fear of what both Eisenhower and Truman called "godless" communism, which soon mounted a nuclear threat. Putting "under God" in
the Pledge of Allegiance was a Cold War move. Proponents of the
change said it was an important way to differentiate Americans from
"Muscovites," who could not pledge allegiance to their country and
name God at the same time. George Doherty, a pastor popular with con-
gressmen, preached that the new pledge proved that "an atheist American is a contradiction in terms" (MM 3. 301–2). And religious strains were
increased dramatically during the brief but bitter ride of Senator Joseph
McCarthy, backed by Irish Catholics in particular (including the father
of John and Robert Kennedy). The sermons of Fulton Sheen were often
aimed against the Soviet Union. God was deployed against Marxists.
The sunny religiosity of the 1950s was partly shadowed by the Bomb.

The other bitter side of euphoria had to do with black Americans.
They too had fought in great numbers, heroically, but with little recognition, in segregated services. President Truman belatedly saw the injustice of this and integrated the armed forces in 1948. Before, in that same
election year, the Democrats put a civil rights plank in their election
platform, leading the South to begin its departure from the Democratic
Party, led by Strom Thurmond as an independent candidate. More
trouble for the South came in 1954, with the Supreme Court decision
integrating public schools (*Brown v. Board of Education*).

The South put up so many practical objections to the implementation of this ruling that the NAACP brought a suit for its immediate fulfillment, leading the Court in 1955 to order that this be done "with all deliberate speed," a phrase that invited foot dragging. As a result, ten years after Brown, only 2 percent of the segregated schools in the South had been integrated. President Eisenhower, while promising compliance with the law, never spoke favorably of the *Brown* decision and did nothing to enforce it until 1957. In that year Governor Orvil Faubus of Arkansas openly refused to allow blacks into the Little Rock public high school. Eisenhower reluctantly sent paratroopers to conduct black students into school. He also signed that year the first civil rights bill to be passed since Reconstruction. But the bill was so weakened with amendments, put there by Southerners in Congress, that some black leaders asked him to veto it. The first rumblings of the civil rights activism of the Sixties were audible in the Montgomery bus boycott of 1955 that brought Rosa Parks and Martin Luther King Jr. onstage.

There were problems in a "religionized" America, even aside from Cold War anxieties and racial tensions. Some thought the popular ministry of Norman Vincent Peale typical of the period's shallow piety. Peale, the pastor of the Marble Collegiate Church in New York, wrote best-sellers like *The Guide to Confident Living* (1948) and *The Power of Positive Thinking* (1952). Was there altogether too much agreement going on? Tocqueville became more popular than he had ever been in America for the passages where he said that Americans are tyrannized into agreement with majority opinion.

Books criticized the organization man, the man in the gray flannel suit, the lonely crowd, and the age of conformity. Will Herberg, who mainly celebrated the ecumenical relations of "the three great faiths," expressed misgivings that people would not be considered American unless they subscribed to one of those faiths—or that Americanness would become the essence of each faith, or that the one shared religious belief would be the American Way of Life.[12] Nathan Glazer feared that the rabbi was becoming just a social organizer: "The synagogues have become 'synagogue centers.'"[13] William Lee Miller claimed that "the faith is not in God but in faith; we worship our own worship."[14]

A particular critic of the time was the Lutheran minister and professor Martin Marty. Writing in 1959, he found that a religionized America was entirely too "inoffensive."[15] He noted that this Awakening (if that is what it was) brought everyone together—as opposed to the old Awakenings, which were contested and divisive. That might be a matter of ecumenically mutual congratulation. On the other hand, it could indicate a flabby way of going along to get along. Was everyone a little too happy with everyone else, and with America, and with the world? He found everywhere "a vague and somewhat sentimental religious syncretism."[16] Of Billy Graham's highly touted encounter with worldly New York in 1957, Marty quotes Roy Eckardt's comment—that David met Goliath and "Goliath yawned."[17] The most striking thing about Graham, for anyone who knows the history of religious figures in America, was "his failure to become unpopular with people outside the churches." He was a darling of the press.

Thanks to the way Graham "packaged God," no one was offended. "Jew, Catholic, 'secularist,' liberal, and fundamentalist somehow failed to get the point that he was talking about a scandal, the offense of the Cross of Jesus Christ."[18] Graham expressed the happiness at religion that people of all faiths seemed to be enjoying: "The utterer of judgments against the nation somehow tended to be a sanctioner of its status quo ante."[19] Marty gives his own sardonic reading of the Will Herberg catechism:

> Who "liked" Billy Graham?
> Protestants. Catholics, Jews.

Why was that? Because "no one was ready to read himself out of the religionized community. . . . No one felt judged."[20] This is what Marty calls "a sleight-of-hand ecumenicity," one that washes away difference in a flow of warmth.[21]

No doubt there was a too easy relaxation into religion as mere comfort and not judgment—despite deeper yearnings expressed in the reading of Tillich and Buber and Maritain. Sydney Ahlstrom noticed that those men, like most of the other profound thinkers being studied in the Fifties, had formed their ides in the more embattled Twenties and Thirties. No new theologians of any depth arose in the balmy 1940s and 1950s—a sign, perhaps, that there was trouble ahead.

> The churches by and large seem to have done little more than
> provide a means of social identification to a mobile people who
> were being rapidly cut loose from the comfort of old contexts,
> whether ethnic or local. Yet with new multitudes entering their
> portals almost unbidden, the churches muffed their chance.
> Put more analytically, the so-called revival led to a sacrifice of
> theological substance which, in the face of the harsh new social
> and spiritual realities of the 1960s, left both clergy and laity
> demoralized and confused. (A 962)

28 | THE RIGHTS REVOLUTION

THE GREAT RELIGIOUS TRUCE of the 1940s and 1950s was called off in the Sixties. People who had complained about the snoozy Eisenhower years, as conformist or apathetic or emptily pious, had reason for nostalgia about such soporific days in the next decade. Even the radical Thirties looked tame in retrospect as various radicalisms sprang up in the Sixties—the Black Panthers, the Nation of Islam, the Weathermen, the Aryan Brotherhood, the Crips, the Bloods, the Blackstone Rangers. It was a time for burning flags, and draft cards, and ROTC buildings, and bras. Also for self-incinerations. There were sit-ins, teach-ins, pray-ins, ride-ins, march-ins, vote-ins, swim-ins (to integrate city pools), and "sip-ins" (to integrate gays in straight bars). That was when the civil rights movement, the feminist movement, and the antiwar movement ignited one another with reciprocal frictions.

The period was darkened by serial assassinations—of John Kennedy, Robert Kennedy, Martin Luther King, Malcolm X, George Lincoln Rockwell, Fred Hampton, Medgar Evers, Herbert Lee, Louis Allen, James Chaney, Andrew Goodman, Michael Schwerner, Jimmie Lee Jackson, James Reeb, Viola Liuzzo, Addie Mae Collins, Denise McNair, Carol Robertson, Jonathan Daniels, Samuel Younge, Vernon Dahmer,

Ben Chester White (these last civil rights martyrs in the South). And there were attempted assassinations—of George Wallace, Gerald Ford, Ronald Reagan, Andy Warhol, Richard Morrisroe (and, some thought, Justice Harry Blackmun).[1]

Authority seemed under siege everywhere—the authority of parents, of teachers, of preachers, of military men, of politicians. The credibility of the nation's leaders was undermined by doubts about the authenticity of official accounts in the Bay of Pigs invasion, the Tonkin Gulf attack, the body counts from Vietnam, the attempted suppression of the Pentagon Papers, the Watergate break-in. Even the great religious consensus seemed ages ago when a fad for the "Death of God" took over the cover of *Time* magazine in 1966 (A 1082–83).

Decades have ragged edges. The Fifties did not end until 1963, with the death of the two Johns—President John Kennedy and Pope John XXIII. President Kennedy's Camelot faded like a dream when his successor had to give up hope for re-election. Pope John's successor brought his renovation of the church to a crashing demise with his 1968 encyclical, *Humanae Vitae*. In the secular sphere, the Kennedy years seemed an Augustan Age till it was undone by Vietnam. In religion, the glories of Second Vatican Council began to look hollow as priests and nuns streamed from their churches and convents. The mainline churches lost members and prestige, while Evangelicals mobilized against the radical developments.

The Sixties would be demonized later by those who think it marks the time when America lost its way. On the other hand, the oral historian Studs Terkel calls the Sixties people "the greatest generation," playing on the title of Tom Brokaw's book about the World War II generation. Terkel's point is that never before, in this or any other country, were human rights taken so seriously or defended so energetically—the rights of women, of blacks, of gays, of Native Americans, of Latino Americans, of the handicapped, of different religions. In the 1940s and 1950s the rights of Catholics and Jews were given greater recognition. The Sixties extended that enlargement to "outsiders." The Sixties did not complete this Rights Revolution, but they made a strong start on it, along a broad front of protests and advocacy, and much of the driving force behind it all was religious.

CIVIL RIGHTS

IN 1965, when a civil rights march was broken up in Selma, Alabama, Martin Luther King Jr. sent out an emergency appeal to religious leaders to help him resume it, against the decree of local authorities and a federal court injunction. Ministers and rabbis, priests and nuns crowded the airplanes to join him. This should not be surprising. For many years, all religious traditions in America had opposed racism. One of the earliest and most effective Jewish activists was Julius Rosenwald, the CEO of Sears, Roebuck, who in the 1920s created over five thousand educational institutions for blacks in the South.[2] A Protestant pioneer was the brilliant Vernon Johns, once president of Virginia Theological Seminary and College, who was a stormy petrel of racial equality in the three decades preceding Dr. King's succession to the pulpit in Atlanta that Johns had once occupied.[3]

A Catholic leader against racism was the Jesuit priest John LaFarge, son of the famous painter of the same name, who was shocked to learn that his Jesuit forebears had owned and sold slaves before the Civil War.[4] He dedicated himself to living down his Order's shame, and his book of 1937, *Interracial Justice*, prompted Pope Pius XI to ask that LaFarge compose an encyclical against another form of racism, that directed against Jews. The pope died before the encyclical could be approved, and his successor, Pius XII, never issued it.[5] But LaFarge continued to work for racial justice in America, setting up the Catholic Interracial Council in 1939.[6] For some later Catholics, his approach was too gradual, but he could still march, at age eighty-three, with Dr. King.

The civil rights movement was led by black religious leaders throughout the 1960s. Many had studied the nonviolent philosophy of Mahatma Gandhi—Howard Thurman (MM 3.383–85), James Farmer, James Lawson (A 389), Martin Luther King Jr., and Andrew Young.

Blacks had already mobilized the Montgomery bus boycott in 1955, using churches as their organizational headquarters. When a wave of protests began in 1960, with the sit-ins to integrate lunch counters, and in 1961, with the Freedom Rides to integrate interstate facilities, ministers were once more prominent. Seminarians like John Lewis and Jesse Jackson were among those sitting in, and the training for their action took place in the nonviolent workshops of Methodist minister James Lawson, a disciple of A. J. Muste as well as of Gandhi. James Farmer, a founder of the Congress of Racial Equality and the leader of the Freedom Rides, was the son of a Methodist minister-professor who had studied in the Divinity Department of Howard University.

As W. E. B. DuBois had recorded long before, black ministers were the natural leaders of Southern black communities, and that was never truer than in the civil rights campaigns. The roll call of them is long, and is certainly not exhausted by mention of Martin Luther King Jr., though he became the best known of many worthy comrades, and the winner of the Nobel Peace Prize. After leading the successful Montgomery bus boycott in 1955, he founded the Southern Christian Leadership Conference (SCLC) in 1957; wrote his defense of nonviolence, "Letter from a Birmingham Jail," and led the huge March on Washington in 1963 (the year when John Kennedy and Pope John died); received the Nobel Prize in 1964; led the March on Montgomery for voting rights and came out against the Vietnam War in 1965; led a Chicago campaign against segregation in 1966; and was organizing a Poor People's Campaign when he was assassinated in 1968.

Black unrest turned violent in the later Sixties, as some grew impatient with King's nonviolent approach. The Black Panthers, the Black Muslims, and the Student Non-Violent Coordinating Committee (SNCC, which forgot the nonviolent part of its original program) made noise but did not make progress. The great strides in the law were fostered and made possible by the nonviolent demonstrators—all the hundreds of men and women, boys and girls, who dramatized injustice by suffering the assaults of police dogs, water hoses, tear gas, clubs, and bombs, awakening the conscience of the nation and leading Congress to pass the Civil Rights Act of 1964 and the Voting Rights Act of 1965.

In terms of this book's theme, the interaction of the two poles of religion, the civil rights movement was clearly an Enlightened project supported by black Evangelicals. The invocation of reason as a critique of racist superstitions and entrenched reaction was in the Enlightenment tradition, and Martin Luther King was a student of Reinhold Niebuhr and Walter Rauschenbusch as well as of Gandhi (MM 3.385). He studied nonviolence at the Highlander Folk School in Tennessee, which had been founded by one of Reinhold Niebuhr's students, Myles Horton—Niebuhr was chairman of its board.[7] The response to King's 1965 call for help from religious leaders brought forth Enlightened heirs to Protestant and Catholics and Jewish traditions—the heirs of Vernon Johns, and John LaFarge, and Julius Rosenwald. Flying into Selma at that moment were people like Robert McAfee Brown, the leading Protestant ethicist, and Rabbi Abraham Heschel, the theologian of Jewish prophecy. At first, Heschel told King that he could not arrive in time because that would involve violating Shabbat. But after study he found that one can break Shabbat to save lives, and he was there when the march began. He said as he marched that he "felt my legs were praying."[8] Catholic nuns were also on the march, and when other Southern churches refused to serve as stopping points in the march, the Catholic Church of Saint Jude welcomed them.[9]

That the civil rights movement was an Enlightened project can be seen from the opposition to it in the white Southern churches, which acted as they had in the Civil War. At that time they either defended slavery or did not denounce it. In the same way, the Southern white churches of the 1960s either defended segregation or did not denounce it. When seminarians tried to take a black colleague into Southern churches, they were excluded or shunned. Congregants in the Episcopal church in Selma refused to share communion with them.[10] The white churches treated the civil rights activists as "outside agitators," bringing in the Northern media to disturb the amicable relations with "their" blacks.[11] In

1965, the year of Dr. King's march on Montgomery, the popular Baptist televangelist Jerry Falwell preached a sermon against marchers to his thousand parishioners, and had it printed up and widely distributed. In it he said: "Nowhere are we commissioned [by the Bible] to reform the externals. . . . I feel that we need to get off the streets and back into the pulpits and into our prayer rooms."[12] The preacher Billy James Hargis called Dr. King "a stinking racial agitator." And Billy Graham, who refused to join Dr. King's march on Washington, derided his "I Have a Dream" speech about children of all races being united: "Only when Christ comes again will the little white children of Alabama walk hand in hand with little black children."[13]

In the civil rights struggle, the Enlightened religion of Niebuhr and Heschel seems to be more just than the conservative one—and, in the short term at least, the more successful, since segregation was beaten back on many fronts. But the deeper theme of the present book is also in evidence—the need for each pole of the religious tradition to call on the other. It was the energy and raw Evangelical eloquence of the black preachers that fired and uplifted the more cerebral theologians of the North. Each force field energized the other. Dr. King, the son of Baptist forebears, inspired the heirs of the Niebuhrs. The framework of the movement was Enlightened. The power of it was Evangelical. The protesters marched to hymns and spirituals. This combination of the best of both elements of American religiosity we have already seen in the abolitionism of the Quakers. Benezet and Woolman used humane reason and Enlightened arguments, but they used them to pious purpose, living out the Sermon on the Mount, making peace, feeding the poor.

WOMEN'S RIGHTS

THE MOST EPIC STRUGGLE in the Rights Revolution, in terms of drama and violent resistance, was clearly the suffering and victories of the African Americans. But the most socially seismic part of the Revolution was that of the women. Blacks were, at the time, little more than a tenth of the nation. Women were and are just over half of the nation, and they play a role in all human relations, affecting all people, of no matter what color or class or religion. Alter the status of women, and you touch the inmost nexus of all society—the relation of wife to husband, of mother to children, of daughter to parents, of sister to siblings, of female employer to employees, of female employee to employers and fellow employees, of woman teacher to student, of woman student to teacher. Literally everything is changed, down to the roots of society and the individual person. That is what made feminism so scary to conservatives. Modern feminism, for the first time in any culture we know of, took the equality of women with men literally and fully. You cannot change half the human race without changing the other half.

I first became aware of the extent of the Rights Revolution in 1992, at the San Francisco meeting of the American Bar Association. The Women's Caucus held a lunch in a crowded ballroom—only a few years earlier the Caucus did not exist, and its existence was widely opposed within the Association. The presider at the dais said that before she introduced the main speakers she would like to ask women in the room to rise in response to a few questions. They went roughly, as I remember, in this vein: Who of you was the first woman to be an editor on your law school journal? The first to make senior partner in a firm? The first woman to open a firm in your town? The first to be dean of a law school? First to be a state or federal district attorney? To be a state or federal judge? Dozens, then hundreds, stood up—emblematic of the many hundreds of others not there. All these "firsts" were recent, within these women's lifetime. The older women there were the pioneers, the younger were their beneficiaries. Those who grew up, as I did, in the first half of the twentieth century know that women had a narrow choice of careers outside marriage—often a choice between no career or a career as a teacher (not a principal) or as a nurse (not a doctor). Girls who have grown up since the Sixties have a vastly expanded horizon.

I reflected on this sudden change in career possibilities for women, and realized that the same change was taking place for them in other fields—in the academy, in medicine, in business, in journalism, in religious ministry, even in the military. And since women are so numerous and so deeply inside all our social transactions, their success affects all the other claimants on rights. The women's revolution was also black women's revolution, so it is part of the civil rights movement. It was part of the gay movement, since lesbians are women—and of the Native American rights movement, or the handicapped rights movement. It was involved in various kinds of religious liberation, since nuns are women, some Protestant ministers are women, and now even some bishops are women. Liberate women, and all other forms of liberation are bound to spread and deepen.

Some have claimed that the women's movement failed, since the Equal Rights Amendment, passed by Congress in 1972, was never ratified by the states—thanks largely to an effective lobbying effort against it by the antifeminist Catholic leader Phyllis Schlafly.[14] Bur Jane Mansbridge points out that the mobilization to get the amendment passed in Congress, and to work for it in the various states, actually accomplished many of its goals. More women were drawn into politics, more men became aware of their grievances, and Congress, local courts, and the Supreme Court passed many antidiscrimination measures to benefit women.[15]

Congressional action included these acts: In 1972, Title IX of the Education Amendments to the Civil Rights Act of 1972 opened up campus activities to women on an equal basis. In 1974, the Equal Opportunity Act prohibited discrimination on the basis of sex for getting consumer credit or public assistance. In 1978, the Pregnancy Discrimination Act protected women from being fired or denied a job or promotion because of their pregnancy. In 1994, the Violence Against Women Act provided special protection for victims of rape or domestic violence.

Court action included these decisions: In 1973, *Roe v. Wade* gave women freedom to choose an abortion. In 1974, *Corning Glass Works v. Brennan* ruled that women could not be paid less because men would not accept the work in question. In 1976, *Planned Parenthood v. Danforth* denied that parents can forbid an abortion. In 1983, *City of Akron v. Akron Center for Reproductive Health, Inc.* said that a waiting period before having an abortion could not be imposed. In 1986, *Meritor Savings Bank v. Vinson* decided that sexual harassment is a form of job discrimination under Title VII of the Civil Rights Act of 1964. In 1986, *Thornburgh v. American College of Obstetricians* denied that a woman can be given an abortion only after detailed instruction on fetus development. In 1989, *Webster v. Reproductive Health Services* ruled against Missouri's restrictions on the right to an abortion.[16] In 1992, *Planned Parenthood v. Casey* ruled against Pennsylvania's attempt to restrict abortion rights.[17]

The women's rights advocates were making their way, despite the defeat of the ERA. Martin Marty notes that religious women were involved historically in this push. Pacifists like Dorothy Day and Georgia Harkness were active in politics early on (MM 3.342–43). The early suffragists were religious women. Protestant women were demanding ordination in their churches (MM 3.234–35). The daughter of a missionary, Nobel Prize–winning author Pearl Buck, had written the feminist *Of Men and Women* as early as 1941. Nuns and other religious women had marched with Dr. King, receiving obscene taunts for doing so. Taylor Branch, throughout his magisterial three-volume series *America in the King Years,* shows how important were women leaders in the movement, especially Septima Clark, Ellen Baker, and Diane Nash. Evangelicals would claim that feminism was an assault on religion, but there were many voices from the churches denying this.

VIETNAM

THE OPPOSITION to the war in Vietnam was heavily religious from the outset, with figures like Dorothy Day, Abraham Heschel, A. J. Muste (ordained in the Dutch Reformed Church), William Sloane Coffin, Daniel Berrigan, Philip Berrigan, and Richard Neuhaus (then an antiwar Lutheran pastor) defending the right to question a dubious authority, even to the point of civil disobedience, as in the civil rights movement. Some of them engaged in the destruction of draft cards to keep young men from serving in the war.

CATHOLIC LIBERATION

IN CALLING for the Second Vatican Council, Pope John XXIII said he
was trying to give his church an updating (*aggiornamento*, "todayify-
ing") and to open the windows to the world. He succeeded in the eyes of
outside beholders—John Kenneth Galbraith said to me, shortly after the
Council, that this was the biggest social change he had seen in his lifetime. He would have changed his view, I am sure, on a later look at the
civil rights and women's movements. But his comment shows just how
dislocating an event the Council was. Its effects amazed and later terri-
fied many conservative Catholics, including John XXIII's successor, the
holy but hapless Paul VI. The Council removed some ugly excrescences
from the church's long history, especially the claim that Jews in general
were Christ killers and that pluralistic democracy was an illicit form of
government. But it also removed, directly or indirectly, many of the
things that gave Catholics their sense of identity—the Latin Mass, the
Friday abstinence from meat, the morning fast before communion, mandatory Sunday church attendance, mandatory annual communion ("the
Easter duty"), traditional liturgical music, the Legion of Decency (rat-
ing movies), the *Index of Forbidden Books*.

Paul VI inadvertently caused the second most unsettling event of this
period (after the Council) in 1968, when he issued an encyclical (*Humanae
Vitae*) reaffirming the ban on contraceptives. To his intense dismay, this
provoked a defiant response on the part of most Catholics (and of many
priests and some bishops). At a Catholic festival of four thousand people
gathered in Essen, Germany, a resolution was passed saying that Catholics
need not comply with the encyclical.[18] Most bishops said that Catholics
should pay respectful attention to what the pope said, but should then follow their own consciences. A Benedictine priest, breaking down diocesan
statements on *Humanae Vitae* in terms of the numbers of the faithful in
each jurisdiction, concluded that 56 percent of Catholics worldwide were
told they could respectfully disagree with the pope, 28 percent were given
equivocal advice, and only 17 percent were told that they must obey.[19]

Polls ever since have shown that a large and growing majority of Catholics do not believe what *Humanae Vitae* says. And even those numbers understate the reality. When the people responding are identified by age, it is clear that the minority of those agreeing are older people, whose views were formed long before the Rights Revolution. In the most extensive poll taken of American Catholics under thirty, the number agreeing with the pope on this point fell within the margin of error—so they are statistically nonexistent.[20] On other questions, Catholics under thirty are just as noncompliant. For instance, only 12 percent think that loving intercourse by unmarried people is sinful. Only 21 percent think that women should be denied ordination as priests. And 22 percent denied that the host at communion contains the actual body and blood of Christ.[21]

Conservative Catholics blame such divergence from past views on the Council. It weakened the authoritative structure and ethos of the church. A more adequate explanation for this, as well as for the mass exodus of priests and nuns from their posts, is the Rights Revolution. All people were reconsidering their roles in a time of individual choice and freedom of action. The Council was a result of this movement, not a cause of it. John XXIII was himself a product of his age, and the age was calling for human rights.

Gay Liberation

The change in the legal and social status of gays would also have been unthinkable before the Rights Revolution. No one could have predicted thirty years ago that openly gay people would hold high political office, be the subject of hit movies and TV shows, have the same work benefits as married people, be the subject of antidiscrimination laws, be legally married in some places and pressing for marriage rights throughout the nation. Gay adoption of children would become commonplace. Once gays began "coming out," people learned how many gays they knew, even in their own families (Phyllis Schlafly's son, Dick Cheney's daughter, George H. W. Bush's commerce secretary Robert

Mosbacher's daughter) or in Right-Wing positions (Maryland congressman Bob Bauman, Conservative PAC head Terry Dolan). Stereotypes about gays began to fall away. A liberal like Barney Frank or a conservative like Andrew Sullivan, a dramatist like Tony Kushner, a comedian like David Sedaris, a novelist like Gregory Maguire brought formidable intelligence to bear on ancient prejudices. It was only a matter of time for gays to win the rest of their rights—including marriage.

Gays date their movement's great leap forward to June of 1969, when three nights of rioting occurred over a police raid on a New York gay bar, the Stonewall Inn. There had been gay marches and protests before, including New York "sip-ins" to integrate straight bars, as sit-ins had integrated lunch counters. The Mattachine Society had existed since 1950. But the raid on the bar led to what became known as the Stonewall Rebellion. The late and sudden raid on the bar took place on the day of Judy Garland's funeral in New York, attended by twenty-thousand people, many of them gays paying homage to their icon. The mood of the bar was emotionally overwrought.[22] Perhaps the police had been upset at seeing so many open gays flood the New York streets. At any rate, the gays decided to make a stand, and a new militancy swept the nation. At once the Gay Liberation Front was formed with a broad agenda.

In 1978 the movement was given an attractive and compelling martyr, Harvey Milk, who became the first openly gay official in any large American city—on the San Francisco Board of Supervisors. The next year he was assassinated by a former member of the board, Dan White, who first killed Mayor George Moscone for not restoring him to the board. When White was condemned to a mere seven years in prison, outcries and riots protested the homophobia expressed in the verdict.[23]

Without the activism of the gay movement, there would not have been the sympathy and support for AIDS victims when that disease struck the gay community so heavily in the 1980s. Act Up staged demonstrations of increasing urgency. Authors like Randy Shilts and Tony Kushner were able to arouse humanitarian reactions that are among the noblest efforts of the Rights Revolution, and the one redeeming feature of that horrible time.

AMERICAN INDIAN RIGHTS

I N 1969, the same year as the Stonewall Revolution, a book that started another mass movement appeared—*Custer Died for Your Sins,* by Vine Deloria. In the Rights Revolution, there were several books recognized as having instant political and policy impact. Three of them, interestingly, appeared in the same year, 1962—Rachel Carson's *Silent Spring,* Jane Jacobs's *The Death and Life of Great American Cities,* and Michael Harrington's *The Other America.* Dr. King's "Letter from a Birmingham Jail," of the next year, was not a book; but it deserves to be among these founding documents. So, perhaps, does James Baldwin's *The Fire Next Time,* which appeared the same year. But a book that certainly deserves to be on the list, though it came out slightly later, is *Custer Died for Your Sins.* It set the agenda for the whole Indian rights movement.

For most Americans, Deloria seemed to come out of nowhere; yet he was rooted deep in one of the most prestigious Indian-rights families. His great-grandfather, a French fur trader named Des Lauriers, married the daughter of a Yankton chief. His grandfather, who changed the family name, was an Episcopal priest who worked in reservation missions and became famous for that. His father, Vine Deloria Sr., was also an Episcopal priest who devoted his life to Indians on the South Dakota mission. This Vine Deloria's sister Ella was a linguist and anthropologist who collaborated with the famous Franz Boas on the study of the indigenous people of the Dakotas. Vine Deloria Jr. (1933–2005) at first intended to be a minister, like his father and grandfather, and took a master's degree in theology. But after serving in the marines, he became the director of the National Congress of American Indians.

Realizing that he could best serve his people in the legal field, he went to the University of Colorado Law School and became an expert on Indian treaties, finding and compiling neglected ones, laying the foundation for many appeals to prevent the termination of them, vindicating Indian fishing rights and land possession. He was on the boards of many civil rights organizations and taught for years as a tenured professor at the University of Colorado. A witty and prolific author who testified before Congress on Indian rights, he is widely recognized as one of the "Big Three" of ethnic civil rights, the other two being Dr. King and Cesar Chavez.

The movement kicked off by Deloria's 1969 book had its first emblematic victory—the equivalent for Indians of the Montgomery bus boycott or the Stonewall Rebellion—in the nineteen-month occupation of Alcatraz as original Indian land (1969–71). This rallied supporters and helped stop the treaty-termination movement of the government. It led to the formation of the American Indian Movement (AIM), which would occupy different symbolic sites over the next two decades. There were skirmishes with the FBI and accusations of violence that most courts failed to vindicate. Criticisms of AIM are strenuously rebuffed by Peter Matthiessen.[24]

AMERICAN LATINO RIGHTS

THE RIGHTS REVOLUTION would not have been complete without a champion of exploited Mexican and Filipino farm workers in the American Southwest. It found such a champion in Cesar Chavez (1927–1993). Chavez learned his organizing techniques from the radical activist Saul Alinsky—which is odd. Alinsky, from his Chicago base, was an urban agitator of contained conflict. But his California extension recruited Chavez to register Latino voters in California, and Chavez learned how to use the urban techniques with the dispersed worker forces in rural California. He was a pious Catholic, backed by his church's bishops, which helped him put pressure on the Catholic governor of California, Edmund "Pat" Brown. When he ran a strike of migrant grape workers in 1966, and his picketers were sprayed with insecticides, he began a march from Delano to the California capital, 250 miles away. This was inspired by the previous year's march of Dr. King to the capital of Alabama.

Chavez's march was a nice blend of militancy and nonviolence. The march's manifesto, the Plan de Delano, was modeled on Emiliano

Zapata's revolutionary Plan de Ayala (1911).[25] But the march went forward under the banner of Our Lady of Guadalupe, the Virgin patroness of poor Mexicans, and it was called a march of penitence, to atone for violence indulged in by some of the picketers. Chavez was a disciple of Gandhi and Tolstoy, and he would fast to do penance when his followers broke out in violence, imitating Gandhi's fasts.

Later he organized nationwide boycotts of California lettuce and grapes, with strong support from people like Robert Kennedy, Walter Mondale, Dr. King, and Ralph Abernathy. In 1975, Governor Brown signed America's first bill of union rights for farm workers. Chavez became a pioneer in agitation against the use of pesticides, whose harmful impact had been identified in Rachel Carson's *Silent Spring*. As a result of his work with others in the United Farm Workers, Brown Pride became a match for Black Pride and Red Pride in this era of a Rights Revolution.

Chavez is another example of the way Enlightened and Evangelical forces can be united. He argued for rights in a rational way, but his own piety and that of his followers centered on devotion to Our Lady of Guadalupe. He won the popular support without which legal arguments would have had little force. Head and heart were united.

A greater sensitivity to the dignity of all human beings has been shown across many areas because of the Rights Revolution. Now pluralism does not mean just respect for Herberg's "three great religions," but for Muslims, Buddhists, Hindus, and other "exotic" creeds. Native American religion won new respect. A regard for the problems of the handicapped has led to increased public access, reconfigured school buildings, reserved parking, new ramps, new elevators, signing for the deaf, closed captioning, and other ways of bringing previously excluded people fully into the broad human community. Much of this action has been scorned. Some say that we are too concerned with human rights. That accusation is, properly, an accolade.

29 | EVANGELICALS COUNTERATTACK

ALMOST EVERY ASPECT of the Rights Revolution of the 1960s was offensive to Evangelicals' values. Abortion is, in their eyes, murder. Gays can have no rights, since sin has no rights. AIDS, they felt, was God's scourge, and those trying to prevent it with condoms were deniers of the tragic truth. The sexual revolution, fostered by FDA adoption of the contraceptive pill in 1960, panders to fornication and adultery. Sex education they consider a form of sex promotion. Public nudity, unisex dress styles, rock music—the whole ethos of the time shocked and revolted Evangelicals. Civil disobedience is forbidden by Paul's injunction to obey those in political office: "Whosoever therefore resisteth the power, resisteth the ordinance of God" (Romans 13.2). Feminism goes against biblical patriarchy: "But I suffer not a woman to teach, nor to usurp authority over the man, but to be in silence" (1 Timothy 2.12). Unless one takes seriously such biblical strictures, one cannot see why Pat Robertson could speak plausibly to Evangelicals in these terms:

The feminist agenda is not about equal rights for women.
It is about a socialist, anti-family political movement that
encourages women to leave their husbands [by divorce], kill
their children [by abortion], practice witchcraft [with New
Age fads], destroy capitalism, and become lesbians.[1]

The Evangelicals had a point. There *was* an alarming lurch into
hedonism during the Sixties. But it was not simply the spirit of the time
that disturbed Evangelicals. They had specific acts they opposed, because
they seemed to impinge on *their* rights. A whole series of Supreme Court
decisions—on school prayer, on the Pledge of Allegiance, on pornography, on Christmas displays, and above all on abortion—they took as
deeply personal assaults. God was swiftly being removed from places
where his presence had been taken for granted all through American
history. Evangelicals responded with a spontaneous indignation that was
gradually organized to become a political force.

When bystanders asked how Fundamentalists, quiet in the immediately preceding period, could enter politics so aggressively, Evangelicals
answered that they were simply defending themselves. The aggression
was on the other side. Long-standing laws and customs were being
undermined at a dizzying rate. They were attacked. They would counterattack. Jerry Falwell, who had attacked all marchers in 1965, was by
1979 issuing marching orders to the Moral Majority. Pat Robertson, who
in 1966 refused as a minister to campaign for his father, the senator from
Virginia—saying "active partisan politics is the wrong path for true
Evangelicals"—was himself running for president by 1988.[2]

The scene for this struggle was imperceptibly being set by the
diminution, then the disappearance, of the Communist menace. Anticommunism had been a powerfully uniting force in the whole postwar
period, and Evangelicals had been out front in raising the alarm. As we
have seen, the Premillennialists saw Russia as the biblical power of "the
North." Protestant preachers like Carl McIntire and Billy James Hargis
backed the Catholic senator Joseph McCarthy in his assaults on "the

enemy within." Grievances between Americans could be deferred while attention was focused on resisting the Soviet Union and its satellites. But when the Berlin Wall fell in 1989, that fall loosened the mortisings of the great Cold War consensus at home. Before then, no matter what others did, they were at least allies in the major moral and military struggle of the time. Now old allies were turning into foes.

THE FIGHT OVER SCHOOLS

EVANGELICALS HAD BEEN jolted into resistance by a rapid-fire series of Supreme Court decisions, rattled off against them like a series of machine gun bursts. Between 1961 and 1971, ten cases hit the Evangelicals blow after blow:

1961: *Torcaso v. Watkins* said a Maryland man could not be refused state appointment because he did not profess a belief in God.

1962: *Engel v. Vitale* knocked down a generic prayer in New York State.

1963: *Abington School District v. Schempp* ruled out Bible readings in Pennsylvania schools.

1963: *Murray v. Curlett* ruled out Bible readings in Maryland schools.

1964: *Chamberlin v. Dade County* reversed a Florida court ruling that allowed Bible readings.

1968: *Board of Education v. Allen* said textbooks could be loaned to religious schools only if secular in content.

1971: *Lemon v. Kurtzman, Earley v. DiCenso,* and *Robinson v. DiCenso* (jointly decided) voided secular aid to religious schools in Pennsylvania and Rhode Island.

1971: *Tilton v. Richardson* allowed aid to construction of buildings for religious schools, but only for colleges, not high schools, and only for secular purposes.

This concentration of cases, suddenly accepted and ruled on by a Court that had not been much interested in the subject before, convinced

Evangelicals that the Court was now waging a war on God.[3] When Billy James Hargis heard of the *Engel* decision, he told his son that "the country had turned its back on God, and that any country that did that could not stand."[4] The preachers were right to think that there was something new going on here. They could not see that this was just one manifestation of the vast Rights Revolution that was the driving force of the time—a realization that students are not to be pressured into religious professions. Instead, the preachers came up with a far-fetched conspiratorial explanation (a scheme hatched by sinister "secular humanists").

Removal of prayer from the classroom was just one of a series of things that made Evangelicals start setting up Christian schools, or homeschooling their children. Reaction to *Brown v. Board of Education* (1954) had already made Southerners, including Jerry Falwell, set up private grade schools.[5] The prayer decisions just accelerated that process.

As did other things—like the teaching of Darwin in the schools. It was noted earlier that the 1925 Scopes trial made a big public stir but quietly left the ban on teaching evolution in place. "A scholarly survey of the content of biology texts up to 1960 found the influence of anti-evolutionist sentiment to be persistent, if undramatic, and showed that the teaching of evolution actually declined after 1925."[6] One thing changed that, the Russian launching of the first man-made space satellite (*Sputnik*) in 1958. There was a great shudder of surprise in America that the Soviet Union had achieved this scientific coup before America did. A startled look at American textbooks showed that they were pitifully inadequate in their treatment of science. Federal money was thrown at the problem, and textbook publishers and schools were quick to snap that up. A whole new science curriculum was created, with Darwinism now mandatory. When Jerry Falwell learned that he could not have anti-Darwinism taught in the biology classes of Liberty College and still qualify for government grants, he set up a separate Center for Creation Studies, and required that all students take a course in it.[7]

Evangelicals tried to evade the new science in various ways, but courts kept knocking down their efforts. At first schools wanted to teach the Bible account of creation *alongside* the Darwinian "hypothesis." They were told that religion could not be injected into the schools. Then they tried to come up with purely "scientific" accounts of a sudden creation, without quoting the Bible. They explained the long record of fossil stratification by attributing all the layers to one event, Noah's flood, a theory spelled out in the founding document of this new "science," *The Genesis Flood* (1960), by Henry Morris. They tried various names for their "science," using "creationism" for a while, then settling on "intelligent design."

Henry Morris, the founder of the new science, teamed up with Tim LaHaye, later famous for his Premillennial "Left Behind" series of novels, to establish Christian Heritage College in 1970. This San Diego institution has, under different names, produced research centers, a creation museum, a journal, and many textbooks and teaching programs, used by the various states that have tried to install creation science in their schools.

Sputnik was responsible for more than the return of Darwin. The overhaul of elementary and secondary education was a task that seemed necessary. In 1970, the National Science Foundation produced a curriculum for the social sciences called "Man: A Course of Study" (MACOS). This was instantly denounced by the Right as relativistic. It focused on comparative studies of various cultures (another effect of the Rights Revolution). Texts that had been celebratory, patriotic, and America-centered were threatened by those that looked at the world at large. Soon it was being denounced as a nefarious plot by "secular humanists." Francis Schaeffer, one of the favorites of the Evangelicals because of his campaigns against abortion, had taught them to fear secular humanism.[8] He pinned this fear on a document few people had read before he alerted the Right against it—the "Humanist Manifesto," written in 1933 and signed by three dozen people, among whom only John Dewey's name is recognizable now.

Another reference that would be forgotten but for the Evangelicals is a footnote by Justice Hugo Black to a Supreme Court case, *Torcaso v. Watkins* (1961), which restored one Roy Torcaso's state job despite his profession that he did not believe in God. In his obiter dictum, Black mentioned, irrelevantly and inaccurately, that some *religions* do not believe in God—he cited "Buddhism, Taoism, Ethical Culture, Secular

Humanism, and others." For the secular humanism reference he cited one obscure group of atheistic humanists—the Fellowship of Humanity—that claimed it had a chapel that should have the same tax exemption given to churches. From these two references, the Evangelicals have built a vast literature on the evils of secular humanism as a religion that has become the established "church" of liberalism. The very obscurity of the sources feeds the view that "conspiracy" keeps them hidden. As some people find Masons or Bilderbergers or Illuminati everywhere, Evangelicals see secular humanism behind everything they hate. The *Christian Harvest Times* of June 1980 proclaimed:

> To understand humanism is to understand women's liberation,
> the ERA, gay rights, children's rights, abortion, sex education,
> the "new" morality, evolution, values clarification, situation
> ethics, the separation of church and state, the loss of patri-
> otism, and many of the other problems that are tearing
> America apart today.[9]

Tim LaHaye, whose "Left Behind" series millions have read, gives an even more sinister reading to the secular humanist program.

> That is why humanist politicians permitted Russia to conquer
> the satellite countries of Europe and turn them into socialist
> prisons. That is why we were not permitted to win in Korea
> and Vietnam and why they voted to give away the Panama
> Canal. That is why Russia was allowed to turn Cuba into an
> armed camp with a submarine base, stationing at least 3,000
> Russian troops.[10]

In 1984, Senator Orrin Hatch attached an amendment to a bill giving federal assistance to "magnet schools," saying that no funds were to be used for "a course of instruction the substance of which is Secular Humanism." Within a year it was found that the addition could not be enforced for want of any agreed definition of secular humanism, and

Hatch withdrew it—though not till Evangelicals had circulated model letters to parents listing all the things their children should not be taught.

The Rights Revolution had struck fear into Christian conservatives. They felt that their country was being taken from them, their children were being turned against them, the Bible was being mocked, the moral foundation of their world was being undermined. This led to popular revolts against what was going on in the schools—sex education, the suppression of prayer, the teaching of evolution. Those who could not flee into the Christian schools, or into homeschooling, decided to change the books and courses and teachers in the schools, by popular protest. The strategy occurred school board by school board, because education is locally controlled, so targeted local drives could take the boards over. The affected local communities were not for a while aware that this was going on, since there was only tepid competition to do boring service on a school board. But once the takeovers occurred, the results were explosive. The three most famous conflicts were in Texas, California, and West Virginia.

Texas

In Longview, Texas, Mel and Norma Gabler read the schoolbooks being taught in the local schools and found them evil in tendency. Beginning in 1961, they insisted that the books must, in every subject, promote Judeo-Christian ethics, saying:

> To the vast majority of Americans, the terms "values" and
> "morals" mean one thing, and one thing only, and that is the
> Christian-Judeo morals, values, and standards as given to us by
> God through His Word written in the Ten Commandments
> and the Bible. . . . After all, according to history these ethics
> have prescribed the only code by which civilization can
> effectively remain in existence.[11]

The Gablers set up a service to grade books for other locales, called the Educational Research Analysts, and became the heroes and models for other Evangelical protesters.

California

Max Rafferty, a former teacher, was California's superintendent of public instruction from 1963 to 1971. He was an opponent of progressive education in all its forms, especially sex education. In a series of writings beginning with *Suffer, Little Children* (1961) he became a Right-Wing favorite. So in 1968, when a Catholic mother, Eleonor Howe, mounted a campaign against the sex education program in Anaheim, he was called on to publicize her effort. Others rushed to join her, including Billy James Hargis. A conservative state senator went to Anaheim to show a movie, *Pavlov's Children*, that claimed UNESCO was using American schools to reduce their students to pawns of communism.[12]

West Virginia

The bitterest textbook war took place in the Kanawha Valley of West Virginia, where another woman, Alice Moore, rose up against the schoolbooks being assigned in 1974. She found evil lurking in every nook and cranny of the texts. A reference to the story of Androcles and the lion as a fable was taken as a hidden attack on the veracity of the Bible's account of Daniel in the lions' den.[13] By distributing exaggerated accounts of what the books contained, she created a popular furor, and conservative heavy hitters rushed to the Valley to support her—the newly founded Heritage Foundation, Max Rafferty, and others. When the school board refused to remove the books, she called for a boycott of school opening in September. This, to her dismay, unleashed a series of violent episodes—a strike in the local mines to support the boycott, bombings of the school and buses, death threats to her and to her foes, Ku Klux Klan interventions, the sentencing of six of her fanatical allies to federal prison for violent acts. The school had to back down and offer a two-track curriculum, for reading the books officially sanctioned and the ones Moore approved of. The two tracks proved unmanageable and the bitterness was not dispelled. This kind of unrest ran through the whole national school system, where schoolbooks were attacked in a fifth of the schools and a third of the school libraries in 1981.[14]

THE NEW RELIGIOUS RIGHT

U NREST SO DEEP, so omnidirectional, was bound to find political expression, and a number of organizations arose to give it shape and impact. The result was described by many as a new rise of the Evangelicals, a surge of piety. Phyllis Schlafly's Eagle Forum beat down the ERA. Morris and LaHaye's works inspired continued school board efforts against Darwin. Beverly LaHaye formed the largest women's organization in modern America, Concerned Women for America, to fight the feminists.[15] Paul Weyrich's Free Congress organization lobbied House and Senate for religious causes. Howard Phillips ran the Conservative Caucus. Bill Bright kept up his Campus Crusade for Christ. Pat Robertson formed his Christian Broadcasting Network. James Dobson's Focus on the Family attracted a daily radio audience exceeded only by those of Paul Harvey and Rush Limbaugh.[16] D. J. Kennedy's *Coral Ridge Hour* was heard on five hundred television stations. Jim and Tammy Faye Bakker ran the PTL (for "Praise the Lord") Club. Randall Terry's Operation Rescue picketed abortion clinics.

The Christian Voice and Donald Wildmon's American Family Association swelled the ranks. The National Right to Life Committee, formed right after the *Roe* decision, claimed it had three thousand chapters.[17] Like other groups, it kept a voting scorecard on every member of Congress, to loose a barrage of letters to any member who strayed from defense of a strict anti-abortion line. Umbrella groups like the Religious Roundtable and the National Religious Broadcasters became favorite venues for addresses by presidents and campaigners for president. Richard Viguerie provided sophisticated direct mail services to the Christian organizations. Christian bookstores and book clubs kept the word circulating. The movement on the Right seemed to be reaching critical mass.

Many Americans first became aware of the growing political clout of the Evangelical movement in 1979, when—at the prompting of Paul Weyrich and Howard Phillips—Jerry Falwell formed the Moral

Majority.[18] Nixon had spoken of a "Silent Majority," but that was a sentiment, not an organization. Falwell made his group, during its ten-year
span, a force in Republican politics. It was becoming clear that Evangelicals, at that time approaching a third of the national electorate, made up
about half of the Republican Party, and their voices had to be heard by
anyone wanting advancement in the party. Falwell's network began beating the drums for Ronald Reagan's candidacy in 1980, and it would take
credit for his election.

When the Moral Majority began to run out of steam, the leading role
on the Right was taken by a new organization, the Christian Coalition,
built on the basis of Pat Robertson's run for president in 1988. Robertson
put Ralph Reed in as managing director of the Coalition. Another body
that took on new importance was the Family Research Council, run in
Washington by Gary Bauer with money provided by James Dobson, of
Focus on the Family. The press paid close, sometimes panicky, attention
to all these developments. Yet the Evangelicals had not succeeded. Their
aim was to cancel the Rights Revolution, or at least to slow or partially
reverse it. That had not happened. *Roe v. Wade* had not been reversed.
Prayer had not returned to the public schools. Evolution had not been
wrenched out of the school curriculum. The progress of the women's
rights movement was growing, as I had seen at the 1992 Bar Association
meeting. Gays were not going back into the closet but on to more and
more TV shows and Broadway hits. Pornography had broken new
ground on the Internet.

The more they organized, the more the Evangelicals expressed an
angry frustration, as national administration after administration disappointed them. The Religious Right had run its own candidates for president—Pat Robertson in 1988, Pat Buchanan in 1992, Howard Phillips in
1996, Gary Bauer in 2000—but that just blurred its focus on affecting the
Republicans' winning candidates. Recognizing that fact, Ralph Reed
helped kill another Pat Buchanan run for the presidency in 1996, mobilizing Christians against him in the South Carolina primary.[19] But that
did not prevent James Dobson from supporting Howard Phillips that
year, on the Taxpayers Party ticket. Buchanan ran again in 2000, as did

Howard Phillips—to protest the poor rewards Republicans were giving their Evangelical supporters. But all they demonstrated was the fecklessness of their cause.

Powerful as this new Religious Right was, then, it had not yet prevailed. Over the years, it had to keep licking its wounds, as it reflected back on a history of Republican failure to meet its demands.

PRESIDENTIAL DISAPPOINTMENTS

1. Richard Nixon

Billy Graham worked closely with Nixon in his 1968 campaign, advised him on relations with the Evangelical community, and vouched for him in that community. It will be recalled that he had played a similar role for President Eisenhower. Then he became a frequent guest of Lyndon Johnson, in the White House and at his Texas ranch.[20] But Johnson's support for Dr. King and his civil rights legislation angered Southern Evangelicals, and there was not much Graham could do about that. He was much closer to Nixon than to either Eisenhower or Johnson, and the Evangelical movement was just beginning to take shape during Nixon's presidency. Even when Nixon was vice president, Graham arranged for him to speak at major gatherings of Baptists, Methodists, or Presbyterians, and wrote at least one speech for him.[21] Nixon became the first president to have regular Sunday prayer services in the White House, initiated by Graham.

Nixon's Southern strategy was generally pleasing to Southern Evangelicals, who were switching from Democratic to Republican ranks. Nixon tried to give them a Southerner on the Supreme Court, but his first two efforts failed (it was hard to find a Southern jurist with a clean record on race), and when he succeeded with a Virginia moderate, Lewis Powell quickly joined the majority decision on *Roe v. Wade.* Admittedly, Nixon also appointed William Rehnquist, who was one of the two justices voting against *Roe.* But before that he had made Warren Burger the chief justice, and Burger assigned the *Roe* opinion to Harry Blackmun, also Nixon's appointee, who defended the right to abortion. Evangelicals felt that Nixon had let them down badly. And then there was the Watergate scandal, and the publication of the profanity-laced Nixon tapes, some of them containing embarrassingly anti-Semitic words by Billy Graham himself.[22]

2. *Jimmy Carter*

Evangelicals were at first elated when one of their own, a born-again Christian, won the White House—though they had been upset during his campaign when he gave an interview to *Playboy* magazine. But once he was elected, he quickly caused disaffection for not trying to change the abortion laws, not promoting school prayer, and supporting the Equal Rights Amendment. Worse in their eyes, he convened a Conference on Families, attended by gays and lesbians, that issued a final document supporting abortion rights, the ERA, and sex education. It was on Carter's watch that Bob Jones University was denied tax exemption, and other schools were threatened by the I.R.S., causing a great upsurge of Evangelical protest.[23]

When the head of the Southern Baptist Conference, the largest Protestant body in America, visited Carter in the White House, he said as he was departing, "We are praying, Mr. President, that you will abandon secular humanism as your religion."[24] In an attempt to mend fences with Evangelicals, Carter invited Jerry Falwell, Jim Bakker, Oral Roberts, Tim LaHaye, and others to breakfast with him in the White House. But that was the breaking point for them. When he defended the ERA and said he would not join the March for Life in Washington that day, they left in total disgust. LaHaye said he was praying as he departed, "God, we have got to get this man out of the White House."[25] Evangelicals as a whole were happy to dump Carter in his re-election bid and flock to Ronald Reagan.

3. *Ronald Reagan*

Evangelicals loved Reagan, though he did nothing to bring about an anti-abortion or school prayer amendment. He mainly pleased them with skillfully delivered gestures. True, he gave them Antonin Scalia on the Court, and appointed many conservatives to lower-level federal benches. But he did not back the conservatives' Family Protection Act, and his wife persuaded him to show some concern for AIDS victims. At that point, he slipped in a *Conservative Digest* poll from being its readers' favorite conservative. Now he came in second after Jerry Falwell. Nancy Reagan slipped, too, as the favorite conservative woman, yielding first place to Phyllis Schlafly.[26]

Fury mounted when the report Reagan had commissioned from his surgeon general, the old Evangelical favorite Everett Koop, recommended the use of condoms and sex education to contain the spread of AIDS. Church people turned on Koop ferociously. Nellie Gray, the head of the anti-abortion March for Life, called for Koop's resignation. Koop recalled that Phyllis Schlafly "went on television and essentially said that she would rather see her children become infected with sexually transmitted disease than to know there was such a thing as condoms."[27] (Her son had not yet told her he is gay.) Schlafly got all the Republican candidates for president to withdraw from their promised attendance at a "Salute to the Surgeon General" dinner.[28]

4. George H. W. Bush

Though Bush was far more faithful in attending church than Reagan, Evangelicals never warmed to him. Asked whether he was "born again," he equivocated.[29] He did give them Clarence Thomas on the Supreme Court, but he angered the religious people when he praised the Hate Crimes Act, which they thought a pro-gay measure. He confirmed their judgment by inviting openly gay and lesbian leaders to the White House for the bill's signing. The outcry on the Right was so great that Doug Wead, the Evangelical spokesman on the White House staff, sent a letter blaming the "mistake" of their invitation on White House staffers. That letter led to Wead's being fired, which made the Evangelicals more angry.[30]

Bush especially alienated Evangelicals when he tried to put pressure on Israel to stop West Bank settlements, since that was biblical land in the eyes of the Premillennialists, given to the Jews by God. When Bush collaborated with Russia, Europe, and the United Nations on a "road map" to a two-state solution of the Israel-Palestine conflict—a plan accepted by Israel itself—the Evangelicals brought thousands to Washington for a Christian Support of Israel rally, demanding "no negotiation with terrorists," and "no dismantling of Jewish communities in biblical Israel," and "no to a Palestinian state." When Bush announced the details of the road map, Garry Bauer, Paul Weyrich, and others mobilized fifty thousand postcards to the White House attacking the plan.[31]

It is not surprising then that Bush was denounced for aiding the Antichrist of the End Time when he said that his Gulf War could bring about a "New World Order" in foreign policy—not so different from his son's later claim that he was going to produce a new era of Middle East democracy. But the Evangelicals were so suspicious of the elder Bush that they saw in this a proclamation of world government, against which Tim LaHaye had warned them in 1984. An alarmed Pat Robertson wrote his book *The New World Order*:

> Indeed, it may well be that men of good will like Woodrow
> Wilson, Jimmy Carter, and George Bush, who sincerely want a
> larger community of nations living at peace in our world, are
> in reality unknowingly and unwittingly carrying out the
> mission and mouthing the phrases of a tightly knit cabal whose
> goal is nothing less than a new order of the human race under
> the domination of Lucifer and his followers.[32]

Stunned by the unexpected fury of the Religious Right, the Bush people leaned over backwards to make their 1992 re-election effort heavily pious. Gary Bauer demanded that the anti-abortion plank stay in the Republican platform, and prime-time speakers at their convention included cultural warriors Pat Robertson, Pat Buchanan, and Marilyn Quayle. But it was too little too late for George Bush, and his son would, in compensation, court Evangelicals as no one in the White House ever had.

5. Bill Clinton

Though Clinton is a Southern Baptist, Evangelicals never hoped for anything from him—except maybe to raise money by making him a devil figure. In fact, he gave them a target larger than anything they had dreamed of—from his bungled effort to legitimate gays in the military, to his veto of the ban on "partial birth abortion," to his affair with Monica Lewinsky. Their only disappointment was that he was not convicted on his impeachment counts. Still, his support for the ERA and abortion rights made him a figure of detestation, and his wife was even more reviled. She had early been an advocate for children's rights, which the Right took as an attack on the family, and she personified everything it hated in the feminist movement. Clinton especially offended Evangelicals when he twice vetoed the ban on abortions they call "partial births." James Dobson told his Focus on the Family radio audience that he and his friend Chuck Colson burst into tears when they heard of the first veto.[33]

Ralph Reed and the Christian Coalition argued that Clinton was so bad that religious people would have to postpone their own favorite causes in the effort to defeat him. He advised the Religious Right to support Newt Gingrich's "Contract with America," though it said nothing about the social issues dear to Evangelicals. Once a Republican majority was voted in, Reed said, then Evangelicals could pressure Congress on abortion, school prayer, and other favorite issues. When Reed argued that the Evangelicals should cooperate with the anti-tax agenda of Grover Norquist, it was not known how close he was to Norquist's ally, the lobbyist Jack Abramoff—Reed had been a protégé of Abramoff since 1981, when "Reed lived in his house, [and] attended [Jewish] services with him."[34]

The Evangelicals, for all the attention they had gained, felt cheated. Ralph Reed said they had won "a place at the table," but that was all. It was not enough, Paul Weyrich decided. In 1999, he said he was giving up on the political front. "We got our people elected, but that did not result in the adoption of our agenda." Instead, America was becoming "an ever-wider sewer." There was nothing left but to "drop out of this culture and find places . . . where we can live godly, righteous, and sober lives."[35] After 2000 he would be saying, with most other Evangelicals, that God had at the last moment sent the man they had been praying for.

X | THE KARL ROVE ERA

30 | FAITH-BASED
GOVERNMENT

THE RIGHT WING in America likes to think that the United States government was, at its inception, highly religious, specifically highly Christian, and—and more to the point—highly biblical. This was not true of that or any later government—until 2000, when the fiction of the past became the reality of the present. George W. Bush was born again, like Jimmy Carter, but his conversion came late and had a political aspect to it—he was converted at the Bush family compound by Billy Graham, who was engaged in a political ministry to his father. Dwight Eisenhower, it is true, was led to baptism by Graham; but Eisenhower was a famous and formed man by then—the principal military figure of World War II, the leader of NATO, the president of Columbia University. George Bush's conversion was a wrenching away from mainly wasted years. He joined a Bible study culture in Texas that was unlike anything Eisenhower bought into.

Bush was a saved alcoholic—and here, too, he had no predecessor in the White House. Ulysses Grant conquered the bottle, but not with the help of Jesus. Other presidents were Evangelicals. Three of them belonged to the Disciples of Christ—James Garfield, Lyndon Johnson, and Ronald Reagan. But none of the three—nor any of the other forty-two presidents preceding Bush (including his father) would have answered a campaign debate question as he did. Asked who was his favorite philosopher, he said "Christ." And why? "Because he changed my life." Bush talks Evangelical talk as no other president has, including Jimmy Carter, who also used the language of the Enlightened culture that Evangelists despise. Bush, as we have seen, told various Evangelicals that he felt God had called him to run for president in 2000.

Bush promised his Evangelical followers faith-based social services, which he called "compassionate conservatism." He went beyond that to give them a faith-based war, faith-based law enforcement, faith-based education, faith-based medicine, and faith-based science. He could deliver on his promises because the agencies handling all these problems were stocked, in large degree, with born-again Christians of his own variety. The Evangelicals had complained for years that they were not able to affect policy because liberals left over from previous administrations were in all the health and education and social service bureaus, at the operational level. They had specific people they objected to, and they had specific people with whom to replace them, and Karl Rove helped them do just that.

It is common knowledge that the Republican White House and Congress let "K Street" lobbyists have a say in the drafting of economic legislation, and on the personnel assigned to carry it out, in areas like oil production, pharmaceutical regulation, medical insurance, and corporate taxes. It is less known that, for social services, Evangelical organizations were given the same right to draft bills and install their implementers. Karl Rove had cultivated the extensive network of Religious Right organizations, and they were consulted at every step of the way as the administration set up its policies on gays, AIDS, condoms, abstinence programs, creationism, and other matters that concerned the Evangelicals. All the Evangelicals' resentments under previous presidents, including Republicans like Reagan and the first Bush, were now being addressed.

The head of the White House Office of Personnel was Kay Cole James, a former dean of Pat Robertson's Regent University and a former vice president of Gary Bauer's Family Research Council.[1] She knew whom to put where, or knew the Religious Right people who knew. An Evangelical was in charge of placing Evangelicals throughout the bureaucracy. The head lobbyist for Gary Bauer's Family Research Council boasted that "a lot of FRC people are in place" in the administration.[2] The Evangelicals knew which positions could affect their agenda, whom to replace there, and whom they wanted appointed. This was true for the Centers for Disease Control, the Food and Drug Administration, and Health and Human Services—agencies that would rule on or administer matters dear to the Evangelical causes.[3]

The White House was alive with piety. Evangelical leaders were in and out on a regular basis. There were Bible study groups in the White House, as in John Ashcroft's Justice Department. Over half of the White House staff attended the meetings. One of the first things David Frum heard someone being asked when he went to work there as a speechwriter: "Missed you at the Bible study."[4] It was said at the time:

> Aside from Rove and Cheney, Bush's inner circle are all deeply
> religious. [Condoleezza] Rice is a minister's daughter, chief of
> staff Andrew Card is a minister's husband, Karen Hughes is a
> church elder, and head speechwriter Michael Gerson is a born-
> again Evangelical, a movement insider.[5]

Other parts of the administration were also pious, with religious services during the lunch hour at the General Services Administration.[6]

FAITH-BASED JUSTICE

THE INFILTRATION of the agencies was invisible to Americans outside the culture of the Religious Right. But even the high-profile appointments made it clear where Bush was taking the country. One of his first appointments, for the office of attorney general, was of the Pentecostal Christian John Ashcroft, a hero to the Evangelicals, many of whom had earlier wanted him to run for president—Pat Robertson had put up money for his campaign. David Kuo, one of Ashcroft's Evangelical speechwriters, said: "In the Evangelical political world he was akin to one of Jesus' disciples."[7] When Ashcroft first became a senator, his Pentecostal father, in Washington for the ceremony, said that scriptural leaders were anointed with oil when they took office. The only oil in Ashcroft's digs was some Crisco—so he was anointed with that.[8]

As a senator, Ashcroft had sponsored a bill to protect unborn life "from [the moment of] fertilization." When he was later nominated to be the attorney general, Gary Bauer's Family Research Council, the Washington branch of James Dobson's Focus on the Family, mobilized women to lobby at Senate offices for his confirmation.[9] The Evangelicals had long been familiar with Ashcroft's piety. He told an audience at Bob Jones University that "we have no king but Jesus," and called the wall of separation between church and state a "wall of oppression."[10]

After his nomination but before his confirmation, Ashcroft promised to put an end to the task force set up by Attorney General Janet Reno to deal with violence against abortion clinics—Evangelicals oppose the very idea of hate crimes. The outcry of liberals against this promise made him back off from it during his confirmation hearings. In 2001, there was a spike in violence against the clinics—790 incidents, as opposed to 209 the year before.[11] That was because the anthrax crimes that year gave abortion opponents the idea of sending threatening powders to the clinics—554 packets were sent. Nonetheless, Ashcroft resisted for a long time the dispatching of marshals to quell the epidemic.[12]

This was one of many signs that the Bush administration thought of abortion as a sin, not as a right to be protected. The president himself called for an amendment to the Constitution outlawing abortion. He called Evangelical leaders around him to celebrate the signing of the bill against "partial-birth abortions." The signing was not held, as usual, at the White House but in the Ronald Reagan Building, as a salute to the hero of younger Evangelicals. Ashcroft moved enforcement of the ban to the Civil Rights Division as a signal that Evangelicals appreciated, implying that the fetus is a person with civil rights to be protected.[13] Then, as a step toward enforcement, Ashcroft subpoenaed hospitals for their files on hundreds of women who had undergone abortions— Democrats in Congress called this a massive invasion of privacy.[14]

Ashcroft's use of the Civil Rights Division for religious purposes was broader than his putting partial-birth abortion under its jurisdiction.

> In 2002, the department established within its Civil Rights Division a separate "religious rights" unit that added a significant new constituency to a division that had long focused on racial injustice. When the Salvation Army—which had been receiving millions of dollars in federal funds—was accused in a private lawsuit of violating federal antidiscrimination laws by requiring employees to embrace Jesus Christ to keep their jobs, the Civil Rights Division for the first time took the side of the alleged discriminators.[15]

In a further step toward faith-based justice, President Bush called for a constitutional amendment banning same-sex marriage. He had resisted this earlier, and his vice president, Dick Cheney (whose daughter is a lesbian), had said that the matter should be left to the states; but in 2003 the Supreme Court knocked down the antisodomy law in Texas (*Lawrence v. Texas*), and the Evangelicals agreed with Justice Scalia's ferocious dissent in ways typified by James Dobson, of Focus on the Family, who said that this was "our D-Day, or Gettysburg, or Stalingrad."[16] The pressure from the Religious Right was now too great for Bush to resist, and he joined the effort to ban gay marriage by constitutional amendment.

FAITH-BASED SOCIAL SERVICES

IN HIS CAMPAIGN FOR the presidency, Bush offered as a proof of his "compassionate conservatism" the plan to give federal aid to church groups that perform social services—the so-called Faith-Based Initiative. The program claimed to have safeguards against using the money to proselytize lest it infringe on the First Amendment. But since large grants went to people who do not believe there is any separation of church and state—Chuck Colson got $2 million and Pat Robertson a million and a half—there was little will to follow the pro forma separation of preaching and aiding. Large grants went to abstinence-only forms of sex education, on the grounds that this was a secular cause, though only religious people were backing it.

The wisdom of the First Amendment was demonstrated by political abuses of the faith-based program. The program was largely targeted to benefit African American ministers. As Matthew Dowd, an adviser to Bush, put it: "The minister is the number one influence in the African American community."[17] The aim was not to win the entire black community away from the Democrats, but to shave a few points off the boost they normally give to Democrats. With that in mind, the administration scheduled conferences to show blacks how to get grants in battleground states just before elections. Thousands of black pastors attended these meetings, including one held in Florida just days before the 2004 presidential election.[18] Local Republican candidates attended, suggesting that religious grants would depend on their election. These events were organized by James Towey, the second man to direct the Faith-Based Initiative.

> Towey, his director of outreach at the time, Jeremy White,
> and other White House staffers also appeared at Republican-
> sponsored events with candidates in half a dozen states. During
> the summer of 2002, for instance, the *Washington Post* reported
> that Towey appeared with numerous other Republicans in
> close races, including Representatives John Shimkus of Illinois,
> Tim Hutchison of Arkansas, and Shelley Moore Capito of
> West Virginia. After a South Carolina event for black ministers,
> participants received a follow-up memo on Republican Party
> letterhead explaining to ministers how they could apply for
> grant money. Of twenty publicly financed trips taken by Towey

between the 2002 and 2004 elections, and publicized through press accounts or releases, sixteen were to battleground states. . . . [In 2002] more than fifteen thousand religious and social service leaders attended free White House conferences in battleground states.[19]

Towey also brought black ministers to the White House to meet the first black woman to become secretary of state, Condoleezza Rice.[20] The fruits of this campaign for black votes could be seen in 2004, when black voters in Milwaukee received fliers from the influential black preacher Bishop Sedgwick Daniels urging them to vote for George Bush because "he shares our values." He also shared with Bishop Daniels a million and a half of taxpayers' funds for faith-based initiatives. Bishop Daniels had always supported Democratic candidates before 2004.[21]

The first leader of the Faith-Based Initiative, a man who had experience in community programs, Catholic political scientist John DiIulio, resigned after complaining of the political uses the program was being put to. His second in command, David Kuo, later resigned for the same reason. As DiIulio explained to a reporter friend:

> In eight months, I heard many, many staff discussions, but not three meaningful, substantive policy discussions. . . . On social policy and related issues, the lack of even basic policy knowledge, and the only casual interest in knowing more, was somewhat breathtaking—discussion by fairly senior people who mean Medicaid but were talking Medicare. . . . On the so-called faith bill, they basically rejected any idea that the president's best political interests—not to mention the best policy of the country—could be served by letting centrist Senate Democrats in on the issue, starting with a bipartisan effort to review the implementation of the kindred law (called "charitable choice") signed in 1996 by Clinton. For a fact, had they done that, six months later they would have had a strongly bipartisan copycat bill to extend that law. But, over-generalizing

the lesson from the politics of the tax cut bill, they winked at
the most far-right Republicans [Rick Santorum and J. C. Watts]
who, in turn, drafted a so-called faith bill (H.R. 7, the Community Solutions Act) that (or so they thought) satisfied certain
fundamentalist leaders. . . . As one senior staff member chided
me at a meeting at which many junior staff were present and
all ears, "John, get a faith bill, any faith bill." Like college
students who fall for the colorful, opinionated, but intellectually third-rate professor, you could see these 20- or 30-
something junior White House staff falling for the Mayberry
Machiavellis.[22]

When the president was unable to get his faith-based bill through Congress, he just launched it by two executive orders, going to Philadelphia
to sign the second one. One of Karl Rove's celebratory signs was unfurled
over the stage: COMPASSION IN ACTION. It should have read RELIGION IN
POLITICS.

FAITH-BASED SCIENCE

DURING THE 2000 presidential campaign, Bush said that "the jury
is still out" on the merits of Darwinism.[23] That is true only if the
jury is not made up of reputable scientists. Bush meant to place religious
figures on the jury to decide a scientific question. As president, he urged
that schools teach "intelligent design" along with Darwinism—that is,
teach religion alongside science in science classes. Gary Bauer, like
other Evangelicals, was delighted when the president said that. His
endorsement proved, he observed, that intelligent design "is not some
backwater view." An executive at the Discovery Institute chimed in:
"President Bush is to be commended for defending free speech on evolution."[24] By that logic, teaching flat-earthism, or the Ptolemaic system
alongside the Copernican system, is a defense of "free speech."

The Discovery Institute claims that it is a scientific, not a religious, enterprise, but that claim was belied when one of its internal documents was discovered. It promised that the Institute would "function as a wedge ... [to] split the trunk [of materialism] at its weakest points" and "replace materialistic explanations with the theistic understanding that nature and human beings are created by God." The Institute is mainly funded with Evangelical money, and its spokespersons are Evangelicals—one, Jonathan Wells, says he was inspired by Unification Church founder Sun Myung Moon to "devote my life to destroying Darwinism." Another, Stephen C. Meyer, is a professor at Palm Beach Atlantic University, whose faculty "must believe in the divine inspiration of the Bible, both the Old and New Testaments."[25]

Since President Bush advocates the teaching of intelligent design, it is not surprising that, in his administration, the National Park Service would authorize the sale of a book at the Grand Canyon claiming the canyon was formed by Noah's flood. A band of scientists protested this endorsement by the government of bogus science. In response to that, the Alliance Defense Fund, set up by James Dobson and other Fundamentalists, threatened a lawsuit if the book was withdrawn from sale at the federal site. As other Religious Right figures chimed in, it was discovered that a draft guide for park interpreters, saying that the canyon was not formed in the time period of the flood, was not released. A survey of Park Service employees in 2003 found that almost nine out of ten felt the scientific message of the service was being skewed for political reasons.[26] The Park Service promised to withdraw the book and conduct a study of the problem. Three years later, no such study had occurred and the book was still for sale, despite a Park Service guideline that said the "history of the earth must be based on the best scientific evidence available, as found in scholarly sources that have stood the test of scientific peer review and criticism." One Park geologist said that sale of the Noah book is like selling a book called *Geysers of Old Faithful: Nostrils of Satan*.[27] The Park Service clearly does not want to anger Dobson and his cadres.

That is the very definition of faith-based science. So is the Bush administration's denial of global warming. The Religious Right would seem to have no stake in this debate, but for whatever reason—the Premillennial lack of concern for the earth's fate as Jesus' coming nears, the "dominion" over the earth given to Adam—Evangelicals have been urgent in denying what most objective scientists have been observing. The White House intervened to have cautions against global warming removed from a 2003 draft report on the environment.[28] Senator James Inhofe of Oklahoma has called reports of global warming "the greatest hoax ever perpetrated on the American people."[29] His hostility to any environmental concerns is such that he has called the Environmental Protection Agency a "Gestapo," and likened its female director to "Tokyo Rose."[30] He is an Evangelical who says that Israel was given the West Bank by God—he claimed that the attack on the World Trade Center was caused by America's weak support of Israel: "One of the reasons I believe the spiritual door was opened for an attack against the United States was that the policy of our government has been to ask the Israelis, and demand it with pressure, not to retaliate against the terrorist strikes that have been launched against them."[31]

FAITH-BASED HEALTH

ONE OF GEORGE W. BUSH's first acts as president—in fact, on his first day in office, signaling its importance to his Evangelical supporters—was to restore a gag rule on aid to international organizations that counsel women on the subject of abortion.[32] Though abortion is legal in this country, the president was able by executive decree to proscribe its mere discussion in other countries if they are to receive money for their population problems. This was just the beginning of the imposition of moral limits on health measures abroad. Though the president was praised for devoting millions of dollars to preventing and treating AIDS in Africa, 30 percent of that money was earmarked for promoting sexual abstinence, and none of it was for condoms.[33] Religion trumped medical findings on what is effective.

Domestically, too, $170 million were lavished on abstinence-only schooling in the year 2005 alone. The Centers for Disease Control removed from its Web site the findings of a panel that abstinence-only programs do not work. A study of the abstinence programs being financed by the federal government showed how little medical knowledge mattered, as opposed to moral dictation.

> In evaluating the curricula of these programs, the report found
> that the vast majority exaggerated the failure rates of condoms,
> spread false claims about abortion's health risks (including
> mental health problems) and perpetuated sexual stereotypes. . . .
> Perhaps most outrageously, one curriculum even claimed that
> sweat and tears could transfer the HIV virus. You might think
> that this would be a fringe claim even on the Right, but Senate
> majority leader Bill Frist, himself a physician, repeatedly
> refused to repudiate the notion of such transmission in an
> interview with ABC's George Stephanopoulos.[34]

The Religious Right had for years been spreading the unfounded claim that abortion causes breast cancer. The National Cancer Institute had correctly reported that no study has proved such a thing, but twenty-seven pro-life members of Congress pressured the NCI to remove that from its online fact sheet.

Another concern of the Religious Right was the morning-after contraceptive pill. Bush put one of the pill's known opponents, David Hager, on the board of the Food and Drug Administration that was to decide whether the pill could be sold without a prescription. Though Hager voted with the minority of three against releasing the pill, against a majority of twenty-four, Hager raised such a clamor about the danger of teenaged girls using the pill that the FDA refused to permit over-the-counter sales, a decision not made on scientific or health grounds but out of a moral imperative. Hager gave himself and God the credit for this, telling an audience at an Evangelical college in Kentucky:

> I argued it from a scientific perspective, and God took that information, and he used it through this minority report [*sic*] to influence the decision. You don't have to wave your Bible to have an effect as a Christian in the public arena. We serve the greatest Scientist. We serve the Creator of all life.[35]

For years the Bush administration could not get a director of the FDA confirmed because the acting director kept up the ban on over-the-counter sale of the morning-after pill and the nominee would not promise to lift the ban. At last, to break the impasse, the nominee said that he would lift the ban, but only for women over eighteen, leaving unsolved all the many unwanted pregnancies of younger girls.

Even after the setback to his administration in the 2006 elections, Bush was busy trying to please the abstinence-only lobby. He appointed a prominent abstinence-only and anti-abortion doctor, Erick Kerouack, to be deputy assistant secretary of population affairs in the Department of Health and Human Services, an office that oversees millions of dollars of funds for family planning. Kerouack is famous for arguing that premarital sex is a form of "germ warfare" that incapacitates a woman for lasting relationships.[36] According to him, it consumes the "bonding" hormone oxytocin. He and a colleague, John Diggs, have called this the sticky-adhesive phenomenon. If you put an adhesive on one arm, then use the same tape on more arms, with each application the adhesive power is weakened, till the tape just falls off when you try to attach it.

Religious views of health determined the first major domestic decision George W. Bush faced as president. The great promise of embryonic stem cell research was beat back by the Evangelicals, who think that embryos are human persons. Bush spent much of his time working out a way to cut off research without seeming to. The Religious Right was consulted all through the decision process, with Jay Lefkowitz as the White House liaison to the Evangelicals.[37] The president decreed that only stem cell lines already being used could be federally funded—those, he said, "where the life and death decision has already been made." He claimed there were over sixty of these, but there turned out to be more like sixteen, most of those unusable by American scientists.[38]

To dramatize his stance against stem cell research, Bush held White House events with "Snowflake" babies. The Snowflake project promotes "adoption" of frozen embryos stored in fertility clinics—who, as full human beings, are all "as unlike as snowflakes"—to be implanted in mothers, rescuing them from research doctors or destruction. The first White House meeting with families who "adopted" Snowflakes was so successful with the Evangelicals that he brought the babies back to be around him as he signed his first veto in five years as president, against the bill authorizing stem cell research. Dismantling an embryo for its stem cells, Bush was suggesting, is like killing one of the little babies around him.

The problem with the Snowflakes project is that only 128 Snowflake babies had been delivered when the president spoke, and they were drawn from a pool of four hundred thousand embryos in cold storage at fertility clinics.[39] There is always overproduction of embryos at such clinics, since a cluster of embryos has to be implanted in the mother to make sure one will embed itself. Besides, some embryos are insufficiently healthy to be used. So four hundred thousand are going to be disposed of if they are not used for research. If one really thinks this is murder, the duty is to make fertility clinics illegal—the Vatican is consistent enough to call for that.[40] But the American public supports fertility clinics, for those who cannot conceive children without them, and even the president has praised them—while condemning their inevitable production of embryos that will never become babies.

Nowhere was a faith-based policy on health more evident than in the massive mobilization of the Bush administration to keep a Florida woman alive. Doctors had pronounced the woman, Terri Schiavo, brain dead; lower courts had approved the removal of life support (which her husband desired); and an autopsy would show that her brain had shrunk to half its normal size. She had long been blind, so the filmed reactions said to be responses to the sight of her parents were impossible. Yet Senator Bill Frist, a physician, after looking at tape sequences of the woman excerpted by the Schiavo parents, declared that she was clearly not brain dead.

Representative Tom DeLay, then still in the House, said: "Terri Schiavo is not dead. She talks and she laughs, and she expresses happiness and discomfort."[41] DeLay's committee issued a subpoena to Schiavo, demanding that she appear before the committee and show her responsiveness. He explained to the Family Research Council that this was to make it impossible to remove her life support, for fear of defying a subpoena. "We have a lot of confidence that they will not pull the feeding tube because of this subpoena."[42] When the subpoena ploy was seen to be not working, DeLay and others rushed through "Terri's Law"— "An Act for the Relief of the Parents of Theresa Marie Schiavo."

The bill, hastily cobbled together, was meant for one case only. It declared: "Nothing in this Act shall constitute a precedent with respect to future legislation, including the provision of private relief bills."[43] The bill gave Schiavo's parents the right to sue before a district court *de novo* (with no reference to local court findings against them). That was a right the Congress could not bestow, according to a unanimous Florida Supreme Court decision that ruled Terri's Law unconstitutional. Yet George Bush, who is reluctant to leave his Texas compound (and did not do so to address the Katrina hurricane crisis), had flown back dramatically to Washington in order to be ready to sign the bill the minute it was completed and delivered to the White House—which happened in the middle of the night, so he got out of bed to sign it. The power of Evangelicals to call the tune for Bush was here as nowhere else confirmed.

With Terri's Law declared unconstitutional, her life support was finally withdrawn (after fifteen years of artificial prolongation). Bumper stickers began appearing on cars: TERRI WAS MURDERED. DeLay, commenting later on the attempted assassination of a Chicago judge, said: "The men responsible for Terri Schiavo's death will have to answer to their behavior." Even when the autopsy proved that she had been in a vegetative state for many years, the Religious Right continued to call her demise murder. Ave Maria University, a conservative Catholic institution funded by Thomas Monaghan, the Domino's Pizza billionaire, offered a Terri Schiavo memorial scholarship to students.[44]

Why was the Schiavo case so important to Evangelicals? They saw her as the oldest and largest fetus. She could not respond, but neither can a fetus. She seemed to have little function left but life itself, and an embryo has initially no human function but life. By Evangelical standards, you have to be pro-life wherever there is life, of whatever sort or quality. Let Terri Schiavo die and you are, by implication, killing millions of the unborn. The Catholic hierarchy for years taught that a person in a permanent vegetative state did not have to be kept alive "by extraordinary means," and taught that intravenous support was "extraordinary." Pope John Paul II, toward the end of his own life, changed that teaching. He said all people, no matter what their condition and what the costs of their care, have to be kept alive by artificial means: "No evaluation of costs can outweigh the value of the fundamental good which we are trying to protect, that of human life." To withdraw life support is the *sin* of euthanasia.[45]

Given the increasing sophistication of artificial means, and their mounting costs, this means that whole peoples and their income could be permanently drained to keep more and more Terri Schiavos alive as their brains go on shriveling year after year. Terri Schiavo was kept alive for fifteen years, and might have lived another fifteen, until she had no brain left at all. The Evangelicals think that is simply a natural corollary to keeping all the millions of aborted fetuses alive. It is a faith-based doctrine on life.

FAITH-BASED WAR

THE DEPUTY UNDERSECRETARY for defense intelligence—General William (Jerry) Boykin, a man leading the search for bin Laden—made headlines during the Iraq war with a slide show lecture he gave in churches. He appeared there not in his dress uniform but in combat gear.

He asked audiences (this was after the 2000 election and before the 2004 one):

> Ask yourself this: why is this man in the White House? The majority of Americans did not vote for him. Why is he there? I tell you this morning he's in the White House because God put him there for such a time as this. God put him there to lead not only this nation but to lead the world in such a time as this.

Then he asked the congregation who the enemy is. He showed slides of Osama bin Laden, Saddam Hussein, Kim Jong Il, and Taliban leaders, asking of each, "Is this man the enemy?" He gave a resounding no to each question, and then revealed the foe's true identity. "The battle this nation is in is a spiritual battle, it's a battle for our soul. And the enemy is a guy called Satan. . . . Satan wants to destroy this nation. He wants to destroy us as a nation, and he wants to destroy us as a Christian nation."[46]

This was not a momentary lapse on Boykin's part. He has been an active translator of war into religion for many years. When he led the failed Black Hawk Down raid on Mogadishu in 1993, he flew over the city taking photographs. When developed, the pictures showed black smears over the city. He showed them to his Sunday-school-teaching mother, and she asked, "Don't you know specifically what you were up against?" Only then did he get the full supernatural meaning of the pictures. "It was a demonic presence in that city, and God revealed it to me as the enemy that I was up against in Mogadishu." He remembered, in this light, the first feeling he had experienced in that non-Christian country: "I could feel the presence of evil. . . . The demonic presence is real in a place that has rejected God." His task was not simply to defeat an enemy force, but to carry Jesus to the benighted. "It is the principalities of darkness. It is a spiritual enemy that will only be defeated if we come against him in the name of Jesus."[47] The Evangelical groups he addressed responded eagerly when he attacked the "godless" courts of his own country. "Don't you worry about what these courts say, our God reigns supreme."[48]

When General Edwin Walker began to promote the John Birch Society to his NATO troops, President Kennedy removed him. What happened to General Boykin after he went around calling Muslims Satanic? He was not silenced, demoted, removed, or even criticized. He continued to work on the Pentagon's special intelligence group. His boss, Secretary of Defense Donald Rumsfeld, said, "This is a free country," and Boykin had "an outstanding record" in his active career as a Delta Force commander. What caused the difference in response between President Kennedy's time and President Bush's? Could it be the power of the Evangelicals? As soon as Boykin became an object of public criticism, the Evangelicals rallied around him.

When President Bush, asked about the content of Boykin's remarks, said, "He doesn't reflect my point of view," Gary Bauer was quick to attack his own leader for this mild expression of difference. He sent a memo to his organization's members:

> I must be missing something. The general has said that
> America is under attack because we are built on a Judeo-
> Christian values system; that ultimately the enemy is not flesh
> and blood, but rather the enemy is Satan, and that God's hand
> of protection prevented September 11 from being worse than it
> was. . . . Precisely which of those statements does the president
> take issue with?

The Christian Coalition directed petitions to Secretary Rumsfeld urging him not to knuckle under to the "intolerant liberal mob [that] has castigated General Boykin, a true American hero." James Dobson, on his radio show, called Boykin a "martyr," and told his listeners to send in their protests to the White House.

There was nothing surprising in this. Boykin was just repeating what other Evangelicals had been saying about the war in Iraq. Charles Stanley, a former president of the Southern Baptist Convention, wrote: "We should offer to serve the war effort in any way possible. . . . God battles with people who oppose him, who fight against him and his followers."

Jerry Falwell put it succinctly in 2004: "God is pro-war." For some Evangelicals, this was a war against the enemies of Israel, who are by definition anti-God. Tim LaHaye called it, therefore, "a focal point of end-time events." For others, it was a chance to spread Christianity to the infidels. An article syndicated on the Southern Baptist Convention's wire service said that "American foreign policy and military might have opened an opportunity for the Gospel in the land of Abraham, Isaac, and Jacob." Franklin Graham, the son of Billy Graham, and Marvin Olasky, the inventor of Bush's "compassionate conservatism," agreed.[49] Boykin's was not a lone voice, then; he was a member in good standing of the community that supported Bush on religious grounds, even in his warfare. Boykin was safe under the sheltering wings of a Religious Right that the White House did not dare to cross. He would not be dropped until his patron, Donald Rumsfeld, was finally extruded after the 2006 elections.

There is one danger with a war that God commands. What if God should lose? That is unthinkable to the Evangelicals. They cannot accept the idea of second-guessing God, and he was the one who led them into war. Thus, in 2006, when two-thirds of the American people told pollsters that the war in Iraq was a mistake, the third of those still standing behind it were mainly Evangelicals (who make up about one-third of the population). It was a faith-based certitude.

31 | ECUMENICAL KARL

THE FAITH-BASED GOVERNMENT of the last chapter was wholly the product of a conceiving Karl Rove and an executing George Bush. No campaign consultant ever went on to be such an arbiter of all things political within an administration as Karl Rove—not even the most famous campaign manager of them all, Mark Hanna. Like Rove with Bush, Hanna ran William McKinley's two successful campaigns for governor before guiding him into the White House—but then Hanna struck off on his own as a powerful United States senator. Rove, who had been the campaign strategist of many Texas state politicians, stayed by Bush's side all through Bush's gubernatorial and presidential years. No major initiative, foreign or domestic, was launched in the Bush White House without "running it by Karl" to be shaped for its political defensibility, its dissemination among the faithful, and its "spin" for the larger public. It is as if Lee Atwater had helped run the White House of Bush's father, or James Carville had stayed by Bill Clinton's side throughout both of his terms.

Bush's own awe for Karl's genius had to be accepted by those in his administration. If anybody on the team felt resentment or envy of Rove, he or she could not express it. Bush called him the "architect" of his re-election in 2004—when Bush won *both* the popular and the electoral majorities, redeeming the loss of the former in 2000. Even as Republicans went into the disastrous (for them) midterm elections of 2006, Bush's aides believed Rove's prediction that they would prevail—and Democrats were so spooked by Rove's legendary prowess that they could not be sure he would not prove right once again. In the very months leading up to the midterms, new books by Thomas Edsall and James Moore and Wayne Slater were describing Rove as virtually unstoppable.[1]

There are various theories about Rove's long string of victories in Texas and on the national scene. Some felt it came from his technological wizardry in targeting and turning out potential Republican voters. Others thought it fumed up from his dark aptitude for denigrating any foes of his clients. Or it came from the prescience with which he foresaw a polarized country and steered Bush away from his promise to be a uniter, not a divider. But on the national scene at least, leaving behind all his Texas work for candidates other than Bush, his real skill lay in finding how to use religion as a political tool. This does not necessarily contradict the other theories. It complements or culminates them. He shaped the hard core of the Republican Party around resentments religious people felt over abortion, homosexuality, Darwinism, women's liberation, pornography, and school prayer. Anyone who reacted strongly against just one of these things could very likely be made to oppose most or even all of the others, and be drawn into an alliance that cut across older patterns of economic, regional, or party ties.

Rove made the executive branch of the United States more openly and avowedly religious than it had ever been, though he had no discernible religious beliefs himself. His own indifference allowed him to be ecumenical in his appeal to Protestants, Catholics, and Jews. That spectrum, which Will Herberg had celebrated in the 1950s as an *inclusive* formula for the country, he put to his own more circumscribed use as an *exclusionary* device. His was an ecumenical effort, but of a tight little constricted ecumenicity. He mobilized any Protestant, Catholic, or Jew who shared, or could be made to see, a common political purpose. He promoted an equal-opportunity Evangelicalism, distancing itself from Enlightened forms of all three religions. He began with a natural advantage so far as Protestants were concerned. Protestant Evangelicals, heavily based in the South, were already staunch Republicans. The trick was to add significant numbers of Right-Wing Jews and Catholics to the mix, since those two groups were historically Democratic in their loyalties.

JEWS

SOME JEWS were already moving to the Right when Rove targeted them—the Orthodox were already there on some issues like abortion. Conservatives in the Right to Life movement included men like Rabbi Barry Freundel, prominent in Washington, and Rabbi Yehuda Levin, a radio presence in New York.[2] The Jewish neocons had also moved to the Right on national security issues—they had made their break in favor of Ronald Reagan's anticommunism. Other Jews were willing to work with Evangelical supporters of Israel. Rove knew many such allies. One rabbi, Daniel Lapin, who was a friend of Rove's fellow Texans Tom DeLay and Richard Armey, would become known as the Right Wing's rabbi in Washington. He is the one who introduced one friend to another—Congressman Tom DeLay to lobbyist Jack Abramoff. Lapin played a role similar to that of Rabbi Baruch Korff, the champion of Richard Nixon who claimed to have raised a million dollars for him.[3]

Lapin became a celebrity among conservatives with his 1999 book, *America's Real War,* saying that a culture war declared by secularists was using the separation of church and state to extinguish religion in America. He also gave a religious spin to the "greed is good" mood of the 1980s, declaring that God wants his followers to be rich and that "the Torah discourages guilt about sex and money."[1] Staying in Abramoff's home on his Washington visits, Lapin was a familiar at the White House and on Capitol Hill, giving Bible lessons to senators and representatives—Congressman Dana Rohrabacher called him "my Rabbi."[5] Daniel Lapin brought his brother and fellow rabbi, David Lapin, into Abramoff's lobbying ventures, where the two were associates of such Abramoff allies as Grover Norquist and Ralph Reed.[6] Rove would find all these people useful for his project, through Norquist even opening an ecumenical effort with Islamists, inviting them to White House events and reaping votes in an unexpected quarter.[7]

PROTESTANTS

R OVE NEVER THOUGHT he could get the votes of many Jews, but he got enough to bolster the larger chunks of the population that were Protestant or Catholic. And his very outreach convinced some of those Protestants and Catholics that the Republican Party was no longer anti-Semitic, boosting their own sense of self-righteousness. If Rove could unite Protestants and Catholics on the Right, they would make up a majority of the Republican vote and a strong plurality of the nation, a base to build on. Evangelicals make up a third of the nation and Catholics a fourth, which makes them the two largest religious groups in America. There is obviously some overlap here, and there were inevitable differences within each group. But Rove had the makings of his power base in the fact that Evangelicals made up 32 percent of the country and 52 percent of the Republican Party.[8] That gave him a good starting bloc for building his ecumenical religious effort.

Most of Rove's Jewish network was mobilized after he got to Washington. But he began earlier to call in national Protestants and Catholics to meet Governor Bush in Texas, for help in organizing his presidential bid in 2000. He sought out new speechwriters for the campaign from Evangelical ranks—Michael Gerson, who had begun by writing speeches for Chuck Colson and Steve Forbes, and David Kuo, who worked for John Ashcroft and for Bill Bennett's Empower America organization. Rove had a recruiting ally with these men, one close to home, a journalism professor at the University of Texas, Marvin Olasky. Though born into a Russian Jewish family in New York, Olasky was a convert to Rousas John Rushdoony's Christian Reconstruction theology—which is also called Dominion Theology. Rushdoony (1916–2001) improbably merged theocracy with the free market. He argued that a religious government based on the Ten Commandments would necessarily be a limited government.

Actually, enforcing the Ten Commandments would take government into the most private areas. (How does the state make you honor your parents?) Rushdoony wanted a return to the government of ancient Israel—he even proposed at one time that homosexuals be stoned, in accord with Leviticus 20.13. He said: "There is not a single text in all of the New Testament to indicate this penalty has been altered or removed."[9] Olasky took up one of Rushdoony's pet projects, homeschooling, and edited over a dozen books in the "Turning Point Christian Worldview" series financed by an ardent follower of Rushdoony, the billionaire Howard Ahmanson.[10]

Olasky was taken up by a wider network of conservatives in 1992, when he published *The Tragedy of American Compassion*, which suggested that the government had tragically neglected religious social services. William Bennett became a great promoter of the book, as did Newt Gingrich. Rove saw the way Olasky's "compassionate conservatism" could give Bush a campaign theme to blunt the idea that conservatives are heartless friends of big business. Some would feel betrayed when the Faith-Based Initiative (FBI to insiders), built on this theme, became just another tool for using and rewarding conservative allies. As was noticed in the last chapter, even the first and second in command of the FBI resigned on just this issue. But the theme had done its work in helping elect Bush as a different kind of Republican. It had earlier been useful in recruiting the two Evangelical speechwriters who would serve Bush in the White House, Michael Gerson and David Kuo.

Gerson became the best known and most respected speechwriter since Peggy Noonan's service with Ronald Reagan. His own sincere Evangelical beliefs greatly strengthened the trust in Bush felt by the Evangelical community—*Time* magazine even listed Gerson among the twenty-five most influential Evangelicals of 2005 (he was number nine).[11] Gerson gave Bush some of his best-known lines. Some were expressly religious. Others promoted domestic policies like the No Child Left Behind education program—Gerson coined the term "soft bigotry of low expectations" to stigmatize the public school system. But Gerson could be as tough as anyone in mounting Bush's aggressive foreign policy. He changed the term "axis of hatred" to "axis of evil" in the 2002 State of the Union address.[12] For the selling of the Iraq war, no phrase was more useful to Bush or to his secretary of state, Condoleezza Rice, than Gerson's "the smoking gun that could come in the form of a mushroom cloud."[13] Gerson was included in the tiny (six-person) group that made Iraq policy, the White House Iraq Group (WHIG).[14] He explained to the *Wall Street Journal* how he, the peace-loving Christian, became such a crusader for war—he thought of it as an extension overseas of "compassionate conservatism."[15]

CATHOLICS

THE RELIGIOUS GROUP Rove most wanted to include in his new Republican majority was made up of Catholics. This sizable bloc included a subset of those he was wooing—Latino Americans. It had been loosened from its historical roots in the Democratic Party by Ronald Reagan's panoptic appeal. And it included prominent Catholics who were already on Rove's side—people like William Bennett, Peggy Noonan, and Robert Novak. While Rove was working on Bush's 1998 re-election campaign for governor, he received a copy of the Catholic magazine *Crisis,* sent him by the magazine's editor, Deal Hudson. Mr. Hudson had commissioned a poll that proved that Catholics who attended Mass regularly were more likely to vote Republican than were the less observant, a finding he reported in an article called "The Catholic Vote: Does It Swing?" Rove would extend the insight of this poll to argue that churchgoers of other faiths were also leaning to the Right. Rove would focus his efforts on expanding this development.

Rove liked the way Hudson thought. He spoke his language—as

when he wrote: "Catholics, at fifty million strong and growing, have emerged as the Holy Grail of coalition politics, and they have the distinction of clustering in states rich in electoral votes, like Florida, Texas, California, New York, Ohio, and Illinois."[16] Rove called Hudson to Austin to meet the governor. Then, as the 2000 presidential campaign got under way, Hudson was appointed to chair the Republican National Committee's Catholic Outreach. Once Bush was elected, Hudson became a regular consultant on Catholic issues. He promoted Catholic appointments, succeeded in placing one assistant as a representative to the U.N., carried White House messages to Cardinal Theodore McCarrick, and was part of the U.S. delegation sent to celebrate John Paul II's twenty-fifth year in the papacy. He showed his power when he got the U.S. Conference of Catholic Bishops to fire an employee for opening a Catholics for Kerry Web site in 2004.[17] But Hudson had to resign from his post at the Republican National Committee and give up the editorship of *Crisis* because an old sex scandal had come to light. As a professor at the Jesuit Fordham College he had seduced a female freshman, for which he lost tenure, was fired, and paid a $30,000 settlement to the young woman.[18]

Hudson might have been missed. But Rove actually had a more useful ally in a Catholic priest who not only mobilized Catholic support of the administration but helped to form the alliance between Catholics and Evangelicals that Rove was fostering. This priest edited a journal, *First Things,* that is more serious and respected than Hudson's *Crisis* ever was. The priest, Richard John Neuhaus, was one of those Rove had invited to Austin while Bush was still governor, and Bush was happier in quoting him than any others on what he called "life issues" like stem cell research. *Time* magazine wrote in its 2005 survey of the nation's most influential Evangelicals:

> When Bush met with journalists from religious publications
> last year, the living authority he cited most often was not a
> fellow evangelical but a man he calls "Father Richard," who, he
> explained, "helps me articulate these religious things."[19]

The *Time* reporter did not realize that one can be, like Neuhaus, a Catholic priest *and* an Evangelical. Neuhaus has made it his business to bring together Catholics and Evangelicals His journal, *First Things,* sponsored a series of meetings between the two groups that produced doctrinal statements of agreement, "Evangelicals and Catholics Together" (familiarly known on the Religious Right as ECT).

The first ECT document (1994) was largely devoted to agreement on abortion, which has been the principal link between the two groups, making it all-important to Rove's strategy. Chuck Colson was the Evangelical who worked most closely with Neuhaus, and the two of them assembled an impressive group of forty leaders to sign the ECT document—twenty Catholics and twenty Evangelicals. The Catholics included New York's John Cardinal O'Connor (since deceased), Archbishop (later Cardinal) Francis George of Chicago, Father (later Cardinal) Avery Dulles, Michael Novak, and George Weigel. The Evangelicals included Pat Robertson, Bill Bright of Campus Crusade for Christ, Richard Mouw, James Packer, and Mark Noll.

Evangelicals had been historically hostile to Catholics, but Francis Schaeffer had long argued that abortion would be the issue to bring them together. Schaeffer, in collaboration with C. Everett Koop (before Koop became surgeon general) had created a famous five-part film series on abortion, dramatizing in 1979 the "Holocaust" brought about by *Roe v. Wade.* The film—*Whatever Happened to the Human Race?*—toured American theaters for three months and then was used by Evangelicals in classes and meetings. The book from the film became a regular seller in Evangelical circles.[20] Schaeffer said that Evangelicals had been slow to react to *Roe.* Catholics had led the way. The two groups should join forces in a "co-belligerency."

Evangelical resistance to Catholics had already been partly blunted by 1979. One reason for the old hostility was a resentment of Catholic schools and their bid for public support. But an Evangelical move toward private schools, to avoid integration and to protest the "godless" lack of school prayer, made the Protestants just as eager for government vouchers and other tax breaks for schools as Catholics had ever been. The growing union between them was seen in the emotional support of both groups for Mel Gibson's movie *The Passion of the Christ* (2004). Even though Gibson drew on the work of a nun who would have been considered "Mariolatrous" by old-time Evangelicals, many Evangelical pastors required attendance at the movie from their congregants.

It was largely because of Pope John Paul II's opposition to abortion that Evangelicals in a 2004 poll placed him higher in their esteem (59 percent) than either Pat Robertson (54 percent) or Jerry Falwell (44 percent).[21] Back in the days of Al Smith, or even of John Kennedy, Protestants would have been horrified at the idea of a Catholic priest advising a president on important matters. But the Evangelicals were now happy to have "Father Richard" doing just that. Neuhaus and *First Things* called for bishops to deny communion to Catholic political candidates who supported abortion rights in the 2004 campaign, though 72 percent of Catholics opposed such action. This was an even higher rate than the general population's opposition (68 percent). Catholics opposed to abortion were against the ban (by 57 percent), though only 41 percent of Evangelical Protestants were opposed.[22] Despite this opposition to what was seen as an extreme blending of religion with politics, Rove's Catholic strategy seemed on track by the re-election of Bush. In 2000, a sizable minority of Catholics (46 percent) voted for Bush, but by 2004 a majority of them (52 percent) did. In close elections, these numbers were vital, and they confirmed Rove's reputation and his master plan.

THE ECUMENICAL ISSUE

FRANCIS SCHAEFFER had predicted that abortion would be the issue to unite Evangelicals and Catholics. As such it was the linchpin of Rove's ecumenical strategy. The *Weekly Standard* editor William Kristol, often considered the principal Republican strategist outside the administration, agreed that abortion was the single most important conservative issue.

> *Roe* and abortion are the test [of the conservative future]. For
> if Republicans are incapable of grappling with this moral and
> political challenge; if they cannot earn a mandate to overturn
> *Roe* and move toward a post-abortion America, then in truth,
> there will be no conservative future. Other issues are impor-
> tant, to be sure, and a governing party will have to show leader-
> ship on those issues as well. But *Roe* is central. . . . The truth is
> that abortion is today the bloody crossroads of American poli-
> tics. It is where judicial liberation (from the Constitution),
> sexual liberation (from traditional mores), and women's
> liberation (from natural distinctions) come together. It is
> the focal point for liberalism's simultaneous assault on self-
> government, morals, and nature.[23]

Rove had to make sure that Bush the candidate would satisfy both
the Evangelicals and the Catholics on this point—and that meant signaling the nomination of pro-life Supreme Court justices. Bush followed
the mantra of presidents when discussing nominees for the Court, saying he would not insist on a "litmus test," but he was careful to add that
he wanted a "strict constructionist," which is a code word for the Religious Right, since they say that only loose construction had allowed
judges to claim there is a "right to privacy" in the Constitution, guaran-
teeing freedom for contraceptives and abortion. Bush made his intentions clear when he told Tim Russert on television that his ideal of a
strict constructionist was met by Antonin Scalia and Clarence Thomas,
the greatest foes of abortion on the Court.[24] He was even more explicit
in the presidential debate of October 8, 2004. Asked what kind of judges
he would nominate, he said he would not favor anyone like the judges
who decided the *Dred Scott* case—of 1857! That puzzled many hearers.
How could any president now have judges available who would enforce
slavery, as *Dred Scott* did? But Evangelicals knew what he was saying.
They frequently compare the *Dred Scott* case to *Roe*, since they contend
(inaccurately) that the former ruled that a slave is not a human person

and the latter says the same thing of the fetus. Bush was telling his followers that he would not nominate a supporter of *Roe*.

What made opposition to abortion so useful to Rove is the fact that it is the ultimate "wedge issue," because it is non-negotiable. Other people may have strong views, but they will not sacrifice everything else to them. The right-to-life people hold that it is as strong a point of religion as any can be. It is religious because the Sixth Commandment (or the Fifth by Catholic count) says, "Thou shalt not kill." For the Evangelicals in general, abortion is murder. That is why what others think, what polls say, what looks practical does not matter for them. One must oppose murder, however much rancor or controversy may ensue. Hitler must be opposed when he murders Jews.

Fair enough. But is abortion murder? Most people think not. The Evangelicals may argue that most people in Germany thought it was all right to kill Jews. But the parallel is not valid. Killing Jews was killing persons. It is not demonstrable that killing fetuses is killing persons. Not even the Evangelicals act as if it were. In that case, the woman seeking the abortion would be the most culpable person. She is committing filicide, killing her own child. She is Medea. But the Evangelical community, which generally believes in the death penalty, does not call for her execution. It does not even call, in most cases, for the death of the doctor involved, but only for fines and imprisonment. In any case, punishing him but not the woman makes no sense—he is just carrying out her intent. He cannot operate without her request and permission.

Furthermore, a fair amount of Evangelicals (10 percent) allow abortion in the case of rape or incest.[25] But the circumstances of the conception should not change the nature of the thing conceived. If it is a human person, killing it is punishing it for something it had nothing to do with. We do not kill people because they had a criminal parent. Moreover, some Evangelicals admit that a fetus can be aborted if the woman's health is threatened. The Greeley-Hout survey of conservative Christians shows that 19 percent of conservative Christians would permit abortion in that case.[26] But why should the mother be preferred over the "child" if both are, equally, persons? And if mere *danger* of death is involved with the mother, why should *certitude* of death be decreed for the other "person"? These exceptions would not arise if, in their minds, removal of a fetus is really murder.

Nor did the Catholic Church treat abortion as murder in the past. If it had, late-term abortions and miscarriages would have called for treatment of the well-formed fetus as a person—calling for its baptism and Christian burial. That was never the practice. And no wonder. The subject of abortion is not scriptural. For those who make it so central to religion in our time, this seems like an odd omission. Abortion is not treated in the Ten Commandments—or anywhere in Jewish Scripture.[27] It is not treated in the Sermon on the Mount—or anywhere in the New Testament. It is not treated in the early creeds. It is not treated in the early ecumenical councils. If it had been part of Scripture, the creeds, or the councils, Saint Augustine in the fifth century would have been given some guidance, since his knowledge of both Jewish and Christian Scriptures was encyclopedic. Yet he says: "I have not been able to discover in the accepted books of Scripture anything at all certain about the origin of the soul."[28]

Lacking scriptural guidance, Saint Thomas Aquinas worked from Aristotle's view of the different kinds of animation—the nutritive (vegetable) soul, the sensing (animal) soul, and the intellectual soul. Some used Aristotle to say that humans therefore have three souls. Others said that the intellectual soul is created by human semen. Thomas denied both positions. He said that a material cause (semen) cannot cause a spiritual product. The intellectual soul (personhood) is directly created by God "at the end of human generation" (*in fine generationis humanae*).[29] This intellectual soul supplants what had preceded it (nutritive and sensory animation). So he denied that personhood arose at fertilization by the semen. God directly infuses the soul at the completion of human formation.

Much of the debate over abortion is based on a misconception, that this is a *religious* issue, that the pro-life advocates are acting out of *religious* conviction. It is not a theological matter at all. There is no theological basis for either defending or condemning abortion. Even the popes have said that it is a matter of natural law, to be decided by natural reason. Well, the pope is not the arbiter of natural law. Natural reason is. John Henry Newman once wrote: "The Pope, who comes of Revelation, has no jurisdiction over nature."[30] The matter must be decided by individual conscience, not by religious fiat; and as Newman, again, said: "I shall drink to the Pope, if you please—still, to conscience first, and to the Pope afterwards."[31] If, on a matter of natural law reachable by natural reason, the majority of experienced and conscientious people do not agree with the religious prescriptionists, then the latter must be relying on something other than natural law.

If we are to decide the matter by natural law, that means, in the terms of this book, that we must turn to reason and science, the realm of Enlightened religion. But that is just what the Evangelicals want to avoid. Who are the relevant experts here? They are philosophers, neurobiologists, embryologists. Those must be excluded, say the Evangelicals, since most of them give answers they do not want to hear. They have only secular expertise, not religious conviction. The experts, admittedly, do not give one answer—they differ among themselves, they are tentative, they qualify. They do not have the certitude that the Religious Right accepts as the sign of truth.

So the Evangelicals take shortcuts. They pin everything on being pro-*life*. But one cannot be indiscriminately pro-life.

> If one claimed, in the manner of Albert Schweitzer, that all life
> deserved moral respect, then plants have rights and it might
> turn out that we would have little if anything to eat. And if
> one were consistently "pro-life," one would have to show (*per
> impossibile*) moral respect for paramecia, insects, tissue excised
> during a medical operation, cancer cells, asparagus, and so on.
> Harvesting carrots, on a consistent pro-life hypothesis, would
> constitute something of a massacre.[32]

Opponents of abortion will say that they are defending only *human* life. It is certainly true that the fetus is human life. But so is the semen before it fertilizes, so is the ovum before it is fertilized. They are both human products, and both are living things. But not even the Evangelicals say that the destruction of one or the other would be murder.

The defenders of the fetus say that life begins only after the semen fertilizes the egg, producing an embryo. But in fact two-thirds of the embryos produced this way fail to live on, because they do not achieve nidation (embedding in the womb wall). Nature is like the fertilization clinics—it produces more embryos than are actually used. That is true of embryos lost during the actual impregnation of a woman, and of embryos inadvertently lost in early miscarriages, which look simply like heavy menstruation. Are all these millions of embryos that fail to be embedded human persons? Then "intelligent design" aborts far more persons than any human abortioners can. God is responsible for this silent holocaust.

The universal mandate to preserve "human life" makes no sense. My hair is human life—it is not canine hair, and it is living. It grows. When it grows too long I have it cut. Is that aborting human life? The same with my growing human fingernails. An Evangelical might respond that my hair does not have the potential to become a person. True. But semen has the potential to become a person, and we do not preserve every bit of semen that is ejaculated but never fertilizes an egg. The question is not whether the fetus is human *life* but whether it is a human *person*, and when it becomes one. Is it when it is capable of thought, or of speech, of recognizing itself as a person, of assuming the responsibilities of a person? Is it when it has a functioning brain? Thomas Aquinas said that the fetus did not become a person until God infused the intellectual soul. A functioning brain is not present in the fetus until the end of the sixth month at the earliest (what *Roe* called the beginning of the third trimester). Only then can the cerebral cortex process information from the various senses.

> To use a helpful metaphor from Morowitz and Trefil, a pile of
> wires and switches is not an electrical circuit, and a collection
> of nerve cells is not a functioning brain. The wires and

switches need to be connected in order to make a circuit or a computer, and the nerve cells in the cortex need to be connected for there to be a functioning brain. In effect, before synapses are sufficiently formed the brain does not function because it is just a collection of nerve (and other) cells. The burst of synapse formation, and hence the start of the cerebral cortex as a functioning entity, occurs between twenty-five and thirty-two weeks.[33]

Not surprisingly, that is the earliest point of viability, the time when a fetus can successfully survive outside the womb.

Whether through serendipity or through some sort of causal connection, it now seems that the onset of a functioning central nervous system with a functioning cerebral cortex and the onset of viability occur around the same time—the end of the second trimester, a time by which 99 percent of all abortions have already occurred.[34]

Opponents of abortion like to show sonograms of the fetus reacting to stimuli. But all living cells have electric and automatic reactions. These are like the reactions of Terri Schiavo when she was in a permanent vegetative state. Remember that Thomas Aquinas called the early stage of fetal development *vegetative* life. The fetus has a face long before it has a brain. It has animation before it has a command center to be aware of its movements or to experience any reaction as pain.

These are difficult matters, on which qualified people differ. It is not enough to say that whatever the woman wants should go. She has a responsibility to consider whether and when she may have a child inside her, not just a fetus. Certainly by the late stages of her pregnancy a child is ready to respond with miraculous celerity to all the personal interchanges with the mother that show a brain in great working order. One cannot read the book *The Scientist in the Crib* without renewed respect for the human being that emerges upon delivery.[35]

Given these uncertainties, who is to make the individual decision to have an abortion? Religious leaders? But they have no special authority in the matter, which is not subject to theological norms or guidance. The state? But its authority is given by the people it represents, and the people are divided on this (though most support the right to an abortion). Doctors? They too differ. The woman is the one closest to the decision. Under *Roe v. Wade,* no woman is forced to have an abortion. But those who have decided to have one are able to. Before that, the woman was forced *not* to have an abortion. She had no choice in the matter, though it affected her most of all.

Some objected to Rove's use of abortion to cement his ecumenical coalition on the grounds that this was injecting religion into politics. The supreme irony is that, properly understood, abortion is not even a religious issue. But that did not matter to Rove. All he cared about was that it worked. For a while.

32 | LIFE AFTER ROVE

I N THE ELECTION OF 2004, George Bush won the religious vote overwhelmingly, Republicans held a strong majority in both houses of Congress, and many governorships and state legislatures stayed or went Republican. Karl Rove spoke of this as the basis for building a permanent Republican majority. A mere two years later, in the midterm elections of 2006, Democrats captured both houses of Congress, ousting some of the most religiously conservative members—Senator Rick Santorum of Pennsylvania, Representative John Hostettler of Indiana, and Representative Jim Ryun of Kansas. The Catholic vote, which had gone 52 percent Republican in 2004, went 55 percent Democratic in 2006. The Latino vote, which Rove had coaxed up to 45 percent for Republicans in the first year, shrank back to 30 percent in the second. Wins in the states gave Democrats 23 legislatures to 17 for Republicans (the rest were divided) and 28 Democratic governors to 22 Republicans.

It would be easy to overstate the change in Rove's fortunes that came in 2006. The principal reason for the Republicans' troubles was not a failure of the religious coalition but distress and disaffection over the war in Iraq. Nonetheless, there were signs that faith-based government had collapsed, and not merely from external blows. There was something shaky about the structure all along. It was a house of cards.

It is an interesting, though merely accidental, fact of our history that the three principal times of great Evangelical influence on the Republic's culture occurred, every one, at the beginning of a century—the Second Great Awakening at the start of the nineteenth century, the Fundamentalist movement of the twentieth, and the faith-based movement of the twenty-first. It may also be coincidental that they ran shorter times from one to the next. The Second Awakening began to fall apart after about thirty years, done in by the schisms over slavery. It took about twenty years for the Fundamentalists to be discredited by the failing of Prohibition and the Scopes trial. It seems like the Rove religious era ran for barely a decade—if in fact it is failing.

But is it? Looking back on it, we can see that it was always less securely based than it looked. Take the initial triumph of Bush's election in 2000. Not only did Bush come in through a disputed election after losing the popular vote. The Democratic Left lost to the Republican Right because it flirted with a candidacy of the elitists, giving just enough votes to Ralph Nader to make Al Gore lose Florida. "The numbers here are compelling. Even if 90 percent of Nader's supporters had stayed home [in Florida] had he not run, the remaining 9,000 voters would have provided an ample margin for Gore, even if they only split 60-40 for Gore over Bush."[1] This means that the voters for Nader are responsible for the war in Iraq, for the huge tax cuts (and resulting deficit), and the whole faith-based government that resulted from the 2000 election.

Many Democrats foresaw this as a possible outcome of Nader's campaign and asked him to withdraw. The *Nation* magazine, which had endorsed him, would not go that far; but it urged him not to campaign energetically in states where he might throw the election to Bush. He rejected the idea and concentrated *especially* on those states. That is where he could get greater attention.[2] He said that depriving Al Gore of office was no great thing, since there was not a real difference between the parties. In fact, it would be a blessing for the Democrats to lose—it might force them to return to principle. After Gore did lose, Nader mocked him as contemptible.[3] Even some of Nader's original followers had told him he could turn over the courts to extreme nominees put forward by Bush—which did not alarm him a bit.

That was a position the Evangelicals would never take, no matter what the circumstances. For them, control of Supreme Court nominations was the most vital issue in the campaign. They blamed the Court for many of their troubles, indeed for all the many things wrong with the country—the godless schools, the free rein to pornography, the protection of women's rights and gay rights; but, above all, the protection of mass murder, which is the way they saw abortion. The Religious Right had watched with sharpest eyes the shrinking of support for abortion on the Court—first 7-2 (*Roe v. Wade*, 1973), then 6-3 (*City of Akron v. Akron Center for Reproductive Rights*, 1983), then 5-4 (*Thornburgh v. American College of Obstetricians and Gynecologists*, 1986), and then a divided majority of 5-3 for supporting a limited *Roe* (*Webster v. Reproductive Health Services*, 1989) and a divided majority of 5-4 for an even more limited *Roe* (*Planned Parenthood v. Casey*, 1992). The Right felt that the Court had reached a tipping point, that all that was needed was one or two more justices to bring down *Roe*, and they knew that their only chance for achieving that was to have a Republican president nominating future justices.

Rove was counting on the intensity and discipline of those concerned with abortion to counter the less focused priorities of leftists and Independents. His whole effort was not to woo Independents, but to keep them apathetic or irrelevant. On many issues—stem cell research, the environment, reasonable gun control, what might be called "Terri Schiavo issues" (living wills, death with dignity)—where the majority was not with him—Rove would not endanger the hold on his righteous core by any gestures of reconciliation with the moderates. By weaving together a chain of marginal concerns he could prevail over a mushier public opinion that was centrist. Grover Norquist, an ally of Rove and a major player on the Right through his Americans for Tax Reform organization, explained the strategy of mobilizing minority groups.

If you want the votes of people who are [simultaneously] good
on guns, good on taxes, and good on faith issues, that is a very
small intersection of voters. But if you say: Give me the votes
of anybody who agrees with you on any of these issues, that is
a much bigger section of the population. . . . And if you add
more things like property rights and home schooling, you can
do even better.[4]

Norquist himself, with his free-market absolutism, represented a key
part of Rove's coalition, the Libertarians. They were not happy with the
social-issues conservatives, who let government interfere with people's
morals. But they were so enamored of Bush's tax cuts, and of opposition
to the regulation of industry, that they were willing to go along with the
Evangelicals to keep Republicans in office cutting taxes.

IGNORING THE MIDDLE

THERE WAS a juggling aspect to Rove's act, the sleight of hand that
kept moralists and Libertarians under the same yoke. On issue after
issue, these insular minorities had to keep defying a more diffuse majority. How, after all, do you keep working with abortion as the linchpin of
your coalition when most Americans want abortion to be safe, rare, and
legal? How long can you count on people not to notice that your groups
want abortions to be safe only because never performed? Decade after
decade roughly two-thirds of the population has opposed the repeal of
Roe v. Wade. Some in this majority were willing to exclude late-term
abortions, and to impose some restrictions, like parental consent for
minors. But on the basic issue of letting a woman choose, rather than
having the state preclude any option but delivery of every conception,
they have solidly held to one view. In a 2003 CBS–*New York Times* poll, 77
percent said that abortion should be legally available, either in unlimited
ways (39 percent) or with some limits (38 percent), as opposed to only 22
percent who said it should be made illegal.[5]

Abortion is so common now that banning it would directly affect the entire population. The Guttmacher Institute finds that 43 percent of American women with unwilled pregnancies will have an abortion, half of those before they are twenty-five. This applies to almost all parts of the population. Those having abortions are 43 percent Protestant and 27 percent Catholic. Since there are three times as many Protestants as Catholics in the population, the Catholics proportionally get many more abortions than the Protestants.[6] Even the Evangelicals are not united in opposition to abortion. The polls analyzed by Andrew Greeley and Michael Hout show that only 10 percent of conservative Christians opposed abortion under all conditions and only 19 percent opposed it when the woman's health was at stake.[7] The others opposed it in limited ways.

If the pro-life forces get their way, it will no doubt be as disastrous for them as Prohibition was for the Fundamentalists. Prohibition demonstrated the difficulty of imposing a moral regime on people who do not agree with the moral principle involved. Prohibition did not stop alcohol consumption, it just drove it underground, where it bred corruption, defiance, and death. More people drank in criminal company and in criminal circumstances, and drank whatever dangerous beverages were available (wood alcohol, bathtub gin, and the like), while bribing officials and rewarding gangsters for making this possible. Why would a law against abortion be any different?

Some predict an idyllic solution to the problem. They say that revocation of *Roe* would not really outlaw abortion. It would just return it to the states, where it should have been in the first place. States where there is a majority opposed to abortion would ban it, and the rest would allow it. But given the overall numbers in favor of abortion, those states banning it would have a sizable proportion determined to flout that law, by illegal operations, collaboration with neighbor states allowing it, or collusion with corruptible authorities. We are back to the Prohibition days. Besides, committed Evangelicals who consider abortion murder would be just as active against it at the state as at the national level.

536 | Head and Heart

Extremism in the Defense of Life

B^Y IGNORING the majority view of abortion, one encourages the tight circle of true believers to ever more extreme views. This had already been proved in 1996 when Richard John Neuhaus, President Bush's adviser on "life issues" and the sponsor of the Evangelicals and Catholics Together movement, sponsored a symposium of essayists in his journal under the heading "The End of Democracy? The Judicial Usurpation of Politics." Essay after essay asked, can a government that lets its courts sanction murder be called legitimate, with a claim on the obedience of its citizens? Robert Bork answered the question: Not for long.

> It seems safe to say that, as our institutional arrangements now
> stand, the Court can never be made a legitimate element of a
> basically democratic polity. . . . Perhaps an elected official will
> one day simply refuse to comply with a Supreme Court
> decision. That suggestion will be regarded as shocking, but it
> should not be.[8]

In his essay for the symposium Chuck Colson, the man who went to jail for Watergate "dirty tricks" and found God there, called the *Roe* decision a "horrendous offense against God." Have we reached the point, he asked, where "government becomes sufficiently corrupt that a believer must resist it"? Not quite, he concluded, but "we are fast approaching that point." Only repeal of *Roe* can keep that point from arriving.[9] Hadley Arkes wrote that "the courts are making the political regime unlivable for serious Christians and Jews."[10] Russell Hittinger warned:

> It is late in the day, and our options have dwindled. Either
> right-minded citizens will have to disobey orders or perhaps
> relinquish offices of public authority, or the new constitutional
> rules will have to be challenged and reformed.[11]

Robert George made the same point in his essay, called simply "The Tyrant State."

Though two members of the *First Things* board—Gertrude Himmelfarb and Walter Berns—resigned in protest at this call for rebellion in the magazine, the Bush White House would later recruit two of the symposiasts—Hadley Arkes and Robert George—to assure conservatives that Bush's nominee for the Court, John Roberts, could be trusted on "life issues."[12] Which is why some of those who have acted violently against clinics and doctors performing abortions compare themselves to Dietrich Bonhoeffer, the pacifist minister who came to justify killing Hitler. The concept of murder in the millions can drive people to extremes. It was probably expectable that a former Presbyterian minister would say that assassinating Supreme Court justices who voted for *Roe* would be a just way of protecting human life.[13]

That former minister, Paul Hill, telephoned the Phil Donahue television show and asked to appear in defense of a man, Michael Griffin, who had just killed a doctor who performed abortions, David Gunn. Hill appeared on the show days after the murder, and told Dr. Gunn's son, as he later said on his Web site, that "I compared killing Dr. Gunn to killing a Nazi concentration camp 'doctor.'" This would be a frequent comparison for the anti-abortionists. The very next year (1994), Hill imitated Griffin, killing another doctor who practiced abortion, along with his escort, and wounding his wife. To defend his act, he posted on his Web site a forty-three-page treatise, riddled with biblical citations, arguing that all good citizens should join him in killing the baby killers.[14]

Church groups led a "Free Paul Hill" campaign.[15] Columnist Michael Kinsley argued that, if their premise is right, they were only being consistent in doing so.[16] If abortion is mass murder, it must be stopped by all means. But is their premise right? Many Evangelicals think it is. That is why four more doctors were killed in America and one in Canada, while many others were wounded in attempted killings. Bombings and attempted bombings of clinics took place in the hundreds, and threats in the thousands (including the 554 anthrax scares in 2001).

THE REVOLT OF THE MODERATES

EVEN BEFORE the 2006 elections, people on the Right were calling for an end to Evangelical extremism. In reaction to the religious campaign for Terri Schiavo's life, the former senator from Missouri John Danforth wrote an op-ed column in the *New York Times* deploring the takeover of the Republican Party by the Religious Right.[17] Danforth is an Episcopal priest with a long record of opposing *Roe v. Wade*—he even took a case against it to the Supreme Court when he was the attorney general of Missouri.[18] He was also a principal supporter of Clarence Thomas's nomination to the Supreme Court. Yet in 2006 he denounced the tactics of the pro-lifers as a call for extreme judicial activism.[19] He went on after that to rebuke religious scaremongers like James Dobson, Pat Robertson, and Jerry Falwell. Danforth favors civil unions and partner benefits for gays, but not the sacrament of marriage. Yet he roundly condemns James Dobson for words like these: "Saying there's a constitutional guarantee for two homosexuals to marry is just a few steps away from saying there's a constitutional guarantee to marry more than one person, or for relatives to marry, even for people to marry their pets."

Danforth responded that there is no sane likelihood that courts will legitimate incest or bestiality. Proclaiming such a danger was done to support the misnamed Protection of Marriage Amendment, as if marriage were endangered by loving gay couples.

> America's divorce rate is now 50 percent, and marriage is under attack from a number of quarters: finances, promiscuity, alcohol and drugs, the pressures of work, cultural acceptance of divorce, et cetera. But it is incomprehensible that one of these threats is [gay marriage]. . . . I think that the only purpose served by the campaign for the ["protection of marriage"] amendment is the humiliation of gay Americans advocated by the Christian Right and eagerly supported by its suitors in the Republican Party. To call it a constitutional amendment

designed to defend marriage makes it seem something loftier
than gay bashing. But in reality it is gay bashing.[20]

Yet forty-eight Republican senators voted for the amendment, which
had no chance of passage and whose only purpose was to allow the senators to be seen in an act of gay bashing.

Danforth's plea for a new civility was taken up by a number of Evangelicals and other conservatives. Jimmy Carter expressed a concern at
the Right's smearing ways in his 2005 book, *Our Endangered Values: America's Moral Crisis*, a work that rose to number one on best-seller lists.
Andrew Sullivan, the Burkean conservative who opposes abortion beyond the first six weeks of pregnancy, was nonetheless scathing on the
"instant of conception" pro-life extremists in his 2006 book *The Conservative Soul: How We Lost It, How to Get It Back*. Joel Hunter, the pastor of a
megachurch in Florida, was elected president of the Christian Coalition,
an organization founded by Pat Robertson in 1989. But on November 22,
2006, he resigned his office because the Coalition's board objected to his
making poverty, the environment, and a living wage important issues, as
well as abortion and gay marriage. According to Hunter, "They pretty
much said, 'These issues are fine, but they're not our issues, that's not our
base.'"[21] Rick Warren, pastor of the large Saddleback Church in California and the author of the wildly popular book *The Purpose-Driven Life*,
has made similar pleas for a Christian concern with the poor and the
suffering.

What caused this reaction on the Rove side of the spectrum was not
so much a disagreement on moral issues, but revulsion at what Danforth
called the bullying (and sometimes mendacious) approach of the Religious Right. Jeffrey Hart, a longtime editor of the conservative *National
Review* (and the author of its official history), joined the revolt:

> The Bush administration has devoted millions to faith-based
> organizations promoting abstinence, but in doing so is telling
> flagrant lies: that condoms fail to prevent HIV 31 percent of the
> time during heterosexual intercourse (2 percent is accurate),

that abortion leads to sterility (elective abortion does not), that
touching a person's genitals can cause pregnancy; that HIV can
be spread through sweat and tears; that a 43-day-old fetus is a
"thinking person"; and that half of gay teenagers have AIDS.
Some grants for faith-based programs stipulate that condoms
be discussed only in connection with their failure.[22]

If this reaction is voiced among conservatives themselves, one can
understand how Independents suddenly mobilized in the 2006 elections.
Some Libertarians were seeing their support of the Rove team as a
devil's bargain. They were already disillusioned by the fact that Bush
had not cut government spending but increased it. Bruce Bartlett, a
Republican stalwart who had worked for the first President Bush, was
fired from a conservative think tank when he published a book in 2006
called *Impostor: How George Bush Bankrupted America and Betrayed the Reagan
Legacy.* Bartlett's conservative credentials were impeccable. He had
worked for and with Jack Kemp, Jude Wanniski, Gary Bauer, and the
Cato Institute. Barlett was not the only conservative who decided that
Bush was a big-government liberal when it came to spending. Peggy
Noonan wrote a *Wall Street Journal* column on May 16, 2006, saying: "If
I'd thought he was a big-spending Rockefeller Republican—that is, if I'd
thought he was a man who could not imagine and had never absorbed
the damage big spending does—I wouldn't have voted for him."

This revolt on the Right was not unconnected with disillusionment
over the Iraq war. Even before he published *Impostor,* Bartlett had written a
"dump Cheney" newspaper column—which was called an ancillary reason for his firing from the National Center for Policy Analysis.[23] And
Peggy Noonan called it a "dreadful mistake" for Bush to reject the advice
of the Baker-Hamilton Iraq Study Group. She said "my heart fell" when
Bush went on television to call for an escalation of the war.[24] The war
course followed by Bush was similar in ethos to his domestic extremism.
As Karl Rove used a tight little chain of minorities to oppose the national
majority, the Dick Cheney team openly ignored and disdained world
opinion to launch a pre-emptive and unilateral war. "The world's only

superpower" had no reason to consult or care for any other nation's views when it decided to impose its will on a whole region like the Middle East.

This go-it-alone attitude fit very well with Rove's refusal to compromise or to build beyond his true-believers base. The scorn heaped on nations like France and Germany, for not joining Bush's rush to war, had the same tone as the Religious Right's contempt for domestic liberals. It should be remembered that the righteousness audible in President Bush's attack on the "axis of evil" was put into his mouth by the Evangelical speechwriter Michael Gerson. Godly attacks on the godless were as much a part of the international policy of the Bush administration as of Karl Rove's domestic initiatives. General Boykin was the supreme symbol of that fact.

This smugness factor was further undercut by scandals that broke out in the months before the 2006 elections. Conservative Republican congressman Mark Foley of Florida was caught sending erotic messages to pageboys, and Pastor Ted Haggard, the president of the National Association of Evangelicals, was expelled from his own Colorado church for his compromising association with a male prostitute. Haggard was a close associate of James Dobson, so conservatives had one more reason to heed John Danforth's criticisms of the Dobson bluster and fearmongering. The impression was also growing that the Religious Right was using religions in a particularly crass way. In the year before the 2006 elections a CBS poll on the Terri Schiavo case found that 82 percent of Americans felt the government had no business entering the case. Just 13 percent said that they thought the intervention came from concern over the woman involved, while 74 percent said it was done for political gain.[25] The suspicion that religion was being used as a cover for politics was confirmed when John DiIulio and David Kuo admitted that the faith-based initiative was such a ploy.

Liberals, looking at the troubles of the Evangelicals, had good reason to fear that they would slip into the same trap. Danforth criticized the Left for trying to counter the God talk of the Right with an equal-but-opposite claim to be conveying God's will to the voters. He explicitly criticized Jim Wallis for calling his 2005 book *God's Politics,* as if only liberalism could be "religious and politically correct." Speaking for moderates, Danforth wrote: "We believe that no one should presume to embody God's truth, including ourselves."[26]

Sobered by the Iraq war, by a collapse of the strutting confidence of the Bush foreign policy team and the Rove domestic preachers, some hoped that the nation was ready to renounce the polarizing absolutisms of its recent past. President Bush had scorned the "kinder, gentler" approach of his own father's presidency. But now a yearning for it had arisen. An event shortly after the 2006 elections might have been a harbinger of this. Rick Warren, the Evangelical pastor of Saddleback Church in California, had been for some time saying that religion was not the monopoly of one party or faction. Asked whether he was Right-Wing or Left-Wing, he said, "I'm for the whole bird. One-winged birds fly in circles." In accord with that stance, Warren invited a Republican senator and a Democratic senator to address his parish on World AIDS Day. Introducing Sam Brownback and Barack Obama, he told his congregation: "I've got two friends here, a Republican and a Democrat. Why? Because you've got to have two wings to fly."[27]

Warren received such heavy criticism from the Right for inviting Obama to his church that Obama offered not to come.[28] But Warren said that dialogue was important, and Obama appeared. Senator Brownback spoke first, and said that in the Evangelical church he felt a different dynamic from the last time he had appeared with Obama—before a black audience. Now, Brownback said, "Welcome to my house." To which Obama responded, when he rose to speak: "This is my house too. This is God's house."[29] The senators were gracious to each other, and both took an HIV test, to help remove the stigma from that procedure. In his speech, which was received with a standing ovation, Senator Obama politely opposed the Evangelicals' opposition to the use of condoms and other measures to prevent the spread of AIDS. His speech was a blend of Enlightened and Evangelical concerns, of reason and apostolic motives:

> I don't think we can deny that there is a moral and spiritual
> component to prevention—that in too many places all over the

world where AIDS is prevalent (including our own country by
the way)—the relationship between men and women, between
sexuality and spirituality, has broken down and needs to be
repaired. . . . These are issues of prevention we cannot walk
away from. When a husband thinks it's acceptable to hide his
infidelity from his wife, it's not only a sin, it's a potential death
sentence. And when rape is still seen as a woman's fault and a
woman's shame, but promiscuity is a man's prerogative, it is a
problem of the heart that no government can solve. It is,
however, a place where local ministries and churches like
Saddleback can and have made a real difference— by providing
people with a moral framework to make better choices. Having
said that, I also believe that we cannot ignore that abstinence
and fidelity may too often be the ideal and not the reality—that
we are dealing with flesh and blood men and women and not
abstractions—and that if condoms, and (potentially)
microbicides can prevent millions of deaths, they should be
made more widely available. I know there are those who, out of
sincere religious conviction, oppose such measures. And with
these folks I must respectfully and unequivocally disagree. I do
not accept the notion that those who make mistakes in their
lives should be given an effective death sentence. Nor am I
willing to stand by and allow those who are entirely innocent —
wives who, because of the culture they live in, often have no
power to refuse sex with their husbands, or children who are
born with the infection as a consequence of their parents'
behavior—suffer when condoms or other measures would have
kept them from harm. . . . The reason for us to step up our
efforts can't simply be instrumental. There are more fundamental reasons to care. Reasons related to our humanity. Reasons of
the soul. Like no other illness, AIDS tests our ability to put ourselves in someone else's shoes—to empathize with the plight of
our fellow man. While most would agree that the AIDS orphan
or the transfusion victim or the wronged wife contracted the

disease though no fault of their own, it has too often been easy
for some to point to the unfaithful husband or the promiscuous
youth or the gay man and say, "This is your fault. You have
sinned." I don't think that a satisfactory response. My faith
reminds me that we all are sinners. My faith also tells me that—
as Pastor Rick has said—it is not a sin to be sick. My Bible tells
me that when God sent his only Son to earth, it was to heal the
sick and comfort the weary; to feed the hungry and clothe the
naked; to befriend the outcast and redeem those who strayed
from righteousness. Living his example is the hardest kind of
faith—but it is surely the most rewarding.

Obama was making a gesture for the Evangelicals to engage in a rea-
soned dialogue. For this to work, liberals should be as ready to address the
religious concerns of their opposite numbers. Danforth, for instance, said
that the Right should not indulge in the "slippery slope" arguments of a
James Dobson—that approval of gay marriage would lead to incest and
bestiality. The Left should not engage in its variant of this approach. Some
said, for instance, that any concession on abortion rights would lead to the
loss of the right to choose. But there are good reasons to consider regulation of late-term abortions (while protecting the health of the mother) or
parental notification of underage girls (while remaining aware that some
pregnancies are caused by a parent's incest). Recognizing valid concerns
like this would not endanger the general right of choice that most people
have long supported. Yet when Senator Hillary Clinton raised such concerns, she was called a traitor to the feminist cause.

Jimmy Carter, who is personally opposed to abortion for religious
reasons (which I have argued are not relevant), made suggestions that
opponents of abortion should accept for the prevention of abortion
short of banning it altogether.

It has long been known that there are fewer abortions in nations
where prospective mothers have access to contraceptives, the

assurance that they and their babies will have good health care, and at least enough income to meet their basic needs. The most notable examples are Belgium and the Netherlands, where only seven abortions occur among each thousand women of childbearing age. In some predominantly Roman Catholic countries, where all abortions are illegal and few social services are available, such as Peru, Brazil, Chile, and Colombia, the abortion rate is fifty per thousand. According to the World Health Organization, this is the highest ratio of unsafe abortions [in the world].[30]

The Religious Right says that the only way to prevent abortion is to end teenage sex. That is the basis of their abstinence-only program, which has failed repeatedly. The reason is not far to seek. Even many religious people now do not think that premarital sex is wrong. Greeley and Hout call this the "partnership revolution" among *conservative* Christians. Although 48 percent of the married conservatives think extramarital sex is always wrong, 76 percent of the unmarried had engaged in sex within the year before the poll.[31] If that is the case for conservative Christians, the rate in the larger and more secular society is clearly higher. For comparative purposes one might look at the attitudes of Catholics under thirty. As far back as 1992, 88 percent of them said that extramarital sex between caring couples is acceptable.[32]

In such a culture, for a supposedly Enlightened government to oppose contraception, sex education, and family planning is sub-primitive. Quoting Carter again:

Canadian and European young people are about equally active sexually; but, deprived of proper sex education, American girls are five times as likely to have a baby as French girls, seven times as likely to have an abortion, and seventy times as likely to have gonorrhea as girls in the Netherlands. Also, the

incidence of HIV/AIDS among American teenagers is five
times that of the same age in Germany.[33]

The way to a post-Rove world is open, if only the American electorate
will follow it. We do not have to think in the absolutes that knotted
American discourse in futile acrimony through the first years of this
century. There is a bigger world out there.

EPILOGUE | SEPARATION NOT SUPPRESSION

W HEN I TAUGHT the history of the Constitution at Johns
Hopkins and Northwestern, I regularly asked my students three
questions: (1) Did they believe in the separation of church and state?
Almost all said yes. (2) Did they believe in the separation of religion and
politics? Most, again, said yes. (3) Did they believe in the separation of
morality and politics? To this none said yes. The answers to (2) and
(3) were inconsistent, since most people's standards of morality are
affected by their religion. Conceptions of what is right and wrong in
politics are a subset of what people think right or wrong in all areas of
their lives. The students were bright enough to say, in that case, that the
answers to (1) and (2) seemed inconsistent as well. How, if religion and
politics are connected, can church and state not be connected?

They can be separated because people's religious views are not
limited to their church membership, and they are not limited to state
action. The highest value of most religious systems is love, which goes
beyond justice. But the state cannot put love above justice. Jesus said to
love one's enemies, turn the other cheek when assailed, and sacrifice

oneself for the love of God and man. The state is not in the self-sacrificing business.

There is a difference, that is, between one's religious motive and one's political argument. An individual may support state aid to the poor because he or she loves Jesus. But the state cannot require a love for Jesus. The basis for its action must be natural justice, as determined by natural reason. John Danforth made this point with regard to "life issues" like abortion or stem cell research. Some people believe that personhood begins at conception, but they have not been able to persuade the majority of Americans on the grounds of natural reason. They are asking, therefore, that their own religious conviction (or what they conceive of as a religious mandate) be enacted into law. "Legislators considering banning such [stem cell] research should realize that they are being asked to establish one religious point of view and to oppose another."[1]

To take another example: John Adams and Thomas Jefferson both said that a belief in the afterlife strengthens morals, but neither would consider it right for the state to improve public morals by mandating a belief in the afterlife. They could encourage the belief, as all citizens can; but Disestablishment blocks any use of the state's coercive force to make the belief a requirement of citizenship. And if the state cannot require belief in an afterlife, it clearly cannot require belief in God as a *political* duty. Danforth, as an Episcopalian priest, distinguished his religious motives for action from the arguments he used in the Senate to back provisions called for by justice, arguments addressed to those of any faith or of none.

The motives of voters can be religious without having those sanctioned by a political orthodoxy. I personally knew many Catholics who voted for John F. Kennedy in 1960 out of pride that one of their own was reaching such a high station, but that did not mean that Catholicism was established as the national religion. Kennedy said himself that he would not govern as a Catholic but as the president of all the people, including the majority that was Protestant (and of all other sects or lack thereof). In various parts of this book I have argued that the separation of church and state has greatly benefited religion, as Madison and Jefferson predicted that it would. It permits the unfettered play of worship, a diversity of denominations, an energetic ministry, a higher level of religious belief and practice than other developed nations enjoy. The separation of the churches from the state has not led to the suppression of religion by the state. Just the opposite. It meant the freeing of religion. We can see in the past how a breaching of the separation led to setbacks for religion. Consider the three times in the Republic's life when Evangelicals had an extraordinary impact on the national culture.

The first time was the period of the great religious surge, the Second Great Awakening. It was more vigorous than the later periods of heightened religiosity. A part of this success probably came from the fact that the religious activities were not based on support from the government. That was the high time of voluntary associations, as Tocqueville noticed, and also a time of minimal government. The result, as we saw, was a "do-it-yourself" religion that flourished from its own resources. If the bitter schisms over slavery had not arisen within the churches in the 1830s and 1840s, there is no telling how long the Awakening would have survived— up to 1860 perhaps, when the Civil War rent all of the social fabric.

At the beginning of the twentieth century, the Fundamentalists had their time in the sun, achieving such milestones as Prohibition, the banning of Darwin in the schools, and Sabbatarian victories like the 1912 closing of post offices on Sunday. This time, religion called on government to enforce or replace its own action—the state banned alcohol when the preachers' sermons and the revivalists' thunderings failed to achieve the same result. And enacting state laws against Darwinism led to the Scopes trial and the discrediting of Fundamentalists. The political disaster of Prohibition was, to some degree, a disaster for religion, which had staked so much on the "glorious experiment."

In the third period of Evangelical hypertropism, that orchestrated by Karl Rove, there was a similar discrediting of religion as a political tool, best exemplified in the national revulsion at the intrusion of preachers and politicians into the family decisions over Terri Schiavo. Senator Danforth deplored the way religion had become a cause of bitter division in America during this era, instead of the champion of amity and reconciliation he thinks the more proper role for religion. The anti-rational attacks on Darwin and doctors and scientific research culminated a growing anti-intellectualism in the Evangelical camp that was deplored by one of their own, Mark Noll: "At this stage in our existence, Evangelicals do not have a lot to offer in intellectual terms as such. We have frittered away a century or more, and have much catching up to do."[2] He found this typified in the attempt to forge a "creation science."

> Creation science has damaged Evangelicalism by making it much more difficult to think clearly about human origins, the age of the earth, and mechanisms of geological or biological change. But it has done more profound damage by undermining the ability to look at the world God has made and to understand what we see when we do look. Fundamentalist habits of mind have been more destructive than individual creationist conclusions. Because those habits of mind are compounded of unreflecting aspects of nineteenth-century procedure alongside tendentious aspects of fundamentalist ideology, they have done serious damage to Christian thinking.[3]

Noll points out that it was not always so. Evangelicals in the nineteenth century drew on aspects of the Enlightenment, keeping their own form of separation from the state, fostering Republicanism and reason in the form of Scottish common-sense epistemology in the colleges and seminaries growing out the Second Great Awakening.[4] In fact, Evangelicalism has been strongest when influenced by Enlightenment. And the opposite holds, too. Separation between church and state does not mean that there should be separation between Enlightened and Evangelical. As I said in the introduction, these are not separate churches or separate religions. They do not excommunicate each other. They are simply two tendencies, two temperaments, and an absolute or sterile division between them is stultifying. There is no reason why Enlightened religion *has* to become desiccated and cerebral, all light and no heat. Nor why the Evangelical *has* be to be mindlessly enthusiastic, all heat and no

light. If fact, at key moments in our history, key and representative figures have combined the best in both tendencies—Anthony Benezet
combining Gospel love with a rational critique of the Bible, or Abraham
Lincoln and Frederick Douglass combining the black churches' biblical
call for freedom with Transcendentalist philosophy. The same dynamic
can be found in some of the most inspiring leaders in our history—Jane
Addams, Martin Luther King Jr., Cesar Chavez, Dorothy Day, A. J.
Muste, and William Sloane Coffin.

Clearly there is a tension between the two force fields I have been
describing in this book. But it can be a creative tension as well as a dis-
ruptive one. And I do not want to exaggerate the different ethos felt
in each one. Even what some have called an extreme of Enlightened
Deism, the religion of Thomas Paine and Thomas Jefferson and John
Adams, left room for a fervent belief in divine providence and the afterlife. Jefferson cannot be considered to emit all light and no heat when he
writes a letter like this, consoling John Adams for the loss of his wife,
Abigail:

> It is of some comfort to us both that the term is not very distant
> at which we are to deposit, in the same cerement, our sorrows
> and suffering bodies, and to ascend in essence to an ecstatic
> meeting with the friends we have loved and lost, and whom we
> shall still love and never lose again.[5]

Similarly, though Transcendentalism is an Enlightened religion, it had a
mystical side that approaches the personalism of the Evangelicals.

On the other hand, even the most extreme Evangelicals—which I
take to mean the doomsday Dispensationalists—yield in wartime to the
optimism and pragmatism that characterize most aspects of American
culture most of the time.

But for long stretches of our history the religion that attracted most
people has been Evangelical—the whole colonial time, for instance, up
to the Enlightenment. And then, after the founding period, there were
three stretches when Evangelicals had their greatest impact on the

national culture—early in each of the succeeding centuries. At the beginning of the nineteenth century, the explosion of Evangelical religions, especially of Methodism, made up what is often called the Second Great Awakening. This was a do-it-yourself religiosity which asked for little governmental assistance. And the churches that provided their own vitality also brought about their own disintegration, into the competing Northern and Southern churches torn apart over slavery in the 1830s and 1840s. It is hard to strike the right balance between the two religious tendencies, and I have described many periods when they got wildly out of balance. But the comforting reflection is that hard self-examination on both sides has brought them back toward the precarious but persisting balance. It is an inspiring thing to watch.

ACKNOWLEDGMENTS

I am grateful to those who read parts of the book and
made valuable suggestions: Martin Marty, Mark Noll,
James Oakes, and Irv Brendlinger. My editor,
Scott Moyers, and my agent, Andrew Wylie,
gave essential support. My editor in chief,
as always, is Natalie.

❖

NOTES

INTRODUCTION

1. His Holiness the Dalai Lama, *The Universe in a Single Atom: The Convergence of Science and Spirituality* (Morgan Road Books, 2005).
2. I capitalize the adjective "Enlightened" because it refers to something arising from a specific era, and that era's effect on America. It is a parallel, therefore, to such phrases as "Renaissance religion," "Reformation religion," or "Reformed religion."
3. *Writings of Professor Bela Bates Edwards* (John P. Jewett, 1853), vol. 2, p. 498.
4. Sydney Ahlstrom quoted in Richard Hofstadter, *Anti-Intellectualism in American Life* (Vintage Books, 1963), p. 119.
5. Sidney E. Mead, *The Old Religion in the Brave New World: Reflections on the Relation Between Christendom and the Republic* (University of California Press, 1977), p. 2.
6. Mark A. Noll, Nathan O. Hatch, and George M. Marsden, *The Search for Christian America*, expanded ed. (Helmers & Howard, 1989), p. 29.
7. Some try to sneak in a reference to God—even more specifically to Jesus—in the chronological convention that dates the Constitution as signed "in the Year of *our Lord* one thousand seven hundred and eighty seven." That introduction to the signatures that follow is separate from the body of the text, is purely conventional, and is usually omitted in copies of the Constitution as currently used, which go directly from the body of the original text to the appended amendments.
8. Mark A. Noll, *America's God: From Jonathan Edwards to Abraham Lincoln* (Oxford University Press, 2002).
9. John M. Murrin, "No Awakening, No Revolution? More Counterfactual Speculations," *Reviews in American History* 11 (June 1983), p. 164.

1. MARY DYER MUST DIE

1. The claim that the Quaker martyrs were suicides was asserted in an October 18, 1659, declaration of the General Court, which pronounced them *felones de se* (M 2.525–26).
2. Dyer would have agreed with Milton that "New presbyter is but old priest writ large" (the final line from the sonnet "On the New Forces of Conscience Under the Long Parliament," 1646).
3. For the death of Mary Dyer, see Nathaniel B. Shurtleff, ed., *Records of the Governor and Company of the Massachusetts Bay in New England, 1628–1686* (Boston, 1853–54), vol. 4, part 1, pp. 383–85, and Horatio Roger, *Mary Dyer of Rhode Island: The Quaker Martyr That Was Hanged on Boston Common, June 1, 1664* (Providence: Preston and Rounds, 1896), pp. 40–62. For the rituals involved, see David D. Hall, *Worlds of Wonder, Days of Judgment: Popular Religious Belief in Early New England* (Harvard University Press, 1985), pp. 178–84.

4. Samuel Willard, quoted in Perry Miller, *Errand into the Wilderness* (Harvard University Press, 1956), p. 145.

5. Nathaniel Ward, *The Simple Cobbler of Aggawam in America*, ed. by P. M. Zall (University of Nebraska Press, 1969), p. 6.

6. Perry Miller, *The New England Mind: From Colony to Province* (Harvard University Press, 1953), p. 123.

7. Richard Mather, *Farewell Exhortation to the Church and People of Dorchester in New England* (Cambridge: Samuel Green, 1657), pp. 5–6.

8. A modern scholar has adopted Cotton Mather's view of "the rantings of the Quakers," of "the depth of their perfidy," prompting them to refuse "the liberty to stay away." Jonathan M. Chu, *Neighbors, Friends, or Madmen: The Puritan Adjustment to Quakerism in Seventeenth-Century Massachusetts Bay* (Greenwood Press, 1985), pp. 44, 50. According to Chu, "Dyer's mad desire to subvert order" must have been "a form of criminal madness" (p. 48).

9. David S. Lovejoy, *Religious Enthusiasm in the New World* (Harvard University Press, 1985), p. 117.

10. The Pilgrims' settlement at Plymouth Bay in 1620 was even sketchier in its authorization than was that of the Massachusetts Bay Company—the Pilgrims claimed to be part of the Virginia Company's domain!

11. Miller, *New England Mind*, p. 167.

12. John Cotton, *A Discourse About Civil Government in a New Plantation Whose Design Is Religion* (Cambridge, 1663), p. 6.

13. Lovejoy, *Religious Enthusiasm*, pp. 125–26.

14. Three Quakers had their ears removed on one day (Chu, *Neighbors*, p. 41).

15. George Francis Dow and Mary G. Thresher, eds., *Records and Files of the Quarterly Courts of Essex Count, Massachusetts, 1636–1696* (Essex Institute, 1911–21), vol. 2, p. 107.

16. Roger, *Mary Dyer*, pp. 37–38.

17. Arthur Worrall, *Quakers in the Colonial Northeast* (University Press of New England, 1980), p. 12.

18. Nathaniel B. Shurtleff, *Records of the Colony of New Plymouth in New England, 1620–1692* (Boston, 1855–61), vol. 10, p. 181. After tolerance had been forced on New England by royal interference, Cotton Mather reluctantly came to the conclusion that the Rhode Island approach would have been better: "I am verily persuaded these miserable Quakers would in a little while (as we have now seen) have come to nothing, if the civil magistrate had not inflicted any civil penalty upon them; nor do I look upon hereticide as an evangelical way for the extinguishing of heresies" (M 2.525). But he took a different view earlier.

19. John Winthrop, *A Short Story of the Rise, Reign, and Ruin of the Antinomians, Familists, and Libertines*, in David D. Hall, ed., *The Antinomian Controversy, 1630–1638* (Duke University Press, 1990), pp. 280–82.

20. *The Complete Writings of Roger Williams* (Russell & Russell, 1963), vol. 5, p. xxi.

21. Worrall, *Quakers*, pp. 32–35.

22. Williams, *Complete Writings*, vol. 5, p. 7.

23. Ibid., pp. 306–7, xxii, 134.

24. Ibid., p. 43. He returns to this offense obsessively—see pp. 28, 59–60, 134, 241–42.

25. Ibid., p. 62. George Fox responded by saying that the Quakers' physical nakedness showed up the spiritual nakedness of their oppressors: "We do believe thee, in that dark persecuting bloody Spirit that thou and the New England priests are bewitched in, you cannot believe that you are naked from God and his clothing, and blind, and therefore had the Lord in his power moved some of his sons and daughters to go naked. And so they were prophets and prophetesses to the nation, as many sober men have confessed since, though you and the old persecuting priests in New England remain in your blindness and nakedness." Fox, *A New England Fire-Brand Quenched* (London: *sine nomine*, 1678), pp. 229–30.

26. Williams, *Complete Writings*, p. 39.

27. Ibid., pp. 44–45.

28. Ibid., p. 261.

29. Edmund Morgan, *Roger Williams: The Church and the State* (Harcourt, Brace & World, 1967), pp. 56–61.

30. Mark A. Noll, George M. Marsden, and Nathan O. Hatch, *The Search for Christian America*, expanded ed. (Helmers & Howard, 1989), p. 36.

31. W 121. Kenneth Silverman notes that this notion of a "plastic" substrate to nature was very common in the physical thinking of the time. "Plastic spirit was a DNA-like program for matter." *The Life and Times of Cotton Mather* (Harper & Row, 1984), p. 122.

32. Silverman, *Life*, pp. 173–78.

33. W. C. Ford, ed., *The Diary of Cotton Mather* (Massachusetts Historical Society, 1912), vol. 1, pp. 86–87.

34. Winthrop, *Short Story*, p. 218.

35. Carla Gardina Pastana, *Quakers and Baptists in Colonial Massachusetts* (Cambridge University Press, 1991), p. 35.

36. Hall, *Worlds of Wonder*, pp. 188–89.

37. Edwin S. Gaustad, *Liberty of Conscience: Roger Williams in America* (Eerdmans, 1998), p. 182.

38. Winthrop, *Short Story*, pp. 280–81.

39. Ibid.

40. Ibid.

41. Ibid., p. 215.

42. Increase Mather, *A Brief History of the War with the Indians in New-England* (John Foster, 1676).

43. Shurtleff, *Records of Massachusetts Bay* (W. White, 1854), vol. 4, part 1, p. 451.

44. Winthrop, *Short Story*, pp. 275–76.

45. Cotton Mather, *Theopolis Americana: An Essay on the Golden City* (B. Green, 1710), p. 3.

46. Richard Bauckham, *Tudor Apocalypse* (Sutton Courtenay, 1978), p. 147.

47. Increase Mather, *Heaven's Alarm to the World*. In *Kometology*, Mather admitted natural explanations for comets' regular appearance, but still found a "speaking voice of Heaven in them."

48. Hall, *Worlds of Wonder*, p. 102.

49. Edward Ward, *A Trip to New England*, in H. W. Troyer, *Five Travel Scripts* (Columbia University Press, 1933), p. 5.

50. Richard Mather, *Farewell*, pp. 2–3.

51. Samuel Sewall to Cotton Mather, Dec. 25, 1684.
52. Cotton Mather, *Theopolis*, p. 43. Also p. 48: "America might be intended as a place where the worshipers of the glorious Jesus may be sheltered while fearful things are doing in the European world."
53. Samuel Sewall, *Proposals Touching the Accomplishment of Prophecies* (1713), pp. 6–7.
54. George Herbert, "The Church Militant."

2. THE PURITAN PSYCHE

1. Increase Mather, *An Essay for the Recording of Illustrious Providences* (Samuel Green, 1684), chapter 8.
2. Keith Thomas, *Religion and the Decline of Magic* (Penguin Books, 1979), pp. 561–62, 589–90.
3. Ibid., p. 594.
4. Ibid., pp. 535–36.
5. Frederick G. Drake, "Witchcraft in the American Colonies, 1647–62," *American Quarterly* 20 (1968), pp. 706, 714.
6. Benjamin Ray, "Salem Witch Trials," University of Virginia Web site; John Demos, *Entertaining Satan: Witchcraft and the Culture of Early New England* (Oxford University Press, 1982), pp. 401–9; Paul Boyer and Stephen Nissenbaum, *Salem-Village Witchcraft: A Documentary Record of Local Conflict in Colonial New England* (Wadsworth Publishing Company, 1993), pp. 375–82.
7. David D. Hall, *Worlds of Wonder, Days of Judgment: Popular Religious Belief in Early New England* (Harvard University Press, 1989), p. 214.
8. Richard Bauckham, *Tudor Apocalypse* (Sutton Courtenay, 1978), p. 96.
9. Ibid., p. 95.
10. See, for instance, Peter Stuyvesant's attempt to expel them from his fledgling province of New Amsterdam in 1654. He called Jews "hateful enemies and blasphemers of the name of Christ." Morris U. Schappes, *A Documentary History of the Jews in the United States, 1654–1875* (Citadel Press, 1950), p. 2.
11. M. Halsey Thomas, *The Diary of Samuel Sewall* (Farrar, Straus and Giroux, 1973), vol. 1, p. 178.
12. Michael Novak, *On Two Wings: Humbler Faith and Common Sense at the American Founding* (Encounter Books, 2002), pp. 7, 17. Novak argues from the concept of a Judeo-Christian America, a concept which was a product of the post–World War II era, as we shall see.
13. For making the nation an idol, see Mark A. Noll, George M. Marsden, and Nathan O. Hatch, *The Search for Christian America* (Helmers & Howard, 1989), pp. 31–36.
14. Jon Butler, *Awash in a Sea of Faith: Christianizing the American People* (Harvard University Press, 1990), p. 157.
15. Albert J. Raboteau, *Slave Religion: The "Invisible Institution" in the Antebellum South* (Oxford University Press, 1978), p. 4.
16. Cotton Mather, *The Negro Christianized* (B. Green, 1706), p. 25.
17. Ibid., pp. 3, 8.
18. Ibid., pp. 14–15.
19. Ibid., p. 26.
20. Ibid., p. 22.

21. Ibid., pp. 2–3; Cotton Mather, *Theopolis Americana: An Essay on the Golden City* (B. Green, 1710), pp. 21–23; Samuel Sewall, *The Selling of Joseph: A Memorial*, ed. Sidney Kaplan (University of Massachusetts Press, 1969), p. 2.

22. William Waller Hening, *The Statutes at Large* (Samuel Pleasants, 1809), vol. 1, p. 57.

23. John Smith, *A True Relation* (Wisconsin Historical Society Digital Archive, 2003), p. 32.

24. George Wilson Pierson, *The Founding of Yale: The Legend of the Forty Folios* (Yale University Press, 1988), p. 14; Samuel Eliot Morison, *The Founding of Harvard College* (Harvard University Press, 1935), pp. 161, 421, 428.

25. John Rolfe to Sir Thomas Dale, 1614, in Franklin J. Jameson, *Narratives of Early Virginia* (Charles Scribner's Sons, 1907), pp. 237–44.

26. Perry Miller, "Religion and Society in the Early Literature of Virginia," in *Errand Into the Wilderness* (Harvard University Press, 1956), pp. 99–140.

27. "New England's First Fruits" (1643), in Morison, *Founding,* pp. 421, 428.

28. Cotton Mather, *The Present State of New England* (Samuel Green, 1690), p. 38.

29. Edmund Morgan, *The Puritan Dilemma: The Story of John Winthrop* (Little, Brown and Company, 1958), p. 122.

30. Increase Mather, *A Brief History of the War with the Indians in New-England* (John Foster, 1676), pp. 3–4.

31. Ibid., p. 45.

32. Ibid., p. 4.

33. John Francis Sprague, *Sebastian Rale: A Maine Tragedy of the Eighteenth Century* (Heintzmann Press, 1906). Francis Parkman has a shrewd chapter (chapter X) on Rasle in *A Half-Century of Conflict* (1892). Parkman also shows that some other French Jesuits were feared and resented by New England almost as much as Rasle was—Jacques Lamberville, for instance. See Parkman, *France and England in North America* (Library of America, 1983), vol. 2, pp. 94–97.

34. Whites regularly took scalps for bounty, but only from Indians. An exception was made for Rasle.

35. Of the roughly 750 individuals whose capture is recorded, about 300 were ransomed and 150 became Catholic converts. Donna M. Campbell, "Early American Captivity Narratives" (Literary Movements Web site, 2000). John Demos tells the moving story of a prominent Puritan minister whose family was captured in 1701, endured years of captivity, and suffered the anguish of seeing its young daughter become a convert, marry an Indian, and raise Catholic children. Demos, *The Unredeemed Captive: A Family Story from Early America* (Alfred A. Knopf, 1994).

36. Hawthorne wrote: "Would that the bloody old [*sic*] hag had been drowned in crossing Contocook River, or that she had sunk over her head and ears in a swamp, and been there buried, and summoned forth to confront her victims at the Day of Judgment." *American Magazine of Useful and Entertaining Knowledge,* May 1836, p. 397.

37. Drake, "Witchcraft," p. 709.

38. Paul Boyer and Stephen Nissenbaum, *The Salem Witchcraft Papers: Verbatim Transcripts of the Legal Documents of the Salem Witchcraft Outbreak of 1692* (Da Capo Press, 1977), vol. 2, p. 611.

39. Marylinne K. Roach, *The Salem Witch Trials: A Day-by-Day Chronicle of a Community Under Siege* (Cooper Square Press, 2002), pp. 337, 390.

40. Boyer and Nissenbaum, *Witchcraft Papers,* vol. 3, p. 768.

41. Roach, *Salem Witch Trials,* pp. 18, 57.

42. Boyer and Nissenbaum, *Witchcraft Papers,* vol. 3, pp. 745–57.

43. Ibid., vol. 1, p. 66.

44. Ibid., vol. 3, p. 769.

45. William Fulke, *A Rejoynder to Bristow's Replies in Defence of Allens Scroll of Article and Booke of Purgatorie* (1581).

46. The *Catholic Encyclopedia* conceded the virtual unanimity of early Protestantism in believing that the pope was Antichrist: "Luther, Calvin, Zwingli, Melanchthon, Bucer, Beza, Calixtus, Bengel, Michaelis, and almost all the Protestant writers of the Continent are cited as upholding this view; the same may be said of the English theologians Cranmer, Latimer, Ridley, Hooper, Hutchinson, Tyndale, Sandys, Philpot, Jewell, Rogers, Fulke, Bradford, King James and Andrewes." These were honored names in Puritan New England. See *Catholic Encyclopedia* (Robert Appleton Company, 1907), vol. 1, s.v. "Antichrist."

47. Peter Lake, "Anti-Popery: The Structure of a Prejudice," in Richard Cust and Ann Hughes, *Conflict in Early Stuart England* (Longman, 1989), p. 73.

48. David D. Hall, *The Antinomian Controversy, 1636–1638: A Documentary History,* 2nd ed. (Duke University Press, 1990), p. 8.

49. Christopher Hill, *The World Turned Upside Down: Radical Ideas During the English Revolution* (Viking Press, 1972).

50. E. Brooks Holifield, *Theology in America: Christian Thought from the Age of the Puritans to the Civil War* (Yale, 2003), pp. 71, 220, 320.

51. Hall, *Antinomian Controversy,* p. 217.

3. THE PURITAN CONSCIENCE

1. See Paul Emanuel Johnson, summarizing earlier studies, in *Psychology of Religion* (Abingdon-Cokesbury Press, 1959).

2. George Marsden, *Jonathan Edwards: A Life* (Yale University Press, 2003), p. 101.

3. Edmund S. Morgan, *The Genuine Article: A Historian Looks at Early America* (W. W. Norton, 2004), pp. 17, 19.

4. Patricia Caldwell, *The Puritan Conversion Narrative: The Beginning of American Expression* (Cambridge University Press, 1983), pp. 50, 66.

5. John H. Ball III, *Chronicling the Soul's Windings: Thomas Hooker and His Morphology of Conversion* (University Press of America, 1992), p. 85 and passim; Sargent Bush Jr., *The Writings of Thomas Hooker: Spiritual Adventures in Two Worlds* (University of Wisconsin Press, 1980), p. 149; Norman Pettit, *The Heart Prepared: Grace and Conversion in Puritan Spiritual Life* (Yale University Press, 1966), pp. 96–101.

6. Bush, *Writings of Thomas Hooker,* p. 49.

7. Caldwell, *Conversion Narrative,* pp. 77–78.

8. Bush, *Writings of Thomas Hooker,* pp. 82–83.

9. David D. Hall, *The Antinomian Controversy, 1636–1638: A Documentary History* (Duke University Press, 1990), pp. 13–14.

10. Edmund Morgan, *Visible Saints: The History of a Puritan Idea* (New York University Press, 1963), pp. 95–102. Patricia Caldwell found more antecedents for the practice, in England and America, than Morgan had, but she grants that Cotton played an

important role in making the practice common in Massachusetts (*Conversion Narrative*, pp. 64–66).

11. Hall, *Antinomian Controversy*, p. 164.
12. Bush, *Writings of Thomas Hooker*, p. 81.
13. Hall, *Antinomian Controversy*, p. 273.
14. Ibid., p. 373
15. Ibid., p. 387.
16. Ibid., p. 300.
17. Bush, *Writings of Thomas Hooker*, p. 78.
18. John Cotton, *The Bloody Tenent, Washed and Made White in the Blood of the Lambe* (London, 1647), part 2, p. 51.
19. Thomas Shepard, *God's Plot: The Paradoxes of Puritan Piety, Being an Autobiography & Journal of Thomas Shepard*, ed. Michael McGiffert (University of Massachusetts Press, 1904), p. 76.
20. Edmund S. Morgan, *Roger Williams: The Church and the State* (Harcourt, Brace & World, 1967), pp. 41–45.
21. Bush, *Writings of Thomas Hooker*, p. 118.
22. Hall, *Antinomian Controversy*, 45.
23. Pettit, *Heart Prepared*, pp. 92–93; Bush, *Writings of Thomas Hooker*, pp. 124–25.
24. Bush, *Writings of Thomas Hooker*, p. 122.
25. Robert G. Pope, *The Half-Way Covenant: Church Membership in Puritan New England* (Princeton University Press, 1969), p. 57.
26. Perry Miller, *The New England Mind: From Colony to Province* (Harvard University Press, 1953), pp. 85–86.
27. Bush, *Writings of Thomas Hooker*, p. 121.
28. Pope, *Half-Way Covenant*, pp. 17–19.
29. Ibid., pp. 28–30, 263.
30. Ibid., pp. 132–39, 264–69.
31. Ibid., pp. 275–78.
32. Edwin S. Gaustad, *Liberty of Conscience: Roger Williams in America* (Eerdmans, 191), p. 88.

4. THE PURITAN INTELLECT

1. George Marsden, *Jonathan Edwards* (Yale University Press, 2003), p. 61.
2. Samuel Eliot Morison, *The Founding of Harvard College* (Harvard University Press, 1935), p. 92. Emmanuel was also the college of the university's eponymous donor, John Harvard.
3. E. Brooks Holifield, *Theology in America: Christian Thought from the Age of the Puritans to the Civil War* (Yale, 2003), p. 27.
4. Ibid.
5. Ibid., p. 26.
6. Michael McGiffert, "Thomas Shepard," in *American National Biography* (Oxford University Press, 1999), p. 795.
7. Samuel Eliot Morison, *Harvard in the Seventeenth Century* (Harvard Universitiy Press, 1936), vol. 1, p. 200.
8. Edwin S. Gaustad, *Liberty of Conscience: Roger Williams in America* (Eerdmans, 1991), p. 180.

9. Ramus (1515–1572) denounced the logic of Aristotle, on which Catholics had based the method of scholasticism.

10. Morison, *Founding*, p. 432.

11. *God's Plot: Puritan Spirituality in Thomas Shepard's Cambridge*, ed. Michael McGiffert (University of Massachusetts Press, 1972), p. 70.

12. George Wilson Pierson, *The Founding of Yale: The Legend of the Forty Folios* (Yale University Press, 1988), p. 157.

13. Ibid., p. 163.

14. Morison, *In the Seventeenth Century* (Harvard University Press, 1936), vol. 1, p. 305.

15. Pierson, *Founding*, pp. 4–13.

16. Edmund Morgan, *The Genuine Article: A Historian Looks at Early America* (W. W. Norton, 2004), pp. 33, 35.

17. G. K. Chesterton, *The Victorian Age in English Literature* (Henry Holt and Company, 1913), p. 13.

18. Sacvan Bercovitch, *The American Jeremiad* (University of Wisconsin Press, 1978), p. 104.

19. Ralph Waldo Emerson, *Collected Essays and Lectures* (Library of America, 1983), pp. 216–17.

20. Ibid., p. 217.

21. Lyman Beecher, *Plea for the West* (Truman and Smith, 1835), p. 40.

22. Ibid., p. 36.

23. Ibid., pp. 9–11.

24. Ibid., p. 54.

25. Ibid., pp. 73, 165.

26. Ibid., pp. 83–84, 147

27. Ibid., p. 60.

28. Alexis de Tocqueville, *De la démocratie en Amérique* (Garnier-Flammarion, 1981), vol. 2, p. 125 (II 2.2): "*L'individualisme est un sentiment réfléchi et paisible qui dispose chacque citoyen à s'isoler de la masse des ses semblables et a se retirer a l'écart avec sa familie et ses amis; de telle sorte que, après s'être ainsi crée une petite societé à son usage, il abandonne volontiers la grande societé à elle-même.*"

29. Steven Lukes, "The Meanings of Individualism," *Journal of the History of Ideas* (January–March, 1971), pp. 46–48; Yehoshua Arieli, *Individualism and Nationalism in American Ideology* (Harvard University Press, 1964), pp. 211–15, 226–34.

30. Alexis de Tocqueville, *The Old Regime and the Revolution*, ed. Francois Furet and Francoise Melonio, trans. Alan S. Kahan (Universiy of Chicago Press, 1998), pp. 162–63.

31. James T. Schleicher finds that Tocqueville first used the word in a favorable "or at least neutral" sense in his 1837 notes toward *Démocratie*, but removed more favorable treatments of it as he went along. Schleicher, *The Making of Tocqueville's "Democracy in America"* (University of North Carolina Press, 1980), pp. 252–59.

32. Tocqueville, *Démocratie*, p. 125: "*L'égoisme desséche le germe de toutes les vertus, l'individualisme ne tarit d'abord que la source des vertus publiques; mais, à la longue, il attaque et détruit toutes les autres et va enfin s'absorber dans l'égoisme.*"

33. Tocqueville, *Démocratie*, II 2.305 (vol. 2, pp. 129–41).

34. Lukes, "Meanings," p. 53.

35. Arieli, *Individualism*, chapter IX.

36. Ibid., p. 198.

37. Ibid., pp. 200–1, 246–56, 344–45.
38. Ibid., pp. 201–2.
39. Mark Hopkins, introduction to Emerson Davis, *The Half Century* (Tappan & Whitemore, 1851).
40. James Bryce, *The American Commonwealth* (Macmillan and Co., 1888), vol. 2, pp. 406–7.
41. Ibid., pp. 340–41.
42. Herbert Spencer, *Principles of Sociology* (1877), vol. 2, p. 211.
43. Arieli, *Individualism*, pp. 330–31.

5. PRECURSORS
1. Thomas M. Davis, "The Traditions of Puritan Typology," in Sacvan Bercovitch, *Typology and Early American Literature* (University of Massachusetts Press, 1972), pp. 33–40.
2. Samuel Eliot Morison, *Harvard in the Seventeenth Century* (Harvard University Press, 1936), vol. 1, pp. 236–51.
3. Winthrop D. Jordan, *White over Black: American Attitudes Toward the Negro, 1550–1812* (University of North Carolina Press, 1968), pp. 17–20, 242–43.
4. See, for instance, Richard Francis, *Judge Sewall's Apology* (Fourth Estate, 2005).
5. Samuel Sewall, *The Selling of Joseph: A Memorial*, ed. Sidney Kaplan (University of Massachusetts Press, 1969).
6. Perry Miller, "Roger Williams: An Essay in Interpretation," in *The Complete Writings of Roger Williams* (Russell & Russell, 1963), vol. 7, p. 9.
7. Ibid., p. 7.
8. Ibid., p. 23.
9. See, among many such statements, Mark De Wolfe Howe, *The Garden and the Wilderness: Religion and Government in American Constitutional History* (University of Chicago Press, 1965), pp. 6–7: "The principle of separation epitomized in Williams's metaphor was predominantly theological. The principle summarized in the same figure when used by Jefferson was primarily political."
10. Miller, "Roger Williams," p. 6.
11. Edmund Morgan, *Roger Williams: The Church and the State* (Harcourt, Brace & World, 1967), pp. 39–44.
12. Ibid., pp. 31, 40, 44.
13. *Boswell's Life of Johnson*, rev. ed. by L. F. Powell (Oxford University Press, 1934), vol. I, p. 397.
14. Morgan, *Roger Williams*, pp. 44–45, 47, 51–52.
15. Ibid., pp. 31–32.
16. Williams, *The Hireling Ministry None of Christ's*, in *Complete Writings*, vol. 7, p. 161.
17. Williams, *Mr. Cotton's Letter Lately Printed, Examined and Answered*, in *Complete Writings*, vol. 1, p. 393.
18. Ibid., p. 352.
19. Once again Morgan parts with his teacher Perry Miller, who wrote of Williams: "His slant was theological, not political" (Miller, "Roger Williams," p. 10).
20. Howe, *Garden*, pp. 10–12.
21. Williams, "To the Town of Providence," in *Complete Writings*, vol. 6, pp. 278–79.
22. Williams, *The Bloody Tenent of Persecution*, in *Complete Writings*, vol. 3, p. 398.

23. Thomas Jefferson, *Notes on the State of Virginia,* Query XVII, in *Thomas Jefferson, Writings,* ed. Merrill D. Peterson (Library of America, 1984), p. 285.

24. Williams, *Complete Writings,* vol. 3, p. 98.

6. SPUR TO ENLIGHTENMENT

1. Perry Miller, *Jonathan Edwards* (William Sloane Associates, 1949), pp. 51–53, 72, 77, 61, 149.

2. Perry Miller, "Jonathan Edwards and the Great Awakening," in *Errand into the Wilderness* (Harvard University Press, 1964), p. 163.

3. Alan Heimert, *Religion and the American Mind* (Harvard University Press, 1966), pp. 9–21, 148, 537–38, 548–52.

4. Sidney Mead, review of Heimert, *Journal of Religion* 48 (July 1968), p. 281. See Edmund Morgan's review of Heimert, *William and Mary Quarterly* (July 1967), p. 459: "The world he offers us has been constructed by reading beyond the lines of what men said; and what he finds beyond the lines is so far beyond, so wrenched from the context, and so at odds with empirical evidence, that his world, to this reviewer at least, partakes more of fantasy than of history."

5. John M. Murrin, "No Awakening, No Revolution? More Counterfactual Speculations," *Reviews in American History* 11 (June 1983), pp. 161–71.

6. Mark A. Noll, *America's God: From Jonathan Edwards to Abraham Lincoln* (Oxford University Press, 2002), p. 162.

7. Ebenezer Frothingham defended the right of women to preach in his *Articles of Faith and Practice* (J. Franklin, 1750).

8. George M. Marsden, *Jonathan Edwards: A Life* (Yale University Press), p. 211.

9. Benjamin Franklin, *The Autobiography,* in *Benjamin Franklin, Writings,* ed. J. A. Leo Lemay (Library of America, 1987), pp. 1, 409.

10. Benjamin Franklin, *Pennsylvania Gazette,* June 12, 1740.

11. Charles Chauncy, *A Letter from a Gentleman in Boston to Mr. George Wishart, One of the Ministers of Edinburgh* (1742), in Richard Bushman, ed., *The Great Awakening: Documents on the Revival of Religion, 1740–1745* (Atheneum, 1969), p. 117.

12. Ibid., p. 119.

13. Gilbert Tennent, *The Danger of an Unconverted Ministry* (1740), in Bushman, *Great Awakening,* p. 90.

14. Ibid., pp. 88, 90.

15. Ibid., p. 92.

16. George Whitefield, *A Continuation of the Reverend Mr. Shitefield's Journal: The Seventh Journal* (W. Strahan, 1741), p. 29.

17. Whitefield, *Continuation,* p. 38.

18. Charles Chauncy, *Seasonable Thoughts on the State of Religion in New-England* (Rogers and Fowle, 1743), p. 166.

19. Catherine A. Brekus, *Strangers and Pilgrims: Female Preaching in America* (University of North Carolina Press, 1998), pp. 23–26.

20. Bushman, *Great Awakening,* pp. 58–60.

21. Ibid., p. 47.

22. Jonathan Edwards, "Sinners in the Hands of an Angry God," in *American Sermons,* ed. Michael Warner (Library of America, 1990), p. 354.

23. Harry S. Stout and Peter Onuf, "James Davenport and the Great Awakening in New London," *Journal of American History* 70 (1981), p. 556.

24. Ibid., p. 575.

25. Bushman, *Great Awakening*, p. 55.

26. Marsden, *Edwards*, pp. 501–2.

27. Norman Fiering, *Jonathan Edwards's Moral Thought and Its British Context* (University of North Carolina Press, 1981), p. 37.

28. Marsden, *Edwards*, p. 546.

29. Ibid., pp. 255–58.

30. Ibid., pp. 292–301.

31. Ibid., p. 338.

32. Ibid., pp. 334–35.

33. Ibid., p. 312.

34. Benjamin Franklin to John Franklin, *The Papers of Benjamin Franklin*, ed. Leonard W. Labaree et al. (Yale University Press, 1963), vol. 3, pp. 26–27.

35. Marsden, *Edwards*, p. 336.

36. Fiering, *Moral Thought*, p. 203.

37. Perry Miller, "The Rhetoric of Sensation," in *Errand Into the Wilderness*, p. 178.

38. Bushman, *Great Awakening*, p. 90.

39. Jonathan Edwards, "Sinners in the Hands of an Angry God," *American Sermons*, p. 356.

40. Passages quoted in Brekus, *Strangers*, p. 40.

41. Marsden, *Edwards*, p. 368.

42. Ibid., p. 166.

43. Joseph Bellamy to Ezra Stiles, in Isabel M. Calder, ed., *Letters and Papers of Ezra Stiles* (Yale University Press, 1933), p. 21.

44. Amy Plantinga Pauw, *The Supreme Harmony of All: The Trinitarian Theology of Jonathan Edwards* (Eerdmans, 2002).

45. Jonathan Edwards, *Miscellanies* #930.

46. Some Presbyterians in Pennsylvania were rejecting the Trinity as nonbiblical as early as 1719. See Leonard J, Trinterud, *The Forming of an American Tradition: A Re-Examination of Colonial Presbyteriansim* (Westminster Press, 1949), pp. 41–44.

47. G. K. Chesterton, *Orthodoxy* (Doubleday, 1959), p. 14.

48. Ibid., p. 142.

49. Even an admirer of Edwards, writing the first full-length book on his Trinitarian thinking, has to admit that he "lapses" into uses of that thinking to underscore "pitiless divine vengeance." Pauw, *Supreme Harmony*, p. 187.

50. Marsden, *Edwards*, pp. 434–35.

51. Mark A. Noll, *America's God: From Jonathan Edwards to Abraham Lincoln* (Oxford University Press, 2002), pp. 135–36.

52. James Tanis, *Dutch Calvinistic Pietism in the Middle Colonies: A Study in the Life and Theology of Theodorus Jacobus Frelinghuysen* (Martinus Nijhoff, 1967), p. 150.

53. Ibid., pp. 68–71.

54. Trinterud, *Forming*, p. 115.

55. Mark A. Noll, *Princeton and the Republic, 1768–1822* (Princeton University Press, 1989), p. 17.

56. Trinterud, *Forming*, pp. 183–95.

7. AGAINST THE AWAKENING

1. E. Brooks Holifield, *Theology in America: Christian Thought from the Age of the Puritans to the Civil War* (Yale University Press, 2003), p. 80.
2. George Marsden, *Jonathan Edwards: A Life* (Yale University Press, 2003), p. 436.
3. Leonard J. Trinterud, *The Forming of an American Tradition: A Re-Examination of Colonial Presbyterianism* (Westminster Press, 1949), p. 195.
4. Holifield, *Theology in America*, p. 80.
5. Ibid., pp. 84–85.
6. John Locke, *An Essay Concerning Human Understanding*, book IV, chapter 19, para. 10.
7. Third Earl of Shaftesbury, *Characteristicks of Men, Manners, Opinions, Times* (1711). Jefferson took from this book a defense of uncensored satire on religious views, a thing he rarely practiced: "Nothing but free argument, raillery, and even ridicule will preserve the purity of religion" (J 1.549).
8. Locke, *Essay*, book IV, chapter 17, para. 2.
9. Arminians is the nickname given to people who preferred the term "Remonstrants." Jacobus Arminius was just one of those propounding this creed, which rejected the Calvinist belief in total depravity of mankind, asserting instead that humans retain enough freedom and virtue to cooperate with the Spirit in their own salvation.
10. John Locke, *The Reasonableness of Christianity*, ed. I. T. Ramsey (Adam & Charles Black, 1958), p. 25. All later references are to this edition.
11. Locke, *Essay*, book IV, chapter 17, para. 23.
12. Socinians were named for the sixteenth-century Italian Fausto Paolo Sozzini (Latinized as Socinus), who popularized this version of Unitarianism.
13. Martin E. Marty, *The Infidel* (Meridian Books, 1961), pp. 33–40.
14. Conrad Wright, *The Beginnings of Unitarianism in America* (Archon Books, 1976), pp. 187–97.
15. John Adams to Thomas Jefferson, Sept. 14, 1813, in Lester J. Cappon, *The Adams Jefferson Letters* (University of North Carolina Press, 1959), vol. 2, pp. 373–74.
16. Wright, *Beginnings*, pp. 213–15.
17. Ibid., pp. 215–16.
18. Ibid., pp. 143–44.
19. Joseph J. Ellis, *The New England Mind in Transition: Samuel Johnson of Connecticut, 1696–1772* (Yale University Press, 1973), p. 79.
20. Henry May, *The Enlightenment in America* (Oxford University Press, 1876), p. 77.
21. Ibid., p. 8.
22. Smith removed the Nicene and Athanasian creeds from the prayer book (Holifield, *Theology in America*, p. 242). Johnson declined speculation on the Trinity (Ellis, *New England Mind*, p. 151).
23. Holifield, *Theology*, p. 121.
24. May, *Enlightenment*, p. 63.
25. Jeffry H. Morrison, *John Witherspoon and the Founding of the American Republic* (University of Notre Dame Press, 2005), p. 4. In one respect Morrison inflates the numbers, since he counts men who served in the House and the Senate under both heads.
26. L. Gordon Tait, *The Piety of John Witherspoon: Pew, Pulpit, and Public Forum* (Geneva Press, 2001), p. 137.

27. Ibid., p. 37: "The doctrine of the Trinity was virtually ignored." Also p. 97: The Trinity "was given short shrift in Witherspoon's rendition of piety."

28. May, *Enlightenment*, p. 62.

29. Ibid., p. 40.

30. Ibid., p. 126. The common-sense school rejected Locke's thesis that the mind was a blank slate filled in by images of the outside world. Reid held that we have an innate ability to know objects directly, without intermediating images. Since this innate mental capability was shared by all, Reid's system seemed more democratic than Locke's, and it was adopted by Americans on that ground.

31. Priestley to Jefferson, May 7, 1803, in Dickenson W. Adams, ed., *Jefferson's Extracts from the Gospels* (Princeton University Press, 1983), pp. 338–40.

32. Adams to Jefferson, July 12, 1813, in Cappon, *Adams-Jefferson Letters*, vol. 2, p. 362.

8. QUAKERS

1. Jefferson to William Baldwin (1910), in *Jefferson's Extracts from the Gospels*, ed. Dickinson W. Adams (Princeton University Press, 1983), p. 346.

2. Thomas Paine, *The Age of Reason*, in *Collected Works*, ed. Eric Fohner (Library of America, 1995), p. 703. Paine honored Quakers who abstained from the Revoutionary War, so long as they did not advocate that others refuse to bear arms. When some did that, he called them not real Quakers: "A religious Quaker is a valuable character, and a political Quaker a real Jesuit" (*The American Crisis*, Number III, *Collected Works*, p. 126).

3. George S. Brookes, *Friend Anthony Benezet* (University of Pennsylvania Press, 1937), p. 98.

4. Ibid., p. 443.

5. Edward Derbyshire Seeber, *Anti-Slavery Opinion in France During the Second Half of the Eighteenth Century* (Johns Hopkins Press, 1937), p. 165.

6. Voltaire, *Letters Concerning the English Nation*, new ed. (London: L. Davis et al., 1760), p. 4.

7. Ibid., p. 24.

8. Ibid., p. 27. Voltaire wrote several articles praising Quaker opposition to slavery (Seeber, *Opinion*, p. 89).

9. George Fox, *Gospel Family-Order* (London 1676).

10. Thomas E. Drake, *Quakers and Slavery* (Yale University Press, 1950), pp. 7–8.

11. Ibid., pp. 23–24.

12. Ibid., p. 19.

13. Ibid., p. 21.

14. Jean R. Soderlund, *Quakers and Slavery: A Divided Spirit* (Princeton University Press, 1985), p. 20.

15. *An Exhortation and Caution to Friends Concerning Buying or Keeping of Negroes* (New York: William Bradford, 1693).

16. Soderlund, *Quakers*, p. 18. A petition by Robert Pyle to the Philadelphia meeting was similarly ignored in 1711 (ibid., pp. 19–20).

17. Ibid., pp. 21–22.

18. Roberts Vaux, *Memoirs of the Lives of Benjamin Lay and Ralph Sundiford* (Philadelphia: W. Phillips, 1816), p. 11.

19. Ibid., p. 18.

20. Ibid., p. 29.

21. Thomas E. Drake, *Quakers and Slavery in America* (Yale University Press, 1950), p. 45.
22. John Woolman, *Journal and Major Essays*, ed. Phillips P. Moulton (Friends United Press, 1971), p. 38.
23. Ibid., pp. 232–39 (*Some Considerations*, part II).
24. Vaux, *Memoirs*, p. 50.
25. Woolman, *Journal and Major Essays*, pp. 60–61 (*Journal*).
26. Ibid., "*A Plea For the Poor*," 1793, in *Journal*, pp. 268–69.
27. Ibid., pp. 127–28 (*Journal*).
28. Ibid., pp. 124–25 (*Journal*).
29. Ibid., p. 14 (*Journal*).
30. Ibid., p. 180 (*Journal*).
31. Ibid., pp. 183–84 (*Journal*).
32. Brookes, *Benezet*, p. 34.
33. Ibid., pp. 38, 57.
34. Ibid., p. 151.
35. Ibid., pp. 67, 70.
36. Ibid., p. 122.
37. Ibid., p. 170.
38. Ibid., p. 99.
39. Ibid., p. 200.
40. Ibid., p. 82.
41. Ibid., p. 85.
42. Ibid., p. 101.
43. Ibid., p. 87.
44. Ibid., p. 91.
45. Ibid., p. 97.
46. Ibid., p. 418.
47. Whitefield to Wesley, Mar. 22, 1751, in Irv A. Brendlinger, *To Be Silent . . . Would Be Criminal: The Antislavery Influence and Writings of Anthony Benezet* (Scarecrow Press, 2007), p. 48.
48. This important work is now most conveniently consulted in the anthology of Benezet's writings included in Brendlinger, *To Be Silent*, and numbers in my text refer to pages in this edition. *Some Historical Account* expands on the material contained in Benezet's earlier and influential tracts *A Short Account of That Part of Africa Inhabited by the Negroes* (1762) and *A Caution and Warning to Great Britain and Her Colonies* (1766).
49. Benezet, *A Mite Cast into the Treasury, Or Obervations on Slave-Keeping* (1771), in Brendlinger, *To Be Silent*, p. 209.
50. *A Mite Cast into the Treasury*, p. 208.
51. Ibid., p. 211.
52. Abraham Lincoln, *Speeches and Writings, 1832–1858*, ed. Don E. Fehrenbacher (Library of America, 1989), p. 686.
53. Roberts Vaux, *Memoirs of the Life of Anthony Benezet* (Philadelphia, 1817), p. 150.
54. Brookes, *Benezet*, p. 170.
55. Ibid., p. 152.
56. Ibid., p. 160.
57. A major flaw in Henry May's otherwise important book on the Enlightenment is its

exclusion of Quakers from the American story. *The Enlightenment in America* (Oxford University Press, 1976), p. 369: "In the interest of brevity, I have reluctantly decided not to treat the Quakers in this book." The Quakers are almost totally ignored, and Benezet is never mentioned, in Mark A. Noll, *America's God: From Jonathan Edwards to Abraham Lincoln* (Oxford University Press, 2002).

9. DEISTS

1. William Lee Miller, *The First Liberty: Religion and the American Republic* (Alfred A. Knopf, 1986), pp. 236–46. Three Christian scholars list Witherspoon and Hamilton among "Bible Christians," along with Roger Williams, John Jay, and Patrick Henry. But Hamilton drew his thought from Enlightenment figures (Montaigne, Montesquieu, Locke, and Hume), and Witherspoon taught his ethics course at Princeton (as the three men admit) from "Hume, Hutcheson and other philosophers of the Scottish Enlightenment." Mark A. Noll, Nathan O. Hatch, and George M. Marsden, *The Search for Christian America*, expanded ed. (Helmers and Howard, 1989) pp. 74–75, 89.

2. Stiles quoted in Martin E. Marty, *The Infidel* (Meridian Books, 1962), p. 47.

3. Martin E. Marty, *The New Shape of American Religion* (Harper & Brothers, 1959), pp. 76–77.

4. Thomas Paine, *Collected Works*, ed. Eric Fohner (Library of America, 1995), pp. 418–19.

5. Ibid., p. 93 (*The American Crisis*, Number 1, 1776). He told one interlocutor that "God almighty is on our side" (ibid., p. 108). His attitude toward his chosen America and his native England was clear: "The will of God hath parted us" (p. 163).

6. Ibid., *Age of Reason*, pp. 719, 712, 687.

7. Ibid., pp. 694, 712, 718.

8. Lester J. Cappon, *The Adams-Jefferson Letters* (University of North Carolina Press, 1959), vol. 2, p. 374.

9. James H. Hutson, *The Founders on Religion* (Princeton University Press, 2005), pp. 170, 220.

10. Paine, *Works*, p. 688.

11. Ibid., p. 817.

12. Ibid., p. 688.

13. Ibid., p. 719.

14. Ibid., p. 821.

15. Ibid., pp. 824–25.

16. Ibid., p. 826.

17. Ibid., p. 829.

18. Ibid., pp. 792, 697.

19. Ibid., pp. 669–70.

20. Ibid., *Age of Reason*, pp. 823–24.

21. Douglas Wilson, ed., *Jefferson's Commonplace Book* (Princeton University Press, 1989), p. 35.

22. For the strong argument that he was referring to his own *Life and Morals of Jesus* in this letter, see Eugene R. Sheridan, Introduction to Dickinson W. Adams, ed., *Jefferson's Extracts from the Gospels* (Princeton University Press, 1985), p. 38.

23. Adams to Jefferson, July 22, 1813 (Cappon, *Adams-Jefferson Letters*, vol. 2, p. 363).

24. Jefferson to Adams, Mar. 11, 1813 (Cappon, vol. 2, p. 369).

25. Adams to Jefferson, Sept. 14, 1813 (Cappon, vol. 2, p. 273).

26. Jefferson to Francis Van der Kemp, Aug. 6, 1816 (Hutson, *Founders*, p. 218).

27. Jefferson to James Smith, Dec. 8, 1822 (ibid., p. 218).
28. Adams to John Quincy Adams, Mar. 28, 1816 (ibid., pp. 220–21).
29. Ibid., p. 220.
30. Jefferson to Benjamin Waterhouse, June 26, 1822 (ibid., p. 221).
31. Jefferson to Adams, Aug. 22, 1813 (Cappon, vol. 2, p. 368).
32. Jefferson to Benjamin Rush, Apr. 21, 1803 (Adams, *Extracts,* p. 332).
33. Jefferson to Priestley, Apr. 9, 1803 (ibid., p. 528).
34. Jefferson to William Short, Aug. 4, 1920 (ibid., p. 398).
35. Ibid., p. 334.
36. Ibid., pp. 332–34.
37. Jefferson's own title page and list of passages to be used have been lost, but a copy of them survives, most likely made by his granddaughter (ibid., p. 46).
38. Jefferson to Adams, Oct. 12, 1813 (Cappon, vol. 2, p 352—also pp. 369, 388).
39. Adams, *Extracts,* pp. 48, 369.
40. Jefferson to Adams, Oct. 12, 1813 (Cappon, vol. 2, p. 352).
41. Michael Novak, *On Two Wings: Humble Faith and Common Sense at the American Founding* (Encounter Books, 2007), p. 65. Another of Novak's "proofs" of Jefferson's religiosity is that he asked Madison for a list of theological books for the library of the University of Virginia (ibid., p. 60). Even on the face of it, this suggests his own lack of familiarity with such works. It also has to be seen in connection with the fact that his university had no chapel, no chaplain, and no department of religion. His interest in having a complete collection for the library was scholarly, not Evangelical.
42. Henry Adams, *History of the United States of America During the Second Administration of Thomas Jefferson, 1805–1809* (Library of America, 1986), p. 605. See also Adams, *Extracts,* p. 28.
43. Jefferson to Benjamin Rush, Apr. 21, 1803 (Adams, *Extracts,* p. 331).
44. Jefferson to Charles Thomson, Jan. 1816 (Adams, p. 32).
45. Adams to Van der Kemp, Oct. 4, 1813 (Hutson, *Founders,* p. 56).
46. Adams to Jefferson, Nov. 4, 1816 (Cappon, vol. 2, pp. 493–94).
47. Adams to Jefferson, Jan. 22, 1815 (Cappon, vol. 2, p. 607).
48. Franklin to Ezra Stiel, Mar. 9, 1790 (Hutson, pp. 122–23).
49. Henry May, *The Enlightenment in America* (Oxford University Press, 1876), p. 131.
50. Ron Chernow, *Alexander Hamilton* (Penguin Press, 2004), pp. 52–52, 706–8.
51. One important exception to this trend would be attempts in the 1850s to try Horace Bushnell for heresy when he adopted a modalist interpretation of the Trinity—that the three Persons were merely manifestations of God's single personality.
52. Marcus Cunliffe, introduction to Mason L. Weems, *The Life of Washington* (Harvard University Press, 1962), p. x.
53. Marcus Cunliffe, *Washington, Man and Monument* (New American Library, 1958), p. 21.
54. Washington, Speech to Delaware Chiefs, May 12, 1779, in *Writings of George Washington,* ed. John C. Fitzpatrick (Library of Congress), vol. 15, p. 55.
55. Hutson, *Founders,* pp. 16–18.
56. Joseph Ellis, *His Excellency: George Washington* (Alfred A. Knopf, 2004), p. 269. Michael Novak and Jana Novak, *Washington's God: Religion, Liberty, and the Father of Our Country* (Basic Books, 2006), pp. 205–10.
57. Ibid. (Novak), pp. 205–10.

58. Cunliffe, *Washington*, p. 60.
59. Paul F. Boller Jr., *George Washington and Religion* (Southern Methodist University Press, 1963), pp. 33–34.
60. Ibid., p. 90.
61. Ibid., p. 89.
62. Ibid.
63. Novak and Novak, *Washington's God*, pp. 230, 237–40.
64. Martin E. Marty, *The New Shape of American Religion* (Harper & Brothers, 1958), p. 3.
65. Mark A. Noll, *The Civil War as a Theological Crisis* (University of North Carolina Press, 2006), p. 14.
66. Peter Gay, *The Enlightenment: An Interpretation* (Norton, 1977), vol. 2, p. 35, and *Voltaire's Politics: The Poet as Realist* (Princeton University Press, 1959), pp. 31–53. Gay quotes Voltaire's satire on Jewish Scripture, one model for Paine's treatment, from (of all things) the article on tolerance in *Questions sur l'Encyclopédie*: "Shall I give him [a Jew] dinner? Yes, provided that during the meal Balaam's ass does not take it into its head to bray; that Ezekiel does not mix his breakfast with our dinner; that a fish does not come to swallow one of the guests and keep him in his belly for three days; that a serpent does not mix into the conversation to seduce my wife; that a prophet does not take it into his head to sleep with her after dinner, as did that good fellow Hoseah for fifteen francs and a bushel of barley; above all, that no Jew make a tour round my house sounding the trumpet, making the walls come down, killing me, my father, my mother, my wife, my children, my cat and my dog, in accord with the former usage of the Jews." Paine's satires on the Jewish Scripture are as well known as his attacks on the New Testament. A. J. Ayer finds irony in the fact that Voltaire devoted so much of his *Treatise on Tolerance* to "mockery of the Old Testament." Ayer, *Voltaire: A Life* (Random House, 1986), p. 167.
67. Adams to Jefferson, Dec. 2, 1813 (Cappon, vol. 2, p. 404).
68. John Courtney Murray, *We Hold These Truths: Catholic Reflections on the American Proposition* (Sheed and Ward, 1960). Father Murray was for some time silenced by the Vatican for challenging Pope Pius IX's condemnation of democracy and Pope Leo XIII's attack on the American separation of church and state. In making his case that Catholics can honor the American system (a case he won at the Second Vatican Council), Murray exaggerated his argument to say that the American system was *inspired* by Catholic principles from the Middle Ages. According to *We Hold These Truths*, the Enlightenment was guilty of "rationalism, individualism, nominalism" (p. 305). Locke was "that most decadent of all philosophical things, a nominalist" (p. 309). Murray claims that these evil Enlightenment principles had not reached America by the time of the founding, making the Founders ignorant of Locke (p. 55), so the Constitution could be based on natural law, as taught by Catholics in the Middle Ages (pp. 30–32). The popes were right in condemning liberalism, since it leads to totalitarianism (p. 68)—but those condemnations do not touch America, founded on Catholic ideals. Murray's exaggerations have been taken up by the authors associated with Richard John Neuhaus's journal, *First Things*.
69. Noll et al., *Search*, p. 17: "We feel that a careful study of the facts of history shows that

early America does not deserve to be considered uniquely, distinctly, or even predominantly Christian, if we mean by the word 'Christian' a state of society reflecting the ideals presented in Scripture."

10. BEYOND TOLERANCE

1. John Locke, *A Letter Concerning Toleration: Latin and English Texts Revised and Edited with Variants and an Introduction* (by Mario Montuori), pp. 7–9. The *Letter* is far less known in Locke's original Latin of 1688 than in the 1689 translation by William Popham, as revised by Locke for its second edition (1690). Popham was a Unitarian poet (the nephew of poet Andrew Marvell). Early editions of Locke's collected works print the English version of the *Letter* rather than the Latin. The English was accepted as so authoritative that translations of the *Letter* into French and Dutch used Popham as their basis, not Locke's original. J. W. Gough made a new translation of the Latin, claiming slightly greater accuracy than Popham—see Raymond Klibansky and J. W. Gough, *John Locke's "Epistula de Tolerantia," A Letter on Toleration* (Oxford University Press, 1965). But the history of political discussion around this text is based on the English version of 1690, and Jefferson's notes on the book were taken from it. That is what is quoted here.
2. *A Decent Respect to the Opinions of Mankind: Congressional State Papers, 1774–1776* (Library of Congress, 1975), p. 56.
3. Ibid., p. 76.
4. The Congress substituted "despotism" for "tyranny" in the official document (J 1.215).
5. Congress, in adopting the draft, changed "colonies" to "states," since Independence had just been declared.
6. Roger Williams, *The Complete Writings* (Russell & Russell, 1963), vol. 3, p. 250.
7. Perry Miller, Introduction to Williams, ibid., vol. 7, p. 10.

11. JEFFERSON'S STATUTE

1. For Jefferson's Statute in his own format, see appendix I.
2. Philip Hamburger, *Separation of Church and State* (Harvard University Press, 2002), pp. 144, 147, 149, 161.
3. Ibid., pp. 161–65.
4. Ibid., p. 166.
5. Ibid., p. 169.
6. Ibid., pp. 170–71.
7. Ibid., pp. 165, 144.
8. Ibid., p. 147.

12. MADISON'S REMONSTRANCE

1. Ralph Ketcham, *James Madison* (University Press of Virginia, 1990), p. 31.
2. For the text as it was originally printed, see appendix II.
3. Jefferson to Gouverneur Morris, Aug. 16, 1793.
4. George Washington, *Writings*, ed. John Rhodehamel (Library of America, 1997), p. 71.
5. Alexander Hamilton, "Report on Manufactures, December 5, 1701," in Jacob E. Cooke, *The Reports of Alexander Hamilton* (Harper Torchbooks, 1964), p. 131.

13. FIRST AMENDMENT

1. Timothy Dwight, *A Discourse in Two Parts,* 2nd ed. (Flagg and Gould, 1813), p. 24.

2. Chauncey Lee, *The Government of God* (Hudson and Goodwin, 1813), p. 43.

3. Max Farrand, *The Records of the Federal Convention of 1787,* rev. ed. (Yale University Press, 1966), vol. 1, pp. 150–52.

4. John Murrin, "Religion and Politics in America from the First Settlements to the Civil War," in Mark A. Noll, ed., *Religion and American Politics: From the Colonial Period to the 1980s* (Oxford University Press, 1990), p. 31.

5. Willmoore Kendall, *The Conservative Affirmation* (Regnery, 1963), pp. 77–82; *Willmoore Kendall Contra Mundum* (Arlington House, 1971), pp. 303–25; Kendall and George W. Carey, *The Basic Symbols of the American Political Tradition* (Louisiana State University Press, 1970), pp. 119–36.

6. Leonard Levy, *Origins of the Bill of Rights* (Yale University Press, 2001), p. 20.

7. Robert Morris to Francis Hopkinson, Aug. 15, 1789, quoted in Helen E. Veit et al., *Creating the Bill of Rights: The Documentary Record from the First Federal Congress* (Johns Hopkins University Press, 1991), p. 278.

8. Patrick Henry to Richard Henry Lere, Aug. 28, 1789, ibid., p. 289.

9. Pierce Butler to James Iredell, Aug. 11, 1789, ibid., p. 274.

10. Robert Morris to Richard Peters, Aug. 24, 1789, ibid., p. 288.

11. Jefferson, Letters of March 1, 1792, in Bernard Schwartz, *The Roots of the Bill of Rights* (Chelsea House Publishers, 1971), vol. 5, p. 1,203.

12. Philip Hamburger, *Separation of Church and State* (Harvard University Press, 2002), p. 206.

13. Kendall, *Kendall Contra Mundum,* p. 323.

14. Veit, *Creating,* p. 158.

15. John Courtney Murray, S. J., *We Hold These Truths: Catholic Reflections on the American Proposition* (Sheed and Ward, 1960), p. 97.

16. William Lee Miller, *The First Liberty: Religion and the American Republic* (Alfred A. Knopf, 1986), p. 219.

17. John Courtney Murray, "Law or Prepossessions?" in *Law and Contemporary Problems* 14 (Duke University Press, 1949), pp. 23–43. Murray's article condemns the *Everson* and *McCollum* decisions against favoring religious schools, decisions in which, he said, "The Supreme Court proceeds to establish a religion—James Madison's" (p. 31). For Murray's denial that "a political society can do without a public religion," and his contention that liberalism came from nineteenth-century "laicism," and led naturally to both fascism and communism, see the passages cited in Robert W. McElroy, *The Search for an American Public Theology: The Contribution of John Courtney Murray* (Paulist Press, 1989), pp. 32–36.

18. Mark Douglas McGarvie, *One Nation Under Law: America's Early National Struggle to Separate Church and State* (Northern Illinois University Press, 2004), pp. 56, 207.

19. *Documentary History of the First Federal Congress of the United States of America* (Johns Hopkins University Press, 1986), vol. 4, p. 17.

20. Ibid., p. 20.

21. Ibid., p. 15.

22. Veit, *Creating,* p. 150.

23. Levy, *Origins,* pp. 86–88.

14. MADISONIAN SEPARATION

1. J. C. A. Stagg et al. *The Papers of James Madison, Presidential Series,* vol. 4 (University Press of Virginia, 1999), p. 581.
2. The Memoranda were discovered by Elizabeth Fleet in the archives of William Cabell Rives, who was the first editor of Madison's papers. She published the document as "Madison's 'Detached Memoranda'" in the *William and Mary Quarterly* (Oct., 1946), pp. 534–68. The parts having to do with religion are on pp. 554–62. Fleet concluded that the Memoranda were "written within a few years of Madison's retirement from the presidency" (p. 534), though Madison made some later additions in different inks. Since Madison used abbreviations and neglected some connectives, I have modernized the pointing of the text.
3. Ibid., pp. 560–62.
4. Leo Pfeffer, "Madison's 'Detached Memoranda': Then and Now," in Merrill D. Peterson and Robert C. Vaughan, *The Virginia Statute for Religious Freedom: Its Evolution and Consequences in American History* (Cambridge University Press, 1988), p. 298.
5. Fleet, "Madison's 'Detached Memoranda,'" pp. 558–59.
6. Ibid., pp. 559–60.
7. Jack N. Rakove, ed., *James Madison: Writings* (Library of America, 1999), p. 685.
8. Ibid., pp. 293–94.
9. Madison's attitude toward church property was probably formed in part by the contentious issue of Anglican property in Virginia. When the state disestablished the church, it initially left church land in the hands of its former holders. When it tried to confiscate the land as having been acquired under a royal establishment, the churches fought back, saying they had a corporate title to them. The case was not resolved until Supreme Court justice Joseph Story decided for the churches in *Terrett v. Taylor* (1815), distinguishing public corporations, such as towns and counties, from private corporations. Madison, who was not a lawyer, seems not to have grasped this distinction. See R. Kent Newmyer, *Supreme Court Justice Joseph Story: Statesman of the Old Republic* (University of North Carolina Press, 1985), pp. 131–32.
10. Fleet, "'Detached Memoranda,'" pp. 556–58.
11. Madison to Jasper Adams, in *Church and State in American History: Key Documents, Decisions, and Commentary from the Past Three Centuries,* ed. John F. Wilson and Donald L. Drakeman (Westview, 2003), p. 77.
12. Madison to Edward Everett, Mar. 19, 1824, in Rakove, *Madison's Writings,* p. 796.
13. Fleet, "'Detached Memoranda,'" p. 555.

15. SCHISM IN NEW ENGLAND

1. Isaiah Berlin, *The Roots of Romanticism* (Princeton University Press, 1999), pp. 1–2.
2. Isaiah Berlin, *Political Ideas in the Romantic Age: Their Rise and Influence on Modern Thought* ed. Henry Hardy (Princeton University Press, 2006), pp. 10–11.
3. Ibid., p. 113.
4. Ibid., pp. 42–43.
5. Henry Adams, *The History of the United States of America During the Administrations of James Madison,* ed. Earl N. Harbert (Library of America, 1986), p. 1309.

6. Ibid., p. 1306.

7. Ibid., p. 1343.

8. Mark DeWolfe Howe, *The Garden and the Wilderness: Religion and Government in American Constitutional History* (University of Chicago Press, 1965), pp. 35–36.

9. What looks like an upside-down version of the *Dedham* case, only with a religious college instead of a church, is *Dartmouth College v. Woodward* (1819). There, the conservative religious group won. Dartmouth College had operated under a royal charter in colonial days, and with state subventions after Independence. When a liberal (Jeffersonian) state government tried to make the college a university with a state-appointed board, it was the new order that carried off the records this time. The old trustees sued this man, William H. Woodward, to get the records back. When the case was appealed up to the Supreme Court, with Daniel Webster arguing for the trustees, the college got back its records. Orthodoxy had prevailed, though Mark Douglas McGarvie says it was a Pyrrhic victory, since secular state universities were given a great impetus by it: *One Nation Under Law: America's Early National Struggle to Separate Church and State* (Northern Illinois University, 2004), pp. 182–88. Chief Justice Marshall's opinion said that religious bodies must be incorporated, since "charitable or public spirited individuals, desirous of making permanent appropriations for charitable or other useful purposes, find it impossible to effect their design securely and certainly without an incorporation act" (17 U.S. 637).

10. Robert D. Richardson Jr., *Emerson, the Mind on Fire* (University of California Press, 1995), p. 249. The group strove to improve its German, Theodore Parker studying with Orestes Brownson; Emily Peabody, the translator of Goethe, correcting Emerson; and several consulting the Göttingen product George Bancroft.

11. "Harvard Divinity School Address," in *Ralph Waldo Emerson, Essays and Lectures,* ed. Joel Porte (Library of America, 1983), p. 60.

12. Richardson, *Emerson,* p. 268.

13. Ibid., p. 338.

14. Margaret Fuller diaries quoted by Henry James in his *Nathaniel Hawthorne:* in James, *Literary Criticism,* ed. Leon Edel (Library of America, 1984), p. 387.

15. Ibid., p. 341.

16. Ibid., p. 337.

17. Nathaniel Hawthorne, *Collected Novels,* ed. Millicent Bell (Library of America, 1983), pp. 645–47.

18. Ibid., p. 693.

19. Among other resemblances they point out that Fuller brought Hawthorne a bowl of broth when he was sick at Brook Farm, as Zenobia does to the narrator at Blithedale; that the real and the fictional characters both die by drowning; that of both it was said that she talked far better than she wrote. Henry James, in his book *Nathaniel Hawthorne,* said of Fuller—"the most distinguished woman of her day"—that "she was a talker, she was *the* talker, she was the genius of talk," and that the fictional woman modeled on her was the most real female character in all of Hawthorne's fiction. Henry James, *Criticism,* pp. 379, 420.

20. Hubert H. Hoeltje, *Inward Sky: The Mind and Heart of Nathaniel Hawthorne* (Duke University Press, 1962), p. 386.

21. Richardson, *Emerson,* p. 398.

22. Ibid., p. 339.
23. Mason Wade, *Margaret Fuller: Whetstone of Genius* (Viking, 1940), pp. 94–95.
24. Ibid., p. 101. It was said of both Emerson and Fuller that they did not like others to talk much when they were holding forth. Henry James quotes the Fuller diaries: "As I am accustomed to deference, however, and need it for the boldness and animation which my part requires, I did not speak with as much force [that day] as usual." James, *Criticism*, p. 386.
25. Walt Whitman, *Poetry and Prose*, ed. Justin Kaplan (Library of America, 1996), p. 1055.
26. Whitman, early manuscript quoted in Justin Kaplan, *Walt Whitman: A Life* (Simon & Schuster, 1980), p. 210.
27. F. O. Matthiesson, *American Renaissance: Art and Expression in the Age of Emerson and Whitman* (Oxford University Press, 1941), p. 522.
28. Ibid., p. 205.
29. David S. Reynalds, *Walt Whitman's America: A Cultural Biography* (Alfred A. Knopf, 1995), p. 342.
30. Whitman, *Poetry and Prose*, pp. 1054–55.

16. EMERSONIANS

1. Catherine Albanese, *Corresponding Motion: Transcendental Religion and the New America* (Temple University Press, 1977), pp. 56–97
2. *The Letters of Ralph Waldo Emerson*, ed. Ralph L. Rusk (Columbia University Press, 1939), vol. 2, p. 741.
3. Ibid., p. 37.
4. Robert Louis Stevenson, "Henry David Thoreau, His Character and Opinions," in *Selected Essays*, ed. George Scott-Moncrieff (Gateway Editions, 1988), p. 136.
5. Henry James, *Literary Criticism*, ed. Leon Edel (Library of America, 1984), p. 380.
6. Ibid., p. 383.
7. The following page references in the text are to Emerson's *Essays and Lectures*, ed. Joel Porte (Library of America, 1983).
8. William H. Gilman et al., *The Journals and Miscellaneous Notebooks of Ralph Waldo Emerson* (Harvard University Press, 1960–82), vol. 7, p. 525.
9. Walt Whitman, *Poetry and Prose*, ed. Justin Kaplan (Library of America, 1984), p. 11.
10. Ibid., pp. 5–7.
11. Emerson, *Essays*, pp. 214–15.
12. Ibid., p. 216.
13. Jonathan Edwards, *Miscellanies* #108, in George Marsden, *Jonathan Edwards: A Life* (Yale University Press, 2003), p. 100.
14. Samuel Sewall, *Phaenomena Quaedam Apocalyptica ad Aspectum Nove Orbi Configurata: Some Few Lines Towards a Description of the New Heaven as It Make to Those Who Stand upon the New Earth* (Bartholomew Green, 1697), p. 59.
15. Emerson, *Essays*, p. 84.
16. Henry Adams, *The Education of Henry Adams*, ed. Ernest Samuels and Jayne N. Samuels (Library of America, 1983), p. 777.
17. Albanese, *Corresponding Motion*, pp. 76–84.
18. Henry Adams, *Esther*, pp. 314–15.

19. Emerson, *Essays*, p. 87.
20. Adams, *Education*, p. 231.
21. Emerson quoted in Henry Mayer, *All on Fire: William Lloyd Garrison and the Abolition of Slavery* (St. Martin's Press, 1995), p. 355.
22. Mayer, ibid., p. 255.
23. *The Journals of Ralph Waldo Emerson*, ed. Edward W. Emerson and Waldo E. Forbes (Houghton Mifflin, 1909–14), vol. 9, pp. 245–46.
24. Ibid., p. 499.
25. Ibid., p. 440.
26. Emerson, "American Civilization," *The Atlantic* 9 (April 1862).
27. Richard Nixon in Garry Wills, *Nixon Agonistes: The Crisis of the Self-Made Man* (Houghton Mifflin, 1970), pp. 164–65.

17. THE SECOND GREAT AWAKENING

1. Mark A. Noll, *America's God: From Jonathan Edwards to Abraham Lincoln* (Oxford University Press, 2002), p. 181.
2. Ibid., p. 166.
3. Nathan O. Hatch, *The Democratization of American Christianity* (Yale University Press, 1989), p. 4.
4. Ibid., p. 4.
5. Noll, *America's God*, p. 169.
6. Ibid., pp. 200–201.
7. Mark A. Noll, *A History of Christianity in the United States and Canada* (William B. Eerdmans, 1992), p. 316.
8. Richard Hofstadter, *Anti-Intellectualism in American Life* (Alfred A. Knopf, 1963), p. 96.
9. Hatch, *Democratization*, pp. 130–33; Richard Carwardine, *Trans-Atlantic Revivalism: Popular Evangelicalism in Britain and America, 1790–1865* (Greenwood Press, 1978), pp. 104–7.
10. Peter Cartwright, *Autobiography*, ed. William Peter Strickland (Carlton & Porter, 1857), p. 79.
11. Hatch, *Democratization*, p. 87.
12. Ibid., p. 86.
13. For Bishop Allen, see W. E. B. DuBois, *The Philadelphia Negro* (University of Pennsylvania Press, 1899), pp. 18–22, and Gary B. Nash, *Forging Freedom: The Formation of Philadelphia's Black Community, 1720–1840* (Harvard University Press, 1988), pp. 95–99, 192–99, 227–33.
14. DuBois, *Philadelphia Negro*, p. 21. This judgment of 1899 would probably have been changed after the civil rights movement.
15. Hatch, *Democratization*, p. 107.
16. W. E. B. DuBois, *The Souls of Black Folk*.
17. Bernard A. Weisberger, *They Gathered at the River: The Story of the Great Revivalists and Their Impact upon Religion in America* (Quadrangle Books, 1958), pp. 34–35.
18. Daniel Walker Howe, "Religion and Politics in the Antebellum North," in Mark A. Noll, ed., *Religion and American Politics: From the Colonial Period to the 1980s* (Oxford University Press, 1990), pp. 124–25.
19. John Murrin, "The Great Inversion, or Court Versus Country: A Comparison of the

Revolution Settlement in England (1688–1721) and America (1776–1816)," in *Three British Revolutions: 1641–1688,* 1776, ed. J. G. A. Pocock (Princeton University Press, 1980), p. 425.

20. Noll, *America's God,* p. 198.

21. Alexis de Tocqueville, *Democracy in America,* trans. Arthur Goldhammer (Library of America, 2004), II.2, chapter 5, p. 595.

22. Ibid., I.2, chapter 9, p. 331.

23. Ibid., II.2, chapter 5, p. 98.

24. Isaiah Berlin, *The Roots of Romanticism* (Princeton University Press, 1999), p. 39.

25. Ibid., p. 38.

26. Gordon S. Wood, *The Radicalism of the American Revolution* (Vintage, 1993), p. 221.

27. Tocqueville, *Democracy,* II.3, chapter 1, p. 658.

28. Ibid., II.2, chapter 5, pp. 595, 598.

29. Mark Twain, *Autobiography,* ed. Charles Neider (HarperCollins, 1990), pp. 117–19.

30. *The Autobiography of Lyman Beecher* (Harvard University Press, 1961), p. 275.

31. *The Memoirs of Charles G. Finney: The Complete Restored Text,* ed. Garth Rosell and Richard A. G. Dupuis (Zondervan Publishing House, 1989), p. 47.

32. Weisberger, *They Gathered,* p. 94.

33. William G. McLoughlin Jr., *Modern Revivalism: Charles Grandison Finney to Billy Graham* (Ronald Press, 1959), p. 55.

34. Finney, *Memoirs,* p. 306.

35. Charles G. Finney, *Lectures on Revivals of Religion,* ed. William G. McLoughlin (Harvard University Press, 1960), pp. 13, 33.

36. Ibid., p. 181.

37. Weisberger, *They Gathered,* p. 101.

38. Hofstadter, *Anti-Intellectualism,* p. 82.

18. SCHISMS OVER SLAVERY

1. Ray Billington, *The Protestant Crusade* (Macmillan, 1938), pp. 68–76.

2. Charles R. Morris, *American Catholic* (Times Books, 1997), p. 60.

3. Billington, *Crusade,* pp. 221–30.

4. Ibid., p. 421.

5. Morris, *American Catholic,* p. 62.

6. M. I. Finley, *Ancient Slavery and Modern Ideology* (Penguin, 1980), p. 57.

7. Among the Tappans' many philanthropies was support for Oberlin College, Berea College, Fisk University, and Howard University.

8. Clement Eaton, *The Freedom-of-Thought Struggle in the Old South,* rev. and enlarged ed. (Harper Torchbooks, 1964), p. 201.

9. Russel B. Nye, *Freedom's Fetters: Civil Liberties and the Slavery Controversy, 1820–1860* (Michigan State College Press, 1949), chapter 5, "The Reign of Mob Law," and William W. Freehling, *The Road to Disunion,* vol. 1, *Secessionists at Bay, 1776–1864* (Oxford University Press, 1990), chapter 6, "Democrats as Lynchers."

10. Eaton, *Struggle,* pp. 216–37. In 1845, Cassius M. Clay, the Kentucky antislavery man, had his newspaper destroyed by a mob. Clay was a hero to blacks, which is why Muhammad Ali was first given his name (though he renounced it, oddly, as "a slave name").

11. Ibid., pp. 222–24.

12. William Lee Miller, *Arguing About Slavery: John Quincy Adams and the Great Battle in the United State Congress* (Viking Press, 1998), pp. 227–29.

13. Jefferson to William Cabell, Jan. 31, 1821.

14. Jefferson to John Taylor, Feb. 14, 1821. See Garry Wills, *Mr. Jefferson's University* (National Geographic Press, 2002), pp, 131–32.

15. Mitchell Snay collects a number of such statements in his *Gospel of Disunion: Religion and Separatism in the Antebellum South* (Cambridge University Press, 1993), pp. 118–22.

16. Ibid., pp. 122–26.

17. Ibid., p. 137.

18. Ibid., pp. 128–29.

19. David Brion Davis, *Inhuman Bondage: The Rise and Fall of Slavery in the New World* (Oxford University Press, 2006), p. 164.

20. Snay, *Gospel*, p. 139.

21. John C. Calhoun, Address to the Senate, Feb. 6, 1837.

22. James W. Silver, *Confederate Morale and Church Propaganda* (Confederate Publishing Company, 1957), p. 102.

23. E. Brooks Holifield, *The Gentlemen Theologians: American Theology in Southern Culture, 1795–1860* (Duke University Press, 1978), pp. 28–29.

24. Ibid., p. 30.

25. B. M. Palmer and W. T. Leacock, *The Rights of the South Defended in the Pulpits* (J. Y. Thompson of Mobile, 1860), p. 3.

26. Ibid., p. 5.

27. Snay, *Gospel*, pp. 37, 81, 93.

28. Ibid., pp. 131, 136, 141, 157.

29. Ibid., pp. 151–58.

30. *Central Presbyterian*, Nov. 17, 1869, cited in Snay, *Gospel*, p. 150.

31. Snay, *Gospel*, pp. 129–30, 133–34, 137.

32. W. T. Leacock, in Palmer and Leacock, *Rights*, p. 16.

19. GOD OF BATTLES

1. Charles Grandison Finney, *Lecture on Revivals of Religion*, ed. William G. McLoughlin (Harvard University Press, 1960), pp. 298–99.

2. Keith J. Hardman, *Charles Grandison Finney, 1792–1875: Revivalist and Reformer* (Syracuse University Press, 1987), p. 274.

3. Ibid., p. 364.

4. Harriet Beecher Stowe, *Uncle Tom's Cabin*, chapter 45 (Modern Library, 1985), pp. 551–52.

5. Henry Timrod, in Mark A. Noll, *A History of Christianity in the United States and Canada* (William B. Eerdmans, 1992), p. 313.

6. Reverend Jeremiah Bell Jeter, in Harry S. Stout, *Upon the Altar of the Nation: A Moral History of the American Civil War* (Viking, 2006), p. 133.

7. *Richmond Daily Dispatch*, Aug. 4, 1864, in Stout, ibid., p. 357.

8. Ward W. Briggs, *Soldier and Scholar: Basil Lanneau Gildersleeve and the Civil War* (University Press of Virginia, 1998), p. 129.

9. Noll, *History*, p. 331.

10. *The Times,* London, Mar. 23, 1863.

11. Benjamin Morgan Palmer, "Slavery a Divine Trust," in *The Rights of the South Defended in the Pulpits* (J. Y. Thomposon of Mobile, 1860), pp. 6–7.

12. For the Southerners' cult of Edmund Burke, see Larry E. Tise, *Proslavery: A History of the Defense of Slavery in America, 1701–1840* (University of Georgia Press, 1987), pp. 341–44, 351–55. These Romantics liked Burke just as they liked the novels of Walter Scott—what Mark Twain called the "Walter Scott disease" that caused the Civil War. Twain, *Mississippi Writings,* ed. Guy Cardwell (Library of America, 1982), pp. 500–502. Wolfgang Schivelbusch describes the South as "Scottland" in *The Culture of Defeat: On National Trauma, Mourning and Recovery,* trans. Jefferson Chase (Henry Holt and Company, 2003), pp. 50–53.

13. Horace Bushnell, "Popular Sovereignty by Divine Right," sermon delivered in the South Church, Hartford, Nov. 24, 1864, published in Bushnell, *Building Eras in Religion* (Charles Scribner's Sons, 1881), p. 306.

14. Ibid., p. 316.

15. Henry W. Bellows sermons in George M. Frederickson, *The Inner Civil War: Northern Intellectuals and the Crisis of the Union* (Harper Torchbooks, 1968), pp. 79, 136.

16. John Weiss, *The Life and Correspondence of Theodore Parker* (D. Appleton, 1864), vol. 2, pp. 170–72.

17. William Beecher and Samuel Scoville, *A Biography of Rev. Henry Ward Beecher* (Charles Wilson, 1888), p. 310.

18. Bushnell, *Building Eras,* p. 317.

19. Bushnell, "Our Obligation to the Dead," sermon preached at Yale, July 20, 1865, ibid., pp. 325–26, 327, 329, 341.

20. Charles Eliot Norton, "The Advantages of Defeat," *The Atlantic* 8 (Sept. 1861), p. 363.

21. Charles Eliot Norton to B. W. Curtis, May 11, 1862, in Fredrickson, *Inner Civil War,* p. 80.

22. *Richmond Daily Dispatch,* in Stout, *Upon the Altar,* pp. 123–24.

23. Ralph Waldo Emerson to Benjamin and Susan Rodman, June 17, 1863, in *The Letters of Ralph Waldo Emerson,* ed. Ralph L. Rusk (Columbia University Press, 1939), vol. 5, p. 332.

24. Fredrickson, *Inner Civil War,* p. 71.

25. *Letters of Francis Parkman,* ed. E. R. Jacobs (University of Oklahoma Press, 1960), vol. 1, p. 143.

26. Fredrickson, *Inner Civil War,* pp. 68–69.

27. Josephine Shaw Lowell, in David Brion Davis, *Inhuman Bondage: The Rise and Fall of Slavery in the New World* (Oxford University Press, 2006), p. 302.

28. Ibid., p. 391.

29. Ibid., p. 675.

30. Davis, *Bondage,* p. 302.

31. *Banner of the Covenant,* Philadelphia, May 31, 1862, cited in Strong, p. 123.

32. Ibid., p. 48.

33. Lawrence Levine, *Black Culture and Black Consciousness: Afro-American Folk Thought from Slavery to Freedom* (Oxford University Press, 1977), p. 52.

34. Ibid., pp. 136–37.

35. Ibid., p. 137.

36. Ibid.

37. James M. McPherson, *Battle Cry of Freedom: The Civil War Era* (Ballantine Books, 1989), pp. 846–47.

38. Levine, *Black Culture*, p. 137.

39. Lincoln, *Speeches and Writings, 1859–1865*, ed. Don E. Fehrenbacher (Library of America, 1989), p. 530.

40. Ibid., p. 361.

41. Stephen Mansfield, *The Faith of George W. Bush* (Tarcher, 2003), pp. 10–11. Bush said the same thing to his Evangelical speechwriter David Kuo when he recruited him for service in the 2000 presidential campaign: Kuo, *Tempting Faith: An Inside Story of Political Seduction* (Free Press, 2006), pp. 111–13.

42. Richard Carwardine, *Lincoln: A Life of Purpose and Power* (Alfred A. Knopf, 2006), p. 227.

43. Ibid., pp. 223–24.

44. Lincoln, *Writings, 1859–1865*, p. 628.

45. Carwardine, *Evangelicals and Politics in Antebellum America* (University of Tennessee Press, 1997).

46. Carwardine, *Lincoln*, p. 32.

47. For instance, "government of all the people, by all the people, for all the people," or "government over all the people, by all the people, and for the sake of all." For Parker's many variations on this formula, see John White Chadwick, *Theodore Parker: Preacher and Reformer* (Houghton Mifflin, 1900), pp. 322–23.

48. William H. Herndon and Jesse W. Weik, *Herndon's Lincoln*, ed. Paul M. Angle (Da Capo Press, 1942), p. 359.

49. Theodore Parker, "Transcendentalism" (1854), in *Works of Theodore Parker* (American Association, 1907), vol. 6, p. 30.

50. Lincoln, "Speech on the Dred Scott Decision" (1857), in *Speeches and Writings, 1832–1858*, ed. Don E. Fehrenbacher (Library of America, 1989), p. 398.

51. See Garry Wills, *Lincoln at Gettysburg: The Words That Remade America* (Simon & Schuster, 1992), chapter 3, "The Transcendental Declaration," pp. 90–120.

52. George Bancroft, *Literary and Historical Miscellanies* (Harper & Brothers, 1885), p. 486.

53. Allen Guelzo also neglects the Transcendentalist connection, but not to shove Lincoln into the Evangelical camp. He treats Lincoln as a Victorian Whig doubter, with a mystical belief in providence: *Abraham Lincoln, Redeemer President* (William B. Eerdmans, 1999), p. 462.

54. Carwardine, *Lincoln*, pp. 225–27.

55. R. Nathaniel Deft, *Religious Folk-Songs of the Negro* (Hampton Institute Press 1927), p. 58.

56. James Weldon Johnson and J. Rosamund Johnson, *The Book of American Negro Spirituals* (Viking, 1925), p. 40.

57. Lincoln to Albert G. Hodges, Apr. 4, 1864, *Writings, 1859–1865*, p. 586.

58. Mark A. Noll, *America's God: From Jonathan Edwards to Abraham Lincoln* (Oxford University Press, 2002), p. 434.

59. Ibid., p. 438. Guelzo too compares Lincoln's religious views to Emily Dickinson's (*Abraham Lincoln*, pp. 17–18, 419, 461).

60. James Oakes, *The Radical and the Republican: Frederick Douglass, Abraham Lincoln, and the Triumph of Antislavery Politics* (W. W. Norton & Company, 2007).

61. *The Autobiographies of Frederick Douglass,* ed. Henry Louis Gates Jr. (Library of America, 1994). For his conversion, see pp. 231–33, 638–40. For the Sabbath school, pp. 298–300, 559–60. For lay preaching, pp. 361–63.

62. Ibid., p. 16.

63. Ibid., p. 233.

64. Ibid., p. 245.

65. Ibid., pp. 1009–10.

20. RELIGION IN THE GILDED AGE

1. Alexander V. G. Allen, *Life and Letter of Phillips Brooks* (E. P. Dutton, 1900), vol. 1, p. 531.

2. Edward Beecher, in H. Richard Niebuhr, *The Kingdom of God in America* (Harper and Row, 1937), p. 157.

3. Confederate States of America, Constitution for the Provisional Government, online at Yale Law School Avalon Project.

4. Harry S. Stout, *Upon the Altar of the Nation: A Moral History of the American Civil War* (Viking, 2006), p. 48.

5. John Adger, "Northern and Southern Views of the Province of the Church," *Southern Presbyterian Review,* Mar 1866, Mark A. Noll, *The Civil War as a Theological Crisis* (University of North Carolina Press, 2006), p. 77.

6. David Brion Davis, *Inhuman Bondage: The Rise and Fall of Slavery in the New World* (Oxford University Press), p. 198.

7. Robert Wiebe, *The Search for Order, 1877–1920* (Hill and Wang, 1967), p. 41, describing "the distended society."

8. Richard Hofstadter, *The Age of Reform* (Vintage Books, 1955), pp. 150–51. Hofstadter quotes a study showing that 39 percent of the governing boards of private institutions were clergymen in 1860, while only 7 percent were in 1930.

9. Noll, *Civil War,* p. 13.

10. Burton J. Bledstein, *The Culture of Professionalism: The Middle Class and the Development of Higher Education in America* (Norton, 1876).

11. Ann Douglas, *The Feminization of American Culture* (Alfred A. Knopf, 1877), pp. 9–12 and passim.

12. Niebuhr, *Kingdom,* p. 193.

13. Mark Twain, *Mississippi Writings,* ed. Guy Cardwell (Library of America, 1982), p. 726.

14. Douglas, *Feminization,* pp. 200–226.

15. See, for instance, Norris Magnuson, *Salvation in the Slums: Evangelical Social Work, 1865–1920* (Baker Book House, 1977), pp. 30–44, and Timothy L. Smith, *Revivalism and Social Reform in Mid-Nineteenth-Century America* (Abingdon Press, 1957), pp. 163–77.

16. Wiebe, *Search,* pp. 133–63.

17. William G. McLoughlin Jr, *Modern Revivalism: Charles Grandison Finney to Billy Graham* (Ronald Press, 1959), p. 166.

18. Bruce J. Evensen, *God's Man for the Gilded Age: D. L. Moody and the Rise of Modern Mass Evangelism* (Oxford University Press, 2003), pp. 11, 16.

19. Don Sweeting, "The Great Turning Point in the Life of D. L. Moody," in Theodore George, ed., *Mr. Moody and the Evangelical Tradition* (T. & T. Clark International, 2004), pp. 43–44.

20. McLoughlin, *Revivalism*, pp. 177–216.
21. Evensen, *God's Man*, pp. 129–34.
22. James J. Findlay Jr., *Dwight L. Moody: American Evangelist, 1837–1899* (University of Chicago Press, 1969), p. 200.
23. McLoughlin, *Revivalism*, pp. 223–27. McLoughlin gives a rundown of the money contributed by these men (pp. 225–27).
24. Ibid., p. 221.
25. Ibid., p. 222.
26. Findlay, *Moody*, pp. 262–66.
27. Richard Hofstadter, *Anti-Intellectualsim in American Life* (Alfred A. Knopf, 1963), p. 110.
28. George Marsden, *Fundamentalism and American Culture*, 2nd ed. (Oxford University Press, 2006), pp. 36–37.
29. McLouglin, *Revivalism*, pp. 254–55.
30. Ibid., p. 265. McLoughlin gives church-growth statistics.
31. Ibid., p. 246.
32. Ibid., p. 253.
33. Marsden, *Fundamentalism*, p. 35.
34. Moody, in Stanley N. Gundry, *Love Them In: The Proclamation Theology of D. L. Moody* (Moody Press, 1976), pp. 217–18.
35. McLoughlin, *Revivalism*, p. 257.
36. Marsden, *Fundamentalism*, p. 35.
37. Ibid., p. 46.
38. Findlay, *Moody*, pp. 349–54.
39. Virginia Lieson Brereton, *Training God's Army: The American Bible School* (Indiana University Press), p. 53.
40. Ibid., p. 78.
41. Ibid.
42. William James, *The Varieties of Religious Experience*, in *Writings*, ed. Bruce Kuklick (Library of America, 1987), p. 93.
43. Evensen, *God's Man*, p. 3.
44. Martin E. Marty, Foreword to Findlay, *Moody*, p. 1.

21. SECOND-COMING THEOLOGY

1. George Marsden, *Fundamentalism and American Culture*, 2nd ed. (Oxford University Press, 2006), p. 33.
2. William G. McLoughlin, *Modern Revivalism: Charles Grandison Finney to Billy Graham* (Ronald Press, 1959), p. 372.
3. Ernest R. Sandeen, *The Roots of Fundamentalism: British and American Millenarianism, 1800–1930* (University of Chicago Press, 1970), pp. 71–73.
4. Ibid., p. 31.
5. Paul Boyer, *When Time Shall Be No More: Prophecy Belief in Modern American Culture* (Harvard University Press, 1992), p. 97.
6. Ibid., p. 98.
7. James Barr, *Fundamentalism* (Westminster Press, 1978), p. 191.
8. Sandeen, *Roots*, pp. 188–91.

9. Ibid., pp. 194–99.

10. Ibid., pp. xiv, 273–74.

11. Some confuse *The Fundamentals* with another statement that came out at the same time, and that was aimed specifically against modernism—the list of Five Points of Fundamental Belief drawn up in 1910 by the General Assembly of the Presbyterian Conference. The five points were (1) biblical inerrancy, (2) virgin birth of Jesus, (3) substitutionary atonement by Christ, (4) physical resurrection of Christ, (5) physical return of Christ.

12. The Premillennialists are less fond of the parallel passage in the Gospel of Luke (17.26–37). That too begins with the story of Noah, but it continues: "I tell you, in that night there shall be two men in one bed; the one shall be taken and the other shall be left" (v. 34). They probably shy from the idea that a gay man can be saved.

13. Peter E. Prescott, *Dispensationalist Eschatology and Its Influence on American and British Religious Movements* (Edwin Mellen Press, 1999), p. 264.

14. Jerry Falwell, 1963 cassette, quoted in Boyer, *When Time*, p. 137.

15. Billy Graham, *World Aflame* (Penguin Books, 1984), p. 149.

22. SECOND-COMING POLITICS

1. Cyrus I. Scofield, *Addresses on Prophecy* (Arno C. Gaebelein Press, n.d.), p. 26.

2. Arno Gaebelein, *Our Hope* 19 (July 1912), p. 50.

3. Eli Reese, in Timothy Weber, *Living in the Shadow of the Second Coming*, enlarged ed. (Academie Books, 1983), p. 94.

4. Paul Boyer, *When Time Shall Be No More: Prophecy Belief in a Modern America Culture* (Harvard University Press, 1992) pp. 119–25, 144–48. For fear of the Aspen Institute see Michael Lienesch, *Redeeming America: Piety and Politics in the New Christian Right* (University of North Carolina Press, 1993), p. 164.

5. Pat Robertson, *New World Order* (Word Publishing, 1991), p. 37.

6. Charles Reihl, "Solution to Prohibition," *The Truth* 15 (1889), pp. 370–75.

7. For limits to Premillennial passivity, or exceptions to it, see Boyer, *When Time*, pp. 290–304.

8. Tim LaHaye, *Battle for the Mind* (Baker Book House, 1980), p. 29.

9. Yaakov Ariel, "How Are Jews and Christians Portrayed in the Left Behind Series?" in Bruce David Forbes and Jeanne Halgren Kilde, *Rapture, Revelation, and the End Times: Exploring the Left Behind Series* (Palgrave Macmillan, 2004), pp. 134–35.

10. Yaakov Ariel, *On Behalf of Israel: American Fundamentalist Attitudes Toward Jews, Judaism, and Zionism, 1865–1945* (Carlson Publishing, 1991), p. 55.

11. Ibid., p. 64.

12. Ibid., p. 96.

13. Ibid., p. 391.

14. Ibid., pp. 62, 67; Boyer, *When Time*, p. 209.

15. Lucy Dawidowicz, "Politics, the Jews, and the '84 Election," *Commentary*, Feb. 1984, p. 28. Dispensationalists make many pilgrimages to Israel, where they are welcomed by high government officials. Tim LaHaye is a special favorite there—see Ariel, "How Are Jews?" pp. 145–46.

16. Ariel, "How Are Jews?" pp. 146–47.

17. Ibid., p. 156.

18. Jonathan Kirsch, *A History of the End of the World: How the Most Controversial Book in the Bible Changed the Course of Western Civilization* (HarperSan Franciso, 2006), p. 238. Falwell apologized for his blunt way of stating his belief but said he held to his belief. Yet he is a welcome visitor to Israel.

19. *Scofield Reference Bible,* note on Revelation 18.2.

20. Ariel, *On Behalf,* pp. 63, 112.

21. Ibid., p. 104.

22. Ibid., pp. 62–63.

23. Ibid., p. 120.

24. Ariel, "How are Jews?" p. 140.

25. Boyer, *When Time,* pp. 193–95.

26. Ariel, "How Are Jews?" pp. 151–55.

27. Ronald Reagan, interview in *Christian Life,* May 1968, quoted in Boyer, *When Time,* p. 162.

28. Boyer, ibid., pp. 154–56.

29. Ibid., p. 162.

30. Ibid., p. 197.

31. Ibid., p. 142.

32. Ibid., p. 135.

33. Ibid., p. 136.

34. Ibid., p. 299.

35. A. G. Mojtabai, *Blessed Assurance: At Home with the Bomb in Amarillo, Texas* (Syracuse University Press, 1986), p. 47.

36. Ibid., p. 167.

37. Ibid., pp. 180–81.

38. Boyer, *When Time,* pp. 134–35, 298–300.

39. Amy Johnson Frykholm, *Rapture Culture: Left Behind in Evangelical America* (Oxford University Press, 2004), p. 20.

40. Mojtabai, *Blessed Assurance,* pp. 94–95.

41. Ibid., p. 177.

42. Barna Research Group, Survey of May 2001, reported in Bruce David Forbes, "How Popular are the Left Behind Books—and Why?" in Forbes and Kilde, *Rapture,* pp. 8–9.

43. Tim LaHaye and Jerry B. Jenkins, *Glorious Appearing* (Tyndale House Publishing, 2004).

23. THE SOCIAL GOSPEL

1. Richard Hofstadter, *The Progressive Historians* (Alfred A. Knopf, 1968).

2. Richard Hofstadter, *The Age of Reform* (Vintage Books, 1955), pp. 131–73.

3. Robert Wiebe, *The Search for Order, 1877–1920* (Hill and Wang, 1967), pp. 111–32.

4. Ibid., p. 208.

5. Hofstadter, *Age of Reform,* p. 152.

6. Wiebe, *Search,* p. 208.

7. Henry F. May, *Protestant Churches and Industrial America* (Harper & Brothers, 1949), pp. 184–93.

8. Ibid., p. 184.

9. Ibid., p. 186.
10. Charles Howard Hopkins, *The Rise of the Social Gospel in American Protestantism, 1865–1915* (Yale University Press, 1940), p. 129.
11. Hopkins, *Rise,* p. 255.
12. May, *Protestant Churches,* pp. 207–13.
13. Ibid., pp. 199–200.
14. William Rainsford, "The National Obligation," *Homiletic Review* 35 (June 1898), p. 518.
15. Josiah Strong, *Our Country: Its Possible Future and Its Present Crisis,* ed. Jurgen Herbst (Harvard University Press, 1963), pp. 172–77.
16. Ibid., p. 212.
17. Ibid., pp. 212–13.
18. Ibid., p. 214.
19. Ibid., p. 217.
20. Ibid., p. 216.
21. Ira V. Brown, *Lyman Abbott: Christian Evolutionist* (Harvard University Press, 1953), p. 178.
22. Ibid., p. 214.
23. Lyman Abbott, *The Rights of Man* (Houghton Mifflin, 1901), p. 219.
24. Lyman Abbott, *The Evolution of Christianity* (Houghton Mifflin, 1892), p. 219.
25. Lyman Abbott, *The Outlook,* Oct. 6, 1900, p. 300.
26. Lyman Abbott, *Reminiscences* (Houghton Mifflin, 1914), pp. 437–38.
27. *The Christian Advocate,* Jan. 22, 1903. The "benevolent assimilation" proclamation was issued Dec. 21, 1898.
28. Stuart Creighton Miller, *"Benevolent Assimilation": The American Conquest of the Philippines, 1899–1903* (Yale University Press, 1982), p. 120.
29. Ibid., pp. 136–39.
30. "Address on the Philippine Question" (1903), in *William James: Writings, 1902–1910,* ed. Bruce Kuklick (Library of America, 1987), p. 1131.
31. Mark Twain, "To the Person Sitting in Darkness," *North American Review,* 1901, reprinted in Frederick Anderson, *A Pen Warmed-Up in Hell: Mark Twain in Protest* (Harper & Row, 1972), p. 75.
32. Ibid., p. 76.

24. Evangelicals Riding High

1. For the Progressives' championing of Prohibition, see James H. Timberlake, *Prohibition and the Progressive Movement, 1900–1920* (Atheneum, 1970). It was the immigrant-fearing "old stock" element among the Progressives that led the way for Prohibition (pp. 126–27). The American Medical Association and the Mayo Clinic were part of this "scientific" initiative (pp. 47–48).
2. K. Austin Kerr, *Organized for Prohibition: A New History of the Anti-Saloon League* (Yale University Press, 1985), pp. 21–24.
3. Sean Dennis Cashman, *Prohibition: The Lie of the Land* (Free Press, 1981), p. 5.
4. Kerr, *Organized,* p. 242.
5. Ibid., p. 4.
6. Ibid., p. 24.
7. Timberlake, *Prohibition,* p. 110.

8. Ruth Bordin, *Frances Willard: A Biography* (University of North Carolina Press, 1986), pp. 65–70.

9. Ibid., pp. 60–65.

10. Ibid., p. 88.

11. Ibid., pp. 87–89.

12. Ibid., pp. 98–102.

13. Ibid., pp. 137–48.

14. Kerr, *Organized,* pp. 54–63.

15. Cashman, *Prohibition,* pp. 7–8.

16. Kerr, *Organized,* pp. 32, 137–38, 173.

17. Wayne Wheeler, interview in the *New York Times,* Mar. 29, 1926.

18. Virginius Dabney, *Dry Messiah: The Life of Bishop Cannon* (Alfred A. Knopf, 1949), pp. 243, 311.

19. Norman H. Clark, *Deliver Us from Evil: An Interpretation of American Prohibition* (W. W. Norton & Company, 1976), p. 114.

20. William McLoughlin, *Billy Sunday Was His Real Name* (University of Chicago Press, 1955), p. 123.

21. Ibid., pp. 49–50.

22. Ibid., pp. 9–12, 42–43, 168–70.

23. Ibid., p. 123.

24. Ibid., p. 138.

25. Bernard A. Weisberger, *They Gathered at the River: The Story of the Great Revivalists and Their Impact upon Religion in America* (Quadrangle, 1958), p. 258.

26. Richard Hofstadter, *Anti-Intellectualism in American Life* (Alfred A. Knopf, 1963), p. 90.

27. McLoughlin, *Billy Sunday,* pp. 44–45, 178.

28. Ibid., p. 163.

29. Weisberger, *They Gathered,* p. 247.

30. McLoughlin, *Billy Sunday,* p. 171.

31. Ibid., p. 175.

32. Ibid., p. 178.

33. Ibid., p. 164.

34. Ibid., pp. 226–53.

35. Ibid., p. 237.

36. Ibid., p. 241.

37. Lyman Abbott, *The Twentieth Century Crusade* (Macmillan, 1918), p. 33.

38. Ira V. Brown, *Lyman Abbott: Christian Evolutionist* (Harvard University Press, 1953), p. 222.

39. Ibid., pp. 222–23.

40. George Marsden, *Fundamentalism and American Culture* (Oxford University Press, 2006), p. 142.

41. Ray H. Abrams, *Preachers Present Arms* (Herald Press, 1933), p. 79.

42. Ibid., p. 112.

43. Ibid., p. 71.

44. Ibid., p. 56.

45. Ibid., p. 57.

46. Marsden, *Fundamentalism,* p. 143.

47. Leo P. Ribuffo, *The Old Christian Right: The Protestant Far Right from the Great Depression to the Cold War* (Temple University Press, 1983), p. 84.
48. Ibid., p. 143.
49. Marsden, *Fundamentalism*, pp. 154–55.
50. Ibid., p. 156.
51. McLoughlin, *Billy Sunday*, p. 276.
52. Marsden, *Fundamentalism*, p. 191.

25. Evangelicals Brought Low

1. Virginius Dabney, *Dry Messiah: The Life of Bishop Cannon* (Alfred A. Knopf, 1949), pp. 49–50, 132–33.
2. K. Austin Kerr, *Organized for Prohibition: A New History of the Anti-Saloon League* (Yale University Press, 1985), pp. 222–24.
3. Ibid., p. 228.
4. Ibid., p. 263.
5. Ibid., pp. 231–39.
6. Justin Steuart, *Wayne Wheeler, Dry Boss* (Fleming H. Revell Company, 1928), p. 14.
7. Herbert Asbury, *The Great Illusion: An Informal History of Prohibition* (Doubleday, 1950), p. 279.
8. Kerr, *Organized*, pp. 230, 255.
9. Norman H. Clark, *Deliver Us From Evil: An Interpretation of American Prohibition* (W. W. Norton & Company, 1976), p. 114.
10. Edward J. Lawson, *Trial and Error: The American Controversy over Creation and Evolution* (Oxford University Press, 1985), p. 28.
11. Robert W. Cherny, *A Righteous Cause: The Life of William Jennings Bryan* (Little, Brown, 1965), pp. 202–3.
12. Carl Bode, *Mencken* (Southern Illinois University Press, 1969), p. 265.
13. William Manchester, *Disturber of the Peace: The Life of H. L. Mencken* (Harper & Row, 1951), p. 144.
14. Joel A. Carpenter makes a strong case that reports of the death of Fundamentalism were exaggerated. He points, for instance, to the popular radio ministry of Charles Fuller, who began broadcasting just before the Scopes trial and went on gathering strength through the Twenties and Thirties: *Revive Us Again: The Reawakening of American Fundamentalism* (Oxford University Press, 1997), pp. 135–40.
15. Mark A. Noll, *The Scandal of the Evangelical Mind* (Eerdmans, 1994), especially chapter 5, "The Intellectual Disaster of Fundamentalism."
16. Dabney, *Dry Messiah*, p. 190.
17. Robert A. Hohner, *Prohibition and Politics: The Life of Bishop James Cannon, Jr.* (University of South Carolina Press, 1999).
18. Ibid., pp. 109–10.
19. Ibid., pp. 110–20.
20. Ibid., pp. 114–18.
21. Dabney, *Dry Messiah*, pp. 151–55.
22. Ibid., p. 183.
23. James R. Sweeney, "Rum, Romanism, and Virginia Democrats: The Party Leaders and

the Campaign of 1928," *Virginia Magazine of History and Biography* 90 (October 1982), pp. 407–22.

24. Michael Williams, *The Shadow of the Pope* (Whittlesey House, 1932), p. 193.

25. Hohner, *Prohibition,* p. 222; Williams, *Shadow,* p. 194.

26. Dabney, *Dry Messiah,* p. 181.

27. Hohner, *Prohibition,* p. 227.

28. Ibid., p. 228.

29. Williams, *Shadow,* p. 250.

30. Dabney, *Dry Messiah,* p. 184.

31. David Burner, *The Politics of Provincialism: The Democratic Party in Transition, 1918–1932* (Alfred A. Knopf, 1968), p. 202.

32. Sweeney, "Rum, Romanism," pp. 419–20.

33. Dabney, *Dry Messiah,* p. 190.

34. Burner, *Politics,* p. 228.

35. Cannon's first biographer, Virginius Dabney, thought Cannon guilty on all points. His most recent biographer, Robert Hohner, defends him on these and all other matters—but the Hohner defense is so strained as to become an inadvertent confirmation of the charges. It is true that Cannon's assistant, who became his wife when Cannon's first wife died, was tricked by Hearst journalists into signing an affidavit that confessed her adultery with the bishop. The document would not be admissible in a court of law on procedural grounds. Still, there the letter is.

36. Dabney, *Dry Messiah,* p. 236.

26. RELIGION IN A RADICAL TIME

1. Leo P. Ribuffo, *The Old Christian Right: The Protestant Far Right from the Great Depression to the Cold War* (Temple University Press, 1983), p. 99.

2. Jonathan Alter, *The Defining Moment: FDR's Hundred Days and the Triumph of Hope* (Simon & Schuster, 2006), p. 6.

3. Ibid., p. 187.

4. Ibid., p. 185.

5. Ibid., p. 186.

6. A. Scott Berg, *Lindbergh* (G. P. Putnam's Sons, 1998), pp. 377–78.

7. Ronald Radosh argues that Lawrence was a Fascist but not a Nazi: *Prophets on the Right: Profiles of Conservative Critics of American Globalism* (Simon & Schuster, 1975), pp. 275 ff. But Lawrence's followers did not grasp the distinction: David H. Bennett, *Demagogues in the Depression: American Radicals and the Union Party, 1932–1936* (Rutgers University Press, 1969), p. 4.

8. Gerald Colby, *Du Pont: Behind the Nylon Curtain* (Prentice-Hall, 1974).

9. Bennett, *Demagogues,* p. 4.

10. Ribuffo, *Old Christian Right,* p. 64. Pelley had been a mediocre novelist and screenplay writer until he had a mystic vision. He argued that Jesus was not a Jew, but FDR was (pp. 59–60). The Silver Shirts had for their emblem a scourge, the one Jesus used to drive the money changers from the temple (p. 64). The House Committee on Un-American Activities, under its chairman, Martin Dies, investigated Pelley, and

he was prosecuted under the World War I Espionage Act, which criminalized opinion, and sent to a federal penitentiary (pp. 74–79). He was not paroled until 1950.

11. Ibid., pp. 80–127.
12. Bennett, *Demagogues*, p. 54.
13. Wallace Stegner, "The Radio Priest and His Flock," in Isabel Leighton, ed., *The Aspirin Age, 1919–1941* (Simon & Schuster, 1949), p. 234.
14. Bennett, *Demagogues*, p. 41.
15. Ibid., p 279.
16. Ibid., p. 80; James A. Farley, *Jim Farley's Story* (McGraw-Hill Book Co., 1948), p. 52; and Thomas Maier, *The Kennedys: America's Emerald Kings* (Basic Books, 2003), pp. 102–9.
17. Bennett, *Demagogues*, p. 180.
18. Ibid., p. 215.
19. Ibid., pp. 269–72.
20. Ibid., pp. 281–82.
21. Ibid., p. 285.
22. Charles R. Morris, *American Catholic: The Saints and Sinners Who Built America's Most Powerful Church* (Random House, 1997), p. 153.
23. Robert I. Gannon, S.J., *The Cardinal Spellman Story* (Doubleday, 1962), p. 153.
24. Ibid., pp. 160–65.
25. Morris, *American Catholic*, p. 231.
26. John Cooney, *The American Pope: The Life and Times of Francis Cardinal Spellman* (Random House, 1984), p. 112.
27. Gannon, *Cardinal Spellman*, p. 154.
28. Cooney, *American Pope*, p. 112.
29. Ibid., pp. 124–34.
30. Mark A. Noll, *The Civil War as a Theological Crisis* (University of North Carolina Press, 2006), p. 23.
31. Geoffrey C. Ward, *A First-Class Temperament: The Emergence of Franklin Roosevelt* (Harper & Row, 1989), p. 254.
32. Ibid.
33. Ibid.
34. Samuel B. Hand, *Counsel and Advise: A Political Biography of Samuel I. Rosenman* (Garland Publishing, Inc., 1979), p. 61.
35. Ibid., p. 100.
36. Ibid., pp. 234–38.
37. Gregory D. Black, *Hollywood Censored: Morality Codes, Catholics, and the Movies* (Cambridge University Press, 1994), p. 33.
38. Ibid., p. 33.
39. Ibid., pp. 156–62.
40. Morris, *American Catholic*, pp. 204–6.
41. Ibid., pp. 165–67.
42. Neal Gabler, *An Empire of Their Own: How the Jews Invented Hollywood* (Doubleday Anchor, 1988), p. 285.

43. Ibid., p. 286.
44. Ibid., p. 287.

27. THE GREAT RELIGIOUS TRUCE

1. Martin E. Marty, *The New Shape of American Religion* (Harper & Brothers, 1959), p. 15.
2. Will Herberg, *Protestant—Catholic—Jew: An Essay in American Religious Sociology*, rev. ed. (Anchor Books, 1960), p. 51.
3. Niebuhr's daughter, Elizabeth Sifton, gives the history of the prayer, and of its many misattributions, in *The Serenity Prayer: Faith and Politics in Times of Peace and War* (W. W. Norton & Company, 2003).
4. George M. Marsden, *Fundamentalism and American Culture* (Oxford University Press, 2006), pp. 143–45.
5. Joel A. Carpenter, *Revive Us Again: The Reawakening of American Fundamentalism* (Oxford University Press, 1997), p. 165.
6. Ibid., pp. 169–70, 225.
7. Herberg, *Protestant*, p. 212.
8. Melvin Konner, *Unsettled: An Anthropology of the Jews* (Viking Compass, 2003), p. 347.
9. Murray Friedman, *The Neoconservative Revolution: Jewish Intellectuals and the Shaping of Public Policy* (Cambridge University Press, 2005), p. 13.
10. Herberg, *Protestant*, pp. 186–88.
11. Ibid., p. 191.
12. Ibid., pp. 75–84.
13. Nathan Glazer, *American Judaism* (University of Chicago Press, 1957), p. 124.
14. William Lee Miller, *Piety Along the Potomac* (Houghton Mifflin, 1964), p. 131.
15. Marty, *New Shape*, p. 7.
16. Ibid., p. 86.
17. Ibid., p. 12.
18. Ibid., p. 21.
19. Ibid., p. 22.
20. Ibid., p. 26.
21. Ibid., p. 27.

28. THE RIGHTS REVOLUTION

1. For the shooting at Blackmun, see Linda Greenhouse, *Becoming Justice Blackmun* (Henry Holt and Company, 2005), p. 182.
2. M. R. Werner, *Julius Rosenwald: The Life of a Practical Humanitarian* (Harper & Brothers, 1939), pp. 127–36.
3. Taylor Branch, *Parting the Waters: America in the King Years, 1954–63* (Simon & Schuster, 1988), pp. 7–25.
4. John LaFarge, S. J., *The Manner Is Ordinary* (Harcourt, Brace and Company, 1954), pp. 184–89.
5. George Passelecq and Bernard Suchecky, *The Hidden Encyclical of Pius XI*, trans. Steven Rendall, with an introduction by Garry Wills (Harcourt Brace, 1997). LaFarge's encyclical had been watered down, by conservative Jesuit superiors in Rome, even before it was submitted to Pius XI.

6. LaFarge, *Manner*, pp. 140–42.
7. Branch, *Parting the Waters*, pp. 121–22.
8. Taylor Branch, *At Canaan's Edge: America in the King Years, 1965–68* (Simon & Schuster, 2006), pp. 134–35, 143.
9. Ibid., p. 154.
10. Ibid., p. 273.
11. William Martin, *With God on Our Side: The Rise of the Religious Right in America* (Broadway Books, 1996), pp. 59–60.
12. Susan Friend Harding, *The Book of Jerry Falwell: Fundamentalist Language and Politics* (Princeton University Press, 2000), p. 22. Falwell, like many Southern preachers, later tried to rewrite the history of his comments on race. He claimed to have repented his 1958 attack on integration "within a year or so," baptizing a black couple and integrating his church. In fact, the first blacks were not admitted to his church for another ten years, and he first baptized a black couple in 1971. Martin, *God on Our Side*, p. 58.
13. Martin, ibid., pp. 79–80.
14. Jane Mansbridge, *Why We Lost the ERA* (University of Chicago Press, 1986), pp. 110–17.
15. Ibid., pp. 188–91.
16. Greenhouse, *Blackmun*, pp. 190–94.
17. Ibid., pp. 200–206.
18. John Horgan, ed. *"Humanae Vitae" and the Bishops: The Encyclical and the Statements of the National Hierarchies* (Irish University Press, 1972), pp. 15–16.
19. Philip Kaufman, *Why You Can Disagree and Remain a Faithful Catholic* (Crossroads, 1991), pp. 72–83.
20. Dean R. Hoge et al., *Young Adult Catholics: Religion in the Culture of Choice* (University of Notre Dame Press, 2001), p. 200.
21. Ibid., pp. 37–38.
22. Martin Duberman, *Stonewall* (Penguin, 1993), pp. 190–91.
23. White was paroled after five years, and committed suicide a year after that. His defense was called the "Twinkie defense" because his lawyers argued that he was mentally disturbed from eating junk food.
24. Peter Mathiessen, *In the Spirit of Crazy Horse* (Viking, 1983).
25. Peter Mathiessen, *Sal Si Puedes: Cesar Chavez and the New American Revolution* (Dell, 1969), p. 128.

29. EVANGELICALS COUNTERATTACK

1. Pat Robertson, in the *Washington Post*, Aug. 23, 1993.
2. William Martin, *With God on Our Side: The Rise of the Religious Right in America* (Broadway Books, 1996), p. 259.
3. As was noticed earlier, the Everson case (1947) had affirmed the wall of separation, but it let federal funds go to busing for parochial students and there was no immediate follow-up. This seemed an isolated case at the time, since there had been only three rulings on church-state relations in the previous fifty-five years. "The modern constitutional law of separation begins with *Everson*.... Between 1951 and 1971, the Court ... decided ten cases bearing directly on the 'no establishment' clause, exactly twice the number it had decided in the preceding 162 years of activity." Frank J. Sorauf,

The Wall of Separation: The Constitutional Politics of Church and State (Princeton University Press, 1976), p. 21.

4. Martin, *With God*, pp. 77–78.

5. Ibid., pp. 70–71.

6. Dorothy Nelkin, *The Creation Controversy: Science or Scripture in the Schools* (W. W. Norton & Company, 1982), p. 33.

7. Susan Friend Harding, *The Book of Jerry Falwell: Fundamentalist Language and Politics* (Princeton University Press, 2000), p. 218.

8. Martin, *With God*, p. 191

9. Ibid., p. 192.

10. Tim LaHaye, *Battle for the Mind* (Baker Book House, 1980), p. 77.

11. Ibid., p. 122.

12. Ibid., p. 107.

13. Ibid., p. 125.

14. Ibid., p. 139.

15. Ibid., p. 164.

16. Ibid., p. 342.

17. Esther Kaplan, *With God on Their Side* (New Press, 2004), p. 131.

18. Murray Friedman, *The Neoconservative Revolution: Jewish Intellectuals and the Shaping of Public Policy* (Camnbridge University Press, 2005), pp. 205–6.

19. Ibid., p. 215.

20. Martin, *With God*, pp. 95–96.

21. Ibid., pp. 41–42.

22. Graham said that Jews "don't really know how I feel about what they're doing to this country," namely that they had a "stranglehold" on the media, so that "they're the ones putting out all the pornography." Alexander Cockburn, *American Journal*, Mar. 12, 2000. When the tapes were published, Graham apologized in the magazine he had founded, *Christianity Today*, Apr. 22, 2002.

23. Martin, *With God*, pp. 169–73.

24. Jimmy Carter, *Our Endangered Values: America's Moral Crisis* (Simon & Schuster, 2005), p. 32.

25. Martin, *With God*, p. 189.

26. Ibid., p. 231.

27. Ibid., p. 251.

28. Ibid., p. 252.

29. Ibid., pp. 263–64.

30. Ibid., pp. 114–16.

31. Kaplan, *With God*, pp. 28–29.

32. Pat Robertson, *New World Order* (Word Publishers, 1991), p. 58.

33. Kaplan, *With God*, p. 130.

34. Friedman, *Neoconservative Revolution*, p. 213.

35. Paul Weyrich, Free Congress Web site, cited in Kaplan, *With God*, p. 2.

30. FAITH-BASED GOVERNMENT

1. Esther Kaplan, *With God on Their Side: How Fundamentalists Trampled Science, Policy, and Democracy in George W. Bush's White House* (New Press, 2004), p. 84.

2. Ibid., p. 83.
3. Ibid., pp. 84–85, 110–12, 120–21, 137–40.
4. David Frum, *The Right Man: The Surprise Presidency of George W. Bush* (Random House, 2003), pp. 3–4.
5. Kaplan, *With God*, p. 83.
6. Hamil R. Harris, "Putting Worship into Their Workday: More Federal Employees Participating in Prayer Services at the Office," *Washington Post*, Nov. 19, 2001.
7. David Kuo, *Tempting Faith: An Inside Story of Political Seduction* (Free Press, 2006), p. 69.
8. Ibid., p. 71.
9. David Johnston and Neil A. Lewis, "Religious Right Made Big Push to Put Ashcroft in Justice Department," *New York Times*, Jan. 7, 2001.
10. Kaplan, *With God*, p. 34.
11. "Violence and Harassment at U.S. Abortion Clinics," Ontario Consultants on Religious Tolerance, Nov. 9, 2004.
12. Ibid., pp. 135–36.
13. Evangelicals have made a concerted effort to assert that the fetus is a person. When Bush set up a new part of Health and Human Services, the Secretary's Advisory Committee on Human Research Protection, its charter spoke of embryos and human fetuses as "human subjects," and the National Right to Life Committee praised it for including "all living members of the species homo sapiens at every stage of their development." Kaplan, *With God*, p. 120.
14. Eric Lichtblau, "Ashcroft Defends Subpoenas," *New York Times*, Feb. 13, 2004.
15. Tom Hamburger and Peter Wallsten, *One Party Country: The Republican Plan for Dominance in the 21st Century* (John Wiley & Sons, 2006), p. 129. Karl Rove also negotiated with the Salvation Army to exempt them from anti-discrimination laws where gays were concerned: Dana Milbank, "Rove Heard Charity Plea on Gay Bias," *Washington Post*, July 12, 2001.
16. Kaplan, *With God*, p. 156.
17. Hamburger and Wallsten, *One Party*, p. 115.
18. Kuo, *Tempting Faith*, p. 252.
19. Ibid., p. 122
20. Ibid., p. 133.
21. Ibid., pp. 129–30.
22. Letter of John DiIulio to Ron Suskind, in *Esquire*, Oct. 2002.
23. Nicholas D. Kristof, "For Bush, His Toughest Call Was the Choice to Run at All," *New York Times*, Oct. 29, 2000.
24. Peter Baker and Peter Slevin, "Bush Remarks on Intelligent Design Theory Fuel Debate," *Washington Post*, Aug. 3, 2005.
25. Chris Mooney, *The Republican War on Science* (Basic Books, 2005), pp. 164–74.
26. Kaplan, *With God*, pp. 91–94.
27. Report of Public Employees for Environmental Responsibility (PEER), Dec. 28, 2006. Park officials claimed that bookstores at the park are like libraries, stocking books without judgment of their content—a claim the service's own guideline denies. Besides, in 2003 the Noah's flood book was the only one approved for sale while twenty-two other books and products were rejected.

28. Ibid., p. 105.
29. Mooney, *Republican War,* pp. 79–101.
30. Michael Barone and Richard E. Cohen, *The Almanac of American Politics, 2006* (National Journal Group, 2006), p. 1, 365.
31. James R. Inhofe, Speech in the Senate, March 4, 2002.
32. Kaplan, *With God,* p. 6.
33. Ibid.
34. Mooney, *Republican War,* p. 213.
35. Ibid., pp. 218–19.
36. Amanda Schaffer, "The Family UN-Planner," Medical Examiner, *Slate,* Nov. 21, 2006. Dr. Kerouack also espouses the discredited views that abortion causes breast cancer and that contraceptives do not work.
37. Kaplan, *With God,* p. 126.
38. Ibid., p. 126. Mooney, *Republican War,* pp. 202–03.
39. Eleonor Clift, "400,000 Frozen Embryos," *Newsweek,* July 21, 2006.
40. Vatican Congregation for the Doctrine of the Faith, *Donum Vitae,* Feb. 22, 1987.
41. DeLay's words reported by Bob Herbert, *New York Times,* June 23, 2005.
42. DeLay to Family Research Council gathering, Mar. 18, 2005. Yet DeLay and his family took his father off life support when doctors declared he would not recover from severe wounds suffered in an accident: "In '88, Accident Forced DeLays to Choose Between Life and Death," *Los Angeles Times,* May 26, 2005.
43. *FindLaw:* "Compromise Bill" *Re:* Terri Schiavo Signed into Law," section 7.
44. Susan Hanson, "Our Lady of Discord," *New York Times,* July 31, 2006.
45. Pope John Paul II, Address to the International Congress on Life-Sustaining Treatments, Mar. 20, 2004.
46. Kaplan, *With God,* p. 21.
47. Richard Leiby, "Christian Soldier," *Washington Post,* Nov. 6, 2003.
48. Ibid.
49. All quotes in this paragraph are from Charles March, "Wayward Christian Soldiers," *New York Times,* Jan. 20, 2005.

31. Ecumenical Karl

1. Thomas B. Edsall, *Building Red America: The New Conservative Coalition and the Drive for Permanent Power* (Basic Books, 2006). After writing this book just before the election, saying Democrats could not win, he became a guest columnist for the *New York Times,* telling how, for a while, they had won. James Moore and Wayne Slater, *The Architect: Karl Rove and the Master Plan for Absolute Power* (Crown Publishers, 2006). These authors, toward the end of the book, hedged their bet, since Rove was still under investigation for leaking the CIA status of Valerie Plame Wilson, but the bulk of the book was clearly written earlier, describing the permanent-power thesis.
2. Matthew Berke, "Jews Choosing Life," *First Things* 90 (February 1999), pp. 35–36.
3. "[Rabbi Korff] Source of Strength," *Time,* July 29, 1974. "'You are our greatest advocate," Nixon told Korff.
4. Hanna Rosin, "The Republicans' Rabbi-in-Arms," *Washington Post,* June 25, 2005.
5. Ibid.

6. Rick Anderson, "Meet the Lapin Brothers," *Seattle Weekly* (the Lapins' hometown newspaper), May 17, 2005.

7. Franklin Foer, "Grover Norquist's Strange alliance with Radical Islam," *New Republic,* Nov. 1, 2001.

8. Andrew Greeley and Michael Hout, *The Truth About Conservative Christians: What They Think and What They Believe* (University of Chicago Press, 2006), pp. 1, 43.

9. Jamie Doward, "Anti-Gay Millionaire Bankrolls Caravaggio Spectacular," *Observer* (U.K.), Mar. 6, 2005; Chris Hedges, *American Fascists: The Christian Right and the War on America* (Free Press, 2006), pp. 12–13.

10. Ahmanson is a heavy donor to the anti-Darwinian Discovery Institute. Both Olasky and Ahmanson have distanced themselves from Rushdoony's call for executing homosexuals. Ahmanson told a *Salon* reporter (Jan. 6, 2004), "Due to my association with Rushdoony, reporters have often assumed that I agree with him in all applications of the penalties of the Old Testament Law, particularly the stoning of homosexuals"— which he then explicitly renounced.

11. *Time,* Feb. 7, 2005.

12. Jeffrey Goldberg, "The Believer," *New Yorker,* Feb. 13, 2006.

13. Michael Isikoff and David Corn, *Hubris: The Inside Story of Spin, Scandal, and the Selling of the Iraq War* (Crown Publishers, 2006), pp. 35, 147.

14. Ibid., p. 29.

15. Naomi Schaefer Riley, "Mr. Compassionate Conservative," *Wall Street Journal,* Oct. 21, 2006.

16. "The Mind of the Catholic Voter," *Crisis,* Nov. 1998.

17. All material on Hudson from Joe Feuerherd, "The Real Deal," *National Catholic Reporter,* Aug. 19, 2004.

18. Ibid. Hudson said his past "mistake" was a private one and should not have been held against his public performance. But when President Clinton was caught having sex with a twenty-one-year-old, Hudson wrote that his own daughter was "being imbued with the lie that a person's private conduct makes no difference to the execution of their public responsibilities. It's this lie, alive in our culture of death, that has shaped the character of Bill Clinton."

19. "The Twenty-Five Most Influential Evangelicals in America," *Time,* Feb. 7, 2005.

20. C. Everett Koop and Francis Schaeffer, *Whatever Happened to the Human Race?* (Fleming H. Revel Co., 1979).

21. Laurie Goodstein, "How the Evangelicals and Catholics Joined Forces," *New York Times,* May 30, 2004.

22. Dalai Sussman, "Poll: Most Americans Think Church Should Steer Clear of Politics," ABC News analysis, June 4, 2004.

23. William Kristol, quoted in Andrew Sullivan, *The Conservative Soul: How We Lost It, How to Get It Back* (HarperCollins, 2006), pp. 138–39.

24. *Meet the Press,* NBC, Nov. 22, 1998.

25. Ibid.

26. Ibid.

27. Though Jewish tradition did not draw any teaching on abortion from Scripture, modern Christians who believe in what they call the Old Testament try to dredge up something on the subject. Here are some of the desperate expedients.

Psalm 139.13–16:
> For thou hast possessed my reins;
> thou hast covered me in my mother's womb.
> I will praise thee, for I am fearfully and wonderfully made:
> marvellous are thy works;
> and that my soul knoweth right well.
> My substance was not hid from thee,
> when I was made in secret,
> and curiously wrought in the lowest parts of the earth.

This says only that God foreknows everything, every stage of a thing's coming into existence—even its primordial patterning in the lowest parts of the earth (whatever that means). That this is not a statement of when a person actually comes into being is seen from Jeremiah 1.5: "*Before I formed thee in the belly* I knew thee."

Exodus 21.22: "If men strive, and hurt a woman with child, so that her fruit depart from her and yet no mischief follow: he shall be surely punished, according as the woman's husband will lay upon him, and he shall pay as the judges determine."

The penalty is not for murder (which calls for the death penalty), but a mere fine to the husband for the possibility of losing an heir. This says nothing of the present status of the fetus, only of its future profit to the male. The woman is not treated as having any stake in the matter. Only the man.

Genesis 38.24–26: Tamar is brought to be executed, but she is pregnant and is spared. But she is not spared because she is pregnant—that was known when she was condemned to death. She is spared because she produces proof that the father is the head of the tribe, Judah.

Actually there is one passage in the Jewish texts that shows God himself inducing an abortion, Numbers 5.11–26 (the Lord is speaking): If a woman is suspected of infidelity, her husband must bring her before a priest, who will make her drink "bitter water" into which he has mingled curses (23). "If she be defiled, and have done trespass against her husband, that the water that causeth the curse shall enter into her, and become bitter, and her belly shall swell, and the women shall be a curse among her people" (27).

28. Epistle 190.5.
29. Thomas Aquinas, *Theological Summary,* Part One, Question 118, Second Article, Second Response.
30. John Henry Newman, *A Letter Addressed to His Grace the Duke of Norfolk* (1875), in Alvan S. Ryan, *Newman and Gladstone: The Vatican Decrees* (University of Notre Dame Press, 1962), p. 133.
31. Ibid., p. 138.
32. Daniel A. Dombrowski and Robert Deltete, *A Brief, Liberal, Catholic Defense of Abortion* (University of Illinois Press, 2000), p. 125.
33. Ibid., p. 13.
34. Ibid., p. 58.

35. Alison Gopnik, Andrew N. Meltzoff, and Patrician K. Kuhl, *The Scientist in the Crib: What Early Learning Tells Us About the Mind* (Willim Morrow & Company, 1999).

32. LIFE AFTER ROVE

1. Henry E. Brady, "Trust the People: Political Party Coalitions and the 2000 Election," in Jack Rakove, *The Unfinished Election of 2000* (Basic Books, 2001), pp. 26–27.
2. Justin Martin, *Ralph Nader: Crusader, Spoiler, Icon* (Basic Books, 2002), pp. 264–67.
3. Ibid., pp. 266–71.
4. John Cassidy, Profile of Grover Norquist, *New Yorker*, Aug. 1, 2005.
5. "Poll: Strong Support for Abortion Rights," CBS News, Jan. 22, 2003. More recent polls only slightly shave points on that one. In a 2005 Pew Research Center poll, 65 percent upheld *Roe* and 29 percent were for its overthrow. In a 2005 ABC News–*Washington Post* poll, 65 percent upheld *Roe*, 32 percent opposed it. In a 2006 CNN–*USA Today* poll, 65 percent were for Roe, 29 percent against. Many of those in the minority opposing abortion would allow it when the woman's health is in danger, or if the pregnancy was caused by rape or incest. Support for *Roe* weakened in the 1990s, when things like late-term abortions ("partial birth") were being debated. It dipped from the sixties to the high fifties, but it went back up to the sixties after 2000, when the possibility of revocation of *Roe* became more imminent. Even the possibility of revoking *Roe* raised people's support for it.
6. *Induced Abortion, Facts in Brief* (Alan Guttmacher Institute, 2002).
7. Andrew Greeley and Michael Hout, *The Truth About Conservative Christians: What They Think and What They Believe* (University of Chicago Press, 2006), p. 53.
8. Robert Bork, "Our Judicial Oligarchy," *First Things*, Nov. 1966.
9. Chuck Colson, "Kingdoms in Conflict," *First Things*, Nov. 1966.
10. Hadley Arkes, "A Culture Corrupted," *First Things*, Nov. 1966.
11. Russell Hittinger, "A Crisis in Legitimacy," *First Thing*, Nov. 1966.
12. David D. Kirkpatrick, "A Year of Work to Sell Roberts to Conservatives," *New York Times*, July 22, 2005.
13. Steve Goldstein, "Paul J. Hill Fatally Shot a Doctor and Escort," *Philadelphia Inquirer*, May 6, 1999.
14. Paul Jennings Hill, "Mix My Blood with the Blood of the Unborn," Aug. 2003.
15. Goldstein, "Paul J. Hill."
16. Michael Kinsley, "Why Not Kill the Baby Killers?" *Time*, Aug. 15, 1994.
17. John Danforth, "In the Name of Politics," *New York Times*, Mar. 30, 2005. Danforth would argue that sincere Christians can take a view of life support very different from that voiced against the termination of Schiavo's support. Danforth and his wife both have living wills allowing each other to end life support when one of them is in a terminal condition. In 1990, he and Senator Edward Kennedy co-sponsored the Patient Self-Determination Act, drafted by Danforth's Catholic legislative assistant, which required hospitals to inform patients of their right to refuse life support and to honor living wills. John Danforth, *Faith and Politics: How the "Moral Values" Debate Divides America and How to Move Forward Together* (Viking, 2005), pp. 70–75.
18. *Planned Parenthood v. Danforth* (1976).

19. Danforth, *Faith and Politics,* pp. 86–88.
20. Ibid., pp. 107–9. The marriage problems Danforth cites are underscored by a headline appearing in the Jan. 15, 2007, *New York Times:* "51% of Women Now Living Without Spouse." It is unlikely that this statistic was in any way caused by talk about gay marriage.
21. "President-Elect of Christian Coalition Resigns," Associated Press, Nov. 24, 2006.
22. Jeffrey Hart, "The Evangelical Effect," *Pittsburgh Post-Gazette,* Apr. 17, 2005.
23. Elizabeth Bumiller, "An Outspoken Conservative Loses His Place at the Table," *New York Times,* Feb. 13, 2006.
24. Peggy Noonan, "The Two Vacuums," *Wall Street Journal,* Jan. 12, 2007.
25. "Political Fallout over Schiavo," CBS News, Mar. 23, 2005.
26. Danforth, *Faith and Politics,* pp. 10, 18.
27. Michael Finnegan, "AIDS Fight Needs Churches, Obama Says," *Los Angeles Times,* Dec. 2, 2006.
28. The Evangelical talk show host Kevin McCullough, on whose show Rick Warren had appeared, denounced "the inhumane, sick, and sinister evil" that Obama represented. Kevin McCullough, "Why is Obama's Evil in Rick Warren's Pulpit?" *Townhall,* Nov. 18, 2006.
29. Tim Grieve, "Left Turn at Saddleback Church," *Salon,* Dec. 2, 2006.
30. Jimmy Carter, *Our Endangered Values: America's Moral Crisis* (Simon & Schuster, 2005), p. 74.
31. Greeley and Hout, *The Truth,* pp. 130–31.
32. Dean Hoge et al., *Young Adult Catholics: Religion in the Culture of Choice* (University of Notre Dame Press, 2002), p. 37.
33. Carter, *Values,* p. 75.

EPILOGUE

1. John Danforth, *Faith and Politics: How the "Moral Values" Debate Divides America and How to Move Forward Together,* p. 97.
2. Mark A. Noll, *The Scandal of the Evangelical Mind* (Eerdmans, 1994), p. 250. It should be said that Noll, along with his fellow Evangelical historians Nathan Hatch and George Marsden, is doing much to repair the loss of intellectual rigor among his fellows.
3. Ibid., p. 196.
4. Ibid., pp. 83–108.
5. Jefferson to Adams, Nov. 13, 1818, in Lester J. Cappon, *The Adams-Jefferson Letters* (University of North Carolina Press, 1959), vol. 2, p. 129.

APPENDIX I

JEFFERSON'S VIRGINIA STATUTE FOR RELIGIOUS FREEDOM

WELL AWARE THAT the opinions and belief of men depend not on their own will, but follow involuntarily the evidence proposed to their minds; that Almighty God hath created the mind free, and manifested his supreme will that free it shall remain by making it altogether insusceptible of restraint; that all attempts to influence it by temporal punishments, or burthens, or by civil incapacitations, tend only to beget habits of hypocrisy and meanness, and are a departure from the plan of the holy author of our religion, who being lord both of body and mind, yet chose not to propagate it by coercions on either, as was in his Almighty power to do, but to extend it by its influence on reason alone; that the impious presumption of legislators and rulers, civil as well as ecclesiastical, who, being themselves but fallible and uninspired men, have assumed dominion over the faith of others, setting up their own opinions and modes of thinking as the only true and infallible, and as such endeavoring to impose them on others, hath established and maintained false religions over the greatest part of the world and through all time: That to compel a man to furnish contributions of money for the propagation of opinions which he disbelieves and abhors, is sinful and tyrannical; that even the forcing him to support this or that teacher of his own religious persuasion, is depriving him of the comfortable liberty of giving his contributions to the particular pastor whose morals he would make his pattern, and whose powers he feels most persuasive to righteousness; and is withdrawing from the ministry those temporary rewards, which proceeding from an approbation of their personal conduct, are an additional incitement to earnest and unremitting labours for the instruction of mankind; that our civil rights have no dependence on our religious opinions, any more than our opinions in physics or geometry; that therefore the proscribing any citizen as unworthy the public confidence by laying upon him an incapacity of being called to offices of trust and emolument, unless he profess or renounce this or that religious opinion, is depriving him injuriously of those privileges and advantages to which, in common with his fellow citizens, he has a natural right; that it tends also to corrupt the principles of that very religion it is meant to encourage, by bribing, with a monopoly of worldly honours and emoluments, those who will externally profess and conform to it; that though indeed these are criminal who do not withstand such temptation, yet neither are those innocent who lay the bait in their way; that the opinions of men are not the object of civil government, nor under its jurisdiction; that to suffer the civil magistrate to intrude his powers into the field of opinion and to restrain the profession or propagation of principles on supposition of their ill tendency is a dangerous fallacy, which at once destroys all religious liberty, because he being of course judge of that tendency will make his opinions the rule of judgment, and approve or condemn the sentiments of others only as they shall square with or differ from his own; that it is time enough for the rightful purposes of civil government for its officers to interfere when principles break out into overt acts against peace and good order; and finally, that truth is great and will prevail if left to herself; that she is the proper and sufficient antagonist to error, and has nothing to fear from the conflict unless by human interposition disarmed of her natural weapons, free argument and debate; errors ceasing to be dangerous when it is permitted freely to contradict them.

We the General Assembly of Virginia do enact that no man shall be compelled to frequent or support any religious worship, place, or ministry whatsoever, nor shall be enforced, restrained, molested, or burthened in his body or goods, nor shall otherwise suffer, on account of his religious opinions or belief; but that all men shall be free to profess, and by argument to maintain, their opinions in matters of religion, and that the same shall in no wise diminish, enlarge, or affect their civil capacities.

And though we well know that this Assembly, elected by the people for the ordinary purposes of legislation only, have no power to restrain the acts of succeeding Assemblies, constituted with powers equal to our own, and that therefore to declare this act irrevocable would be of no effect in law; yet we are free to declare, and do declare, that the rights hereby asserted are of the natural rights of mankind, and that if any act shall be hereafter passed to repeal the present or to narrow its operation, such act will be an infringement of natural right.

APPENDIX II

MADISON'S *MEMORIAL AND REMONSTRANCE AGAINST RELIGIOUS ASSESSMENTS*
1785

TO THE HONORABLE THE GENERAL ASSEMBLY OF THE COMMONWEALTH OF VIRGINIA
A MEMORIAL AND REMONSTRANCE AGAINST RELIGIOUS ASSESSMENTS
WE THE SUBSCRIBERS, citizens of the said Commonwealth, having taken into serious consideration, a Bill printed by order of the last Session of General Assembly, entitled "A Bill establishing a provision for Teachers of the Christian Religion," and conceiving that the same if finally armed with the sanctions of a law, will be a dangerous abuse of power, are bound as faithful members of a free State to remonstrate against it, and to declare the reasons by which we are determined. We remonstrate against the said Bill,

1. Because we hold it for a fundamental and undeniable truth, "that religion or the duty which we owe to our Creator and the manner of discharging it, can be directed only by reason and conviction, not by force or violence." The Religion then of every man must be left to the conviction and conscience of every man; and it is the right of every man to exercise it as these may dictate. This right is in its nature an unalienable right. It is unalienable, because the opinions of men, depending only on the evidence contemplated by their own minds cannot follow the dictates of other men: It is unalienable also, because what is here a right towards men, is a duty towards the Creator. It is the duty of every man to

render to the Creator such homage and such only as he believes to be acceptable to him. This duty is precedent, both in order of time and in degree of obligation, to the claims of Civil Society. Before any man can be considered as a member of Civil Society, he must be considered as a subject of the Governour of the Universe: And if a member of Civil Society, do it with a saving of his allegiance to the Universal Sovereign. We maintain therefore that in matters of Religion, no man's right is abridged by the institution of Civil Society and that Religion is wholly exempt from its cognizance. True it is, that no other rule exists, by which any question which may divide a Society, can be ultimately determined, but the will of the majority; but it is also true that the majority may trespass on the rights of the minority.

2. Because Religion be exempt from the authority of the Society at large, still less can it be subject to that of the Legislative Body. The latter are but the creatures and vicegerents of the former. Their jurisdiction is both derivative and limited: it is limited with regard to the co-ordinate departments, more necessarily is it limited with regard to the constituents. The preservation of a free Government requires not merely, that the metes and bounds which separate each department of power be invariably maintained; but more especially that neither of them be suffered to overleap the great Barrier which defends the rights of the people. The Rulers who are guilty of such an encroachment, exceed the commission from which they derive their authority, and are Tyrants. The People who submit to it are governed by laws made neither by themselves nor by an authority derived from them, and are slaves.

3. Because it is proper to take alarm at the first experiment on our liberties. We hold this prudent jealousy to be the first duty of Citizens, and one of the noblest characteristics of the late Revolution. The free men of America did not wait till usurped power had strengthened itself by exercise, and entangled the question in precedents. They saw all the consequences in the principle, and they avoided the consequences by denying the principle. We revere this lesson too much soon to forget it. Who does not see that the same authority which can establish Christianity, in exclusion of all other Religions, may establish with the same ease any

particular sect of Christians, in exclusion of all other Sects? that the same authority which can force a citizen to contribute three pence only of his property for the support of any one establishment, may force him to conform to any other establishment in all cases whatsoever?

4. Because the Bill violates the equality which ought to be the basis of every law, and which is more indispensable, in proportion as the validity or expediency of any law is more liable to be impeached. If "all men are by nature equally free and independent," all men are to be considered as entering into Society on equal conditions; as relinquishing no more, and therefore retaining no less, one than another, of their natural rights. Above all are they to be considered as retaining an "equal title to the free exercise of Religion according to the dictates of Conscience." Whilst we assert for ourselves a freedom to embrace, to profess and to observe the Religion which we believe to be of divine origin, we cannot deny an equal freedom to those whose minds have not yet yielded to the evidence which has convinced us. If this freedom be abused, it is an offence against God, not against man: To God, therefore, not to man, must an account of it be rendered. As the Bill violates equality by subjecting some to peculiar burdens, so it violates the same principle, by granting to others peculiar exemptions. Are the Quakers and Mennonists the only sects who think a compulsive support of their Religions unnecessary and unwarrantable? Can their piety alone be entrusted with the care of public worship? Ought their Religions to be endowed above all others with extraordinary privileges by which proselytes may be enticed from all others? We think too favorably of the justice and good sense of these denominations to believe that they either covet pre-eminences over their fellow citizens or that they will be seduced by them from the common opposition to the measure.

5. Because the Bill implies either that the Civil Magistrate is a competent Judge of Religious Truth; or that he may employ Religion as an engine of Civil policy. The first is an arrogant pretension falsified by the contradictory opinions of Rulers in all ages, and throughout the world: the second an unhallowed perversion of the means of salvation.

6. Because the establishment proposed by the Bill is not requisite for

the support of the Christian Religion. To say that it is, is a contradiction to the Christian Religion itself, for every page of it disavows a dependence on the powers of this world: it is a contradiction to fact; for it is known that this Religion both existed and flourished, not only without the support of human laws, but in spite of every opposition from them, and not only during the period of miraculous aid, but long after it had been left to its own evidence and the ordinary care of Providence. Nay, it is a contradiction in terms; for a Religion not invented by human policy, must have pre-existed and been supported, before it was established by human policy. It is moreover to weaken in those who profess this Religion a pious confidence in its innate excellence and the patronage of its Author; and to foster in those who still reject it, a suspicion that its friends are too conscious of its fallacies to trust it to its own merits.

7. Because experience witnesseth that ecclesiastical establishments, instead of maintaining the purity and efficacy of Religion, have had a contrary operation. During almost fifteen centuries has the legal establishment of Christianity been on trial. What have been its fruits? More or less in all places, pride and indolence in the Clergy, ignorance and servility in the laity, in both, superstition, bigotry and persecution. Enquire of the Teachers of Christianity for the ages in which it appeared in its greatest lustre; those of every sect, point to the ages prior to its incorporation with Civil policy. Propose a restoration of this primitive State in which its Teachers depended on the voluntary rewards of their flocks, many of them predict its downfall. On which Side ought their testimony to have greatest weight, when for or when against their interest?

8. Because the establishment in question is not necessary for the support of Civil Government. If it be urged as necessary for the support of Civil Government only as it is a means of supporting Religion, and it be not necessary for the latter purpose, it cannot be necessary for the former. If Religion be not within the cognizance of Civil Government how can its legal establishment be necessary to Civil Government? What influence in fact have ecclesiastical establishments had on Civil Society? In some instances they have been seen to erect a spiritual tyranny on the

ruins of the Civil authority; in many instances they have been seen upholding the thrones of political tyranny: in no instance have they been seen the guardians of the liberties of the people. Rulers who wished to subvert the public liberty, may have found an established Clergy convenient auxiliaries. A just Government instituted to secure & perpetuate it needs them not. Such a Government will be best supported by protecting every Citizen in the enjoyment of his Religion with the same equal hand which protects his person and his property; by neither invading the equal rights of any Sect, nor suffering any Sect to invade those of another.

9. Because the proposed establishment is a departure from the generous policy, which, offering an Asylum to the persecuted and oppressed of every Nation and Religion, promised a lustre to our country, and an accession to the number of its citizens. What a melancholy mark is the Bill of sudden degeneracy? Instead of holding forth an Asylum to the persecuted, it is itself a signal of persecution. It degrades from the equal rank of Citizens all those whose opinions in Religion do not bend to those of the Legislative authority. Distant as it may be in its present form from the Inquisition, it differs from it only in degree. The one is the first step, the other the last in the career of intolerance. The magnanimous sufferer under this cruel scourge in foreign Regions, must view the Bill as a Beacon on our Coast, warning him to seek some other haven, where liberty and philanthropy in their due extent, may offer a more certain repose from his Troubles.

10. Because it will have a like tendency to banish our Citizens. The allurements presented by other situations are every day thinning their number. To superadd a fresh motive to emigration by revoking the liberty which they now enjoy, would be the same species of folly which has dishonoured and depopulated flourishing kingdoms

11. Because it will destroy that moderation and harmony which the forbearance of our laws to intermeddle with Religion has produced among its several sects. Torrents of blood have been spilt in the old world, by vain attempts of the secular arm, to extinguish Religious discord, by proscribing all difference in Religious opinion. Time has

at length revealed the true remedy. Every relaxation of narrow and rigorous policy, wherever it has been tried, has been found to assuage the disease. The American Theatre has exhibited proofs that equal and compleat liberty, if it does not wholly eradicate it, sufficiently destroys its malignant influence on the health and prosperity of the State. If with the salutary effects of this system under our own eyes, we begin to contract the bounds of Religious freedom, we know no name that will too severely reproach our folly. At least let warning be taken at the first fruits of the threatened innovation. The very appearance of the Bill has transformed "that Christian forbearance, love and charity," which of late mutually prevailed, into animosities and jealousies, which may not soon be appeased. What mischiefs may not be dreaded, should this enemy to the public quiet be armed with the force of a law?

12. Because the policy of the Bill is adverse to the diffusion of the light of Christianity. The first wish of those who enjoy this precious gift ought to be that it may be imparted to the whole race of mankind. Compare the number of those who have as yet received it with the number still remaining under the dominion of false Religions; and how small is the former! Does the policy of the Bill tend to lessen the disproportion? No; it at once discourages those who are strangers to the light of revelation from coming into the Region of it; and countenances by example the nations who continue in darkness, in shutting out those who might convey it to them. Instead of Levelling as far as possible, every obstacle to the victorious progress of Truth, the Bill with an ignoble and unchristian timidity would circumscribe it with a wall of defence against the encroachments of error.

13. Because attempts to enforce by legal sanctions, acts obnoxious to so great a proportion of Citizens, tend to enervate the laws in general, and to slacken the bands of Society. If it be difficult to execute any law which is not generally deemed necessary or salutary, what must be the case, where it is deemed invalid and dangerous? And what may be the effect of so striking an example of impotency in the Government, on its general authority?

14. Because a measure of such singular magnitude and delicacy ought not to be imposed, without the clearest evidence that it is called for by a majority of citizens, and no satisfactory method is yet proposed by which the voice of the majority in this case may be determined, or its influence secured. The people of the respective counties are indeed requested to signify their opinion respecting the adoption of the Bill to the next Session of Assembly. But the representatives of the Counties will be that of the people. Our hope is that neither of the former will, after due consideration, espouse the dangerous principle of the Bill. Should the event disappoint us, it will still leave us in full confidence, that a fair appeal to the latter will reverse the sentence against our liberties.

15. Because finally, "the equal right of every citizen to the free exercise of his Religion according to the dictates of conscience" is held by the same tenure with all our other rights. If we recur to its origin, it is equally the gift of nature; if we weigh its importance, it cannot be less dear to us; if we consult the "Declaration of those rights which pertain to the good people of Virginia, as the basis and foundation of Government," it is enumerated with equal solemnity, or rather studied emphasis. Either then, we must say, that the Will of the Legislature is the only measure of their authority; and that in the plenitude of this authority, they may sweep away all our fundamental rights; or, that they are bound to leave this particular right untouched and sacred: Either we must say, that they may control the freedom of the press, may abolish the Trial by Jury, may swallow up the Executive and Judiciary Powers of the State; nay that they may despoil us of our very right of suffrage, and erect themselves into an independent and hereditary Assembly or, we must say, that they have no authority to enact into the law the Bill under consideration. We the Subscribers say, that the General Assembly of this Commonwealth have no such authority: And that no effort may be omitted on our part against so dangerous an usurpation, we oppose to it, this remonstrance; earnestly praying, as we are in duty bound, that the Supreme Lawgiver of the Universe, by illuminating those to whom it is addressed, may on the one hand, turn their Councils from every act

which would affront his holy prerogative, or violate the trust committed to them: and on the other, guide them into every measure which may be worthy of his [blessing, may re]dound to their own praise, and may establish more firmly the liberties, the prosperity and the happiness of the Commonwealth.

INDEX

Equal Rights Amendment (ERA), 472, 473, 485, 488, 491, 494
Era of Good Feelings, 297, 303, 453
Essay Concerning Human Understanding, An (Locke), 127
Esther (Adams), 280, 339
Evangelicals, 2–7, 9, 154, 156, 167, 170, 171, 207, 241, 287, 288, 289, 298, 335, 339, 356, 357, 363, 368, 379, 413–14, 415, 453, 466, 532, 550–52
 anti-intellectualism among, 550
 black, 291–92, 331, 469, 470
 Bush and, 498
 camp meetings and, 294
 Chavez and, 479
 civil rights movement and, 470
 Douglass and, 334
 Enlightenment united with, 470, 479, 550–51
 feminism and, 473
 in Gilded Age, 341–42
 Great Awakening and, 101
 Lincoln and, 328, 330, 331, 333
 Niebuhr and, 454
 in 1940s and 1950s, 455–56
 presidents as, 497–98
 Prohibition and, 399–406
 reason and, 423
 Rights Revolution and, 480–81, 483, 489
 schools and, 481, 482–87
 slavery and, 316
 see also Fundamentalism; Religious Right; revivals
Everett, Edward, 248
evolution, *see* Darwinism

Faith-Based Initiative (FBI), 502–4, 519
Falwell, Jerry, 367, 372, 380, 470, 481, 483, 488–89, 491, 492, 514, 523, 538
Family Research Council (FRC), 489, 499, 500, 510
Farley, James, 433
Farmer, James, 467, 468
Farmer, John, 138
fascism, 430–31
Faubus, Orvil, 462
Fell, Jesse, 328–29
feminism, *see* women's rights
Fiering, Norman, 106, 109
Fifth Amendment, 231
Finley, Samuel, 116, 117
Finney, Charles Grandison, 299–302, 316–17, 343, 344, 345, 346, 348
Finney, Samuel, 116
First Amendment, 6, 93, 134, 197–98, 200, 202, 203, 207, 222, 223–35, 237, 242, 246, 502

as nonpreferential, rather than against religion in general, 225, 234–35
 as not based on matter of principle, 225, 232–34
 Pinckney Resolution and, 306
 and religion at state level, 7, 225, 229–32, 249
 as unimportant, 225–29
First Great Awakening, *see* Great Awakening
First Things, 521, 522, 523, 537
Fitzhugh, George, 312
Fletcher, Robert, 317
Focus on the Family, 488, 489, 494, 500, 501
Foley, Mark, 541
Ford, Henry, 373, 435
Ford, Henry, II, 457
Fosdick, Harry Emerson, 414
Fourteenth Amendment, 246
Fourth Amendment, 418
Fowler, Charles, 402
Fox, George, 23, 27, 40, 52, 136, 137
France, 133–34, 154
 Quakers and, 135, 136
 Revolution in, 78–79, 133, 154, 176, 319, 320
Francis, Convers, 263, 264
Franco, Francisco, 438, 439
Frankfurter, Felix, 441, 442
Franklin, Benjamin, 2, 86, 103, 130–31, 136, 147, 153, 166
 immigration and, 216–17
 prayer and, 108, 224
 slavery and, 139
Frelinghuysen, Theodorus, 102, 103, 115
Frémont, John C., 307
French and Indian War, 140, 141–42, 147, 180
Freneau, Philip, 153
Frist, Bill, 507, 510
frontier, *see* West and frontier
Frum, David, 499
Frykholm, Amy Johnson, 379
Fulke, William, 51
Fuller, Margaret, 263–68, 272, 277, 282
Fundamentalism, 347, 363, 364, 382, 383, 384, 410, 413–14, 532, 549
 Moody's contribution to, 355
 Scopes trial and, 368, 413, 415, 420–23, 453, 455, 532
 September 11 attacks and, 389
 world government and, 369
 see also Evangelicals; Premillennialism; Religious Right
Fundamentals, The, 358, 364

Gabler, Mel and Norma, 486
Gabler, Neal, 445
Gaebelein, Arno C., 361, 362, 369, 373, 412, 413–14

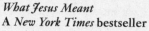

What Jesus Meant
A *New York Times* bestseller
In what are billed "culture wars," people on the political right and the political left cite Jesus as endorsing their views. Garry Wills argues that Jesus subscribed to no political program. He was far more radical than that. In a fresh reading of the gospels, Wills explores the meaning of the "reign of heaven" Jesus not only promised for the future but brought with him into this life. It is only by dodges and evasions that people misrepresent what Jesus plainly had to say against power, the wealthy, and religion itself. But Wills is just as critical of those who would make Jesus a mere ethical teacher, ignoring or playing down his divinity. An illuminating analysis for believers and nonbelievers alike, *What Jesus Meant* is a brilliant addition to our national conversation on religion.   *ISBN 978-0-14-303880-1*

What Paul Meant
A *New York Times* bestseller
All through history, Christians have debated Paul's influence on the church. Writings attributed to Peter and James charge Paul, in the second century, with being a tool of Satan. In later centuries, Paul became a target of ridicule for writers such as Thomas Jefferson, George Bernard Shaw, and Nietzsche. However, as Wills argues eloquently in this masterly analysis, what Paul meant was not something contrary to what Jesus meant. Rather, the best way to know Jesus is to discover Paul. Wills illuminates how Paul, writing on the road and in the heat of the moment, and often in the midst of controversy, galvanized a movement and offers us the best reflection of those early times.   *ISBN 978-0-14-311263-1*

The Rosary
The Christian rosary arranges beads so that one can contemplate different episodes in the life of Christ. Though some think of the rosary as a form of piety, sentimental if not superstitious, Wills argues that it is deeply grounded in scripture and theology, a way by which Christians participate in the life of Christ's mystical body. He supplies the texts from the gospels that are meditated on, with some suggested reflections and a series of exquisite Tintoretto paintings to concentrate the mind. The result is an illuminating and profound exploration of the power of prayer.   *ISBN 978-0-14-303797-2*

Saint Augustine
Garry Wills brings the same fresh scholarship, lively prose, and critical appreciation that characterize his books on religion and American history to this outstanding biography of one of the most influential Christian philosophers. *Saint Augustine* examines this famed fourth century bishop and seminal thinker whose grounding in classical philosophy informed his influential interpretation of the Christian doctrines of mind, wisdom, and God.   *ISBN 978-0-14-303598-5*

Explaining America
In 1787 and 1788, Alexander Hamilton and James Madison published what remains perhaps the greatest example of political journalism in the English language—the *Federalist Papers*. Written to urge ratification of the Constitution, the eighty-five essays—trenchant in thought and graceful in expression—defended the Constitution not merely as a theoretical statement but as a practical instrument of rule. Now updated with a new introduction, Garry Wills's classic study subjects these essays to rigorous analysis, illuminating, as only he can, their significance in the development of the philosophy on which our government is based.   *ISBN 978-0-14-029839-0*

Also Available from Penguin Classics

Confessions
Saint Augustine
Translated by Garry Wills
Garry Wills is an exceptionally gifted translator and one of our best writers on religion today. His bestselling translations of individual chapters of Saint Augustine's *Confessions* have received widespread and glowing reviews. Now for the first time, Wills's translation of the entire work is available in a Penguin Classics Deluxe Edition. Removed by time and place but not by spiritual relevance, Augustine's *Confessions* continues to influence contemporary religion, language, and thought. Reading with fresh, keen eyes, Wills brings his superb gifts of analysis and insight to this ambitious translation of the entire book.

This Penguin Classics Deluxe Edition features a new introduction by the translator and luxurious packaging.   *ISBN 978-0-14-303951-8*

Now Available from Viking

What the Gospels Meant
Hailed as "one of the most intellectually interesting and doctrinally heterodox Christians writing today" by *The New York Times Book Review*, Garry Wills now turns his remarkable gift for biblical analysis to the four gospels of Matthew, Mark, Luke, and John. Brilliantly examining how their particular goals, methods, and styles shaped the gospels' messages, Wills guides readers through the maze of meanings that have accrued around these foundational texts to reveal their essential Christian truths. *What the Gospels Meant* will prove to be a valuable source of wisdom and inspiration for all.
ISBN 978-0-670-01871-0

Coming from Viking in November 2008

Martial's Epigrams
A Selection
From acclaimed author Garry Wills comes a selection of Martial's *Epigrams*, exquisitely translated. One of literature's greatest satirists, Martial earned his livelihood by excoriating the follies and vices of his time, and set a pattern that satirists have admired and imitated across the ages. Born in Spain, Marcus Valerius Martialis (c. 40–102 CE), known in English as Martial, went to Rome as a young man to win fame and fortune. At the height of his career he published a book of scathing social commentary every year—1,500 poems in all, of which Wills translates about a third.
ISBN 978-0-670-02039-3